Microsoft Silverlight Edition: Programming Windows Phone 7

Charles Petzold

PUBLISHED BY
Microsoft Press
A Division of Microsoft Corporation
One Microsoft Way
Redmond, Washington 98052-6399

Library of Congress Control Number: 2010941604
ISBN: 978-0-7356-5667-3

Printed and bound in the United States of America.

Microsoft Press books are available through booksellers and distributors worldwide. For further information about international editions, contact your local Microsoft Corporation office or contact Microsoft Press International directly at fax (425) 936-7329. Tell us what you think of this book at http://www.microsoft.com/learning/booksurvey. Send comments to mspinput@microsoft.com.

Microsoft and the trademarks listed at http://www.microsoft.com/about/legal/en/us/IntellectualProperty/Trademark/EN-US.aspx are trademarks of the Microsoft group of companies. All other marks are the property of their respective owners.

The example companies, organizations, products, domain names, e-mail addresses, logos, people, places, and events depicted herein are fictitious. No association with any real company, organization, product, domain name, e-mail address, logo, person, place, or event is intended or should be inferred.

This book expresses the author's views and opinions. The information contained in this book is provided without any express, statutory, or implied warranties. Neither the authors, Microsoft Corporation, nor its resellers, or distributors will be held liable for any damages caused or alleged to be caused either directly or indirectly by this book.

Acquisitions Editor: Devon Musgrave
Developmental Editor: Devon Musgrave
Project Editor: Devon Musgrave
Editorial Production: Ashley Schneider, S4Carlisle Publishing Services
Technical Reviewer: Per Blomqvist; Technical Review Services provided by Content Master, a member of CM Group, Ltd.

Body Part No. X17-35780

Contents at a Glance

Table of Contents

What do you think of this book? We want to hear from you!

Microsoft is interested in hearing your feedback so we can continually improve our
books and learning resources for you. To participate in a brief online survey, please visit:

microsoft.com/learning/booksurvey

Introduction

> **Important** This book and *Microsoft XNA Framework Edition: Programming Windows Phone 7* are fully indexed, print-book versions of a single free, electronic edition titled *Programming Windows Phone 7,* which you can find on the Microsoft Press blog: *http://blogs.msdn.com/b/ microsoft_press/.* No changes have been made to the original edition's text, including references to the color of the original images, which appear black and white in this book. What follows is the Introduction that originally appeared in *Programming Windows Phone 7;* "Code Samples" is the only section in this Introduction that has been updated.

This book is a gift from the Windows Phone 7 team at Microsoft to the programming community, and I am proud to have been a part of it. Within the pages that follow, I show you the basics of writing applications for Windows Phone 7 using the C# programming language with the Silverlight and XNA 2D frameworks.

Yes, *Programming Windows Phone 7* is truly a free download, but for those readers who still love paper—as I certainly do—this book will also be available (for sale) divided into two fully-indexed print editions: *Microsoft Silverlight Edition: Programming Windows Phone 7* and *Microsoft XNA Framework Edition: Programming Windows Phone 7.*

With the money you've saved downloading this book, please buy other books. Despite the plethora of information available online, books are still the best way to learn about programming within a coherent and cohesive tutorial narrative. Every book sale brings a tear of joy to an author's eye, so please help make them weep overflowing rivers.

In particular, you might want to buy other books to *supplement* the material in this book. For example, I barely mention Web services in this book, and that's a serious deficiency because Web services are likely to become increasingly important in Windows Phone 7 applications. My coverage of XNA is limited to 2D graphics and while I hope to add several 3D chapters in the next edition of this book, I don't really get into the whole Xbox LIVE community aspect of game development. Nor do I discuss any programming tools beyond Visual Studio—not even Expression Blend.

My publisher Microsoft Press has a couple additional Windows Phone 7 books coming soon: *Windows Phone 7 Silverlight Development Step by Step* by Andy Wigley & Peter Foot offers a more tools-oriented approach. Although Michael Stroh's *Windows Phone 7 Plain & Simple* is a guide to *using* the phone rather than developing for it, I suspect it will give developers some insights and ideas.

Moreover, I also hear that my old friend Doug Boling is working hard on a Windows Phone 7 enterprise-programming book that is likely to be considered his masterpiece. Be sure to check out that one.

Organization

This book is divided into three parts. The first part discusses basic concepts of Windows Phone 7 programming using example programs that target both Silverlight and the XNA framework. It is likely that many Windows Phone 7 developers will choose either one platform or the other, but I think it's important for all developers who have at least a *little* knowledge of the alternative to their chosen path.

The second part of this book focuses entirely on Silverlight, and the third part on XNA 2D. For your convenience, the chapters in each part build upon previous knowledge in a progressive tutorial narrative, and hence are intended to be read sequentially.

My Assumptions About You

I assume that you know the basic principles of .NET programming and you have a working familiarity with the C# programming language. If not, you might benefit from reading my free online book *.NET Book Zero: What the C or C++ Programmer Needs to Know about C# and the .NET Framework*, available from my website at *www.charlespetzold.com/dotnet*.

System Requirements

To use this book properly you'll need to download and install the Windows Phone Developer Tools, which includes Visual Studio 2010 Express for Windows Phone, XNA Game Studio 4.0, and an on-screen Windows Phone Emulator to test your programs in the absence of an actual device. Get the latest information and downloads at *http://developer .windowsphone.com*.

You can install these tools on top of Visual Studio 2010, in effect enhancing Visual Studio 2010 for phone development. That's the configuration I used.

Although you can do quite a bit with the phone emulator, at some point you'll want to deploy your programs to an actual Windows Phone 7 device. You can register as a phone developer at *http://developer.windowsphone.com* and then have the ability to unlock your phone so you can deploy your programs from Visual Studio.

Since late July 2010, I've had an LG GW910 phone to test the programs in this book. For the record, the final build I installed was 7.0.7003.0.

Using the Phone Emulator

Windows Phone 7 supports multi-touch, and working with multi-touch is an important part of developing programs for the phone. When using the Windows Phone Emulator, mouse clicks and mouse movement on the PC can mimic touch on the emulator, but for only one finger. You can test out multi-touch for real on the phone emulator if you have a multi-touch monitor running under Windows 7.

In the absence of a multi-touch monitor, you might want to explore simulating multi-touch with multiple mouse devices. The site *http://multitouchvista.codeplex.com* has the download you'll need and includes a link to *http://michaelsync.net/2010/04/06/step-by-step-tutorial-installing-multi-touch-simulator-for-silverlight-phone-7* that provides instructions.

Windows Phone 7 devices also have a built-in accelerometer, which can be *very* difficult to simulate in an emulator. Per Blomqvist, the Technical Reviewer for this book, found an application at *http://accelkit.codeplex.com* that utilizes the webcam and ARToolkit to emulate the accelerometer sensor and feed that data into the Windows Phone 7 emulator through a TCP/HTTP Server, and although neither of us have tried it out, it sounds quite intriguing.

Code Samples

To illustrate Silverlight and XNA programming concepts, this book describes about 190 complete programs. Many of them are small and simple, but others are larger and more interesting.

Some people like to learn new programming environments by re-creating the projects in Visual Studio and typing in the source code themselves from the pages of the book. Others prefer to study the code and run the pre-existing programs to see what the code does. If you fall into the latter category, you can download all the source code in a ZIP file via the Companion Content link at *http://oreilly.com/catalog/0790145316707/.*

If you find something in the code that is useful in your own software project, feel free to use the code without restriction—either straight up or modified in whatever way you want. That's what it's there for.

Last-Minute Items

As I was nearing the completion this book, the first version of the Silverlight for Windows Phone Toolkit was released with some additional elements and controls, and is available for downloading at *http://silverlight.codeplex.com*. Historically, these Silverlight toolkits very often contain previews of elements and controls that are incorporated into later Silverlight releases. I regret that I could not include a discussion of the toolkit contents in the appropriate chapters of this book.

With XNA programs, sometimes Visual Studio complains that it can't build or deploy the program. If you encounter that problem, in the Solution Platforms drop-down list on the standard toolbar, select "Windows Phone" rather than "Any CPU". Or, invoke the

Configuration Manager from the Build menu, and in the Active Solution Platform drop-down select "Windows Phone" rather than "Any CPU".

The *www.charlespetzold.com/phone* page on my website will contain information about this book and perhaps even some information about a future edition. I also hope to blog about Windows Phone 7 programming as much as possible.

The Essential People

This book owes its existence to Dave Edson—an old friend from the early 1990s era of *Microsoft Systems Journal*—who had the brilliant idea that I would be the perfect person to write a tutorial on Windows Phone 7. Dave arranged for me to attend a technical deep dive on the phone at Microsoft in December 2009, and I was hooked. Todd Brix gave the thumbs up on the book, and Anand Iyer coordinated the project with Microsoft Press.

At Microsoft Press, Ben Ryan launched the project and Devon Musgrave had the unenviable job of trying to make my code and prose resemble an actual book. (We all go way back: You'll see Ben and Devon's names on the bottom of the copyright page of *Programming Windows*, fifth edition, published in 1998.)

My Technical Reviewer was the diligent Per Blomqvist, who apparently tested all the code in both the sample files and as the listings appear in the book, and who in the process caught several errors on my part that were truly, well, shocking.

Dave Edson also reviewed some chapters and served as conduit to the Windows Phone team to deal with my technical problems and questions. Early on, Aaron Stebner provided essential guidance; Michael Klucher reviewed chapters, and Kirti Deshpande, Charlie Kindel, Casey McGee, and Shawn Oster also had important things to tell me. Thanks to Bonnie Lehenbauer for reviewing a chapter.

I am also indebted to Shawn Hargreaves for his XNA expertise, and Yochay Kiriaty and Richard Bailey for the lowdown on tombstoning.

My wife Deirdre Sinnott has been a marvel of patience and tolerance over the past months as she dealt with an author given to sudden mood swings, insane yelling at the computer screen, and the conviction that the difficulty of writing a book relieves one of the responsibility of performing basic household chores.

Alas, I can't blame any of them for bugs or other problems that remain in this book. Those are all mine.

Charles Petzold
New York City and Roscoe, New York
October 22, 2010

Errata & Book Support

We've made every effort to ensure the accuracy of this book and its companion content. If you do find an error, e-mail Microsoft Press Book Support at *mspinput@microsoft.com*. (Please note that product support for Microsoft software is not offered through this address.)

We Want to Hear from You

At Microsoft Press, your satisfaction is our top priority, and your feedback our most valuable asset. Please tell us what you think of this book at:

http://www.microsoft.com/learning/booksurvey

The survey is short, and we read *every one* of your comments and ideas. Thanks in advance for your input.

Stay in Touch

Let's keep the conversation going! We're on Twitter: *http://twitter.com/MicrosoftPress*

Part I
The Basics

Chapter 1
Hello, Windows Phone 7

Sometimes it becomes apparent that previous approaches to a problem haven't quite worked the way you anticipated. Perhaps you just need to clear away the smoky residue of the past, take a deep breath, and try again with a new attitude and fresh ideas. In golf, it's known as a "mulligan"; in schoolyard sports, it's called a "do-over"; and in the computer industry, we say it's a "reboot."

A reboot is what Microsoft has initiated with its new approach to the mobile phone market. With its clean look, striking fonts, and new organizational paradigms, Microsoft Windows Phone 7 not only represents a break with the Windows Mobile past but also differentiates itself from other smartphones currently in the market. Windows Phone 7 devices will be made by several manufacturers and available with a variety of cell providers.

For programmers, Windows Phone 7 is also exciting, for it supports two popular and modern programming platforms: Silverlight and XNA.

Silverlight—a spinoff of the client-based Windows Presentation Foundation (WPF)—has already given Web programmers unprecedented power to develop sophisticated user interfaces with a mix of traditional controls, high-quality text, vector graphics, media, animation, and data binding that run on multiple platforms and browsers. Windows Phone 7 extends Silverlight to mobile devices.

XNA—the three letters stand for something like "XNA is Not an Acronym"—is Microsoft's game platform supporting both 2D sprite-based and 3D graphics with a traditional game-loop architecture. Although XNA is mostly associated with writing games for the Xbox 360 console, developers can also use XNA to target the PC itself, as well as Microsoft's classy audio player, the Zune HD.

Either Silverlight or XNA would make good sense as the sole application platform for the Windows Phone 7, but programmers have a choice. And this we call "an embarrassment of riches."

Targeting Windows Phone 7

All programs for Windows Phone 7 are written in .NET managed code. Although the sample programs in this book are written in the C# programming language, it is also possible to write Windows Phone 7 applications in Visual Basic .NET. The free downloadable Microsoft Visual Studio 2010 Express for Windows Phone includes XNA Game Studio 4.0 and an on-screen phone emulator, and also integrates with Visual Studio 2010. You can develop visuals and animations for Silverlight applications using Microsoft Expression Blend.

The Silverlight and XNA platforms for Windows Phone 7 share some libraries, and you can use some XNA libraries in a Silverlight program and vice versa. But you can't create a program that mixes visuals from both platforms. Maybe that will be possible in the future, but not now. Before you create a Visual Studio project, you must decide whether your million-dollar idea is a Silverlight program or an XNA program.

Generally you'll choose Silverlight for writing programs you might classify as applications or utilities. These programs are built from a combination of markup and code. The markup is the Extensible Application Markup Language, or XAML and pronounced "zammel." The XAML mostly defines a layout of user-interface controls and panels. Code-behind files can also perform some initialization and logic, but are generally relegated to handling events from the controls. Silverlight is great for bringing to the Windows Phone the style of Rich Internet Applications (RIA), including media and the Web. Silverlight for Windows Phone is a version of Silverlight 3 excluding some features not appropriate for the phone, but compensating with some enhancements.

XNA is primarily for writing high-performance games. For 2D games, you define sprites and backgrounds based around bitmaps; for 3D games you define models in 3D space. The action of the game, which includes moving graphical objects around the screen and polling for user input, is synchronized by the built-in XNA game loop.

The differentiation between Silverlight-based applications and XNA-based games is convenient but not restrictive. You can certainly use Silverlight for writing games and you can even write traditional applications using XNA, although doing so might sometimes be challenging.

In particular, Silverlight might be ideal for games that are less graphically oriented, or use vector graphics rather than bitmap graphics, or are paced by user-time rather than clock-time. A Tetris-type program might work quite well in Silverlight. You'll probably find XNA to be a bit harder to stretch into Silverlight territory, however. Implementing a list box in XNA might be considered "fun" by some programmers but a torture by many others.

The first several chapters in this book describe Silverlight and XNA together, and then the book splits into different parts for the two platforms. I suspect that some developers will stick with either Silverlight or XNA exclusively and won't even bother learning the other environment. I hope that's not a common attitude. The good news is that Silverlight and XNA are so dissimilar that you can probably bounce back and forth between them without confusion!

Microsoft has been positioning Silverlight as the front end or "face" of the cloud, so cloud services and Windows Azure form an important part of Windows Phone 7 development. The Windows Phone is "cloud-ready." Programs are location-aware and have access to maps and other data through Bing and Windows Live. One of the available cloud services is Xbox Live, which allows XNA-based programs to participate in online multiplayer games, and can also be accessed by Silverlight applications.

Programs you write for the Windows Phone 7 will be sold and deployed through the Windows Phone Marketplace, which provides registration services and certifies that programs meet minimum standards of reliability, efficiency, and good behavior.

I've characterized Windows Phone 7 as representing a severe break with the past. If you compare it with past versions of Windows Mobile, that is certainly true. But the support of Silverlight, XNA, and C# are not breaks with the past, but a balance of continuity and innovation. As young as they are, Silverlight and XNA have already proven themselves as powerful and popular platforms. Many skilled programmers are already working with either one framework or the other—probably not so many with both just yet—and they have expressed their enthusiasm with a wealth of online information and communities. C# has become the favorite language of many programmers (myself included), and developers can use C# to share libraries between their Silverlight and XNA programs as well as programs for other .NET environments.

The Hardware Chassis

Developers with experience targeting Windows Mobile devices of the past will find significant changes in Microsoft's strategy for the Windows Phone 7. Microsoft has been extremely proactive in defining the hardware specification, often referred to as a "chassis."

Initial releases of Windows Phone 7 devices will have one consistent screen size. (A second screen size is expected in the future.) Many other hardware features are guaranteed to exist on each device.

The front of the phone consists of a multi-touch display and three hardware buttons generally positioned in a row below the display. From left to right, these buttons are called Back, Start, and Search:

- **Back** Programs can use this button for their own navigation needs, much like the Back button on a Web browser. From the home page of a program, the button causes the program to terminate.
- **Start** This button takes the user to the start screen of the phone; it is otherwise inaccessible to programs running on the phone.
- **Search** The operating system uses this button to initiate a search feature.

The initial releases of Windows Phone 7 devices have a display size of 480 × 800 pixels. In the future, screens of 320 × 480 pixels are also expected. There are no other screen options for Windows Phone 7, so obviously these two screen sizes play a very important role in phone development.

In theory, it's usually considered best to write programs that adapt themselves to any screen size, but that's not always possible, particularly with game development. You will probably find yourself specifically targeting these two screen sizes, even to the extent of having conditional code paths and different XAML files for layout that is size-dependent.

I will generally refer to these two sizes as the "large" screen and the "small" screen. The greatest common denominator of the horizontal and vertical dimensions of both screens is 160, so you can visualize the two screens as multiples of 160-pixel squares:

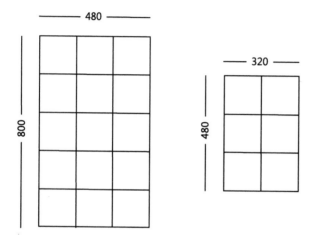

I'm showing these screens in portrait mode because that's usually the way smartphones are designed. The screen of the original Zune is 240 × 320 pixels; the Zune HD is 272 × 480.

Of course, phones can be rotated to put the screen into landscape mode. Some programs might require the phone to be held in a certain orientation; others might be more adaptable.

You have complete control over the extent to which you support orientation. By default, Silverlight applications appear in portrait mode, but you'll probably want to write your Silverlight applications so they adjust themselves to orientation changes. New events are available specifically for the purpose of detecting orientation change, and some orientation shifts are handled automatically. In contrast, game programmers can usually impose a particular orientation on the user. XNA programs use landscape mode by default, but it's easy to override that.

In portrait mode, the small screen is half of an old VGA screen (that is, 640 × 480). In landscape mode, the large screen has a dimension sometimes called WVGA ("wide VGA"). In landscape mode, the small screen has an aspect ratio of 3:2 or 1.5; the large screen has an aspect ratio of 5:3 or 1.66.... Neither of these matches the aspect ratio of television, which for standard definition is 4:3 or 1.33... and for high-definition is 16:9 or 1.77.... The Zune HD screen has an aspect ratio of 16:9.

Like many recent phones and the Zune HD, the Windows Phone 7 displays will likely use OLED ("organic light emitting diode") technology, although this isn't a hardware requirement. OLEDs are different from flat displays of the past in that power consumption is proportional to the light emitted from the display. For example, an OLED display consumes less than half the power of an LCD display of the same size, but only when the screen is mostly black. For an all-white screen, an OLED consumes more than three times the power of an LCD.

Because battery life is extremely important on mobile devices, this characteristic of OLED displays implies an aesthetic of mostly black backgrounds with sparse graphics and light-stroked fonts. Regardless, Windows Phone 7 users can choose between two major color themes: light text on a dark background, or dark text on a light background.

Most user input to a Windows Phone 7 program will come through multi-touch. The screens incorporate capacitance-touch technology, which means that they respond to a human fingertip but not to a stylus or other forms of pressure. Windows Phone 7 screens are required to respond to at least four simultaneous touch-points.

A hardware keyboard is optional. Keep in mind that phones can be designed in different ways, so when the keyboard is in use, the screen might be in either portrait mode or landscape mode. A Silverlight program that uses keyboard input *must* respond to orientation changes so that the user can both view the screen and use the keyboard without wondering what idiot designed the program sideways. An on-screen keyboard is also provided, known in Windows circles as the Soft Input Panel or SIP. XNA programs also have access to the hardware keyboard and SIP.

Sensors and Services

A Windows Phone 7 device is required to contain several other hardware features—sometimes called sensors—and provide some software services, perhaps through the assistance of hardware. These are the ones that affect developers the most:

- **Wi-Fi**   The phone has Wi-Fi for Internet access to complement 3G data access through the cell provider. Software on the phone includes a version of Internet Explorer.

- **Camera**   The phone has at least a 5-megapixel camera with flash. Programs can invoke the camera program for their own input, or register themselves as a Photos Extra Application and appear on a menu to obtain access to photographed images, perhaps for some image processing.

- **Accelerometer**   An accelerometer detects acceleration, which in physics is a change in velocity. When the camera is still, the accelerometer responds to gravity. Programs can obtain a three-dimensional vector that indicates how the camera is oriented with respect to the earth. The accelerometer can also detect sharp movements of the phone.

- **Location**   If the user so desires, the phone can use multiple strategies for determining where it is geographically located. The phone supplements a hardware GPS device with information from the Web or cell phone towers. If the phone is moving, course and speed might also be available.

- **Vibration**   The phone can be vibrated through program control.

- **FM Radio**   An FM Radio is available and accessible through program control.

- **Push Notifications**   Some Web services would normally require the phone to frequently poll the service to obtain updated information. This can drain battery **life. To** help out, a push notification service has been developed that will allow any required polling to occur outside the phone and for the phone to receive notifications only when data has been updated.

File | New | Project

I'll assume that you have Visual Studio 2010 Express for Windows Phone installed, either by itself or supplementing a regular version of Visual Studio 2010. For convenience, I'm going to refer to this development environment simply as "Visual Studio."

The traditional "hello, world" program that displays just a little bit of text might seem silly to nonprogrammers, but programmers have discovered that such a program serves at least two useful purposes: First, the program provides a way to examine how easy (or ridiculously complex) it is to display a simple text string. Second, it gives the programmer an opportunity to experience the process of creating, compiling, and running a program without a lot of distractions. When developing programs that run on a mobile device, this process is a little more complex than customary because you'll be creating and compiling programs on the PC but you'll be deploying and running them on an actual phone or at least an emulator.

This chapter presents programs for both Microsoft Silverlight and Microsoft XNA that display the text "Hello, Windows Phone 7!"

Just to make these programs a little more interesting, I want to display the text in the center of the display. The Silverlight program will use the background and foreground colors selected by the user in the Themes section of the phone's Settings screen. In the XNA program, the text will be white on a dark background to use less power on OLED.

If you're playing along, it's time to bring up Visual Studio and from the File menu select New and then Project.

A First Silverlight Phone Program

In the New Project dialog box, on the left under Installed Templates, choose Visual C# and then Silverlight for Windows Phone. In the middle area, choose Windows Phone Application. Select a location for the project, and enter the project name: SilverlightHelloPhone.

As the project is created you'll see an image of a large-screen phone in portrait mode with a screen area 480 × 800 pixels in size. This is the design view. Although you can interactively pull controls from a toolbox to design the application, I'm going to focus instead on showing you how to write your own code and markup.

Several files have been created for this SilverlightHelloPhone project and are listed under the project name in the Solution Explorer over at the right. In the Properties folder are three files that you can usually ignore when you're just creating little sample Silverlight programs for the phone. Only when you're actually in the process of making a real application do these files become important.

However, you might want to open the WMAppManifest.xml file. In the App tag near the top, you'll see the attribute:

```
Title="SilverlightHelloPhone"
```

That's just the project name you selected. Insert some spaces to make it a little friendlier:

```
Title="Silverlight Hello Phone"
```

This is the name used by the phone and the phone emulator to display the program in the list of installed applications presented to the user. If you're really ambitious, you can also edit the ApplicationIcon.png and Background.png files that the phone uses to visually symbolize the program. The SplashScreenImage.jpg file is what the program displays as it's initializing.

In the standard Visual Studio toolbar under the program's menu, you'll see a drop-down list probably displaying "Windows Phone 7 Emulator." The other choice is "Windows Phone 7 Device." This is how you deploy your program to either the emulator or an actual phone connected to your computer via USB.

Just to see that everything's working OK, select Windows Phone 7 Emulator and press F5 (or select Start Debugging from the Debug menu). Your program will quickly build and in the status bar you'll see the text "Connecting to Windows Phone 7 Emulator…" The first time you use the emulator during a session, it might take a little time to start up. If you leave the emulator running between edit/build/run cycles, Visual Studio doesn't need to establish this connection again.

Soon the phone emulator will appear on the desktop and you'll see the opening screen, followed soon by this little do-nothing Silverlight program as it is deployed and run on the emulator. On the phone you'll see pretty much the same image you saw in the design view.

The phone emulator has a little floating menu at the upper right that comes into view when you move the mouse to that location. You can change orientation through this menu, or change the emulator size. By default, the emulator is displayed at 50% actual size, about the same size as the image on this page. When you display the emulator at 100%, it becomes enormous, and you might wonder "How will I ever fit a phone this big into my pocket?"

The difference involves pixel density. Your computer screen probably has about 100 pixels per inch. (By default, Windows assumes that screens are 96 DPI.) The screen on an actual Windows Phone 7 device is more than 2½ times that. When you display the emulator at 100%, you're seeing all the pixels of the phone's screen, but at about 250% their actual size.

You can terminate execution of this program and return to editing the program either though Visual Studio (using Shift-F5 or by selecting Stop Debugging from the Debug menu) or by clicking the Back button on the emulator.

Don't exit the emulator itself by clicking the X at the top of the floating menu! Keeping the emulator running will make subsequent deployments go much faster.

While the emulator is still running, it retains all programs deployed to it. If you click the arrow at the upper-right of the Start screen, you'll get a list that will include this program identified by the text "Silverlight Hello Phone" and you can run the program again. The program will disappear from this list when you exit the emulator.

If you have a Windows Phone 7 device, you'll need to register for the marketplace at the Windows Phone 7 portal, *http://developer.windowsphone.com*. After you're approved, you'll to connect the phone to your PC and run the Zune desktop software. You can unlock the phone for development by running the Windows Phone Developer Registration program and entering your Windows Live ID. You can then deploy programs to the phone from Visual Studio.

The Standard Silverlight Files

With the project loaded in Visual Studio, take a look at the Solution Explorer for the project. You'll see two pairs of skeleton files: App.xaml and App.xaml.cs, and MainPage.xaml and MainPage.xaml.cs. The App.xaml and MainPage.xaml files are Extensible Application Markup Language (XAML) files, while App.xaml.cs and MainPage.xaml.cs are C# code files. This peculiar naming scheme is meant to imply that the two C# code files are "code-behind" files associated with the two XAML files. They provide code in support of the markup. This is a basic Silverlight concept.

I want to give you a little tour of these four files. If you look at the App.xaml.cs file, you'll see a namespace definition that is the same as the project name and a class named *App* that derives from the Silverlight class *Application*. Here's an excerpt showing the general structure:

Silverlight Project: **SilverlightHelloPhone**   File: **App.xaml.cs** (excerpt)

```
namespace SilverlightHelloPhone
{
    public partial class App : Application
    {
        public App()
        {
            . . .
            InitializeComponent();
            . . .
        }
        . . .
    }
}
```

All Silverlight programs contain an *App* class that derives from *Application*; this class performs application-wide initialization, startup, and shutdown chores. You'll notice this class is defined as a *partial* class, meaning that the project should probably include another C# file that contains additional members of the *App* class. But where is it?

The project also contains an App.xaml file, which has an overall structure like this:

Silverlight Project: SilverlightHelloPhone File: **App.xaml (excerpt)**

```
<Application
    x:Class="SilverlightHelloPhone.App"
    xmlns="http://schemas.microsoft.com/winfx/2006/xaml/presentation"
    xmlns:x="http://schemas.microsoft.com/winfx/2006/xaml"
    xmlns:phone="clr-namespace:Microsoft.Phone.Controls;assembly=Microsoft.Phone"
    xmlns:shell="clr-namespace:Microsoft.Phone.Shell;assembly=Microsoft.Phone">
    ...
</Application>
```

You'll recognize this file as XML, but more precisely it is a XAML file, which is an important part of Silverlight programming. In particular, developers often use the App.xaml file for storing *resources* that are used throughout the application. These resources might include color schemes, gradient brushes, styles, and so forth.

The root element is *Application*, which is the Silverlight class that the *App* class derives from. The root element contains four XML namespace declarations. Two are common in all Silverlight applications; two are unique to the phone.

The first XML namespace declaration ("xmlns") is the standard namespace for Silverlight, and it helps the compiler locate and identify Silverlight classes such as *Application* itself. As with most XML namespace declarations, this URI doesn't actually point to anything; it's just a URI that Microsoft owns and which it has defined for this purpose.

The second XML namespace declaration is associated with XAML itself, and it allows the file to reference some elements and attributes that are part of XAML rather than specifically Silverlight. By convention, this namespace is associated with a prefix of "x" (meaning "XAML").

Among the several attributes supported by XAML and referenced with this "x" prefix is *Class*, which is often pronounced "x class." In this particular XAML file *x:Class* is assigned the name *SilverlightHelloPhone.App*. This means that a class named *App* in the .NET *SilverlightHelloPhone* namespace derives from the Silverlight *Application* class, the root element. It's the same class definition you saw in the App.xaml.cs file but with very different syntax.

The App.xaml.cs and App.xaml files really define two halves of the same *App* class. During compilation, Visual Studio parses App.xaml and generates another code file named App.g.cs. The "g" stands for "generated." If you want to look at this file, you can find it in the \obj\ Debug subdirectory of the project. The App.g.cs file contains another partial definition of the *App* class, and it contains a method named *InitializeComponent* that is called from the constructor in the App.xaml.cs file.

You're free to edit the App.xaml and App.xaml.cs files, but don't mess around with App.g.cs. That file is recreated when you build the project.

When a program is run, the *App* class creates an object of type *PhoneApplicationFrame* and sets that object to its own *RootVisual* property. This frame is 480 pixels wide and 800 pixels tall and occupies the entire display surface of the phone. The *PhoneApplicationFrame* object then behaves somewhat like a web browser by navigating to an object called *MainPage*.

MainPage is the second major class in every Silverlight program and is defined in the second pair of files, MainPage.xaml and MainPage.xaml.cs. In smaller Silverlight programs, it is in these two files that you'll be spending most of your time.

Aside from a long list of *using* directives, the MainPage.xaml.cs file is very simple:

Silverlight Project: SilverlightHelloPhone   File: MainPage.xaml.cs (excerpt)

```
using System;
using System.Collections.Generic;
using System.Linq;
using System.Net;
using System.Windows;
using System.Windows.Controls;
using System.Windows.Documents;
using System.Windows.Input;
using System.Windows.Media;
using System.Windows.Media.Animation;
using System.Windows.Shapes;
using Microsoft.Phone.Controls;

namespace SilverlightHelloPhone
{
    public partial class MainPage : PhoneApplicationPage
    {
        // Constructor
        public MainPage()
        {
            InitializeComponent();
        }
    }
}
```

The *using* directives for namespaces that begin with the words *System.Windows* are for the Silverlight classes; sometimes you'll need to supplement these with some other *using* directives as well. The *Microsoft.Phone.Controls* namespace contains extensions to Silverlight for the phone, including the *PhoneApplicationPage* class.

Again, we see another *partial* class definition. This one defines a class named *MainPage* that derives from the Silverlight class *PhoneApplicationPage*. This is the class that defines the visuals you'll actually see on the screen when you run the SilverlightHelloPhone program.

The other half of this *MainPage* class is defined in the MainPage.xaml file. Here's the nearly complete file, reformatted a bit to fit the printed page, and excluding a section that's commented out at the end, but still a rather frightening chunk of markup:

Silverlight Project: SilverlightHelloPhone   File: MainPage.xaml (almost complete)

```
<phone:PhoneApplicationPage
    x:Class="SilverlightHelloPhone.MainPage"
    xmlns="http://schemas.microsoft.com/winfx/2006/xaml/presentation"
    xmlns:x="http://schemas.microsoft.com/winfx/2006/xaml"
    xmlns:phone="clr-namespace:Microsoft.Phone.Controls;assembly=Microsoft.Phone"
    xmlns:shell="clr-namespace:Microsoft.Phone.Shell;assembly=Microsoft.Phone"
    xmlns:d="http://schemas.microsoft.com/expression/blend/2008"
    xmlns:mc="http://schemas.openxmlformats.org/markup-compatibility/2006"
    mc:Ignorable="d" d:DesignWidth="480" d:DesignHeight="768"
    FontFamily="{StaticResource PhoneFontFamilyNormal}"
    FontSize="{StaticResource PhoneFontSizeNormal}"
    Foreground="{StaticResource PhoneForegroundBrush}"
    SupportedOrientations="Portrait" Orientation="Portrait"
    shell:SystemTray.IsVisible="True">

    <!--LayoutRoot is the root grid where all page content is placed-->
    <Grid x:Name="LayoutRoot" Background="Transparent">
        <Grid.RowDefinitions>
            <RowDefinition Height="Auto"/>
            <RowDefinition Height="*"/>
        </Grid.RowDefinitions>

        <!--TitlePanel contains the name of the application and page title-->
        <StackPanel x:Name="TitlePanel" Grid.Row="0" Margin="12,17,0,28">
            <TextBlock x:Name="ApplicationTitle" Text="MY APPLICATION"
                    Style="{StaticResource PhoneTextNormalStyle}"/>
            <TextBlock x:Name="PageTitle" Text="page name" Margin="9,-7,0,0"
                    Style="{StaticResource PhoneTextTitle1Style}"/>
        </StackPanel>

        <!--ContentPanel - place additional content here-->
        <Grid x:Name="ContentPanel" Grid.Row="1" Margin="12,0,12,0">
        </Grid>
    </Grid>
</phone:PhoneApplicationPage>
```

The first four XML namespace declarations are the same as in App.xaml. As in the App .xaml file, an *x:Class* attribute also appears in the root element. Here it indicates that the *MainPage* class in the *SilverlightHelloPhone* namespace derives from the Silverlight *PhoneApplicationPage* class. This *PhoneApplicationPage* class requires its own XML namespace declaration because it is not a part of standard Silverlight.

The "d" (for "designer") and "mc" (for "markup compatibility") namespace declarations are for the benefit of XAML design programs, such as Expression Blend and the designer in

Visual Studio itself. The *DesignerWidth* and *DesignerHeight* attributes are ignored during compilation.

The compilation of the program generates a file name MainPage.g.cs that contains another partial class definition for *MainPage* (you can look at it in the \obj\Debug subdirectory) with the *InitializeComponent* method called from the constructor in MainPage.xaml.cs.

In theory, the App.g.cs and MainPage.g.cs files generated during the build process are solely for internal use by the compiler and can be ignored by the programmer. However, sometimes when a buggy program raises an exception, one of these files comes popping up into view. It might help your understanding of the problem to have seen these files before they mysteriously appear in front of your face. However, don't try to edit these files to fix the problem! The real problem is probably somewhere in the corresponding XAML file.

In the root element of MainPage.xaml you'll see settings for *FontFamily*, *FontSize*, and *Foreground* that apply to the whole page. I'll describe *StaticResource* and this syntax in Chapter 7.

The body of the MainPage.xaml file contains several nested elements named *Grid*, *StackPanel*, and *TextBlock* in a parent-child hierarchy.

Notice the word I used: *element*. In Silverlight programming, this word has two related meanings. It's an XML term used to indicate items delimited by start tags and end tags. But it's also a word used in Silverlight to refer to visual objects, and in fact, the word *element* shows up in the names of two actual Silverlight classes.

Many of the classes you use in Silverlight are part of this important class hierarchy:

Object
  DependencyObject (abstract)
    UIElement (abstract)
      FrameworkElement (abstract)

Besides *UIElement*, many other Silverlight classes derive from *DependencyObject*. But *UIElement* has the distinction of being the class that has the power to appear as a visual object on the screen and to receive user input. (In Silverlight, all visual objects can receive user input.) Traditionally, this user input comes from the keyboard and mouse; on the phone, most user input comes from touch.

The only class that derives from *UIElement* is *FrameworkElement*. The distinction between these two classes is a historical artifact of the Windows Presentation Foundation. In WPF, it is possible for developers to create their own unique frameworks by deriving from *UIElement*. In Silverlight this is not possible, so the distinction is fairly meaningless.

One of the classes that derives from *FrameworkElement* is *Control*, a word more common than *element* in traditional graphical user-interface programming. Some objects commonly referred to as *controls* in other programming environments are more correctly referred to as *elements* in Silverlight. Control derivatives include buttons and sliders that I'll discuss in Chapter 10.

Another class that derives from *FrameworkElement* is *Panel*, which is the parent class to the *Grid* and *StackPanel* elements you see in MainPage.xaml. Panels are elements that can host multiple children and arrange them in particular ways on the screen. I'll discuss panels in more depth in Chapter 9.

Another class that derives from *FrameworkElement* is *TextBlock*, the element you'll use most often in displaying blocks of text up to about a paragraph in length. The two *TextBlock* elements in MainPage.xaml display the two chunks of title text in a new Silverlight program.

PhoneApplicationPage, *Grid*, *StackPanel*, and *TextBlock* are all Silverlight classes. In Markup these become XML elements. Properties of these classes become XML attributes.

The nesting of elements in MainPage.xaml is said to define a *visual tree*. In a Silverlight program for Windows Phone 7, the visual tree always begins with an object of type *PhoneApplicationFrame*, which occupies the entire visual surface of the phone. A Silverlight program for Windows Phone 7 always has one and only one instance of *PhoneApplicationFrame*, referred to informally as the *frame*.

In contrast, a program can have multiple instances of *PhoneApplicationPage*, referred to informally as a *page*. At any one time, the frame hosts one page, but lets you navigate to the other pages. By default, the page does not occupy the full display surface of the frame because it makes room for the system tray (also known as the status bar) at the top of the phone.

Our simple application has only one page, appropriately called *MainPage*. This *MainPage* contains a *Grid*, which contains a *StackPanel* with a couple *TextBlock* elements, and another *Grid*, all in a hierarchical tree. The visual tree of a Silverlight program creates by Visual Studio is:

PhoneApplicationFrame
    PhoneApplicationPage
        Grid named "LayoutRoot"
            StackPanel named "TitlePanel"
                TextBlock named "ApplicationTitle"
                TextBlock named "PageTitle"
            Grid named "ContentPanel"

Our original goal was to create a Silverlight program that displays some text in the center of the display, but given the presence of a couple titles, let's amend that goal to displaying the text in the center of the page apart from the titles. The area of the page for program content is the *Grid* towards the bottom of the file preceded by the comment "ContentPanel - place additional content here." This *Grid* has a name of "ContentPanel" and I'm going to refer to it informally as the "content panel" or "content grid". The area of the screen corresponding to this *Grid* apart from the titles I'll often refer to as the "content area".

In the content grid, you can insert a new *TextBlock*:

Silverlight Project: SilverlightHelloPhone   File: MainPage.xaml (excerpt)

```
<Grid x:Name="ContentPanel" Grid.Row="1" Margin="12,0,12,0">
    <TextBlock Text="Hello, Windows Phone 7!"
               HorizontalAlignment="Center"
               VerticalAlignment="Center" />
</Grid>
```

Text, HorizontalAlignment, and *VerticalAlignment* are all properties of the *TextBlock* class. The *Text* property is of type *string*. The *HorizontalAlignment* and *VerticalAlignment* properties are of numeration types HorizontalAlignment and *VerticalAlignment*, respectively. When you reference an enumeration type in XAML, you only need the member name.

While you're editing MainPage.xaml you might also want to fix the other *TextBlock* elements so that they aren't so generic. Change

```
<TextBlock ... Text="MY APPLICATION" ... />
```

to

```
<TextBlock ... Text="SILVERLIGHT HELLO PHONE" ... />
```

and

```
<TextBlock ... Text="page title" ... />
```

to:

```
<TextBlock ... Text="main page" ... />
```

It doesn't make much sense to have a page title in a Silverlight application with only a single page, and you can delete that second *TextBlock* if you'd like. The changes you make to this XAML file will be reflected in the design view. You can now compile and run this program:

This screen shot—and most of the remaining screen shots in this book—are shown on the pages of this book with a size that approximates the size of the actual phone, surrounded by some simple "chrome" that symbolizes either the actual phone or the phone emulator.

As simple as it is, this program demonstrates some essential concepts of Silverlight programming, including dynamic layout. The XAML file defines a layout of elements in a visual tree. These elements are capable of arranging themselves dynamically. The *HorizontalAlignment* and *VerticalAlignment* properties can put an element in the center of another element, or (as you might suppose) along one of the edges or in one of the corners. *TextBlock* is one of a number of possible elements you can use in a Silverlight program; others include bitmap images, movies, and familiar controls like buttons, sliders, and list boxes.

Color Themes

From the Start screen of the phone or phone emulator, click or touch the right arrow at the upper right and navigate to the Settings page and then select Theme. A Windows Phone 7 theme consists of a Background and an Accent color. For the Background you can select either Dark (light text on a dark background, which you've been seeing) or Light (the opposite). Select the Light theme, run SilverlightHelloPhone again, and express some satisfaction that the theme colors are automatically applied:

Although these colors are applied automatically, you're not stuck with them in your application. If you'd like the text to be displayed in a different color, you can try setting the *Foreground* attribute in the *TextBlock* tag, for example:

```
Foreground="Red"
```

You can put it anywhere in the tag as long as you leave spaces on either side. As you type this attribute, you'll see a list of colors pop up. Silverlight supports the 140 color names supported by many browsers, as well as a bonus 141st color, *Transparent*.

In a real-world program, you'll want to test out any custom colors with the available themes so text doesn't mysteriously disappear or becomes hard to read.

Points and Pixels

Another property of the *TextBlock* that you can easily change is *FontSize*:

```
FontSize="36"
```

But what exactly does this mean?

All dimensions in Silverlight are in units of pixels, and the *FontSize* is no exception. When you specify 36, you get a font that from the top of its ascenders to the bottom of its descenders measures approximately 36 pixels.

But fonts are never this simple. The resultant *TextBlock* will actually have a height more like 48 pixels—about 33% higher than the *FontSize* would imply. This additional space (called *leading*) prevents successive lines of text from jamming against each other.

Traditionally, font sizes are expressed in units of *points*. In classical typography, a point is very close to 1/72nd inch but in digital typography the point is often assumed to be exactly 1/72nd inch. A font with a size of 72 points measures approximately an inch from the top of its characters to the bottom. (I say "approximately" because the point size indicates a typographic design height, and it's really the creator of the font who determines exactly how large the characters of a 72-point font should be.)

How do you convert between pixels and points? Obviously you can't except for a particular output device. On a 600 dots-per-inch (DPI) printer, for example, the 72-point font will be 600 pixels tall.

Desktop video displays in common use today usually have a resolution somewhere in the region of 100 DPI. For example, consider a 21" monitor that displays 1600 pixels horizontally and 1200 pixels vertically. That's 2000 pixels diagonally, which divided by 21" is about 95 DPI.

By default, Microsoft Windows assumes that video displays have a resolution of 96 DPI. Under that assumption, font sizes and pixels are related by the following formulas:

points = ¾ × pixels

pixels = 4/3 × points

Although this relationship applies only to common video displays, people so much enjoy having these conversion formulas, they show up in Windows Phone 7 programming as well.

So, when you set a *FontSize* property such as

```
FontSize="36"
```

you can also claim to be setting a 27-point font.

For a particular point size, increase by 33% to get a pixel size. This is what you set to the *FontSize* property of *TextBlock*. The resultant *TextBlock* will then be another 33% taller than the *FontSize* setting.

The issue of font size becomes more complex when dealing with high-resolution screens found on devices such as Windows Phone 7. The 480 × 800 pixel display has a diagonal of 933 pixels. The phone I used for this book has a screen with about 3½" for a pixel density closer to 264 DPI. (Screen resolution is usually expressed as a multiple of 24.) Roughly that's 2½ times the resolution of conventional video displays.

This doesn't necessarily mean that all the font sizes used on a conventional screen need to be increased by 2½ times on the phone. The higher resolution of the phone—and the closer viewing distance common with phones—allows smaller font sizes to be more readable.

When running in a Web browser, the default Silverlight *FontSize* is 11 pixels, corresponding to a font size of 8.25 points, which is fine for a desktop video display but a little too small for the phone. For that reason, Silverlight for Windows Phone defines a collection of common font sizes that you can use. (I'll describe how these work in Chapter 7.) The standard MainPage .xaml file includes the following attribute in the root element:

```
FontSize="{StaticResource PhoneFontSizeNormal}"
```

This *FontSize* is inherited through the visual tree and applies to all *TextBlock* elements that don't set their own *FontSize* properties. It has a value of 20 pixels—almost double the default Silverlight *FontSize* on the desktop. Using the standard formulas, this 20-pixel *FontSize* corresponds to 15 points, but as actually displayed on the phone, it's about 2/5 the size that a 15-point font would appear in printed text.

The actual height of the *TextBlock* displaying text with this font is about 33% more than the *FontSize*, in this case about 27 pixels.

The XAP is a ZIP

If you navigate to the \bin\Debug directory of the Visual Studio project for SilverlightHelloPhone, you'll find a file named SilverlightHelloPhone.xap. This is commonly referred to as a XAP file, pronounced "zap." This is the file that is deployed to the phone or phone emulator.

The XAP file is a package of other files, in the very popular compression format known as ZIP. (Shouting "The XAP is a ZIP" in a crowded room will quickly attract other Silverlight programmers.) If you rename SilverlightHelloPhone.xap to SilverlightHelloPhone.zip, you can look inside. You'll see several bitmap files that are part of the project, an XML file, a XAML file, and a SilverlightHelloPhone.dll file, which is the compiled binary of your program.

Any assets that your program needs can be made part of the Visual Studio project and added to this XAP file. Your program can access these files at runtime. I'll discuss some of the concepts in Chapter 4.

An XNA Program for the Phone

Next up on the agenda is an XNA program that displays a little greeting in the center of the screen. While text is often prevalent in Silverlight applications, it is less common in graphical games. In games, text is usually relegated to describing how the game works or displaying the score, so the very concept of a "hello, world" program doesn't quite fit in with the whole XNA programming paradigm.

In fact, XNA doesn't even have any built-in fonts. You might think that an XNA program running on the phone can make use of the same native fonts as Silverlight programs, but this is not so. Silverlight uses vector-based TrueType fonts and XNA doesn't know anything about such exotic concepts. To XNA, everything is a bitmap, including fonts.

If you wish to use a particular font in your XNA program, that font must be embedded into the executable as a collection of bitmaps for each character. XNA Game Studio (which is integrated into Visual Studio) makes the actual process of font embedding very easy, but it raises some thorny legal issues. You can't legally distribute an XNA program unless you can also legally distribute the embedded font, and with most of the fonts distributed with Windows itself or Windows applications, this is not the case.

To help you out of this legal quandary, Microsoft licensed some fonts from Ascender Corporation specifically for the purpose of allowing you to embed them in your XNA programs. Here they are:

Kootenay	Lindsey
Miramonte	Pescadero
Miramonte Bold	**Pescadero Bold**
Pericles	Segoe UI Mono
Pericles Light	**Segoe UI Mono Bold**

Notice that the Pericles font uses small capitals for lower-case letters, so it's probably suitable only for headings.

From the File menu of Visual Studio select New and Project. On the left of the dialog box, select Visual C# and XNA Game Studio 4.0. In the middle, select Windows Phone Game (4.0). Select a location and enter a project name of XnaHelloPhone.

Visual Studio creates two projects, one for the program and the other for the program's content. XNA programs usually contain lots of content, mostly bitmaps and 3D models, but fonts as well. To add a font to this program, right-click the Content project (labeled "XnaHelloPhoneContent (Content)" and from the pop-up menu choose Add and New Item. Choose Sprite Font, leave the filename as SpriteFont1.spritefont, and click Add.

The word "sprite" is common in game programming and usually refers to a small bitmap that can be moved very quickly, much like the sprites you might encounter in an enchanted forest. In XNA, even fonts are sprites.

You'll see SpriteFont1.spritefont show up in the file list of the Content directory, and you can edit an extensively commented XML file describing the font.

XNA Project: XnaHelloPhone   File: **SpriteFont1.spritefont** (complete w/o comments)

```
<XnaContent xmlns:Graphics="Microsoft.Xna.Framework.Content.Pipeline.Graphics">
  <Asset Type="Graphics:FontDescription">
    <FontName>Segoe UI Mono</FontName>
    <Size>14</Size>
    <Spacing>0</Spacing>
    <UseKerning>true</UseKerning>
    <Style>Regular</Style>
    <CharacterRegions>
      <CharacterRegion>
        <Start>&#32;</Start>
        <End>&#126;</End>
      </CharacterRegion>
    </CharacterRegions>
  </Asset>
</XnaContent>
```

Within the *FontName* tags you'll see Segoe UI Mono, but you can change that to one of the other fonts I listed earlier. If you want Pericles Light, put the whole name in there, but if you want Miramonte Bold or Pescadero Bold or Segoe UI Mono Bold, use just Miramonte or Pescadero or Segoe UI Mono, and enter the word Bold between the Style tags. You can use Bold for the other fonts as well, but for the other fonts, bold will be synthesized, while for Miramonte or Pescadero or Segoe UI Mono, you'll get the font actually designed for bold.

The *Size* tags indicate the point size of the font. In XNA as in Silverlight, you deal almost exclusively with pixel coordinates and dimensions, but the conversion between points and pixels used within XNA is based on 96 DPI displays. The point size of 14 becomes a pixel size of 18-2/3 within your XNA program. This is very close to the 15-point and 20-pixel "normal" *FontSize* in Silverlight for Windows Phone.

The *CharacterRegions* section of the file indicates the ranges of hexadecimal Unicode character encodings you need. The default setting from 0x32 through 0x126 includes all the non-control characters of the ASCII character set.

The filename of SpriteFont1.spritefont is not very descriptive. I like to rename it to something that describes the actual font; if you're sticking with the default font settings, you can rename it to Segoe14.spritefont. If you look at the properties for this file—right-click the filename and select Properties—you'll see an Asset Name that is also the filename without the extension: Segoe14. This Asset Name is what you use to refer to the font in your program to load the font. If you want to confuse yourself, you can change the Asset Name independently of the filename.

In its initial state, the XNAHelloPhone project contains two C# code files: Program.cs and Game1.cs. The first is very simple and turns out to be irrelevant for Windows Phone 7 games! A preprocessor directive enables the *Program* class only if a symbol of WINDOWS or XBOX is defined. When compiling Windows Phone programs, the symbol WINDOWS_PHONE is defined instead.

For most small games, you'll be spending all your time in the Game1.cs file. The *Game1* class derives from *Game* and in its pristine state it defines two fields: *graphics* and *spriteBatch*. To those two fields I want to add three more:

XNA Project: XnaHelloPhone   File: **Game1.cs (excerpt showing fields)**

```
namespace XnaHelloPhone
{
    public class Game1 : Microsoft.Xna.Framework.Game
    {
        GraphicsDeviceManager graphics;
        SpriteBatch spriteBatch;
        string text = "Hello, Windows Phone 7!";
        SpriteFont segoe14;
        Vector2 textPosition;
        ...
    }
}
```

These three new fields simply indicate the text that the program will display, the font it will use to display it, and the position of the text on the screen. That position is specified in pixel coordinates relative to the upper-left corner of the display. The *Vector2* structure has two fields named *X* and *Y* of type *float*. For performance purposes, all floating-point values in XNA are single-precision. (Silverlight is all double-precision.) The *Vector2* structure is often used for two-dimensional points, sizes, and even vectors.

When the game is run on the phone, the *Game1* class is instantiated and the *Game1* constructor is executed. This standard code is provided for you:

XNA Project: XnaHelloPhone   File: **Game1.cs (excerpt)**

```
public Game1()
{
    graphics = new GraphicsDeviceManager(this);
    Content.RootDirectory = "Content";

    // Frame rate is 30 fps by default for Windows Phone.
    TargetElapsedTime = TimeSpan.FromTicks(333333);
}
```

The first statement initializes the *graphics* field. In the second statement, *Content* is a property of *Game* of type *ContentManager*, and *RootDirectory* is a property of that class.

Setting this property to "Content" is consistent with the Content directory that is currently storing the 14-point Segoe font. The third statement sets a time for the program's game loop, which governs the pace at which the program updates the video display. The Windows Phone 7 screen is refreshed at 30 frames per second.

After *Game1* is instantiated, a *Run* method is called on the *Game1* instance, and the base *Game* class initiates the process of starting up the game. One of the first steps is a call to the *Initialize* method, which a *Game* derivative can override. XNA Game Studio generates a skeleton method to which I won't add anything:

XNA Project: XnaHelloPhone   File: Game1.cs (excerpt)

```
protected override void Initialize()
{
    base.Initialize();
}
```

The *Initialize* method is not the place to load the font or other content. That comes a little later when the base class calls the *LoadContent* method.

XNA Project: XnaHelloPhone   File: Game1.cs (excerpt)

```
protected override void LoadContent()
{
    spriteBatch = new SpriteBatch(GraphicsDevice);

    segoe14 = this.Content.Load<SpriteFont>("Segoe14");
    Vector2 textSize = segoe14.MeasureString(text);
    Viewport viewport = this.GraphicsDevice.Viewport;

    textPosition = new Vector2((viewport.Width - textSize.X) / 2,
                               (viewport.Height - textSize.Y) / 2);

}
```

The first statement in this method is provided for you. You'll see shortly how this *spriteBatch* object is used to shoot sprites out to the display.

The other statements are ones I've added, and you'll notice I tend to preface property names like *Content* and *GraphicsDevice* with the keyword *this* to remind myself that they're properties and not a static class. As I mentioned, the *Content* property is of type *ContentManager*. The generic *Load* method allows loading content into the program, in this case content of type *SpriteFont*. The name in quotation marks is the Asset Name as indicated in the content's properties. This statement stores the loaded font in the *segoe14* field of type *SpriteFont*.

In XNA, sprites (including text strings) are usually displayed by specifying the pixel coordinates relative to the upper-left corner or the sprite relative to the upper-left corner of the display. To calculate these coordinates, it's helpful to know both the screen size and the size of the text when displayed with a particular font.

The *SpriteFont* class has a very handy method named *MeasureString* that returns a *Vector2* object with the size of a particular text string in pixels. (For the 14-point Segoe UI Mono font, which has an equivalent height of 18-2/3 pixels, the *MeasureString* call returns a height of 28 pixels.)

An XNA program generally uses the *Viewport* property of the *GraphicsDevice* class to obtain the size of the screen. This is accessible through the *GraphicsDevice* property of *Game* and provides *Width* and *Height* properties.

It is then straightforward to calculate *textPosition*—the point relative to the upper-left corner of the viewport where the upper-left corner of the text string is to be displayed.

The initialization phase of the program has now concluded, and the real action begins. The program enters the *game loop*. In synchronization with the 30 frame-per-second refresh rate of the video display, two methods in your program are called: *Update* followed by *Draw*. Back and forth: *Update, Draw, Update, Draw, Update, Draw*.... (It's actually somewhat more complicated than this if the *Update* method requires more than 1/30th of a second to complete, but I'll discuss these timing issues in more detail in a later chapter.)

In the *Draw* method you want to draw on the display. But that's *all* you want to do. If you need to perform some calculations in preparation for drawing, you should do those in the *Update* method. The *Update* method prepares the program for the *Draw* method. Very often an XNA program will be moving sprites around the display based on user input. For the phone, this user input mostly involves fingers touching the screen. All handling of user input should also occur during the *Update* method. You'll see an example in Chapter 3.

You should write your *Update* and *Draw* methods so that they execute as quickly as possible. That's rather obvious, I guess, but here's something very important that might not be so obvious:

You should avoid code in *Update* and *Draw* that routinely allocates memory from the program's local heap. Eventually the .NET garbage collector will want to reclaim some of this memory, and while the garbage collector is doing its job, your game might stutter a bit. Throughout the chapters on XNA programming, you'll see techniques to avoid allocating memory from the heap.

Your *Draw* methods probably won't contain any questionable code; it's usually in the *Update* method where trouble lurks. Avoid any *new* expressions involving classes. These always cause memory allocation. Instantiating a structure is fine, however, because structure instances are stored on the stack and not in the heap. (XNA uses structures rather than classes for many types of objects you'll often need to create in *Update*.) But heap allocations can also occur without explicit *new* expressions. For example, concatenating two strings creates another string on the heap. If you need to perform string manipulation in *Update*, you should use *StringBuilder*. Conveniently, XNA provides methods to display text using *StringBuilder* objects.

In XnaHelloPhone, however, the *Update* method is trivial. The text displayed by the program is anchored in one spot. All the necessary calculations have already been performed in the *LoadContent* method. For that reason, the *Update* method will be left simply as XNA Game Studio originally created it:

XNA Project: XnaHelloPhone   File: Game1.cs (excerpt)

```
protected override void Update(GameTime gameTime)
{
    if (GamePad.GetState(PlayerIndex.One).Buttons.Back == ButtonState.Pressed)
        this.Exit();

    base.Update(gameTime);
}
```

The default code uses the static *GamePad* class to check if the phone's hardware Back button has been pressed and uses that to exit the game.

Finally, there is the *Draw* method. The version created for you simply colors the background with a light blue:

XNA Project: XnaHelloPhone   File: Game1.cs (excerpt)

```
protected override void Draw(GameTime gameTime)
{
    GraphicsDevice.Clear(Color.CornflowerBlue);

    base.Draw(gameTime);
}
```

The color known as CornflowerBlue has achieved iconic status in the XNA programming community. When you're developing an XNA program, the appearance of the light blue screen is very comforting because it means the program has at least gotten as far as *Draw*. But if you want to conserve power on OLED displays, you want to go with darker backgrounds. In my revised version, I've compromised by setting the background to a darker blue. As in Silverlight, XNA supports the 140 colors that have come to be regarded as standard. The text is colored white:

XNA Project: XnaHelloPhone   File: Game1.cs (excerpt)

```
protected override void Draw(GameTime gameTime)
{
    GraphicsDevice.Clear(Color.Navy);

    spriteBatch.Begin();
    spriteBatch.DrawString(segoe14, text, textPosition, Color.White);
    spriteBatch.End();

    base.Draw(gameTime);
}
```

Sprites get out on the display by being bundled into a *SpriteBatch* object, which was created during the call to *LoadContent*. Between calls to *Begin* and *End* there can be multiple calls to *DrawString* to draw text and *Draw* to draw bitmaps. Those are the only options. This particular *DrawString* call references the font, the text to display, the position of the upper-left corner of the text relative to the upper-left corner of the screen, and the color. And here it is:

Oh, that's interesting! By default, Silverlight programs come up in portrait mode, but XNA programs come up in landscape mode. Let's turn the phone or emulator sideways:

Much better!

But this raises a question: Do Silverlight programs always run in portrait mode and XNA programs always run in landscape mode?

Is program biology destiny?

Chapter 2
Getting Oriented

By default, Silverlight programs for Windows Phone 7 run in portrait mode, and XNA programs run in landscape mode. This chapter discusses how to transcend those defaults and explores other issues involving screen sizes, element sizes, and events.

Silverlight and Dynamic Layout

If you run the SilverlightHelloPhone program from the last chapter, and you turn the phone or emulator sideways, you'll discover that the display doesn't change to accommodate the new orientation. That's easy to fix. In the root *PhoneApplicationPage* tag, of MainPage.xaml change the attribute

```
SupportedOrientations="Portrait"
```

to:

```
SupportedOrientations="PortraitOrLandscape"
```

SupportedOrientations is a property of *PhoneApplicationPage*. It's set to a member of the *SupportedPageOrientation* enumeration, either *Portrait*, *Landscape*, or *PortraitOrLandscape*.

Recompile. Now when you turn the phone or emulator sideways, the contents of the page shift around accordingly:

The *SupportedOrientations* property also allows you to restrict your program to *Landscape* if you need to.

This response to orientation really shows off dynamic layout in Silverlight. Everything has moved around and some elements have changed size. Silverlight originated in WPF and the desktop, so historically it was designed to react to changes in window sizes and aspect ratios. This facility carries well into the phone.

Two of the most important properties in working with dynamic layout are *HorizontalAlignment* and *VerticalAlignment*. In the last chapter, using these properties to center text in a Silverlight program was certainly easier than performing calculations based on screen size and text size that XNA required.

On the other hand, if you now needed to stack a bunch of text strings, you would probably find it straightforward in XNA, but not so obvious in Silverlight.

Rest assured that there are ways to organize elements in Silverlight. A whole category of elements called *panels* exist solely for that purpose. You can even position elements based on pixel coordinates, if that's your preference. But a full coverage of panels won't come until Chapter 9.

In the meantime, you can try putting multiple elements into the content grid. Normally a *Grid* organizes its content into cells identified by row and column, but this program puts nine *TextBlock* elements in a single-cell *Grid* to demonstrate the use of *HorizontalAlignment* and *VerticalAlignment* in nine different combinations:

Silverlight Project: SilverlightCornersAndEdges   File: MainPage.xaml

```
<Grid x:Name="ContentPanel" Grid.Row="1" Margin="12,0,12,0">
    <TextBlock Text="Top-Left"
               VerticalAlignment="Top"
               HorizontalAlignment="Left" />

    <TextBlock Text="Top-Center"
               VerticalAlignment="Top"
               HorizontalAlignment="Center" />

    <TextBlock Text="Top-Right"
               VerticalAlignment="Top"
               HorizontalAlignment="Right" />

    <TextBlock Text="Center-Left"
               VerticalAlignment="Center"
               HorizontalAlignment="Left" />

    <TextBlock Text="Center"
               VerticalAlignment="Center"
               HorizontalAlignment="Center" />

    <TextBlock Text="Center-Right"
               VerticalAlignment="Center"
               HorizontalAlignment="Right" />
```

```
            <TextBlock Text="Bottom-Left"
                       VerticalAlignment="Bottom"
                       HorizontalAlignment="Left" />

            <TextBlock Text="Bottom-Center"
                       VerticalAlignment="Bottom"
                       HorizontalAlignment="Center"  />

            <TextBlock Text="Bottom-Right"
                       VerticalAlignment="Bottom"
                       HorizontalAlignment="Right" />
    </Grid>
```

As with many of the simpler Silverlight programs in this book, I've set the
SupportedOrientations property of *MainPage* to *PortraitOrLandscape*. And here it is turned
sideways:

Although this screen appears to show all the combinations, the program does *not* actually
show the *default* settings of the *HorizontalAlignment* and *VerticalAlignment* properties. The
default settings are enumeration members named *Stretch*. If you try them out, you'll see that
the *TextBlock* sits in the upper-left corner, just as with values of *Top* and *Left*. But what won't
be so obvious is that the *TextBlock* occupies the entire interior of the *Grid*. The *TextBlock* has
a transparent background (and you can't set an alternative) so it's a little difficult to tell the
difference. But I'll demonstrate the effect in the next chapter.

Obviously the *HorizontalAlignment* and *VerticalAlignment* properties are very important
in the layout system in Silverlight. So is *Margin*. Try adding a *Margin* setting to the first
TextBlock in this program:

```
<TextBlock Text="Top-Left"
           VerticalAlignment="Top"
           HorizontalAlignment="Left"
           Margin="100" />
```

Now there's a 100-pixel breathing room between the *TextBlock* and the left and top edges of the client area. The *Margin* property is of type *Thickness*, a structure that has four properties named *Left*, *Top*, *Right*, and *Bottom*. If you specify only one number in XAML, that's used for all four sides. You can also specify two numbers like this:

```
Margin="100 200"
```

The first applies to the left and right; the second to the top and bottom. With four numbers

```
Margin="100 200 50 300"
```

they're in the order left, top, right, and bottom. Watch out: If the margins are too large, the text or parts of the text will disappear. Silverlight preserves the margins even at the expense of truncating the element.

If you set both *HorizontalAlignment* and *VerticalAlignment* to *Center*, and set *Margin* to four different numbers, you'll notice that the text is no longer visually centered in the content area. Silverlight bases the centering on the size of the element including the margins.

TextBlock also has a *Padding* property:

```
<TextBlock Text="Top-Left"
           VerticalAlignment="Top"
           HorizontalAlignment="Left"
           Padding="100 200" />
```

Padding is also of type *Thickness*, and when used with the *TextBlock*, *Padding* is visually indistinguishable from *Margin*. But they are definitely different: *Margin* is space on the outside of the *TextBlock*; *Padding* is space inside the *TextBlock* not occupied by the text itself. If you were using *TextBlock* for touch events (as I'll demonstrate in the next chapter), it would respond to touch in the *Padding* area but not the *Margin* area.

The *Margin* property is defined by *FrameworkElement*; in real-life Silverlight programming, almost everything gets a non-zero *Margin* property to prevent the elements from being jammed up against each other. The *Padding* property is rarer; it's defined only by *TextBlock*, *Border*, and *Control*.

It's possible to use *Margin* to position multiple elements within a single-cell *Grid*. It's not common—and there are better ways to do the job—but it is possible. I'll have an example in Chapter 5.

What's crucial to realize is what we're *not* doing. We're not explicitly setting the *Width* and *Height* of the *TextBlock* like in some antique programming environment:

```
<TextBlock Text="Top-Left"
           VerticalAlignment="Top"
           HorizontalAlignment="Left"
           Width="100"
           Height="50" />
```

You're second guessing the size of the *TextBlock* without knowing as much about the element as the *TextBlock* itself. In some cases, setting *Width* and *Height* is appropriate, but not here.

The *Width* and *Height* properties are of type *double*, and the default values are those special floating-point values called Not a Number or NaN. If you need to get the *actual* width and height of an element as it's rendered on the screen, access the properties named *ActualWidth* and *ActualHeight* instead. (But watch out: These values will have non-zero values only when the element has been rendered on the screen.)

Some useful events are also available for obtaining information involving element sizes. The *Loaded* event is fired when visuals are first arranged on the screen; *SizeChanged* is supported by elements to indicate when they've changed size; *LayoutUpdated* is useful when you want notification that a layout cycle has occurred, such as occurs when orientation changes.

The SilverlightWhatSize project demonstrates the use of the *SizeChanged* method by displaying the sizes of several elements in the standard page. It's not often that you need these precise sizes, but they might be of interest occasionally.

You can associate a particular event with an event handler right in XAML, but the actual event handler must be implemented in code. When you type an event name in XAML (such as *SizeChanged*) Visual Studio will offer to create an event handler for you. That's what I did with the *SizeChanged* event for the content grid:

SilverlightProject: SilverlightWhatSize   File: **MainPage.xaml (excerpt)**

```
<Grid x:Name="ContentPanel" Grid.Row="1" Margin="12,0,12,0"
        SizeChanged="ContentPanel_SizeChanged">
    <TextBlock Name="txtblk"
                HorizontalAlignment="Center"
                VerticalAlignment="Center" />
</Grid>
```

I also assigned the *TextBlock* property *Name* to "txtblk." The *Name* property plays a very special role in Silverlight. If you compile the program at this point and look inside MainPage.g.cs—the code file that the compiler generates based on the MainPage.xaml file— you'll see a bunch of fields in the *MainPage* class, among them a field named *txtblk* of type *TextBlock*:

```
internal System.Windows.Controls.TextBlock txtblk;
```

You'll also notice that this field is assigned from code in the *InitializeComponent* method:

```
this.txtblk = ((System.Windows.Controls.TextBlock)(this.FindName("txtblk")));
```

This means that anytime after the constructor in MainPage.xaml.cs calls *InitializeComponent*, any code in the *MainPage* class can reference that *TextBlock* element in the XAML file using the *txtblk* variable stored as a field in the class.

You'll notice that several of the elements in the MainPage.xaml file are assigned names with *x:Name* rather than *Name*. As used in XAML, these two attributes are basically equivalent. *Name* only works with elements (that is, instances of classes that derive from *FrameworkElement* because that's where the *Name* property is defined) but *x:Name* works with everything.

This means that code in the MainPage class in MainPage.xaml.cs has a field available named *ContentPanel* to reference the standard *Grid* that appears in MainPage.xaml, and similarly for the other elements in MainPage.xaml.

Assigning names to elements is one of two primary ways in which code and XAML interact. The second way is for the element defined in XAML to fire an event that is handled in code. Here's the handler for the *SizeChanged* event of the content grid as Visual Studio created it:

SilverlightProject: **SilverlightWhatSize**   File: **MainPage.xaml.cs (excerpt)**

```
private void ContentPanel_SizeChanged(object sender, SizeChangedEventArgs e)
{

}
```

I usually don't like the way Visual Studio creates these handlers. Normally I remove the keyword *private*, I rename the event handlers to start them with the word *On,* and I eliminate underscores. This one I'd call *OnContentPanelSizeChanged*. I also tend to change the event arguments from *e* to *args*.

But for this program I'll leave it as is. On entry to the method, the *sender* argument is the element that fired the event, in this case the *Grid* named *ContentPanel*. The second argument contains information specific to the event.

I added a body to this method that just sets the *Text* property of *txtblk* to a longish multi-line string:

SilverlightProject: **SilverlightWhatSize**   File: **MainPage.xaml.cs (excerpt)**

```
private void ContentPanel_SizeChanged(object sender, SizeChangedEventArgs e)
{
    txtblk.Text = String.Format("ContentPanel size: {0}\n" +
                                "TitlePanel size: {1}\n" +
                                "LayoutRoot size: {2}\n" +
                                "MainPage size: {3}\n" +
```

```
                                        "Frame size: {4}",
                                        e.NewSize,
                                        new Size(TitlePanel.ActualWidth, TitlePanel.
ActualHeight),
                                        new Size(LayoutRoot.ActualWidth, LayoutRoot.
ActualHeight),
                                        new Size(this.ActualWidth, this.ActualHeight),
                                        Application.Current.RootVisual.RenderSize);
        }
```

The five items are of type *Size*, a structure with *Width* and *Height* properties. The size of the *ContentPanel* itself is available from the *NewSize* property of the event arguments. For the next three, I used the *ActualWidth* and *ActualHeight* properties.

Notice the last item. The static property *Application.Current* returns the *Application* object associated with the current process. This is the *App* object created by the program. It has a property named *RootVisual* that references the frame, but the property is defined to be of type *UIElement*. The *ActualWidth* and *ActualHeight* properties are defined by *FrameworkElement*, the class that derives from *UIElement*. Rather than casting, I chose to use a property of type *Size* that *UIElement* defines.

The first *SizeChanged* event occurs when the page is created and laid out, that is, when the content grid changes size from 0 to a finite value:

The 32-pixel difference between the *MainPage* size and the frame size accommodates the system tray at the top. You can prevent that tray from appearing while your application is running (and in effect, get access to the entire screen) by changing an attribute in the root element of MainPage.xaml from:

```
shell:SystemTray.IsVisible="True"
```

to

```
shell:SystemTray.IsVisible="False"
```

The syntax of this attribute might seem a little peculiar. *SystemTray* is a class in the *Microsoft .Phone.Shell* namespace and *IsVisible* is a property of that class, and both the class and property appear together because it's a special kind of property called an *attached property*.

The topmost *Grid* named *LayoutRoot* is the same size as *MainPage*. The vertical size of the *TitlePanel* (containing the two titles) and the vertical size of *ContentPanel* don't add up to the vertical size of *LayoutRoot* because of the 45-pixel vertical margin (17 pixels on the top and 28 pixels on the bottom) of the *TitlePanel*.

Subsequent *SizeChanged* events occur when something in the visual tree causes a size change, or when the phone changes orientation:

Notice that the frame doesn't change orientation. In the landscape view, the system tray takes away 72 pixels of width from *MainPage*.

Orientation Events

In many of the simpler Silverlight programs in this book, I'll set *SupportedOrientations* to *PortraitOrLandscape*, and try to write orientation-independent applications. For Silverlight programs that get text input, it's crucial for the program to be aligned with the hardware keyboard (if one exists) and the location of that keyboard can't be anticipated.

Obviously there is more to handling orientation changes than just setting the *SupportedOrientations* property! In some cases, you might want to manipulate your layout from code in the page class. If you need to perform any special handling, both *PhoneApplicationFrame* and *PhoneApplicationPage* include *OrientationChanged* events. *PhoneApplicationPage* supplements that event with a convenient and equivalent protected overridable method called *OnOrientationChanged*.

The *MainPage* class in the SilverlightOrientationDisplay project shows how to override *OnOrientationChanged*, but what it does with this information is merely to display the current orientation. The content grid in this project contains a simple *TextBlock*:

SilverlightProject: SilverlightOrientationDisplay   File: **MainPage.xaml** (excerpt)

```
<Grid x:Name="ContentPanel" Grid.Row="1" Margin="12,0,12,0">
    <TextBlock Name="txtblk"
               HorizontalAlignment="Center"
               VerticalAlignment="Center" />
</Grid>
```

Here's the complete code-behind file. The constructor initializes the *TextBlock* text with the current value of the *Orientation* property, which is a member of the *PageOrientation* enumeration:

SilverlightProject: SilverlightOrientationDisplay   File: **MainPage.xaml.cs**

```
using System.Windows.Controls;
using Microsoft.Phone.Controls;

namespace SilverlightOrientationDisplay
{
    public partial class MainPage : PhoneApplicationPage
    {
        public MainPage()
        {
            InitializeComponent();
            txtblk.Text = Orientation.ToString();
        }

        protected override void OnOrientationChanged(OrientationChangedEventArgs args)
        {
            txtblk.Text = args.Orientation.ToString();
            base.OnOrientationChanged(args);
        }
    }
}
```

The *OnOrientationChanged* method obtains the new value from the event arguments.

XNA Orientation

By default, XNA for Windows Phone is set up for a landscape orientation, perhaps to be compatible with other screens on which games are played. Both landscape orientations are supported, and the display will automatically flip around when you turn the phone from one landscape orientation to the other. If you prefer designing your game for a portrait display, it's easy to do that. In the constructor of the *Game1* class of XnaHelloPhone, try inserting the following statements:

```
graphics.PreferredBackBufferWidth = 320;
graphics.PreferredBackBufferHeight = 480;
```

The *back buffer* is the surface area on which XNA constructs the graphics you display in the *Draw* method. You can control both the size and the aspect ratio of this buffer. Because the buffer width I've specified here is smaller than the buffer height, XNA assumes that I want a portrait display:

Look at that! The back buffer I specified is not the same aspect ratio as the Windows Phone 7 display, so the drawing surface is letter-boxed! The text is larger because it's the same pixel size but now the display resolution has been reduced.

Although you may not be a big fan of the retro graininess of this particular display, you should seriously consider specifying a smaller back buffer if your game doesn't need the high resolution provided by the phone. Performance will improve and battery consumption will decrease. You can set the back buffer to anything from 240 × 240 up to 480 × 800 (for portrait mode) or 800 × 480 (for landscape). XNA uses the aspect ratio to determine whether you want portrait or landscape.

Setting a desired back buffer is also an excellent way to target a specific display dimension in code but allow for devices of other sizes that may come in the future.

By default the back buffer is 800 × 480, but it's actually not displayed at that size. It's scaled down a bit to accommodate the system tray. To get rid of the system tray (and possibly annoy your users who like to always know what time it is) you can set

```
graphics.IsFullScreen = true;
```

in the *Game1* constructor.

It's also possible to have your XNA games respond to orientation changes, but they'll definitely have to be restructured a bit. The simplest type of restructuring to accommodate orientation changes is demonstrated in the XnaOrientableHelloPhone project. The fields now include a *textSize* variable:

XNA Project: XnaOrientableHelloPhone   File: **Game1.cs** (excerpt showing fields)

```
public class Game1 : Microsoft.Xna.Framework.Game
{
    GraphicsDeviceManager graphics;
    SpriteBatch spriteBatch;
    string text = "Hello, Windows Phone 7!";
    SpriteFont segoe14;
    Vector2 textSize;
    Vector2 textPosition;
    . . .
}
```

The *Game1* constructor includes a statement that sets the *SupportedOrientations* property of the *graphics* field:

XNA Project: XnaOrientableHelloPhone   File: **Game1.cs** (excerpt)

```
public Game1()
{
    graphics = new GraphicsDeviceManager(this);
    Content.RootDirectory = "Content";
```

```
        // Allow portrait mode as well
        graphics.SupportedOrientations = DisplayOrientation.Portrait |
                                         DisplayOrientation.LandscapeLeft |
                                         DisplayOrientation.LandscapeRight;

        // Frame rate is 30 fps by default for Windows Phone.
        TargetElapsedTime = TimeSpan.FromTicks(333333);
    }
```

You can also use *SupportedOrientation* to restrict the phone to just one of the two landscape orientations. The statement to support both portrait and landscape looks simple, but there are repercussions. When the orientation changes, the graphics device is effectively reset (which generates some events) and the back buffer dimensions are swapped. You can subscribe to the *OrientationChanged* event of the *GameWindow* class (accessible through the *Window* property) or you can check the *CurrentOrientation* property of the *GameWindow* object.

I chose a little different approach. Here's the new *LoadContent* method, which you'll notice obtains the text size and stores it as a field, but does not get the viewport.

XNA Project: XnaOrientableHelloPhone   File: Game1.cs (excerpt)

```
protected override void LoadContent()
{
    spriteBatch = new SpriteBatch(GraphicsDevice);
    segoe14 = this.Content.Load<SpriteFont>("Segoe14");
    textSize = segoe14.MeasureString(text);
}
```

Instead, the viewport is obtained during the *Update* method because the dimensions of the viewport reflect the orientation of the display.

XNA Project: XnaOrientableHelloPhone   File: Game1.cs (excerpt)

```
protected override void Update(GameTime gameTime)
{
    // Allows the game to exit
    if (GamePad.GetState(PlayerIndex.One).Buttons.Back == ButtonState.Pressed)
        this.Exit();

    Viewport viewport = this.GraphicsDevice.Viewport;
    textPosition = new Vector2((viewport.Width - textSize.X) / 2,
                               (viewport.Height - textSize.Y) / 2);
    base.Update(gameTime);
}
```

Whatever the orientation currently is, the *Update* method calculates a location for the text. The *Draw* method is the same as several you've seen before.

XNA Project: XnaOrientableHelloPhone   File: Game1.cs (excerpt)

```
protected override void Draw(GameTime gameTime)
{
    GraphicsDevice.Clear(Color.Navy);

    spriteBatch.Begin();
    spriteBatch.DrawString(segoe14, text, textPosition, Color.White);
    spriteBatch.End();

    base.Draw(gameTime);
}
```

Now the phone or emulator can be turned between portrait and landscape, and the display will switch as well.

If you need to obtain the size of the phone's display independent of any back buffers or orientation (but taking account of the system tray), that's available from the *ClientBounds* property of the *GameWindow* class, which you can access from the *Window* property of the *Game* class:

```
Rectangle clientBounds = this.Window.ClientBounds;
```

Simple Clocks (*Very* Simple Clocks)

So far in this chapter I've described two Silverlight events—*SizeChanged* and *OrientationChanged*—but used them in different ways. For *SizeChanged*, I associated the event with the event handler in XAML, but for *OrientationChanged*, I overrode the equivalent *OnOrientationChanged* method.

Of course, you can attach handlers to events entirely in code as well. One handy class for Silverlight programs is *DispatcherTimer*, which periodically nudges the program with a *Tick* event and lets the program do some work. A timer is essential for a clock program, for example.

The content grid of the SilverlightSimpleClock project contains just a centered *TextBlock*:

Silverlight Project: **SilverlightSimpleClock**   File: **MainPage.xaml** (excerpt)

```
<Grid x:Name="ContentPanel" Grid.Row="1" Margin="12,0,12,0">
    <TextBlock Name="txtblk"
               HorizontalAlignment="Center"
               VerticalAlignment="Center" />
</Grid>
```

Here's the entire code-behind file. Notice the *using* directive for the *System.Windows. Threading* namespace, which isn't included by default. That's the namespace where *DispatcherTimer* resides:

Silverlight Project: SilverlightSimpleClock   File: MainPage.xaml.cs

```
using System;
using System.Windows.Threading;
using Microsoft.Phone.Controls;

namespace SilverlightSimpleClock
{
    public partial class MainPage : PhoneApplicationPage
    {
        public MainPage()
        {
            InitializeComponent();

            DispatcherTimer tmr = new DispatcherTimer();
            tmr.Interval = TimeSpan.FromSeconds(1);
            tmr.Tick += OnTimerTick;
            tmr.Start();
        }

        void OnTimerTick(object sender, EventArgs args)
        {
            txtblk.Text = DateTime.Now.ToString();
        }
    }
}
```

The constructor initializes the *DispatcherTimer*, instructing it to call *OnTimerTick* once every second. The event handler simply converts the current time to a string to set it to the *TextBlock*.

Although *DispatcherTimer* is defined in the *System.Windows.Threading* namespace, the *OnTimerTick* method is called in the same thread as the rest of the program. If that was not the case, the program wouldn't be able to access the *TextBlock* directly. Silverlight elements and related objects are not thread safe, and they will prohibit access from threads that did not create them. I'll discuss the procedure for accessing Silverlight elements from secondary threads in Chapter 5.

The clock is yet another Silverlight program in this chapter that changes the *Text* property of a *TextBlock* dynamically during runtime. The new value shows up rather magically without any additional work. This is a very different from older graphical environments like Windows API programming or MFC programming, where a program draws "on demand," that is, when an area of a window becomes invalid and needs to be repainted, or when a program deliberately invalidates an area to force painting.

A Silverlight program often doesn't seem to draw at all! Deep inside of Silverlight is a visual composition layer that operates in a retained graphics mode and organizes all the visual elements into a composite whole. Elements such as *TextBlock* exist as actual entities inside this composition layer. At some point, *TextBlock* is rendering itself—and re-rendering itself when one of its properties such as *Text* changes—but what it renders is retained along with the rendered output of all the other elements in the visual tree.

In contrast, an XNA program is actively drawing during every frame of the video display. This is conceptually different from older Windows programming environments as well as Silverlight. It is very powerful, but I'm sure you know quite well what must also come with great power.

Sometimes an XNA program's display is static; the program might not need to update the display every frame. To conserve power, it is possible for the *Update* method to call the *SuppressDraw* method defined by the *Game* class to inhibit a corresponding call to *Draw*. The *Update* method will still be called 30 times per second because it needs to check for user input, but if the code in *Update* calls *SuppressDraw*, *Draw* won't be called during that cycle of the game loop. If the code in *Update* doesn't call *SuppressDraw*, *Draw* will be called.

An XNA clock program doesn't need a timer because a timer is effectively built into the normal game loop. However, the clock I want to code here won't display milliseconds so the display only needs to be updated every second. For that reason it uses the *SuppressDraw* method to inhibit superfluous *Draw* calls.

Here are the XnaSimpleClock fields:

XNA Project: XnaSimpleClock   File: Game1.cs (excerpt showing fields)

```
public class Game1 : Microsoft.Xna.Framework.Game
{
    GraphicsDeviceManager graphics;
    SpriteBatch spriteBatch;
    SpriteFont segoe14;
    Viewport viewport;
    Vector2 textPosition;
    StringBuilder text = new StringBuilder();
    DateTime lastDateTime;
    ...
}
```

Notice that instead of defining a field of type *string* named *text*, I've defined a *StringBuilder* instead. If you're creating new strings in your *Update* method for display during *Draw* (as this program will do), you should use *StringBuilder* to avoid the heap allocations associated with the normal *string* type. This program will only be creating a new string every second, so I really didn't need to use *StringBuilder* here, but it doesn't hurt to get accustomed to it. *StringBuilder* requires a *using* directive for the *System.Text* namespace.

Notice also the *lastDateTime* field. This is used in the *Update* method to determine if the displayed time needs to be updated.

The *LoadContent* method gets the font and the viewport of the display:

XNA Project: XnaSimpleClock   File: Game1.cs (excerpt)

```
protected override void LoadContent()
{
    spriteBatch = new SpriteBatch(GraphicsDevice);
    segoe14 = this.Content.Load<SpriteFont>("Segoe14");
    viewport = this.GraphicsDevice.Viewport;
}
```

The logic to compare two *DateTime* values to see if the time has changed is just a little tricky because *DateTime* objects obtained during two consecutive *Update* calls will *always* be different because they have will have different *Millisecond* fields. For this reason, a new *DateTime* is calculated based on the current time obtained from *DateTime.Now*, but subtracting the milliseconds:

XNA Project: XnaSimpleClock   File: Game1.cs (excerpt)

```
protected override void Update(GameTime gameTime)
{
    // Allows the game to exit
    if (GamePad.GetState(PlayerIndex.One).Buttons.Back == ButtonState.Pressed)
        this.Exit();

    // Get DateTime with no milliseconds
    DateTime dateTime = DateTime.Now;
    dateTime = dateTime - new TimeSpan(0, 0, 0, 0, dateTime.Millisecond);

    if (dateTime != lastDateTime)
    {
        text.Remove(0, text.Length);
        text.Append(dateTime);
        Vector2 textSize = segoe14.MeasureString(text);
        textPosition = new Vector2((viewport.Width - textSize.X) / 2,
                                   (viewport.Height - textSize.Y) / 2);
        lastDateTime = dateTime;
    }
    else
    {
        SuppressDraw();
    }

    base.Update(gameTime);
}
```

At that point it's easy. If the time has changed, new values of *text*, *textSize*, and *textPosition* are calculated. Because *text* is a *StringBuilder* rather than a *string*, the old contents are removed and the new contents are appended. The *MeasureString* method of *SpriteFont* has an overload for *StringBuilder*, so that call looks exactly the same.

If the time has not changed, *SuppressDraw* is called. The result: *Draw* is called only once per second.

DrawString also has an overload for *StringBuilder*:

XNA Project: XnaSimpleClock   File: Game1.cs (excerpt)

```
protected override void Draw(GameTime gameTime)
{
    GraphicsDevice.Clear(Color.Navy);

    spriteBatch.Begin();
    spriteBatch.DrawString(segoe14, text, textPosition, Color.White);
    spriteBatch.End();

    base.Draw(gameTime);
}
```

And here's the result:

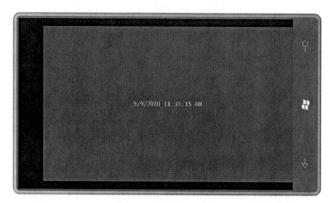

SuppressDraw can be a little difficult to use—I've found it particularly tricky during the time that the program is first starting up—but it's one of the primary techniques used in XNA to reduce the power requirements of the program.

Chapter 3
An Introduction to Touch

Even for experienced Silverlight and XNA programmers, Windows Phone 7 comes with a feature that is likely to be new and unusual. The screen on the phone is sensitive to touch. And not like old touch screens that basically mimic a mouse, or the tablet screens that recognize handwriting.

The multi-touch screen on a Windows Phone 7 device can detect at least four simultaneous fingers. It is the interaction of these fingers that makes multi-touch so challenging for programmers. For this chapter, however, I have much a less ambitious goal. I want only to introduce the touch interfaces in the context of sample programs that respond to simple taps.

For testing critical multi-touch code, an actual Windows Phone 7 device is essential. In the interim, the phone emulator will respond to mouse activity and convert it to touch input. If you run the emulator under Windows 7 with a multi-touch display and a Windows 7 driver, you can also use touch directly on the emulator.

The programs in this chapter look much like the "Hello, Windows Phone 7!" programs in the first chapter, except that when you tap the text with your finger, it changes to a random color, and when you tap outside the area of the text, it goes back to white (or whatever color the text was when the program started up).

In a Silverlight program, touch input is obtained through events. In an XNA program, touch input comes through a static class polled during the *Update* method. One of the primary purposes of the XNA *Update* method is to check the state of touch input and make changes that affect what goes out to the screen during the *Draw* method.

Low-Level Touch Handling in XNA

The multi-touch input device is referred to in XNA as a *touch panel*. You use methods in the static *TouchPanel* class to obtain this input. Although you can obtain gestures, let's begin with the lower-level touch information.

It is possible (although not necessary) to obtain information about the multi-touch device itself by calling the static *TouchPanel.GetCapabilities* method. The *TouchPanelCapabilities* object returned from this method has two properties:

- *IsConnected* is *true* if the touch panel is available. For the phone, this will always be *true*.
- *MaximumTouchCount* returns the number of touch points, at least 4 for the phone.

For most purposes, you just need to use one of the other two static methods in *TouchPanel*. To obtain low-level touch input, you'll probably be calling this method during every call to *Update* after program initialization:

```
TouchCollection touchLocations = TouchPanel.GetState();
```

The *TouchCollection* is a collection of zero or more *TouchLocation* objects. *TouchLocation* has three properties:

- *State* is a member of the *TouchLocationState* enumeration: *Pressed*, *Moved*, *Released*.

- *Position* is a *Vector2* indicating the finger position relative to the upper-left corner of the viewport.

- *Id* is an integer identifying a particular finger from *Pressed* through *Released*.

If no fingers are touching the screen, the *TouchCollection* will be empty. When a finger first touches the screen, *TouchCollection* contains a single *TouchLocation* object with *State* equal to *Pressed*. On subsequent calls to *TouchPanel.GetState*, the *TouchLocation* object will have *State* equal to *Moved* even if the finger has not physically moved. When the finger is lifted from the screen, the *State* property of the *TouchLocation* object will equal *Released*. On subsequent calls to *TouchPanel.GetState*, the *TouchCollection* will be empty.

One exception: If the finger is tapped and released on the screen very quickly—that is, within a 1/30th of a second—it's possible that the *TouchLocation* object with *State* equal to *Pressed* will be followed with *State* equal to *Released* with no *Moved* states in between.

That's just one finger touching the screen and lifting. In the general case, multiple fingers will be touching, moving, and lifting from the screen independently of each other. You can track particular fingers using the *Id* property. For any particular finger, that *Id* will be the same from *Pressed*, through all the *Moved* values, to *Released*.

Very often when dealing with low-level touch input, you'll use a *Dictionary* object with keys based on the *Id* property to retain information for a particular finger.

TouchLocation also has a very handy method called *TryGetPreviousLocation*, which you call like this:

```
TouchLocation previousTouchLocation;
bool success = touchLocation.TryGetPreviousLocation(out previousTouchLocation);
```

Almost always, you will call this method when *touchLocation.State* is *Moved* because you can then obtain the previous location and calculate a difference. If *touchLocation.State* equals *Pressed*, then *TryGetPreviousLocation* will return *false* and *previousTouchLocation.State* will equal the enumeration member *TouchLocationState.Invalid*. You'll also get these results if you use the method on a *TouchLocation* that itself was returned from *TryGetPreviousLocation*.

The program I've proposed changes the text color when the user touches the text string, so the processing of *TouchPanel.GetStates* will be relatively simple. The program will examine only *TouchLocation* objects with *State* values of *Pressed*.

This project is called XnaTouchHello. Like the other XNA projects you've seen so far, it needs a font, which I've made a little larger so it provides a more substantial touch target. A few more fields are required:

XNA Project: XnaTouchHello File: **Game1.cs (excerpt showing fields)**

```
public class Game1 : Microsoft.Xna.Framework.Game
{
    GraphicsDeviceManager graphics;
    SpriteBatch spriteBatch;

    Random rand = new Random();
    string text = "Hello, Windows Phone 7!";
    SpriteFont segoe36;
    Vector2 textSize;
    Vector2 textPosition;
    Color textColor = Color.White;
    ...

}
```

The *LoadContent* method is similar to earlier versions except that *textSize* is saved as a field because it needs to be accessed in later calculations:

XNA Project: XnaTouchHello File: **Game1.cs (excerpt)**

```
protected override void LoadContent()
{
    spriteBatch = new SpriteBatch(GraphicsDevice);

    segoe36 = this.Content.Load<SpriteFont>("Segoe36");
    textSize = segoe36.MeasureString(text);
    Viewport viewport = this.GraphicsDevice.Viewport;
    textPosition = new Vector2((viewport.Width - textSize.X) / 2,
                               (viewport.Height - textSize.Y) / 2);
}
```

As is typical with XNA programs, much of the "action" occurs in the *Update* method. The method calls *TouchPanel.GetStates* and then loops through the collection of *TouchLocation* objects to find only those with *State* equal to *Pressed*.

XNA Project: XnaTouchHello   File: Game1.cs (excerpt)

```
protected override void Update(GameTime gameTime)
{
    if (GamePad.GetState(PlayerIndex.One).Buttons.Back == ButtonState.Pressed)
        this.Exit();

    TouchCollection touchLocations = TouchPanel.GetState();

    foreach (TouchLocation touchLocation in touchLocations)
    {
        if (touchLocation.State == TouchLocationState.Pressed)
        {
            Vector2 touchPosition = touchLocation.Position;

            if (touchPosition.X >= textPosition.X &&
                touchPosition.X < textPosition.X + textSize.X &&
                touchPosition.Y >= textPosition.Y &&
                touchPosition.Y < textPosition.Y + textSize.Y)
            {
                textColor = new Color((byte)rand.Next(256),
                                      (byte)rand.Next(256),
                                      (byte)rand.Next(256));
            }
            else
            {
                textColor = Color.White;
            }
        }
    }

    base.Update(gameTime);
}
```

If the *Position* is inside the rectangle occupied by the text string, the *textColor* field is set to a random RGB color value using one of the constructors of the *Color* structure. Otherwise, *textColor* is set to *Color.White*.

The *Draw* method looks very similar to the versions you've seen before, except that the text color is a variable:

XNA Project: XnaTouchHello   File: Game1.cs (excerpt)

```
protected override void Draw(GameTime gameTime)
{
    this.GraphicsDevice.Clear(Color.Navy);

    spriteBatch.Begin();
    spriteBatch.DrawString(segoe36, text, textPosition, textColor);
```

```
        spriteBatch.End();

        base.Draw(gameTime);
    }
```

One problem you might notice is that touch is not quite as deterministic as you might like. Even when you touch the screen with a single finger, the finger might make contact with the screen in more than one place. In some cases, the same *foreach* loop in *Update* might set *textColor* more than once!

The XNA Gesture Interface

The *TouchPanel* class also includes gesture recognition, which is demonstrated by the XnaTapHello project. The fields of this project are the same as those in XnaTouchHello, but the *LoadContent* method is a little different:

XNA Project: XnaTapHello   File: Game1.cs (excerpt)

```
protected override void LoadContent()
{
    spriteBatch = new SpriteBatch(GraphicsDevice);

    segoe36 = this.Content.Load<SpriteFont>("Segoe36");
    textSize = segoe36.MeasureString(text);
    Viewport viewport = this.GraphicsDevice.Viewport;
    textPosition = new Vector2((viewport.Width - textSize.X) / 2,
                               (viewport.Height - textSize.Y) / 2);

    TouchPanel.EnabledGestures = GestureType.Tap;
}
```

Notice the final statement. *GestureType* is an enumeration with members *Tap, DoubleTap, Flick, Hold, Pinch, PinchComplete, FreeDrag, HorizontalDrag, VerticalDrag,* and *DragComplete,* defined as bit flags so you can combine the ones you want with the C# bitwise OR operator.

The *Update* method is very different.

XNA Project: XnaTapHello   File: Game1.cs (excerpt)

```
protected override void Update(GameTime gameTime)
{
    // Allows the game to exit
    if (GamePad.GetState(PlayerIndex.One).Buttons.Back == ButtonState.Pressed)
        this.Exit();
```

```
while (TouchPanel.IsGestureAvailable)
{
    GestureSample gestureSample = TouchPanel.ReadGesture();

    if (gestureSample.GestureType == GestureType.Tap)
    {
        Vector2 touchPosition = gestureSample.Position;

        if (touchPosition.X >= textPosition.X &&
            touchPosition.X < textPosition.X + textSize.X &&
            touchPosition.Y >= textPosition.Y &&
            touchPosition.Y < textPosition.Y + textSize.Y)
        {
            textColor = new Color((byte)rand.Next(256),
                                  (byte)rand.Next(256),
                                  (byte)rand.Next(256));
        }
        else
        {
            textColor = Color.White;
        }
    }
}

base.Update(gameTime);
}
```

Although this program is interested in only one type of gesture, the code is rather generalized. If a gesture is available, it is returned from the *TouchPanel.ReadGesture* method as an object of type *GestureSample*. Besides the *GestureType* and *Position* used here, a *Delta* property provides movement information in the form of a *Vector2* object. For some gestures (such as *Pinch*), the *GestureSample* also reports the status of a second touch point with *Position2* and *Delta2* properties.

The *Draw* method is the same as the previous program, but you'll find that the program behaves a little differently from the first one: In the first program, the text changes color when the finger touches the screen; in the second, the color change occurs when the finger lifts from the screen. The gesture recognizer needs to wait until that time to determine what type of gesture it is.

Low-Level Touch Events in Silverlight

Like XNA, Silverlight also supports two different programming interfaces for working with multi-touch, which can be most easily categorized as low-level and high-level. The low-level interface is based around the static *Touch.FrameReported* event, which is very similar to the XNA *TouchPanel* except that it's an event and it doesn't include gestures.

The high-level interface consists of three events defined by the *UIElement* class: *ManipulationStarted*, *ManipulationDelta*, and *ManipulationCompleted*. The *Manipulation* events, as they're collectively called, consolidate the interaction of multiple fingers into movement and scaling factors.

The core of the low-level touch interface in Silverlight is a class called *TouchPoint*, an instance of which represents a particular finger touching the screen. *TouchPoint* has four get-only properties:

- *Action* of type *TouchAction*, an enumeration with members *Down*, *Move*, and *Up*.

- *Position* of type *Point*, relative to the upper-left corner of a particular element. Let's call this element the *reference* element.

- *Size* of type *Size*. This is supposed to represent the touch area (and, hence, finger pressure, more or less) but Windows Phone 7 doesn't return useful values.

- *TouchDevice* of type *TouchDevice*.

The *TouchDevice* object has two get-only properties:

- *Id* of type *int*, used to distinguish between fingers. A particular finger is associated with a unique *Id* for all events from *Down* through *Up*.

- *DirectlyOver* of type *UIElement*, the topmost element underneath the finger.

As you can see, the Silverlight *TouchPoint* and *TouchDevice* objects give you mostly the same information as the XNA *TouchLocation* object, but the *DirectlyOver* property of *TouchDevice* is often very useful for determining what element the user is touching.

To use the low-level touch interface, you install a handler for the static *Touch.FrameReported* event:

```
Touch.FrameReported += OnTouchFrameReported;
```

The *OnTouchFrameReported* method looks like this:

```
void OnTouchFrameReported(object sender, TouchFrameEventArgs args)
{
   . . .
}
```

The event handler gets all touch events throughout your application. The *TouchFrameEventArgs* object has a *TimeStamp* property of type *int*, plus three methods:

- *GetTouchPoints(refElement)* returns a *TouchPointCollection*

- *GetPrimaryTouchPoint(refElement)* returns one *TouchPoint*

- *SuspendMousePromotionUntilTouchUp()*

In the general case, you call *GetTouchPoints*, passing to it a reference element. The *TouchPoint* objects in the returned collection have *Position* properties relative to that element. You can pass *null* to *GetTouchPoints* to get *Position* properties relative to the upper-left corner of the application.

The reference element and the *DirectlyOver* element have no relationship to each other. The event always gets all touch activity for the entire program. Calling *GetTouchPoints* or *GetPrimaryTouchPoints* with a particular element does *not* limit the events to only those events involving that element. All that it does is cause the *Position* property to be calculated relative to that element. (For that reason, *Position* coordinates can easily be negative if the finger is to the left of or above the reference element.) The *DirectlyOver* element indicates the element under the finger.

A discussion of the second and third methods requires some background: The *Touch. FrameReported* event originated on Silverlight for the desktop, where it is convenient for the mouse logic of existing controls to automatically use touch. For this reason, touch events are "promoted" to mouse events.

But this promotion only involves the "primary" touch point, which is the activity of the first finger that touches the screen when no other fingers are touching the screen. If you don't want the activity of this finger to be promoted to mouse events, the event handler usually begins like this:

```
void OnTouchFrameReported(object sender, TouchFrameEventArgs args)
{
    TouchPoint primaryTouchPoint = args.GetPrimaryTouchPoint(null);

    if (primaryTouchPoint != null && primaryTouchPoint.Action == TouchAction.Down)
    {
        args.SuspendMousePromotionUntilTouchUp();
    }
    . . .
}
```

The *SuspendMousePromotionUntilTouchUp* method can only be called when a finger first touches the screen when no other fingers are touching the screen.

On Windows Phone 7, such logic presents something of a quandary. As written, it basically wipes out all mouse promotion throughout the application. If your phone application incorporates Silverlight controls that were originally written for mouse input but haven't been upgraded to touch, you're basically disabling those controls.

Of course, you can also check the *DirectlyOver* property to suspend mouse promotion selectively. But on the phone, no elements should be processing mouse input except for those controls that don't process touch input! So it might make more sense to *never* suspend mouse promotion.

I'll leave that matter for your consideration and your older mouse-handling controls. Meanwhile, the program I want to write is only interested in the primary touch point when it has a *TouchAction* of *Down*, so I can use that same logic.

The SilverlightTouchHello project has a *TextBlock* in the XAML file:Silverlight Project:

SilverlightTouchHello   File: **MainPage.xaml** (excerpt)

```
<Grid x:Name="ContentPanel" Grid.Row="1" Margin="12,0,12,0">
    <TextBlock Name="txtblk"
            Text="Hello, Windows Phone 7!"
            Padding="0 34"
            HorizontalAlignment="Center"
            VerticalAlignment="Center" />
</Grid>
```

Notice the *Padding* value. I know that the font displayed here has a *FontSize* property of 20 pixels, which actually translates into a *TextBlock* that is about 27 pixels tall. I also know that it's recommended that touch targets not be smaller than 9 millimeters. If the resolution of the phone display is 264 DPI, then 9 millimeters is 94 pixels. (The calculation is 9 millimeters divided by 25.4 millimeters to the inch, times 264 pixels per inch.) The *TextBlock* is short by 67 pixels. So I set a *Padding* value that puts 34 more pixels on both the top and bottom (but not the sides).

I used *Padding* rather than *Margin* because *Padding* is space *inside* the *TextBlock*. The *TextBlock* actually becomes larger than the text size would imply. *Margin* is space *outside* the *TextBlock*. It's not part of the *TextBlock* itself and is excluded for purposes of hit-testing.

Here's the complete code-behind file. The constructor of *MainPage* installs the *Touch.FrameReported* event handler.

Silverlight Project: **SilverlightTouchHello**   File: **MainPage.xaml.cs**

```
using System;
using System.Windows.Input;
using System.Windows.Media;
using Microsoft.Phone.Controls;

namespace SilverlightTouchHello
{
    public partial class MainPage : PhoneApplicationPage
    {
        Random rand = new Random();
        Brush originalBrush;

        public MainPage()
        {
            InitializeComponent();
            originalBrush = txtblk.Foreground;
            Touch.FrameReported += OnTouchFrameReported;
        }
```

```
        void OnTouchFrameReported(object sender, TouchFrameEventArgs args)
        {
            TouchPoint primaryTouchPoint = args.GetPrimaryTouchPoint(null);

            if (primaryTouchPoint != null && primaryTouchPoint.Action == TouchAction.
Down)
            {
                if (primaryTouchPoint.TouchDevice.DirectlyOver == txtblk)
                {
                    txtblk.Foreground = new SolidColorBrush(
                            Color.FromArgb(255, (byte)rand.Next(256),
                                                (byte)rand.Next(256),
                                                (byte)rand.Next(256)));
                }
                else
                {
                    txtblk.Foreground = originalBrush;
                }
            }
        }
    }
}
```

The event handler is only interested in primary touch points with an *Action* of *Down*. If the *DirectlyOver* property is the element named *txtblk*, a random color is created. Unlike the *Color* structure in XNA, the Silverlight *Color* structure doesn't have a constructor to set a color from red, green, and blue values, but it does have a static *FromArgb* method that creates a *Color* object based on alpha, red, green, and blue values, where alpha is opacity. Set the alpha channel to 255 to get an opaque color. Although it's not obvious at all in the XAML files, the *Foreground* property is actually of type *Brush*, an abstract class from which *SolidColorBrush* descends.

If *DirectlyOver* is not *txtblk*, then the program doesn't change the color to white, because that wouldn't work if the user chose a color theme of black text on a white background. Instead, it sets the *Foreground* property to the brush originally set on the *TextBlock*. This is obtained in the constructor.

The Manipulation Events

The high-level touch interface in Silverlight involves three events: *ManipulationStarted*, *ManipulationDelta*, and *ManipulationCompleted*. These events don't bother with reporting the activity of individual fingers. Instead, they consolidate the activity of multiple fingers into translation and scaling operations. The events also accumulate velocity information, so while they don't support inertia directly, they can be used to implement inertia.

The *Manipulation* events will receive more coverage in the chapters ahead. In this chapter I'm going to stick with *ManipulationStarted* just to detect contact of a finger on the screen, and I won't bother with what the finger does after that.

While *Touch.FrameReported* delivered touch information for the entire application, the *Manipulation* events are based on individual elements, so in SilverlightTapHello1, a *ManipulationStarted* event handler can be set on the *TextBlock*:

Silverlight Project: SilverlightTapHello1   File: MainPage.xaml (excerpt)

```
<Grid x:Name="ContentPanel" Grid.Row="1" Margin="12,0,12,0">
    <TextBlock Text="Hello, Windows Phone 7!"
               Padding="0 34"
               HorizontalAlignment="Center"
               VerticalAlignment="Center"
               ManipulationStarted="OnTextBlockManipulationStarted" />
</Grid>
```

The MainPage.xaml.cs contains this event handler:

Silverlight Project: SilverlightTapHello1   File: MainPage.xaml.cs (excerpt)

```
public partial class MainPage : PhoneApplicationPage
{
    Random rand = new Random();

    public MainPage()
    {
        InitializeComponent();
    }
    void OnTextBlockManipulationStarted(object sender,
                                        ManipulationStartedEventArgs args)
    {
        TextBlock txtblk = sender as TextBlock;

        Color clr = Color.FromArgb(255, (byte)rand.Next(256),
                                        (byte)rand.Next(256),
                                        (byte)rand.Next(256));

        txtblk.Foreground = new SolidColorBrush(clr);

        args.Complete();
    }
}
```

The event handler is able to get the element generating the message from the *sender* argument. That will always be the *TextBlock*. The *TextBlock* is also available from the *args. OriginalSource* property and the *args.ManipulationContainer* property.

Notice the call to the *Complete* method of the event arguments at the end. This is not required but effectively tells the system that further *Manipulation* events involving this finger won't be necessary.

This program is flawed: If you try it out, you'll see that it works only partially. Touching the *TextBlock* changes the text to a random color. But if you touch outside the *TextBlock*, the text does *not* go back to white. Because this event was set on the *TextBlock*, the event handler is called only when the user touches the *TextBlock*. No other *Manipulation* events are processed by the program.

A program that functions correctly according to my original specification needs to get touch events occurring *anywhere* on the page. A handler for the *ManipulationStarted* event needs to be installed on *MainPage* rather than just on the *TextBlock*.

Although that's certainly possible, there's actually an easier way. The *UIElement* class defines all the *Manipulation* events. But the *Control* class (from which *MainPage* derives) supplements those events with protected virtual methods. You don't need to install a handler for the *ManipulationStarted* event on *MainPage*; instead you can override the *OnManipulationStarted* virtual method.

This approach is implemented in the SilverlightTapHello2 project. The XAML file doesn't refer to any events but gives the *TextBlock* a name so that it can be referred to in code:

Silverlight Project: SilverlightTapHello2   File: MainPage.xaml (excerpt)

```
<Grid x:Name="ContentPanel" Grid.Row="1" Margin="12,0,12,0">
    <TextBlock Name="txtblk"
               Text="Hello, Windows Phone 7!"
               Padding="0 34"
               HorizontalAlignment="Center"
               VerticalAlignment="Center" />
</Grid>
```

The *MainPage* class overrides the *OnManipulationStarted* method:

Silverlight Project: SilverlightTapHello2   File: MainPage.xaml.cs (excerpt)

```
public partial class MainPage : PhoneApplicationPage
{
    Random rand = new Random();
    Brush originalBrush;

    public MainPage()
    {
        InitializeComponent();
        originalBrush = txtblk.Foreground;
    }
```

```
    protected override void OnManipulationStarted(ManipulationStartedEventArgs args)
    {
        if (args.OriginalSource == txtblk)
        {
            txtblk.Foreground = new SolidColorBrush(
                    Color.FromArgb(255, (byte)rand.Next(256),
                                        (byte)rand.Next(256),
                                        (byte)rand.Next(256)));
        }
        else
        {
            txtblk.Foreground = originalBrush;
        }

        args.Complete();
        base.OnManipulationStarted(args);
    }
}
```

In the *ManipulationStartedEventArgs* a property named *OriginalSource* indicates where this event began—in other words, the topmost element that the user tapped. If this equals the *txtblk* object, the method creates a random color for the *Foreground* property. If not, then the *Foreground* property is set to the original brush.

In this *OnManiulationStarted* method we're handling events for *MainPage*, but that *OriginalSource* property tells us the event actually originated lower in the visual tree. This is part of the benefit of the Silverlight feature known as *routed event handling*.

Routed Events

In Microsoft Windows programming, keyboard and mouse input always go to particular controls. Keyboard input always goes to the control with the input focus. Mouse input always goes to the topmost enabled control under the mouse pointer. Stylus and touch input is handled similarly to the mouse. But sometimes this is inconvenient. Sometimes the control underneath needs the user-input more than the control on top.

To be a bit more flexible, Silverlight implements a system called *routed event handling*. Most user input events—including the three *Manipulation* events—do indeed originate using the same paradigm as Windows. The *Manipulation* events originate at the topmost enabled element touched by the user. However, if that element is not interested in the event, the event then goes to that element's parent, and so forth up the visual tree ending at the *PhoneApplicationFrame* element. Any element along the way can grab the input and do something with it, and also inhibit further progress of the event up the tree.

This is why you can override the *OnManipulationStarted* method in *MainPage* and also get manipulation events for the *TextBlock*. By default the *TextBlock* isn't interested in those events.

The event argument for the *ManipulationStarted* event is *ManipulationStartedEventArgs*, which derives from *RoutedEventArgs*. It is *RoutedEventArgs* that defines the *OriginalSource* property that indicates the element on which the event began.

But this suggests another approach that combines the two techniques shown in SilverlightTapHello1 and SilverlightTapHello2. Here's the XAML file of SilverlightTapHello3:

Silverlight Project: SilverlightTapHello3   File: MainPage.xaml (excerpt)

```
<Grid x:Name="ContentPanel" Grid.Row="1" Margin="12,0,12,0">
    <TextBlock Name="txtblk"
               Text="Hello, Windows Phone 7!"
               Padding="0 34"
               HorizontalAlignment="Center"
               VerticalAlignment="Center"
               ManipulationStarted="OnTextBlockManipulationStarted" />
</Grid>
```

The *TextBlock* has a *Name* as in the first program. A handler for the *ManipulationStarted* event is set on the *TextBlock* as in the first program. Both the event handler and an override of *OnManipulationStarted* appear in the code-behind file:

Silverlight Project: SilverlightTapHello3   File: MainPage.xaml.cs (excerpt)

```
public partial class MainPage : PhoneApplicationPage
{
    Random rand = new Random();
    Brush originalBrush;

    public MainPage()
    {
        InitializeComponent();
        originalBrush = txtblk.Foreground;
    }

    void OnTextBlockManipulationStarted(object sender,
                                    ManipulationStartedEventArgs args)
    {
        txtblk.Foreground = new SolidColorBrush(
                    Color.FromArgb(255, (byte)rand.Next(256),
                                        (byte)rand.Next(256),
                                        (byte)rand.Next(256)));
        args.Complete();
        args.Handled = true;
    }
```

```
    protected override void OnManipulationStarted(ManipulationStartedEventArgs args)
    {
        txtblk.Foreground = originalBrush;

        args.Complete();
        base.OnManipulationStarted(args);
    }
}
```

The logic has been split between the two methods, making the whole thing rather more elegant, I think. The *OnTextBlockManipulationStarted* method only gets events when the *TextBlock* is touched. The *OnManipulationStarted* event gets all events for *MainPage*.

At first there might seem to be a bug here. After *OnTextBlockManipulationStarted* is called, the event continues to travel up the visual tree and *OnManipulationStarted* sets the color back to white. But that's not what happens: The crucial statement that makes this work right is this one at the end of the *OnTextBlockManipulationStarted* handler for the *TextBlock*:

```
args.Handled = true;
```

That statement says that the event has now been handled and it should *not* travel further up the visual tree. Remove that statement and the *TextBlock* never changes from its initial color—at least not long enough to see.

Some Odd Behavior?

Now try this. In many of the Silverlight programs I've shown so far, I've centered the *TextBlock* within the content grid by setting the following two attributes:

```
HorizontalAlignment="Center"
VerticalAlignment="Center"
```

Delete them from SilverlightTapHello3, and recompile and run the program. The text appears at the upper-left corner of the *Grid*. But now if you touch *anywhere* within the large area below the *TextBlock*, the text will change to a random color, and only by touching the title area above the text can you change it back to white.

By default the *HorizontalAlignment* and *VerticalAlignment* properties are set to enumeration values called *Stretch*. The *TextBlock* is actually filling the *Grid*. You can't see it, of course, but the fingers don't lie.

With other elements—those that display bitmaps, for example—this stretching effect is much less subtle.

Chapter 4
Bitmaps, Also Known as Textures

Aside from text, one of the most common objects to appear in both Silverlight and XNA applications is the *bitmap*, formally defined as a two-dimensional array of bits corresponding to the pixels of a graphics display device.

In Silverlight, a bitmap is sometimes referred to as an *image*, but that's mostly a remnant of the Windows Presentation Foundation, where the word *image* refers to both bitmaps and vector-based drawings. In both WPF and Silverlight, the *Image* element displays bitmaps but the *Image* element is not the bitmap itself.

In XNA, a bitmap has a data type of *Texture2D* and hence is often referred to as a *texture*, but that term is mostly related to 3D programming where bitmaps are used to cover surfaces of 3D solids. In XNA 2D programming, bitmaps are often used as sprites.

Bitmaps are also used to symbolize your application on the phone. A new XNA or Silverlight project in Visual Studio results in the creation of three bitmaps for various purposes.

The native Windows bitmap format has an extension of BMP but it's become less popular in recent years as compressed formats have become widespread. At this time, the three most popular bitmap formats are probably:

- JPEG (Joint Photography Experts Group)
- PNG (Portable Network Graphics)
- GIF (Graphics Interchange File)

XNA supports all three (and more). Silverlight supports only JPEG and PNG. (And if you're like most Silverlight programmers, you'll not always remember this simple fact and someday wonder why your Silverlight program simply refuses to display a GIF or a BMP.)

The compression algorithms implemented by PNG and GIF do not result in the loss of any data. The original bitmap can be reconstituted exactly. For that reason, these are often referred to as "lossless" compression algorithms.

JPEG implements a "lossy" algorithm by discarding visual information that is less perceptible by human observers. This type of compression works well for real-world images such as photographs, but is less suitable for bitmaps that derive from text or vector-based images, such as architectural drawings or cartoons.

Both Silverlight and XNA allow manipulating bitmaps at the pixel level for generating bitmaps—or altering existing bitmaps—interactively or algorithmically. This chapter will focus more on the techniques of obtaining bitmaps from various sources, including the program itself, the Web, the phone's built-in camera, and the phone's photo library.

XNA Texture Drawing

Because XNA 2D programming is almost entirely a process of moving sprites around the screen, you might expect that loading and drawing bitmaps in an XNA program is fairly easy, and you would be correct.

The first project is called XnaLocalBitmap, so named because this bitmap will be stored as part of the program's content. To add a new bitmap to the program's content project, right-click the XnaLocalBitmapContent project name, select Add and then New Item, and then Bitmap File. You can create the bitmap right in Visual Studio.

Or, you can create the bitmap in an external program, as I did. Windows Paint is often convenient, so for this exercise I created the following bitmap with a dimension of 320 pixels wide and 160 pixels high:

I saved it under the name Hello.png.

To add this file as part of the program's content, right-click the XnaLocalBitmapContent project in Visual Studio, select Add and Existing Item, and then navigate to the file. Once the file shows up, you can right-click it to display Properties, and you'll see that it has an Asset Name of "Hello."

The goal is to display this bitmap centered on the screen. Define a field in the Game1.cs file to store the *Texture2D* and another field for the position:

XNA Project: XnaLocalBitmap   File: **Game1.cs** (excerpt showing fields)

```
public class Game1 : Microsoft.Xna.Framework.Game
{
    GraphicsDeviceManager graphics;
    SpriteBatch spriteBatch;
    Texture2D helloTexture;
    Vector2 position;
    ...
}
```

Both fields are set during the *LoadContent* method. Use the same generic method to load the *Texture2D* as you use to load a *SpriteFont*. The *Texture2D* class has properties named *Width* and *Height* that provide the dimensions of the bitmap in pixels. As with the programs that centered text in the Chapter 1, the *position* field indicates the pixel location on the display that corresponds to the upper-left corner of the bitmap:

XNA Project: XnaLocalBitmap   File: **Game1.cs** (excerpt)

```
protected override void LoadContent()
{
    spriteBatch = new SpriteBatch(GraphicsDevice);
    helloTexture = this.Content.Load<Texture2D>("Hello");
    Viewport viewport = this.GraphicsDevice.Viewport;
    position = new Vector2((viewport.Width - helloTexture.Width) / 2,
                          (viewport.Height - helloTexture.Height) / 2);
}
```

The *SpriteBatch* class has seven *Draw* methods to render bitmaps. This one is certainly the simplest:

XNA Project: XnaLocalBitmap   File: **Game1.cs** (excerpt)

```
protected override void Draw(GameTime gameTime)
{
    GraphicsDevice.Clear(Color.Navy);

    spriteBatch.Begin();
    spriteBatch.Draw(helloTexture, position, Color.White);
    spriteBatch.End();

    base.Draw(gameTime);
}
```

The final argument to Draw is a color that can be used to attenuate the existing colors in the bitmap. Use *Color.White* if you want the bitmap's colors to display without any alteration.

And here it is:

The Silverlight *Image* Element

The equivalent program in Silverlight is even simpler. Let's create a project named SilverlightLocalBitmap. First create a directory in the project to store the bitmap. This isn't strictly required but it makes for a tidier project. Programmers usually name this directory Images or Media or Assets depending on the types of files that might be stored there. Right-click the project name and choose Add and then New Folder. Let's name it Images. Then right-click the folder name and choose Add and Existing Item. Navigate to the Hello. png file. (If you've created a different bitmap on your own, keep in mind that Silverlight supports only JPEG and PNG files.)

From the Add button choose either Add or Add as Link. If you choose Add, a copy will be made and the file will be physically copied into a subdirectory of the project. If you choose Add as Link, only a file reference will be retained with the project but the file will still be copied into the executable.

The final step: Right-click the bitmap filename and display Properties. Note that the Build Action is Resource. It's possible to change that Build Action to Content, but let's leave it for now and I'll discuss the difference shortly.

In Silverlight, you use the *Image* element to display bitmaps just as you use the *TextBlock* element to display text. Set the *Source* property of *Image* to the folder and filename of the bitmap within the project:

Silverlight Project: SilverlightLocalBitmap   File: **MainPage.xaml** (excerpt)

```
<Grid x:Name="ContentPanel" Grid.Row="1" Margin="12,0,12,0">
    <Image Source="Images/Hello.png" />
</Grid>
```

The display looks a little different than the XNA program, and it's not just the titles. By default, the *Image* element expands or contracts the bitmap as much as possible to fill its container (the content grid) while retaining the correct aspect ratio. This is most noticeable if you set the *SupportedOrientations* attribute of the *PhoneApplicationPage* start tag to *PortraitOrLandscape* and turn the phone sideways:

If you want to display the bitmap in its native pixel size, you can set the *Stretch* property of Image to *None*:

```
<Image Source="Images/Hello.png"
       Stretch="None" />
```

Images Via the Web

One feature that's really nice about the *Image* element is that you can set the *Source* property to a URL, such as in this Silverlight project:

Silverlight Project: SilverlightWebBitmap   File: **MainPage.xaml** (excerpt)

```
<Grid x:Name="ContentPanel" Grid.Row="1" Margin="12,0,12,0">
    <Image Source="http://www.charlespetzold.com/Media/HelloWP7.jpg" />
</Grid>
```

Here it is:

This is certainly easy enough, and pulling images off the Web rather than binding them into the application certainly keeps the size of the executable down. But an application running on Windows Phone 7 is not guaranteed to have an Internet connection, and you're undoubtedly associated with other problems associated with downloading. The *Image* element has two events named *ImageOpened* and *ImageFailed* that you can use to determine if the download was successful or not.

For Windows Phone 7 programs that display a lot of bitmaps, you need to do some hard thinking. You can embed the bitmaps into the executable and have their access guaranteed, or you can save space and download them when necessary.

In XNA, downloading a bitmap from the Web is not quite as easy, but a .NET class named *WebClient* makes the job relatively painless. It's somewhat easier to use than the common alternative (*HttpWebRequest* and *HttpWebResponse*) and is often the preferred choice for downloading individual items.

You can use *WebClient* to download either strings (commonly XML files) or binary objects. The actual transfer occurs asynchronously and then *WebClient* calls a method in your program to indicate completion or failure. This method call is in your program's thread, so you get the benefit of an asynchronous data transfer without explicitly dealing with secondary threads.

To use *WebClient* in an XNA program, you'll need to add a reference to the System.Net library: In the Solution Explorer, under the project name, right click References and select Add Reference. In the .NET table, select System.Net. (Silverlight programs get a reference to System.Net automatically.)

The Game1.cs file of the XnaWebBitmap project also requires a *using* directive for the *System .Net* namespace. The program defines the same fields as the earlier program:

XNA Project: XnaWebBitmap   File: Game1.cs (excerpt showing fields)

```
public class Game1 : Microsoft.Xna.Framework.Game
{
    GraphicsDeviceManager graphics;
    SpriteBatch spriteBatch;
    Texture2D helloTexture;
    Vector2 position;
    ...
}
```

The *LoadContent* method creates an instance of *WebClient*, sets the callback method, and then initiates the transfer:

XNA Project: XnaWebBitmap   File: Game1.cs (excerpt)

```
protected override void LoadContent()
{
    spriteBatch = new SpriteBatch(GraphicsDevice);

    WebClient webClient = new WebClient();
    webClient.OpenReadCompleted += OnWebClientOpenReadCompleted;
    webClient.OpenReadAsync(new Uri("http://www.charlespetzold.com/Media/HelloWP7.
jpg"));
}
```

The *OnWebClientOpenReadCompleted* method is called when the entire file has been downloaded. You'll want to check if the download hasn't been cancelled and that no error has been reported. If everything is OK, the *Result* property of the event arguments is of type *Stream*. You can use that *Stream* with the static *Texture2D.FromStream* method to create a *Texture2D* object:

XNA Project: XnaWebBitmap   File: Game1.cs (excerpt)

```
void OnWebClientOpenReadCompleted(object sender, OpenReadCompletedEventArgs args)
{
    if (!args.Cancelled && args.Error == null)
    {
        helloTexture = Texture2D.FromStream(this.GraphicsDevice, args.Result);
        Viewport viewport = this.GraphicsDevice.Viewport;
        position = new Vector2((viewport.Width - helloTexture.Width) / 2,
                               (viewport.Height - helloTexture.Height) / 2);
    }
}
```

The *Texture2D.FromStream* method supports JPEG, PNG, and GIF.

By default, the *AllowReadStreamBuffering* property of *WebClient* is *true*, which means that the entire file will have been downloaded when the *OpenReadCompleted* event is raised. The *Stream* object available in the *Result* property is actually a memory stream, except that it's an instance of a class internal to the .NET libraries rather than *MemoryStream* itself.

If you set *AllowReadStreamBuffering* to *false*, then the *Result* property will be a network stream. The *Texture2D* class will not allow you to read from that stream on the main program thread.

Normally the *LoadContent* method of a *Game* derivative is called before the first call to the *Update* or *Draw* method, but it is essential to remember that a gap of time will separate *LoadContent* from the *OnWebClientOpenReadCompleted* method. During that time an asynchronous read is occurring, but the *Game1* class is proceeding as normal with calls to *Update* and *Draw*. For that reason, you should only attempt to access the *Texture2D* object when you know that it's valid:

XNA Project: XnaWebBitmap   File: Game1.cs (excerpt)

```
protected override void Draw(GameTime gameTime)
{
    GraphicsDevice.Clear(Color.Navy);

    if (helloTexture != null)
    {
        spriteBatch.Begin();
        spriteBatch.Draw(helloTexture, position, Color.White);
        spriteBatch.End();
    }

    base.Draw(gameTime);
}
```

In a real program, you'd also want to provide some kind of notification to the user if the bitmap could not be downloaded.

Image and ImageSource

Although you can certainly use *WebClient* in a *Silverlight* application, it's not generally necessary with bitmaps because the bitmap-related classes already implement asynchronous downloading.

However, once you begin investigating the *Image* element, it may seem a little confusing. The *Image* element is not the bitmap; the *Image* element merely displays the bitmap. In the uses you've seen so far, the *Source* property of *Image* has been set to a relative file path or a URL:

```
<Image Source="Images/Hello.png" />
<Image Source="http://www.charlespetzold.com/Media/HelloWP7.jpg" />
```

You might have assumed that this *Source* property was of type *string*. Sorry, not even close! You're actually seeing XAML syntax that hides some extensive activity behind the scenes. The *Source* property is really of type *ImageSource*, an abstract class from which derives *BitmapSource*, another abstract class but one that defines a method named *SetSource* that allows loading the bitmap from a *Stream* object.

From *BitmapSource* derives *BitmapImage*, which supports a constructor that accepts a *Uri* object and also includes a *UriSource* property of type *Uri*. The SilverlightTapToDownload1 project mimics a program that needs to download a bitmap whose URL is known only at runtime. The XAML contains an *Image* element with no bitmap to display:

Silverlight Project: SilverlightTapToDownload1   File: MainPage.xaml (excerpt)

```
<Grid x:Name="ContentPanel" Grid.Row="1" Margin="12,0,12,0">
    <Image Name="img" />
</Grid>
```

BitmapImage requires a *using* directive for the *System.Windows.Media.Imaging* namespace. When *MainPage* gets a tap, it creates a *BitmapImage* from the *Uri* object and sets that to the *Source* property of the *Image*:

Silverlight Project: SilverlightTapToDownload1   File: MainPage.xaml.cs (excerpt)

```
protected override void OnManipulationStarted(ManipulationStartedEventArgs args)
{
    Uri uri = new Uri("http://www.charlespetzold.com/Media/HelloWP7.jpg");
    BitmapImage bmp = new BitmapImage(uri);
    img.Source = bmp;

    args.Complete();
    args.Handled = true;
    base.OnManipulationStarted(args);
}
```

Remember to tap the screen to initiate the download!

The *BitmapImage* class defines *ImageOpened* and *ImageFailed* events (which the *Image* element also duplicates) and also includes a *DownloadProgess* event.

If you want to explicitly use *WebClient* in a Silverlight program, you can do that as well, as the next project demonstrates. The SilverlightTapToDownload2.xaml file is the same as SilverlightTapToDownload1.xaml. The code-behind file uses *WebClient* much like the earlier XNA program:

Silverlight Project: SilverlightTapToDownload2   File: MainPage.xaml.cs (excerpt)

```
protected override void OnManipulationStarted(ManipulationStartedEventArgs args)
{
    WebClient webClient = new WebClient();
    webClient.OpenReadCompleted += OnWebClientOpenReadCompleted;
    webClient.OpenReadAsync(new Uri("http://www.charlespetzold.com/Media/HelloWP7.jpg"));

    args.Complete();
    args.Handled = true;
    base.OnManipulationStarted(args);
}

void OnWebClientOpenReadCompleted(object sender, OpenReadCompletedEventArgs args)
{
    if (!args.Cancelled && args.Error == null)
    {
        BitmapImage bmp = new BitmapImage();
        bmp.SetSource(args.Result);
        img.Source = bmp;
    }
}
```

Notice the use of *SetSource* to create the bitmap from the *Stream* object.

Loading Local Bitmaps from Code

In a Silverlight program, you've seen that a bitmap added to the project as a resource is bound into the executable. It's so customary to reference that local bitmap directly from XAML that very few experienced Silverlight programmers could tell you offhand how to do it in code. The SilverlightTapToLoad project shows you how.

Like the other Silverlight programs in this chapter, the SilverlightTapToLoad project contains an *Image* element in its content grid. The Hello.png bitmap is stored in the Images directory and has a Build Action of Resource.

The MainPage.xaml.cs file requires a *using* directive for the *System.Windows.Media.Imaging* namespace for the *BitmapImage* class. Another *using* directive for *System.Windows.Resources* is required for the *StreamResourceInfo* class.

When the screen is tapped, the event handler accesses the resource using the static *GetResourceStream* method defined by the *Application* class:

Silverlight Project: SilverlightTapToLoad   File: MainPage.xaml.cs

```
protected override void OnManipulationStarted(ManipulationStartedEventArgs args)
{
    Uri uri = new Uri("/SilverlightTapToLoad;component/Images/Hello.png", UriKind
.Relative);
    StreamResourceInfo resourceInfo = Application.GetResourceStream(uri);
    BitmapImage bmp = new BitmapImage();
    bmp.SetSource(resourceInfo.Stream);
    img.Source = bmp;

    args.Complete();
    args.Handled = true;
    base.OnManipulationStarted(args);
}
```

Notice how complicated that URL is! It begins with the name of the program followed by a semicolon, followed by the word "component" and then the folder and filename of the file. If you change the Build Action of the Hello.png file to Content rather than Resource, you can simplify the syntax considerably:

```
Uri uri = new Uri("Images/Hello.png", UriKind.Relative);
```

What's the difference?

Navigate to the *Bin/Debug* subdirectory of the Visual Studio project and find the SilverlightTapToLoad.xap file that contains your program. If you rename it the file to a ZIP extension you can look inside. The bulk of the file will be SilverlightTapToLoad.dll, the compiled binary.

In both cases, the bitmap is obviously stored somewhere within the XAP file. The difference is this:

- With a Build Action of Resource for the bitmap, it is stored inside the SilverlightTapToLoad.dll file along with the compiled program

- With a Build Action of Content, the bitmap is stored external to the SilverlightTapToLoad.dll file but within the XAP file, and when you rename the XAP file to a ZIP file, you can see the *Images* directory and the file.

Which is better?

In a document entitled "Creating High Performance Silverlight Applications for Windows Phone," Microsoft has recommending using a Build Action of Content rather than Resource for assets included in your application to minimize the size of the binary and startup time. However, if these assets are in a Silverlight library that the program references, then it is better for them to be embedded in the binary with a Build Action of Resource.

If you have a number of images in your program, and you don't want to include them all in the XAP file, but you're nervous about downloading the images, why not do a little of both? Include low resolution (or highly compressed) images in the XAP file, but download better versions asynchronously while the application is running.

Capturing from the Camera

Besides embedding bitmaps in your application or accessing them from the web, Windows Phone 7 also allows you to acquire images from the built-in camera.

Your application has no control over the camera itself. For reasons of security, your program cannot arbitrarily snap a picture, or "see" what's coming through the camera lens. Your application basically invokes a standard camera utility, the user points and shoots, and the picture is returned back to your program.

The classes you use for this job are in the *Microsoft.Phone.Tasks* namespace, which contains several classes referred to as *choosers* and *launchers*. Conceptually, these are rather similar, except that choosers return data to your program but launchers do not.

The *CameraCaptureTask* is derived from the generic *ChooserBase* class which defines a *Completed* event and a *Show* method. Your program attaches a handler for the *Completed* event and calls *Show*. When the *Completed* event handler is called, the *PhotoResult* event argument contains a *Stream* object to the photo. From there, you already know what to do.

Like the earlier programs in this chapter, the SilverlightTapToShoot program contains an *Image* element in the content grid of its MainPage.xaml file. Here's the entire code-behind file:

Silverlight Project: SilverlightTapToShoot   File: MainPage.xaml.cs

```
using System.Windows.Input;
using System.Windows.Media.Imaging;
using Microsoft.Phone.Controls;
using Microsoft.Phone.Tasks;

namespace SilverlightTapToShoot
{
```

```
    public partial class MainPage : PhoneApplicationPage
    {
        CameraCaptureTask camera = new CameraCaptureTask();;

        public MainPage()
        {
            InitializeComponent();

            camera.Completed += OnCameraCaptureTaskCompleted;
        }

        protected override void OnManipulationStarted(ManipulationStartedEventArgs
    args)
        {
            camera.Show();

            args.Complete();
            args.Handled = true;
            base.OnManipulationStarted(args);
        }

        void OnCameraCaptureTaskCompleted(object sender, PhotoResult args)
        {
            if (args.TaskResult == TaskResult.OK)
            {
                BitmapImage bmp = new BitmapImage();
                bmp.SetSource(args.ChosenPhoto);
                img.Source = bmp;
            }
        }
    }
}
```

You can run this program on the phone emulator. When you tap the emulator screen, the call to *Show* causes the camera task to start up and you'll navigate to a page that resembles the actual camera. You can "shoot" a photo by tapping an icon in the upper-right corner of the screen. The simulated "photo" just looks like a large white square with a small black square inside one of the edges. Then you need to click the Accept button.

You can also run this program on the phone itself, of course, but not when the phone is tethered to the PC and the Zune software is running. After deploying the application to the phone using Visual Studio, you'll need to close the Zune software before testing the program.

If you need to use Visual Studio to debug an application that uses the camera while the application is running on the phone, you can use a little command-line program called WPDTPTConnect32.exe or WPDTPTConnect64.exe (depending on whether your development machine is 32-bit or 64-bit). These program is an alternative to the Zune software for allowing the Visual Studio debugger to control your program as it's running on the phone. The Zune software must be closed before you use these programs.

In either case, when you press the Accept button, the camera goes away and the program's *OnCameraCaptureTaskCompleted* method takes over. It creates a *BitmapImage* object, sets the input stream from *args.ChoosenPhoto*, and then sets the *BitmapImage* object to the *Image* element, displaying the photo on the screen.

The whole process seems fairly straightforward. Conceptually it seems as if the program is spawning the camera process, and then resuming control when that camera process terminates.

However, the Windows Phone 7 documentation that I'm consulting warns that this is not the case. There's something else going on that is not so evident at first and which you will probably find somewhat unnerving.

When the SilverlightTapToShoot program calls the *Show* method on the *CameraCaptureTask* object, the SilverlightTapToShoot program is terminated. (Not immediately, though. The *OnManipulationStarted* method is allowed to return back to the program, and a couple other events are fired, but then the program is definitely terminated.)

The camera utility then runs. When the camera utility has done its job, the SilverlightTapToShoot program is re-executed. It's a new instance of the program. The program starts up from the beginning, the *MainPage* constructor is eventually called which sets the *Completed* event of the *CameraCaptureTask* to *OnCameraCaptureTaskCompleted*, and then that method is called.

For these reasons, the documentation advises that when you use a chooser or launcher such as *CameraCaptureTask*, the object must be defined as a field, and the handler for the *Completed* event must be attached in the program's constructor, and as late in the constructor as possible because once the handler is attached when the program starts up again, it will be called.

This termination and re-execution of your program is a characteristic of Windows Phone 7 programming call *tombstoning*. When the program is terminated as the camera task begins, sufficient information is retained by the phone operating system to start the program up again when the camera finishes. However, not enough information is retained to restore the program entirely to its pre-tombstone state. That's your responsibility.

Running a launcher or chooser is one way tombstoning can occur. But it also occurs when the user leaves your program by pressing the Start button on the phone. Eventually the user could return to your program by pressing the Back button, and your program needs to be re-executed from its tombstoned state. Tombstoning also takes place when a lack of activity on the phone causes it to go into a lock state.

Tombstoning does *not* occur when your program is running and the user presses the Back button. The Back button simply terminates the program normally.

When tombstoning occurs, obviously you'll want to save some of the state of your program so you can restore that state when the program starts up again, and obviously Windows Phone 7 has facilities to help you out. That's in Chapter 6.

With all that said, in later versions of the Windows Phone 7 operating system, including the one I'm using as I'm finishing the chapters for this book, I am not seeing tombstoning occur when using *CameraCaptureTask*. But it doesn't hurt to prepare for it.

The Phone's Photo Library

As you take pictures with the phone and synchronize your phone with the PC, the phone accumulates a photo library. A program running on the phone can access this library in one of two ways:

- From the perspective of your program, the *PhotoChooserTask* is much like the *CameraCaptureTask* except it takes the user to the photo library and allows the user to choose one photo, which is then returned to the program.

- The XNA namespace *Microsoft.Xna.Framework.Media* has a *MediaLibrary* and related classes that let a program obtain collections of all the photos stored in the photo library, and present these to the user.

I'm going to show you these two approaches with two programs. Just for variety (and to demonstrate how to use XNA classes in a Silverlight program), I'll use XNA for the first approach and Silverlight for the second.

You can run these two programs on the phone emulator. The emulator includes a small collection of photos specifically for testing programs such as these. When testing the programs on the actual phone, however, the phone must be untethered from the PC or the Zune software must be closed, because the Zune software won't allow simultaneous access to the phone's photo library. After you close Zune, you can run WPDTPTConnect32.exe or WPDTPTConnect64.exe program to allow Visual Studio to debug the program running on the phone.

The XnaTapToBrowse program requires a *using* directive for *Microsoft.Phone.Tasks*. It creates a *PhotoChooserTask* object along with the other fields:

Silverlight Project: XnaTapToBrowse   File: **Game1.cs (excerpt showing fields)**

```
public class Game1 : Microsoft.Xna.Framework.Game
{
    GraphicsDeviceManager graphics;
    SpriteBatch spriteBatch;
    Texture2D texture;
    PhotoChooserTask photoChooser = new PhotoChooserTask();
    . . .
}
```

In compliance with the recommendations of the documentation, the class attaches a handler for the *Completed* event in the constructor:

Silverlight Project: XnaTapToBrowse   File: Game1.cs (excerpt)

```
public Game1()
{
    graphics = new GraphicsDeviceManager(this);
    Content.RootDirectory = "Content";

    // Frame rate is 30 fps by default for Windows Phone.
    TargetElapsedTime = TimeSpan.FromTicks(333333);

    TouchPanel.EnabledGestures = GestureType.Tap;
    photoChooser.Completed += OnPhotoChooserCompleted;
}
```

As usual, the *Update* method checks for user input. If a tap has occurred, the method calls the *Show* event of the *PhotoChooserTask* object:

Silverlight Project: XnaTapToBrowse   File: Game1.cs (excerpt)

```
protected override void Update(GameTime gameTime)
{
    // Allows the game to exit
    if (GamePad.GetState(PlayerIndex.One).Buttons.Back == ButtonState.Pressed)
        this.Exit();

    while (TouchPanel.IsGestureAvailable)
        if (TouchPanel.ReadGesture().GestureType == GestureType.Tap)
            photoChooser.Show();

    base.Update(gameTime);
}

void OnPhotoChooserCompleted(object sender, PhotoResult args)
{
    if (args.TaskResult == TaskResult.OK)
        texture = Texture2D.FromStream(this.GraphicsDevice, args.ChosenPhoto);
}
```

The handler for the *Completed* event then creates a *Texture2D* from the stream available from the *ChosenPhoto* property. The *Draw* override doesn't attempt to render this object until it's available:

Silverlight Project: XnaTapToBrowse   File: **Game1.cs** (excerpt)

```
protected override void Draw(GameTime gameTime)
{
    GraphicsDevice.Clear(Color.Navy);

    if (texture != null)
    {
        spriteBatch.Begin();
        spriteBatch.Draw(texture, this.GraphicsDevice.Viewport.Bounds, Color.White);
        spriteBatch.End();
    }

    base.Draw(gameTime);
}
```

I'm using a slight variation of the *Draw* method of *SpriteBatch* here. Rather than provide a position for the *Texture2D* in the second argument, I'm providing a whole rectangle equal to the size of the viewport. This causes the photo to expand (or, more likely, shrink) in size, very possibly distorting the image by not taking account of the original aspect ratio. More sophisticated code can handle those problems, of course.

The SilverlightAccessLibrary program requires a reference to the Microsoft.Xna.Framework DLL, and you'll probably get a warning about including an XNA library in your Silverlight program. It's OK! The content area in the MainPage.xaml file contains both a bitmap-less *Image* and a text-less *TextBlock* in the *Grid*:

Silverlight Project: SilverlightAccessLibrary   File: **MainPage.xaml** (excerpt)

```
<Grid x:Name="ContentPanel" Grid.Row="1" Margin="12,0,12,0">
    <Image Name="img" />

    <TextBlock Name="txtblk"
               TextWrapping="Wrap"
               TextAlignment="Center"
               VerticalAlignment="Bottom" />
</Grid>
```

Rather than present the entire photo library to the user (a task that would be a little difficult with only the rudimentary Silverlight layout elements I've described so far), the program picks one at random, and picks another when the user taps the screen:

Silverlight Project: SilverlightAccessLibrary   File: MainPage.xaml.cs (excerpt)

```
public partial class MainPage : PhoneApplicationPage
{
    MediaLibrary mediaLib = new MediaLibrary();
    Random rand = new Random();

    public MainPage()
    {
        InitializeComponent();
        GetRandomPicture();
    }

    protected override void OnManipulationStarted(ManipulationStartedEventArgs args)
    {
        GetRandomPicture();

        args.Complete();
        base.OnManipulationStarted(args);
    }

    void GetRandomPicture()
    {
        PictureCollection pictures = mediaLib.Pictures;

        if (pictures.Count > 0)
        {
            int index = rand.Next(pictures.Count);
            Picture pic = pictures[index];

            BitmapImage bmp = new BitmapImage();
            bmp.SetSource(pic.GetImage());
            img.Source = bmp;

            txtblk.Text = String.Format("{0}\n{1}\n{2}",
                                        pic.Name, pic.Album.Name, pic.Date);
        }
    }
}
```

The XNA *MediaLibrary* class is instantiated as a field. In the *GetRandomPicture* method, the program obtains a *PictureCollection* object from the *MediaLibrary* class and picks one at random. The *Picture* object has a *GetImage* method that returns a stream, and a *Name*, *Album*, and *Data* information that the program displays in the overlaying *TextBlock*.

A Windows Phone 7 program can also save a bitmap back into the library. All such bitmaps go into a special album called Saved Pictures. I'll show you how to do that in Chapters 14 and 22.

Chapter 5
Sensors and Services

This chapter covers two of the facilities in Windows Phone 7 that provide information about the outside world. With the user's permission, the location service lets your application obtain the phone's location on the earth in the traditional geographic coordinates of longitude and latitude, whereas the accelerometer tells your program which way is down.

The accelerometer and location service are related in that neither of them will work very well in outer space.

Although the accelerometer and the location service are ostensibly rather easy, this chapter also explores issues involved with working with secondary threads of execution, handling asynchronous operations, and accessing web services.

Accelerometer

Windows Phones contain an accelerometer—a small hardware device that essentially measures force, which elementary physics tells us is proportional to acceleration. When the phone is held still, the accelerometer responds to the force of gravity, so the accelerometer can tell your application the direction of the Earth relative to the phone.

A simulation of a bubble level is an archetypal application that makes use of an accelerometer, but the accelerometer can also provide a basis for interactive animations. For example, you might pilot a messenger bike through the streets of Manhattan by tilting the phone left or right to indicate steering.

The accelerometer also responds to sudden movements such as shakes or jerks, useful for simulations of dice or some other type of randomizing activity. Coming up with creative uses of the accelerometer is one of the many challenges of phone development.

It is convenient to represent the accelerometer output as a vector in three-dimensional space. Vectors are commonly written in boldface, so the acceleration vector can be symbolized as **(x, y, z)**. XNA defines a three-dimensional vector type; Silverlight does not.

While a three-dimensional point (x, y, z) indicates a particular location in space, the vector **(x, y, z)** encapsulates instead a direction and a magnitude. Obviously the point and the vector are related: The direction of the vector **(x, y, z)** is the direction from the point $(0, 0, 0)$ to the point (x, y, z). But the vector **(x, y, z)** is definitely not the line from $(0, 0, 0)$ to (x, y, z). It's only the direction of that line.

The magnitude of the vector **(x, y, z)** is calculable from the three-dimensional form of the Pythagorean Theorem:

$$Magnitude = \sqrt{x^2 + y^2 + z^2}$$

For working with the accelerometer, you can imagine the phone as defining a three-dimensional coordinate system. No matter how the phone is oriented, the positive Y axis points from the bottom of the phone (with the buttons) to the top, the positive X axis points from left to right,

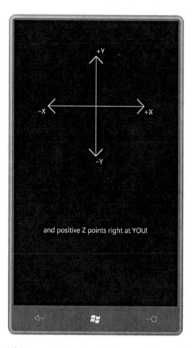

This is a traditional three-dimensional coordinate system, the same coordinate system used in XNA 3D programming. It's termed a *right-hand* coordinate system: Point the index finger of your right hand to increasing X, the middle finger to increase Y, and your thumb points to increasing Z. Or, curve the fingers of your right hand from the positive X axis to the positive Y axis. Your thumb again points to increasing Z.

This coordinate system remains fixed relative to the phone regardless how you hold the phone, and regardless of the orientation of any programs running on the phone. In fact, as you might expect, the accelerometer is the basis for performing orientation changes of Windows Phone 7 applications.

When the phone is still, the accelerometer vector points towards the Earth. The magnitude is 1, meaning 1 *g*, which is the force of gravity on the earth's surface. When holding your phone in the upright position, the acceleration vector is **(0, –1, 0)**, that is, straight down.

Turn the phone 90° counter-clockwise (called landscape left) and the acceleration vector becomes **(–1, 0, 0)**, upside down it's **(0, 1, 0)**, and another 90° counter-clockwise turn brings you to the landscape right orientation and an accelerometer value of **(1, 0, 0)**. Sit the phone down on the desk with the display facing up, and the acceleration vector is **(0, 0, –1)**. (That final value is what the Windows Phone 7 emulator always reports.)

Of course, the acceleration vector will *rarely* be those exact values, and even the magnitude won't be exact. For a still phone, the magnitude may vary by a few percentage points with different orientations. When you visit the Moon with your Windows Phone 7, you can expect acceleration vector magnitudes in the region of 0.17 but limited cell phone reception.

I've been describing values of the acceleration vector when the device is still. The acceleration vector can point in other directions (and the magnitude can become larger or smaller) when the phone is accelerating, that is, gaining or losing velocity. For example, if you jerk the phone to the left, the acceleration vector points to the right but only when the device is gaining velocity. As the velocity stabilizes, the acceleration vector again registers only gravity. When you decelerate this jerk to the left, the acceleration vector goes to the left briefly as the device comes to a stop.

If the phone is in free fall, the magnitude of the accelerometer vector should theoretically go down to zero.

To use the accelerometer, you'll need a reference to the Microsoft.Devices.Sensors library, and a *using* directive for the *Microsoft.Devices.Sensors* namespace. In WMAppManifest.xml, you need

```
<Capability Name="ID_CAP_SENSORS" />
```

This is set by default.

In your program you create an instance of the *Accelerometer* class, set an event handler for the *ReadingChanging* event, and call *Start*.

And then it gets a little tricky. Let's take a look at a project named SilverlightAccelerometer. that simply displays the current reading in its content grid. A centered *TextBlock* is defined in the XAML file:

Silverlight Project: SilverlightAccelerometer   File: MainPage.xaml (excerpt)

```
<Grid x:Name="ContentPanel" Grid.Row="1" Margin="12,0,12,0">
    <TextBlock Name="txtblk"
               HorizontalAlignment="Center"
               VerticalAlignment="Center" />
</Grid>
```

This is a program that will display the accelerometer vector throughout its lifetime, so it creates the *Accelerometer* class in its constructor and calls *Start*:

Silverlight Project: **SilverlightAccelerometer**   File: **MainPage.xaml.cs** (excerpt)

```
public MainPage()
{
    InitializeComponent();

    Accelerometer acc = new Accelerometer();
    acc.ReadingChanged += OnAccelerometerReadingChanged;

    try
    {
        acc.Start();
    }
    catch (Exception exc)
    {
        txtblk.Text = exc.Message;
    }
}
```

The documentation warns that calling *Start* might raise an exception, so the program protects itself against that eventuality. The *Accelerometer* also supports *Stop* and *Dispose* methods, but this program doesn't make use of them. A *State* property is also available if you need to know if the accelerometer is available and what it's currently doing.

A *ReadingChanged* event is accompanied by the *AccelerometerReadingEventArgs* event arguments. The object has properties named *X*, *Y*, and *Z* of type *double* and *TimeStamp* of type *DateTimeOffset*. In the SilverlightAccelerometer program, the job of the event handler is to format this information into a string and set it to the *Text* property of the *TextBlock*.

The catch here is that the event handler (in this case *OnAccelerometerReadingChanged*) is called on a different thread of execution, and this means it must be handled in a special way.

A little background: All the user-interface elements and objects in a Silverlight application are created and accessed in a main thread of execution often called the *user interface thread* or the *UI thread*. These user-interface objects are not thread safe; they are not built to be accessed simultaneously from multiple threads. For this reason, Silverlight will not allow you to access a user-interface object from a non-UI thread.

This means that the *OnAccelerometerReadingChanged* method cannot directly access the *TextBlock* element to set a new value to its *Text* property.

Fortunately, there's a solution involving a class named *Dispatcher* defined in the *System. Windows.Threading* namespace. Through the *Dispatcher* class, you can post jobs from a non-UI thread on a queue where they are later executed by the UI thread. This process sounds complex, but from the programmer's perspective it's fairly easy because these jobs take the form of simple method calls.

An instance of this *Dispatcher* is readily available. The *DependencyObject* class defines a property named *Dispatcher* of type *Dispatcher*, and many Silverlight classes derive from *DependencyObject*. Instances of all of these classes can be accessed from non-UI threads because they all have *Dispatcher* properties. You can use any *Dispatcher* object from any *DependencyObject* derivative created in your UI thread. They are all the same.

The *Dispatcher* class defines a method named *CheckAccess* that returns *true* if you can access a particular user interface object from the current thread. (The *CheckAccess* method is also duplicated by *DependencyObject* itself.) If an object can't be accessed from the current thread, then *Dispatcher* provides two versions of a method named *Invoke* that you use to post the job to the UI thread.

The SilverlightAccelerometer project implements a syntactically elaborate version of the code, but then I'll show you how to chop it down in size.

The verbose version requires a delegate and a method defined in accordance with that delegate. The delegate (and method) should have no return value, but as many arguments as you need to do the job, in this case the job of setting a string to the *Text* property of a *TextBlock*:

Project: SilverlightAccelerometer   File: MainPage.xaml.cs (excerpt)

```
delegate void SetTextBlockTextDelegate(TextBlock txtblk, string text);

void SetTextBlockText(TextBlock txtblk, string text)
{
    txtblk.Text = text;
}
```

The *OnAccelerometerReadingChanged* is responsible for calling *SetTextBlockText*. It first makes use of *CheckAccess* to see if it can just call the *SetTextBlockText* method directly. If not, then the handler calls the *BeginInvoke* method. The first argument is an instantiation of the delegate with the *SetTextBlockText* method; this is followed by all the arguments that *SetTextBlockText* requires:

Project: SilverlightAccelerometer   File: MainPage.xaml.cs (excerpt)

```
void OnAccelerometerReadingChanged(object sender, AccelerometerReadingEventArgs args)
{
    string str = String.Format("X = {0:F2}\n" +
                               "Y = {1:F2}\n" +
```

```
                                  "Z = {2:F2}\n\n" +
                                  "Magnitude = {3:F2}\n\n" +
                                  "{4}",
                                  args.X, args.Y, args.Z,
                                  Math.Sqrt(args.X * args.X + args.Y * args.Y +
                                                            args.Z * args.Z),
                                  args.Timestamp);

        if (txtblk.CheckAccess())
        {
            SetTextBlockText(txtblk, str);
        }
        else
        {
            txtblk.Dispatcher.BeginInvoke(new SetTextBlockTextDelegate(SetTextBlockText),
                                txtblk, str);
        }
    }
```

This is not too bad, but the need for the code to jump across threads has necessitated an additional method and a delegate. Is there a way to do the whole job right in the event handler?

Yes! The *BeginInvoke* method has an overload that accepts an *Action* delegate, which defines a method that has no return value and no arguments. You can create an anonymous method right in the *BeginInvoke* call. The complete code following the creation of the string object looks like this:

```
if (txtblk.CheckAccess())
{
    txtblk.Text = str;
}
else
{
    txtblk.Dispatcher.BeginInvoke(delegate()
    {
        txtblk.Text = str;
    });
}
```

The anonymous method begins with the keyword *delegate* and concludes with the curly brace following the method body. The empty parentheses following the *delegate* keyword are not required.

The anonymous method can also be defined using a lambda expression:

```
if (txtblk.CheckAccess())
{
    txtblk.Text = str;
}
```

```
else
{
    txtblk.Dispatcher.BeginInvoke(() =>
    {
        txtblk.Text = str;
    });
}
```

The duplicated code that sets the *Text* property of *TextBlock* to *str* looks a little ugly here (and would be undesirable if it involved more than just one statement), but you don't really need to call *CheckAccess*. You can just call *BeginInvoke* and nothing bad will happen even if you are calling it from the UI thead.

The Windows Phone 7 emulator doesn't contain any actual accelerometer, so it always reports a value of (0, 0, –1), which indicates the phone is lying on a flat surface. The program only makes sense when running on an actual phone:

The values here indicate the phone is roughly upright but tilted back a bit, which is a very natural orientation in actual use.

A Simple Bubble Level

One handy tool found in any workshop is a bubble level, also called a spirit level. A little bubble always floats to the top of a liquid, so it visually indicates whether something is parallel or orthogonal to the earth, or tilted in some way.

The XnaAccelerometer project includes a 48-by-48 pixel bitmap named Bubble.bmp that consists of a red circle:

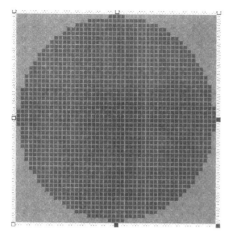

The magenta on the corners makes those areas of the bitmap transparent when XNA renders it.

As with the Silverlight program, you'll need a reference to the Microsoft.Devices.Sensors library and a using directive for the *Microsoft.Devices.Sensors* namespace.

The fields in the *Game1* class mostly involve variables necessary to position that bitmap on the screen:

XNA Project: XnaAccelerometer   File: Game1.cs (excerpt showing fields)

```
public class Game1 : Microsoft.Xna.Framework.Game
{
    const float BUBBLE_RADIUS_MAX = 25;
    const float BUBBLE_RADIUS_MIN = 12;

    GraphicsDeviceManager graphics;
    SpriteBatch spriteBatch;

    Vector2 screenCenter;
    float screenRadius;        // less BUBBLE_RADIUS_MAX

    Texture2D bubbleTexture;
    Vector2 bubbleCenter;
    Vector2 bubblePosition;
    float bubbleScale;

    Vector3 accelerometerVector;
    object accelerometerVectorLock = new object();
    ...

}
```

Towards the bottom you'll see a field named *accelerometerVector* of type *Vector3*. The *OnAccelerometerReadingChanged* event handler will store a new value in that field, and the *Update* method will utilize the value in calculating a position for a bitmap.

OnAccelerometerReadingChanged and *Update* run in separate threads. One is setting the field; the other is accessing the field. This is no problem if the field is set or accessed in a single machine code instruction. That would be the case if *Vector3* were a class, which is a reference type and basically referenced with something akin to a pointer. But *Vector3* is a structure (a value type) consisting of three properties of type *float*, each of which occupies four bytes, for a total of 12 bytes or 96 bits. Setting or accessing this *Vector3* field requires this many bits to be transferred.

A Windows Phone 7 device contains at least a 32-bit ARM processor, and a brief glance at the ARM instruction set does not reveal any machine code that would perform a 12-byte memory transfer in one instruction. This means that the accelerometer thread storing a new *Vector3* value could be interrupted midway in the process by the *Update* method in the program's main thread when it retrieves that value. The resultant value might have *X*, *Y*, and *Z* values mixed up from two readings.

While that could hardly be classified as a catastrophe in this program, let's play it entirely safe and use the C# *lock* statement to make sure the *Vector3* value is stored and retrieved by the two threads without interruption. That's the purpose of the *accelerometerVectorLock* variable among the fields.

I chose to create the *Accelerometer* object and set the event handler in the *Initialize* method:

XNA Project: XnaAccelerometer   File: Game1.cs (excerpt)

```
protected override void Initialize()
{
    Accelerometer accelerometer = new Accelerometer();
    accelerometer.ReadingChanged += OnAccelerometerReadingChanged;

    try
    {
        accelerometer.Start();
    }
    catch
    {
    }

    base.Initialize();
}

void OnAccelerometerReadingChanged(object sender, AccelerometerReadingEventArgs args)
{
```

```
    lock (accelerometerVectorLock)
    {
        accelerometerVector = new Vector3((float)args.X, (float)args.Y, (float)
args.Z);
    }
}
```

Notice that the event handler uses the *lock* statement to set the *accelerometerVector* field. That prevents code in the *Update* method from accessing the field during this short duration.

The *LoadContent* method loads the bitmap used for the bubble and initializes several variables used for positioning the bitmap:

XNA Project: XnaAccelerometer   File: Game1.cs (excerpt)

```
protected override void LoadContent()
{
    spriteBatch = new SpriteBatch(GraphicsDevice);

    Viewport viewport = this.GraphicsDevice.Viewport;
    screenCenter = new Vector2(viewport.Width / 2, viewport.Height / 2);
    screenRadius = Math.Min(screenCenter.X, screenCenter.Y) - BUBBLE_RADIUS_MAX;

    bubbleTexture = this.Content.Load<Texture2D>("Bubble");
    bubbleCenter = new Vector2(bubbleTexture.Width / 2, bubbleTexture.Height / 2);
}
```

When the *X* and *Y* properties of accelerometer are zero, the bubble is displayed in the center of the screen. That's the reason for both *screenCenter* and *bubbleCenter*. The *screenRadius* value is the distance from the center when the magnitude of the *X* and *Y* components is 1.

The *Update* method safely access the *accelerometerVector* field and calculates *bubblePosition* based on the *X* and *Y* components. It might seem like I've mixed up the *X* and *Y* components in the calculation, but that's because the default screen orientation is portrait in XNA, so it's opposite the coordinates of the acceleration vector. Because both landscape modes are supported by default, it's also necessary to multiply the acceleration vector values by –1 when the phone has been tilted into the *LandscapeRight* mode:

XNA Project: XnaAccelerometer   File: Game1.cs (excerpt)

```
protected override void Update(GameTime gameTime)
{
    // Allows the game to exit
    if (GamePad.GetState(PlayerIndex.One).Buttons.Back == ButtonState.Pressed)
        this.Exit();
```

```
Vector3 accVector;

lock (accelerometerVectorLock)
{
    accVector = accelerometerVector;
}

int sign = this.Window.CurrentOrientation ==
                            DisplayOrientation.LandscapeLeft ? 1 : -1;

bubblePosition = new Vector2(screenCenter.X + sign * screenRadius * accVector.Y,
                            screenCenter.Y + sign * screenRadius * accVector.X);
float bubbleRadius = BUBBLE_RADIUS_MIN + (1 - accVector.Z) / 2 *
                            (BUBBLE_RADIUS_MAX - BUBBLE_RADIUS_MIN);
bubbleScale = bubbleRadius / (bubbleTexture.Width / 2);

base.Update(gameTime);
}
```

In addition, a *bubbleScale* factor is calculated based on the *Z* component of the vector. The idea is that the bubble is largest when the screen is facing up and smallest when the screen is facing down, as if the screen is really one side of a rectangular pool of liquid that extends below the phone, and the size of the bubble indicates how far it is from the surface.

The *Draw* override uses a long version of the *Draw* method of *SpriteBatch*.

XNA Project: XnaAccelerometer   File: Game1.cs (excerpt)

```
protected override void Draw(GameTime gameTime)
{
    GraphicsDevice.Clear(Color.Navy);

    spriteBatch.Begin();
    spriteBatch.Draw(bubbleTexture, bubblePosition, null, Color.White, 0,
                    bubbleCenter, bubbleScale, SpriteEffects.None, 0);
    spriteBatch.End();
    base.Draw(gameTime);
}
```

Notice the *bubbleScale* argument, which scales the bitmap to a particular size. The center of scaling is provided by the previous argument to the method, *bubbleCenter*. That point is also aligned with the *bubblePosition* value relative to the screen.

The program doesn't look like much, and is even more boring running on the emulator. Here's an indication that the phone is roughly upright and tilted back a bit:

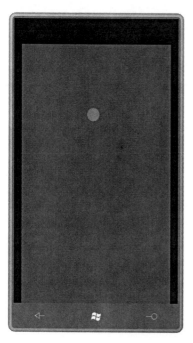

You'll discover that the accelerometer is very jittery and cries out for some data smoothing.

Geographic Location

With the user's permission, a Windows Phone 7 program can obtain the geographic location of the phone using a technique called Assisted-GPS or A-GPS.

The most accurate method of determining location is accessing signals from Global Positioning System (GPS) satellites. However, GPS can be slow. It doesn't work well in cities or indoors, and it's considered expensive in terms of battery use. To work more cheaply and quickly, an A-GPS system can attempt to determine location from cell-phone towers or the network. These methods are faster and more reliable, but less accurate.

The core class involved in location detection is *GeoCoordinateWatcher*. You'll need a reference to the System.Device assembly and a *using* direction for the *System.Device. Location* namespace. The WMAppManifest.xml file requires the tag:

```
<Capability Name="ID_CAP_LOCATION" />
```

This is included by default.

The *GeoCoordinateWatcher* constructor optionally takes a member of the *GeoPositionAccuracy* enumeration:

- *Default*

- *High*

After creating a *GeoCoordinateWatcher* object, you'll want to install a handler for the *PositionChanged* event and call *Start*. The *PositionChanged* event delivers a *GeoCoordinate* object that has eight properties:

- *Latitude*, a *double* between –90 and 90 degrees

- *Longitude*, a *double* between –180 and 180 degrees

- *Altitude* of type *double*

- *HorizontalAccuracy* and *VerticalAccuracy* of type *double*

- *Course*, a *double* between 0 and 360 degrees

- *Speed* of type *double*

- *IsUnknown*, a Boolean that is *true* if the *Latitude* or *Longitude* is not a number

If the application does not have permission to get the location, then *Latitude* and *Longitude* will be *Double.NaN*, and *IsUnknown* will be *true*.

In addition, *GeoCoordinate* has a *GetDistanceTo* method that calculates the distance between two *GeoCoordinate* objects.

I'm going to focus on the first two properties, which together are referred to as *geographic coordinates* to indicate a point on the surface of the Earth. Latitude is the angular distance from the equator. In common usage, latitude is an angle between 0 and 90 degrees and followed with either N or S meaning north or south. For example, the latitude of New York City is approximately 40°N. In the *GeoCoordinate* object, latitudes north of the equator are positive values and south of the equator are negative values, so that 90° is the North Pole and –90° is the South Pole.

All locations with the same latitude define a *line of latitude*. Along a particular line of latitude, longitude is the angular distance from the Prime Meridian, which passes through the Royal Observatory at Greenwich England. In common use, longitudes are either east or west. New York City is 74°W because it's west of the Prime Meridian. In a *GeoCoordinate* object, positive longitude values denote east and negative values are west. Longitude values of 180 and –180 meet up at the International Date Line.

Although the *System.Device.Location* namespace includes classes that use the geographic coordinates to determine civic address (streets and cities), these are not implemented in the initial release of Windows Phone 7.

The XnaLocation project simply displays numeric values.

XNA Project: XnaLocation   File: **Game1.cs (excerpt showing fields)**

```
public class Game1 : Microsoft.Xna.Framework.Game
{
    GraphicsDeviceManager graphics;
    SpriteBatch spriteBatch;
    SpriteFont segoe14;
    string text = "Obtaining location...";
    Viewport viewport;
    Vector2 textPosition;
    ...
}
```

As with the accelerometer, I chose to create and initialize the *GeoCoordinateWatcher* in the *Initialize* override. The event handler is called in the same thread, so nothing special needs to be done to format the results in a string:

XNA Project: XnaLocation   File: **Game1.cs (excerpt)**

```
protected override void Initialize()
{
    GeoCoordinateWatcher geoWatcher = new GeoCoordinateWatcher();
    geoWatcher.PositionChanged += OnGeoWatcherPositionChanged;
    geoWatcher.Start();

    base.Initialize();
}

void OnGeoWatcherPositionChanged(object sender,
                        GeoPositionChangedEventArgs<GeoCoordinate> args)
{
    text = String.Format("Latitude: {0:F3}\r\n" +
                         "Longitude: {1:F3}\r\n" +
                         "Altitude: {2}\r\n\r\n" +
                         "{3}",
                         args.Position.Location.Latitude,
                         args.Position.Location.Longitude,
                         args.Position.Location.Altitude,
                         args.Position.Timestamp);
}
```

The *LoadContent* method simply obtains the font and saves the *Viewport* for later text positioning:

XNA Project: XnaLocation   File: Game1.cs (excerpt)

```
protected override void LoadContent()
{
    spriteBatch = new SpriteBatch(GraphicsDevice);
    segoe14 = this.Content.Load<SpriteFont>("Segoe14");
    viewport = this.GraphicsDevice.Viewport;
}
```

The size of the displayed string could be different depending on different values. That's why the position of the string is calculated from its size and the *Viewport* values in the *Update* method:

XNA Project: XnaLocation   File: Game1.cs (excerpt)

```
protected override void Update(GameTime gameTime)
{
    // Allows the game to exit
    if (GamePad.GetState(PlayerIndex.One).Buttons.Back == ButtonState.Pressed)
        this.Exit();

    Vector2 textSize = segoe14.MeasureString(text);
    textPosition = new Vector2((viewport.Width - textSize.X) / 2,
                               (viewport.Height - textSize.Y) / 2);
    base.Update(gameTime);
}
```

The *Draw* method is trivial:

XNA Project: XnaLocation   File: Game1.cs (excerpt)

```
protected override void Draw(GameTime gameTime)
{
    GraphicsDevice.Clear(Color.Navy);

    spriteBatch.Begin();
    spriteBatch.DrawString(kootenay14, text, textPosition, Color.White);
    spriteBatch.End();

    base.Draw(gameTime);
}
```

Because the *GeoCoordinateWatcher* is left running for the duration of the program, it should update the location as the phone is moved. Here's where I live:

With the phone emulator, however, the *GeoCoordinateWatcher* program might not work. With some beta software releases of Windows Phone 7 development tools, the Accelerometer always returned the coordinates of a spot in Princeton, New Jersey, perhaps as a subtle reference to the college where Alan Turing earned his PhD.

Using a Map Service

Of course, most people curious about their location prefer to see a map rather than numeric coordinates. The Silverlight demonstration of the location service displays a map that comes to the program in the form of bitmaps.

In a real phone application, you'd probably be using Bing Maps, particularly considering the existence of a Bing Maps Silverlight Control tailored for the phone. Unfortunately, making use of Bing Maps in a program involves opening a developer account, and getting a maps key and a credential token. This is all free and straightforward but it doesn't work well for a program that will be shared among all the readers of a book.

For that reason, I'll be using an alternative that doesn't require keys or tokens. This alternative is Microsoft Research Maps, which you can learn all about at *msrmaps.com*. The aerial images are provided by the United States Geological Survey (USGS). Microsoft Research Maps makes these images available through a web service called MSR Maps Service, but still sometimes referred to by its old name of TerraService.

The downside is that the images are not quite state-of-the-art and the service doesn't always seem entirely reliable.

MSR Maps Service is a SOAP (Simple Object Access Protocol) service with the transactions described in a WSDL (Web Services Description Language) file. Behind the scenes, all the transactions between your program and the web service are in the form of XML files. However, to avoid programmer anguish, generally the WSDL file is used to generate a *proxy*, which is a collection of classes and structures that allow your program to communicate with the web service with method calls and events.

You can generate this proxy right in Visual Studio. Here's how I did it: I first created an Windows Phone 7 project in Visual Studio called SilverlightLocationMapper. In the Solution Explorer, I right-clicked the project name and selected Add Service Reference. In the Address field I entered the URL of the MSR Maps Service WSDL file: *http://MSRMaps.com/ TerraService2.asmx*.

(You might wonder if the URL should be *http://msrmaps.com/TerraService2.asmx?WSDL* because that's how WSDL files are often referenced. That address will actually seem to work at first, but you'll get files containing obsolete URLs.)

After you've entered the URL in the Address field, press Go. Visual Studio will access the site and report back what it finds. There will be one service, called by the old name of TerraService.

Next you'll want to enter a name in the Namespace field to replace the generic ServiceReference1. I used MsrMapsService and pressed OK.

You'll then see MsrMapsService show up under the project in the Solution Explorer. If you click the little Show All Files icon at the top of the Solution Explorer, you can view the generated files. In particular, nested under MsrMapsService and Reference.svcmap, you'll see Reference.cs, a big file (over 4000 lines) with a namespace of XnaLocationMapper. MsrMapsService, which combines the original project name and the name you selected for the web service.

This Reference.cs file contains all the classes and structures you need to access the web service, and which are documented on the *msrmaps.com* web site. To access these classes in your program, add a *using* direction:

```
using SilverlightLocationMapper.MsrMapsService;
```

You also need a reference to the System.Device assembly and *using* directives for the *System.Device.Location*, *System.IO*, and *System.Windows.Media.Imaging* namespacess.

In the MainPage.xaml file, I left the *SupportedOrientations* property at its default setting of *Portrait*, I removed the page title to free up more space, and I moved the title panel below the content grid just in case there was a danger of something spilling out of the content grid and obscuring the title. Moving the title panel below the content grid in the XAML file ensures that it will be visually on top.

Here's the content grid:

```
Silverlight Project: SilverlightLocationMapper   File: MainPage.xaml (excerpt)

<Grid x:Name="ContentPanel" Grid.Row="1" Margin="12,0,12,0">
    <TextBlock Name="statusText"
               HorizontalAlignment="Center"
               VerticalAlignment="Center"
               TextWrapping="Wrap" />

    <Image Source="Images/usgslogoFooter.png"
           Stretch="None"
           HorizontalAlignment="Right"
           VerticalAlignment="Bottom" />
</Grid>
```

The *TextBlock* is used to display status and (possibly) errors; the *Image* displays a logo of the United States Geological Survey.

The map bitmaps will be inserted between the *TextBlock* and *Image* so they obscure the *TextBlock* but the *Image* remains on top.

The code-behind file has just two fields, one for the *GeoCoordinateWatcher* that supplies the location information, and the other for the proxy class created when the web service was added:

```
Silverlight Project: SilverlightLocationMapper   File: MainPage.xaml.cs (excerpt)

public partial class MainPage : PhoneApplicationPage
{
    GeoCoordinateWatcher geoWatcher = new GeoCoordinateWatcher();
    TerraServiceSoapClient proxy = new TerraServiceSoapClient();
    ...
}
```

You use the proxy by calling its methods, which make network requests. All these methods are asynchronous. For each method you call, you must also supply a handler for a completion event that is fired when the information you requested has been transferred to your application.

The completion event is accompanied by event arguments: a *Cancelled* property of type *bool*, an *Error* property that is *null* if there is no error, and a *Result* property that depends on the request.

I wanted the process to begin after the program was loaded and displayed, so I set a handler for the *Loaded* event. That *Loaded* handler sets the handlers for the two completion events I'll require of the proxy, and also starts up the *GeoCoordinateWatcher*:

Silverlight Project: SilverlightLocationMapper   File: MainPage.xaml.cs (excerpt)

```
public MainPage()
{
    InitializeComponent();
    Loaded += OnMainPageLoaded;
}

void OnMainPageLoaded(object sender, RoutedEventArgs args)
{
    // Set event handlers for TerraServiceSoapClient proxy
    proxy.GetAreaFromPtCompleted += OnProxyGetAreaFromPtCompleted;
    proxy.GetTileCompleted += OnProxyGetTileCompleted;

    // Start GeoCoordinateWatcher going
    statusText.Text = "Obtaining geographic location...";
    geoWatcher.PositionChanged += OnGeoWatcherPositionChanged;
    geoWatcher.Start();
}
```

When coordinates are obtained, the following *OnGeoWatcherPositionChanged* method is called. This method begins by turning off the *GeoCoordinateWatcher*. The program is not equipped to continuously update the display, so it can't do anything with any additional location information. It appends the longitude and latitude to the *TextBlock* called *ApplicationTitle* displayed at the top of the screen.

Silverlight Project: SilverlightLocationMapper   File: MainPage.xaml.cs (excerpt)

```
void OnGeoWatcherPositionChanged(object sender,
                        GeoPositionChangedEventArgs<GeoCoordinate> args)
{
    // Turn off GeoWatcher
    geoWatcher.PositionChanged -= OnGeoWatcherPositionChanged;
    geoWatcher.Stop();

    // Set coordinates to title text
    GeoCoordinate coord = args.Position.Location;
    ApplicationTitle.Text += ": " + String.Format("{0:F2}°{1} {2:F2}°{3}",
                                        Math.Abs(coord.Latitude),
                                        coord.Latitude > 0 ? 'N' : 'S',
                                        Math.Abs(coord.Longitude),
                                        coord.Longitude > 0 ? 'E' : 'W');
```

```
    // Query proxy for AreaBoundingBox
    LonLatPt center = new LonLatPt();
    center.Lon = args.Position.Location.Longitude;
    center.Lat = args.Position.Location.Latitude;

    statusText.Text = "Accessing Microsoft Research Maps Service...";
    proxy.GetAreaFromPtAsync(center, 1, Scale.Scale16m,
(int)ContentPanel.ActualWidth,

(int)ContentPanel.ActualHeight);
    }
```

The method concludes by making its first call to the proxy. The *GetAreaFromPtAsync* call requires a longitude and latitude as a center point, but some other information as well. The second argument is 1 to get an aerial view and 2 for a map (as you'll see at the end of this chapter). The third argument is the desired scale, a member of the *Scale* enumeration. The member I've chosen means that each pixel of the returned bitmaps is equivalent to 16 meters.

Watch out: Some scaling factors—in particular, *Scale2m*, *Scale8m*, and *Scale32m*—result in GIF files being returned. Remember, remember, remember that Silverlight doesn't do GIF! For the other scaling factors, JPEGS are returned.

The final arguments to *GetAreaFromPtAsync* are the width and height of the area you wish to cover with the map.

All the bitmaps you get back from the MSR Maps Service are 200 pixels square. Almost always, you'll need multiple bitmaps to tile a complete area. For example, if the last two arguments to *GetAreaFromPtAsync* are 400 and 600, you'll need 6 bitmaps to tile the area.

Well, actually not: An area of 400 pixels by 600 pixels will require 12 bitmaps, 3 horizontally and 4 vertically.

Here's the catch: These bitmaps aren't specially created when a program requests them. They already exist on the server in all the various scales. The geographic coordinates where these bitmaps begin and end are fixed. So if you want to cover a particular area of your display with a tiled map, and you want the center of this area to be precisely the coordinate you specify, the existing tiles aren't going to fit exactly. You want sufficient tiles to cover your area, but the tiles around the boundary are going to hang over the edges.

What you get back from the *GetAreaFromPtAsync* call (in the following *OnProxyGetAreaFromPtCompleted* method) is an object of type *AreaBoundingBox*. This is a rather complex structure that nonetheless has all the information required to request the individual tiles you need and then assemble them together in a grid.

Silverlight Project: SilverlightLocationMapper File: **MainPage.xaml.cs (excerpt)**

```csharp
void OnProxyGetAreaFromPtCompleted(object sender, GetAreaFromPtCompletedEventArgs
args)
{
    if (args.Error != null)
    {
        statusText.Text = args.Error.Message;
        return;
    }

    statusText.Text = "Getting map tiles...";

    AreaBoundingBox box = args.Result;
    int xBeg = box.NorthWest.TileMeta.Id.X;
    int yBeg = box.NorthWest.TileMeta.Id.Y;
    int xEnd = box.NorthEast.TileMeta.Id.X;
    int yEnd = box.SouthWest.TileMeta.Id.Y;

    // Loop through the tiles
    for (int x = xBeg; x <= xEnd; x++)
        for (int y = yBeg; y >= yEnd; y--)
        {
            // Create Image object to display tile
            Image img = new Image();
            img.Stretch = Stretch.None;
            img.HorizontalAlignment = HorizontalAlignment.Left;
            img.VerticalAlignment = VerticalAlignment.Top;
            img.Margin = new Thickness((x - xBeg) * 200 -
box.NorthWest.Offset.XOffset,
                                        (yBeg - y) * 200 -
box.NorthWest.Offset.YOffset,
                                        0, 0);

            // Insert after TextBlock but before Image with logo
            ContentPanel.Children.Insert(1, img);

            // Define the tile ID
            TileId tileId = box.NorthWest.TileMeta.Id;
            tileId.X = x;
            tileId.Y = y;

            // Call proxy to get the tile (Notice that Image is user object)
            proxy.GetTileAsync(tileId, img);
        }
}
```

I won't discuss the intricacies of *AreaBoundingBox* because it's more or less documented on the *msrmaps.com* web site, and I was greatly assisted by some similar logic on the site written for Windows Forms (which I suppose dates it a bit).

Notice that the loop creates each *Image* object to display each tile. Each of these *Image* objects has the same *Stretch*, *HorizontalAlignment*, and *VerticalAlignment* properties, but a different *Margin*. This *Margin* is how the individual tiles are positioned within the content grid. The *XOffset* and *YOffset* values cause the tiles to hang off the top and left edges of the content grid. The content grid doesn't clip its contents, so these tiles possibly extend to the top of the program's page.

Notice also that each *Image* object is passed as a second argument to the proxy's *GetTileAsync* method. This is called the *UserState* argument. The proxy doesn't do anything with this argument except return it as the *UserState* property of the completion arguments, as shown here:

Silverlight Project: **SilverlightLocationManager**   File: **MainPage.xaml.cs** (excerpt)

```
void OnProxyGetTileCompleted(object sender, GetTileCompletedEventArgs args)
{
    if (args.Error != null)
    {
        return;
    }

    Image img = args.UserState as Image;
    BitmapImage bmp = new BitmapImage();
    bmp.SetSource(new MemoryStream(args.Result));
    img.Source = bmp;
}
```

That's how the method links up the particular bitmap tile with the particular *Image* element already in place in the content grid.

It is my experience that in most cases, the program doesn't get all the tiles it requests. If you're very lucky—and you happen to be running the program somewhere in my neighborhood—your display might look like this:

If you change the second argument of the *proxy.GetAreaFromPtAsync* call from a 1 to a 2, you get back images of an actual map rather than an aerial view:

It has a certain retro charm—and I love the watercolor look—but I'm afraid that modern users are accustomed to something just a little more 21st century.

Chapter 6
Issues in Application Architecture

A Silverlight application for Windows Phone 7 consists of several standard classes:

- an *App* class that derives from *Application*;

- an instance of the *PhoneApplicationFrame* class; and

- one or more classes that derive from *PhoneApplicationPage*.

This chapter is partially about the "or more" of that last item. The programs you've seen so far have consisted of a single class named *MainPage* that derives from *PhoneApplicationPage*. In more complex applications, you might want to have multiple pages and allow the user to navigate among them, much like navigating among Web pages.

Page navigation would seem to be an advanced Silverlight programming topic, and a topic that applies only to Silverlight programming rather than XNA programming. However, there are issues involved with navigation that are related to the very important topic of *tombstoning*, which is what happens to your Windows Phone 7 application when the user navigates to another application through the phone's Start screen. Tombstoning is very much an issue that also affects XNA programmers.

Basic Navigation

The SilverlightSimpleNavigation project begins as usual with a *MainPage* class, and as usual I set the two *TextBlock* elements for the titles:

Silverlight Project: SilverlightSimpleNavigation   **File: MainPage.xaml (excerpt)**

```
<StackPanel x:Name="TitlePanel" Grid.Row="0" Margin="12,17,0,28">
    <TextBlock x:Name="ApplicationTitle" Text="SIMPLE NAVIGATION" ... />
    <TextBlock x:Name="PageTitle" Text="main page" ... />
</StackPanel>
```

The content area of MainPage.xaml contains only a *TextBlock* that sets a handler for its *ManipulationStarted* event:

Silverlight Project: SilverlightSimpleNavigation   File: MainPage.xaml (excerpt)

```
<Grid x:Name="ContentPanel" Grid.Row="1" Margin="12,0,12,0">
    <TextBlock Text="Navigate to 2nd Page"
               HorizontalAlignment="Center"
               VerticalAlignment="Center"
               Padding="0 34"
               ManipulationStarted="OnTextBlockManipulationStarted" />
</Grid>
```

Notice the *Text* property on the *TextBlock*: "Navigate to 2nd page." The code-behind file contains the handler for *ManipulationStarted* but also overrides the *OnManipulationStarted* method for the whole page:

Silverlight Project: SilverlightSimpleNavigation   File: MainPage.xaml.cs (excerpt)

```
public partial class MainPage : PhoneApplicationPage
{
    Random rand = new Random();

    public MainPage()
    {
        InitializeComponent();
    }

    void OnTextBlockManipulationStarted(object sender, ManipulationStartedEventArgs
args)
    {
        this.NavigationService.Navigate(new Uri("/SecondPage.xaml",
UriKind.Relative));

        args.Complete();
        args.Handled = true;
    }

    protected override void OnManipulationStarted(ManipulationStartedEventArgs args)
    {
        ContentPanel.Background = new SolidColorBrush(
            Color.FromArgb(255, (byte)rand.Next(255),
                                (byte)rand.Next(255),
                                (byte)rand.Next(255)));

        base.OnManipulationStarted(args);
    }
}
```

If you touch anywhere on the page outside of the *TextBlock*, the background of the *ContentPanel* is set to a random color. Touch the *TextBlock*, and the handler accesses the *NavigationService* property of the page. This is an object of type *NavigationService* that contains properties, methods, and events related to navigation, including the crucial *Navigate* method:

```
this.NavigationService.Navigate(new Uri("/SecondPage.xaml", UriKind.Relative));
```

The argument is an object of type *Uri*. Notice the slash in front of SecondPage.xaml, and notice the use of *UriKind.Relative* to indicate a URI relative to MainPage.xaml.

I created a second page in the SilverlightSimpleNavigation project by right-clicking the project name in the Visual Studio solution explorer, and selecting Add and New Item. From the Add New Item dialog box, I picked Windows Phone Portrait Page and gave it a name of SecondPage.xaml.

This process creates not only SecondPage.xaml but also the code-behind file SecondPage.cs. The two SecondPage files are virtually identical to the two MainPage files that Visual Studio customarily creates. Like *MainPage*, *SecondPage* derives from *PhoneApplicationPage*.

I gave the titles In SecondPage.xaml the same application name as FirstPage.xaml but a page title of "second page":

Silverlight Project: SilverlightSimpleNavigation   File: SecondPage.xaml (excerpt)

```
<StackPanel x:Name="TitlePanel" Grid.Row="0" Margin="12,17,0,28">
    <TextBlock x:Name="ApplicationTitle" Text="SIMPLE NAVIGATION" ... />
    <TextBlock x:Name="PageTitle" Text="second page" ... />
</StackPanel>
```

The content area of SecondPage.xaml is very much like MainPage.xaml but the *TextBlock* reads "Go Back to 1st Page":

Silverlight Project: SilverlightSimpleNavigation   File: SecondPage.xaml (excerpt)

```
<Grid x:Name="ContentPanel" Grid.Row="1" Margin="12,0,12,0">
    <TextBlock Text="Go Back to 1st Page"
            HorizontalAlignment="Center"
            VerticalAlignment="Center"
            Padding="0 34"
            ManipulationStarted="OnTextBlockManipulationStarted" />
</Grid>
```

The code-behind file of the *SecondPage* class is also very much like the *FirstPage* class:

```
Silverlight Project: SilverlightSimpleNavigation   File: SecondPage.xaml.cs (excerpt)

public partial class SecondPage : PhoneApplicationPage
{
    Random rand = new Random();

    public SecondPage()
    {
        InitializeComponent();
    }

    void OnTextBlockManipulationStarted(object sender, ManipulationStartedEventArgs
args)
    {
        this.NavigationService.GoBack();

        args.Complete();
        args.Handled = true;
    }

    protected override void OnManipulationStarted(ManipulationStartedEventArgs args)
    {
        ContentPanel.Background = new SolidColorBrush(
            Color.FromArgb(255, (byte)rand.Next(255),
                                (byte)rand.Next(255),
                                (byte)rand.Next(255)));

        base.OnManipulationStarted(args);
    }
}
```

Once again, when you touch anywhere on the page except the *TextBlock*, the background changes to a random color. When you touch the *TextBlock*, the handler calls another method of *NavigationService*:

```
this.NavigationService.GoBack();
```

This call causes the program to go back to the page that navigated to SecondPage.xaml, in this case, MainPage.xaml. Take a look at the *Navigate* call in MainPage.cs again:

```
this.NavigationService.Navigate(new Uri("/SecondPage.xaml", UriKind.Relative));
```

Navigation in a Silverlight program is based around XAML files in much the same way that navigation in a traditional Web environment is based around HTML files. The actual instance of the *SecondPage* class is created behind the scenes. The *PhoneApplicationFrame* instance in the application handles many of the actual mechanics of navigation, but the public interface of *PhoneApplicationFrame* also involves *Uri* objects and XAML files rather than instances of *PhoneApplicationPage* derivatives.

Let's run the program. The program begins with the main page, and you can touch the screen to change the color:

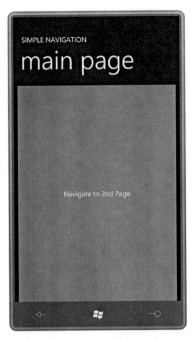

Now touch the *TextBlock* that says "Navigate to 2nd Page" and the second page comes into view:

You can touch that screen to change to a different color:

Now touch the *TextBlock* that says "Go Back to 1st Page". (Alternatively, you can press the phone's hardware Back button.) You'll be whisked back to the main page with the color just as you left it:

Now touch the *TextBlock* again to navigate to the second page:

The background is black. The second page does *not* display the color you set when you last visited the second page. This is very obviously a brand new instance of the *SecondPage* class.

The navigation system in Silverlight for Windows Phone is based around the metaphor of the last-in-first-out data structure called the *stack*. I'll sometimes refer to the page calling *Navigate* as the *source* page and the page being navigated to as the *destination* page. When the source page calls *Navigate*, the source page is put on the stack and a new instance of the destination page is created and displayed. When a page calls *GoBack*—or when the user presses the phone's hardware Back button—that page is abandoned, and the page at the top of the stack is popped off and displayed.

Within a Silverlight application, the phone's Back button performs the same function as a call to *GoBack* except if you're at the initial page of the program, in which case the hardware Back button terminates the application.

Try this: Replace the *GoBack* call in SecondPage.xaml.cs with the following:

```
this.NavigationService.Navigate(new Uri("/MainPage.xaml", UriKind.Relative));
```

This is not the same as the *GoBack* call. You won't go back to the original instance of *MainPage*. This call causes *SecondPage* to navigate to a *new* instance of *MainPage*, and if you keep pressing the *TextBlock* on each on the pages, you'll build up a whole stack of alternating *MainPage* and *SecondPage* instances, each of which can have its own unique color. You'll need to use the hardware Back button on the phone to back up through all these pages and finally terminate the application.

Navigate and *GoBack* are the two basic methods of *NavigationService*, and it's unlikely you'll need to use anything beyond these for your applications. Keep in mind that you're coding for a phone, and it doesn't make a lot of sense to have very complex navigation schemes within your program without also some way of reminding the user how the current page was arrived at and how to unwind the process.

Perhaps the most important use of secondary pages in a Silverlight application for the phone is to serve as dialog boxes. When a program needs some information from the user, it navigates to a new page to collection that information. The user enters the information, and then goes back to the main page.

Passing Data to Pages

The possible use of pages as dialog boxes provokes two questions:

- How do I pass data from a source page to a destination page?
- How do I return data when going back to the original page?

Interestingly, a facility is provided specifically for the first item but not for the second. I'll show you this facility and then look at more generalized solutions to the second problem.

The following project is called SilverlightPassData. It is very much like the first project in this chapter except that when *MainPage* navigates to *SecondPage*, it provides *SecondPage* with its current background color, and *SecondPage* initializes itself with that color.

Here's the content area of MainPage.xaml, the same as in the previous program:

Silverlight Project: SilverlightPassData   File: MainPage.xaml (excerpt)

```
<Grid x:Name="ContentPanel" Grid.Row="1" Margin="12,0,12,0">
    <TextBlock Text="Navigate to 2nd Page"
               HorizontalAlignment="Center"
               VerticalAlignment="Center"
               Padding="0 34"
               ManipulationStarted="OnTextBlockManipulationStarted" />
</Grid>
```

I won't show you the *OnManipulationStarted* override because it's the same as in the previous program, but the *ManipulationStarted* event handler for the *TextBlock* is a bit enhanced:

Silverlight Project: SilverlightPassData   File: **MainPage.xaml.cs** (excerpt)

```
void OnTextBlockManipulationStarted(object sender, ManipulationStartedEventArgs args)
{
    string destination = "/SecondPage.xaml";

    if (ContentPanel.Background is SolidColorBrush)
    {
        Color clr = (ContentPanel.Background as SolidColorBrush).Color;
        destination += String.Format("?Red={0}&Green={1}&Blue={2}",
                                     clr.R, clr.G, clr.B);
    }

    this.NavigationService.Navigate(new Uri(destination, UriKind.Relative));

    args.Complete();
    args.Handled = true;
}
```

If the *Background* brush of the *ContentPanel* is a *SolidColorBrush*, then the handler gets the *Color* and formats the red, green, and blue values into a string that is appended to the name of the destination page. The URI now looks something like this:

"/SecondPage.xaml?Red=244&Green=43&Blue=91"

You'll recognize this as a common format of an HTML query string.

The SilverlightPassData project also contains a *SecondPage* class that is the same as the one in the first project except that the code-behind file contains an override of the *OnNavigatedTo* method:

Silverlight Project: SilverlightPassData   File: **SecondPage.xaml.cs** (excerpt)

```
protected override void OnNavigatedTo(NavigationEventArgs args)
{
    IDictionary<string, string> parameters = this.NavigationContext.QueryString;

    if (parameters.ContainsKey("Red"))
    {
        byte R = Byte.Parse(parameters["Red"]);
        byte G = Byte.Parse(parameters["Green"]);
        byte B = Byte.Parse(parameters["Blue"]);

        ContentPanel.Background =
            new SolidColorBrush(Color.FromArgb(255, R, G, B));
    }

    base.OnNavigatedTo(args);
}
```

You'll need a *using* directive for the *System.Windows.Navigation* namespace for the *NavigationEventArgs* class.

The *OnNavigatedTo* method is defined by *Page*, the class from which *PhoneApplicationPage* derives. The method is called right after the page has been created. When *OnNavigatedTo* is called, the page's constructor has already executed, of course, but not much else has happened.

The destination class can access the query strings used to invoke the page through the page's *NavigationContext* property. This property is of type *NavigationContext*, a class that has only one public property named *QueryString*, which returns a dictionary that I've saved in a variable called *parameters*. The code here assumes that if the "Red" query string is present, the "Blue" and "Green" must exist as well. It passes all the strings to the *Byte.Parse* method and reconstructs the color.

Now as you navigate from *MainPage* to *SecondPage*, the background color remains the same. As you go back, however, that's not the case. There is no built-in facility like the query string to return data from one page to another.

Sharing Data Among Pages

Keep in mind that all the pages in your program have convenient access to the *App* class that derives from *Application*. The static *Application.Current* property returns the *Application* object associated with the program, and you can simply cast that to *App*. This means that you can use the *App* class for storing data you want to share among multiple pages of the application.

In the SilverlightShareData project, I defined a simple public property in the *App* class:

Silverlight Project: SilverlightShareData   **File: App.xaml.cs (excerpt)**

```
public partial class App : Application
{
    // public property for sharing data among pages
    public Color? SharedColor { set; get; }

    . . .

}
```

I defined this property of type nullable *Color* rather than just *Color* for those cases where a *SolidColorBrush* has not been set on the *Background* property of *ContentPanel*. In those cases, the *Background* property is *null* and there shouldn't be a *Color* stored in this property. If the property were of type *Color*, then a *Color* would be stored by default; that *Color* value would be transparent black, and that's wrong. Even non-transparent black is wrong if the user has selected the Light color scheme.

Much of the program remains the same, except that when you touch the *TextBlock* in *MainPage*, the handler first attempts to save a color in the new *App* class property before navigating to *SecondPage*:

Silverlight Project: SilverlightShareData   File: MainPage.xaml.cs (excerpt)

```
void OnTextBlockManipulationStarted(object sender, ManipulationStartedEventArgs args)
{
    if (ContentPanel.Background is SolidColorBrush)
        (Application.Current as App).SharedColor =
                    (ContentPanel.Background as SolidColorBrush).Color;

    this.NavigationService.Navigate(new Uri("/SecondPage.xaml", UriKind.Relative));

    args.Complete();
    args.Handled = true;
}
```

The *OnNavigatedTo* override in *SecondPage* than accesses that property:

Silverlight Project: SilverlightShareData   File: SecondPage.xaml.cs (excerpt)

```
protected override void OnNavigatedTo(NavigationEventArgs args)
{
    Color? sharedColor = (Application.Current as App).SharedColor;

    if (sharedColor != null)
        ContentPanel.Background =
                new SolidColorBrush(sharedColor.Value);

    base.OnNavigatedTo(args);
}
```

Similarly, when you press the *TextBlock* on *SecondPage*, the handler saves whatever color the background now happens to be back in the *App* class before calling *GoBack*:

Silverlight Project: SilverlightShareData   File: SecondPage.xaml.cs (excerpt)

```
void OnTextBlockManipulationStarted(object sender, ManipulationStartedEventArgs args)
{
    if (ContentPanel.Background is SolidColorBrush)
        (Application.Current as App).SharedColor =
                    (ContentPanel.Background as SolidColorBrush).Color;

    this.NavigationService.GoBack();
```

```
        args.Complete();
        args.Handled = true;
    }
```

The *MainPage* class also overrides *OnNavigatedTo* so it too can retrieve the stored color and set it to the background of the grid:

Silverlight Project: SilverlightShareData   File: MainPage.xaml.cs (excerpt)

```
protected override void OnNavigatedTo(NavigationEventArgs args)
{
    Color? sharedColor = (Application.Current as App).SharedColor;

    if (sharedColor != null)
        ContentPanel.Background =
                new SolidColorBrush(sharedColor.Value);

    base.OnNavigatedTo(args);
}
```

Now as you navigate between the pages they always share the same color.

Using the *App* class as a repository for shared data among pages is so convenient that you might find yourself using it exclusively. But you should really consider more structured solutions that involve only the pages navigating between each other and not some third-party class like *App*.

Besides the *OnNavigatedTo* virtual method, *Page* also defines an *OnNavigatedFrom* method, which at first seems much less useful. After all, a page knows that it's navigating from itself because it's just called *Navigate* or *GoBack*.

However, both *OnNavigatedFrom* and *OnNavigatedTo* have event arguments of type *NavigationEventArgs*, which defines two properties: *Uri* of type *Uri*, and *Content* of type *object*. These always indicate the page being navigated to.

For example, *MainPage* calls *Navigate* with an argument of "/SecondPage.xaml". The *OnNavigatedFrom* method in *MainPage* is called with event arguments with a *Uri* property indicating "/SecondPage.xaml" and a *Content* property of type *SecondPage*. This is the newly created instance of *SecondPage* that is about to be displayed, and this is the most convenient way to obtain that instance. The *OnNavigatedTo* method of *SecondPage* is then called with the same event arguments indicating a *Uri* of "/SecondPage.xaml" and the *SecondPage* object.

Similarly, when *SecondPage* calls *GoBack*, its *OnNavigatedFrom* method is called with event arguments that include a *Uri* property indicating "/MainPage.xaml" and a *Content* property with the *MainPage* instance. The *OnNavigatedTo* method of *MainPage* is then called with those same event arguments.

This means that during the *OnNavigatedFrom* method, a class has an opportunity to set a property or call a method in the class of the destination page.

Let's look at an example called SilverlightInsertData. The project has two pages named *MainPage* and *SecondPage* and the XAML files are the same as those you've already seen. The *MainPage* class doesn't have any logic to randomly change its color. Instead, it uses *SecondPage* to obtain a color for it. You can think of *SecondPage* as a dialog box that returns a random color to *MainPage*.

Here's most of the code-behind file in *MainPage*:

Silverlight Project: SilverlightInsertData   File: MainPage.xaml.cs (excerpt)

```
public partial class MainPage : PhoneApplicationPage
{
    public MainPage()
    {
        InitializeComponent();
    }

    public Color? ReturnedColor { set; get; }

    void OnTextBlockManipulationStarted(object sender, ManipulationStartedEventArgs
args)
    {
        this.NavigationService.Navigate(new Uri("/SecondPage.xaml", UriKind.
Relative));

        args.Complete();
        args.Handled = true;
    }
    ...
}
```

Notice the *ReturnedColor* property, of type nullable *Color* just like the property in the *App* class in the previous program.

Here's the *SecondPage* code-behind file:

Silverlight Project: SilverlightInsertData   File: SecondPage.xaml.cs (excerpt)

```
public partial class SecondPage : PhoneApplicationPage
{
    Random rand = new Random();

    public SecondPage()
    {
        InitializeComponent();
    }
```

```
    void OnTextBlockManipulationStarted(object sender, ManipulationStartedEventArgs
args)
    {
        this.NavigationService.GoBack();

        args.Complete();
        args.Handled = true;
    }

    protected override void OnManipulationStarted(ManipulationStartedEventArgs args)
    {
        ContentPanel.Background = new SolidColorBrush(
            Color.FromArgb(255, (byte)rand.Next(255),
                                (byte)rand.Next(255),
                                (byte)rand.Next(255)));

        base.OnManipulationStarted(args);
    }

    protected override void OnNavigatedFrom(NavigationEventArgs args)
    {
        if (ContentPanel.Background is SolidColorBrush)
        {
            Color clr = (ContentPanel.Background as SolidColorBrush).Color;

            if (args.Content is MainPage)
                (args.Content as MainPage).ReturnedColor = clr;
        }

        base.OnNavigatedFrom(e);
    }
}
```

As in the previous programs, *SecondPage* changes its background to a random color
when touched, and calls *GoBack* when the *TextBlock* is touched. The new code is in the
OnNavigatedFrom override, which is called shortly after the class calls *GoBack*. If there's
a valid *SolidColorBrush* available, the method checks if it's navigating to an object of type
MainPage. If so, then it saves the *Color* object in the *ReturnedColor* property of *MainPage*.

MainPage can retrieve the value of that property in its *OnNavigatedTo* override:

Silverlight Project: SilverlightInsertData   File: MainPage.xaml.cs (excerpt)

```
public partial class MainPage : PhoneApplicationPage
{
    ...
    protected override void OnNavigatedTo(NavigationEventArgs args)
    {
        if (ReturnedColor != null)
```

```
        ContentPanel.Background =
              new SolidColorBrush(ReturnedColor.Value);

     base.OnNavigatedTo(args);
   }
 }
```

In a sense, *MainPage* invokes *SecondPage* to obtain a *Color* value, just like a real dialog box. But if you navigate to *SecondPage* subsequent times, it always starts out with a black screen (or white if you've selected the Light color theme).

Interestingly, *SecondPage* can't initialize itself from any property in *MainPage* because the *OnNavigatedTo* call that *SecondPage* receives doesn't reference the source page. To work in a symmetrical manner, *SecondPage* would need to define its own public *Color* property, and *MainPage* would need to initialize that property in its own *OnNavigatedFrom* override.

You might consider a little variation on this program where *SecondPage* defines the *ReturnedColor* property. When *MainPage* navigates to *SecondPage* the *OnNavigatedFrom* method in *MainPage* is called, and the method saves the instance of *SecondPage* being navigated to in a field in *MainPage*. When *SecondPage* is finished, it saves the *Color* value in its *ReturnedColor* property and calls *GoBack*. The *OnNavigatedTo* method in *MainPage* is then called. *MainPage* can use the *SecondPage* instance saved as a field to access the *ReturnedColor* property.

This scheme sounds fine, but it won't always work. The problem is that *MainPage* can't be assured that the *SecondPage* instance it navigates to will be the same *SecondPage* instance that navigates back to *MainPage*. You'll have a better sense of this problem soon.

Retaining Data across Instances

Every time *MainPage* navigates to *SecondPage*, it's a different instance of *SecondPage*. That's why *SecondPage* always starts out the same. It's always a new instance.

If we want *SecondPage* to "remember" the last color it was set to, something outside of *SecondPage* must be responsible for saving that data. That could be *MainPage*.

Or, *SecondPage* could save its state in *isolated storage*. Isolated storage is much like regular disk storage. To access it, you use classes in the *System.IO.IsolatedStorage* namespace. Every Windows Phone 7 application has access to isolated storage but only to files that the application itself has created. Isolated storage allows an application to save data between multiple executions, and is ideal for saving application settings.

I'll present examples of isolated storage later in this chapter.

A third solution is provided by a class named *PhoneApplicationService*, defined in the *Microsoft.Phone.Shell* namespace. An instance of *PhoneApplicationService* is created in the standard App.xaml file:

```
<Application.ApplicationLifetimeObjects>
    <!--Required object that handles lifetime events for the application-->
    <shell:PhoneApplicationService
        Launching="Application_Launching" Closing="Application_Closing"
        Activated="Application_Activated" Deactivated="Application_Deactivated"/>
</Application.ApplicationLifetimeObjects>
```

Following the *PhoneApplicationService* tag are four events being associated with handlers; you'll see examples of these events later in this chapter. Don't create a new *PhoneApplicationService*. You can obtain this existing *PhoneApplicationService* with the static *PhoneApplicationService.Current* property.

PhoneApplicationService contains a property named *State*, which is a dictionary that lets you save and restore data. This *State* property is of type *IDictionary<string, object>*. You store objects in this dictionary using text keys. This data is only retained while the application is running, so it's not suitable for application settings that must be preserved between multiple executions of a program. Data retained by the applicaton only when it's running is sometimes known as "transient" data.

Any object you store in this *State* dictionary must be serializable, that is, it must be possible to convert the object into XML, and recreate the object from XML. It must have a public parameterless constructor, and all its public properties must either be serializable or be of types that have *Parse* methods to convert the strings back to objects.

It's not always obvious what objects are serializable and which ones are not. When I first started experimenting, I tried to store *SolidColorBrush* objects in the *State* dictionary. The program raised an exception that said "Type 'System.Windows.Media.Transform' cannot be serialized." It took awhile to remember that *Brush* has a property named *Transform* of type *Transform*, an abstract class. I had to serialize the *Color* instead.

Let's modify the previous program so that *SecondPage* uses this *State* property. In the SilverlightRetainData project, everything is the same except for a *using* directive for the *Microsoft.Phone.Shell* namespace and two overrides in *SecondPage*. Here they are:

Silverlight Project: SilverlightRetainData   File: SecondPage.xaml.cs (excerpt)

```
protected override void OnNavigatedFrom(NavigationEventArgs args)
{
    if (ContentPanel.Background is SolidColorBrush)
    {
        Color clr = (ContentPanel.Background as SolidColorBrush).Color;
```

```
            if (args.Content is MainPage)
                (args.Content as MainPage).ReturnedColor = clr;

            // Save color
            PhoneApplicationService.Current.State["Color"] = clr;
        }

        base.OnNavigatedFrom(args);
    }

    protected override void OnNavigatedTo(NavigationEventArgs args)
    {
        // Retrieve color
        if (PhoneApplicationService.Current.State.ContainsKey("Color"))
        {
            Color clr = (Color)PhoneApplicationService.Current.State["Color"];
            ContentPanel.Background = new SolidColorBrush(clr);
        }

        base.OnNavigatedTo(args);
    }
```

During the *OnNavigatedFrom* call, if there's a valid *Color* object available, then it's saved in the *State* dictionary with a key of "Color":

```
PhoneApplicationService.Current.State["Color"] = clr;
```

During the *OnNavigatedTo* override, if the key exists, then the *Color* value is loaded from the dictionary and *SolidColorBrush* is made from the *Color*. The key will not exist if you've just started running the program and you've navigated to *SecondPage* for the first time. But on subsequent navigations to *SecondPage*, the page is restored to the color you last set.

Every time you exit the program by pressing the Back button on the main page, the *State* dictionary is discarded with the rest of the *PhoneApplicationService*. This *State* dictionary is only suitable for saving transient data that a program needs to retain while it's running. If you need to save data between multiple executions of a program, use isolated storage.

Now try this: Navigate to *SecondPage*. Touch the screen to change the color. Now press the phone's hardware Start button. You've left the SilverlightRetainData program. From the phone's start screen, you can navigate to other programs, but eventually you'll want to press the phone's Back button to return to the SilverlightRetainData program and *SecondPage*. The color is still there.

Now go back to *MainPage*. The color you set in *SecondPage* is displayed. From *MainPage*, press the phone's hardware Start button, leaving the program. Navigate around a bit if you want but eventually start pressing the Back button to come back to SilverlightRetainData and *MainPage*.

Lo and behold, the screen has lost its color! What happened?

The Multitasking Ideal

Over the past few decades, it's been a common desire that our personal computers be able to do more than one thing at a time. But when user interfaces are involved, multitasking is never quite as seamless as we'd like. The Terminate-and-Stay-Resident (TSR) programs of MS-DOS and the cooperative multitasking of early Windows were only the first meager attempts in an ongoing struggle. In theory, process switching is easy. But sharing resources—including the screen and a handful of various input devices—is very hard.

While the average user might marvel at the ability of modern Windows to juggle many different applications at once, we programmers still wrestle with the difficulties of multitasking— carefully coding our UI threads to converse amicably with our non-UI threads, always on the lookout for the hidden treachery of asynchronous operations.

Every new application programming interface we encounter makes a sort of awkward accommodation with the ideals of multitasking, and as we become familiar with the API we also become accustomed to this awkward accommodation, and eventually we might even consider this awkward accommodation to be a proper solution to the problem.

On Windows Phone 7, that awkward accommodation is known as *tombstoning*.

Task Switching on the Phone

We want our phones to be much like our other computers. We want to have a lot of applications available. We want to start up a particular application as soon as we conceive a need for it. While that application is running, we want it to be as fast as possible and have access to unlimited resources. But we want this application to coexist with other running applications because we want to be able to jump among multiple applications running on the machine.

Arbitrarily jumping among multiple running applications is somewhat impractical on the phone. It would require some kind of display showing all the currently running applications, much like the Windows taskbar. Either this taskbar would have to be constantly visible—taking valuable screen space away from the active applications—or a special button or command would need to be assigned to display the taskbar or task list.

Instead, Windows Phone 7 manages multiple active applications by implementing a stack. In a sense, this application stack extends the page stack within a single Silverlight program. You can think of the phone as an old-fashioned web browser with no tab feature and no Forward button. But it does have a Back button and it also has a Start button, which brings you to the Start screen and allows you to launch a new program.

Suppose you choose to launch a program called Analyze. You work a little with Analyze and then decide you're finished. You press the Back button. The Analyze program is terminated and you're back at the Start screen. That's the simple scenario.

Later you decide you need to run Analyze again. While you're using Analyze, you need to check something on the Web. You press the Start button to get to the Start screen and select Internet Explorer. While you're browsing, you remember you haven't played any games recently. You press the Start button, select Backgammon and play a little of that. While playing Backgammon, you wonder about the odds of a particular move, so you press the Start button again and run Calc. Then you feel guilty about not doing any work, so you press the Start button again and run Draft.

Draft is a Silverlight program with multiple pages. From the main page, you navigate to several other pages.

Now start pressing the Back button. You go backwards through all the pages in the page stack of the Draft, then Draft is terminated as you go back to Calc. Calc still displays the remnants of your work, and Calc is terminated as you go back to Backgammon, which shows a game in progress, and Backgammon is terminated as you go back to Internet Explorer, and again you go backwards through any Web pages you may have navigated through, and IE is terminated as you go back to Analyze, and Analyze is terminated as you go back to the Start screen. The stack is now empty.

This type of navigation is a good compromise for small devices, and it's consistent with users' experiences in web browsing. The stack is conceptually very simple: The Start button pushes the current application on the stack so a new application can be run; the Back button terminates the current application and pops one off the top of the stack.

However, the limited resources of the phone convinced the Windows Phone 7 developers that applications on the stack should have as minimum a footprint as possible. For this reason, an application put on the stack does not continue plugging away at work. It's not even put into a suspended state of some sort. Something more severe than that happens. The process is actually terminated. When this terminated program comes off the stack, it is then re-executed from scratch.

This is tombstoning. The application is killed but then allowed to come back to life.

You've probably seen enough movies to know that re-animating a corpse can be a very scary proposition. Almost always the hideous thing that arises out of the filthy grave is not the clean and manicured loved one who went in.

The trick here is to persuade the disinterred program to look and feel much the same as when it was last alive and the user interacted with it. This process is a collaboration between you and Windows Phone 7. The phone gives you the tools (events and a place to put some data); your job is to use the tools to restore your program to a presentable state. Ideally the user should have no idea that it's a completely new process.

For some applications, resurrection doesn't have to be 100% successful. We all have experience with navigating among Web pages to know what's acceptable and what's not.

For example, suppose you visit a long Web page, and you scroll down a ways, then you navigate to another page. When you go back to the original page, it's not too upsetting if it's lost your place and you're back at the top of the page.

On the other hand, if you've just spent 10 minutes filling out a large form, you definitely do *not* want to see all your work gone after another page tells you that you've made one tiny error.

Let's nail down some terminology that's consistent with some events I'll discuss later:

- When an application is run from the Start screen, it is said to be *launched*.

- When an application is terminated as a result of the Back button, it is *closed*.

- When the program is running and the user presses the Start button, the program is said to be *deactivated*, even though it really is quite dead. This is the tombstoned state.

- When a program comes out of tombstoning as the user navigates back to it, it is said to be *activated*, even though it's really starting up from scratch.

Page State

The *SilverlightFlawedTombstoning* project is a simple Silverlight program with just one page. The program responds to taps on the screen by changing the background of *ContentGrid* to a random color, and displaying the total number of taps in its page title. Everything of interest happens in the code-behind file:

Silverlight Project: SilverlightFlawedTombstoning   File: MainPage.xaml.cs (excerpt)

```
public partial class MainPage : PhoneApplicationPage
{
    Random rand = new Random();
    int numTaps = 0;

    public MainPage()
    {
        InitializeComponent();
        UpdatePageTitle(numTaps);
    }

    protected override void OnManipulationStarted(ManipulationStartedEventArgs args)
    {
        ContentPanel.Background =
            new SolidColorBrush(Color.FromArgb(255, (byte)rand.Next(256),
                                                    (byte)rand.Next(256),
                                                    (byte)rand.Next(256)));
        UpdatePageTitle(++numTaps);
```

```
        args.Complete();
        base.OnManipulationStarted(args);
    }

    void UpdatePageTitle(int numTaps)
    {
        PageTitle.Text = String.Format("{0} taps total", numTaps);
    }
}
```

The little *UpdatePageTitle* method is called from both the program's constructor (where it always results in displaying a value of 0) and from the *OnManipulationStarted* override.

Build and deploy the program to the phone or phone emulator by pressing F5 (or selecting Start Debugging from the Debug menu). Arrange Visual Studio so you can see the Output window. When the program starts up, tap the screen several times to change the color and bump up the tap count. Now press the phone's Start button. You can see from Visual Studio that two threads in the program end and the program has terminated, but to the phone the program has actually been deactivated and tombstoned.

Now press the Back button to return to the program. You'll see a blank screen with the word "Resuming…" and the Output window in Visual Studio shows libraries being loaded. That's the program coming back to life.

However, when the program comes back into view, you'll see that the color and the number of taps have been lost. All your hard work! Totally gone! This is not a good way for a program to emerge from tombstoning. It is this state data that we want to preserve when the program is flat-lined.(Now you may see why the approach I described after the SilverlightInsertData program would not always work. That scheme involved saving the instance of *SecondPage* when *MainPage* navigated to that page. But if the user goes to the Start screen from *SecondPage* and then returned, that would be a new instance of *SecondPage* and not the one that *FrontPage* saved.)

An excellent opportunity to save and reload state data for a page is through overrides of the *OnNavigatedTo* and *OnNavigatedFrom* methods defined by the *Page* class from which *PhoneApplicationPage* derives. As you've seen, these methods are called when a page is brought into view by being loaded by the frame, and when the page is detached from the frame.

Using these methods is particularly appropriate if your Silverlight application will have multiple pages that the user can navigate among. You've already discovered that a new instance of *PhoneApplicationPage* is created every time a user navigates to a page, so you'll probably want to save and reload page state data for normal navigation anyway. By overriding *OnNavigatedTo* and *OnNavigatedFrom* you're effectively solving two problems with one solution.

Although Windows Phone 7 leaves much of the responsibility for restoring a tombstoned application to the program itself, it will cause the correct page to be loaded on activation, so it's possible that a page-oriented Silverlight program that saves and restores page state data using the *State* property of *PhoneApplicationSerivce* class during *OnNavigatedTo* and *OnNavigatedFrom* will need no special processing for tombstoning. The phone operating system preserves this *State* property during the time a program is deactivated and tombstoned, but gets rid of it when the program closes and is terminated for real.

The code-behind file for SilverlightBetterTombstoning includes a *using* directive for *Microsoft.Phone.Shell* and uses this *State* dictionary. Here's the complete class:

Silverlight Project: SilverlightBetterTombstoning   File: MainPage.xaml.cs (excerpt)

```
public partial class MainPage : PhoneApplicationPage
{
    Random rand = new Random();
    int numTaps = 0;
    PhoneApplicationService appService = PhoneApplicationService.Current;

    public MainPage()
    {
        InitializeComponent();
        UpdatePageTitle(numTaps);
    }

    protected override void OnManipulationStarted(ManipulationStartedEventArgs args)
    {
        ContentPanel.Background =
            new SolidColorBrush(Color.FromArgb(255, (byte)rand.Next(256),
                                                    (byte)rand.Next(256),
                                                    (byte)rand.Next(256)));
        UpdatePageTitle(++numTaps);

        args.Complete();
        base.OnManipulationStarted(args);
    }

    void UpdatePageTitle(int numTaps)
    {
        PageTitle.Text = String.Format("{0} taps total", numTaps);
    }

    protected override void OnNavigatedFrom(NavigationEventArgs args)
    {
        appService.State["numTaps"] = numTaps;

        if (ContentPanel.Background is SolidColorBrush)
        {
            appService.State["backgroundColor"] =
                            (ContentPanel.Background as SolidColorBrush).Color;
        }

        base.OnNavigatedFrom(args);
    }
```

```
    protected override void OnNavigatedTo(NavigationEventArgs args)
    {
        // Load numTaps
        if (appService.State.ContainsKey("numTaps"))
        {
            numTaps = (int)appService.State["numTaps"];
            UpdatePageTitle(numTaps);
        }

        // Load background color
        object obj;

        if (appService.State.TryGetValue("backgroundColor", out obj))
            ContentPanel.Background = new SolidColorBrush((Color)obj);

        base.OnNavigatedTo(args);
    }
}
```

Notice the *appService* field set to *PhoneApplicationService.Current*. That's just for convenience for accessing the *State* property. You can use the long *PhoneApplicationService.Current.State* instead if you prefer.

Storing items in the *State* dictionary is easier than getting them out. The syntax:

```
appService.State["numTaps"] = numTaps;
```

replaces an existing item if the "numTaps" key exists, or adds a new item if the key does not exist. Saving the background color is a little trickier: By default the *Background* property of *ContentPanel* is *null*, so the code checks for a non-*null* value before attempting to save the *Color* property.

To get items out of the dictionary, you can't use similar syntax. You'll raise an exception if the key does not exist. (And these keys will *not* exist when the application is launched.) The *OnNavigatedTo* method shows two different standard ways of accessing the items: The first checks if the dictionary contains the key; the second uses *TryGetValue*, which returns *true* if the key exists.

In a real program, you'll probably want to use *string* variables for the keys to avoid accidently typing inconsistent values. (If your typing is impeccable, don't worry about the multiple identical strings taking up storage: Strings are interned, and identical strings are consolidated into one.) You'll probably also want to write some standard routines that perform these jobs.

Try running this program like you ran the earlier one: Press F5 to deploy it to the phone or phone emulator from Visual Studio. Tap the screen a few times. Press the Start button as if you're going to start a new program. Visual Studio indicates that the process has terminated. Now press the Back button. When the program resumes the settings have been saved and the corpse looks as good as new!

As you experiment, you'll discover that the settings are saved when the application is tombstoned (that is, when you navigate away from the application with the Start button and then return) but not when a new instance starts up from the Start list. This is correct behavior. The operating system discards the *State* dictionary when the program terminates for real. The State dictionary is only for transient data and not for data that affects other instances of the same application.

If you want some similar data shared among all instances of a program, you probably want to implement what's often called *application settings*. You can do that as well.

Isolated Storage

Every program installed on Windows Phone 7 has access to its own area of permanent disk storage referred to as *isolated storage*, which the program can access using classes in the *System.IO.IsolatedStorage* namespace. Whole files can be read and written to in isolated storage, and I'll show you how to do that in the program that concludes this chapter. For the program that following I'm going to focus instead on a special use of isolated storage for storing application settings. The *IsolatedStorageSettings* class exists specifically for this purpose.

For application settings, you should be thinking in terms of the whole application rather than a particular page. Perhaps some of the application settings apply to multiple pages. Hence, a good place to deal with these application settings is in the program's *App* class.

Not coincidentally, it is the App.xaml file that creates a *PhoneApplicationService* object (the same *PhoneApplicationService* object used for saving transient data) and assigns event handlers for four events:

```
<shell:PhoneApplicationService Launching="Application_Launching"
                               Closing="Application_Closing"
                               Activated="Application_Activated"
                               Deactivated="Application_Deactivated"/>
```

The *Launching* event is fired when the program is first executed from the Start screen. The *Deactivated* event occurs when the program is tombstoned, and the *Activated* event occurs when the program is resurrected from tombstoning. The *Closing* event occurs when the program is really terminated, probably by the user pressing the Back button.

So, when a program starts up, it gets either a *Launching* event or an *Activated* event (but never both), depending whether it's being started from the Start screen or coming out of a tombstoned state. When a program ends, it gets either a *Deactivated* event or a *Closing* event, depending whether it's being tombstoned or terminated for real.

A program should load application settings during the *Launching* event and save them in response to the *Closing* event. That much is obvious. But a program should also save application settings during the *Deactivated* event because the program really doesn't know if it will ever be resurrected. And if it is resurrected, it should load application settings during the *Activated* event because otherwise it won't know about those settings.

Conclusion: application settings should be loaded during the *Launching* and *Activated* events and saved during the *Deactivated* and *Closing* events.

For the SilverlightIsolatedStorage program, I decided that the number of taps should continue to be treated as transient data—part of the state of the page. But the background color should be an application setting and shared among all instances.

In App.xaml.cs I defined the following public property:

Silverlight Project: **SilverlightIsolatedStorage**   File: **App.xaml.cs (excerpt)**

```
public partial class App : Application
{
    // Application settings
    public Brush BackgroundBrush { set; get; }
    . . .
}
```

Conceivably this can be one of many application settings that are accessible throughout the application.

App.xaml.cs already has empty event handlers for all the *PhoneApplicationService* events. I gave each handler a body consisting of a single method call:

Silverlight Project: **SilverlightIsolatedStorage**   File: **App.xaml.cs (excerpt)**

```
private void Application_Launching(object sender, LaunchingEventArgs e)
{
    LoadSettings();
}

private void Application_Activated(object sender, ActivatedEventArgs e)
{
    LoadSettings();
}

private void Application_Deactivated(object sender, DeactivatedEventArgs e)
{
    SaveSettings();
}

private void Application_Closing(object sender, ClosingEventArgs e)
{
    SaveSettings();
}
```

Here are the *LoadSettings* and *SaveSettings* methods. Both methods obtain an *IsolatedStorageSettings* object. Like the *State* property of *PhoneApplicationService*, the *IsolatedStorageSettings* object is a dictionary. One method in the program loads (and the other saves) the *Color* property of the *BackgroundBrush* property with code that is similar to what you saw before.

Silverlight Project: SilverlightIsolatedStorage   File: App.xaml.cs (excerpt)

```
void LoadSettings()
{
    IsolatedStorageSettings settings = IsolatedStorageSettings.ApplicationSettings;

    Color clr;

    if (settings.TryGetValue<Color>("backgroundColor", out clr))
        BackgroundBrush = new SolidColorBrush(clr);
}

void SaveSettings()
{
    IsolatedStorageSettings settings = IsolatedStorageSettings.ApplicationSettings;

    if (BackgroundBrush is SolidColorBrush)
    {
        settings["backgroundColor"] = (BackgroundBrush as SolidColorBrush).Color;
        settings.Save();
    }
}
```

And finally, here's the new MainPage.xaml.cs file. This file—and any other class in the program—can get access to the *App* object using the static *Application.Current* property and casting it to an *App*. The constructor of *MainPage* obtains the *BackgroundBrush* property from the *App* class, and the *OnManipulationStarted* method sets that *BackgroundBrush* property.

Silverlight Project: SilverlightIsolatedStorage   File: MainPage.xaml.cs (excerpt)

```
public partial class MainPage : PhoneApplicationPage
{
    Random rand = new Random();
    int numTaps = 0;
    PhoneApplicationService appService = PhoneApplicationService.Current;

    public MainPage()
    {
        InitializeComponent();
        UpdatePageTitle(numTaps);
```

```
        // Access App class for isolated storage setting
        Brush brush = (Application.Current as App).BackgroundBrush;

        if (brush != null)
            ContentPanel.Background = brush;
    }

    protected override void OnManipulationStarted(ManipulationStartedEventArgs args)
    {
        SolidColorBrush brush =
            new SolidColorBrush(Color.FromArgb(255, (byte)rand.Next(256),
                                                    (byte)rand.Next(256),
                                                    (byte)rand.Next(256)));
        ContentPanel.Background = brush;

        // Save to App class for isolated storage setting
        (Application.Current as App).BackgroundBrush = brush;

        UpdatePageTitle(++numTaps);

        args.Complete();
        base.OnManipulationStarted(args);
    }

    void UpdatePageTitle(int numTaps)
    {
        PageTitle.Text = String.Format("{0} taps total", numTaps);
    }

    protected override void OnNavigatedFrom(NavigationEventArgs args)
    {
        appService.State["numTaps"] = numTaps;

        base.OnNavigatedFrom(args);
    }

    protected override void OnNavigatedTo(NavigationEventArgs args)
    {
        // Load numTaps
        if (appService.State.ContainsKey("numTaps"))
        {
            numTaps = (int)appService.State["numTaps"];
            UpdatePageTitle(numTaps);
        }
    }
}
```

Because that background color has been upgraded from transient page data to an application setting, references to it have been removed in the *OnNavigatedFrom* and *OnNavigatedTo* overrides.

Xna Tombstoning and Settings

XNA applications aren't normally built around pages like Silverlight applications. If you wanted, however, you could certainly implement your own page-like structure within an XNA program. You'll recall that the state of the phone's Back button is checked during every call to the standard *Update* override. You can use this logic for navigational purposes as well as for terminating the program. But that's something I'll let you work out on your own.

An XNA program can also make use of the same *PhoneApplicationService* class used by Silverlight programs for saving transient state information during tombstoning. An XNA program can also use this class to install handlers for the four *PhoneApplicationService* events: *Launching*, *Activated*, *Deactivated*, and *Closing*. You'll need references both to the Microsoft.Phone library (for *PhoneApplicationService* itself) and System.Windows (for the *IApplicationService* interface that *PhoneApplicationService* implements). Within the Game1.cs file you'll want a *using* directive for *Microsoft.Phone.Shell*.

In the constructor of the *Game1* class you can obtain the *PhoneApplicationService* instance associated with the application through the static *PhoneApplicationService.Current* property.

The *Game* class also defines a couple handy virtual methods named *OnActivated* and *OnDeactivated* that are also useful for handling tombstoning. The *OnActivated* method is called during launching and re-activation, and *OnDeactivated* is called during deactivation and program closing, much like the *OnNavigatedTo* and *OnNavigatedFrom* virtual methods of a Silverlight page.

In the XnaTombstoning program that concludes this chapter I've tried to mimic the functionality and structure of the SilverlightIsolatedStorage program. The program uses the *PhoneApplicationService* events for saving and restoring application settings (a *Color*), and overrides of the *OnDeactivated* and *OnActivated* events for retaining transient data (the number of taps).

But I went a little further in providing a more generalized solution for application settings. I gave the *XnaTombstoning* project a dedicated *Settings* class that uses the more generalized features of isolated storage that involve real files rather than just simple settings. You'll need a reference to System.Xml.Serialization library for this class as well *using* directives for the *System.IO*, *System.IO.IsolatedStorage*, and *System.Xml.Serialization* namespaces.

Silverlight Project: XnaTombstoning   File: **Settings.cs** (excerpt)

```
public class Settings
{
    const string filename = "settings.xml";
```

```
    // Application settings
    public Color BackgroundColor { set; get; }

    public Settings()
    {
        BackgroundColor = Color.Navy;
    }

    public void Save()
    {
        IsolatedStorageFile storage = IsolatedStorageFile.GetUserStoreForApplication();
        IsolatedStorageFileStream stream = storage.CreateFile(filename);
        XmlSerializer xml = new XmlSerializer(GetType());
        xml.Serialize(stream, this);
        stream.Close();
        stream.Dispose();
    }

    public static Settings Load()
    {
        IsolatedStorageFile storage = IsolatedStorageFile.GetUserStoreForApplication();
        Settings settings;

        if (storage.FileExists(filename))
        {
            IsolatedStorageFileStream stream =
                    storage.OpenFile("settings.xml", FileMode.Open);
            XmlSerializer xml = new XmlSerializer(typeof(Settings));
            settings = xml.Deserialize(stream) as Settings;
            stream.Close();
            stream.Dispose();
        }
        else
        {
            settings = new Settings();
        }

        return settings;
    }
}
```

The idea here is that an instance of this *Settings* class itself is serialized and saved in isolated storage in the *Save* method, and then retrieved from isolated storage and deserialized in the *Load* method. Notice that the *Load* method is static and returns an instance of the *Settings* class.

When an instance of this *Settings* class is serialized, all its public properties are serialized. This class has exactly one public property of type *Color* named *BackgroundColor* but it would be very easy to add more properties to this class as the application develops and gets more sophisticated.

In the *Save* method, the area of isolated storage reserved for this application is obtained from the static *IsolatedStorageFile.GetUserStoreForApplication* method. This method returns an object of type *IsolatedStorageFile* but the name is a little misleading. This *IsolatedStorageFile* object is closer in functionality to a *file system* than a *file*. You use the object to maintain directories, and to create and open files. A call to *CreateFile* returns an *IsolatedStorageFileStream* which here is used with an *XmlSerializer* object to serialize and save the file.

The *Load* method is a bit more complex because it's possible that the program is being run for the very first time and the settings.xml file does not exist. In that case, the *Load* method creates a new instance of *Settings*.

Notice the constructor that initializes the properties to their default values, which in this case only involves the single public property named *BackgroundColor*. If you add a second public property for another application setting at some point, you'll want to also specify a default value of that property in the constructor. The first time you run the new version of the program, that new property will be initialized in the constructor, but the *Load* method will retrieve a file that doesn't have that property, so the new version smoothly integrates with the previous version.

Here's another consideration: This scheme only works if the properties representing application settings are serializable. For a more complex program, that might not be the case. For objects that are not serializable but still must be saved to isolated storage, you can still include a property for that object in this file but you'll want to flag that property definition with the *[XmlIgnore]* attribute. The property will be ignored for serialization purposes. Instead you'll need to handle that property with special code in the *Save* and *Load* methods.

The remainder of the XnaTombstoning project lets you tap the screen and responds by displaying a new random background color and a count of the number of taps. The background color is treated as an application setting (as is evident by its inclusion in the *Settings* class) and the number of taps is a transient setting.

Here's an excerpt of the *Game1* class showing the fields, constructor, and *PhoneApplicationService* events:

Silverlight Project: XnaTombstoning   File: Game1.cs (excerpt)

```
public class Game1 : Microsoft.Xna.Framework.Game
{
    GraphicsDeviceManager graphics;
    SpriteBatch spriteBatch;

    Settings settings;
    SpriteFont segoe14;
```

```
Viewport viewport;
Random rand = new Random();
StringBuilder text = new StringBuilder();
Vector2 position;
int numTaps = 0;

public Game1()
{
    graphics = new GraphicsDeviceManager(this);
    Content.RootDirectory = "Content";

    // Frame rate is 30 fps by default for Windows Phone.
    TargetElapsedTime = TimeSpan.FromTicks(333333);

    TouchPanel.EnabledGestures = GestureType.Tap;

    PhoneApplicationService appService = PhoneApplicationService.Current;
    appService.Launching += OnAppServiceLaunching;
    appService.Activated += OnAppServiceActivated;
    appService.Deactivated += OnAppServiceDeactivated;
    appService.Closing += OnAppServiceClosing;
}

...

void OnAppServiceLaunching(object sender, LaunchingEventArgs args)
{
    settings = Settings.Load();
}

void OnAppServiceActivated(object sender, ActivatedEventArgs args)
{
    settings = Settings.Load();
}

void OnAppServiceDeactivated(object sender, DeactivatedEventArgs args)
{
    settings.Save();
}

void OnAppServiceClosing(object sender, ClosingEventArgs args)
{
    settings.Save();
}
}
```

A *Settings* object named *settings* is saved as a field. The constructor attaches handlers for the four events of *PhoneApplicationService* and it is in the handlers for these events that the application settings are saved and loaded.

The *LoadContent* override contains nothing surprising:

Silverlight Project: XnaTombstoning   File: Game1.cs (excerpt)

```
protected override void LoadContent()
{
    spriteBatch = new SpriteBatch(GraphicsDevice);
    segoe14 = this.Content.Load<SpriteFont>("Segoe14");
    viewport = this.GraphicsDevice.Viewport;
}
```

The *Update* method reads taps, updates the *numTaps* field, determines a new random color, and also prepares a *StringBuilder* object for displaying the number of taps:

Silverlight Project: XnaTombstoning   File: Game1.cs (excerpt)

```
protected override void Update(GameTime gameTime)
{
    // Allows the game to exit
    if (GamePad.GetState(PlayerIndex.One).Buttons.Back == ButtonState.Pressed)
        this.Exit();

    while (TouchPanel.IsGestureAvailable)
        if (TouchPanel.ReadGesture().GestureType == GestureType.Tap)
        {
            numTaps++;
            settings.BackgroundColor =  new Color((byte)rand.Next(255),
                                                  (byte)rand.Next(255),
                                                  (byte)rand.Next(255));
        }

    text.Remove(0, text.Length);
    text.AppendFormat("{0} taps total", numTaps);
    Vector2 textSize = segoe14.MeasureString(text.ToString());
    position = new Vector2((viewport.Width - textSize.X) / 2,
                           (viewport.Height - textSize.Y) / 2);

    base.Update(gameTime);
}
```

Notice that the new color is saved not as a field, but as the *BackgroundColor* property of the *Settings* instance. That property is then referenced in the *Draw* override:

Silverlight Project: XnaTombstoning   File: Game1.cs (excerpt)

```
protected override void Draw(GameTime gameTime)
{
    GraphicsDevice.Clear(settings.BackgroundColor);

    spriteBatch.Begin();
    spriteBatch.DrawString(segoe14, text, position, Color.White);
    spriteBatch.End();

    base.Draw(gameTime);
}
```

The transient value of the *numTaps* field is saved to and restored from the *State* dictionary of the *PhoneApplicationService* in overrides of *OnActivated* and *OnDeactivated*:

Silverlight Project: XnaTombstoning   File: Game1.cs (excerpt)

```
protected override void OnActivated(object sender, EventArgs args)
{
    if (PhoneApplicationService.Current.State.ContainsKey("numTaps"))
        numTaps = (int)PhoneApplicationService.Current.State["numTaps"];

    base.OnActivated(sender, args);
}

protected override void OnDeactivated(object sender, EventArgs args)
{
    PhoneApplicationService.Current.State["numTaps"] = numTaps;
    base.OnDeactivated(sender, args);
}
```

It might seem a little arbitrary to save and restore application settings in one set of event handlers, and save and restore transient settings in another set of overrides to virtual methods, and in a practical sense it is arbitrary. The program will get a call to *OnActivated* about the same time the *Launching* and *Activated* events are fired, and a call to *OnDeactivated* about the same time the *Deactivated* and *Closing* events are fired. The differentiation is more conceptual in that *OnActivated* and *OnDeactivated* are associated with the *Game* instance, so they should be used for properties associated with the game rather than overall application settings.

It's possible that you'll need to save an unserializable object as a transient setting, but because it's not serializable, you can't use the *State* dictionary of the *PhoneApplicationService* class. You'll need to use isolated storage for such an object, but you don't want to accidently retrieve that object and reuse it when the program is run again. In this case, you'll use a flag in the *State* dictionary indicating whether you need to load the transient object from isolated storage.

Testing and Experimentation

Programmers at Microsoft who have been writing Windows Phone 7 applications longer than many of us report that dealing with tombstoning can be one of the trickier aspects of phone development. The techniques I've shown you in this chapter illustrate a good starting point but all applications will have slightly different requirements. Surely you'll want to do a lot of testing in your own programs, and it always helps to know exactly what methods of a program are being called and in what order. For this job, the *Debug.WriteLine* method of the *System.Diagnostics* namespace can be very helpful.

Part II
Silverlight

Chapter 7
XAML Power and Limitations

As you've seen, a Silverlight program is generally a mix of code and XAML. Most often, you'll use XAML for defining the layout of the visuals of your application, and you'll use code for event handling, including all user-input events and all events generated by controls as a result of processing user-input events.

Much of the object creation and initialization performed in XAML would traditionally be done in the constructor of a page or window class. This might make XAML seem just a tiny part of the application, but it turns out to be much more than that. As the name suggests, XAML is totally compliant XML, so it's instantly toolable—machine writable and machine readable as well as human writable and human readable.

Although XAML is usually concerned with object creation and initialization, certain features of Silverlight provide much more than object initialization would seem to imply. One of these features is data binding, which involves connections between controls, or between controls and underlying data, so that properties are automatically updated without the need for explicit event handlers. Entire animations can also be defined in XAML.

Although XAML is sometimes referred to as a "declarative language," it is certainly not a complete programming language. You can't perform arithmetic in any generalized manner in XAML, and you can't dynamically create objects in XAML.

Experienced programmers encountering XAML for the first time are sometimes resistant to it. I know I was. Everything that we value in a programming language such as C#—required declarations, strong typing, array-bounds checking, tracing abilities for debugging—largely goes away when everything is reduced to XML text strings. Over the years, however, I've gotten very comfortable with XAML, and I find it very liberating in using XAML for the visuals of the application. In particular I like how the parent-child relationship of controls on the surface of a window is mimicked by the parent-child structure inherent in XML. I also like the ability to experiment with XAML—even just in the Visual Studio designer.

Everything you need to do in Silverlight can be allocated among these three categories:

- Stuff you can do in either code or XAML
- Stuff you can do only in code (e.g., event handling and methods)
- Stuff you can do only in XAML (e.g., templates)

In both code and XAML you can instantiate classes and structures, and set the properties of these objects. A class or structure instantiated in XAML must be defined as public (of course), but it must also have a parameterless constructor. When XAML instantiates the class, it has no way of passing anything to the constructor. In XAML you can associate a particular event with an event handler, but the event handler itself must be implemented in code. You can't make method calls in XAML because, again, there's no way to pass arguments to the method.

If you want, you can write *almost* all of your Silverlight application entirely in code. However, page navigation is based around the existence of XAML files for classes that derive from *PhoneApplicationPage*, and there also is a very important type of job that *must* be done in XAML. This is the construction of *templates*. You use templates in two ways: First, to visually display data using a collection of elements and controls, and secondly, to redefine the visual appearance of a control while maintaining its functionality. You can write alternatives to templates in code, but you can't write the templates themselves.

After some experience with Silverlight programming, you might decide that you want to use a design program such as Expression Blend to generate XAML for you. But I urge you—speaking programmer to programmer—*to learn how to write XAML by hand*. At the very least you need to know how to read the XAML that design programs generate for you.

One of the very nice features of XAML is that you can experiment with it in a very interactive manner, and by experimenting with XAML you can learn a lot about Silverlight. Programming tools designed specifically for experimenting with XAML are available. These programs take advantage of a static method named *XamlReader.Load* that can convert XAML text into an object at runtime. In Chapter 13 you'll see an application that lets you experiment with XAML right on the phone!

Until then, however, you can experiment with XAML in the Visual Studio designer. Generally the designer responds promptly and accurately to changes you make in the XAML. Only when things get a bit complex will you actually need to build and deploy the application to see what it's doing.

A *TextBlock* in Code

Before we get immersed in experimenting with XAML, however, I must issue another warning: As you get accustomed to using XAML exclusively for certain common chores, it's important not to forget how to write C#!

You'll recall the XAML version of the *TextBlock* in the *Grid* from Chapter 2:

```
<Grid x:Name="ContentPanel" Grid.Row="1" Margin="12,0,12,0">
    <TextBlock Text="Hello, Windows Phone 7!"
            HorizontalAlignment="Center"
            VerticalAlignment="Center" />
</Grid>
```

Elements in XAML such as *TextBlock* are actually classes. Attributes of these elements (such as *Text*, *HorizontalAlignment*, and *VerticalAlignment*) are properties of the class. Let's see how easy it is to write a *TextBlock* in code, and to also use code to insert the *TextBlock* into the XAML *Grid*.

The TapForTextBlock project creates a new *TextBlock* in code every time you tap the screen. The MainPage.xaml file contains a TextBlock centered with the content grid:

Silverlight Project: TapForTextBlock   File: **MainPage.xaml** (excerpt)

```
<Grid x:Name="ContentPanel" Grid.Row="1" Margin="12,0,12,0">
    <TextBlock Name="txtblk"
               Text="Hello, Windows Phone 7!"
               HorizontalAlignment="Center"
               VerticalAlignment="Center" />
</Grid>
```

The code-behind file for *MainPage* creates an additional *TextBlock* whenever you tap the screen. It uses the dimensions of the existing *TextBlock* to set a *Margin* property on the new *TextBlock* element to randomly position it within the content grid:

Silverlight Project: TapForTextBlock   File: **MainPage.xaml.cs** (excerpt)

```
public partial class MainPage : PhoneApplicationPage
{
    Random rand = new Random();

    public MainPage()
    {
        InitializeComponent();
    }

    protected override void OnManipulationStarted(ManipulationStartedEventArgs args)
    {
        TextBlock newTextBlock = new TextBlock();
        newTextBlock.Text = "Hello, Windows Phone 7!";
        newTextBlock.HorizontalAlignment = HorizontalAlignment.Left;
        newTextBlock.VerticalAlignment = VerticalAlignment.Top;
        newTextBlock.Margin = new Thickness(
            (ContentPanel.ActualWidth - txtblk.ActualWidth) * rand.NextDouble(),
            (ContentPanel.ActualHeight - txtblk.ActualHeight) * rand.NextDouble(),
            0, 0);

        ContentPanel.Children.Add(newTextBlock);

        args.Complete();
        args.Handled = true;
        base.OnManipulationStarted(args);
    }
}
```

You don't need to perform the steps precisely in this order: You can add the *TextBlock* to *ContentPanel* first and then set the *TextBlock* properties.

But this is the type of thing you simply can't do in XAML. XAML can't respond to events, it can't arbitrarily create new instances of elements, it can't make calls to the *Random* class, and it certainly can't perform calculations.

You can also take advantage of a feature introduced in C# 3.0 to instantiate a class and define its properties in a block:

```
TextBlock newTextBlock = new TextBlock
{
    Text = "Hello, Windows Phone 7!",
    HorizontalAlignment = HorizontalAlignment.Left,
    VerticalAlignment = VerticalAlignment.Top,
    Margin = new Thickness(
            (ContentPanel.ActualWidth - txtblk.ActualWidth) * rand.NextDouble(),
            (ContentPanel.ActualHeight - txtblk.ActualHeight) * rand.NextDouble(),
            0, 0)
};

ContentPanel.Children.Add(newTextBlock);
```

That makes the code look a *little* more like the XAML (except for the calculations and method calls to *rand.NextDouble*), but you can still see that XAML provides several shortcuts. In code the *HorizontalAlignment* and *VerticalAlignment* properties must be set to members of the *HorizontalAlignment* and *VerticalAlignment* enumerations, respectively. In XAML, you need only specify the member name.

Just looking at the XAML, it is not so obvious that the *Grid* has a property named *Children*, and that this property is a collection, and nesting the *TextBlock* inside the *Grid* effectively adds the *TextBlock* to the *Children* collection. The process of adding the *TextBlock* to the *Grid* must be more explicit in code.

Property Inheritance

To experiment with some XAML, it's convenient to create a project specifically for that purpose. Let's call the project XamlExperiment, and put a *TextBlock* in the content grid:

Silverlight Project: XamlExperiment   File: **MainPage.xaml (excerpt)**

```
<Grid x:Name="ContentPanel" Grid.Row="1" Margin="12,0,12,0">
    <TextBlock Text="Hello, Windows Phone 7!" />
</Grid>
```

The text shows up in the upper-left corner of the page's client area. Let's make the text italic. You can do that by setting the *FontStyle* property in the *TextBlock*:

```
<TextBlock Text="Hello, Windows Phone 7!"
           FontStyle="Italic" />
```

Alternatively, you can put that *FontStyle* attribute in the *PhoneApplicationPage* tag:

```
<phone:PhoneApplicationPage ... FontStyle="Italic" ...
```

This *FontStyle* attribute can go anywhere in the *PhoneApplicationPage* tag. Notice that setting the property in this tag affects *all* the *TextBlock* elements on the page. This is a feature known as *property inheritance*. Certain properties—not many more than *Foreground* and the font-related properties *FontFamily, FontSize, FontStyle, FontWeight*, and *FontStretch*—propagate through the visual tree. This is how the *TextBlock* gets the *FontFamily, FontSize*, and *Foreground* properties (and now the *FontStyle* property) set on the *PhoneApplicationPage*.

You can visualize property inheritance beginning at the *PhoneApplicationPage* object. The *FontStyle* is set on that object and then it's inherited by the outermost *Grid*, and then the inner *Grid* objects, and finally by the *TextBlock*. This is a good theory. The problem with this theory is that *Grid* doesn't have a *FontStyle* property! If you try setting *FontStyle* in a *Grid* element, Visual Studio will complain. Property inheritance is somewhat more sophisticated than a simple handing off from parent to child, and it is one of the features of Silverlight that is intimately connected with the role of *dependency properties*, which you'll learn about in Chapter 11.

While keeping the *FontStyle* property setting to *Italic* in the *PhoneApplicationPage* tag, add a *FontStyle* setting to the *TextBlock*:

```
<TextBlock Text="Hello, Windows Phone 7!"
           FontStyle="Normal" />
```

Now the text in this particular *TextBlock* goes back to normal. Obviously the *FontStyle* setting on the *TextBlock*—which is referred to as a *local value* or a *local setting*—has precedence over property inheritance. A little reflection will convince you that this behavior is as it should be. Both property inheritance and the local setting have precedence over the default value. We can express this relationship in a simple chart:

Local Settings have precedence over

Property Inheritance, which has precedence over

Default Values

This chart will grow in size as we examine all the ways in which properties can be set.

Property-Element Syntax

Let's remove any *FontStyle* settings that might stil be around, set the *TextBlock* attributes to these values:

```
<TextBlock Text="Hello, Windows Phone 7!"
           FontSize="36"
           Foreground="Red" />
```

Because this is XML, we can separate the *TextBlock* tag into a start tag and end tag with nothing in between:

```
<TextBlock Text="Hello, Windows Phone 7!"
           FontSize="36"
           Foreground="Red">
</TextBlock>
```

But you can also do something that will appear quite strange initially. You can remove the *FontSize* attribute from the start tag and set it like this:

```
<TextBlock Text="Hello, Windows Phone 7!"
           Foreground="Red">
    <TextBlock.FontSize>
        36
    </TextBlock.FontSize>
</TextBlock>
```

Now the *TextBlock* has a child element called *TextBlock.FontSize*, and within the *TextBlock.FontSize* tags is the value.

This is called *property-element* syntax, and it's an extremely important part of XAML. The introduction of property-element syntax also allows nailing down some terminology that unites .NET and XML. This single *TextBlock* element now contains three types of identifiers:

- *TextBlock* is an *object element*—a .NET object based on an XML element.
- *Text* and *Foreground* are *property attributes*—.NET properties set with XML attributes.
- *FontSize* is now a *property element*—a .NET property expressed as an XML element.

When I first saw the property-element syntax, I wondered if it was some kind of XML extension. Of course it's not. The period is a legal character for XML tags, so in terms of nested XML tags, these are perfectly legitimate. That they happen to consist of a class name and a property name is something known only to XAML parsers (machine and human alike).

One restriction, however: It is illegal for anything else to appear in a property-element tag:

```
<TextBlock Text="Hello, Windows Phone 7!"
           Foreground="Red">
    <!-- Not a legal property-element tag! -->
```

```
    <TextBlock.FontSize absolutely nothing else goes in here!>
        36
    </TextBlock.FontSize>
</TextBlock>
```

Also, you can't have both a property attribute and a property element for the same property, like this:

```
<TextBlock Text="Hello, Windows Phone 7!"
        FontSize="36"
        Foreground="Red">
    <TextBlock.FontSize>
        36
    </TextBlock.FontSize>
</TextBlock>
```

This is an error because the *FontSize* property is set twice.

If you look towards the top of MainPage.xaml, you'll see another property element:

```
<Grid.RowDefinitions>
```

RowDefinitions is a property of *Grid*. In App.xaml, you'll see two more:

```
<Application.Resources>
<Application.ApplicationLifetimeObjects>
```

Both *Resources* and *ApplicationLIfeTimeObjects* are properties of *Application*.

Colors and Brushes

Let's return the *TextBlock* to its pristine condition:

```
<Grid x:Name="ContentPanel" Grid.Row="1" Margin="12,0,12,0">
    <TextBlock Text="Hello, Windows Phone 7!" />
</Grid>
```

The text shows up as white (or black, depending on the theme your selected) because the *Foreground* property is set on the root element in MainPage.xaml. You can override the user's preferences by setting *Background* for the *Grid* and *Foreground* for the *TextBlock*:

```
<Grid x:Name="ContentPanel" Background="Blue" Grid.Row="1" Margin="12,0,12,0">
    <TextBlock Text="Hello, Windows Phone 7!"
            Foreground="Red" />
</Grid>
```

The *Grid* has a *Background* property but no *Foreground* property. The *TextBlock* has a *Foreground* property but no *Background* property. The *Foreground* property is inheritable through the visual tree, and it may sometimes seem that the *Background* property is as well, but it is not. The default value of *Background* is *null*, which makes the background transparent. When the background is transparent, the parent background shows through, and that makes it seem as if the property is inherited.

A *Background* property set to *null* is visually the same as a *Background* property set to *Transparent*, but the two settings affect hit-testing differently, which affects how the element responds to touch. A *Grid* with its *Background* set to the default value of *null* cannot detect touch input! If you want a *Grid* to have no background color on its own but still respond to touch, set *Background* to *Transparent*. You can also do the reverse: You can make an element with a non-*null* background unresponsive to touch by setting the *IsHitTestVisible* property to *false*.

Besides the standard colors, you can write the color as a string of red, green, and blue one-byte hexadecimal values ranging from 00 to FF. For example:

```
Foreground="#FF0000"
```

That's also red. You can alternatively specify *four* two-digit hexadecimal numbers where the first one is an alpha value indicating transparency: The value 00 is completely transparent, FF is opaque, and values in between are partially transparent. Try this value:

```
Foreground="#80FF0000"
```

The text will appear a somewhat faded magenta because the blue background shows through.

If you preface the pound sign with the letters *sc* you can use values between 0 and 1 for the red, blue, and green components:

```
Foreground="sc# 1 0 0"
```

You can also precede the three numbers with an alpha value between 0 and 1.

These two methods of specifying color numerically are not equivalent, as you can verify by putting these two *TextBlocks* in the same *Grid*:

```
<Grid x:Name="ContentPanel" Background="Blue" Grid.Row="1" Margin="12,0,12,0">
    <TextBlock Text="RGB COLOR"
               HorizontalAlignment="Left"
               Foreground="#808080" />

    <TextBlock Text="scRGB COLOR"
               HorizontalAlignment="Right"
               Foreground="sc# 0.5 0.5 0.5" />
</Grid>
```

Both color specifications seem to suggest medium gray, except that the one on the right is much lighter than the one on the left.

The colors you get with the hexadecimal specification are probably most familiar. The one-byte values of red, green, and blue are directly proportional to the voltages sent to the pixels of the video display. Although the light intensity of video displays is not linear with respect to voltage, the human eye is not linear with respect to light intensity either. These two non-linearities cancel each other out (approximately) so the text on the left appears somewhat medium.

With the scRGB color space, you specify values between 0 and 1 that are proportional to light intensity, so the non-linearity of the human eye makes the color seem off. If you really want a medium gray in scRGB you need values much lower than 0.5, such as:

```
Foreground="sc# 0.2 0.2 0.2"
```

Let's go back to one *TextBlock* in the *Grid*:

```
<Grid x:Name="ContentPanel" Background="Blue" Grid.Row="1" Margin="12,0,12,0">
    <TextBlock Text="Hello, Windows Phone 7!"
               Foreground="Red" />
</Grid>
```

Just as I did earlier with the *FontSize* property, break out the *Foreground* property as a property element:

```
<TextBlock Text="Hello, Windows Phone 7!">
    <TextBlock.Foreground>
        Red
    </TextBlock.Foreground>
</TextBlock>
```

When you specify a *Foreground* property in XAML, a *SolidColorBrush* is created for the element behind the scenes. You can also explicitly create the *SolidColorBrush* in XAML:

```
<TextBlock Text="Hello, Windows Phone 7!">
    <TextBlock.Foreground>
        <SolidColorBrush Color="Red" />
    </TextBlock.Foreground>
</TextBlock>
```

You can also break out the *Color* property as a property element:

```
<TextBlock Text="Hello, Windows Phone 7!">
    <TextBlock.Foreground>
        <SolidColorBrush>
            <SolidColorBrush.Color>
                Red
            </SolidColorBrush.Color>
        </SolidColorBrush>
    </TextBlock.Foreground>
</TextBlock>
```

And you can go even further:

```
<TextBlock Text="Hello, Windows Phone 7!">
    <TextBlock.Foreground>
        <SolidColorBrush>
            <SolidColorBrush.Color>
                <Color>
                    <Color.A>
                        255
                    </Color.A>
                    <Color.R>
                        #FF
                    </Color.R>
                </Color>
            </SolidColorBrush.Color>
        </SolidColorBrush>
    </TextBlock.Foreground>
</TextBlock>
```

Notice that the *A* property of the *Color* structure needs to be explicitly set because the default value is 0, which means transparent.

This excessive use of property elements might not make much sense for simple colors and *SolidColorBrush*, but the technique becomes essential when you need to use XAML to set a property with a value that can't be expressed as a simple text string—for example, when you want to use a gradient brush rather than a *SolidColorBrush*.

Let's begin with a simple solid *TextBlock* but with the *Background* property of the Grid broken out as a property element:

```
<Grid x:Name="ContentPanel" Grid.Row="1" Margin="12,0,12,0">
    <Grid.Background>
        <SolidColorBrush Color="Blue" />
    </Grid.Background>

    <TextBlock Text="Hello, Windows Phone 7!"
               Foreground="Red" />
</Grid>
```

Remove that *SolidColorBrush* and replace it with a *LinearGradientBrush*:

```
<Grid x:Name="ContentPanel" Grid.Row="1" Margin="12,0,12,0">
    <Grid.Background>
        <LinearGradientBrush>
        </LinearGradientBrush>
    </Grid.Background>

    <TextBlock Text="Hello, Windows Phone 7!"
               Foreground="Red" />
</Grid>
```

The *LinearGradientBrush* has a property of type *GradientStops*, so let's add property element tags for the *GradientStops* property:

```
<Grid x:Name="ContentPanel" Grid.Row="1" Margin="12,0,12,0">
    <Grid.Background>
        <LinearGradientBrush>
            <LinearGradientBrush.GradientStops>
            </LinearGradientBrush.GradientStops>
        </LinearGradientBrush>
    </Grid.Background>

    <TextBlock Text="Hello, Windows Phone 7!"
            Foreground="Red" />
</Grid>
```

The *GradientStops* property is of type *GradientStopCollection*, so let's add tags for that:

```
<Grid x:Name="ContentPanel" Grid.Row="1" Margin="12,0,12,0">
    <Grid.Background>
        <LinearGradientBrush>
            <LinearGradientBrush.GradientStops>
                <GradientStopCollection>
                </GradientStopCollection>
            </LinearGradientBrush.GradientStops>
        </LinearGradientBrush>
    </Grid.Background>

    <TextBlock Text="Hello, Windows Phone 7!"
            Foreground="Red" />
</Grid>
```

Now let's put a couple *GradientStop* objects in there. The *GradientStop* has properties named *Offset* and *Color*:

```
<Grid x:Name="ContentPanel" Grid.Row="1" Margin="12,0,12,0">
    <Grid.Background>
        <LinearGradientBrush>
            <LinearGradientBrush.GradientStops>
                <GradientStopCollection>
                    <GradientStop Offset="0" Color="Blue" />
                    <GradientStop Offset="1" Color="Green" />
                </GradientStopCollection>
            </LinearGradientBrush.GradientStops>
        </LinearGradientBrush>
    </Grid.Background>

    <TextBlock Text="Hello, Windows Phone 7!"
            Foreground="Red" />
</Grid>
```

And with the help of property elements, that is how you create a gradient brush in markup. It looks like this:

The *Offset* values range from 0 to 1 and they are relative to the element being colored with the brush. You can use more than two:

```
<Grid x:Name="ContentPanel" Grid.Row="1" Margin="12,0,12,0">
    <Grid.Background>
        <LinearGradientBrush>
            <LinearGradientBrush.GradientStops>
                <GradientStopCollection>
                    <GradientStop Offset="0" Color="Blue" />
                    <GradientStop Offset="0.5" Color="White" />
                    <GradientStop Offset="1" Color="Green" />
                </GradientStopCollection>
            </LinearGradientBrush.GradientStops>
        </LinearGradientBrush>
    </Grid.Background>

    <TextBlock Text="Hello, Windows Phone 7!"
               Foreground="Red" />
</Grid>
```

Conceptually the brush knows the size of the area that it's coloring and adjusts itself accordingly.

By default the gradient starts at the upper-left corner and goes to the lower-right corner, but that's only because of the default settings of the *StartPoint* and *EndPoint* properties of *LinearGradientBrush*. As the names suggest, these are coordinate points relative to the upper-left corner of the element being colored. For *StartPoint* the default value is the point (0, 0), meaning the upper-left, and for *EndPoint* (1, 1), the lower-right. If you change them to (0, 0) and (0, 1), for example, the gradient goes from top to bottom:

```
<Grid x:Name="ContentPanel" Grid.Row="1" Margin="12,0,12,0">
    <Grid.Background>
        <LinearGradientBrush StartPoint="0 0" EndPoint="0 1">
            <LinearGradientBrush.GradientStops>
                <GradientStopCollection>
                    <GradientStop Offset="0" Color="Blue" />
                    <GradientStop Offset="0.5" Color="White" />
                    <GradientStop Offset="1" Color="Green" />
                </GradientStopCollection>
            </LinearGradientBrush.GradientStops>
        </LinearGradientBrush>
    </Grid.Background>

    <TextBlock Text="Hello, Windows Phone 7!"
            Foreground="Red" />
</Grid>
```

Each point is just two numbers separated by space or a comma. There are also properties that determine what happens outside the range of the lowest and highest *Offset* values if they don't go from 0 to 1.

LinearGradientBrush derives from *GradientBrush*. Another class that derives from *GradientBrush* is *RadialGradientBrush*. Here's markup for a larger *TextBlock* with a *RadialGradientBrush* set to its *Foreground* property:

```
<TextBlock Text="GRADIENT"
            FontFamily="Arial Black"
            FontSize="72"
            HorizontalAlignment="Center"
            VerticalAlignment="Center">
    <TextBlock.Foreground>
        <RadialGradientBrush>
            <RadialGradientBrush.GradientStops>
                <GradientStopCollection>
                    <GradientStop Offset="0" Color="Transparent" />
                    <GradientStop Offset="1" Color="Red" />
                </GradientStopCollection>
            </RadialGradientBrush.GradientStops>
        </RadialGradientBrush>
    </TextBlock.Foreground>
</TextBlock>
```

And here's what the combination looks like:

Content and Content Properties

Everyone knows that XML can be a little "wordy." However, the markup I've shown you with the gradient brushes is a little wordier than it needs to be. Let's look at the *RadialGradientBrush* I originally defined for the *TextBlock*:

```
<TextBlock.Foreground>
    <RadialGradientBrush>
        <RadialGradientBrush.GradientStops>
            <GradientStopCollection>
                <GradientStop Offset="0" Color="Transparent" />
                <GradientStop Offset="1" Color="Red" />
            </GradientStopCollection>
        </RadialGradientBrush.GradientStops>
    </RadialGradientBrush>
</TextBlock.Foreground>
```

First, if you have at least one item in a collection, you can eliminate the tags for the collection itself. This means that the tags for the *GradientStopCollection* can be removed:

```
<TextBlock.Foreground>
    <RadialGradientBrush>
        <RadialGradientBrush.GradientStops>
            <GradientStop Offset="0" Color="Transparent" />
            <GradientStop Offset="1" Color="Red" />
```

```
        </RadialGradientBrush.GradientStops>
    </RadialGradientBrush>
</TextBlock.Foreground>
```

Moreover, many classes that you use in XAML have something called a *ContentProperty* attribute. This word "attribute" has different meanings in .NET and XML; here I'm talking about the .NET attribute, which refers to some additional information that is associated with a class or a member of that class. If you look at the documentation for the *GradientBrush* class—the class from which both *LinearGradientBrush* and *RadialGradientBrush* derive—you'll see that the class was defined with an attribute of type *ContentPropertyAttribute*:

```
[ContentPropertyAttribute("GradientStops", true)]
public abstract class GradientBrush : Brush
```

This attribute indicates one property of the class that is assumed to be the content of that class, and for which the property-element tags are not required. For *GradientBrush* (and its descendents) that one property is *GradientStops*. This means that the *RadialGradientBrush. GradientStops* tags can be removed from the markup:

```
<TextBlock.Foreground>
    <RadialGradientBrush>
        <GradientStop Offset="0" Color="Transparent" />
        <GradientStop Offset="1" Color="Red" />
    </RadialGradientBrush>
</TextBlock.Foreground>
```

Now it's not quite as wordy but it's still comprehensible. The two *GradientStop* objects are the content of the *RadialGradientBrush* class.

Earlier in this chapter I created a *TextBlock* in code and added it to the *Children* collection of the *Grid*. In XAML, we see no reference to this *Children* collection. That's because the *ContentProperty* attribute of *Panel*—the class from which *Grid* derives—defines the *Children* property as the content of the *Panel*:

```
[ContentPropertyAttribute("Children", true)]
public abstract class Panel : FrameworkElement
```

If you want to get more explicit in your markup, you can include a property element for the *Children* property:

```
<Grid x:Name="ContentPanel" Grid.Row="1" Margin="12,0,12,0">
    <Grid.Children>
        <TextBlock Text="Hello, Windows Phone 7!" />
    </Grid.Children>
</Grid>
```

Similarly, *PhoneApplicationPage* derives from *UserControl*, which also has a *ContentProperty* attribute:

```
[ContentPropertyAttribute("Content", true)]
public class UserControl : Control
```

The *ContentProperty* attribute of *UserControl* is the *Content* property. (That sentence makes more sense when you see it on the page rather than when you read it out load!)

Suppose you want to put two *TextBlock* elements in a *Grid*, and you want the *Grid* to have a *LinearGradientBrush* for its *Background*. You can put the *Background* property element first within the *Grid* tags followed by the two *TextBlock* elements:

```
<Grid x:Name="ContentPanel" Grid.Row="1" Margin="12,0,12,0">
    <Grid.Background>
        <LinearGradientBrush>
            <GradientStop Offset="0" Color="LightCyan" />
            <GradientStop Offset="1" Color="LightPink" />
        </LinearGradientBrush>
    </Grid.Background>

    <TextBlock Text="TextBlock #1"
            HorizontalAlignment="Left" />

    <TextBlock Text="TextBlock #2"
            HorizontalAlignment="Right" />
</Grid>
```

It's also legal to put the two *TextBlock* elements first and the *Background* property element last:

```
<Grid x:Name="ContentPanel" Grid.Row="1" Margin="12,0,12,0">
    <TextBlock Text="TextBlock #1"
            HorizontalAlignment="Left" />

    <TextBlock Text="TextBlock #2"
            HorizontalAlignment="Right" />

    <Grid.Background>
        <LinearGradientBrush>
            <GradientStop Offset="0" Color="LightCyan" />
            <GradientStop Offset="1" Color="LightPink" />
        </LinearGradientBrush>
    </Grid.Background>
</Grid>
```

But putting the *Background* property element between the two *TextBlock* elements simply won't work:

```
<Grid x:Name="ContentPanel" Grid.Row="1" Margin="12,0,12,0">
    <TextBlock Text="TextBlock #1"
            HorizontalAlignment="Left" />

    <!-- Not a legal place for the property element! -->
    <Grid.Background>
        <LinearGradientBrush>
            <GradientStop Offset="0" Color="LightCyan" />
            <GradientStop Offset="1" Color="LightPink" />
        </LinearGradientBrush>
    </Grid.Background>
```

```
    <TextBlock Text="TextBlock #2"
               HorizontalAlignment="Right" />
</Grid>
```

The precise problem with this syntax is revealed when you put in the missing property elements for the *Children* property of the *Grid*:

```
<Grid x:Name="ContentPanel" Grid.Row="1" Margin="12,0,12,0">
    <Grid.Children>
        <TextBlock Text="TextBlock #1"
                   HorizontalAlignment="Left" />
    </Grid.Children>

    <!-- Not a legal place for the property element! -->
    <Grid.Background>
        <LinearGradientBrush>
            <GradientStop Offset="0" Color="LightCyan" />
            <GradientStop Offset="1" Color="LightPink" />
        </LinearGradientBrush>
    </Grid.Background>

    <Grid.Children>
        <TextBlock Text="TextBlock #2"
                   HorizontalAlignment="Right" />
    </Grid.Children>
</Grid>
```

Now it's obvious that the *Children* property is being set twice—and that's clearly illegal.

The Resources Collection

In one sense, computer programming is all about the avoidance of repetition. (Or at least repetition by us humans. We don't mind if our machines engage in repetition. We just want it to be efficient repetition.) XAML would seem to be a particularly treacherous area for repetition because it's just markup and not a real programming language, You can easily imagine situations where a bunch of elements have the same *HorizontalAlignment* or *VerticalAlignment* or *Margin* settings, and it would certainly be convenient if there were a way to avoid a lot of repetitive markup. If you ever needed to change one of these properties, changing it just once is much better than changing it scores or hundreds of times.

Fortunately XAML has been designed by programmers who (like the rest of us) prefer not to type in the same stuff over and over again.

The most generalized solution to repetitive markup is the Silverlight *style*. But a prerequisite to styles is a more generalized sharing mechanism. This is called the *resource*, and right away we need to distinguish between the resources I'll be showing you here, and the resources encountered in Chapter 4 when embedding images into the application. Whenever there's a chance of confusion, I will refer to the resources in this chapter as XAML resources, even though they can exist in code as well.

XAML resources are always instances of a particular .NET class or structure, either an existing class or structure or a custom class. When a particular class is defined as a XAML resource, only one instance is made, and that one instance is shared among everybody using that resource.

The sharing of resources immediately disqualifies many classes from being defined as XAML resources. For example, a single instance of *TextBlock* can't be used more than once because the *TextBlock* must have a unique parent and a unique location within that parent. And that goes for any other element as well. Anything derived from *UIElement* is probably not going to show up as a resource because it can't be shared.

However, it is very common to share brushes. This is a typical way to give a particular application a certain consistent and distinctive visual appearance. Animations are also candidates for sharing. It's also possible to share text strings and numbers. Think of these as the XAML equivalents of string or numeric constants in a C# program. When you need to change one of them, you can just change the single resource rather than hunting through the XAML to change a bunch of individual occurrences.

To support the storage of resources, *FrameworkElement* defines a property named *Resources* of type *ResourceDictionary*. On any element that derives from *FrameworkElement*, you can define *Resources* as a property element. By converntion this appears right under the start tag. Here's a *Resources* collection for a page class that derives from *PhoneApplicationPage*:

```
<phone:PhoneApplicationPage ... >

    <phone:PhoneApplicationPage.Resources>
        . . .
    </phone:PhoneApplicationPage.Resources>


    . . .
</phone:PhoneApplicationPage>
```

The collection of resources within those *Resources* tags is sometimes called a *resource section*, and anything in that particular *PhoneApplicationPage* can then use those resources.

The *Application* class also defines a *Resources* property, and the App.xaml file that Visual Studio creates for you in a new Silverlight application already includes an empty resource section:

```
<Application ... >
    <Application.Resources>
    </Application.Resources>
    . . .
</Application>
```

The resources defined in the *Resources* collection on a *FrameworkElement* are available only within that element and nested elements; the resources defined in the *Application* class are available throughout the application.

Sharing Brushes

Let's suppose your page contains several *TextBlock* elements, and you want to apply the same *LinearGradientBrush* to the *Foreground* of each of them. This is an ideal use of a resource.

The first step is to define a *LinearGradientBrush* in a resource section of a XAML file. If you're defining the resource in a *FrameworkElement*-derivative, the resource must be defined before it is used, and it can only be accessed by the same element or a nested element.

```
<phone:PhoneApplicationPage.Resources>
    <LinearGradientBrush x:Key="brush">
        <GradientStop Offset="0" Color="Pink" />
        <GradientStop Offset="1" Color="SkyBlue" />
    </LinearGradientBrush>
</phone:PhoneApplicationPage.Resources>
```

Notice the *x:Key* attribute. Every resource must have a key name. There are only four keywords that must be prefaced with "x" and you've already seen three of them: Besides *x:Key* they are *x:Class*, *x:Name* and *x:Null*.

Accessing that resource is possible with a couple kinds of syntax. The rather verbose way is to break out the *Foreground* property of the *TextBlock* as a property element and set it to an object of type *StaticResource* referencing the key name:

```
<TextBlock Text="Hello, Windows Phone 7!">
    <TextBlock.Foreground>
        <StaticResource ResourceKey="brush" />
    </TextBlock.Foreground>
</TextBlock>
```

There is, however, a shortcut syntax that makes use of what is called a *XAML markup extension*. A markup extension is always delimited by curly braces. Here's what the *StaticResource* markup extension looks like:

```
<TextBlock Text="Hello, Windows Phone 7!"
           Foreground="{StaticResource brush}" />
```

Notice that within the markup extension the word "brush" is not in quotation marks. Quotation marks within a markup extension are always prohibited.

Suppose you want to share a *Margin* setting. The *Margin* is of type *Thickness*, and in XAML you can specify it with 1, 2, or 4 numbers. Here's a *Thickness* resource:

```
<Thickness x:Key="margin">
    12 96
</Thickness>
```

Suppose you want to share a *FontSize* property. That's of type *double*, and you're going to need a little help. The *Double* structure, which is the basis for the *double* C# data type, is defined in the *System* namespace, but the XML namespace declarations in a typical XAML file only refer to Silverlight classes in Silverlight namespaces. What's needed is an XML namespace declaration for the *System* namespace in the root element of the page, and here it is:

```
xmlns:system="clr-namespace:System;assembly=mscorlib"
```

This is the standard syntax for associating an XML namespace with a .NET namespace. First, make up an XML namespace name that reminds you of the .NET namespace. The word "system" is good for this one; some programmers use "sys" or just "s." The hyphenated "clr-namespace" is followed by a colon and the .NET namespace name. If you're interested in referencing objects that are in the current assembly, you're done. Otherwise you need a semicolon followed by "assembly=" and the assembly, in this case the standard mscorlib.lib ("Microsoft Common Runtime Library").

Now you can have a resource of type *double*:

```
<system:Double x:Key="fontsize">
    48
</system:Double>
```

The ResourceSharing project defines all three of these resources and references them in two *TextBlock* elements. Here's the complete resource section:

Silverlight Project: ResourceSharing   File: MainPage.xaml (excerpt)

```
<phone:PhoneApplicationPage.Resources>
    <LinearGradientBrush x:Key="brush">
        <GradientStop Offset="0" Color="Pink" />
        <GradientStop Offset="1" Color="SkyBlue" />
    </LinearGradientBrush>

    <Thickness x:Key="margin">
        12 96
    </Thickness>

    <system:Double x:Key="fontsize">
        48
    </system:Double>
</phone:PhoneApplicationPage.Resources>
```

The content grid contains the two *TextBlock* elements:

Silverlight Project: ResourceSharing   File: MainPage.xaml (excerpt)

```
<Grid x:Name="ContentPanel" Grid.Row="1" Margin="12,0,12,0">
    <TextBlock Text="Whadayasay?"
               Foreground="{StaticResource brush}"
               Margin="{StaticResource margin}"
```

```
                    FontSize="{StaticResource fontsize}"
                    HorizontalAlignment="Left"
                    VerticalAlignment="Top" />

    <TextBlock Text="Fuhgedaboudit!"
                    Foreground="{StaticResource brush}"
                    Margin="{StaticResource margin}"
                    FontSize="{StaticResource fontsize}"
                    HorizontalAlignment="Right"
                    VerticalAlignment="Bottom" />
</Grid>
```

The screen shot demonstrates that it works:

The *Resources* property is a dictionary, so within any resource section the key names must be unique. However, you can re-use key names in different resource collections. For example, try inserting the following markup right after the start tag of the content grid:

```
<Grid.Resources>
    <Thickness x:Key="margin">96</Thickness>
</Grid.Resources>
```

This resource will override the one defined on *MainPage*. Resources are searched going up the visual tree for a matching key name, and then the *Resources* collection in the *App* class is searched. For this reason, the *Resources* collection in App.xaml is an excellent place to put resources that are used throughout the application.

If you put that little piece of markup in the *Grid* named "LayoutRoot" it will also be accessible to the *TextBlock* elements because this *Grid* is an ancestor. But if you put the markup in the *StackPanel* entitled "TitlePanel," (and changing *Grid* to *StackPanel* in the process) it will be ignored. Resources are searched going up the visual tree, and that's another branch.

This little piece of markup will also be ignored if you put it in the content grid but *after* the two *TextBlock* elements. Now it's not accessible because it's lexicographically after the reference.

x:Key and x:Name

If you need to reference a XAML resource from code, you can simply index the *Resources* property with the resource name. For example, in the MainPage.xaml.cs code-behind file, this code will retrieve the resource named "brush" stored in the *Resources* collection of *MainPage*:

```
this.Resources["brush"]
```

You would then probably cast that object to an appropriate type, in this case either *Brush* or *LinearGradientBrush*. Because the *Resources* collection isn't built until the XAML is processed, you can't access the resource before the *InitializeComponent* call in the constructor of the code-behind file.

If you have resources defined in other *Resource* collections in the same XAML file, you can retrieve those as well. For example, if you've defined a resource named "margin" in the *Resources* collection of the content grid, you can access that resource using:

```
ContentPanel.Resources["margin"]
```

If no resource with that name is found in the *Resources* collection of an element, then the *Resources* collection of the *App* class is searched. If the resource is not found there, then the indexer returns *null*.

Due to a legacy issue involving Silverlight 1.0, you can use *x:Name* rather than using *x:Key* to identify a resource:

```
<phone:PhoneApplicationPage.Resources>
    <LinearGradientBrush x:Name="brush">
    . . .
</phone:PhoneApplicationPage.Resources>
```

There is one big advantage to this: The name is stored as a field in the generated code file so you can reference the resource in the code-behind file just like any other field:

```
txtblk.Foreground = brush;
```

This is a much better syntax for sharing resources between XAML and code. However, if you use *x:Name* for a resource, that name must be unique in the XAML file.

An Introduction to Styles

One very common item in a *Resources* collection is a *Style*, which is basically a collection of property assignments for a particular element type. Besides a key, the *Style* also requires a *TargetType*:

```
<Style x:Key="txtblkStyle"
       TargetType="TextBlock">
    ...
</Style>
```

Between the start and end tags go one or more *Setter* definitions. *Setter* has two properties: One is actually called *Property* and you set it to a property name. The other is *Value*. A few examples:

```
<Style x:Key="txtblkStyle"
       TargetType="TextBlock">
    <Setter Property="HorizontalAlignment" Value="Center" />
    <Setter Property="VerticalAlignment" Value="Center" />
    <Setter Property="Margin" Value="12 96" />
    <Setter Property="FontSize" Value="48" />
</Style>
```

Suppose you also want to include a *Setter* for the *Foreground* property but it's a *LinearGradientBrush*. There are two ways to do it. If you have a previously defined resource with a key of "brush" (as in the ResourceSharing project) you can reference that:

```
<Setter Property="Foreground" Value="{StaticResource brush}" />
```

Or, you can use property-element syntax with the *Value* property to embed the brush right in the *Style* definition. That's how it's done in the *Resources* collection of the StyleSharing project:

Silverlight Project: StyleSharing   File: MainPage.xaml (excerpt)

```
<phone:PhoneApplicationPage.Resources>
    <Style x:Key="txtblkStyle"
           TargetType="TextBlock">
        <Setter Property="HorizontalAlignment" Value="Center" />
        <Setter Property="VerticalAlignment" Value="Center" />
        <Setter Property="Margin" Value="12 96" />
        <Setter Property="FontSize" Value="48" />
        <Setter Property="Foreground">
            <Setter.Value>
                <LinearGradientBrush>
                    <GradientStop Offset="0" Color="Pink" />
                    <GradientStop Offset="1" Color="SkyBlue" />
                </LinearGradientBrush>
            </Setter.Value>
        </Setter>
    </Style>
</phone:PhoneApplicationPage.Resources>
```

To apply this style to an element of type *TextBlock*, set the *Style* property (which is defined by *FrameworkElement* so every kind of element has it):

Silverlight Project: StyleSharing File: MainPage.xaml (excerpt)

```
<Grid x:Name="ContentPanel" Grid.Row="1" Margin="12,0,12,0">
    <TextBlock Text="Whadayasay?"
               Style="{StaticResource txtblkStyle}"
               HorizontalAlignment="Left"
               VerticalAlignment="Top" />

    <TextBlock Text="Fuhgedaboudit!"
               Style="{StaticResource txtblkStyle}"
               HorizontalAlignment="Right"
               VerticalAlignment="Bottom" />
</Grid>
```

The display looks the same as the previous program, which teaches an important lesson. Notice that values of *HorizontalAlignment* and *VerticalAlignment* are defined in the *Style*, yet these are overridden by local settings in the two *TextBlock* elements. But the *Foreground* set in the *Style* overrides the value normally inherited through the visual tree.

That means that the little chart I started earlier in this chapter can now be enhanced slightly.

Local Settings have precedence over

Style Settings, which have precedence over

Property Inheritance, which has precedence over

Default Values

Style Inheritance

Styles can enhance or modify other styles through the process of inheritance. Set the *Style* property *BasedOn* to a previously defined *Style*. Here's the *Resources* collection of the StyleInheritance project:

Silverlight Project: StyleInheritance File: MainPage.xaml (excerpt)

```
<phone:PhoneApplicationPage.Resources>
    <Style x:Key="txtblkStyle"
           TargetType="TextBlock">
        <Setter Property="HorizontalAlignment" Value="Center" />
```

```
        <Setter Property="VerticalAlignment" Value="Center" />
        <Setter Property="Margin" Value="12 96" />
        <Setter Property="FontSize" Value="48" />
        <Setter Property="Foreground">
            <Setter.Value>
                <LinearGradientBrush>
                    <GradientStop Offset="0" Color="Pink" />
                    <GradientStop Offset="1" Color="SkyBlue" />
                </LinearGradientBrush>
            </Setter.Value>
        </Setter>
    </Style>

    <Style x:Key="upperLeftStyle"
           TargetType="TextBlock"
           BasedOn="{StaticResource txtblkStyle}">
        <Setter Property="HorizontalAlignment" Value="Left" />
        <Setter Property="VerticalAlignment" Value="Top" />
    </Style>

    <Style x:Key="lowerRightStyle"
           TargetType="TextBlock"
           BasedOn="{StaticResource txtblkStyle}">
        <Setter Property="HorizontalAlignment" Value="Right" />
        <Setter Property="VerticalAlignment" Value="Bottom" />
    </Style>
</phone:PhoneApplicationPage.Resources>
```

The two new *Style* definitions at the end override the *HorizontalAlignment* and
VerticalAlignment properties set in the earlier style. This allows the two *TextBlock* elements to
reference these two different styles:

Silverlight Project: StyleInheritance   File: MainPage.xaml (excerpt)

```
<Grid x:Name="ContentPanel" Grid.Row="1" Margin="12,0,12,0">
    <TextBlock Text="Whadayasay?"
               Style="{StaticResource upperLeftStyle}" />

    <TextBlock Text="Fuhgedaboudit!"
               Style="{StaticResource lowerRightStyle}" />
</Grid>
```

Implicit styles, which were introduced into Silverlight 4, are not supported in Silverlight for
Windows Phone.

Themes

Windows Phone 7 predefines many resources that you can use throughout your application with the *StaticResource* markup extension. There are predefined colors, brushes, font names, font sizes, margins, and text styles. Some of them show up in the root element of MainPage .xaml to supply the defaults for the whole page:

```
FontFamily="{StaticResource PhoneFontFamilyNormal}"
FontSize="{StaticResource PhoneFontSizeNormal}"
Foreground="{StaticResource PhoneForegroundBrush}"
```

You can find all these predefined themes in the Themes section of the Windows Phone 7 documentation. You should try to use these resources particularly for foreground and background brushes so you comply with the user's wishes, and you don't inadvertently cause your text to become invisible. Some of the predefined font sizes may be different when the small-screen phone is released, and these differences might help you port your large-screen programs to the new device.

What happens if the user navigates to the Settings page of the phone and sets a different theme while your program is running? Well, the only way this can happen is if your program is tombstoned at the time, and when your program is reactivated, it starts up from scratch and hence references the new colors automatically.

The color theme that the user selects includes a foreground and background (either white on a black background or black on a white background) but also an accent color: magenta, purple, teal, lime, brown, pink, orange, blue (the default), red, or green. This color is available as the PhoneAccentColor resource, and a brush based on this color is available as PhoneAccentBrush.

Gradient Accents

You might want to use the user's preferred accent color in your program, but as a gradient brush. In other words, you want the same hue, but you want to get darker or lighter versions. In code, this is fairly easy by manipulating the red, green, and blue components of the color.

It's also fairly easy in XAML, as the GradientAccent project demonstrates:

Silverlight Project: GradientAccent   File: MainPage.xaml (excerpt)

```
<Grid x:Name="ContentPanel" Grid.Row="1" Margin="12,0,12,0">
    <Grid.Background>
        <LinearGradientBrush StartPoint="0 0" EndPoint="0 1">
            <GradientStop Offset="0" Color="White" />
            <GradientStop Offset="0.5" Color="{StaticResource PhoneAccentColor}" />
```

```
            <GradientStop Offset="1" Color="Black" />
        </LinearGradientBrush>
    </Grid.Background>
</Grid>
```

Here it is:

You can get a more subtle affect by changing the gradient offsets. These can actually be set outside the range of 0 to 1, perhaps like this:

```
<LinearGradientBrush StartPoint="0 0" EndPoint="1 0">
    <GradientStop Offset="-1" Color="White" />
    <GradientStop Offset="0.5" Color="{StaticResource PhoneAccentColor}" />
    <GradientStop Offset="2" Color="Black" />
</LinearGradientBrush>
```

Now the gradient goes from White at an offset of –1 to the accent color at 0.5 to Black at 2. But you're only seeing the section of the gradient between 0 and 1, so the White and Black extremes are not here:

It's just another little suggestion that XAML can be more powerful than it might at first seem.

Chapter 8
Elements and Properties

You've already seen several examples of *TextBlock* and *Image*, which are surely two of the most important elements supported by Silverlight. This chapter explores text and bitmaps in more depth, and also describes other common elements and some important properties you can apply to all these elements, including transforms. This lays the groundwork for the subject of *Panel* elements that provide the basis of Silverlight's dynamic layout system (in the next chapter) and then the huge subject of controls (Chapter 10).

Basic Shapes

The *System.Windows.Shapes* namespace includes elements for displaying vector graphics—the use of straight lines and curves for drawing and defining filled areas. Although the subject of vector graphics awaits us in Chapter 13, two of the classes in this namespace—*Ellipse* and *Rectangle*—are a little different from the others in that you can use them without specifying any coordinate points.

Go back to the XamlExperiment program from the Chapter 7 and insert this *Ellipse* element into the content grid:

```
<Grid x:Name="ContentPanel" Grid.Row="1" Margin="12,0,12,0">
    <Ellipse Fill="Blue"
             Stroke="Red"
             StrokeThickness="50" />
</Grid>
```

You'll see a blue ellipse with a red outline fill the *Grid*:

Now try setting *HorizontalAlignment* and *VerticalAlignment* to *Center*. The *Ellipse* disappears. What happened?

This *Ellipse* has no intrinsic minimum size. When allowed to, it will assume the size of its container, but if it's forced to become small, it will become as small as possible, which is nothing at all. This is one case where explicitly setting *Width* and *Height* properties of an element is appropriate and often necessary.

The terms *stroke* and *fill* are common in vector graphics. The basis of vector graphics is the use of coordinate points to define straight lines and curves. These are mathematical entities that only become visible by being *stroked* with a particular color and line thickness. The lines and curves might also defined enclosed areas, in which case this area can be *filled*. Both the *Fill* property and the *Stroke* property of *Ellipse* are of type *Brush*, so you can set either or both to gradient brushes.

It is very common to set the *Width* property of an *Ellipse* to the *Height* to create a circle. The *Fill* can then be set to a *RadialGradientBrush* that starts at White in the center and then goes to a gradient color at the perimeter. Normally the gradient center is the point (0.5, 0.5) relative to the ball's dimension, but you can offset that like so:

```
<Grid x:Name="ContentPanel" Grid.Row="1" Margin="12,0,12,0">
    <Ellipse Width="300"
             Height="300">
        <Ellipse.Fill>
            <RadialGradientBrush Center="0.4 0.4"
                                 GradientOrigin="0.4 0.4">
                <GradientStop Offset="0" Color="White" />
                <GradientStop Offset="1" Color="Red" />
            </RadialGradientBrush>
        </Ellipse.Fill>
    </Ellipse>
</Grid>
```

The offset white spot looks like reflection from a light source, suggesting a three dimensional shape:

The *Rectangle* has the same properties as *Ellipse* except that *Rectangle* also defines *RadiusX* and *RadiusY* properties for rounding the corners.

Transforms

Until the advent of the Windows Presentation Foundation and Silverlight, transforms were mostly the tools of the graphics mavens. Mathematically speaking, transforms apply a simple formula to all the coordinates of a visual object and cause that object to be shifted to a different location, or change size, or be rotated.

In Silverlight, you can apply transforms to any object that descends from *UIElement*, and that includes text, bitmaps, movies, panels, and all controls. The property defined by *UIElement* that makes transforms possible is *RenderTransform*, which you set to an object of type *Transform*. *Transform* is an abstract class, but it is the parent class to seven non-abstract classes:

- *TranslateTransform* to shift location
- *ScaleTransform* to increase or decrease size
- *RotateTransform* to rotate around a point
- *SkewTransform* to shift in one dimension based on another dimension
- *MatrixTransform* to express transforms with a standard matrix
- *TransformGroup* to combine multiple transforms
- *CompositeTransform* to specify a series of transforms in a fixed order

The whole subject of transforms can be quite complex, particularly when transforms are combined, so I'm really only going to show the basics here. Very often, transforms are used in combination with animations. Animating a transform is the most efficient way that an animation can be applied to a visual object.

Suppose you have a *TextBlock* and you want to make it twice as big. That's easy: Just double the *FontSize*. Now suppose you want to make the text twice as wide but three times taller. The *FontSize* won't help you there. You need to break out the *RenderTransform* property as a property element and set a *ScaleTransform* to it:

```
<TextBlock ... >
    <TextBlock.RenderTransform>
        <ScaleTransform ScaleX="2" ScaleY="3" />
    </TextBlock.RenderTransform>
</TextBlock>
```

Most commonly, you'll set the *RenderTransform* property of an object of type *TranslateTransform*, *ScaleTransform*, or *RotateTransform*. If you know what you're doing, you can combine multiple transforms in a *TransformGroup*. In two dimensions, transforms are expressed as 3×3 matrices, and combining transforms is equivalent to matrix multiplication. It is well known that matrix multiplication is not commutative, so the order that transforms are multiplied makes a difference in the overall effect.

Although *TransformGroup* is normally an advanced option, I have nevertheless used *TransformGroup* in a little project named TransformExperiment that allows you to play with the four standard of transforms. It begins with all the properties set to their default values;

Silverlight Project: TransformExperiment   File: MainPage.xaml (excerpt)

```xml
<Grid x:Name="ContentPanel" Grid.Row="1" Margin="12,0,12,0">
    <TextBlock Text="Transform Experiment"
               HorizontalAlignment="Center"
               VerticalAlignment="Center">
        <TextBlock.RenderTransform>
            <TransformGroup>
                <ScaleTransform ScaleX="1" ScaleY="1"
                                CenterX="0" CenterY="0" />
                <SkewTransform AngleX="0" AngleY="0"
                               CenterX="0" CenterY="0" />
                <RotateTransform Angle="0"
                                 CenterX="0" CenterY="0" />
                <TranslateTransform X="0" Y="0" />
            </TransformGroup>
        </TextBlock.RenderTransform>
    </TextBlock>
</Grid>
```

You can experiment with this program right in Visual Studio. At first you'll want to try out each type of transform independently of the others. Although it's at the bottom of the group, try *TranslateTransform* first. By setting the *X* property you can shift the text right or (with negative values) to the left. The *Y* property makes the text go down or up. Set *Y* equal to −400 or so and the text goes up into the title area!

TranslateTransform is useful for making drop shadows. and effects where the text seems embossed or engraved. Simply put two *TextBlock* elements in the same location with the same text, and all the same text properties, but different *Foreground* properties. Without any transforms, the second *TextBlock* sits on top of the first *TextBlock*. On one or the other, apply a small *ScaleTransform* and the result is magic. The EmbossedText project demonstrates this technique. Here are two *TextBlock* elements in the same *Grid*:

Silverlight Project: EmbossedText   File: MainPage.xaml (excerpt)

```xml
<Grid x:Name="ContentPanel" Grid.Row="1" Margin="12,0,12,0">
    <TextBlock Text="EMBOSS"
               Foreground="{StaticResource PhoneForegroundBrush}"
               FontSize="96"
               HorizontalAlignment="Center"
               VerticalAlignment="Center" />
```

```
            <TextBlock Text="EMBOSS"
                       Foreground="{StaticResource PhoneBackgroundBrush}"
                       FontSize="96"
                       HorizontalAlignment="Center"
                       VerticalAlignment="Center">
                <TextBlock.RenderTransform>
                    <TranslateTransform X="2" Y="2" />
                </TextBlock.RenderTransform>
            </TextBlock>
        </Grid>
```

Notice I've used theme colors for the two *Foreground* properties. With the default dark theme, the *TextBlock* underneath is white, and the one on top is black like the background but shifted a little to let the white one peak through a bit:

Generally this technique is applied to black text on a white background, but it looks pretty good with this color scheme as well.

Back in the TransformExperiment project, set the *TranslateTransform* properties back to the default values of 0, and experiment a bit with the *ScaleX* and *ScaleY* properties of the *ScaleTransform*. The default values are both 1. Larger values make the text larger in the horizontal and vertical directions; values smaller than 1 shrink the text. You can even use negative values to flip the text around its horizontal or vertical axes.

All scaling is relative to the upper-left corner of the text. In other words, as the text gets larger or smaller, the upper-left corner of the text remains in place. This might be a little hard to see because the upper-left corner that remains in place is actually a little *above* the horizontal stroke of the first 'T' in the text string, in the area reserved for diacritics such as accent marks and heavy-metal umlauts.

Suppose you want to scale the text relative to another point, perhaps the textt's center. That's the purpose of the *CenterX* and *CenterY* properties of the *ScaleTransform*. For scaling around the center of the text, you can estimate the size of the text (or obtain it in code using the

ActualWidth and *ActualHeight* properties of the *TextBlock*), divide the values by 2 and set *CenterX* and *CenterY* to the results. For the text string in TransformExperiment, try 96 and 13, respectively. Now the scaling is relative to the center.

But there's a much easier way: *TextBlock* itself has a *RenderTansformOrigin* property that it inherits from *UIElement*. This property is a point in *relative coordinates* where (0, 0) is the upper-left corner, (1, 1) is the lower-right corner, and (0.5, 0.5) is the center. Set *CenterX* and *CenterY* in the *ScaleTransform* back to 0, and set *RenderTransformOrigin* in the *TextBlock* like so:

```
RenderTransformOrigin="0.5 0.5"
```

Leave *RenderTransformOrigin* at this value when you set the *ScaleX* and *ScaleY* properties of *ScaleTransform* back to the default values of 1, and play around with *RotateTransform*. As with scaling, rotation is always relative to a point. You can use *CenterX* and *CenterY* to set that point in absolute coordinates relative to the object being rotated, or you can use *RenderTransformOrigin* to use relative coordinates. The *Angle* property is in degrees, and positive angles rotate clockwise. Here's rotation of 45 degrees around the center.

The *SkewTransform* is hard to describe but easy to demonstrate. Here's the result when *AngleX* is set to 30 degrees:

The *X* coordinates are shifted to the right based on values of *Y* so as *Y* becomes larger (at the bottom of the text) values of *X* also increase. Use a negative angle to simulate oblique (italic-like) text. Setting *AngleY* causes vertical shifting based on increasing X coordinates. Here's *AngleY* set to 30 degrees:

All the transforms that derive from *Transform* are categorized as affine ("non-infinite") transforms. A rectangle will never be transformed into anything other than a parallelogram.

It's easy to convince yourself that the order of the transforms makes a difference. For example, in TransformExperiment on the *ScaleTransform* set *ScaleX* and *ScaleY* to 4, and on the *TranslateTransform* set *X* and *Y* to 100. The text is being scaled by a factor of 4 and then translated 100 pixels. Now cut and paste the markup to move the *TranslateTransform* above the *ScaleTransform*. Now the text is first translated by 100 pixels and then scaled, but the scaling applies to the original translation factors as well, so the text is effectively translated by 400 pixels.

It is sometimes tempting to put a *Transform* in a *Style*, like so:

```
<Setter Property="RenderTransform">
    <Setter.Value>
        <TranslateTransform />
    </Setter.Value>
</Setter>
```

You can then manipulate that transform from code, perhaps. But watch out: resources are shared. There will be only one instance of the *TranslateTransform* that is shared among all elements that use the *Style*. Hence, changing the transform for one element will also affect the others! If that's what you want, sharing the transform through the *Style* is ideal.

If you have a need to combine transforms in the original order that I had them in TransformExperiment—the order scale, skew, rotate, translate—you can use *CompositeTransform* to set them all in one convenient class.

Let's make a clock. It won't be a digital clock, but it won't be entirely an analog clock either. That's why I call it HybridClock. The hour, minute, and second hands are actually *TextBlock* objects that are rotated around the center of the content grid. Here's the XAML:

Silverlight Project: HybridClock   File: MainPage.xaml (excerpt)

```
<Grid Name="ContentPanel" Grid.Row="1" Margin="12,0,12,0"
      SizeChanged="OnContentPanelSizeChanged">
    <TextBlock Name="referenceText"
            Text="THE SECONDS ARE 99"
            Foreground="Transparent" />
```

```
        <TextBlock Name="hourHand">
            <TextBlock.RenderTransform>
                <CompositeTransform />
            </TextBlock.RenderTransform>
        </TextBlock>

        <TextBlock Name="minuteHand">
            <TextBlock.RenderTransform>
                <CompositeTransform />
            </TextBlock.RenderTransform>
        </TextBlock>

        <TextBlock Name="secondHand">
            <TextBlock.RenderTransform>
                <CompositeTransform />
            </TextBlock.RenderTransform>
        </TextBlock>
    </Grid>
```

Notice the *SizeChanged* handler on the *Grid*. The code-behind file will use this to make calculation adjustments based on the size of the *Grid*, which will depend on the orientation.

Of the four *TextBlock* elements in the same *Grid*, the first is transparent and used solely by the code part of the program for measurement. The other three *TextBlock* elements are colored through property inheritance, and have default *CompositeTransform* objects attached to their *RenderTransform* properties. The code-behind file defines a few fields that will be used throughout the program, and the constructor sets up a *DispatcherTimer*, for which you'll need a *using* directive for *System.Windows.Threading*:

Silverlight Project: HybridClock   File: MainPage.xaml.cs (excerpt)

```
public partial class MainPage : PhoneApplicationPage
{
    Point gridCenter;
    Size textSize;
    double scale;

    public MainPage()
    {
        InitializeComponent();

        DispatcherTimer tmr = new DispatcherTimer();
        tmr.Interval = TimeSpan.FromSeconds(1);
        tmr.Tick += OnTimerTick;
        tmr.Start();
    }
```

```
void OnContentPanelSizeChanged(object sender, SizeChangedEventArgs args)
{
    gridCenter = new Point(args.NewSize.Width / 2,
                           args.NewSize.Height / 2);

    textSize = new Size(referenceText.ActualWidth,
                        referenceText.ActualHeight);

    scale = Math.Min(gridCenter.X, gridCenter.Y) / textSize.Width;

    UpdateClock();
}

void OnTimerTick(object sender, EventArgs e)
{
    UpdateClock();
}

void UpdateClock()
{
    DateTime dt = DateTime.Now;
    double angle = 6 * dt.Second;
    SetupHand(secondHand, "THE SECONDS ARE " + dt.Second, angle);
    angle = 6 * dt.Minute + angle / 60;
    SetupHand(minuteHand, "THE MINUTE IS " + dt.Minute, angle);
    angle = 30 * (dt.Hour % 12) + angle / 12;
    SetupHand(hourHand, "THE HOUR IS " + (((dt.Hour + 11) % 12) + 1), angle);
}

void SetupHand(TextBlock txtblk, string text, double angle)
{
    txtblk.Text = text;
    CompositeTransform xform = txtblk.RenderTransform as CompositeTransform;
    xform.CenterX = textSize.Height / 2;
    xform.CenterY = textSize.Height / 2;
    xform.ScaleX = scale;
    xform.ScaleY = scale;
    xform.Rotation = angle - 90;
    xform.TranslateX = gridCenter.X - textSize.Height / 2;
    xform.TranslateY = gridCenter.Y - textSize.Height / 2;
}
}
```

HybridClock uses the *SizeChanged* handler to determine the center of the *ContentPanel*, and the size of the *TextBlock* named *referenceText*. (The latter item won't change for the duration of the program.) From these two items the program can calculate a scaling factor that will expand the *referenceText* so it is exactly as wide as half the smallest dimension of the *Grid*, and the other *TextBlock* elements proportionally.

The timer callback obtains the current time and calculates the angles for the second, minute, and hour hands relative to their high-noon positions. Each hand gets a call to *SetupHand* to do all the remaining work.

The *CompositeTransform* must perform several chores. The translation part must move the *TextBlock* elements so the beginning of the text is positioned in the center of the *Grid*. But I don't want the upper-left corner of the text to be positioned in the center. I want a point that is offset by that corner by half the height of the text. That explains the *TranslateX* and *TranslateY* properties. Recall that in the *CompositeTransform* the translation is applied last; that's why I put these properties at the bottom of the method, even though the order that these properties are set is irrelevant.

Both *ScaleX* and *ScaleY* are set to the scaling factor calculated earlier. The *angle* parameter passed to the method is relative to the high-noon position, but the *TextBlock* elements are positioned at 3:00. That's why the *Rotation* angle offsets the *angle* parameter by −90 degrees. Both scaling and rotation are relative to *CenterX* and *CenterY*, which is a point at the left end of the text, but offset from the upper-left corner by half the text height. Here's the clock in action:

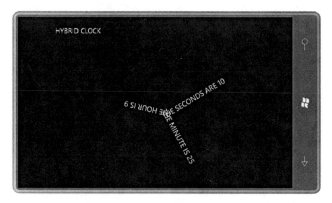

Windows Phone also supports the *Projection* transform introduced in Silverlight 3, but it's almost exclusively used in connection with animations, so I'll hold off on *Projection* until Chapter 15.

Animating at the Speed of Video

The use of the *DispatcherTimer* with a one-second interval makes sense for the HybridClock program because the positions of the clock hands need to be updated only once per second. But switching to a sweep second hand immediately raises the question: How often should the clock hands be updated? Considering that the second hand only needs to move a few pixels per second, setting the timer for 250 milliseconds would probably be fine, and 100 milliseconds would be more than sufficient.

It's helpful to keep in mind that the video display of Windows Phone 7 devices is refreshed about 30 times per second, or once every 33-1/3 milliseconds. Therefore, the use of a timer with a tick rate shorter than 33-1/3 milliseconds makes no sense whatsoever for video animations.

A timer that is synchronous with the video refresh rate is ideal for animations, and Silverlight provides one in the very easy-to-use *CompositionTarget.Rendering* event. The event handler looks something like this:

```
void OnCompositionTargetRendering(object sender, EventArgs args)
{
    TimeSpan renderingTime = (args as RenderingEventArgs).RenderingTime;
    . . .
}
```

Although the event handler must be defined with an *EventArgs* argument, the argument is actually a *RenderingEventArgs* object. If you cast the argument to a *RenderingEventArgs*, you can get a *TimeSpan* object that indicates the elapsed time since the application began running.

CompositionTarget is a static class with only one public member, which is the *Rendering* event. Install the event handler like so:

```
CompositionTarget.Rendering += OnCompositionTargetRendering;
```

Unless you're coding a very animation-laden game, you probably don't want this event handler installed for the duration of your program, so uninstall it when you're done:

```
CompositionTarget.Rendering -= OnCompositionTargetRendering;
```

The RotatingText project contains a *TextBlock* in the center of its content grid:

Project: RotatingText   File: MainPage.xaml (excerpt)

```
<Grid x:Name="ContentPanel" Grid.Row="1" Margin="12,0,12,0">
    <TextBlock Text="ROTATE!"
            FontSize="96"
            HorizontalAlignment="Center"
            VerticalAlignment="Center"
            RenderTransformOrigin="0.5 0.5">
        <TextBlock.RenderTransform>
            <RotateTransform x:Name="rotate" />
        </TextBlock.RenderTransform>
    </TextBlock>
</Grid>
```

Notice the *x:Name* attribute on the *RotateTransform*. You can't use *Name* here because that's defined by *FrameworkElement*. The code-behind file starts a *CompositionTarget.Rendering* event going in its constructor:

Project: RotatingText   File: MainPage.xaml.cs (except)

```
public partial class MainPage : PhoneApplicationPage
{
    TimeSpan startTime;

    public MainPage()
    {
        InitializeComponent();
        CompositionTarget.Rendering += OnCompositionTargetRendering;
    }

    void OnCompositionTargetRendering(object sender, EventArgs args)
    {
        TimeSpan renderingTime = (args as RenderingEventArgs).RenderingTime;

        if (startTime.Ticks == 0)
        {
            startTime = renderingTime;
        }
        else
        {
            TimeSpan elapsedTime = renderingTime - startTime;
            rotate.Angle = 180 * elapsedTime.TotalSeconds % 360;
        }
    }
}
```

The event handler uses the *renderingTime* to pace the animation so there's one revolution every two seconds.

For simple repetitive animations like this, the use of Silverlight's built-in animation facility (which I'll discuss in Chapter 15) is greatly preferred over *CompositionTarget.Rendering*.

Handling Manipulation Events

Transforms are also a good way to handle manipulation events. Here's a ball sitting in the middle of the content grid:

Silverlight Project: DragAndScale   File: Page.xaml

```
<Grid x:Name="ContentPanel" Grid.Row="1" Margin="12,0,12,0">
    <Ellipse Width="200"
```

```
            Height="200"
            RenderTransformOrigin="0.5 0.5"
            ManipulationDelta="OnEllipseManipulationDelta">
    <Ellipse.Fill>
        <RadialGradientBrush Center="0.4 0.4"
                             GradientOrigin="0.4 0.4">
            <GradientStop Offset="0" Color="White" />
            <GradientStop Offset="1" Color="{StaticResource PhoneAccentColor}" />
        </RadialGradientBrush>
    </Ellipse.Fill>

    <Ellipse.RenderTransform>
        <CompositeTransform  />
    </Ellipse.RenderTransform>
    </Ellipse>
</Grid>
```

Notice the *CompositeTransform*. It has no name so the code will have to reference it through the *Ellipse* element. (This is a good strategy to use if you're handling more than one element in a single event handler.)

The code-behind file just handles the *ManipulationDelta* event from the *Ellipse*:

```
void OnEllipseManipulationDelta(object sender, ManipulationDeltaEventArgs args)
{
    Ellipse ellipse = sender as Ellipse;
    CompositeTransform xform = ellipse.RenderTransform as CompositeTransform;

    if (args.DeltaManipulation.Scale.X > 0 || args.DeltaManipulation.Scale.Y > 0)
    {
        double maxScale = Math.Max(args.DeltaManipulation.Scale.X,
                                   args.DeltaManipulation.Scale.Y);
        xform.ScaleX *= maxScale;
        xform.ScaleY *= maxScale;
    }

    xform.TranslateX += args.DeltaManipulation.Translation.X;
    xform.TranslateY += args.DeltaManipulation.Translation.Y;

    args.Handled = true;
}
```

For handling anything other than taps, the *ManipulationDelta* event is crucial. This is the event that consolidates one or more fingers on an element into translation and scaling information. The *ManipulationDeltaEventArgs* has two properties named *CumulativeManipulation* and *DeltaManipulation*, both of type *ManipulationDelta*, which has two properties named *Translation* and *Scale*.

Using *DeltaManipulation* is often easier than *CumulativeManipulation*. If only one finger is manipulating the element, then only the *Translation* factors are valid, and these can just be added to the *TranslateX* and *TranslateY* properties of the *CompositeTransform*. If two fingers are touching the screen, then the *Scale* values are non-zero, although they could be negative and they're often unequal. To keep the circle a circle, I use the maximum and multiply by the existing scaling factors of the transform. This enables "pinch" and "stretch" manipulations.

The XAML file sets the transform center to the center of the ellipse; in theory it should be based on the position and movement of the two fingers, but this is a rather more difficult thing to determine.

The *Border* Element

The *TextBlock* doesn't include any kind of border that you can draw around the text. Fortunately Silverlight has a *Border* element that you can use to enclose a *TextBlock* or any other type of element. The *Border* has a property named *Child* of type *UIElement*, which means you can only put one element in a *Border*; however, the element you put in the *Border* can be a panel, and you can then add multiple elements to that panel.

If you load the XamlExperiment program from the last chapter into Visual Studio, you can put a *TextBlock* in a *Border* like so:

```
<Grid x:Name="ContentPanel" Grid.Row="1" Margin="12,0,12,0">
    <Border Background="Navy"
            BorderBrush="Blue"
            BorderThickness="16"
            CornerRadius="25">
        <Border.Child>
            <TextBlock Text="Hello, Windows Phone 7!" />
        </Border.Child>
    </Border>
</Grid>
```

The *Child* property is the *ContentProperty* attribute of *Border* so the *Border.Child* tags are not required. Without setting any *HorizontalAlignment* and *VerticalAlignment* properties, the *Border* element occupies the entire area of the *Grid*, and the *TextBlock* occupies the entire area of the *Border*, even though the text itself sits at the upper-left corner. You can center the *TextBlock* within the *Border*:

```
<Grid x:Name="ContentPanel" Grid.Row="1" Margin="12,0,12,0">
    <Border Background="Navy"
            BorderBrush="Blue"
            BorderThickness="16"
            CornerRadius="25">
        <TextBlock Text="Hello, Windows Phone 7!"
                   HorizontalAlignment="Center"
                   VerticalAlignment="Center" />
    </Border>
</Grid>
```

Or, you can center the *Border* within the *Grid*:

```
<Grid x:Name="ContentPanel" Grid.Row="1" Margin="12,0,12,0">
    <Border Background="Navy"
            BorderBrush="Blue"
            BorderThickness="16"
            CornerRadius="25"
            HorizontalAlignment="Center"
            VerticalAlignment="Center">
        <TextBlock Text="Hello, Windows Phone 7!" />
    </Border>
</Grid>
```

At this point, the *Border* contracts in size to become only large enough to fit the *TextBlock*. You can also set the *HorizontalAlignment* and *VerticalAlignment* properties of the *TextBlock* but they would now have no effect. You can give the *TextBlock* a little breathing room inside the border by either setting the *Margin* or *Padding* property of the *TextBlock*, or the *Padding* property of the *Border*:

And now we have an attractive *Border* surrounding the *TextBlock*. The *BorderThickness* property is of type *Thickness*, the same structure used for *Margin* or *Padding*, so you can potentially have four different thicknesses for the four sides. The *CornerRadius* property is of type *CornerRadius*, a structure that also lets you specify four different values for the four corners. The *Background* and *BorderBrush* properties are of type *Brush*, so you can use gradient brushes.

If you want a *Border* with a "normal" thickness, you can use one of the pre-defined resources:

```
<Border BorderThickness="{StaticResource PhoneBorderThickness}"
```

This is 3 pixels in width. The PhoneStrokeThickness resource also provides that same value.

What happens if you set a *RenderTransform* on the *TextBlock*? Try this:

```
<Grid x:Name="ContentPanel" Grid.Row="1" Margin="12,0,12,0">
    <Border Background="Navy"
            BorderBrush="Blue"
            BorderThickness="16"
            CornerRadius="25"
```

```
            HorizontalAlignment="Center"
            VerticalAlignment="Center"
            Padding="20">
        <TextBlock Text="Hello, Windows Phone 7!"
                RenderTransformOrigin="0.5 0.5">
            <TextBlock.RenderTransform>
                <RotateTransform Angle="45" />
            </TextBlock.RenderTransform>
        </TextBlock>
    </Border>
</Grid>
```

Here's what you get:

The *RenderTransform* property is called a *render* transform for a reason: It only affects rendering. It does *not* affect how the element is perceived in the layout system. (The Windows Presentation Foundation has a second property named *LayoutTransform* that does affect layout. If you were coding in WPF and set the *LayoutTransform* in this case, the *Border* would expand to fit the rotated text, although it wouldn't be rotated itself. But Silverlight does not yet have a *LayoutTransform* and, yes, it is sometimes sorely missed.)

Your spirits might perk up, however, when you try moving the *RenderTransform* (and *RenderTransformOrigin*) from the *TextBlock* to the *Border*, like this:

```
<Grid x:Name="ContentPanel" Grid.Row="1" Margin="12,0,12,0">
    <Border Background="Navy"
            BorderBrush="Blue"
            BorderThickness="16"
            CornerRadius="25"
            HorizontalAlignment="Center"
            VerticalAlignment="Center"
            Padding="20"
            RenderTransformOrigin="0.5 0.5">
        <Border.RenderTransform>
            <RotateTransform Angle="45" />
        </Border.RenderTransform>

        <TextBlock Text="Hello, Windows Phone 7!" />
    </Border>
</Grid>
```

Transforms affect not only the element to which they are applied, but all child elements as this screen shot makes clear:

This means that you can apply transforms to whole sections of the visual tree, and within that transformed visual tree you can have additional compounding transforms.

TextBlock Properties and Inlines

Although I've been talking about the *TextBlock* since the early pages of this book, it's time to look at it in just a little bit more detail. The *TextBlock* element has five font-related properties: *FontFamily*, *FontSize*, *FontStretch*, *FontStyle*, and *FontWeight*.

As you saw earlier, you can set *FontStyle* to either *Normal* or *Italic*. In theory, you can set *FontStretch* to values such as *Condensed* and *Expanded* but I've never seen these work in Silverlight. Generally you'll set *FontWeight* to *Normal* or *Bold*, although there are other options like *Black*, *SemiBold*, and *Light*.

TextBlock also has a *TextDecorations* property. Although this property seems to be very generalized, in Silverlight there is only one option:

```
TextDecorations="Underline"
```

The *TextBlock* property I've used most, of course, is *Text* itself. The string you set to the *Text* property can include embedded Unicode characters in the standard XML format, for example:

```
Text="&#x03C0; is approximately 3.14159"
```

If the *Text* property is set to a very long string, you might not be able to see all of it. You can insert the codes for carriage return or line feed characters ( or
) or you can set

```
TextWrapping="Wrap"
```

and *TextAlignment* to *Left*, *Right*, or *Center* (but not *Justify*). You can also set the text as a content of the *TextBlock* element:

```
<TextBlock>
    This is some text.
</TextBlock>
```

However, you might be surprised to learn that the *ContentProperty* attribute of *TextBlock* is not the *Text* property but an entirely different property named *Inlines*. This *Inlines* property is of type *InlineCollection*—a collection of objects of type *Inline*, namely *LineBreak* and *Run*. These make *TextBlock* much more versatile. The use of *LineBreak* is simple:

```
<TextBlock>
    This is some text<LineBreak />This is some more text.
</TextBlock>
```

Run is interesting because it too has *FontFamily*, *FontSize*, *FontStretch*, *FontStyle*, *FontWeight*, *Foreground*, and *TextDecorations* properties, so you can make your text very fancy:

```
<TextBlock FontSize="36"
           TextWrapping="Wrap">
    This is
    some <Run FontWeight="Bold">bold</Run> text and
    some <Run FontStyle="Italic">italic</Run> text and
    some <Run Foreground="Red">red</Run> text and
    some <Run TextDecorations="Underline">underlined</Run> text
    and some <Run FontWeight="Bold"
                  FontStyle="Italic"
                  Foreground="Cyan"
                  FontSize="72"
                  TextDecorations="Underline">big</Run> text.
</TextBlock>
```

In the Visual Studio design view, you might see the text within the *Run* tags not properly separated from the text outside the *Run* tags. This is an error. When you actually run the program in the emulator, it looks fine:

These are vector-based TrueType fonts, and the actual vectors are scaled to the desired font size before the font characters are rasterized, so regardless how big the characters get, they still seem smooth.

Although you might think of a *TextBlock* as sufficient for a paragraph of text, it doesn't provide all the features that a proper *Paragraph* class provides, such as first-line text indenting or a hanging first line where the rest of the paragraph is indented. I don't know of a way to accomplish the second feat, but the first one is actually fairly easy, as I'll demonstrate in the next chapter.

The use of the *Inlines* property allows us to write a program that explores the *FontFamily* property. In XAML you can set *FontFamily* to a string. (In code you need to create an instance of the *FontFamily* class.) The default is called "Portable User Interface". On the phone emulator, this default font maps seems to map to Segoe WP—a Windows Phone variant of the Segoe font that is a frequently found in Microsoft products and printed material, including this very book.

The FontFamilies program lists all the *FontFamily* values that Visual Studio's Intellisense tells us are valid:

Silverlight Project: FontFamilies   File: MainPage.xaml

```
<Grid x:Name="ContentPanel" Grid.Row="1" Margin="12,0,12,0">
    <TextBlock FontSize="24">
        <Run FontFamily="Arial">Arial</Run><LineBreak />
        <Run FontFamily="Arial Black">Arial Black</Run><LineBreak />
        <Run FontFamily="Calibri">Calibri</Run><LineBreak />
        <Run FontFamily="Comic Sans MS">Comic Sans MS</Run><LineBreak />
        <Run FontFamily="Courier New">Courier New</Run><LineBreak />
        <Run FontFamily="Georgia">Georgia</Run><LineBreak />
        <Run FontFamily="Lucida Sans Unicode">Lucida Sans Unicode</Run><LineBreak />
        <Run FontFamily="Portable User Interface">Portable User Interface</
Run><LineBreak />
        <Run FontFamily="Segoe WP">Segoe WP</Run><LineBreak />
        <Run FontFamily="Segoe WP Black">Segoe WP Black</Run><LineBreak />
        <Run FontFamily="Segoe WP Bold">Segoe WP Bold</Run><LineBreak />
        <Run FontFamily="Segoe WP Light">Segoe WP Light</Run><LineBreak />
        <Run FontFamily="Segoe WP Semibold">Segoe WP Semibold</Run><LineBreak />
        <Run FontFamily="Segoe WP SemiLight">Segoe WP SemiLight</Run><LineBreak />
        <Run FontFamily="Tahoma">Tahoma</Run><LineBreak />
        <Run FontFamily="Times New Roman">Times New Roman</Run><LineBreak />
        <Run FontFamily="Trebuchet MS">Trebuchet MS</Run><LineBreak />
        <Run FontFamily="Verdana">Verdana</Run><LineBreak />
        <Run FontFamily="Webdings">Webdings</Run> (Webdings)
    </TextBlock>
</Grid>
```

Here's the result:

If you misspell a name that you assign to *FontFamily*, nothing bad will happen; you'll just get the default.

The predefined resources include four keys that return objects of type *FontFamily*: PhoneFontFamilyNormal, PhoneFontFamilyLight, PhoneFontFamilySemiLight, and PhoneFontFamilySemiBold. These return the corresponding Segoe WP fonts.

More on Images

As you saw in Chapter 4, a Silverlight program can display bitmaps in the JPEG and PNG formats with the *Image* element. Let's explore the *Image* element a little more.

The ImageExperiment project contains a folder named Images containing a file named BuzzAldrinOnTheMoon.png, which is the famous photograph taken with a Hasselblad camera by Neil Armstrong on July 21st, 1969. The photo is 288 pixels square.

The file is referenced in the MainPage.xaml file like this:

Silverlight Project: ImageExperiment   File: MainPage.xaml (excerpt)

```
<Grid x:Name="ContentPanel" Grid.Row="1" Margin="12,0,12,0"
      Background="{StaticResource PhoneAccentBrush}">
    <Image Source="Images/BuzzAldrinOnTheMoon.png" />
</Grid>
```

I've also give the content grid a *Background* brush of the accent color just to make the photo stand out a little better. Here's how it appears in landscape mode:

By default, the bitmap expands to the size of its container (the content grid in this case) while maintaining the correct aspect ratio. Depending on the dimensions and aspect ratio of the container, the image is centered either horizontally or vertically. You can move it to one side or the other with the *HorizontalAlignment* and *VerticalAlignment* properties.

The stretching behavior is governed by a property defined by the *Image* element named *Stretch*, which is set to a member of the *Stretch* enumeration. The default value is *Uniform*, which you can set explicitly like this:

```
<Image Source="Images/BuzzAldrinOnTheMoon.png"
       Stretch="Uniform" />
```

The term "uniform" here means equally in both directions so the image is not distorted.

You can also set *Stretch* to *Fill* to make the image fill its container by stretching unequally.

A compromise is *UniformToFill*:

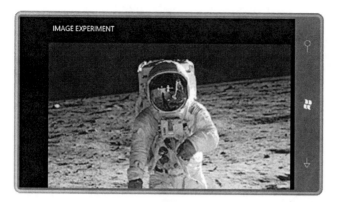

Now the *Image* both fills the container and stretches uniformly to preserve the aspect ratio. How can both goals be accomplished? Well, in general the only way that can happen is by cropping the image. You can govern which edge gets cropped with the *HorizontalAlignment* and *VerticalAlignment* properties. What setting you use really depends on the particular image.

The fourth option is *None* for no stretching. Now the image is displayed in its native size of 288 pixels square:

If you want to display the image in a particular size at the correct aspect ratio, you can set either an explicit *Width* or *Height* property. If you want to stretch non-uniformly to a particular dimension, specify both *Width* and *Height* and set *Stretch* to *Fill*.

You can set transforms on the *Image* element with the same ease that you set them on *TextBlock* elements:

```
<Image Source="Images/BuzzAldrinOnTheMoon.png"
       RenderTransformOrigin="0.5 0.5">
   <Image.RenderTransform>
```

```
            <RotateTransform Angle="30" />
        </Image.RenderTransform>
    </Image>
```

Here it is:

Playing Movies

Almost as easy as displaying bitmaps is playing a movie. However, due to their size, video files are almost never included in an executable and almost always are played from a web connection. You can play a movie from my Web site in ImageExperiment by replacing the *Image* element with a *MediaElement*:

```
<Grid x:Name="ContentGrid" Grid.Row="1" Margin="12,0,12,0"
      Background="{StaticResource PhoneAccentBrush}">
    <MediaElement Source=http://www.charlespetzold.com/Media/Walrus.wmv />
</Grid>
```

The default value of the *AutoPlay* property defined by *MediaElement* is *true*, so the movie begins playing as soon as a sufficient amount has been buffered.

In Chapter 10 I'll show you how to use *MediaPlayer* with buttons that allow controlling it like a DVD player.

Modes of Opacity

UIElement defines an *Opacity* property that you can set to a value between 0 and 1 to make an element (and its children) more or less transparent. But a somewhat more interesting property is *OpacityMask*, which can "fade out" part of an element. You set the *OpacityMask* to an object of type *Brush*; most often you'll use one of the two *GradientBrush* derivatives.

The actual color of the brush is ignored. Only the alpha channel is used to govern the opacity of the element.

For example, you can apply a *RadialGradientBrush* to the *OpacityMask* property of an *Image* element:

```
<Image Source="Images/BuzzAldrinOnTheMoon.png">
    <Image.OpacityMask>
        <RadialGradientBrush>
            <GradientStop Offset="0" Color="White" />
            <GradientStop Offset="0.8" Color="White" />
            <GradientStop Offset="1" Color="Transparent" />
        </RadialGradientBrush>
    </Image.OpacityMask>
</Image>
```

Notice that the *RadialGradientBrush* is opaque in the center, and continues to be opaque until a radius of 0.8, at which point the gradient goes to fully transparent at the edge of the circle. Here's the result, a very nice effect that looks much fancier than the few lines of XAML would seem to imply:

Here's a popular technique that uses two identical elements but one of them gets both a *ScaleTransform* to flip it upside down, and an *OpacityMask* to make it fade out:

```
<Image Source="Images/BuzzAldrinOnTheMoon.png"
       Stretch="None"
       VerticalAlignment="Top" />
<Image Source="Images/BuzzAldrinOnTheMoon.png"
       Stretch="None"
       VerticalAlignment="Top"
       RenderTransformOrigin="0.5 1">
    <Image.RenderTransform>
        <ScaleTransform ScaleY="-1" />
    </Image.RenderTransform>
    <Image.OpacityMask>
```

```
    <LinearGradientBrush StartPoint="0 0" EndPoint="0 1">
        <GradientStop Offset="0" Color="#00000000" />
        <GradientStop Offset="1" Color="#40000000" />
    </LinearGradientBrush>
    </Image.OpacityMask>
</Image>
```

The two *Image* elements are the same size and aligned at the top and center. Normally the second one would be positioned on top of the other. But the second one has a *RenderTransform* set to a *ScaleTransform* that flips the image around the horizontal axis. The *RenderTransformOrigin* is set at (0.5, 1), which is the bottom of the element. This causes the scaling to flip the image around its bottom edge. Then a *LinearGradientBrush* is applied to the *OpacityMask* property to make the reflected image fade out:

Notice that the *GradientStop* values apply to the unreflected image, so that full transparency (the #00000000 value) seems to be at the top of the picture and then is reflected to the bottom of the composite display.

It is often little touches like these that make a program's visuals pop out just a little more and endear themselves to the user. But indiscriminate use of *OpacityMask*—particularly in combination with complex animations—is discouraged because it sometimes tends to cripple performance. The general rule is: Only use *OpacityMask* if the effect is really, really cool.

Non-Tiled Tile Brushes

You've seen examples of *SolidColorBrush*, *LinearGradientBrush*, and *RadialGradientBrush*. This class hierarchy is complete from *Brush* on down:

Object

        DependencyObject (abstract)

                Brush (abstract)

                        SolidColorBrush (sealed)

                        GradientBrush (abstract)

                                LinearGradientBrush (sealed)

                                RadialGradientBrush (sealed)

                        TileBrush (abstract)

                                ImageBrush (sealed)

                                VideoBrush (sealed)

                      ImplicitInputBrush (sealed)

However, the only other brush supported under Windows Phone 7 is *ImageBrush*, and although it derives from *TileBrush*, you can't create a tiled pattern with it. (You can in the Windows Presentation Foundation, and perhaps someday in Silverlight.) Basically, *ImageBrush* lets you set any property of type *Brush* to a bitmap. Here's ImageExperiment again but with the *Image* element replaced with an *ImageBrush* set to the *Background* property of the content grid:

```
<Grid x:Name="ContentGrid" Grid.Row="1" Margin="12,0,12,0">
    <Grid.Background>
        <ImageBrush ImageSource="Images/BuzzAldrinOnTheMoon.png" />
    </Grid.Background>
</Grid>
```

Like *Image*, *TileBrush* defines a *Stretch* property, but the default value is *Fill*, so the image fills the area without regard to aspect ratio.

Chapter 9
The Intricacies of Layout

One of the most important classes in all of Silverlight is *Panel*—the class that plays a starring role in the Silverlight layout system. You might expect such a crucial class to define many properties and events, but *Panel* defines only three properties on its own:

- *Background* of type *Brush*
- *Children* of type *UIElementCollection*
- *IsItemsHost* of type *bool*

The first one is simple, and the third one is get-only and involves its role in *ListBox* and related classes.

The big one is the *Children* property. In the previous chapter you saw that the *Border* class defines a property named *Child* of type *UIElement*. This *Children* property defined by the *Panel* is of type *UIElementCollection*. Huge difference!

The *Border* doesn't have a whole lot of decision-making regarding its single child. The child element is inside the *Border* and that's about it. But a panel can host multiple children, and it can do this in a variety of ways. Perhaps the panel aligns the children in a stack, or a grid, or perhaps it docks the children on its edges, or puts them in a circle, or displays them like a fanned deck of cards, or arranges them in a carousel.

For this reason, the *Panel* class itself is abstract. This class hierarchy is complete from *Panel* onwards:

```
Object
        DependencyObject (abstract)
                UIElement (abstract)
                        FrameworkElement (abstract)
                                Panel (abstract)
                                        Canvas
                                                InkPresenter (sealed)
                                        Grid
                                        StackPanel
                                        VirtualizingPanel (abstract)
                                                VirtualizingStackPanel
                                        PanoramaPanel
                                        MapLayerBase (abstract)
                                                MapLayer (sealed)
```

The three standard types of panels provided by Silverlight for Windows Phone are *StackPanel* (probably the simplest kind of panel), *Grid* (which is the first choice for most routine layout), and *Canvas*, which should be ignored for most routine layout jobs, but has some special characteristics that make it handy sometimes.

The Silverlight for Windows Phone Toolkit includes a *WrapPanel*, which is rather similar to the right side of Windows Explorer.

I'll show you a sample program using *InkPresenter* in the next chapter. The *VirtualizingPanel* option is discussed in Chapter 17 in connection with items controls, and the others (as their names suggest) are for specialized purposes in connection with the *Panorama* and *Map* controls.

You've already seen the *Grid* and *StackPanel* in the standard MainPage.xaml, and you've probably deduced that panels can be nested. Panels are the primary architectural elements of the Silverlight page.

You can also write your own panels. I'll show you the basics in this chapter, and then more sophisticated panels in the chapters ahead.

The Single-Cell *Grid*

A *Grid* is generally arranged in rows and columns, but you've seen in previous chapters that you can put multiple children in a single-cell *Grid*. Here's a simple example for reference purposes:

Silverlight Project: GridWithFourElements   File: MainPage.xaml (excerpt)

```xaml
<Grid x:Name="ContentPanel" Grid.Row="1" Margin="12,0,12,0">
    <TextBlock Text="TextBlock aligned at right bottom"
               HorizontalAlignment="Right"
               VerticalAlignment="Bottom" />

    <Image Source="Images/BuzzAldrinOnTheMoon.png" />

    <Ellipse Stroke="{StaticResource PhoneAccentBrush}"
             StrokeThickness="24" />

    <TextBlock Text="TextBlock aligned at left top"
               HorizontalAlignment="Left"
               VerticalAlignment="Top" />
</Grid>
```

All four elements are given the entire content area in which to reside:

With regard to size, the elements here are all a little different. The sizes of the two *TextBlock* elements are governed by the text being displayed and the size of the font. The *Image* element displays the bitmap in the maximum size allowed by the dimensions of the *Grid* but maintaining the proper aspect rate. The *Ellipse* just sprawls out as much as it can.

The elements overlap in the order in which they appear in the markup, which is the order that they are added to the *Children* collection of the *Grid*. I've set the *SupportedOrientations* property on the *Page* to *PortraitOrLandscape* so you can turn the phone sideways and the elements shift around:

The *StackPanel* Stack

Here are the same four elements in a *StackPanel*, which is nested in the content grid:

Silverlight Project: **StackPanelWithFourElements**   File: **MainPage.xaml (excerpt)**

```
<Grid x:Name="ContentPanel" Grid.Row="1" Margin="12,0,12,0">
    <StackPanel Name="stackPanel"
                Orientation="Vertical">
        <TextBlock Text="TextBlock aligned at right bottom"
                   HorizontalAlignment="Right"
                   VerticalAlignment="Bottom" />

        <Image Source="Images/BuzzAldrinOnTheMoon.png" />

        <Ellipse Stroke="{StaticResource PhoneAccentBrush}"
                 StrokeThickness="12" />

        <TextBlock Text="TextBlock aligned at left top"
                   HorizontalAlignment="Left"
                   VerticalAlignment="Top" />
    </StackPanel>
</Grid>
```

By default, the *StackPanel* arranges its children in a stack from top to bottom. The children do not overlap:

The text displayed by the two *TextBlock* elements now seems a little peculiar: The first *TextBlock* is at the top of the display because that's the first one in the *Children* collection. The *HorizontalAlignment* property moves it over to the right, but the *VerticalAlignment* property (which indicates *Bottom*) is obviously being ignored, and similarly for the other *TextBlock*. The width of the *Image* element occupies the full width of the *StackPanel*. It still has the correct aspect ratio, and now only requires enough vertical space to accommodate its height.

Both the *TextBlock* and *Image* elements only occupy the minimum vertical space that they require, and the *Ellipse* … well, the *Ellipse* has totally disappeared. You might find that shocking, but reasonable. The *Ellipse* doesn't really *require* any vertical space at all, and that's exactly what it's received. (If you set the *Height* property of *Ellipse* to a positive number, you'll bring it back into view.)

Changing the orientation of the phone provides the *Image* with a greater width that it matches with a height that preserves the aspect ratio of the bitmap, but in doing so pushes most of the bitmap off the screen, together with the second *TextBlock*:

As you know, the ability of the page to respond to portrait and landscape orientation changes is governed by the *SupportedOrientations* property of the *PhoneApplicationPage* class. The property is set to a member of the *SupportedPageOrientation* enumeration. *PhoneApplicationPage* defines another property named *Orientation* which is set to a member of the *PageOrientation* enumeration to indicate whether the orientation of the phone is currently portrait or landscape.

The *StackPanel* has its own *Orientation* property, but it has nothing to do with page orientation. The *Orientation* property of *StackPanel* is set to a member of the *Orientation* enumeration, either *Horizontal* or *Vertical*. The default is *Vertical*, but the

StackPanelWithFourElements program toggles the *StackPanel* orientation when you tap the screen. Here's the code to do it:

Silverlight Project: StackPanelWithFourElements   File: MainPage.xaml.cs (excerpt)

```
protected override void OnManipulationStarted(ManipulationStartedEventArgs args)
{
    stackPanel.Orientation =
        stackPanel.Orientation == System.Windows.Controls.Orientation.Vertical ?
                        System.Windows.Controls.Orientation.Horizontal :
                        System.Windows.Controls.Orientation.Vertical;
    args.Complete();
    args.Handled = true;
    base.OnManipulationStarted(args);
}
```

The *Orientation* enumeration has to be fully qualified or the compiler thinks you're referring to the *Orientation* property defined by *PhoneApplicationPage*.

One tap and the elements are arranged from left to right:

The *HorizontalAlignment* of the first *TextBlock* is now ignored, and the *VerticalAlignment* puts it down at the bottom. The *Image* gets such a big height that most of it is off screen. We can get a little better view (including the second *TextBlock*) by turning the phone sideways:

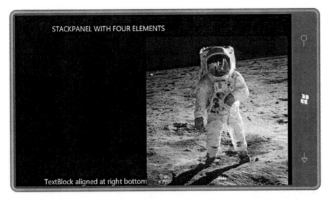

The *StackPanel* occupies the full interior of the content grid, even if that that's more than what its children require. You can easily verify this by setting a *Background* on the *StackPanel*. The StackPanel fills its parent container because the default values of the *HorizontalAlignment* and *VerticalAlignment* properties are the default values of *Stretch*.

You can set other *HorizontalAlignment* or *VerticalAlignment* properties on the *StackPanel* to force it to use only as much space as necessary, and position it within the content grid. Here's a *Background* of Pink and a *VerticalAlignment* property of *Center*:

In this particular program, the *HorizontalAlignment* property of the *StackPanel* has no effect.

Text Concatenation with *StackPanel*

A *StackPanel* with a horizontal orientation can concatenate text. This is demonstrated in the TextConcatenation project:

Silverlight Project: TextConcatenation   File: MainPage.xaml (excerpt)

```
<Grid x:Name="ContentPanel" Grid.Row="1" Margin="12,0,12,0">
    <StackPanel Orientation="Horizontal"
                HorizontalAlignment="Center"
                VerticalAlignment="Center"
                Background="{StaticResource PhoneAccentBrush}">
        <TextBlock Text="Two " />
        <TextBlock Text="plus " />
        <TextBlock Text="two " />
        <TextBlock Text="equals " />
        <TextBlock Text="four!" />
    </StackPanel>
</Grid>
```

Here it is:

It might seem rather silly to concatenate text in this way, but it's actually a very useful technique. Sometimes a program has some fixed text defined in XAML, mixed with some variable text from code or a data binding. The *StackPanel* does a nice job of piecing it together without any extraneous spacing. (In some cases you can alternatively use a *TextBlock* with its *Inlines* property set to multiple *Run* objects, but you'll see in Chapter 12 that *Run* can't be used with data bindings.)

Suppose you wanted the background color of the concatenated text to extend a little further beyond the boundaries of the text. You can't do it with a *Margin* property on the *StackPanel* because that's space outside the element. *StackPanel* doesn't have a *Padding* property (alas), so you'd need to set *Margin* properties or *Padding* properties on all the individual *TextBlock* elements, and that doesn't sound like fun.

An easier solution is to put the *StackPanel* in a *Border* element, and move all the alignment and *Background* settings to that *Border*:

```
<Grid x:Name="ContentPanel" Grid.Row="1" Margin="12,0,12,0">
    <Border Background="{StaticResource PhoneAccentBrush}"
            Padding="12"
            CornerRadius="24"
            HorizontalAlignment="Center"
            VerticalAlignment="Center">
        <StackPanel Orientation="Horizontal">
            <TextBlock Text="Two " />
            <TextBlock Text="plus " />
            <TextBlock Text="two " />
            <TextBlock Text="equals " />
            <TextBlock Text="four!" />
        </StackPanel>
    </Border>
</Grid>
```

Now you get a nice comfortable background with rounded corners:

Nested Panels

It's possible to nest one *StackPanel* in another, which makes most sense if they're of different orientations. Here's a program with two verticals in one horizontal:

Silverlight Project: StackPanelTable   File: MainPage.xaml (excerpt)

```
<Grid x:Name="ContentPanel" Grid.Row="1" Margin="12,0,12,0">
    <StackPanel Orientation="Horizontal"
                HorizontalAlignment="Center"
                VerticalAlignment="Center">
        <StackPanel>
            <TextBlock Text="Panel" FontWeight="Bold"
                                    TextDecorations="Underline" />
            <TextBlock Text="StackPanel" />
            <TextBlock Text="Canvas" />
            <TextBlock Text="Grid" />
        </StackPanel>

        <StackPanel Margin="12 0 0 0">
            <TextBlock Text="Properties" FontWeight="Bold"
                                    TextDecorations="Underline" />
            <TextBlock Text="Orientation" />
            <TextBlock Text="Left, Top, ZIndex" />
            <TextBlock Text="RowDefinitions, ColumnDefinitions, etc" />
        </StackPanel>
    </StackPanel>
</Grid>
```

The single *Margin* setting serves to separate the two columns just a bit:

Notice that each vertical *StackPanel* is as wide as its widest child, and as tall as the sum of the heights of its children. The horizontal *StackPanel* is aligned in the center of the display and is as wide as the sum of its two children.

This is not the best way to make a table! It only seems to work reasonably well because the *TextBlock* elements are all of equal height. If they weren't, then the rows would not line up as well as they do.

Visibility and Layout

The *UIElement* class defines a property named *Visibility* that's handy for temporariliy hiding elements that you don't want to be visible all the time. The *Visibility* property is not a Boolean, however. It's of type *Visibility*, an enumeration with two members, *Visible* and *Collapsed*.

In the previous program, set the *Visibility* property on one of the elements:

```
<TextBlock Text="Left, Top, ZIndex" Visibility="Collapsed" />
```

The value of *Collapsed* causes the element to have a zero size, and it effectively no longer participates in layout. In some cases that's exactly what you want, but in this particular case it results in a table with rows that no longer line up correctly:

If you want to hide an element but you still want it to have a non-zero size in the layout, don't use the *Visibility* property. Use *Opacity* instead:

```
<TextBlock Text="Left, Top, ZIndex" Opacity="0" />
```

Now the *TextBlock* has the correct size but is otherwise invisible:

That's *almost* correct. One possible problem is that the *TextBlock* will still respond to touch input. If you want to completely hide it from both sight and touch, use:

```
<TextBlock Text="Left, Top, ZIndex"
           Opacity="0"
           IsHitTestVisible="False" />
```

Opacity is not nearly as efficient as *Visibility* when used for layout purposes, so try to avoid it if you're doing something that requires frequent layout cycles. (And if you're wondering why *Visibility* is not a Boolean, it's because of the Windows Presentation Foundation. In WPF, the *Visibility* enumeration has a third member named *Invisible*, which hides the element visually but retains its size for layout purposes.)

The *Visibility* and *Opacity* properties apply to an element and the element's children, so if you set these properties on a panel, they apply to the panel's children as well.

If you set a *RenderTransform* property on a panel, the panel's children will also be affected by the transform. However, if you set a *RenderTransform* on a child of a panel, then the parent panel will ignore any effects the *RenderTransform* has when laying out its children.

Two *ScrollViewer* Applications

If the *StackPanel* has more elements than can be displayed on the screen (or in whatever container the *StackPanel* happens to find itself), the elements towards the bottom (or right) won't be displayed.

If you fear that the phone's screen is not large enough to fit all the children of your *StackPanel*, you can put the *StackPanel* in a *ScrollViewer*, a control that determines how large its content needs to be, and provides a scrollbar or two.

Actually, on Windows Phone 7, the scrollbars are more virtual than real. You don't actually scroll the *ScrollViewer* with the scrollbars. You use your fingers instead. Still, it's convenient to refer to scrollbars, so I will continue to do so.

By default, the vertical scrollbar is visible and the horizontal scrollbar is hidden, but you can change that with the *VerticalScrollBarVisibility* and *HorizontalScrollBarVisibility* properties. The options are members of the *ScrollBarVisibility* enumeration: *Visible*, *Hidden*, *Auto* (visible only if needed), and *Disabled* (visible but not responsive).

The next program is an ebook reader. Well, not exactly an *ebook* reader. It's more like an *eshort* reader, and I guess it's not very versatile: It displays a little humor piece written by Mark Twain in 1880 and believed to be the first description of the experience of listening to a person talk on the telephone without hearing the other side of the conversation. (The woman talking on the telephone is Mark Twain's wife, Olivia.)

I enhanced the customary application title a little bit to put it in a different color and make it two lines:

Silverlight Project: TelephonicConversation File: MainPage.xaml (excerpt)

```
<StackPanel x:Name="TitlePanel" Grid.Row="0" Margin="24,24,0,12">
    <TextBlock x:Name="ApplicationTitle"
            Style="{StaticResource PhoneTextNormalStyle}"
            TextAlignment="Center"
            Foreground="{StaticResource PhoneAccentBrush}">
        "A Telephonic Conversation"<LineBreak />by Mark Twain
    </TextBlock>
</StackPanel>
```

The content grid includes its own *Resources* collection with a *Style* defined. The *Grid* contains a *ScrollViewer*, which contains a *StackPanel*, which contains all the *TextBlock* elements of the story, one for each paragraph. Notice the strict division of labor: The *TextBlock* elements display the text; the *StackPanel* provides the stacking; the *ScrollViewer* provides the scrolling:

Silverlight Project: TelephonicConversation File: MainPage.xaml (excerpt)

```
<Grid x:Name="ContentPanel" Grid.Row="1" Margin="12,0,12,0">
    <Grid.Resources>
        <Style x:Key="paragraphStyle"
```

```
                    TargetType="TextBlock">
                <Setter Property="TextWrapping" Value="Wrap" />
                <Setter Property="Margin" Value="5" />
                <Setter Property="FontSize" Value="{StaticResource PhoneFontSizeSmall}" />
            </Style>
        </Grid.Resources>

        <ScrollViewer Padding="5">
            <StackPanel>
                <TextBlock Style="{StaticResource paragraphStyle}">
                     I consider that a conversation by telephone – when you are
                    simply sitting by and not taking any part in that conversation –
                    is one of the solemnest curiosities of this modern life.
                    Yesterday I was writing a deep article on a sublime philosophical
                    subject while such a conversation was going on in the
                    room. I notice that one can always write best when somebody
                    is talking through a telephone close by. Well, the thing began
                    in this way. A member of our household came in and asked
                    me to have our house put into communication with Mr. Bagley's,
                    down town. I have observed, in many cities, that the sex
                    always shrink from calling up the central office themselves. I
                    don't know why, but they do. So I touched the bell, and this
                    talk ensued: –
                </TextBlock>
                <TextBlock Style="{StaticResource paragraphStyle}">
                     <Run FontStyle="Italic">Central Office.</Run>
                    [Gruffly.] Hello!
                </TextBlock>
                <TextBlock Style="{StaticResource paragraphStyle}">
                     <Run FontStyle="Italic">I.</Run> Is it the Central Office?
                </TextBlock>

                ...

                <TextBlock Style="{StaticResource paragraphStyle}"
                        TextAlignment="Right">
                    – <Run FontStyle="Italic">Atlantic Monthly</Run>, June 1880
                </TextBlock>
            </StackPanel>
        </ScrollViewer>
    </Grid>
```

This is not the whole file, of course. The bulk of the story has been replaced by an ellipsis (…).

ScrollViewer is given a *Padding* value of 5 pixels so the *StackPanel* doesn't go quite to the edges; in addition, each *TextBlock* gets a *Margin* property of 5 pixels through the *Style*. The result of padding and margin contributes to a composite space on both the left and right sides of 10 pixels, and 10 pixels also separate each *TextBlock*, making them look more like distinct paragraphs and aiding readability

I also put a Unicode character   at the beginning of each paragraph. This is the Unicode em-space and effectively indents the first line by about a character width.

By default, *ScrollViewer* provides vertical scrolling. The control responds to touch, so you can easily scroll through and read the whole story.

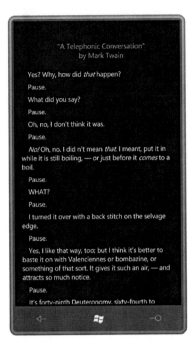

The PublicClasses program coming up next also has a *ScrollViewer* containing a vertical *StackPanel*, but it fills up that *StackPanel* entirely in code. Using reflection, the code-behind file obtains all the public classes exposed by the System.Windows, Microsoft .Phone, Microsoft.Phone.Controls, and Microsoft.Phone.Controls.Maps assemblies, and lists them in a class hierarchy.

In preparation for this job, the XAML file contains an empty *StackPanel* identified by name:

Silverlight Project: PublicClasses   File: MainPage.xaml (excerpt)

```
<Grid x:Name="ContentPanel" Grid.Row="1" Margin="12,0,12,0">
    <ScrollViewer HorizontalScrollBarVisibility="Auto">
        <StackPanel Name="stackPanel" />
    </ScrollViewer>
</Grid>
```

By default, the *VerticalScrollBarVisibility* is *Visible*, but I've given the *HorizontalScrollBarVisibility* property a value of *Auto*. If any line of text in the *StackPanel* is too long to be displayed on the screen, horizontal scrolling will be allowed to bring it into view.

This horizontal scrolling represents a significant difference between this program and the previous one. You don't want horizontal scrolling when text is wrapped into paragraphs as it is in the TelephonicConversation project. But in this program, non-wrapped lines are displayed that might be wider than the width of the display, so horizontal scrollbar is desirable.

The code-behind file makes use of a separate little class named *ClassAndChildren* to store the tree-structured classes:

Silverlight Project: PublicClasses   File: ClassAndChildren.cs

```
using System;
using System.Collections.Generic;

namespace PublicClasses
{
    class ClassAndChildren
    {
        public ClassAndChildren(Type parent)
        {
            Type = parent;
            SubClasses = new List<ClassAndChildren>();
        }

        public Type Type { set; get; }
        public List<ClassAndChildren> SubClasses { set; get; }
    }
}
```

The program creates a *ClassAndChildren* object for each class that is displayed in the tree, and each *ClassAndChildren* object contains a *List* object with all the classes that derive from that class.

Here's the complete code portion of the *MainPage* class. It needs a using directive for *System.Reflection*.

Silverlight Project: PublicClasses   File: MainPage.xaml.cs (excerpt)

```
public partial class MainPage : PhoneApplicationPage
{
    Brush accentBrush;

    public MainPage()
    {
        InitializeComponent();
        accentBrush = this.Resources["PhoneAccentBrush"] as Brush;
```

```csharp
    // Get all assemblies
    List<Assembly> assemblies = new List<Assembly>();
    assemblies.Add(Assembly.Load("System.Windows"));
    assemblies.Add(Assembly.Load("Microsoft.Phone"));
    assemblies.Add(Assembly.Load("Microsoft.Phone.Controls"));
    assemblies.Add(Assembly.Load("Microsoft.Phone.Controls.Maps"));

    // Set root object (use DependencyObject for shorter list)
    Type typeRoot = typeof(object);

    // Assemble total list of public classes
    List<Type> classes = new List<Type>();
    classes.Add(typeRoot);

    foreach (Assembly assembly in assemblies)
        foreach (Type type in assembly.GetTypes())
            if (type.IsPublic && type.IsSubclassOf(typeRoot))
                classes.Add(type);

    // Sort those classes
    classes.Sort(TypeCompare);

    // Now put all those sorted classes into a tree structure
    ClassAndChildren rootClass = new ClassAndChildren(typeRoot);
    AddToTree(rootClass, classes);

    // Display the tree
    Display(rootClass, 0);
}

int TypeCompare(Type t1, Type t2)
{
    return String.Compare(t1.Name, t2.Name);
}


// Recursive method
void AddToTree(ClassAndChildren parentClass, List<Type> classes)
{
    foreach (Type type in classes)
    {
        if (type.BaseType == parentClass.Type)
        {
            ClassAndChildren subClass = new ClassAndChildren(type);
            parentClass.SubClasses.Add(subClass);
            AddToTree(subClass, classes);
        }
    }
}


// Recursive method
void Display(ClassAndChildren parentClass, int indent)
{
    string str1 = String.Format("{0}{1}{2}{3}",
```

```
                                new string(' ', indent * 4),
                                parentClass.Type.Name,
                                parentClass.Type.IsAbstract ? " (abstract)" : "",
                                parentClass.Type.IsSealed ? " (sealed)" : "");

        string str2 = " " + parentClass.Type.Namespace;

        TextBlock txtblk = new TextBlock();
        txtblk.Inlines.Add(str1);
        txtblk.Inlines.Add(new Run
        {
            Text = str2,
            Foreground = accentBrush
        });

        stackPanel.Children.Add(txtblk);

        foreach (ClassAndChildren child in parentClass.SubClasses)
            Display(child, indent + 1);
    }
}
```

The constructor starts out storing all the public classes from the major Silverlight assemblies in a big collection. These are then sorted by name, and apportioned into *ClassAndChildren* objects in a recursive method. A second recursive method adds *TextBlock* elements to the *StackPanel*. Notice that each *TextBlock* element has an *Inlines* collection with two *Run* objects. An earlier version of the program wasn't very easy to read, so I decided the namespace name should be in a different color, and for convenience I used the accent color chosen by the user.

Here's the portion of the class hierarchy showing *Panel* and its derivatives:

The Mechanism of Layout

I want you to perform a little experiment. Go into the XAML file of the TelephonicConversation project and insert the following setting into the *ScrollViewer* tag:

```
HorizontalScrollBarVisibility="Visible"
```

Almost immediately you'll see a startling change. All the *TextBlock* elements become long single lines of text with no wrapping. What happened? How does setting a property on the *ScrollViewer* have such a profound effect on the individual *TextBlock* elements?

In a sense, this behavior shouldn't be surprising: If the *ScrollViewer* has a horizontal scrollbar, it must exist for some purpose, and it has no purpose if the words of each *TextBlock* wrap into paragraphs. If the horizontal scrollbar is to have some function, then the paragraphs should consist of single lines.

But it would be nice to have a better grasp on this actual mechanism, and not only to understand this particular peculiarity. Getting a good feel for the layout system is one of the most important Silverlight programming skills you can acquire. The layout system is very powerful, but for the uninitiated, it can also seem quite strange.

Layout in Silverlight is a two-pass process starting at the top of the visual tree and working down through all the elements' children. In a Silverlight phone application, it begins with the *PhoneApplicationFrame*, then the *PhoneApplicationPage*, then most likely a *Grid* and then (usually) a *StackPanel* and a second *Grid*. In Telephonic Conversation, the process continues into the *ScrollViewer*, which probably contains its own *Border*, and then eventually the *StackPanel*, and finally the *TextBlock* elements. These *TextBlock* elements have no children so that's the end of the line.

During the first pass, every element in the tree is responsible for querying its children to obtain their desired size. In the second pass, elements are responsible for arranging their children relative to their surface. The arrangement can be trivial or complex. For example, a *Border* has only one child and need only take account of its own *BorderThickness* to determine where to position that child relative to itself. But *Panel* derivatives must arrange their children in unique ways.

When a parent queries the size of its children, it effectively says "Here's an available size for you. How big do you want to be?" and each child calculates its desired size. All sizes are in the form of a *Size* structure with *Width* and *Height* properties. If that child itself has children, then the child must determine its own size by querying its children's sizes, until the process gets down to elements like *TextBlock* that have no children.

Elements determine their own size in various ways depending on the nature of the element. A *TextBlock*, for example, might be displaying a long piece of text and might have its *TextWrapping* property set to *Wrap*. In that case, the *TextBlock* looks at the *Width* property of the available size and determines where lines should break. It then knows how many lines it needs to display and how much vertical space is required for all those lines. This is how the *TextBlock* calculates its desired size.

But there's also an odd complication: A parent presents its children with an available size using the *Size* structure, which has two properties named *Width* and *Height* of type *double*. Sometimes the parent could set the *Width* or *Height* (or both) to that special floating-point value *Double.PositiveInfinity*. The parent is basically saying: "Child, I am offering you an infinite width [or an infinite height, or both] to play around in. How much of that do you need?"

The child cannot respond "I want it all!" as children sometimes tend to do. That's not allowed. The child must claim a desired size that is finite and non-negative.

This is how the *StackPanel* queries the size of its children. A vertical *StackPanel* offers to each of its child an available size with a width that is equal to its own width, but a height of infinity.

But there's a paradox here: Some elements, such as the *TextBlock* and *Image*, have some kind of intrinsic size, which is the size of the formatted text or the size of the unscaled bitmap. Others, like the *Ellipse*, do not have an intrinsic size. When an *Ellipse* is given a specific size, it will display itself at that size. But when the *Ellipse* is offered an infinite size, it has no choice but to shrink itself into nothingness.

To understand the precise mechanism at work here, it will be extremely useful to actually create some simple panels.

Inside the Panel

Panels are written entirely in code. There is no XAML involved. When you write a *Panel* derivative, you'll probably be defining a couple properties to make the panel more flexible. Because these properties are almost always dependency properties, I'll wait until Chapter 11 to show you how to write panels with their own properties.

Apart from defining those custom properties, a panel always overrides two methods: *MeasureOverride* and *ArrangeOverride*, which correspond to the two passes of layout. The first pass is for each parent to determine the size of its children; the second pass is for the parent to arrange its children relative to itself.

For both these jobs, the panel accesses the *Children* property that your panel inherits from *Panel*. (The *Children* property is of type *UIElementCollection*, but you can't instantiate a *UIElementCollection* yourself, and the object performs some special jobs under the covers that you don't know about, so you really can't create your own *Panel*-like class without deriving from *Panel*. If you need an element that can host multiple children in a flexible manner, derive from *Panel*.)

The big mystery regarding panels is: Who would ever make up names like *MeasureOverride* and *ArrangeOverride* for protected virtual methods? Why is the C# keyword *override* in the method name?

I don't know. The names originated in the Windows Presentation Foundation and involve the difference between the *UIElement* class and the *FrameworkElement* class. *UIElement* implements a comparatively simple layout system, and to support that layout system, it has two methods named *Measure* and *Arrange*. These methods are still vitally important in layout (as you'll see) but *FrameworkElement* needed to add some more complicated concepts to layout, namely *HorizontalAlignment*, *VerticalAlignment*, and *Margin*. These concepts make the layout system rather messier, so *FrameworkElement* added two new methods called *MeasureOverride* and *ArrangeOverride* to supersede the *Measure* and *Arrange* methods in *UIElement*.

MeasureOverride and *ArrangeOverride* are protected virtual methods. *Measure* and *Arrange* are public sealed methods. Your panel overrides *MeasureOverride* and *ArrangeOverride*. In *MeasureOverride*, the panel calls *Measure* on all its children; within *ArrangeOverride* the panel calls *Arrange* on all its children. These *Measure* and *Arrange* methods in each child then internally call the *MeasureOverride* and *ArrangeOverride* methods in the child, which continues the process down the tree.

A panel does *not* need to worry about the following properties that might be set on itself or its children:

- *HorizontalAlignment* and *VerticalAlignment*
- *Margin*
- *Visibility*
- *Opacity* (does not affect layout at all)
- *RenderTransform* (does not affect layout at all)
- *Height*, *MinHeight*, and *MaxHeight*
- *Width*, *MinWidth*, and *MaxWidth*

These properties are all handled automatically in various ways.

A Single-Cell *Grid* Clone

Perhaps the simplest panel of all is the *Grid* that contains no rows or columns, commonly referred to as a "single-cell *Grid*." I've been using the *Grid* named *ContentPanel* as a single-cell *Grid*; as you've seen, the *Grid* can host multiple children, but they overlap within the same area.

Let's duplicate the functionality of a single-cell *Grid* with a class named *SingleCellGrid*.

In a new project named SingleCellGridDemo, I right-clicked the project name, selected Add and New Item from the menu, and picked Class from the dialog box, naming it SingleCellGrid.cs. In the file, I made sure the class was public and derived from *Panel*.

Silverlight Project: SingleCellGridDemo **File: SingleCellGrid.cs (excerpt)**

```
namespace SingleCellGridDemo
{
    public class SingleCellGrid : Panel
    {
        . . .
    }
}
```

Like all panels, this class overrides the two methods *MeasureOverride* and *ArrangeOverride*. Here's the first:

Silverlight Project: SingleCellGridDemo **File: SingleCellGrid.cs (excerpt)**

```
protected override Size MeasureOverride(Size availableSize)
{
    Size compositeSize = new Size();

    foreach (UIElement child in Children)
    {
        child.Measure(availableSize);
        compositeSize.Width = Math.Max(compositeSize.Width, child.DesiredSize.Width);
        compositeSize.Height = Math.Max(compositeSize.Height, child.DesiredSize.
Height);
    }

    return compositeSize;
}
```

The argument to *MeasureOverride* is called *availableSize* of type *Size*, a structure that has two properties named *Width* and *Height* of type *double*. This is the size that the panel is getting from its parent. One or both of these dimensions might be infinite.

The *MeasureOverride* method has two fundamental jobs:

The first job is to call *Measure* on all its children. This is essential; otherwise, the children will have no size and will not appear on the screen. *MeasureOverride* almost always performs this job by enumerating through the *Children* collection with a *foreach* loop.

The second job of the *MeasureOverride* method is to return a size that the panel wants to be. In this *MeasureOverride* method, that size is the variable called *compositeSize*. This size must have finite non-negative dimensions. The *MeasureOverride* method cannot simply return the *availableSize* argument under the assumption that it wants all the space it's being offered because the *availableSize* argument might have infinite dimensions.

By the time the *MeasureOverride* method is called, this *availableSize* argument has been adjusted in some ways. If the panel has a *Margin* set on it, this *availableSize* excludes that *Margin*. If any of the *Width*, *MinWidth*, *MaxWidth*, *Height*, *MinHeight*, or *MaxHeight* properties are set on the panel, then the *availableSize* is constrained by those values.

The two jobs of *MeasureOverride* are usually performed in concert: When the panel calls *Measure* on each of its children, it offers to each child an available size. This size might have infinite dimensions. The *Size* argument passed to the *Measure* method depends on the paradigm of the particular panel. In this particular case, the *SingleCellGrid* offers to each of its children its own *availableSize*:

```
child.Measure(availableSize);
```

The panel is allowing each child to exist in the same area as itself. It's no problem if this *availableSize* argument has infinite dimensions.

When *Measure* returns, the child's *DesiredSize* property has been set and has a valid value. This is how the parent determines the size the child wants to be. This *DesiredSize* property was calculated by the child's *Measure* method after calling its own *MeasureOverride* method, which possibly interrogated its own children's sizes. The *MeasureOverride* method doesn't need to bother itself with *Margin* settings, or explicit *Width* or *Height* settings. The *Measure* method does that, and adjusts *DesiredSize* appropriately. If the child has a *Margin* setting, for example, the *DesiredSize* includes that additional amount.

Some examples: The *MeasureOverride* method of a *TextBlock* returns the size of the text displayed in a particular font. The *MeasureOverride* method of an *Image* element returns the native pixel dimensions of the bitmap. The *MeasureOverride* method of an *Ellipse* returns a size of zero.

The *DesiredSize* property is always finite. The *MeasureOverride* method in *SingleCellGrid* uses each child's *DesiredSize* property to determine a maximum size that it stores in the local variable *compositeSize*:

```
compositeSize.Width = Math.Max(compositeSize.Width, child.DesiredSize.Width);
compositeSize.Height = Math.Max(compositeSize.Height, child.DesiredSize.Height);
```

This size reflects the largest width of all the children and the largest height.

The other method required in a *Panel* derivative is *ArrangeOverride*. Here's the one in the *SingleCellGrid* class:

Silverlight Project: SingleCellGridDemo   File: SingleCellGrid.cs (excerpt)

```
protected override Size ArrangeOverride(Size finalSize)
{
    foreach (UIElement child in Children)
    {
        child.Arrange(new Rect(new Point(), finalSize));
    }

    return base.ArrangeOverride(finalSize);
}
```

The *ArrangeOverride* method receives an argument called *finalSize*. This is the area that the panel has been given by its parent. It always has finite dimensions.

The job of the *ArrangeOverride* method is to arrange its children on its surface. This is accomplished by enumerating through all its children and calling *Arrange* on them. The *Arrange* method requires an argument of type *Rect*—a rectangle defined by a *Point* indicating an upper-left corner and a *Size* indicating a width and height. This is normally the only appearance of a *Rect* in the layout process. The *Rect* specifies both the location of the child relative to the upper-left corner of the parent, and the size of the child.

In this particular case, all children are positioned at the upper-left corner of the panel and given a size of *finalSize*, the same size as the panel itself.

You might think that the size passed to *Arrange* should be the *DesiredSize* of the child, but that's not correct (at least for this particular panel). Very often this *finalSize* will be larger than the *DesiredSize* of the child. (In an extreme case, consider an *Ellipse* with a *DesiredSize* of zero.) This is how adjustments are made in the child's *Arrange* method for *HorizontalAlignment* and *VerticalAlignment*. In *SingleCellGrid*, the child's *Arrange* method is called with a size of *finalSize*:

```
child.Arrange(new Rect(new Point(), finalSize));
```

The *Arrange* method compares that size with the child's own *DesiredSize*, and then calls the child's *ArrangeOverride* method with an altered size and position based on the *HorizontalAlignment* and *VerticalAlignment* settings. That's how the *Ellipse* gets a non-zero size when its *DesiredSize* is zero.

The *ArrangeOverride* method almost always returns the *finalSize* argument, which is the value returned from the method in the base *Panel* class.

Now to test it out. The MainPage.xaml file in the SingleCellGridDemo project needs to reference this custom class. In the root element, an XML namespace declaration associates the name "local" with the .NET namespace used by the project:

```
xmlns:local="clr-namespace:SingleCellGridDemo"
```

The MainPage.xaml file nests the *SingleCellGrid* in the content grid, and then fills it with the same four elements from the first two programs in this chapter:

Silverlight Project: SingleCellGridDemo   File: MainPage.xaml (excerpt)

```
<Grid x:Name="ContentPanel" Grid.Row="1" Margin="12,0,12,0">
    <local:SingleCellGrid>
        <TextBlock Text="TextBlock aligned at right bottom"
                   HorizontalAlignment="Right"
                   VerticalAlignment="Bottom" />

        <Image Source="Images/BuzzAldrinOnTheMoon.png" />

        <Ellipse Stroke="{StaticResource PhoneAccentBrush}"
                 StrokeThickness="24" />

        <TextBlock Text="TextBlock aligned at left top"
                   HorizontalAlignment="Left"
                   VerticalAlignment="Top" />
    </local:SingleCellGrid>
</Grid>
```

You'll discover that this program displays the elements the same way as the earlier GridWithFourElements program.

A Custom Vertical *StackPanel*

The next *Panel* derivative I'll show you is the *StackPanel*, and you'll see how it differs from the single-cell *Grid*. To keep the code simple, and to avoid defining properties, I'm going to call this custom class *VerticalStackPanel*. Here's the *MeasureOverride* method:

Silverlight Project: VerticalStackPanelDemo   File: VerticalStackPanel.cs (exerpt)

```
protected override Size MeasureOverride(Size availableSize)
{
    Size compositeSize = new Size();

    foreach (UIElement child in Children)
    {
        child.Measure(new Size(availableSize.Width, Double.PositiveInfinity));
        compositeSize.Width = Math.Max(compositeSize.Width, child.DesiredSize.Width);
        compositeSize.Height += child.DesiredSize.Height;
    }
    return compositeSize;
}
```

As usual, the *MeasureOverride* method loops through all its children and calls *Measure* on each of them. But notice that the *Size* offered to each child here consists of the width of the *VerticalStackPanel* itself and a height of infinity.

The children are essentially being asked how tall they need to be. For *TextBlock*, this is easy: It's the height of the text. The *Ellipse* is easy as well: It's zero. The *Image* element, however, calculates a height based on maintaining the correct aspect ratio with the specified width, which might be a different size than in the single-cell *Grid*.

As in the *SingleCellGrid* version of *MeasureOverride*, the *Width* property of the local *compositeSize* variable is based on the maximum child width. But in this panel the *Height* property of *compositeSize* is accumulated. The *VerticalStackPanel* needs to be as tall as the sum of the heights of all its children.

If *VerticalStackPanel* is itself in a *StackPanel* with a *Horizontal* orientation, then the *Width* property of *availableSize* will be infinite, and *Measure* will be called on each child with a size that is infinite in both directions. This is fine, and it's not something that needs to be handled as a special case.

In *SingleCellGrid*, the *ArrangeOverride* method positioned each of its children in the same location. The *VerticalStackPanel* needs to stack its children. For that reason, it defines local variables named *x* and *y*:

Silverlight Project: VerticalStackPanelDemo   File: VerticalStackPanel.cs (exerpt)

```
protected override Size ArrangeOverride(Size finalSize)
{
    double x = 0, y = 0;

    foreach (UIElement child in Children)
    {
        child.Arrange(new Rect(x, y, finalSize.Width, child.DesiredSize.Height));
        y += child.DesiredSize.Height;
    }
    return base.ArrangeOverride(finalSize);
}
```

The *x* variable remains 0 throughout but the *y* variable is incremented based on the *Height* property of each child's *DesiredSize*. The *Arrange* measure is called with *x* and y indicating the location of the child relative to the panel's upper-left corner. The *Width* property of this *Rect* is the *Width* property of *finalSize*, but the *Height* property is the *Height* of the child's *DesiredSize*. This is how much vertical space was previously allocated for each child in the *MeasureOverride* method. Giving the child its own desired height in the *Arrange* method essentially voids any *VerticalAlignment* property set on the child—an effect we discovered empirically in earlier explorations of the vertical *StackPanel*.

In general, for either the horizontal or vertical dimension or both, if you offer a child an infinite dimension in *MeasureOverride*, you'll be sizing that dimension of the child based on *DesiredSize* in *ArrangeOverride*.

The MainPage.xaml file in the VerticalStackPanelDemo project is the same as the one I showed at the outset of this chapter but using *VerticalStackPanel*:

Silverlight Project: VerticalStackPanelDemo   File: **MainPage.xaml** (exerpt)

```xml
<Grid x:Name="ContentPanel" Grid.Row="1" Margin="12,0,12,0">
    <local:VerticalStackPanel>
        <TextBlock Text="TextBlock aligned at right bottom"
                   HorizontalAlignment="Right"
                   VerticalAlignment="Bottom" />

        <Image Source="Images/BuzzAldrinOnTheMoon.png" />

        <Ellipse Stroke="{StaticResource PhoneAccentBrush}"
                 StrokeThickness="24" />

        <TextBlock Text="TextBlock aligned at left top"
                   HorizontalAlignment="Left"
                   VerticalAlignment="Top" />
    </local:VerticalStackPanel>
</Grid>
```

The display is the same as the earlier program.

When this *VerticalStackPanel* is inside the content grid, its *MeasureOverride* method gets the same dimensions as the content grid itself (less any *Margin* that might be set on the *VerticalStackPanel*). This is a finite dimension that you actually saw in the SilverlightWhatSize program in Chapter 2.

But put the *VerticalStackPanel* (or a vertical *StackPanel*) in a *ScrollViewer* and something quite different happens. By default, the *ScrollViewer* displays a vertical scrollbar, so the *ScrollViewer* (or rather, one of its children) calls *Measure* on the *StackPanel* with a finite width but an infinite height. The *DesiredHeight* of the vertical *StackPanel* then gives *ScrollViewer* the information it needs for the vertical scrollbar parameters.

When you set the *HorizontalScrollBarVisibility* property of *ScrollViewer* to *Visible* or *Auto*, the *ScrollViewer* calls *Measure* on the *StackPanel* with an infinite width to determine the desired width of the panel. The *ScrollViewer* uses this information to set its horizontal scrollbar parameters. The *StackPanel* then passes this infinite width to the *MeasureOverride* calls to its own children. This has the potential of affecting children of the *StackPanel* in perhaps unanticipated ways.

For example, when a *TextBlock* has its *TextWrapping* property set to *Wrap*, it uses the *availableSize.Width* value in its own *MeasureOverride* call to determine how many lines will result from text wrapping. But if *availableSize.Width* is infinite—as it will be if the *TextBlock* is somewhere inside a *ScrollViewer* that has an enabled horizontal scrollbar—then *TextBlock* has no choice but to return a size with the text not wrapped at all.

This is why, in the TelephonicConversation program, it's not a good idea to enable the horizontal scrollbar on the *ScrollViewer*.

The Retro *Canvas*

The *Canvas* is certainly the most old-fashioned sort of panel. To position elements within the *Canvas* you supply horizontal and vertical coordinates relative to the top-left corner.

The *Canvas* has two unusual characteristics:

- In its *MeasureOverride* method, *Canvas* always calls *Measure* on its children with a size consisting of both an infinite width and an infinite height. (Accordingly, in *ArrangeOverride*, *Canvas* sizes each child based on the child's *DesiredSize*.)

- From its *MeasureOverride* method, *Canvas* returns a size consisting of a zero width and a zero height.

The first item means that children of a *Canvas* are always displayed in their smallest possible sizes, which is nothing at all for an *Ellipse* and *Rectangle*, and the native pixel size of a bitmap for an *Image*. Any *HorizontalAlignment* of *VerticalAlignment* properties set on children of a *Canvas* have no effect.

The second item implies that *Canvas* has no footprint of its own in the Silverlight layout system. (You can override that with explicit *Width* or *Height* settings on the *Canvas*.) This is actually very useful in some circumstances where you want an element to exist somewhere "outside" of the layout system and not affect the positioning of other elements.

Here's a program that uses a *Canvas* to display seven *Ellipse* elements in a type of overlapping chain in the shape of a catenary. A *Style* object (defined in the *Resources* collection of the *Canvas* itself) gives each *Ellipse* a finite *Width* and *Height*; otherwise they would not show up at all.

Silverlight Project: EllipseChain   File: MainPage.xaml (excerpt)

```
<Grid x:Name="ContentPanel" Grid.Row="1">
    <Canvas>
        <Canvas.Resources>
            <Style x:Key="ellipseStyle"
                   TargetType="Ellipse">
                <Setter Property="Width" Value="100" />
                <Setter Property="Height" Value="100" />
```

```
                    <Setter Property="Stroke" Value="{StaticResource PhoneAccentBrush}" />
                    <Setter Property="StrokeThickness" Value="10" />
            </Style>
        </Canvas.Resources>

        <Ellipse Style="{StaticResource ellipseStyle}"
                 Canvas.Left="0" Canvas.Top="0" />

        <Ellipse Style="{StaticResource ellipseStyle}"
                 Canvas.Left="52" Canvas.Top="53" />

        <Ellipse Style="{StaticResource ellipseStyle}"
                 Canvas.Left="116" Canvas.Top="92" />

        <Ellipse Style="{StaticResource ellipseStyle}"
                 Canvas.Left="190" Canvas.Top="107" />

        <Ellipse Style="{StaticResource ellipseStyle}"
                 Canvas.Left="263" Canvas.Top="92" />

        <Ellipse Style="{StaticResource ellipseStyle}"
                 Canvas.Left="326" Canvas.Top="53" />

        <Ellipse Style="{StaticResource ellipseStyle}"
                 Canvas.Left="380" Canvas.Top="0" />
    </Canvas>
</Grid>
```

Notice I've removed the *Margin* on the content panel so the math comes out to 480. Here's what it look like:

The *Canvas* is ideal for the arbitrary positioning of elements, which of course is much more associated with vector graphics programming than with control layout.

But get a load of that odd-looking syntax, rather different from anything in XAML I've yet described:

```
<Ellipse Style="{StaticResource ellipseStyle}"
         Canvas.Left="190" Canvas.Top="107" />
```

Those *Left* and *Top* properties position the upper-right corner of the element relative to the upper-right corner of the *Canvas*. The properties appear to be defined by the *Canvas* class, and yet they are set on the *Ellipse* element! When I first saw this syntax many years ago, I was baffled. Why does the *Canvas* class need to define *Left* and *Top* properties? Shouldn't *FrameworkElement* define these properties?

Of course, in graphical programming environments of days gone by, everybody has *Left* and *Top* properties because that's how the system works.

But it doesn't quite make sense for Silverlight. *Canvas* needs for its children to have *Left* and *Top* properties set, but other panels do not. In fact, other panels—including custom panels that you have yet to write or even conceive—might need quite different properties set on their children.

For this reason, Silverlight supports the concept of *attached properties*. The *Left* and *Top* properties are indeed defined by the *Canvas* class (and you'll see exactly how in Chapter 11) but you set these properties on the children on the *Canvas*. (You can set them on elements that are not actually children of a *Canvas*, but they will be ignored.)

It's instructive to look at a program that sets these attached properties in code. The EllipseMesh program creates a bunch of overlapping ellipses in the content grid. The XAML file has an empty *Canvas* with a *SizeChanged* event handler assigned:

Silverlight Project: EllipseMesh   File: MainPage.xaml (excerpt)

```
<Grid x:Name="ContentPanel" Grid.Row="1" Margin="12,0,12,0">
    <Canvas Name="canvas"
            SizeChanged="OnCanvasSizeChanged" />
</Grid>
```

Although *Canvas* has no footprint in the layout system, it still has a size and a *SizeChanged* event. With every *SizeChanged* call, the event handler empties out the *Canvas* (just for convenience) and fills it up again with new *Ellipse* objects:

Silverlight Project: EllipseMesh   File: MainPage.xaml.cs (excerpt)

```
public partial class MainPage : PhoneApplicationPage
{
    public MainPage()
    {
        InitializeComponent();
    }

    void OnCanvasSizeChanged(object sender, SizeChangedEventArgs args)
    {
        canvas.Children.Clear();

        for (double y = 0; y < args.NewSize.Height; y += 75)
            for (double x = 0; x < args.NewSize.Width; x += 75)
            {
                Ellipse ellipse = new Ellipse
                {
                    Width = 100,
                    Height = 100,
                    Stroke = this.Resources["PhoneAccentBrush"] as Brush,
                    StrokeThickness = 10
                };

                Canvas.SetLeft(ellipse, x);
                Canvas.SetTop(ellipse, y);

                canvas.Children.Add(ellipse);
            }
    }
}
```

Here's what it looks like:

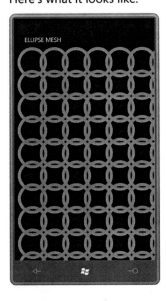

These two statements set the *Left* and *Top* attached properties:

```
Canvas.SetLeft(ellipse, x);
Canvas.SetTop(ellipse, y);
```

These are two static methods defined by the *Canvas* class. You can call these methods either before or after you add the child to the *Children* collection of the *Canvas*. Because these methods are static, you can even call them when a *Canvas* object does not yet exist.

Even more revealing is knowing how these two static methods are defined in the *Canvas* class. Right in the EllipseMesh program you can replace the two static method calls with the following statements:

```
ellipse.SetValue(Canvas.LeftProperty, x);
ellipse.SetValue(Canvas.TopProperty, y);
```

These equivalent calls make it clear that something is actually being set on the *Ellipse* objects. The *SetValue* method is defined by *DependencyObject*—a very basic class in the Silverlight class hierarchy—and *LeftProperty* and *RightProperty* are (despite their names) actually static fields of type *DependencyProperty* defined by *Canvas*.

My guess is that *SetValue* accesses an internal dictionary created and maintained by *DependencyObject* where the first argument to *SetValue* is the dictionary key and the second is the value. When *Canvas* is laying out its children in its *ArrangeOverride* method, it can access these values for a particular *child* element using either:

```
double x = GetLeft(child);
double y = GetTop(child);
```

or the equivalent:

```
double x = (double)child.GetValue(LeftProperty);
double y = (double)child.GetValue(TopProperty);
```

The *GetValue* method accesses the internal dictionary in the child and returns an object of type *object* that needs to be cast here to a *double*.

I'll show you a *Canvas* clone in Chapter 11 and you'll see how to define your own attached properties.

Watch out: I described how to replace the *Canvas.SetLeft* and *Canvas.SetTop* calls in EllipseMesh with equivalent calls to *SetValue*. But this call:

```
Canvas.SetLeft(ellipse, 57);
```

is *not* equivalent to this call:

```
ellipse.SetValue(Canvas.LeftProperty, 57);
```

The second argument of *Canvas.SetLeft* is defined to be of type *double* but the second argument of the general-purpose *SetValue* method is defined to be of type *object*. When the C# compiler parses that *SetValue* call it will assume the number is an *int*. Only at runtime will the error be caught. You can avoid the problem by making it explicitly a *double*:

```
ellipse.SetValue(Canvas.LeftProperty, 57.0);
```

Although we speak of the *Left* and *Top* attached properties of *Canvas*, nothing defined by *Canvas* is actually named *Left* or *Top*! *Canvas* defines static fields named *LeftProperty* and *TopProperty*, and static methods named *SetLeft*, *SetTop*, *GetLeft* and *GetTop*, but nothing named *Left* or *Top*. The XAML syntax shown here

```
<Ellipse Style="{StaticResource ellipseStyle}"
         Canvas.Left="190" Canvas.Top="107" />
```

is actually rendered by making calls to *Canvas.SetLeft* and *Canvas.SetTop*.

You'll see other attached properties around. The standard MainPage.xaml file has an attached property set on its root element:

```
shell:SystemTray.IsVisible="True"
```

In fact, the entire *SystemTray* class exists for the sole purpose of defining this attached property so you can set it on the *PhoneApplicationPage* derivative. It's probably the *PageApplicationFrame* that hunts for this property on each page to determine whether the system tray should be visible.

Canvas and ZIndex

The *Canvas* has a third attached property named *ZIndex* that you can use to override the default layering of elements.

As you've seen, elements in a panel are layered by the order in which they appear in the *Children* collection. The earlier elements in the collection are covered by the later elements.

You can alter this behavior by setting the *Canvas.ZIndex* attached property on one or more children. The name refers to the imaginary Z axis that extends out from the screen. Elements with higher Z indices appear on top of (and might even completely obscure) siblings with lower Z indices. If two siblings have the same *Canvas.ZIndex* attached property—and by default no element has a *Canvas.ZIndex* value and hence is assumed to have a value of zero—then the ordering in the *Children* collection is used instead.

Although this *Canvas.ZIndex* attached property is defined by the *Canvas* class, it actually works with any type of panel. If you're writing a custom panel class, handling Z indices is not something you have to worry about. It's taken care of automatically by the layout system.

The *Canvas* and Touch

In Chapter 8 I showed you how to move elements around the screen in response to touch by altering transform objects set to the *RenderTransform* property. You can also move elements around a *Canvas* by setting the *Left* and *Top* attached properties in code.

Here's a simple program called TouchCanvas. A *Canvas* hosts three *Ellipse* elements colored red, green, and blue:

Silverlight Project: TouchCanvas   File: MainPage.xaml (excerpt)

```
<Grid x:Name="ContentPanel" Grid.Row="1" Margin="12,0,12,0">
    <Canvas Name="canvas">
        <Ellipse Canvas.Left="50"
                 Canvas.Top="50"
                 Width="100"
                 Height="100"
                 Fill="Red" />

        <Ellipse Canvas.Left="150"
                 Canvas.Top="150"
                 Width="100"
                 Height="100"
                 Fill="Green" />

        <Ellipse Canvas.Left="250"
                 Canvas.Top="250"
                 Width="100"
                 Height="100"
                 Fill="Blue" />
    </Canvas>
</Grid>
```

The code file overrides the *OnManipulationStarted* and *OnManipulationDelta* methods in *MainPage*. Setting the *ManipulationContainer* property to the *Canvas* in the first override isn't strictly required.

Silverlight Project: TouchCanvas   File: MainPage.xaml.cs (excerpt)

```
public partial class MainPage : PhoneApplicationPage
{
    public MainPage()
    {
        InitializeComponent();
    }
```

```
protected override void OnManipulationStarted(ManipulationStartedEventArgs args)
{
    args.ManipulationContainer = canvas;
    base.OnManipulationStarted(args);
}

protected override void OnManipulationDelta(ManipulationDeltaEventArgs args)
{
    UIElement element = args.OriginalSource as UIElement;
    Point translation = args.DeltaManipulation.Translation;
    Canvas.SetLeft(element, Canvas.GetLeft(element) + translation.X);
    Canvas.SetTop(element, Canvas.GetTop(element) + translation.Y);

    args.Handled = true;
    base.OnManipulationDelta(args);
}
```

The *OnManipulationDelta* override moves one of the ellipses by obtaining its *Left* and *Top* settings, adding the delta translation factors, and then setting them back, all in fairly short and clean statements.

The Mighty *Grid*

The *Grid* should be your default choice of panel. It is both flexible and powerful, both simple and versatile. I'm only going to show you one sample program using the *Grid* in this chapter, but that's only because the rest of the book has plenty more.

The *Grid* is somewhat reminiscent of an HTML table, but with several differences: Unlike the HTML table, the *Grid* doesn't do formatting. It's strictly for layout. There's no concept of headers, for example, or built-in cell dividers. Also, unlike the HTML table, the use of the *Grid* is actually encouraged.

A *Grid* has a certain number of rows and columns; rows can be different heights; columns can be different widths. A child of the *Grid* normally occupies a particular row and column but it can also span multiple rows and multiple columns. This sounds versatile (and it is), but it comes with something of a price. Although you can arbitrarily add children to a *StackPanel* or a *Canvas*, with a *Grid* you really need to know how many rows and columns you need to accommodate all the children. You can add rows and columns from code at runtime, but if you're defining the *Grid* entirely in XAML you need to know beforehand.

Nesting *Grid* panels is common, but don't get carried away, particularly if something is going on in your program that frequently generates layout cycles. Overly complex nesting can bog down layout.

The *Grid* defines two properties named *RowDefinitions* and *ColumnDefinitions*. These are, respectively, collections of *RowDefinition* and *ColumnDefinition* objects. These objects define the height of each row and the width of each column, and you have three choices:

- the word "Auto"
- a fixed amount in pixels
- an asterisk, or a number followed by an asterisk (called "star")

The first and the last are most common. The first indicates that the cell is sized to fit the element in the cell. (The *Grid* interrogates the size of that element in its *MeasureOverride* method using infinite dimensions.) Rows and columns marked with asterisks are used to divide remaining space proportionally.

As you've seen, it's common that *StackPanel* elements contain more children than can be displayed on the screen; the *Grid* is usually defined so that doesn't happen.

You indicate the particular row and column of an element with the attached properties *Grid.Row* and *Grid.Column*. Row and column numbers begin with zero at the upper-left. You can specify that a particular element occupies additional rows or additional columns with attached properties *Grid.RowSpan* and *Grid.ColumnSpan*.

Here's an example:

Silverlight Project: SimpleGrid   File: MainPage.xaml (excerpt)

```
<Grid x:Name="ContentPanel" Grid.Row="1" Margin="12,0,12,0">
    <Grid.RowDefinitions>
        <RowDefinition Height="Auto" />
        <RowDefinition Height="*" />
        <RowDefinition Height="Auto" />
    </Grid.RowDefinitions>

    <Grid.ColumnDefinitions>
        <ColumnDefinition Width="2*" />
        <ColumnDefinition Width="*" />
    </Grid.ColumnDefinitions>

    <TextBlock Grid.Row="0"
               Grid.Column="0"
               Grid.ColumnSpan="2"
               Text="Heading at top of Grid"
               HorizontalAlignment="Center" />

    <Image Grid.Row="1"
           Grid.Column="0"
           Source="Images/BuzzAldrinOnTheMoon.png" />
```

```
    <Ellipse Grid.Row="1"
            Grid.Column="1"
            Stroke="{StaticResource PhoneAccentBrush}"
            StrokeThickness="6" />

    <TextBlock Grid.Row="2"
            Grid.Column="0"
            Grid.ColumnSpan="2"
            Text="Footer at bottom of Grid"
            HorizontalAlignment="Center" />
</Grid>
```

I just added the row and column definitions to the existing content grid. Each element in the *Grid* has explicit *Grid.Row* and *Grid.Column* settings, but you can omit them for values of zero. Both the *TextBlock* at the top and *TextBlock* at the bottom span the two columns to be centered in the whole grid.

The two columns were apportioned so the first column is twice as wide as the second. The width of that first column determines the size of the *Image*, which is then centered vertically in the cell:

The rows and columns change size when the phone is tilted, but the overall layout remains the same:

Try setting *HorizontalAlignment* and *VerticalAlignment* properties on this *Grid*. You'll discover that the size of the grid is constrained by the native pixel dimensions of the bitmap.

The *Grid* named *ContentPanel* itself has a setting of the *Grid.Row* attached property, but this refers to the second row of its parent *Grid*—the one named *LayoutRoot*. The first row of that *Grid* is occupied by the *StackPanel* with the two titles.

And now, finally, we have reached the point in the accumulation of knowledge of Silverlight and XAML where nothing in MainPage.xaml should be a mystery.

Chapter 10
The App Bar and Controls

You won't be surprised to learn that Silverlight for Windows Phone supports several standard controls, including a *ScrollBar* and *Slider* for selecting from a continuous range of values, a *TextBox* for entering and editing text, and the common array of buttons, including *CheckBox* (for on/off options), *RadioButton* (for a group of mutually-exclusive options), and the basic *Button* for initiating commands.

At this point, you're probably more than ready to dive into Silverlight controls, particularly since a couple of the programs in this chapter are actually useful and might even be classified as "real" Windows Phone 7 applications.

But before I discuss the standard controls, I want to explore an alternative to these controls. When programming for Windows Phone 7, basic program commands and options might best be implemented in a mechanism developed specifically for the phone and which is intended to provide a consistent user experience for phone users.

This is known as the *ApplicationBar* and commonly referred to as the *app bar*.

ApplicationBar Icons

The *ApplicationBar* serves the same role as a menu or toolbar that you might find in a conventional Windows program. It also shares some visual and functional similarities with those older structures. If you only need a couple buttons in your program for some common commands, and perhaps a little menu, the *ApplicationBar* is what you should use. There is no conventional menu or toolbar defined in Silverlight at all (although you can certainly make one yourself).

The *ApplicationBar* and related classes (*ApplicationBarIconButton* and *ApplicationBarMenuItem*) are defined in the *Microsoft.Phone.Shell* namespace. These classes derive from *Object* and exist entirely apart from the whole *DependencyObject, UIElement*, and *FrameworkElement* class hierarchy of conventional Silverlight programming. Strictly speaking, the *ApplicationBar* is *not* part of the visual tree of your page.

An *ApplicationBar* object is always set to the *ApplicationBar* property of a *PhoneApplicationPage*. When the phone is held upright, the *ApplicationBar* always appears at the bottom of the page, and stays in the same location when the phone is turned sideways or upside down. The *ApplicationBar* is not at all customizable.

An *ApplicationBar* can contain up to four buttons. These are sometimes referred to as *icons* and they always display images. These images are generally PNG files; the bitmaps themselves should be 48 pixels square and mostly transparent. The actual image should be white and occupy a 26-pixels square area in the middle of the bitmap. A collection of suitable bitmaps can be downloaded from *http://www.microsoft.com/downloads/details. aspx?FamilyID=369b20f7-9d30-4cff-8a1b-f80901b2da93*. You should study these images before designing your own.

I'll assume you've downloaded the bitmaps. They are stored in two folders named *light* (black images on white backgrounds) and *dark* (white images on transparent background). Although the bitmaps in the *light* folder are easier to see in Windows Explorer, in your programs you should always use the corresponding files from the *dark* folder.

The MoviePlayer project contains a *MediaElement* to play a movie, and the *ApplicationBar* contains icons for Play, Pause, rewind to the beginning, and go to the end.

When creating a project in Visual Studio that uses the *ApplicationBar*, you'll want a folder in the project for the icons. Right click the project name and choose Add and New Folder. (Or pick Add New Folder from the Project menu.) Name the folder *Images* or something like that. Right click that folder name, choose Add and Existing Item, and navigate to the *dark* folder of the bitmaps you've downloaded. For MoviePlayer I selected:

- appbar.transport.ff.rest.png

- appbar.transport.pause.rest.png

- appbar.transport.play.rest.png

- appbar.transport.rew.rest.png

These are the four standard images associated with a videotape "transport" device metaphor.

This is crucial: Click each of these files as listed under the *Images* directory to display its Properties page. (You might have to right-click the file and select Properties.) Set the Build Action field to Content. The *ApplicationBar* is not smart enough to find the images if the Build Action is Resource.

The *ApplicationBar* is not part of standard Silverlight, so an XML namespace declaration needs to associate the XML "shell" namespace with the .NET namespace *Microsoft.Phone. Shell*. The standard MainPage.xaml file provides this for you already:

```
xmlns:shell="clr-namespace:Microsoft.Phone.Shell;assembly=Microsoft.Phone"
```

MainPage.xaml will also have a sample *ApplicationBar* at the bottom of the file. You can uncomment and alter that one, or add your own right before the *phone:PhoneApplicationPage* end tag:

```
<phone:PhoneApplicationPage.ApplicationBar>
    <shell:ApplicationBar>
        <shell:ApplicationBarIconButton
                IconUri="Images/appbar.transport.rew.rest.png"
                Text="rewind" />

        <shell:ApplicationBarIconButton
                IconUri="Images/appbar.transport.play.rest.png"
                Text="play" />

        <shell:ApplicationBarIconButton
                IconUri="Images/appbar.transport.pause.rest.png"
                Text="pause" />

        <shell:ApplicationBarIconButton
                IconUri="Images/appbar.transport.ff.rest.png"
                Text="to end" />
    </shell:ApplicationBar>
</phone:PhoneApplicationPage.ApplicationBar>
```

ApplicationBar has a property named *Buttons* which is the content property for the class.
The *Buttons* collection can contain no more than four *ApplicationBarIconButton* objects.
The *IconUri* and *Text* fields are required! The text description should be short; it is converted
to lower-case for display purposes.

Build and deploy the program as it exists at this point. Here's what it looks like. (I've also
removed the page title.)

As you press each icon, it flashes and wiggles a bit for feedback. If you press the ellipsis, the buttons rise up to display the explanatory *Text* property:

When you turn the phone sideways, the *ApplicationBar* stays in the same place relative to the phone, but if you've set the *SupportedOrientations* property to *PortraitOrLandscape*, the images themselves turn sideways:

Watch out for this feature: Don't use icons that will cause user disorientation when the phone is oriented sideways. If you have one icon with a horizontal bar, and another with a vertical bar, you're going to confuse your users and, quite possibly, yourself.

If you'd like to define an *ApplicationBar* in XAML but you don't want it to be initially displayed, you can set the *IsVisible* property to *false*:

```
<shell:ApplicationBar IsVisible="False">
```

You can later set that property to *true* in code. But don't bother setting the *x:Name* attribute on the *ApplicationBar* to access it from code. Inexplicably, you can't reference an *ApplicationBar* object in code by name. Instead, get at it through the *ApplicationBar* property of *MainPage*:

```
this.ApplicationBar.IsVisible = true;
```

ApplicationBar also defines *ForegroundColor* and *BackgroundColor* properties that you should probably ignore. By default the *ApplicationBar* colors will be properly swapped if you change the color theme of the phone.

ApplicationBar also defines an *Opacity* property, whose familiar name disguises an unconventional effect. The *Opacity* property involves the background of the *ApplicationBar* rather than the foreground; it never affects the icon images themselves.

The *Opacity* property is 1 by default, which means that the background of the *ApplicationBar* is opaque. The background is colored using the resource referenced as *PhoneChromeBrush*—a very darkish gray for the dark theme, and a very lightish gray for the light theme.

With an *Opacity* property of 1, the *ApplicationBar* takes space away from the rest of the content of the page. For any other *Opacity* values, other content on the page shares the space with the *ApplicationBar*. The *ApplicationBar* is always on top, and when *Opacity* goes down to 0, the *ApplicationBar* has an entirely transparent background and the icons are displayed on top of whatever happens to be in that area of the content grid. Documentation recommends you stick to *Opacity* values of 1, 0.5, or 0.

If a particular icon is not valid at a particular time, you can set the *IsEnabled* property of *ApplicationBarIconButton* to *false*. For example, the Play and Pause buttons shouldn't both be enabled at the same time. Here's how to disable the Pause button at startup:

```
<shell:ApplicationBarIconButton
        IconUri="Images/appbar.transport.pause.rest.png"
        Text="Pause"
        IsEnabled="False" />
```

Now it looks like this:

You'll probably want to enable that button in code later on, but once again, you can't use *x:Name*. Because this is the third button (and hence has an index in the *Buttons* collection of 2) you can set the *IsEnabled* property in code like this:

```
(this.ApplicationBar.Buttons[2] as ApplicationBarIconButton).IsEnabled = true;
```

You'll probably be disabling the Play button at the same time:

```
(this.ApplicationBar.Buttons[1] as ApplicationBarIconButton).IsEnabled = false;
```

Actually, if the movie is accessed over the Internet, you'll probably want to disable all the buttons until you've actually opened the media and know you're going to be able to play the movie!

The program also needs to know when a user has clicked an enabled button. Set the *Click* event to a handler:

```
<shell:ApplicationBarIconButton
       IconUri="Images/appbar.transport.play.rest.png"
       Text="Play"
       Click="OnAppBarPlayClick" />
```

In the code-behind file, the handler is based on the *EventHandler* delegate:

```
void OnAppbarPlayClick(object sender, EventArgs args)
{
    . . .
}
```

The final MoviePlayer project has an *ApplicationBar* defined like this:

Silverlight Project: MoviePlayer   File: MainPage.xaml (excerpt)

```
<phone:PhoneApplicationPage.ApplicationBar>
    <shell:ApplicationBar x:Name="appbar">
        <shell:ApplicationBarIconButton
                x:Name="appbarRewindButton"
                IconUri="Images/appbar.transport.rew.rest.png"
                Text="rewind"
                IsEnabled="False"
                Click="OnAppbarRewindClick" />

        <shell:ApplicationBarIconButton
                x:Name="appbarPlayButton"
                IconUri="Images/appbar.transport.play.rest.png"
                Text="play"
                IsEnabled="False"
                Click="OnAppbarPlayClick" />

        <shell:ApplicationBarIconButton
                x:Name="appbarPauseButton"
                IconUri="Images/appbar.transport.pause.rest.png"
                Text="pause"
                IsEnabled="False"
                Click="OnAppbarPauseClick" />

        <shell:ApplicationBarIconButton
                x:Name="appbarEndButton"
                IconUri="Images/appbar.transport.ff.rest.png"
                Text="to end"
                IsEnabled="False"
                Click="OnAppbarEndClick" />
    </shell:ApplicationBar>
</phone:PhoneApplicationPage.ApplicationBar>
```

Yes, I have assigned *x:Name* attributes to all the buttons, but you'll see shortly that I've also reassigned them in code.

The content grid contains the *MediaElement* to play the movie and two *TextBlock* elements for some status and error messages:

Silverlight Project: MoviePlayer   File: MainPage.xaml (excerpt)

```
<Grid x:Name="ContentPanel" Grid.Row="1" Margin="12,0,12,0">
    <MediaElement Name="mediaElement"
            Source="http://www.charlespetzold.com/Media/Walrus.wmv"
            AutoPlay="False"
            MediaOpened="OnMediaElementMediaOpened"
```

```
                     MediaFailed="OnMediaElementMediaFailed"
                     CurrentStateChanged="OnMediaElementCurrentStateChanged"  />

    <TextBlock Name="statusText"
               HorizontalAlignment="Left"
               VerticalAlignment="Bottom" />

    <TextBlock Name="errorText"
               HorizontalAlignment="Right"
               VerticalAlignment="Bottom"
               TextWrapping="Wrap" />
</Grid>
```

Notice that the *AutoPlay* property on the *MediaElement* is set to *false* so the movie doesn't start playing when it's loaded. That's all handled in the code-behind file.

The constructor of the *MainPage* assigns *x:Name* attributes to the appropriate *ApplicationBarIconButton* so they can be conveniently referenced in the rest of the class:

Silverlight Project: MoviePlayer   File: MainPage.xaml.cs (excerpt)

```
public MainPage()
{
    InitializeComponent();

    // Re-assign names already in the XAML file
    appbarRewindButton = this.ApplicationBar.Buttons[0] as ApplicationBarIconButton;
    appbarPlayButton = this.ApplicationBar.Buttons[1] as ApplicationBarIconButton;
    appbarPauseButton = this.ApplicationBar.Buttons[2] as ApplicationBarIconButton;
    appbarEndButton = this.ApplicationBar.Buttons[3] as ApplicationBarIconButton;
}
```

The four handlers for the *ApplicationBar* buttons have just one line of code each:

Silverlight Project: MoviePlayer   File: MainPage.xaml.cs (excerpt)

```
void OnAppbarRewindClick(object sender, EventArgs args)
{
    mediaElement.Position = TimeSpan.Zero;
}

void OnAppbarPlayClick(object sender, EventArgs args)
{
    mediaElement.Play();
}
```

```
void OnAppbarPauseClick(object sender, EventArgs args)
{
    mediaElement.Pause();
}

void OnAppbarEndClick(object sender, EventArgs args)
{
    mediaElement.Position = mediaElement.NaturalDuration.TimeSpan;
}
```

The messy part of a movie-playing program involves the enabling and disabling of the
buttons. Because the primary purpose of this program is to demonstrate the use of the
ApplicationBar, I've taken a very simple approach here: The Rewind and End buttons
are enabled when the media is opened, and the Play and Pause buttons are enabled based
on the *CurrentState* property of the *MediaElement:*

Silverlight Project: MoviePlayer   File: MainPage.xaml.cs (excerpt)

```
void OnMediaElementMediaFailed(object sender, ExceptionRoutedEventArgs args)
{
    errorText.Text = args.ErrorException.Message;
}

void OnMediaElementMediaOpened(object sender, RoutedEventArgs args)
{
    appbarRewindButton.IsEnabled = true;
    appbarEndButton.IsEnabled = true;
}

void OnMediaElementCurrentStateChanged(object sender, RoutedEventArgs args)
{
    statusText.Text = mediaElement.CurrentState.ToString();

    if (mediaElement.CurrentState == MediaElementState.Stopped ||
        mediaElement.CurrentState == MediaElementState.Paused)
    {
        appbarPlayButton.IsEnabled = true;
        appbarPauseButton.IsEnabled = false;
    }
    else if (mediaElement.CurrentState == MediaElementState.Playing)
    {
        appbarPlayButton.IsEnabled = false;
        appbarPauseButton.IsEnabled = true;
    }
}
```

Jot and Application Settings

The Jot program I'll be discussing next is one of three programs in this chapter that you might find useful on the phone in daily life. The idea for it arose out of the QuickNotes program described later in this chapter. QuickNotes is basically a big *TextBox* control but it retains the contents of this *TextBox* in isolated storage. Every time you open the program, you get the same text you left in there the last time you used the program. You can add text and delete text. It's good for taking quick notes (as the program name suggests) because you don't have to load or save any files. That's all done automatically.

But I'll discuss QuickNotes in more detail at the end of this chapter. For now, the Jot program is similar and rather easier to use because it doesn't require a virtual or actual keyboard. You just use your finger for writing or drawing.

As you'll see, QuickNotes makes do with just one text document because you can easily scroll through and insert text wherever you want. But Jot is more canvas-oriented, and the fixed size of this canvas seemed to imply that the program should support multiple pages for multiple canvases.

Jot displays finger input using a class named *InkPresenter*, which originated with tablet interfaces. *InkPresenter* derives from the *Canvas* panel, which means you could use the *Children* property of *InkPresenter* to design a background image (a yellow legal pad, for example). Or you can ignore the *Canvas* part of *InkPresenter*.

InkPresenter exists primarily for displaying "ink," which is represented as multiple series of connected short lines—*polylines* in graphics speak but called *strokes* in this context.

A particular point on the display surface is a *StylusPoint*, a structure defined in the *System .Windows.Input* namespace with *X* and *Y* properties as well as a *PressureFactor* for devices that support pressure. (Windows Phone 7 does not support touch pressure.)

When you draw on a screen with a finger (on touch screens) or stylus (on tablets), you might create a bunch of crazy curves, but regardless how complex the curves are, they are always represented by a collection of *StylusPoint* objects that together mimic the complex curve. This collection of *StylusPoint* objects representing a continuous line is encapsulated in a *Stroke*, a class defined in the *System.Windows.Ink* namespace. The *Stroke* object encapsulates not only the points of this line; but also its color and width with these two properties:

- *StylusPoints* of type *StylusPointCollection*
- *DrawingAttributes* of type *DrawingAttributes*

A *Stroke* is a continuous line created when the user touches the screen, moves the finger, and lifts. Touching the screen again begins another *Stroke*. Multiple *Stroke* objects are stored in a *StrokeCollection*. And that's what the *InkPresenter* stores: *InkPresenter* defines a *Strokes* property of type *StrokeCollection* and renders those strokes, each of which forms a continuous line.

My Jot program supports multiple pages, so it will need yet another collection to store a *StrokeCollection* for each page.

You need to know all this up front because I'm going to begin my discussion of the Jot program with the application settings. The whole idea of the program is that it always brings you back to where you last left off. Jot doesn't need any transient data for tombstoning because it treats tombstoning the same way as normal program launching and closing. Jot needs to use isolated storage to save the same data when it's deactivated (tombstoned) as when it's closed, and it needs to load this data when it's both launched and activated (that is, revived after tombstoning).

The application settings for Jot are encapsulated in a class specifically for that purpose called *JotAppSettings*. An instance of *JotAppSettings* is serialized and saved in isolated storage. The class also contains methods to save and load the settings. The project needs a reference to the System.Xml.Serialization library, and *JotAppSettings* needs several non-standard *using* directives for *System.Collection.Generic*, *System.IO*, *System.IO.IsolatedStorage*, and *System.Xml.Serialization*.

Here are the public properties of *JotAppSettings* that constitute application settings:

Silverlight Project: Jot   File: JotAppSettings.cs (excerpt)

```
public List<StrokeCollection> StrokeCollections { get; set; }
public int PageNumber { set; get; }
public Color Foreground { set; get; }
public Color Background { set; get; }
public int StrokeWidth { set; get; }
```

There is one *StrokeCollection* for each page that Jot displays; hence the program needs to save a collection of *StrokeCollection* objects. The program initially displays a particular page indicated by *PageNumber*.

The first time Jot is run, it picks up the *Foreground* and *Background* colors from the system theme. However, the program implements an option to swap those colors for drawing purposes, under the assumption that you might prefer a white-on-black theme for most of the phone, but black-on-white drawing for Jot. For that reason, it saves and loads explicit colors. The *StokeWidth* property starts out as 3 (the default with *InkPresenter*) but can be set by the user to 1 or 5 instead.

I tried using the *IsolatedStorageSettings* class to save these items, but I couldn't get it to work, so I switched to the regular isolated storage facility. Here's the *Save* method:

Silverlight Project: Jot   File: JotAppSettings.cs (excerpt)

```
public void Save()
{
    IsolatedStorageFile iso = IsolatedStorageFile.GetUserStoreForApplication();
    IsolatedStorageFileStream stream = iso.CreateFile("settings.xml");
    StreamWriter writer = new StreamWriter(stream);

    XmlSerializer ser = new XmlSerializer(typeof(JotAppSettings));
    ser.Serialize(writer, this);

    writer.Close();
    iso.Dispose();
}
```

The *Save* method creates (or re-creates) a file in the program's isolated storage named settings.xml, obtains a *StreamWriter* associated with that file, and then uses the *XmlSerializer* class to serialize this particular instance of the *JotAppSettings* class.

The *Load* method is static because it must create an instance of *JotAppSettings* by deserializing the file in isolated storage. If that file doesn't exist—which means the program is being run for the first time—then it simply creates a new instance.

Silverlight Project: Jot   File: JotAppSettings.cs (excerpt)

```
public static JotAppSettings Load()
{
    JotAppSettings settings;
    IsolatedStorageFile iso = IsolatedStorageFile.GetUserStoreForApplication();

    if (iso.FileExists("settings.xml"))
    {
        IsolatedStorageFileStream stream = iso.OpenFile("settings.xml", FileMode.
Open);
        StreamReader reader = new StreamReader(stream);

        XmlSerializer ser = new XmlSerializer(typeof(JotAppSettings));
        settings = ser.Deserialize(reader) as JotAppSettings;

        reader.Close();
    }
```

```
    else
    {
        // Create and initialize new JotAppSettings object
        settings = new JotAppSettings();
        settings.StrokeCollections = new List<StrokeCollection>();
        settings.StrokeCollections.Add(new StrokeCollection());
    }

    iso.Dispose();
    return settings;
}
```

The constructor of the class sets some (but not all) of the properties to default values:

Silverlight Project: Jot   File: JotAppSettings.cs (excerpt)

```
public JotAppSettings()
{
    this.PageNumber = 0;
    this.Foreground = (Color)Application.Current.Resources["PhoneForegroundColor"];
    this.Background = (Color)Application.Current.Resources["PhoneBackgroundColor"];
    this.StrokeWidth = 3;
}
```

This constructor is called both when the *Load* method explicitly creates a new instance when the program is run for the first time, and when the file in isolated storage is deserialized. In the latter case, the default values in the constructor are all replaced. However, it's a good idea to keep these settings in the constructor in case you later add a new application setting to the program. That setting will not be in the existing file in isolated storage, but will be set to a default value in this constructor.

Originally I also put the initialization of the *StrokeCollection* collection in the constructor:

```
settings.StrokeCollections = new List<StrokeCollection>();
settings.StrokeCollections.Add(new StrokeCollection());
```

However, I discovered that the *Deserialize* method of *XmlSerializer* would then avoid creating a new *List* object and simply add to the one created in the constructor, leaving me with one new empty *StrokeCollection* in the *List* every time I ran the program! That's why I moved this code to the *Load* method.

The *Save* and *Load* methods of *JotAppSettings* are called only from App.xaml.cs while handling the four *PhoneApplicationService* events that I discussed in Chapter 6. These events signal when the program is being launched, deactivated, activated, and closed. App.xaml.cs also exposes the application settings as a public property:

Silverlight Project: Jot File: App.xaml.cs (excerpt)

```
public partial class App : Application
{
    // Application Settings
    public JotAppSettings AppSettings { set; get; }

    ...

    private void Application_Launching(object sender, LaunchingEventArgs e)
    {
        AppSettings = JotAppSettings.Load();
    }

    private void Application_Activated(object sender, ActivatedEventArgs e)
    {
        AppSettings = JotAppSettings.Load();
    }

    private void Application_Deactivated(object sender, DeactivatedEventArgs e)
    {
        AppSettings.Save();
    }

    private void Application_Closing(object sender, ClosingEventArgs e)
    {
        AppSettings.Save();
    }
}
```

Within *MainPage*, all references to the properties that comprise application settings are through that *AppSettings* property of the *App* class.

Jot and Touch

The content area of Jot is tiny but significant:

Silverlight Project: Jot File: MainPage.xaml (excerpt)

```
<Grid x:Name="ContentPanel" Grid.Row="1" Margin="12,0,12,0">
    <InkPresenter Name="inkPresenter" />
</Grid>
```

As the name suggests, the *InkPresenter* renders virtual ink that comes from stylus or touch input. The *InkPresenter* doesn't collect that ink on its own. That's your responsibility. (And Silverlight has no built-in handwriting recognition, although there's nothing to prevent you from adding your own.)

The code-behind file requires a *using* directive for the *System.Windows.Ink* namespace and defines just two private fields:

Silverlight Project: Jot   File: MainPage.xaml.cs (excerpt)

```
public partial class MainPage : PhoneApplicationPage
{
    JotAppSettings appSettings = (Application.Current as App).AppSettings;
    Dictionary<int, Stroke> activeStrokes = new Dictionary<int, Stroke>();

    public MainPage()
    {
        InitializeComponent();

        inkPresenter.Strokes = appSettings.StrokeCollections[appSettings.PageNumber];
        inkPresenter.Background = new SolidColorBrush(appSettings.Background);
        ...
        TitleAndAppbarUpdate();

        Touch.FrameReported += OnTouchFrameReported;
    }
    ...
}
```

The first field provides convenient access to the application settings exposed by the *App* class. The second is for maintaining multi-touch data. The constructor initializes both the *Strokes* and *Background* property of the *InkPresenter* from application data, and concludes by setting a handler for the low-level *Touch.FrameReported* event. (I'll discuss the *TitleAndAppbarUpdate* method a little later.)

I chose to use low-level touch input because the program isn't manipulating anything. It's only interested in getting points corresponding to finger movement. With *Touch.FrameReported*, the program can get input from multiple fingers at once, but of course, it's a little tricky in actual practice.

You'll recall that with *Touch.FrameReported* event, each finger is identified with an integer ID from the moment it touches the screen to the time it lifts off. In this program, the activity of that finger generates a new *Stroke* for the *Strokes* property of *InkPresenter*. Keeping a finger's ID associated with its *Stroke* is the purpose of that *Dictionary* named *activeStrokes*:

```
Dictionary<int, Stroke> activeStrokes = new Dictionary<int, Stroke>();
```

Here's the *OnTouchFrameReported* handler:

Silverlight Project: Jot   File: MainPage.xaml.cs (excerpt)

```
void OnTouchFrameReported(object sender, TouchFrameEventArgs args)
{
    TouchPoint primaryTouchPoint = args.GetPrimaryTouchPoint(null);

    if (primaryTouchPoint != null && primaryTouchPoint.Action == TouchAction.Down)
        args.SuspendMousePromotionUntilTouchUp();

    TouchPointCollection touchPoints = args.GetTouchPoints(inkPresenter);

    foreach (TouchPoint touchPoint in touchPoints)
    {
        Point pt = touchPoint.Position;
        int id = touchPoint.TouchDevice.Id;

        switch (touchPoint.Action)
        {
            case TouchAction.Down:
                Stroke stroke = new Stroke();
                stroke.DrawingAttributes.Color = appSettings.Foreground;
                stroke.DrawingAttributes.Height = appSettings.StrokeWidth;
                stroke.DrawingAttributes.Width = appSettings.StrokeWidth;
                stroke.StylusPoints.Add(new StylusPoint(pt.X, pt.Y));

                inkPresenter.Strokes.Add(stroke);
                activeStrokes.Add(id, stroke);
                break;

            case TouchAction.Move:
                activeStrokes[id].StylusPoints.Add(new StylusPoint(pt.X, pt.Y));
                break;

            case TouchAction.Up:
                activeStrokes[id].StylusPoints.Add(new StylusPoint(pt.X, pt.Y));
                activeStrokes.Remove(id);

                TitleAndAppbarUpdate();
                break;
        }
    }
}
```

When the finger first touches the screen (signaled by an *Action* property of *TouchAction*
.*Down*), the method creates a new *Stroke* object. This is added to the *Strokes* collection of
the *InkPresenter,* and it is re-rendered by *InkPresenter* with each new point added to it. That
Stroke object is also stored in the *activeStrokes* dictionary along with the ID. That allows
the *Stroke* to be built up with each *TouchAction.Move* event. The entry is removed from the
dictionary when the finger leaves the screen.

Jot and the *ApplicationBar*

The *ApplicatonBar* in Jot defines four buttons: for adding a new page, going to the previous page, going to the next page, and deleting the current page. (If the current page is the only page, then only the strokes are deleted from the page.) Each button has its own *Click* handler:

Silverlight Project: Jot   File: MainPage.xaml (excerpt)

```xml
<phone:PhoneApplicationPage.ApplicationBar>
    <shell:ApplicationBar IsVisible="True" IsMenuEnabled="True">
        <shell:ApplicationBarIconButton x:Name="appbarAddButton"
                                        IconUri="/Images/appbar.add.rest.png"
                                        Text="add page"
                                        Click="OnAppbarAddClick" />

        <shell:ApplicationBarIconButton x:Name="appbarLastButton"
                                        IconUri="/Images/appbar.back.rest.png"
                                        Text="last page"
                                        Click="OnAppbarLastClick" />

        <shell:ApplicationBarIconButton x:Name="appbarNextButton"
                                        IconUri="/Images/appbar.next.rest.png"
                                        Text="next page"
                                        Click="OnAppbarNextClick" />

        <shell:ApplicationBarIconButton x:Name="appbarDeleteButton"
                                        IconUri="/Images/appbar.delete.rest.png"
                                        Text="delete page"
                                        Click="OnAppbarDeleteClick" />
        <shell:ApplicationBar.MenuItems>
            <shell:ApplicationBarMenuItem Text="swap colors"
                                          Click="OnAppbarSwapColorsClick" />

            <shell:ApplicationBarMenuItem Text="light stroke width"
                                          Click="OnAppbarSetStrokeWidthClick" />

            <shell:ApplicationBarMenuItem Text="medium stroke width"
                                          Click="OnAppbarSetStrokeWidthClick" />

            <shell:ApplicationBarMenuItem Text="heavy stroke width"
                                          Click="OnAppbarSetStrokeWidthClick" />
        </shell:ApplicationBar.MenuItems>
    </shell:ApplicationBar>
</phone:PhoneApplicationPage.ApplicationBar>
```

A menu is also included with a collection of *ApplicationBarMenuItem* objects in the *MenuItems* property element. The menu items are displayed when you press the ellipsis on the *ApplicationBar*. They consist solely of short text strings in lower-case. (You should keep menu items to five or fewer, and keep the text to a maximum of 20 characters or so.)

The first menu item (to swap the colors) has its own *Click* handler; the other three share a *Click* handler.

Here are the *Click* handlers for the four buttons:

Silverlight Project: Jot   File: MainPage.xaml.cs (excerpt)

```
void OnAppbarAddClick(object sender, EventArgs args)
{
    StrokeCollection strokes = new StrokeCollection();
    appSettings.PageNumber += 1;
    appSettings.StrokeCollections.Insert(appSettings.PageNumber, strokes);
    inkPresenter.Strokes = strokes;
    TitleAndAppbarUpdate();
}

void OnAppbarLastClick(object sender, EventArgs args)
{
    appSettings.PageNumber -= 1;
    inkPresenter.Strokes = appSettings.StrokeCollections[appSettings.PageNumber];
    TitleAndAppbarUpdate();
}

void OnAppbarNextClick(object sender, EventArgs args)
{
    appSettings.PageNumber += 1;
    inkPresenter.Strokes = appSettings.StrokeCollections[appSettings.PageNumber];
    TitleAndAppbarUpdate();
}

void OnAppbarDeleteClick(object sender, EventArgs args)
{
    MessageBoxResult result = MessageBox.Show("Delete this page?", "Jot",
                                       MessageBoxButton.OKCancel);

    if (result == MessageBoxResult.OK)
    {
        if (appSettings.StrokeCollections.Count == 1)
        {
            appSettings.StrokeCollections[0].Clear();
        }
        else
        {
            appSettings.StrokeCollections.RemoveAt(appSettings.PageNumber);

            if (appSettings.PageNumber == appSettings.StrokeCollections.Count)
                appSettings.PageNumber -= 1;

            inkPresenter.Strokes = appSettings.StrokeCollections[appSettings.
PageNumber];
        }
        TitleAndAppbarUpdate();
    }
}
```

The only one just a little complex is the deletion of a page, but notice that it begins by asking for a confirmation from the user with a call to *MessageBox.Show*! A message box seems very archaic in this context, but the most important characteristic of *MessageBox.Show* on the phone is that it works with a minimum of hassle. If you just need to inform the user of something with an OK button, or if you need to ask a question with OK and Cancel, nothing beats it.

The message box is displayed at the top of the screen and disables the rest of the application until you make it go away:

I'll show you a more sophisticated dialog later in this chapter and others in Chapter 14.

The four menu items are handled here:

Silverlight Project: Jot   File: MainPage.xaml.cs (excerpt)

```
void OnAppbarSwapColorsClick(object sender, EventArgs args)
{
    Color foreground = appSettings.Background;
    appSettings.Background = appSettings.Foreground;
    appSettings.Foreground = foreground;
    inkPresenter.Background = new SolidColorBrush(appSettings.Background);

    foreach (StrokeCollection strokeCollection in appSettings.StrokeCollections)
        foreach (Stroke stroke in strokeCollection)
            stroke.DrawingAttributes.Color = appSettings.Foreground;
}
```

```
void OnAppbarSetStrokeWidthClick(object sender, EventArgs args)
{
    ApplicationBarMenuItem item = sender as ApplicationBarMenuItem;

    if (item.Text.StartsWith("light"))
        appSettings.StrokeWidth = 1;

    else if (item.Text.StartsWith("medium"))
        appSettings.StrokeWidth = 3;

    else if (item.Text.StartsWith("heavy"))
        appSettings.StrokeWidth = 5;
}
```

When swapping colors, the new colors must be saved in application settings, but the existing colors of all the *Stroke* objects on every page must also be changed. Fortunately, it's just a couple nested *foreach* loops.

The *OnAppbarSetStrokeWidthClick* method accommodates three related menu items. Notice that the *sender* object is the particular *ApplicationBarMenuItem* that's been clicked. The logic here is simple, but it depends on the *Text* properties of the three items. You might prefer using a technique that is independent of that text, such as three separate handlers.

You've already seen several references to *TitleAndAppbarUpdate*, the final method in the *MainPage* code-behind file. Here it is:

Silverlight Project: Jot   File: MainPage.xaml.cs (excerpt)

```
void TitleAndAppbarUpdate()
{
    pageInfoTitle.Text = String.Format(" - PAGE {0} OF {1}",
                                    appSettings.PageNumber + 1,
                                    appSettings.StrokeCollections.Count);

    appbarLastButton.IsEnabled = appSettings.PageNumber > 0;
    appbarNextButton.IsEnabled =
                appSettings.PageNumber < appSettings.StrokeCollections.Count - 1;
    appbarDeleteButton.IsEnabled = (appSettings.StrokeCollections.Count > 1) ||
                                    (appSettings.StrokeCollections[0].Count > 0);
}
```

The last three statements disable various buttons on the *ApplicationBar* if they aren't valid. (The handlers for the buttons rely on the fact that they won't be called if the option is invalid.) These statements are able to reference the names assigned to the three buttons in the XAML file because I reassigned those names in the *MainPage* constructor:

Silverlight Project: Jot   File: MainPage.xaml.cs (excerpt)

```
public MainPage()
{
    InitializeComponent();
    ...
    appbarLastButton = this.ApplicationBar.Buttons[1] as ApplicationBarIconButton;
    appbarNextButton = this.ApplicationBar.Buttons[2] as ApplicationBarIconButton;
    appbarDeleteButton = this.ApplicationBar.Buttons[3] as ApplicationBarIconButton;
    ...
}
```

The first statement in *TitleAndAppbarUpdate* references a *TextBlock* that I added to the application title in the XAML file:

Silverlight Project: Jot   File: MainPage.xaml (excerpt)

```
<StackPanel x:Name="TitlePanel" Grid.Row="0" Margin="24,24,0,12"
            Orientation="Horizontal">
    <TextBlock x:Name="ApplicationTitle" Text="JOT"
               Style="{StaticResource PhoneTextNormalStyle}"
               Margin="12 0 0 0" />
    <TextBlock Name="pageInfoTitle"
               Style="{StaticResource PhoneTextNormalStyle}"
               Margin="0" />
</StackPanel>
```

Jot is one program that is not enabled for landscape mode. Once you've jotted something on an *InkPresenter* of a particular size and aspect ratio, you don't want it flipped around so that some of what you've done is now off-screen. But Jot is also a program you can use sideways without the program itself being aware of the orientation change:

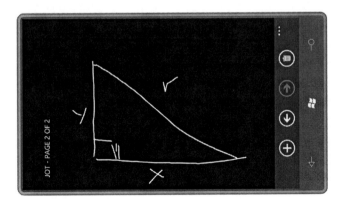

Elements and Controls

ApplicationBar exists entirely outside of the normal Silverlight class hierarchy in a very lonely corner of Silverlight for Windows Phone. The remainder of this chapter returns to a more familiar realm of classes.

Most of the visual objects that I've discussed so far in this book are often referred to as *elements*, primarily because they derive from *FrameworkElement* in this class hierarchy:

Object
> *DependencyObject* (abstract)
>> *UIElement* (abstract)
>>> *FrameworkElement* (abstract)

These derivatives of *FrameworkElement* include *TextBlock, Image, Border, MediaElement, Shape* (which is the parent class to *Rectangle* and *Ellipse*), and *Panel*, which is the parent class to *Grid, StackPanel,* and *Canvas.*

For the remainder of this chapter I'm going to focus on some classes that derive from *Control*:

Object
> *DependencyObject* (abstract)
>> *UIElement* (abstract)
>>> *FrameworkElement* (abstract)
>>>> *Control* (abstract)

Most *Control* derivatives are found in the *System.Windows.Controls* namespace, but others hide out in *System.Windows.Controls.Primitives.*

To programmers with experience in graphical environments the word *control* is much more familiar and *element*. And this raises a question: If visual objects that might normally be called *controls* are more properly referred to as *elements* in Silverlight, then what's the difference between elements and the visual objects that really *are* Silverlight controls?

One convenient distinction is that elements are usually relegated to *presentation* while controls are for *interaction*. In Silverlight, *Control* is the ancestor to classes such as *Button, Slider,* and *TextBox,* so this distinction certainly seems plausible. You might also notice that *Control* implements an *IsEnabled* property, as well as three properties involved in keyboard navigation using the tab key: *IsTabStop, TabIndex,* and *TabNavigation.*

On the other hand, user-input events for the keyboard, mouse, stylus, and touch are actually defined by *UIElement,* so elements such as *TextBlock* and *Image* can receive user input and—with the proper support from markup or code—respond to that input.

Perhaps a more significant difference is that controls are built from elements. You can think of elements as *visual primitives*. Controls are assemblages of these elements and other controls. A *Button*, for example, is not much more than a *Border* with some content inside, usually (but not limited to) a *TextBlock*. A *Slider* is not much more than a couple of *Rectangle* elements and some special *RepeatButton* controls.

The visuals of a *Control* are always defined by a visual tree of *FrameworkElement* derivatives. This visual tree can also contain objects that also derive from *Control*, but these objects are then defined by a visual tree of other *FrameworkElement* and *Control* derivatives.

Although the visuals of a *Control* are always a tree of *FrameworkElement* derivatives, this tree is not fixed. You can replace this tree to entirely redefine the visuals of the control. The *Control* class defines a property named *Template* of type *ControlTemplate*, and you'll see how to replace the template in Chapter 16.

Redefining the visuals of a control with a template is a powerful tool for control customization. But it's hard to see how one would redefine the visuals of a *FrameworkElement* derivative. Surely a *TextBlock* has a different appearance depending on the *Text*, *FontFamily FontSize* and *Foreground* properties, but there's no sensible way to make a *TextBlock* visually different independent of these properties. In contrast, think how the basic *Button* has changed its visual appearance in many different versions of Windows over the years.

You can't derive from *FrameworkElement* in Silverlight. (Well, you actually can, but you can't do anything useful in the derived class.) And except for *Panel*, most *FrameworkElement* derivatives are sealed. *Shape* isn't sealed, but you can't derive from it, and all the derived classes of *Shape* are sealed.

But you can derive from *Control* and you can derive from many *Control* derivatives. One *Control* derivative named *UserControl* exists solely for the purpose of creating custom classes. So not only can you customize the visuals of an existing control using templates, you can create your own controls. But no matter how you do it, the visuals of the control will always be defined as a tree of elements and other controls.

If you look at the documentation for *Control*, you'll see that the class adds a number of convenient properties to *FrameworkElement*. These include several text-related properties usually associated with *TextBlock*: *FontSize*, *FontFamily*, *FontStyle*, *FontWeight*, and *FontStretch*. *Control* also adds a few properties found in the *Border* class: *BorderBrush*, *BorderThickness*, *Background*, and *Padding*, and two other properties associated with control content: *HorizontalContentAlignment* and *VerticalContentAlignment*. The *Control* class itself doesn't use these properties. The properties are defined solely for the convenience of classes that descend from *Control*.

Similarly, *Control* defines a bunch of protected virtual methods corresponding to user input events defined by *UIElement*. For Windows Phone 7 programmers, certainly the most important of these methods are those for multi-touch: *OnManipulationStarted*, *OnManipulationDelta*, and *OnManipulationCompleted*.

RangeBase and *Slider*

You've probably already grasped that scrollbars and sliders are not required as much on multi-touch screens as they are in mouse-based environments. The *ScrollViewer* in the last chapter responds directly to touch rather than any manipulation of its scrollbars, which barely even exist except as concepts.

Still, scrollbars and sliders are sometimes useful for jobs that allow the user to select from a continuous range of values. These controls are found in this little corner of the class hierarchy:

Control (abstract)
　　　　RangeBase (abstract)
　　　　　　　　ProgressBar
　　　　　　　　ScrollBar (sealed)
　　　　　　　　Slider

The *RangeBase* class defines *Minimum*, *Maximum*, *SmallChange*, and *LargeChange* properties to define the parameters of scrolling, plus a *Value* property for the user's selection and a *ValueChanged* event that signals when *Value* has changed. (Notice that *ProgressBar* also derives from *RangeBase*, but the *Value* property is always controlled programmatically rather than being set by the user.)

I'm going to focus on the *Slider* here because the version in Windows Phone 7 seems a little more tailored to the phone than the *ScrollBar*. The goal is to use three *Slider* controls to create a program called ColorScroll that looks like this:

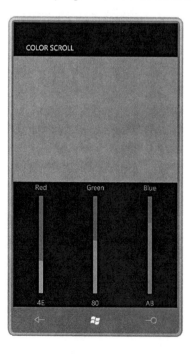

You scroll the red, green, and blue *Slider* controls to define a composite color. To make it more interesting, when the phone is turned sideways, I want the visuals to re-orient themselves slightly so it looks like this:

The easiest way to architect such a display is with nested grids. One grid has three rows and three columns containing the three *Slider* controls and six *TextBlock* elements. That *Grid* is in another *Grid* with just two cells. The other cell holds a *Rectangle* element whose *Fill* property is set to a *SolidColorBrush* based on the color selected from the sliders.

That larger *Grid* with the two cells is the familiar *Grid* named *ContentPanel*. Whether those two cells are two rows or two columns is determined by the code-behind file based on the current *Orientation* property.

The XAML file contains a *Resources* collection with *Style* definitions for both *TextBlock* and *Slider*:

Silverlight Project: ColorScroll   File: MainPage.xaml (excerpt)

```
<phone:PhoneApplicationPage.Resources>
    <Style x:Key="textStyle" TargetType="TextBlock">
        <Setter Property="HorizontalAlignment" Value="Center" />
    </Style>

    <Style x:Key="sliderStyle" TargetType="Slider">
        <Setter Property="Minimum" Value="0" />
        <Setter Property="Maximum" Value="255" />
        <Setter Property="Orientation" Value="Vertical" />
    </Style>
</phone:PhoneApplicationPage.Resources>
```

A *Style* with just one *Setter* seems a bit ostentatious, but it's nice to have if you ever want to add another *Setter* for the *Margin* or *FontSize*. The default range of a *Slider* is 0 to 10; I've changed that to make the range appropriate for a one-byte value.

ScrollBar and *Slider* have their own *Orientation* properties, entirely unrelated to the *Orientation* property of *PhoneApplicationPage* but somewhat related to the *Orientation* property of *StackPanel* because they both share the same *Orientation* enumeration with values of *Horizontal* and *Vertical*.

The default *Orientation* of a *Slider* is *Horizontal*. (For a *ScrollBar* it's *Vertical*, a difference I've never quite understood.)

By default, the top of a vertical *Slider* is associated with the *Maximum* value. That's OK for this program but you can change it by setting the *IsDirectionReversed* property to *true*.

Here's the whole content panel:

Silverlight Project: ColorScroll   File: MainPage.xaml (excerpt)

```xml
<Grid x:Name="<Grid x:Name="ContentPanel" Grid.Row="1" Margin="12,0,12,0">
    <Grid.RowDefinitions>
        <RowDefinition Height="*" />
        <RowDefinition Height="*" />
    </Grid.RowDefinitions>

    <Rectangle Name="rect"
               Grid.Row="0"
               Grid.Column="0" />

    <Grid Name="controlGrid"
          Grid.Row="1"
          Grid.Column="0">
        <Grid.RowDefinitions>
            <RowDefinition Height="Auto" />
            <RowDefinition Height="*" />
            <RowDefinition Height="Auto" />
        </Grid.RowDefinitions>

        <Grid.ColumnDefinitions>
            <ColumnDefinition Width="*" />
            <ColumnDefinition Width="*" />
            <ColumnDefinition Width="*" />
        </Grid.ColumnDefinitions>

        <!-- Red column -->
        <TextBlock Grid.Column="0"
                   Grid.Row="0"
                   Text="Red"
                   Foreground="Red"
                   Style="{StaticResource textStyle}" />

        <Slider Name="redSlider"
                Grid.Column="0"
                Grid.Row="1"
                Foreground="Red"
```

```xml
                    Style="{StaticResource sliderStyle}"
                    ValueChanged="OnSliderValueChanged" />

          <TextBlock Name="redText"
                     Grid.Column="0"
                     Grid.Row="2"
                     Text="0"
                     Foreground="Red"
                     Style="{StaticResource textStyle}" />

          <!-- Green column -->
          <TextBlock Grid.Column="1"
                     Grid.Row="0"
                     Text="Green"
                     Foreground="Green"
                     Style="{StaticResource textStyle}" />

          <Slider Name="greenSlider"
                  Grid.Column="1"
                  Grid.Row="1"
                  Foreground="Green"
                  Style="{StaticResource sliderStyle}"
                  ValueChanged="OnSliderValueChanged" />

          <TextBlock Name="greenText"
                     Grid.Column="1"
                     Grid.Row="2"
                     Text="0"
                     Foreground="Green"
                     Style="{StaticResource textStyle}" />

          <!-- Blue column -->
          <TextBlock Grid.Column="2"
                     Grid.Row="0"
                     Text="Blue"
                     Foreground="Blue"
                     Style="{StaticResource textStyle}" />

          <Slider Name="blueSlider"
                  Grid.Column="2"
                  Grid.Row="1"
                  Foreground="Blue"
                  Style="{StaticResource sliderStyle}"
                  ValueChanged="OnSliderValueChanged" />

          <TextBlock Name="blueText"
                     Grid.Column="2"
                     Grid.Row="2"
                     Text="0"
                     Foreground="Blue"
                     Style="{StaticResource textStyle}" />
     </Grid>
</Grid>
```

All the *Slider* controls have their *ValueChanged* events set to the same handler. This handler really takes an easy way out by not bothering to determine which *Slider* actually raised the event:

Silverlight Project: ColorScroll   File: MainPage.xaml.cs (excerpt)

```
void OnSliderValueChanged(object sender, RoutedPropertyChangedEventArgs<double> args)
{
    Color clr = Color.FromArgb(255, (byte)redSlider.Value,
                                    (byte)greenSlider.Value,
                                    (byte)blueSlider.Value);

    rect.Fill = new SolidColorBrush(clr);

    redText.Text = clr.R.ToString("X2");
    greenText.Text = clr.G.ToString("X2");
    blueText.Text = clr.B.ToString("X2");
}
```

You may have noticed that the XAML file doesn't initialize the *Value* property of any *Slider*. Here's why:

As the page is being constructed, various elements and controls are created, event handlers are linked to events, and properties are set. When a new *Value* property is set to a *Slider* in the construction of this page, the *Slider* fires the *ValueChanged* event. It is extremely likely that the *OnSliderValueChanged* method in *MainPage* will be called before the page has been entirely constructed. But *OnSliderValueChanged* references other elements in the visual tree. If those element do not yet exist, a runtime exception will result.

Want to see it happen? Try setting

```
<Setter Property="Value" Value="128" />
```

in the *Style* definition for the *Slider*.

Causing an event to be fired while the visual tree is being constructed is a common pitfall. You can either bullet-proof your event handlers by checking for *null* elements and controls, or you can do what I do in ColorScroll: Properties that trigger events in the page are safely set in the class's constructor after the call to *InitializeComponent* when the visual tree has been entirely built:

Silverlight Project: ColorScroll   File: MainPage.xaml.cs (excerpt)

```
public MainPage()
{
    InitializeComponent();
```

```
        redSlider.Value = 128;
        greenSlider.Value = 128;
        blueSlider.Value = 128;
    }
```

To handle orientation changes in the phone, *MainPage* overrides its *OnOrientationChanged* method. The event arguments include a property named *Orientation* of type *PageOrientation*.

It helps to know that the *PageOrientation* enumeration values are bit flags with the following values:

None	0000–0000
Portrait	0000–0001
Landscape	0000–0010
PortraitUp	0000–0101
PortraitDown	0000–1001
LandscapeLeft	0001–0010
LandscapeRight	0010–0010

You can check for portrait or landscape by performing a bitwise OR operation between the *Orientation* property and the *Portrait* or *Landscape* members, and then checking for a non-zero result. It makes the code just a little simpler:

Silverlight Project: ColorScroll   File: MainPage.xaml.cs (excerpt)

```
protected override void OnOrientationChanged(OrientationChangedEventArgs args)
{
    ContentPanel.RowDefinitions.Clear();
    ContentPanel.ColumnDefinitions.Clear();

    // Landscape
    if ((args.Orientation & PageOrientation.Landscape) != 0)
    {
        ColumnDefinition coldef = new ColumnDefinition();
        coldef.Width = new GridLength(1, GridUnitType.Star);
        ContentPanel.ColumnDefinitions.Add(coldef);

        coldef = new ColumnDefinition();
        coldef.Width = new GridLength(1, GridUnitType.Star);
        ContentPanel.ColumnDefinitions.Add(coldef);

        Grid.SetRow(controlGrid, 0);
        Grid.SetColumn(controlGrid, 1);
    }
```

```
        // Portrait
        else
        {
            RowDefinition rowdef = new RowDefinition();
            rowdef.Height = new GridLength(1, GridUnitType.Star);
            ContentPanel.RowDefinitions.Add(rowdef);

            rowdef = new RowDefinition();
            rowdef.Height = new GridLength(1, GridUnitType.Star);
            ContentPanel.RowDefinitions.Add(rowdef);

            Grid.SetRow(controlGrid, 1);
            Grid.SetColumn(controlGrid, 0);
        }
        base.OnOrientationChanged(args);
    }
```

The *ContentPanel* object needs to be switched between two rows for portrait mode and two columns for landscape mode, so it creates the *GridDefinition* and *ColumnDefinition* objects for the new orientation. (Alternatively, it could create these collections ahead of time and just switch back and forth. Or it could create a 2-cell by 2-cell *Grid* in the XAML file and set the unused row or column to a zero height or width.)

The *Rectangle* element is always in the cell with *Grid.Row* and *Grid.Column* settings of zero. But the *Grid* named *controlGrid* must have its *Grid.Row* and *Grid.Column* attached properties set using the syntax I discussed in the previous chapter.

In the next chapter, I'll show you how to derive from *UserControl* to modularize this program and turn it into a control.

The Basic *Button*

The standard Silverlight *Button* is much more flexible than the *ApplicationBar* buttons, as well as being easier to use. You can put a *Button* in the content *Grid* as simply as this:

```
<Grid x:Name="ContentPanel" Grid.Row="1" Margin="12,0,12,0">
    <Button Content="Click me!" />
</Grid>
```

By default, the *Button* fills the *Grid*:

It has a simple white border and displays the text string assigned to its *Content* property. If you put the *Button* in a horizontal *StackPanel*, it will be only as wide as it needs to be to fit the content; the opposite effect happens when you switch the *StackPanel* orientation to *Vertical*. Or you can set the *HorizontalAlignment* and *VerticalAlignment* properties to anything other than *Stretch*:

Obviously the basic *Button* has been redesigned a bit for the phone. It has a little more space around its border to provide a larger touch target.

The border in the *Button* is an actual *Border* and the content of the *Button* (in this example) is an actual *TextBlock*. Earlier I mentioned that the *Control* class defines a bunch of properties normally associated with the *Border* and the *TextBlock*. You can set some of those properties like so:

```
<Grid x:Name="ContentPanel" Grid.Row="1" Margin="12,0,12,0">
    <Button Content="Click me!"
            FontSize="48"
            FontStyle="Italic"
            Foreground="Red"
            Background="Blue"
            BorderThickness="10"
            BorderBrush="Yellow"
            Padding="20"
            HorizontalAlignment="Center"
            VerticalAlignment="Center" />
</Grid>
```

As you might hope (or perhaps fear), these property settings are reflected in the button's appearance:

The *Control* class also defines *HorizontalContentAlignment* and *VerticalContentAlignment* and *Padding* properties that you can set like so:

```
<Grid x:Name="ContentPanel" Grid.Row="1" Margin="12,0,12,0">
    <Button Content="Click me!"
```

```
            Padding="50 100"
            HorizontalContentAlignment="Right"
            VerticalContentAlignment="Bottom" />
</Grid>
```

Now the content is positioned at the lower-right corner but 50 pixels from the right and 100 pixels from the bottom:

The *Control* class defines an *IsEnabled* property; when set to *false*, the *Button* is grayed and does not respond to touch.

Almost always you'll want to set a handler for the *Click* property of the *Button* to know when it's been pressed. The *Click* event is generated only when the user presses the *Button* and then releases the finger without moving away. Setting the *ClickMode* property to *Press* causes the *Button* to fire the *Click* event when the finger first meets the screen.

The Concept of *Content*

Button derives from *Control* but it also derives from *ContentControl*, which is the class that provides the button's *Content* property. You can pull out the *Content* property as a property element:

```
<Button>
    <Button.Content>

    </Button.Content>
</Button>
```

But oddly enough you can't put text in there:

```
<!-- Doesn't work! -->
<Button>
    <Button.Content>
        Click this button!
    </Button.Content>
</Button>
```

There's nothing ostensibly wrong with that syntax but Silverlight doesn't allow it. If you really want to do something like this you'll need an XML namespace declaration for the *System* namespace:

```
xmlns:system="clr-namespace:System;assembly=mscorlib"
```

You can then put the string between tags that explicitly tell the XAML parser than the string is truly a *String*:

```
<Button>
    <Button.Content>
        <system:String>Click this button</system:String>
    </Button.Content>
</Button>
```

As with any *ContentControl* derivative, you can omit the explicit property-element tags for the *Content* property:

```
<Button>
    <system:String>Click this button</system:String>
</Button>
```

The *Content* property is of type *object*, and you really *can* set the *Content* property to pretty much anything:

```
<Button>
    <system:Double>1E5</system:Double>
</Button>
```

You'll realize it's being interpreted as a number when it displays inside the *Button* as 10000. Or try this:

```
<Button>
    <system:DateTime>October 1, 2010, 9:30 PM</system:DateTime>
</Button>
```

That will display as 10/1/2010 9:30:00 PM. The text is parsed by the *Parse* method of *Double* or *DateTime* to be inserted into the *Button*, and then the object's *ToString* method is used to get a text rendition of that *Double* or *DateTime* object.

You can put a *Color* in the *Button*:

```
<Button>
    <Color>Cyan</Color>
</Button>
```

But what you'll see in the button is the textual hexadecimal representation of that color: "#FF00FFFF." You can also try a *SolidColorBrush* in the *Button*:

```
<Button>
    <SolidColorBrush Color="Cyan" />
</Button>
```

But that's even worse. Now you'll get the text "System.Windows.Media.SolidColorBrush". *SolidColorBrush* doesn't define a *ToString* so the fully qualified class name is displayed instead. A brush is fine for the *Foreground*, *Background*, or *BorderBrush* properties of *Button* but usually not *Content*.

Yet, there is a reason why the *Content* property is of type *object* and you'll discover in Chapter 16 how you can create a *DataTemplate* to display objects such as *SolidColorBrush* in more interesting ways. But for now, if you want the *Button* to display something other than just plain text, you'll need to set the *Content* property to anything that derives from *FrameworkElement*. For example, you can set the *Content* property to an explicit *TextBlock* if you'd like to do a little internal formatting:

```
<Button>
    <TextBlock>
        Click <Run FontStyle="Italic">this</Run> button!
    </TextBlock>
</Button>
```

Or you can put an *Image* element in there:

```
<Button HorizontalAlignment="Center"
        VerticalAlignment="Center">
    <Image Source="Images/BuzzAldrinOnTheMoon.png"
           Stretch="None" />
</Button>
```

Here's what you get:

The *Content* property is of type *object*, so you can't set the *Content* property to multiple objects, but you can set the *Content* property to a *Panel* of some sort:

```
<Button HorizontalAlignment="Center"
        VerticalAlignment="Center">
    <StackPanel>
        <Image Source="Images/BuzzAldrinOnTheMoon.png"
               Stretch="None" />
        <TextBlock Text="Click this button!"
                   TextAlignment="Center" />
    </StackPanel>
</Button>
```

And that's how you get a picture and some text in the same button:

And yes, you can put a *Button* inside another *Button* or a *Slider* in a *Button* if you think your users are ready for it.

You've seen *ContentControl* derivatives before *Button*: The *ScrollViewer* that you met in the last chapter is derived from *ContentControl*. The *Content* property of a *ScrollViewer* is very often set to a *StackPanel* but you can also set *Content* to an *Image* element with a larger bitmap The *PhoneApplicationFrame* also derives from *ContentControl* by way of *Frame*, but it's generally used a little differently from most *ContentControl* derivatives because it needs to manage page navigation.

ContentControl is not the only class that defines a property named *Content*. *UserControl*—the class from which *PhoneApplicationPage* derives by way of *Page*—also defines a *Content* property. It's natural to assume that *ContentControl* and *UserControl* are related in some way, but it's actually a sibling relationship as this partial class hierarchy shows:

Control (abstract)
      ContentControl
          Frame
               PhoneApplicationFrame
      UserControl
          Page
               PhoneApplicationPage

The *Content* property defined by *ContentControl* is of type *object*; the *Content* property defined by *UserControl* is of type *UIElement* and hence is just a bit less versatile.

It is very common to derive from *UserControl* (as the name might suggest) and I'll show you how to do it in the next chapter.

Theme Styles and Precedence

Here's an interesting little experiment. Put a simple *TextBlock* in the content grid with a very large *FontSize* set:

```
<Grid x:Name="ContentPanel" Grid.Row="1" Margin="12,0,12,0">
    <TextBlock Text="Hello!"
               FontSize="96"
               HorizontalAlignment="Center"
               VerticalAlignment="Center" />
</Grid>
```

As you know, you can move that *FontSize* setting from the *TextBlock* to the *PhoneApplicationPage* tag (replacing the existing *FontSize* setting) and you'll get the same effect:

```
<phone:PhoneApplicationPage ...
                            FontSize="96"
                            ... >
    ...
        <Grid x:Name="ContentPanel" Grid.Row="1" Margin="12,0,12,0">
            <TextBlock Text="Hello!"
                       HorizontalAlignment="Center"
                       VerticalAlignment="Center" />
        </Grid>
    ...
</phone:PhoneApplicationPage>
```

That's property inheritance at work. Now put the *TextBlock* in a *Button*. You can make the text very large by setting the *FontSize* on the *TextBlock*:

```
<Grid x:Name="ContentPanel" Grid.Row="1" Margin="12,0,12,0">
    <Button HorizontalAlignment="Center"
            VerticalAlignment="Center">
        <TextBlock Text="Hello!"
                   FontSize="96" />
    </Button>
</Grid>
```

Or, you can achieve the same effect by setting the *FontSize* on the *Button* itself:

```
<Grid x:Name="ContentPanel" Grid.Row="1" Margin="12,0,12,0">
    <Button HorizontalAlignment="Center"
            VerticalAlignment="Center"
            FontSize="96">
        <TextBlock Text="Hello!" />
    </Button>
</Grid>
```

But what doesn't work is setting the *FontSize* on the *PhoneApplicationPage*. It seems as if property inheritance should cause the value to trickle down to the *TextBlock*:

```
<phone:PhoneApplicationPage ...
                            FontSize="96"
                            ... >
    ...
        <Grid x:Name="ContentPanel" Grid.Row="1" Margin="12,0,12,0">
            <Button HorizontalAlignment="Center"
                    VerticalAlignment="Center">
                <TextBlock Text="Hello!" />
            </Button>
        </Grid>
    ...
</phone:PhoneApplicationPage>
```

But it doesn't work. Something is blocking the *TextBlock* from inheriting that *FontSize* value.

Button is defined in the System.Windows library, and that library also contains a default style and template for the *Button*. This is known as a *theme style*, and for the *Button* it includes a style setting for the *FontSize* property. In regular Silverlight, that's not the case, but the developers of Windows Phone 7 apparently decided that text in a *Button* needed to be a little larger by default to provide a more substantial touch target. So they gave this default theme style a *FontSize* property, and that setting has precedence over property inheritance.

You might recall the table of property precedence in Chapter 7. That table can now be enpanded:

Local Settings have precedence over

Style Settings, which have precedence over the

Theme Style, which has precedence over

Property Inheritance, which has precedence over

Default Values

The Button Hierarchy

This class hierarchy is complete beginning with the *ButtonBase* class:

Control (abstract)
 ContentControl
  ButtonBase (abstract)
   Button
   HyperlinkButton
   RepeatButton (sealed)
   ToggleButton
    CheckBox
    RadioButton

It's actually *ButtonBase* that defines the *Click* event and the *ClickMode* property.

The ButtonCornucopia project creates instances of all these buttons with nearly as few superfluous properties as possible:

Silverlight Project: ButtonCornucopia   File: MainPage.xaml

```xml
<Grid x:Name="ContentPanel" Grid.Row="1" Margin="12,0,12,0">
    <StackPanel>
        <Button Content="Button" HorizontalAlignment="Center" />
        <HyperlinkButton Content="HyperlinkButton" HorizontalAlignment="Center" />
        <RepeatButton Content="RepeatButton" HorizontalAlignment="Center" />
        <ToggleButton Content="ToggleButton" HorizontalAlignment="Center" />
        <CheckBox Content="CheckBox" HorizontalAlignment="Center" />

        <Border BorderBrush="White"
                BorderThickness="1"
                HorizontalAlignment="Center">
            <StackPanel>
                <RadioButton Content="RadioButton1" />
                <RadioButton Content="RadioButton2" />
                <RadioButton Content="RadioButton3" />
            </StackPanel>
        </Border>
    </StackPanel>
</Grid>
```

The buttons may seem a bit large with too much space around them, but keep in mind that they need to provide adequate touch targets:

The *HyperlinkButton* is used in connection with Silverlight page navigation, and includes a *NavigateUri* property for that purpose. *RepeatButton* generates multiple *Click* events when the button is held down; its primary purpose is in the *ScrollBar* and *Slider*, and it's rarely used elsewhere.

There is no functional difference between the *ToggleButton* and *CheckBox*. The difference is only visual, and that's something that can be changed with a template (as I'll demonstrate in Chapter 16). The Silverlight for Windows Phone Toolkit adds a *ToggleButton* derivative named *ToggleSwitchButton* that you've probably seen in the Settings section of a Windows Phone.

When checked, the *RadioButton* causes all its siblings to become unchecked. There is no special container for the *RadioButton*. Just put two or more in a panel (almost always a *StackPanel*) and they will turn off by themselves. *RadioButton* defines a *GroupName* property that allows you to differentiate multiple groups of mutually exclusive buttons that might be children of the same panel.

Normally the *ToggleButton* and *CheckBox* are physical manifestations of a Boolean. They turn on and off with successive clicks. But *ToggleButton* defines an *IsThreeState* property that optionally provides a third "indeterminate" state. Generally this is used only in connection with the *CheckBox*; the *ToggleButton* doesn't even have a unique visual appearance for the indeterminate state.

Consequently, the *IsChecked* property defined by *ToggleButton* is not of type *bool*. It's of type *Nullable<bool>* (also written as *bool?*) with three possible values: *true*, *false*, and *null*. If you need to set the *IsChecked* property to a *null* value in XAML you can use a special markup extension:

```
IsChecked="{x:Null}"
```

For conventional two-state toggling purposes, *IsChecked* usually needs to be cast to *bool*.

ToggleButton defines three events: *Checked* is fired when the button becomes checked, *Unchecked* when it becomes unchecked, and *Indeterminate* when it's going into the third state. In most cases, a program using a *ToggleButton* or *CheckBox* needs to handle both the *Checked* and *Unchecked* events, but you can use the same handler for both events.

Toggling a *Stopwatch*

One handy application on a phone is a stopwatch—an ideal use for a *ToggleButton* as well as the *Stopwatch* class defined in the *System.Diagnostics* namespace.

I deliberately spelled the name of the StopWatch project in camel case to avoid confusion with the .NET *Stopwatch* class. To make the program a little more interesting, I decided that the elapsed time should be displayable in three different formats, corresponding to the members of this enumeration:

Silverlight Project: StopWatch   File: ElapsedTimeFormat.cs

```
namespace StopWatch
{
    public enum ElapsedTimeFormat
    {
        HourMinuteSecond,
        Seconds,
        Milliseconds
    }
}
```

This elapsed time format is an application setting in StopWatch, so it is exposed as a public property in the *App* class. As usual with application settings, it is saved to isolated storage when the program is deactivated or closed, and retrieved when the program is launched or activated:

Silverlight Project: StopWatch   File: App.xaml.cs (excerpt)

```
public partial class App : Application
{
    // Application Setting
    public ElapsedTimeFormat ElapsedTimeFormat { set; get; }

    ...

    private void Application_Launching(object sender, LaunchingEventArgs e)
    {
        LoadSettings();
    }

    private void Application_Activated(object sender, ActivatedEventArgs e)
    {
        LoadSettings();
    }

    private void Application_Deactivated(object sender, DeactivatedEventArgs e)
    {
        SaveSettings();
    }

    private void Application_Closing(object sender, ClosingEventArgs e)
    {
        SaveSettings();
    }

    void LoadSettings()
    {
        IsolatedStorageSettings settings = IsolatedStorageSettings.ApplicationSettings;

        if (settings.Contains("elapsedTimeFormat"))
            ElapsedTimeFormat = (ElapsedTimeFormat)settings["elapsedTimeFormat"];
        else
            ElapsedTimeFormat = ElapsedTimeFormat.HourMinuteSecond;
    }

    void SaveSettings()
    {
        IsolatedStorageSettings settings = IsolatedStorageSettings.ApplicationSettings;
        settings["elapsedTimeFormat"] = ElapsedTimeFormat;
        settings.Save();
    }
}
```

The content area in the XAML file is a bit more extensive than you might expect because it includes a type of "dialog box" that's used by the user to select the elapsed time format.

So as not to overwhelm you, only the portion of the content area devoted to the operation of the stopwatch is shown here. It consists of just a *ToggleButton* to turn the stopwatch on and off, and a *TextBlock* to display the elapsed time.

Silverlight Project: StopWatch   File: MainPage.xaml (excerpt)

```xml
<Grid x:Name="ContentPanel" Grid.Row="1" Margin="12,0,12,0">

    <!-- Stopwatch display -->
    <Grid VerticalAlignment="Center"
          Margin="25 0">
        <Grid.RowDefinitions>
            <RowDefinition Height="Auto" />
            <RowDefinition Height="Auto" />
        </Grid.RowDefinitions>

        <TextBlock Name="elapsedText"
                   Text="0"
                   Grid.Row="0"
                   FontFamily="Arial"
                   FontSize="{StaticResource PhoneFontSizeExtraLarge}"
                   TextAlignment="Center"
                   Margin="0 0 0 50"/>

        <ToggleButton Name="startStopToggle"
                      Content="Start"
                      Grid.Row="1"
                      Checked="OnToggleButtonChecked"
                      Unchecked="OnToggleButtonChecked" />
    </Grid>

    <!-- Rectangle to simulate disabling -->
    ...
    <!-- "Dialog Box" to select TimeSpan formatting -->
    ...
</Grid>
```

The code-behind file defines just three fields; *using* directives are required for *System.Diagnostics* and *System.Globaliztion*.

Silverlight Project: StopWatch   File: MainPage.xaml.cs (excerpt)

```csharp
public partial class MainPage : PhoneApplicationPage
{
    Stopwatch stopwatch = new Stopwatch();
    TimeSpan suspensionAdjustment = new TimeSpan();
    string decimalSeparator = NumberFormatInfo.CurrentInfo.NumberDecimalSeparator;
```

```
public MainPage()
{
    InitializeComponent();
    DisplayTime();
}
...
void DisplayTime()
{
    TimeSpan elapsedTime = stopwatch.Elapsed + suspensionAdjustment;
    string str = null;

    switch ((Application.Current as App).ElapsedTimeFormat)
    {
        case ElapsedTimeFormat.HourMinuteSecond:
            str = String.Format("{0:D2} {1:D2} {2:D2}{3}{4:D2}",
                                elapsedTime.Hours, elapsedTime.Minutes,
                                elapsedTime.Seconds, decimalSeparator,
                                elapsedTime.Milliseconds / 10);
            break;

        case ElapsedTimeFormat.Seconds:
            str = String.Format("{0:F2} sec", elapsedTime.TotalSeconds);
            break;

        case ElapsedTimeFormat.Milliseconds:
            str = String.Format("{0:F0} msec", elapsedTime.TotalMilliseconds);
            break;
    }
    elapsedText.Text = str;
}
...
}
```

The most important field is an instance of the *Stopwatch*. Programmers customarily use this class to determine how long a program spends in a particular method. It's not often used as an actual stopwatch!

You'll see shortly how the *suspensionAdjustment* field is used in connection with tombstoning.

The .NET *Stopwatch* object provides an elapsed time in the form of a *TimeSpan* object. I couldn't quite persuade the *TimeSpan* object to display the elapsed time in precisely the format I wanted, so I ended up doing my own formatting. The *decimalSeparator* field represents a tiny nod to internationalization.

The *DisplayTime* method is devoted to setting the *Text* property of the *TextBlock*. It accesses the *Elapsed* property of the *Stopwatch* and adds the *suspensionAdjustment*. This is formatted in one of three ways depending on the *ElapsedTimeFormat* property of the *App* class.

When pressed, the *ToggleButton* fires *Checked* and *Unchecked* events, which are both handled by the *OnToggleButtonChecked* method. This method uses the *IsChecked* property of the *ToggleButton* to start or stop the *Stopwatch* object and also to change the text displayed by the button. To keep the display promptly updated, a *CompositionTarget.Rendering* event simply calls *DisplayTime*:

Silverlight Project: StopWatch   File: MainPage.xaml.cs (excerpt)

```
void OnToggleButtonChecked(object sender, RoutedEventArgs e)
{
    if ((bool)startStopToggle.IsChecked)
    {
        stopwatch.Start();
        startStopToggle.Content = "Stop";
        CompositionTarget.Rendering += OnCompositionTargetRendering;
    }
    else
    {
        stopwatch.Stop();
        startStopToggle.Content = "Start";
        CompositionTarget.Rendering -= OnCompositionTargetRendering;
    }
}

void OnCompositionTargetRendering(object sender, EventArgs args)
{
    DisplayTime();
}
```

Here it is in action:

As you can see, the program also contains an *ApplicationBar*. The two buttons are labeled "format" and "reset." Here's the definition of the *ApplicationBar* in the XAML file:

Silverlight Project: StopWatch   File: MainPage.xaml (excerpt)

```
<phone:PhoneApplicationPage.ApplicationBar>
    <shell:ApplicationBar>
        <shell:ApplicationBarIconButton IconUri="/Images/appbar.feature.settings.rest.
png"
                                        Text="format"
                                        Click="OnAppbarFormatClick" />

        <shell:ApplicationBarIconButton IconUri="/Images/appbar.refresh.rest.png"
                                        Text="reset"
                                        Click="OnAppbarResetClick" />
    </shell:ApplicationBar>
</phone:PhoneApplicationPage.ApplicationBar>
```

The simpler of the two *Click* methods is the one for resetting the stopwatch. Resetting the .NET *Stopwatch* object also causes it to stop, so the *ToggleButton* is explicitly unchecked and *suspensionAdjustment* is set to zero:

Silverlight Project: StopWatch   File: MainPage.xaml.cs (excerpt)

```
void OnAppbarResetClick(object sender, EventArgs args)
{
    stopwatch.Reset();
    startStopToggle.IsChecked = false;
    suspensionAdjustment = new TimeSpan();
    DisplayTime();
}
```

Selecting the elapsed time format is a little more complex. I chose to handle this not with menu items on the *ApplicationBar* but with something resembling a little dialog box. This dialog box is defined right in the XAML file in the same *Grid* cell as the main display:

Silverlight Project: StopWatch   File: MainPage.xaml.cs (excerpt)

```
<Grid x:Name="ContentPanel" Grid.Row="1" Margin="12,0,12,0">

    <!-- Stopwatch display -->
    ...
    <!-- Rectangle to simulate disabling -->
    <Rectangle Name="disableRect"
               Fill="#80000000"
               Visibility="Collapsed" />
```

```xml
<!-- "Dialog Box" to select TimeSpan formatting -->
<Border Name="formatDialog"
        Background="{StaticResource PhoneChromeBrush}"
        BorderBrush="{StaticResource PhoneForegroundBrush}"
        BorderThickness="3"
        HorizontalAlignment="Center"
        VerticalAlignment="Center"
        Visibility="Collapsed">
    <Grid>
        <Grid.RowDefinitions>
            <RowDefinition Height="Auto" />
            <RowDefinition Height="Auto" />
        </Grid.RowDefinitions>

        <Grid.ColumnDefinitions>
            <ColumnDefinition Width="*" />
            <ColumnDefinition Width="*" />
        </Grid.ColumnDefinitions>

        <StackPanel Name="radioButtonPanel"
                    Grid.Row="0"
                    Grid.Column="0"
                    Grid.ColumnSpan="2"
                    HorizontalAlignment="Center">

            <RadioButton Content="Hour/Minute/Seconds"
                         Tag="HourMinuteSecond" />

            <RadioButton Content="Seconds"
                         Tag="Seconds" />

            <RadioButton Content="Milliseconds"
                         Tag="Milliseconds" />
        </StackPanel>

        <Button Grid.Row="1" Grid.Column="0"
                Content="ok"
                Click="OnOkButtonClick" />

        <Button Grid.Row="1" Grid.Column="1"
                Content="cancel"
                Click="OnCancelButtonClick" />
    </Grid>
</Border>
</Grid>
```

Notice that both the *Rectangle* and the *Border* have *Visibility* settings of *Collapsed* so they are normally absent from the display. The *Rectangle* covers the entire content area and is used solely to "gray out" the background. The *Border* is structured much like a traditional dialog box, with three *RadioButton* controls and two *Button* controls labeled "ok" and "cancel."

Notice that the *RadioButton* controls do not have handlers set for their *Checked* events, but they do have text strings set to their *Tag* properties. The *Tag* property is defined by

FrameworkElement and is available to attach arbitrary data on elements and controls. It's no coincidence that the text strings I've set to these *Tag* properties are exactly the members of the *ElapsedTimeFormat* enumeration.

When the user presses the *ApplicationBar* button labeled "format," the *OnAppbarFormatClick* method takes over, making the *disableRect* and *formatDialog* elements visible:

Silverlight Project: StopWatch   File: MainPage.xaml.cs (excerpt)

```
void OnAppbarFormatClick(object sender, EventArgs args)
{
    disableRect.Visibility = Visibility.Visible;
    formatDialog.Visibility = Visibility.Visible;

    // Initialize radio buttons
    ElapsedTimeFormat currentFormat = (Application.Current as App).ElapsedTimeFormat;

    foreach (UIElement child in radioButtonPanel.Children)
    {
        RadioButton radio = child as RadioButton;
        ElapsedTimeFormat radioFormat =
            (ElapsedTimeFormat)Enum.Parse(typeof(ElapsedTimeFormat),
                                          radio.Tag as string, true);
        radio.IsChecked = currentFormat == radioFormat;
    }
}
```

The logic sets the *IsChecked* property of a particular *RadioButton* if its *Tag* property (when converted into an *ElapsedTimeFormat* enumeration member) equals the *ElapsedTimeFormat* stored as an application setting. (Easier logic would have been possible if the *Tag* properties were simply set to 0, 1, and 2 for the integer values of the enumeration members.)

Here's the displayed dialog box:

No event handlers are attached to the *RadioButton* controls. After the dialog is display, the next event the program will receive signals whether the user has press the "ok" or "cancel" button:

Silverlight Project: StopWatch   File: MainPage.xaml.cs (excerpt)

```
void OnOkButtonClick(object sender, RoutedEventArgs args)
{
    foreach (UIElement child in radioButtonPanel.Children)
    {
        RadioButton radio = child as RadioButton;
        if ((bool)radio.IsChecked)
            (Application.Current as App).ElapsedTimeFormat =
                (ElapsedTimeFormat)Enum.Parse(typeof(ElapsedTimeFormat),
                                        radio.Tag as string, true);
    }
    OnCancelButtonClick(sender, args);
}

void OnCancelButtonClick(object sender, RoutedEventArgs args)
{
    disableRect.Visibility = Visibility.Collapsed;
    formatDialog.Visibility = Visibility.Collapsed;
    DisplayTime();
}
```

The routine for the "ok" button checks which *RadioButton* is now clicked and then sets the application setting with that value. It also calls the "cancel" handler, which "dismisses" the "dialog box" by setting the *Visibility* properties of *disableRect* and *formatDialog* back to *Collapsed*.

A program such as this presents a bit of a challenge with respect to tombstoning. I decided to ignore issues involving the dialog box. If someone navigates away from the program with the dialog box displayed, it's no big deal if it's no longer there when the user returns.

But ideally, you want an active stopwatch to continue running if the user navigates to another application. Of course, it can't *really* keep running because in reality the program is terminated.

What the program *can* do, however, is save the current elapsed time and the clock time as it is being tombstoned. When the program returns, it can use that information to adjust the time shown on the stopwatch. This occurs in the *OnNavigatedFrom* and *OnNavigatedTo* methods:

Silverlight Project: StopWatch   File: MainPage.xaml.cs (excerpt)

```
protected override void OnNavigatedFrom(NavigationEventArgs args)
{
    PhoneApplicationService service = PhoneApplicationService.Current;
    service.State["stopWatchRunning"] = (bool)startStopToggle.IsChecked;
```

```
        service.State["suspensionAdjustment"] = suspensionAdjustment + stopwatch.Elapsed;
        service.State["tombstoneBeginTime"] = DateTime.Now;

        base.OnNavigatedFrom(args);
    }

    protected override void OnNavigatedTo(NavigationEventArgs args)
    {
        PhoneApplicationService service = PhoneApplicationService.Current;

        if (service.State.ContainsKey("stopWatchRunning"))
        {
            suspensionAdjustment = (TimeSpan)service.State["suspensionAdjustment"];

            if ((bool)service.State["stopWatchRunning"])
            {
                suspensionAdjustment += DateTime.Now -
                                        (DateTime)service.State["tombstoneBeginTime"];
                startStopToggle.IsChecked = true;
            }
            else
            {
                DisplayTime();
            }
        }
        base.OnNavigatedTo(args);
    }
```

Whenever the program starts up again, the .NET *Stopwatch* object always begins at an elapsed time of zero. That *Stopwatch* object can't be adjusted directly. Instead, the *suspensionAdjustment* field represents the time that elapsed when the program was tombstoned plus the elapsed time of the *Stopwatch* when tombstoning began. A user could navigate away several times while the stopwatch is running, so this field could be the accumulation of several periods of tombstoning.

For *OnNavigatedTo*, the simplest case is when the stopwatch is not actively running. All that's necessary is to set the *suspensionAdjustment* from the saved value. But if the stopwatch has conceptually been running all this time, then the *suspensionAdjustment* must be increased by the period of time that elapsed based on the value returned by *DateTime.Now*.

In actual use, the StopWatch program will appear to be running and keeping track of elapsed time even when it's not, and it's that illusion that make the program much more useful than it would be otherwise.

Buttons and Styles

The *Style* property is defined by *FrameworkElement* so of course it's inherited by *Control* and *ButtonBase* and *Button*. Here's a program that defines a *Style* for *Button* in the *Resources* section of the page:

Project: **ButtonStyles**   File: **MainPage.xaml** (excerpt)

```
<phone:PhoneApplicationPage.Resources>
    <Style x:Key="btnStyle" TargetType="Button">
        <Setter Property="Foreground" Value="SkyBlue" />
        <Setter Property="FontSize" Value="36" />
        <Setter Property="HorizontalAlignment" Value="Center" />
        <Setter Property="Margin" Value="12" />
    </Style>
</phone:PhoneApplicationPage.Resources>
```

As usual, the *Style* has an *x:Key* attribute and a *TargetType*. Three *Button* controls are arranged in a *StackPanel*. Each has a reference to the *Style* resource:

Project: **ButtonStyles**   File: **MainPage.xaml** (excerpt)

```
<Grid x:Name=" ContentPanel" Grid.Row="1" Margin="12,0,12,0">
    <StackPanel>
        <Button Content="Button No. 1"
                Style="{StaticResource btnStyle}" />

        <Button Content="Button No. 2"
                Style="{StaticResource btnStyle}" />

        <Button Content="Button No. 3"
                Style="{StaticResource btnStyle}" />
    </StackPanel>
</Grid>
```

Here's what it looks like:

Now change one of those three *Button* objects to a *ToggleButton*:

```
<ToggleButton Content="Button No. 2"
              Style="{StaticResource btnStyle}" />
```

This causes a runtime error because you're attempting to set a *ToggleButton* from a *Style* whose *TargetType* is *Button*.

But if you look at the class hierarchy, you'll see that both *Button* and *ToggleButton* derive from *ButtonBase*. Try setting that as the *TargetType* in the *Style*:

```
<Style x:Key="btnStyle" TargetType="ButtonBase">
    <Setter Property="Foreground" Value="SkyBlue" />
    <Setter Property="FontSize" Value="36" />
    <Setter Property="HorizontalAlignment" Value="Center" />
    <Setter Property="Margin" Value="12" />
</Style>
```

Now it works again. You can even change the *TargetType* to *Control*, but that's about as far back as you can go with the particular example. If you change the *TargetType* to *FrameworkElement* you'll get a runtime error because *FrameworkElement* doesn't have *Foreground* or *FontSize* properties.

As a general rule, it makes sense to set *TargetType* to be the most general class that has all the properties you're defining in the *Style*. You can inherit from styles based on derived classes. For example, you can begin with a *Style* with a *TargetType* of *ButtonBase* and then have two derived styles for a *TargetType* of *Button* and a *TargetType* of *ToggleButton*.

TextBox and Keyboard Input

The two types of text-entry controls available in Silverlight for Windows Phone are *TextBox*, which allows typing and editing single-line or multiline plain unformatted text, and *PasswordBox*, which briefly displays each letter you type but then replaces it with another character, by default an asterisk.

These are the only two ways your program can get input from the hardware keyboard of the phone (if it exists) or invoke the Software Input Panel (SIP), the virtual on-screen keyboard.

Let's just jump right into a program. The OneTimeText program is designed to let you send an SMS (Short Message Service) text message to a particular phone number. The program requires you to type in that phone number but doesn't save it anywhere. That's why I called the program "one time" text.

Here's the content area:

Silverlight Project: OneTimeText   File: **MainPage.xaml** (excerpt)

```xml
<Grid x:Name="ContentPanel" Grid.Row="1" Margin="12,0,12,0">
    <Grid Margin="24">
        <Grid.RowDefinitions>
            <RowDefinition Height="Auto" />
            <RowDefinition Height="Auto" />
            <RowDefinition Height="Auto" />
            <RowDefinition Height="*" />
            <RowDefinition Height="Auto" />
        </Grid.RowDefinitions>

        <TextBlock Grid.Row="0"
                   Text="phone number"
                   Style="{StaticResource PhoneTextSmallStyle}" />

        <TextBox Name="toTextBox"
                 Grid.Row="1"
                 InputScope="TelephoneNumber"
                 TextChanged="OnTextBoxTextChanged" />

        <TextBlock Grid.Row="2"
                   Text="text message"
                   HorizontalAlignment="Left"
                   Style="{StaticResource PhoneTextSmallStyle}" />

        <TextBlock Name="charCountText"
                   Grid.Row="2"
                   HorizontalAlignment="Right"
                   Style="{StaticResource PhoneTextSmallStyle}" />

        <TextBox Name="bodyTextBox"
                 Grid.Row="3"
                 MaxLength="160"
                 TextWrapping="Wrap"
                 VerticalScrollBarVisibility="Auto"
                 TextChanged="OnTextBoxTextChanged" />

        <Button Name="sendButton"
                Grid.Row="4"
                Content="send"
                IsEnabled="False"
                HorizontalAlignment="Center"
                Click="OnSendButtonClick" />
    </Grid>
</Grid>
```

The first *TextBox* control is for the phone number so it only needs a single line. The second *TextBox* is for the body of the message. It takes up the remainder of the Grid not used by any of the other siblings; the *TextWrapping* property set to *Wrap* turns on the multi-line feature, which is generally used in conjunction with vertical scrolling.

The *Button* labeled "send" is initially disabled because nothing is typed into either *TextBox* yet. That's one reason why the *TextChanged* event is set on both.

The first *TextBox* has its *InputScope* property set to *TelephoneNumber.* When you press on that *TextBox*, a numeric keypad pops up:

The second doesn't have its *InputScope* property set so a standard general-purpose keyboard comes up:

The *MaxLength* property is set on this second *TextBox* so you can't enter more than 160 characters—the maximum for SMS.

The various names you can use with *InputScope* are documented in the *InputScopeNameValue* enumeration defined in the *System.Windows.Input* namespace. If you prefer to invoke Intellisense in Visual Studio for helping you out, you need to break out the *InputScope* as a property element and set it like this:

```
<TextBox Name="toTextBox"
         Grid.Row="1"
         TextChanged="OnTextBoxTextChanged">
    <TextBox.InputScope>
        <InputScope>
            <InputScopeName NameValue="TelephoneNumber" />
        </InputScope>
    </TextBox.InputScope>
</TextBox>
```

Once you type the equal sign after *NameValue*, you'll get a list of the possible choices.

The XAML doesn't show the most important property of the *TextBox*, which is the property named *Text* of type *string*. At any time, you can programmatically access the *Text* property to see what's in there, or you can set the *Text* property to initialize the contents. It's also possible to insert something into the existing contents of the *TextBox*, or delete something: Get the current *Text* property, use normal methods of the *String* class to create a new string containing the new text, and then set that string back to the *Text* property.

Here's a good chunk of the *MainPage* code-behind file:

Silverlight Project: **OneTimeText**   File: **MainPage.xaml.cs (excerpt)**

```
public partial class MainPage : PhoneApplicationPage
{
    PhoneApplicationService appService = PhoneApplicationService.Current;
    SmsComposeTask smsTask;

    public MainPage()
    {
        InitializeComponent();

        smsTask = new SmsComposeTask();
    }

    void OnTextBoxTextChanged(object sender, TextChangedEventArgs args)
    {
        if (sender == bodyTextBox)
            charCountText.Text = String.Format("{0} chars", bodyTextBox.Text.Length);

        sendButton.IsEnabled = toTextBox.Text.Length > 0 && bodyTextBox.Text.Length >
0;
    }
```

```
void OnSendButtonClick(object sender, RoutedEventArgs e)
{
    smsTask.To = toTextBox.Text;
    smsTask.Body = bodyTextBox.Text;
    smsTask.Show();
}
...
}
```

The single *TextChanged* handler can differentiate between the two *TextBox* controls by comparing the *sender* argument with the names defined in the XAML file. For the second *TextBox*, a display is updated showing how many characters are typed. The "send" *Button* remains disabled if either *TextBox* is empty of text.

When that *Button* is pressed, the program invokes *SmsComposeTask*, which is the standard texting program on the phone. At this point, the user has a somewhat friendlier interface to send this text, to edit it, or to send other texts.

At some point the user might return to the OneTimeText program. The *SmsComposeTask* object doesn't return anything to the program that invoked it—it's a *launcher* rather than a *chooser*—but it would still be nice for the user to see the text previously entered. For this reason, the program overrides the *OnNavigationFrom* and *OnNavigationTo* methods to save and restore that program state:

Silverlight Project: OneTimeText   File: MainPage.xaml.cs (excerpt)

```
protected override void OnNavigatedFrom(NavigationEventArgs args)
{
    appService.State["toText"] = toTextBox.Text;
    appService.State["bodyText"] = bodyTextBox.Text;

    base.OnNavigatedFrom(args);
}

protected override void OnNavigatedTo(NavigationEventArgs args)
{
    object text;

    if (appService.State.TryGetValue("toText", out text))
        toTextBox.Text = text as string;

    if (appService.State.TryGetValue("bodyText", out text))
        bodyTextBox.Text = text as string;

    base.OnNavigatedTo(args);
}
```

The last sample program in this chapter is called QuickNotes. It is intended to provide a quick way to type some notes and be assured that they'll be retained without any explicit saving or loading. It's basically a Windows Phone 7 version of Notepad but only capable of working with a single file.

The program also allows changing the font size, so the *QuickNotesSettings* class for the program's application settings has two public properties named *Text* and *FontSize*, plus methods to save and load those properties in isolated storage:

Silverlight Project: QuickNotes   File: QuickNotesSettings.cs

```
public class QuickNotesSettings
{
    public QuickNotesSettings()
    {
        this.Text = "";
        this.FontSize = (double)Application.Current.Resources["PhoneFontSizeMediumLar
ge"];
    }

    public string Text { set; get; }
    public double FontSize { set; get; }

    public static QuickNotesSettings Load()
    {
        IsolatedStorageSettings isoSettings = IsolatedStorageSettings.
ApplicationSettings;
        QuickNotesSettings settings;

        if (!isoSettings.TryGetValue<QuickNotesSettings>("settings", out settings))
            settings = new QuickNotesSettings();

        return settings;
    }

    public void Save()
    {
        IsolatedStorageSettings isoSettings = IsolatedStorageSettings.
ApplicationSettings;
        isoSettings["settings"] = this;
    }
}
```

As with the Jot program, these setting are saved, loaded, and exposed in the *App* class:

Silverlight Project: QuickNotes   File: App.xaml.cs

```
public partial class App : Application
{
    // Application settings
    public QuickNotesSettings AppSettings { set; get; }

    ...

    private void Application_Launching(object sender, LaunchingEventArgs e)
    {
        AppSettings = QuickNotesSettings.Load();
    }

    private void Application_Activated(object sender, ActivatedEventArgs e)
    {
        AppSettings = QuickNotesSettings.Load();
    }

    private void Application_Deactivated(object sender, DeactivatedEventArgs e)
    {
        AppSettings.Save();
    }

    private void Application_Closing(object sender, ClosingEventArgs e)
    {
        AppSettings.Save();
    }
    ...
}
```

The XAML file creates a multiline *TextBox* the size of the content area. Besides setting *TextWrapping* for multiline editing, the markup also sets *AcceptsReturn* to *true* so that the Enter key will go to a new line, which I thought was appropriate for this program. (In the context of a dialog box, you usually want the Enter key to instead invoke the OK button, even if a *TextBox* is currently getting input from the user.)

Silverlight Project: QuickNotes   File: MainPage.xaml

```
<Grid x:Name="ContentPanel" Grid.Row="1" Margin="12,0,12,0">
    <TextBox Name="txtbox"
             TextWrapping="Wrap"
             AcceptsReturn="True"
             VerticalScrollBarVisibility="Auto"
             TextChanged="OnTextBoxTextChanged" />
</Grid>
```

The XAML file also contains an *ApplicationBar* with two buttons I designed myself for increasing and decreasing the size of the font:

Silverlight Project: QuickNotes   File: MainPage.xaml

```
<phone:PhoneApplicationPage.ApplicationBar>
    <shell:ApplicationBar>
        <shell:ApplicationBarIconButton IconUri="/Images/littleletter.icon.png"
                                        Text="smaller font"
                                        Click="OnAppBarSmallerFontClick" />

        <shell:ApplicationBarIconButton IconUri="/Images/bigletter.icon.png"
                                        Text="larger font"
                                        Click="OnAppBarLargerFontClick" />
    </shell:ApplicationBar>
</phone:PhoneApplicationPage.ApplicationBar>
```

With all this preparation, the actual code file for *MainPage* is rather short and straightforward:

Silverlight Project: QuickNotes   File: MainPage.xaml.cs

```
public partial class MainPage : PhoneApplicationPage
{
    QuickNotesSettings appSettings = (Application.Current as App).AppSettings;

    public MainPage()
    {
        InitializeComponent();

        txtbox.Text = appSettings.Text;
        txtbox.FontSize = appSettings.FontSize;
    }

    void OnTextBoxTextChanged(object sender, TextChangedEventArgs args)
    {
        appSettings.Text = txtbox.Text;
    }

    void OnAppBarSmallerFontClick(object sender, EventArgs args)
    {
        txtbox.FontSize = Math.Max(12, txtbox.FontSize - 1);
        appSettings.FontSize = txtbox.FontSize;
    }

    void OnAppBarLargerFontClick(object sender, EventArgs args)
    {
        txtbox.FontSize = Math.Min(48, txtbox.FontSize + 2);
        appSettings.FontSize = txtbox.FontSize;
    }
}
```

Whenever the text in the *TextBox* changes, the *OnTextBoxChanged* method saves the new version in application settings. The two methods to increase and decrease the font size similarly save the new setting but also use it to set the *FontSize* property of the *TextBox*. Here's the program in action:

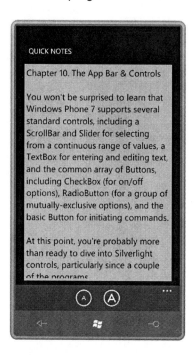

What the program does not do is save the text insertion point (visually indicated by the *TextBox* caret), so whenever the program starts up, you need to tap on the screen to indicate where you want to continue typing. It's possible that you left off at the end of the file, but QuickNotes will always bring you back to the top.

I toyed around with fixing this problem. The insertion point is available as the *SelectionStart*, property, and as the name suggests, it's used in conjunction with text selection. There's also a *SelectionLength* property, which has a value of 0 if no text is selected. (You can also access or set the selected text using the *SelectedText* property.)

TextBox also has a *SelectionChanged* event, so it's certainly possible for QuickNotes to save the new value of *SelectionStart* in application settings every time it changes. Then it would be a simple matter to set the *SelectionStart* property along with *Text* and *FontSize* in the constructor of *MainPage*.

But that doesn't quite work. When you launch QuickNotes or return to it after navigating away, the *TextBox* doesn't have input focus. You need to tap on the screen to give the *TextBox* focus and start typing something in. But by tapping on the screen, you're also setting a new insertion point!

The solution to that little problem is to give input focus to the *TextBox* programmatically. It doesn't work in the constructor to *MainPage*, but if you install a handler for the *Loaded* event, you can do it there:

```
txtbox.Focus();
```

But doing that creates quite a dramatic entrance to the program! As soon as the program starts up, the virtual keyboard pops up! I struggled with the propriety of doing that, and at last I decided it was just too intrusive.

But who knows? Maybe I'll put that feature back in at a later time. That's why they call it *software.*

Chapter 11
Dependency Properties

This chapter is about creating custom control classes in Silverlight, optionally making them available in dynamic link libraries, and referencing them in code and markup.

Deriving one class from another is such a basic aspect of object-oriented programming that devoting a whole chapter to the topic hardly seems necessary. And in one sense, you don't need to do anything special to derive a custom class from an existing Silverlight class. You can reference that class in XAML just by providing an XML namespace declaration to associate an XML prefix with your .NET namespace. I demonstrated as much in Chapter 9 in the two projects that showed how to create custom panels.

On the other hand, if you're creating a custom control class, and that class defines new properties, and if you want those properties to be set through styles, or you want those properties to be set through data bindings, or you want those properties to be the target of animations, then you need to do something very special with those properties.

You need to make them *dependency properties*,

The Problem Illustrated

To illustrate the difference that dependency properties make, let's first look at a custom control class perhaps coded by a naïve programmer.

Suppose you want to use a bunch of buttons whose foregrounds are colored with various linear gradient brushes, and you figure it would be convenient for you to specify the two colors as properties of the buttons, perhaps properties named *Color1* and *Color2*. So you open a project named NaiveGradientButtonDemo and add a new class named *NaiveGradientButton*. Here's that class:

Silverlight Project: **NaiveGradientButtonDemo**   File: **NaiveGradientButton.cs** (excerpt)

```
public class NaiveGradientButton : Button
{
    GradientStop gradientStop1, gradientStop2;

    public NaiveGradientButton()
    {
        LinearGradientBrush brush = new LinearGradientBrush();
        brush.StartPoint = new Point(0, 0);
        brush.EndPoint = new Point(1, 0);
```

```
        gradientStop1 = new GradientStop();
        gradientStop1.Offset = 0;
        brush.GradientStops.Add(gradientStop1);

        gradientStop2 = new GradientStop();
        gradientStop2.Offset = 1;
        brush.GradientStops.Add(gradientStop2);

        Foreground = brush;
    }

    public Color Color1
    {
        set { gradientStop1.Color = value; }
        get { return (Color)gradientStop1.Color; }
    }

    public Color Color2
    {
        set { gradientStop2.Color = value; }
        get { return (Color)gradientStop2.Color; }
    }
}
```

As expected, *NaiveGradientButton* derives from *Button* and has two new properties of type *Color* named *Color1* and *Color2*. The constructor creates a *LinearGradientBrush*, sets the *StartPoint* and *EndPoint* properties, creates two *GradientStop* objects that are stored as fields, adds those to the *LinearGradientBrush*, and then sets the brush to the button's *Foreground* property.

This class will not prevent the *Foreground* property of the *GradientBrush* from being re-set in code or XAML after the object has been created, but because the code that sets the *Foreground* here is considered to be a local setting, it will prevent inheritance of the *Foreground* property, and won't be affected by a *Style* that targets the *Foreground* property.

As you can see, the set and get accessors of the *Color1* and *Color2* properties are implemented simply to access the *Color* property in the corresponding *GradientStop*.

The MainPage.xaml file in the NaiveGradientButtonDemo project references this class. The root element includes an XML namespace declaration that associates the namespace prefix "local" with the CLR namespace of *NaiveGradientButton*:

```
xmlns:local="clr-namespace:NaiveGradientButtonDemo"
```

The *Resources* collection in MainPage.xaml defines a *Style* for *NaiveGradientButton*:

Silverlight Project: NaiveGradientButtonDemo   File: **MainPage.xaml** (excerpt)

```
<phone:PhoneApplicationPage.Resources>
    <Style x:Key="gradientButtonStyle"
           TargetType="local:NaiveGradientButton">
        <Setter Property="HorizontalAlignment" Value="Center" />

        <!--
        <Setter Property="Color1" Value="Cyan" />
        <Setter Property="Color2" Value="Pink" />
        -->

    </Style>
</phone:PhoneApplicationPage.Resources>
```

Notice the style *TargetType* referencing the custom class by prefacing the class name with the XML namespace.

You'll also notice that I've commented out *Setter* tags that target the *Color1* and *Color2* properties. (Perhaps I'm not as naïve as I sometimes pretend to be.)

The content area of the XAML file has four instances of *NaiveGradientButton* with their *Color1* and *Color2* properties set in a variety of different ways:

Silverlight Project: NaiveGradientButtonDemo   File: **MainPage.xaml** (excerpt)

```
<Grid x:Name="ContentPanel" Grid.Row="1" Margin="12,0,12,0">
    <StackPanel>
        <local:NaiveGradientButton Content="Naive Gradient Button #1"
                                   HorizontalAlignment="Center" />

        <local:NaiveGradientButton Content="Naive Gradient Button #2"
                                   Color1="Blue" Color2="Red"
                                   HorizontalAlignment="Center" />

        <local:NaiveGradientButton Content="Naive Gradient Button #3"
                                   Color1="{StaticResource PhoneForegroundColor}"
                                   Color2="{StaticResource PhoneBackgroundColor}"
                                   HorizontalAlignment="Center" />

        <local:NaiveGradientButton Content="Naive Gradient Button #4"
                                   Style="{StaticResource gradientButtonStyle}" />
    </StackPanel>
</Grid>
```

The first button uses the default values of *Color1* and *Color2*; the second uses explicit colors; the third references theme colors, and the fourth references the *Style* defined in the *Resources* collection.

When you run the program, you'll discover that the second and third buttons are fine, but the first and fourth seem to have no content:

There are no default values for *Color1* and *Color2*. If they're not explicitly set, the colors in the gradient will have all the *A*, *R*, *G*, and *B* properties set to 0, a color known as transparent black.

Try uncommenting the two *Setter* tags in the *Style*. The Visual Studio error window will tell you "Object reference not set to an instance of an object" (certainly one of my favorite error messages) and if you try to run the program under the debugger, a *XamlParseException* will be raised with the message "Invalid attribute value Color1 for property Property." That's a little better: It's telling you that in the *Setter* tag, you can't set *Property* to *Color1*.

What the error message should really say is: "Don't be so naïve. Use dependency properties."

The Dependency Property Difference

In Silverlight, properties can be set in several ways. We have empirically discovered that a strict precedence is established when the same property is set from property inheritance, or from a theme, or a style, or a local setting. A little chart created in Chapter 7 reads:

Local Settings have precedence over

Style Settings, which have precedence over the

Theme Style, which has precedence over

Property Inheritance, which has precedence over

Default Values

In chapters ahead you'll see that properties can be set from animations and templates, and these also fit into the precedence chart.

This strict precedence is required to avoid a lot of fighting and squabbles among styles and animations and everything else. It would be chaos otherwise, and that violates our fundamental desire that code be completely deterministic.

What Silverlight providesis an infrastructure to manage all the different ways properties can be set and to impose some kind of order. Dependency properties are a major part of this infrastructure. They're called dependency properties because the properties *depend* on a bunch of different external forces, which are then mediated.

Dependency properties are built on top of existing .NET properties, and there's some grunt work involved, and some extra typing, but you'll be coding dependency properties automatically before you know it.

Among other things, dependency properties provide the property-setting precedence. It occurs way under the covers and it's not something you can mess with. Dependency properties also provide a very structured way to give properties a default value, and to provide callback methods that are invoked when the value of the property changes.

Almost all the properties of the Silverlight classes encountered so far have actually been dependency properties. It's easier listing the exceptions to this rule! Two that come to mind are the *Children* property of *Panel* and the *Text* property of *Run*.

Any class that implements dependency properties must derive from *DependencyObject*, which is a very basic class in the Silverlight class hierarchy. Many classes in Silverlight derive from *DependencyObject*, including the big one: *UIElement*. That means *Button* derives from *DependencyObject*, which of course means that any class that derives from *Button* can implement dependency properties.

A *BetterGradientButton* class with dependency properties starts off normally:

```
public class BetterGradientButton : Button
{

}
```

As with *NaiveGradientButton*, *BetterGradientButton* defines two properties named *Color1* and *Color2*. A dependency property begins with a public field of type *DependencyProperty* that has the same name as the property but with the word *Property* appended. So in the *BetterGradientButton* class, the first step to defining a *Color1* property is to define a public field of type *DependencyProperty* named *Color1Property*.

```
public class BetterGradientButton : Button
{
    public static readonly DependencyProperty Color1Property =
        DependencyProperty.Register("Color1",
            typeof(Color),
            typeof(BetterGradientButton),
            new PropertyMetadata(Colors.Black, OnColorChanged));
}
```

Not only is it a field, but it's a *public static* field, and it's customarily defined as *readonly* as well, which means it can't be changed after it's defined. Once a *DependencyProperty* is created for a particular class, it doesn't change, and it's shared among all instances of that class.

Generally you create an object of type *DependencyProperty* by calling the static *DependencyProperty.Register* method. (The only exception is for attached properties.) The first argument is a text string of the property name; the second argument is the type of the property, in this case *Color*; the third argument is the class defining the property, in this case *BetterGradientButton*.

The final argument is an object of type *PropertyMetadata*, and there are only two possible pieces of information you supply in the *PropertyMetadata* constructor. One is the default value of the property—the value of the property if it's not otherwise assigned. If you don't supply this default value for a reference type, it will be assumed to be *null*. For a value type, it's the type's default.

I've decided that the *Color1* property should have a default value of *Colors.Black*.

The second part of the *PropertyMetadata* constructor is the name of a handler that is called when the property changes. This handler is only called if the property really changes. For example, if the property has a default value of *Colors.Black*, and the property is then set to a value of *Colors.Black*, the property changed handler will *not* be called.

I know it seems weird for something called a *dependency property* with a type of *DependencyProperty* and a name of *Color1Property* to be defined as a field, but there it is.

It's easy to confuse the two classes *DependencyObject* and *DependencyProperty*. Any class that has dependency properties must descend from *DependencyObject*, just as normal classes descend from *Object*. The class then creates objects of type *DependencyProperty* just as a normal class might define regular properties.

It's not necessary to define the entire *DependencyProperty* in the static field. Some programmers prefer instead to initialize the *DependencyProperty* field in the static constructor:

```
public class BetterGradientButton : Button
{
    public static readonly DependencyProperty Color1Property;

    static BetterGradientButton()
    {
        Color1Property = DependencyProperty.Register("Color1",
                         typeof(Color),
                         typeof(BetterGradientButton),
                         new PropertyMetadata(Colors.Black, OnColorChanged));
    }
}
```

There's really no difference between these two techniques.

Besides the static field of type *DependencyProperty* you need a regular .NET property definition for the *Color1* property:

```
public class BetterGradientButton : Button
{
    public static readonly DependencyProperty Color1Property =
        DependencyProperty.Register("Color1",
            typeof(Color),
            typeof(BetterGradientButton),
            new PropertyMetadata(Colors.Black, OnColorChanged));

    public Color Color1
    {
        set { SetValue(Color1Property, value); }
        get { return (Color)GetValue(Color1Property); }
    }
}
```

This definition of the *Color1* property is standard. The *set* accessor calls *SetValue* referencing the *Color1Property* dependency property, and the *get* accessor calls *GetValue* also referencing *Color1Property*.

Where did these two methods *SetValue* and *GetValue* come from? *SetValue* and *GetValue* are two public methods defined by *DependencyObject* and inherited by all derived classes. Notice that the second argument to *SetValue* is the value to which the property is being set. The return value of *GetValue* is of type *object* so it must be explicitly cast to a *Color*.

In connection with dependency properties, the *Color1* property definition is said to be the definition of the *CLR property*—the .NET Common Language Runtime property—to distinguish it from the *DependencyProperty* object defined as a public static field. It is sometimes said that the CLR property named *Color1* is "backed by" the dependency property named *Color1Property*. That terminology is convenient when you want to distinguish the property definition from the definition of the public static field. But just as often, both pieces—the public static field and the property definition—are collectively referred to as "the dependency property" or (if you're really cool) "the DP."

It is very important that your CLR property does nothing more than call *SetValue* and *GetValue*. This is not the place for any kind of validity checking or property-changed processing. The reason is that you never really know how a dependency property is being set. You might think the property is always set like this:

```
btn.Color1 = Colors.Red;
```

However, the *SetValue* and *GetValue* methods defined by *DependencyObject* are public, so some code could just as easily set the property like this:

```
btn.SetValue(GradientButton2.Color1Property, Colors.Red);
```

Or, the property could be set in a way that is known only to the Silverlight internals.

On the other hand, don't mistakenly omit the CLR property. Sometimes if you just define the *DependencyProperty* field and forget the CLR property, some things will work but others will not.

Here's the class with a *DependencyProperty* and CLR property for *Color2* as well:

```
public class BetterGradientButton : Button
{
    public static readonly DependencyProperty Color1Property =
        DependencyProperty.Register("Color1",
            typeof(Color),
            typeof(BetterGradientButton),
            new PropertyMetadata(Colors.Black, OnColorChanged));

    public static readonly DependencyProperty Color2Property =
        DependencyProperty.Register("Color2",
            typeof(Color),
            typeof(BetterGradientButton),
            new PropertyMetadata(Colors.White, OnColorChanged));

    public Color Color1
    {
        set { SetValue(Color1Property, value); }
        get { return (Color)GetValue(Color1Property); }
    }

    public Color Color2
    {
        set { SetValue(Color2Property, value); }
        get { return (Color)GetValue(Color2Property); }
    }
}
```

In the *DependencyProperty* definition for *Color2*, I set the default value to *Colors.White*.

Both *DependencyProperty* fields refer to a property-changed handler named *OnColorChanged*. Because this method is referred to in the definition of a static field, the method itself must be static and here's what it look like:

```
static void OnColorChanged(DependencyObject obj,
                           DependencyPropertyChangedEventArgs args)
{
    . . .
}
```

This is a static method so it's the same method for all instances of *BetterGradientButton*, and that's a little problem. Normally in a static method you can't access any non-static properties or methods, so at first you might assume that this method can't refer to anything involving a particular instance of *BetterGradientButton*.

But notice that the first argument to this property-changed handler is of type *DependencyObject*. This argument is actually the particular instance of *BetterGradientButton* whose property is being changed. This means that you can safely cast this first argument to an object of type *BetterGradientButton*:

```
static void OnColorChanged(DependencyObject obj,
                           DependencyPropertyChangedEventArgs args)
{
    BetterGradientButton btn = obj as BetterGradientButton;
    . . .
}
```

You can then use that *btn* variable to access all the instance properties and instance methods in the class.

The second argument to the handler gives you specific information on the particular property that's being changed, and the old and new values of that property.

Here's the complete *BetterGradientButton* class:

SilverlightProject: BetterGradientButtonDemo   **File: BetterGradientButton.cs (excerpt)**

```
public class BetterGradientButton : Button
{
    GradientStop gradientStop1, gradientStop2;

    public static readonly DependencyProperty Color1Property =
        DependencyProperty.Register("Color1",
            typeof(Color),
            typeof(BetterGradientButton),
            new PropertyMetadata(Colors.Black, OnColorChanged));
```

```
    public static readonly DependencyProperty Color2Property =
        DependencyProperty.Register("Color2",
            typeof(Color),
            typeof(BetterGradientButton),
            new PropertyMetadata(Colors.White, OnColorChanged));

    public BetterGradientButton()
    {
        LinearGradientBrush brush = new LinearGradientBrush();
        brush.StartPoint = new Point(0, 0);
        brush.EndPoint = new Point(1, 0);

        gradientStop1 = new GradientStop();
        gradientStop1.Offset = 0;
        gradientStop1.Color = Color1;
        brush.GradientStops.Add(gradientStop1);

        gradientStop2 = new GradientStop();
        gradientStop2.Offset = 1;
        gradientStop2.Color = Color2;
        brush.GradientStops.Add(gradientStop2);

        Foreground = brush;
    }

    public Color Color1
    {
        set { SetValue(Color1Property, value); }
        get { return (Color)GetValue(Color1Property); }
    }

    public Color Color2
    {
        set { SetValue(Color2Property, value); }
        get { return (Color)GetValue(Color2Property); }
    }

    static void OnColorChanged(DependencyObject obj,
                              DependencyPropertyChangedEventArgs args)
    {
        BetterGradientButton btn = obj as BetterGradientButton;

        if (args.Property == Color1Property)
            btn.gradientStop1.Color = (Color)args.NewValue;

        if (args.Property == Color2Property)
            btn.gradientStop2.Color = (Color)args.NewValue;
    }
}
```

Like the earlier *NaiveGradientButton* class, the class has two private instance fields of type *gradientStop1* and *gradientStop2*. The constructor is also quite similar to the earlier version, but this one has a significant difference: The *Color* property of each *GradientStop* object is initialized from the *Color1* and *Color2* properties:

```
gradientStop1.Color = Color1;
```

```
gradientStop2.Color = Color2;
```

Accessing those *Color1* and *Color2* properties causes calls to *GetValue* with the *Color1Property* and *Color2Property* arguments. *GetValue* returns the default values defined in the *DependencyProperty* field: *Colors.Black* and *Colors.White*. That's how the *LinearGradientBrush* is created with the default colors.

There are numerous ways to code the property-changed handler down at the bottom of the class. In the *BetterGradientButton* class, I've made use of two properties in *DependencyPropertyChangedEventArgs*: The property named *Property* of type *DependencyProperty* indicates the particular dependency property being changed. This is very handy if you're sharing a property-changed handler among multiple properties as I am here.

DependencyPropertyChangedEventArgs also defines *OldValue* and *NewValue* properties. These two values will always be different. The property-changed handler isn't called unless the property is actually changing.

By the time the property-changed handler has been called, the property has already been changed, so the handler can be implemented by accessing those properties directly. Here's a simple alternative:

```
static void OnColorChanged(DependencyObject obj,
                           DependencyPropertyChangedEventArgs args)
{
    BetterGradientButton btn = obj as BetterGradientButton;

    btn.gradientStop1.Color = btn.Color1;
    btn.gradientStop2.Color = btn.Color2;
}
```

This version doesn't check which property is changing, so for any particular call to *OnColorChanged*, one of those two statements is superfluous. You'll be comforted to know that *GradientStop* derives from *DependencyObject*, and the *Color* property is a dependency property, so the property-changed handler in *GradientStop* doesn't get called if one of the properties is not actually changing.

Here's something I do quite often, and I'm a much happier programmer as a result:

Rather than warp my brain by using a reference to a particular instance of a class within a static method, I use the static method for the sole purpose of calling an instance method with the same name. Here's how my technique would look in *BetterGradientBrush*:

```
static void OnColorChanged(DependencyObject obj,
                           DependencyPropertyChangedEventArgs args)
```

```
{
    (obj as BetterGradientButton).OnColorChanged(args);
}

void OnColorChanged(DependencyPropertyChangedEventArgs args)
{
    if (args.Property == Color1Property)
        gradientStop1.Color = (Color)args.NewValue;

    if (args.Property == Color2Property)
        gradientStop2.Color = (Color)args.NewValue;
}
```

This instance method can do everything the static method can do but without the hassle of carrying around a reference to a particular instance of the class.

Let's see this new class in action. It would be a shame if all this hard work didn't improve things. As in the earlier program, the *Resources* collection in MainPage.xaml has a *Style* element targeting the custom button. But now the *Setter* tags for *Color1* and *Color2* have been optimistically uncommented:

SilverlightProject: **BetterGradientButtonDemo** File: **MainPage.xaml** (excerpt)

```
<phone:PhoneApplicationPage.Resources>
    <Style x:Key="gradientButtonStyle"
            TargetType="local:BetterGradientButton">
        <Setter Property="HorizontalAlignment" Value="Center" />
        <Setter Property="Color1" Value="Cyan" />
        <Setter Property="Color2" Value="Pink" />
    </Style>
</phone:PhoneApplicationPage.Resources>
```

The content area is basically the same:

SilverlightProject: **BetterGradientButtonDemo** File: **MainPage.xaml** (excerpt)

```
<Grid x:Name="ContentPanel" Grid.Row="1" Margin="12,0,12,0">
    <StackPanel>
        <local:BetterGradientButton Content="Better Gradient Button #1"
                                    HorizontalAlignment="Center" />

        <local:BetterGradientButton Content="Better Gradient Button #2"
                                    Color1="Blue" Color2="Red"
                                    HorizontalAlignment="Center" />

        <local:BetterGradientButton Content="Better Gradient Button #3"
                                    Color1="{StaticResource PhoneForegroundColor}"
                                    Color2="{StaticResource PhoneBackgroundColor}"
```

```
                                    HorizontalAlignment="Center" />

        <local:BetterGradientButton Content="Better Gradient Button #4"
                                    Style="{StaticResource gradientButtonStyle}" />
    </StackPanel>
</Grid>
```

The really great news is in the screen shot:

The first button shows the effect of the defaults, a concept built into dependency properties, and the last button shows that the *Style* works.

A few miscellaneous notes:

Notice that you don't have direct access to the actual values of the dependency properties. They are obviously stored somewhere private that is accessible only through *SetValue* and *GetValue*. Presumably *DependencyObject* maintains a dictionary to store a collection of dependency properties and their values. It must be a dictionary because it's possible to use *SetValue* to store certain types of dependency properties—specifically, attached properties—in any *DependencyObject*.

Watch out for the first argument to the *PropertyMetadata* constructor. It is defined as type *object*. Suppose you're creating a *DependencyProperty* for a property of type *double* and you want to set a default value of 10:

```
public static readonly DependencyProperty MyDoubleProperty =
    DependencyProperty.Register("MyDouble",
        typeof(double),
        typeof(SomeClass),
        new PropertyMetadata(10, OnMyDoubleChanged));
```

The C# compiler will interpret that value of 10 as an *int*, and generate code to pass an integer value of 10 to the *PropertyMetadata* constructor, which will try to store an integer value for a dependency property of type *double*. That's a runtime error. Make the data type explicit:

```
public static readonly DependencyProperty MyDoubleProperty =
    DependencyProperty.Register("MyDouble",
        typeof(double),
        typeof(SomeClass),
        new PropertyMetadata(10.0, OnMyDoubleChanged));
```

You might have cause to create a read-only dependency property. (For example, the *ActualWidth* and *ActualHeight* properties defined by *FrameworkElement* have get accessors only.) At first, it seems easy:

```
public double MyDouble
{
    private set { SetValue(MyDoubleProperty, value); }
    get { return (double)GetValue(MyDoubleProperty); }
}
```

Now only the class itself can set the property.

But wait! As I mentioned earlier, the *SetValue* method is public, so any class can call *SetValue* to set the value of this property. To protect a read-only dependency property from unauthorized access you'll need to raise an exception if the property is being set from code external to the class. The easiest logic probably entails setting a private flag when you set the property from within the class and then checking for that private flag in the property-changed handler.

You can easily tell from the documentation if a particular property of an existing class is backed by a dependency property. Just look in the Fields section for a static field of type *DependencyProperty* with the same name as the property but with the word *Property* attached.

The existence of the static *DependencyProperty* field allows code or markup to refer to a particular property defined by a class independent of any instance of that class, even if an instance of that class has not yet been created. Some methods—for example, the *SetBinding* method defined by *FrameworkElement*—have arguments that allow you to refer to a particular property, and the dependency property is ideal for this.

Finally, don't feel obligated to make *every* property in your classes a dependency property. If a particular property will never be the target of a style, or a data binding, or an animation, there's no problem if you just make it a regular property.

For example, if you plan to use multiple *RadioButton* controls to let the user select an object of type *Color*, you could derive from *RadioButton* and define a property for associating a *Color* object with each *RadioButton*:

```
public class ColorRadioButton : RadioButton
{
    public Color ColorTag { set; get; }
}
```

You could then set that property in XAML and reference it later in code for easily determining what *Color* each *RadioButton* represents. You don't need a dependency property for a simple application like this.

Deriving from *UserControl*

As you've seen, it's possible to derive from a class that derives from *Control* to add some additional properties. It's also possible to derive directly from *Control* to create entirely new controls (or to derive from *ContentControl* if the control needs to have a *Content* property). However, deriving from *Control* or *ContentControl* in a proper and cordial manner involves creating a default template in XAML that describes the control's visual appearance, and allowing that template to be replaced to redefine the visuals of the control.

This is not inherently difficult, but often requires giving deep thought to how the control will be customized. You'll see some of the issues involved in Chapter 16.

If you're in the control-writing business, the custom controls that you develop and market should derive from *Control* or *ContentControl* or *ItemsControl* (Chapter 17). A replaceable template is an essential feature for commercial-grade controls.

But some custom controls don't require additional visual customization: For controls specific to a particular project, or used only by one programmer or a programming team within a company, or controls that have an inherent visual appearance, it's usually not necessary to allow the control's template to be replaced.

For such controls, deriving from *UserControl* is often an ideal solution. (The *User* in *UserControl* is you—the programmer.) Moreover, you already have experience deriving from *UserControl*! The *PhoneApplicationPage* class derives from *Page*, which derives from *UserControl*.

UserControl has a property named *Content* of type *UIElement*. When deriving from *UserControl* you generally define new properties in code (and often methods and events as well), but you define your visuals in XAML by assigning a visual tree to that *Content* property. This makes the *Content* property unusable for other purposes. If your *UserControl* derivative requires a *Content* property, you should define a new property named *Child* or something similar to serve the same purpose.

Making liberal use of *UserControl* is an ideal way to modularize the visuals of your program.

For example, the *ColorScroll* program in the previous chapter had a lot of repetition in the XAML file. The three rows contained a *Slider* and two *TextBlock* elements each. If you wanted to adapt the concept of *ColorScroll* to a reusable control, you might begin by deriving a class named *ColorColumn* from *UserControl*, and then putting three *ColorColumn* controls together in a *UserControl* derivative named *RgbColorScroller*.

ColorColumn and *RgbColorScroller* can both be found in a dynamic link library (DLL) project called Petzold.Phone.Silverlight. Creating a DLL in Visual Studio for your Windows Phone programs is easy: In the New Project dialog, select Silverlight for Windows Phone at the left and Windows Phone Class Library in the middle area. (To facilitate testing, you'll probably want a second application project in the same solution as the library; or you might want to develop custom classes in an application project and then move them to the library when you know they're working right.)

Within the Petzold.Phone.Silverlight project (or any other library project), you can add a new item by right-clicking the project name in the Solution Explorer and selecting Add and New Item.

To make a new *UserControl* in either an application project or a library project. From the Add New Item dialog box, select Windows Phone User Control and give it a name. You'll get two files: a XAML file and a code-behind file.

The XAML file is rather simpler than the one created for a *PhoneApplicationPage* class. The root element is *UserControl*. It contains an *x:Class* attribute indicating the derived class, and the only nested element is a *Grid* named *LayoutRoot*. You don't need to retain that *Grid* but it's usually convenient.

The root element contains attributes to set these properties:

```
FontFamily="{StaticResource PhoneFontFamilyNormal}"
FontSize="{StaticResource PhoneFontSizeNormal}"
Foreground="{StaticResource PhoneForegroundBrush}"
```

You'll almost certainly want to delete those attributes. These three properties are inherited through the visual tree, so the *UserControl* will normally get the settings of these properties from *MainPage*. By setting these properties here, you're disabling any markup (or code) that sets these properties on the control that you're creating. Keep these properties in the *UserControl* only if your control relies on them.

I also deleted the designer-related attributes, so here's the complete ColorColumn.xaml file. Notice I've also changed the *Background* property on the *Grid* from a *StaticResource* referencing *PhoneChromeBrush* to *Transparent*:

Silverlight Project: Petzold.Phone.Silverlight   File: ColorColumn.xaml

```
<UserControl
    x:Class="Petzold.Phone.Silverlight.ColorColumn"
    xmlns="http://schemas.microsoft.com/winfx/2006/xaml/presentation"
    xmlns:x="http://schemas.microsoft.com/winfx/2006/xaml">

    <Grid x:Name="LayoutRoot" Background="Transparent">
        <Grid.RowDefinitions>
            <RowDefinition Height="Auto" />
            <RowDefinition Height="*" />
            <RowDefinition Height="Auto" />
        </Grid.RowDefinitions>

        <TextBlock Name="colorLabel"
                Grid.Row="0"
                TextAlignment="Center" />

        <Slider Name="slider"
                Grid.Row="1"
                Orientation="Vertical"
                Minimum="0"
                Maximum="255"
                ValueChanged="OnSliderValueChanged" />

        <TextBlock Name="colorValue"
                Grid.Row="2"
                Text="00"
                TextAlignment="Center" />
    </Grid>
</UserControl>
```

The *Grid* has three rows with a *TextBlock* at the top with a name of *colorLabel*, a *Slider* with a range of 0 to 255, and another *TextBlock* with a name of *colorValue*. The *Slider* has an event handler set on its *OnSliderValueChanged* event.

In the ColorScroll program from the previous chapter, the *Slider* controls and *TextBlock* elements were all colored red, green, and blue through the *Foreground* property. Because the *Foreground* property is inherited through the visual tree, it should be sufficient to set it once on any instance of *ColumnColumn* and let it trickle down through the tree.

The text displayed by the *TextBlock* named *colorLabel* will indicate that color, but I decided I wanted to handle that text a little differently, with a property specifically for that purpose.

This means the *ColorColumn* class defines two properties—a *Label* property for the text above the *Slider* as well as the more expected *Value* property corresponding to the *Slider* position. Like the *Slider* itself, the *ColorColumn* class also defines an event named *ValueChanged* to indicate when the *Slider* value has changed.

Generally a *UserControl* derivative will define its own properties and events, and very often these properties and events will parallel properties and events of elements in its visual tree. It's typical for a class like *ColorColumn* to have a *Label* property corresponding to the *Text* property of a *TextBlock*, and a *Value* property corresponding to the *Value* property of the *Slider*, and a *ValueChanged* event corresponding to the *ValueChanged* event of the *Slider*.

Here's the portion of the *ColorColumn* code-behind file devoted to the *Label* property for the text above the *Slider*:

Silverlight Project: **Petzold.Phone.Silverlight**   File: **ColorColumn.xaml.cs** (excerpt)

```
public partial class ColorColumn : UserControl
{
    ...
    public static readonly DependencyProperty LabelProperty =
        DependencyProperty.Register("Label",
            typeof(string),
            typeof(ColorColumn),
            new PropertyMetadata(OnLabelChanged));
    ...
    public string Label
    {
        set { SetValue(LabelProperty, value); }
        get { return (string)GetValue(LabelProperty); }
    }
    ...
    static void OnLabelChanged(DependencyObject obj,
                              DependencyPropertyChangedEventArgs args)
    {
        (obj as ColorColumn).colorLabel.Text = args.NewValue as string;
    }
}
```

The property-changed handler for *Label* simply sets the value to the *Text* property of the *TextBlock* in the visual tree named *colorLabel*. This is one way that a property defined on the custom control is transferred to a property on an element in the visual tree. I'll demonstrate a simpler approach using data bindings in the next chapter.

The *Value* property in *ColorColumn* is a little more complex because it needs to fire a *ValueChanged* event. This *Value* property is eventually used in the calculation of a *Color*, so I thought it should be of type *byte* rather than *double*. Here's the code in the class pertaining to the *Value* property and *ValueChanged* event:

Silverlight Project: Petzold.Phone.Silverlight   File: ColorColumn.xaml.cs (excerpt)

```
public partial class ColorColumn : UserControl
{
    public static readonly DependencyProperty ValueProperty =
        DependencyProperty.Register("Value",
            typeof(byte),
            typeof(ColorColumn),
            new PropertyMetadata((byte)0, OnValueChanged));
    ...
    public event RoutedPropertyChangedEventHandler<byte> ValueChanged;
    ...
    public byte Value
    {
        set { SetValue(ValueProperty, value); }
        get { return (byte)GetValue(ValueProperty); }
    }
    ...
    static void OnValueChanged(DependencyObject obj,
                              DependencyPropertyChangedEventArgs args)
    {
        (obj as ColorColumn).OnValueChanged((byte)args.OldValue, (byte)args.NewValue);
    }

    protected virtual void OnValueChanged(byte oldValue, byte newValue)
    {
        slider.Value = newValue;
        colorValue.Text = newValue.ToString("X2");

        if (ValueChanged != null)
            ValueChanged(this,
                new RoutedPropertyChangedEventArgs<byte>(oldValue, newValue));
    }
    ...
}
```

To define the *ValueChanged* event I chose to use the generic *RoutedPropertyChangedEventHandler* and the corresponding *RoutedPropertyChangedEventArgs*.) This is a good choice for signaling when dependency properties change because it accommodates old and new values.

The static *OnValueChanged* method calls a protected virtual instance method also named *OnValueChanged* but with arguments indicating the old and new property values. (My design was inspired by the *OnValueChanged* method in *RangeBase*.) This instance method sets the *Slider* and the *TextBlock* indicating the current value and fires the *ValueChanged* event.

The only code of *ColorColumn* not yet discussed encompass the constructor and the handler for the *ValueChanged* event of the *Slider*. This event handler simply casts the *Value* property of the *Slider* to a *byte* and sets it to the *Value* property of the *ColorColumn* class.

Silverlight Project: Petzold.Phone.Silverlight   File: ColorColumn.xaml.cs (excerpt)

```
public partial class ColorColumn : UserControl
{
    ...
    public ColorColumn()
    {
        InitializeComponent();
    }
    ...
    void OnSliderValueChanged(object sender,
                        RoutedPropertyChangedEventArgs<double> args)
    {
        Value = (byte)args.NewValue;
    }
}
```

And now you may detect an infinite loop: The user manipulates the *Slider*. The *Slider* fires a *ValueChanged* event. The *OnSliderValueChanged* method sets the *Value* property of *ColorColumn*. The static property-changed handler *OnValueChanged* is called. The static method calls the instance *OnValueChanged* method, which sets the *Value* property of the *Slider*, which fires another *ValueChanged* event, and so forth.

In reality, this doesn't happen because at some point one of these *Value* properties—either the *Value* property of the *Slider* or the *Value* property of *ColorColumn*—will be set to its existing value, and no property-changed event will be fired. The infinite loop grinds to a halt.

The *RgbColorScoller* class also derives from *UserControl* and consists of three *ColorColumn* controls. Here's the complete XAML file:

Silverlight Project: Petzold.Phone.Silverlight   File: RgbColorScroller.xaml

```
<UserControl
    x:Class="Petzold.Phone.Silverlight.RgbColorScroller"
    xmlns="http://schemas.microsoft.com/winfx/2006/xaml/presentation"
    xmlns:x="http://schemas.microsoft.com/winfx/2006/xaml"
    xmlns:petzold="clr-namespace:Petzold.Phone.Silverlight">

    <Grid x:Name="LayoutRoot" Background="Transparent">
        <Grid.ColumnDefinitions>
            <ColumnDefinition Width="*" />
            <ColumnDefinition Width="*" />
            <ColumnDefinition Width="*" />
        </Grid.ColumnDefinitions>
```

```
          <petzold:ColorColumn x:Name="redColumn"
                               Grid.Column="0"
                               Foreground="Red"
                               Label="Red"
                               ValueChanged="OnColorColumnValueChanged" />

          <petzold:ColorColumn x:Name="greenColumn"
                               Grid.Column="1"
                               Foreground="Green"
                               Label="Green"
                               ValueChanged="OnColorColumnValueChanged" />

          <petzold:ColorColumn x:Name="blueColumn"
                               Grid.Column="2"
                               Foreground="Blue"
                               Label="Blue"
                               ValueChanged="OnColorColumnValueChanged" />
      </Grid>
  </UserControl>
```

Each of the three *ColorColumn* controls has its *Foreground* property set to one of the three colors, and its *Label* property to the same value but a *string* rather than a *Color*.

Notice each *ColorColumn* is identified with *x:Name* rather than *Name*. I normally use *Name* but *Name* is not allowed for referencing a class from the same assembly, and both *ColorColumn* and *RgbColorScroller* are in the Petzold.Phone.Silverlight assembly.

The *RgbColorScroller* class defines one property named *Color* (of type *Color*, of course) and an event named *ColorChanged*. Here's the whole class in one shot:

Silverlight Project: Petzold.Phone.Silverlight   File: RgbColorScroller.xaml.cs (excerpt)

```
public partial class RgbColorScroller : UserControl
{
    public static readonly DependencyProperty ColorProperty =
        DependencyProperty.Register("Color",
            typeof(Color),
            typeof(RgbColorScroller),
            new PropertyMetadata(Colors.Gray, OnColorChanged));

    public event RoutedPropertyChangedEventHandler<Color> ColorChanged;

    public RgbColorScroller()
    {
        InitializeComponent();
    }
```

```
public Color Color
{
    set { SetValue(ColorProperty, value); }
    get { return (Color)GetValue(ColorProperty); }
}

void OnColorColumnValueChanged(object sender,
                RoutedPropertyChangedEventArgs<byte> args)
{
    Color = Color.FromArgb(255, redColumn.Value,
                                greenColumn.Value,
                                blueColumn.Value);
}

static void OnColorChanged(DependencyObject obj,
                    DependencyPropertyChangedEventArgs args)
{
    (obj as RgbColorScroller).OnColorChanged((Color)args.OldValue,
                                (Color)args.NewValue);
}

protected virtual void OnColorChanged(Color oldValue, Color newValue)
{
    redColumn.Value = newValue.R;
    greenColumn.Value = newValue.G;
    blueColumn.Value = newValue.B;

    if (ColorChanged != null)
        ColorChanged(this,
            new RoutedPropertyChangedEventArgs<Color>(oldValue, newValue));
}
}
```

The two *OnColorChanged* methods are called when the *Color* property changes. These are responsible for breaking down the *Color* property into bytes, setting the *Value* properties of the individual *ColorColumn* objects, and firing the *ColorChanged* event.

The *OnColorColumnValueChanged* handler is called when any of the three *ColorColumn* controls fires a *ValueChanged* event. This handler is responsible for assembling the individual bytes from the three *ColorColumn* controls into a single *Color*.

Again, it looks like an infinite loop might result but in reality it doesn't happen.

To use this *RgbColorScroller* class from the Petzold.Phone.Silverlight library, create a new application project. Let's call it SelectTwoColors. Right-click the References header under the project name in the Solution Explorer, and select Add Reference. In the Add Reference dialog box, select the Browse tag. Navigate to the DLL file (in this case Petzold.Phone.Silverlight.dll) and select it.

In the MainPage.xaml file you'll need a XML namespace declaration for the library. Because the library is a separate assembly, this namespace declaration requires an assembly section to refer to the DLL file:

```
xmlns:petzold="clr-namespace:Petzold.Phone.Silverlight;assembly=Petzold.Phone.Silverlight"
```

The SelectTwoColors XAML file has two *RgbColorScroller* controls, each inside a *Border* with a *Rectangle* element between them. Each *RgbColorScroll* has its *ColorChanged* event attached to the same handler:

Silverlight Project: SelectTwoColors   File: MainPage.xaml (excerpt)

```
<Grid x:Name="ContentPanel" Grid.Row="1" Margin="12,0,12,0">
    <Grid.ColumnDefinitions>
        <ColumnDefinition Width="*" />
        <ColumnDefinition Width="*" />
        <ColumnDefinition Width="*" />
    </Grid.ColumnDefinitions>

    <Border Grid.Column="0"
            BorderBrush="{StaticResource PhoneForegroundBrush}"
            BorderThickness="2"
            Margin="12"
            Padding="12">

        <petzold:RgbColorScroller
                Name="colorScroller1"
                ColorChanged="OnColorScrollerColorChanged" />
    </Border>

    <Rectangle Name="rectangle"
            Grid.Column="1"
            StrokeThickness="24"
            Margin="12" />

    <Border Grid.Column="2"
            BorderBrush="{StaticResource PhoneForegroundBrush}"
            BorderThickness="2"
            Margin="12"
            Padding="12">

        <petzold:RgbColorScroller
                Name="colorScroller2"
                ColorChanged="OnColorScrollerColorChanged" />

    </Border>
</Grid>
```

The constructor of the code-behind file initializes the two *RgbColorScroller* controls with two colors, which causes the first *ColorChanged* events to fire, which are then processed by the event handler to set colors on the *Rectangle*:

Silverlight Project: **SelectTwoColors**   File: **MainPage.xaml.cs (excerpt)**

```
public partial class MainPage : PhoneApplicationPage
{
    public MainPage()
    {
        InitializeComponent();

        colorScroller1.Color = Color.FromArgb(0xFF, 0xC0, 0x80, 0x40);
        colorScroller2.Color = Color.FromArgb(0xFF, 0x40, 0x80, 0xC0);
    }

    void OnColorScrollerColorChanged(object sender,
                                RoutedPropertyChangedEventArgs<Color> args)
    {
        Brush brush = new SolidColorBrush(args.NewValue);

        if (sender == colorScroller1)
            rectangle.Stroke = brush;

        else if (sender == colorScroller2)
            rectangle.Fill = brush;
    }
}
```

And here it is in landscape mode:

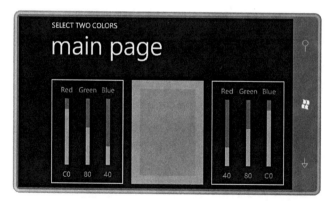

Notice that the labels have picked up the *Foreground* property set to each *ColorColumn* control through property inheritance, but not the *Slider*. I suspect the *Foreground* property is set in the theme style for the *Slider* and that's blocking property inheritance. If getting that color was really important, I'd probably define a new *Color* property on *ColorColumn* and use that to programmatically set the *Foreground* property on the *Slider*.

I deliberately designed the layout of SelectTwoColors so it wouldn't work quite well in portrait mode:

As you can see, the text runs together. But all is not lost. All that's necessary is to set a smaller *FontSize* property directly on the two *RgbColorScroller* controls:

```
FontSize="12"
```

That one property setting affects all six *TextBlock* elements in each control. The text becomes very small, of course, but it's no longer overlapping:

A New Type of Toggle

You've probably noticed a new style of toggle button in some Windows Phone 7 screens. Here they are on the page that lets you set date and time, blown up to almost double size:

If you experiment with these controls a bit, you'll find that you can toggle the switch just by tapping it, but you can also move the larger block back and forth with your finger, although it will tend to snap into position either at the left or right.

I'm not going to try to duplicate that more complex movement. My version will respond only to taps. For that reason I call it *TapSlideToggle*. The button is a *UserControl* derivative in the *Petzold.Phone.Silverlight* library. (I should note that something similar could be implemented entirely in a template applied to the existing *ToggleButton*, and the Silverlight for Windows Phone Toolkit implements this control under the name *ToggleSwitchButton*.) Here's the complete XAML file of my version:

Silverlight Project: Petzold.Phone.Silverlight   File: TapSlideToggle.xaml

```
<UserControl x:Class="Petzold.Phone.Silverlight.TapSlideToggle"
             xmlns="http://schemas.microsoft.com/winfx/2006/xaml/presentation"
             xmlns:x="http://schemas.microsoft.com/winfx/2006/xaml"
             xmlns:d="http://schemas.microsoft.com/expression/blend/2008"
             xmlns:mc="http://schemas.openxmlformats.org/markup-compatibility/2006"
             mc:Ignorable="d"
             d:DesignHeight="36" d:DesignWidth="96">

    <Grid x:Name="LayoutRoot"
          Background="Transparent"
          Width="96" Height="36">

        <Border BorderBrush="{StaticResource PhoneForegroundBrush}"
                BorderThickness="2"
                Margin="4 2"
                Padding="4">
            <Rectangle Name="fillRectangle"
```

```
                                Fill="{StaticResource PhoneAccentBrush}"
                                Visibility="Collapsed" />
        </Border>

        <Border Name="slideBorder"
                BorderBrush="{StaticResource PhoneBackgroundBrush}"
                BorderThickness="4 0"
                HorizontalAlignment="Left">
            <Rectangle Stroke="{StaticResource PhoneForegroundBrush}"
                       Fill="White"
                       StrokeThickness="2"
                       Width="20" />
        </Border>
    </Grid>
</UserControl>
```

The button is given a specific size in the *Grid*. If you want a control to have a specific size, here's the place to do it rather than with the *Height* and *Width* properties of the control itself. I also changed the designer-related attributes and left them in so I could get a little sense of what the controls looks like in the design view.

I must confess that I'm not entirely happy with the approach I took here: To keep it simple, I restricted myself to two *Border* elements each containing a *Rectangle*, but to mimic the gap between the larger sliding block and the wide background, I gave the second *Border* a *BorderBrush* colored with the background color. The button will not look right if it's on a surface that is not colored with the *PhoneBackgroundBrush* resource.

To somewhat mimic the normal *ToggleButton* (but without the three-state option) the code-behind file defines an *IsChecked* dependency property of type *bool* and two events named *Checked* and *Unchecked*. One or the other of these events is fired when the *IsChecked* property changes value:

Silverlight Project: Petzold.Phone.Silverlight   File: TapSlideToggle.xaml.cs (excerpt)

```
public partial class TapSlideToggle : UserControl
{
    public static readonly DependencyProperty IsCheckedProperty =
        DependencyProperty.Register("IsChecked",
            typeof(bool),
            typeof(TapSlideToggle),
            new PropertyMetadata(false, OnIsCheckedChanged));

    public event RoutedEventHandler Checked;
    public event RoutedEventHandler Unchecked;
```

```
public TapSlideToggle()
{
    InitializeComponent();
}

public bool IsChecked
{
    set { SetValue(IsCheckedProperty, value); }
    get { return (bool)GetValue(IsCheckedProperty); }
}

...

static void OnIsCheckedChanged(DependencyObject obj,
                               DependencyPropertyChangedEventArgs args)
{
    (obj as TapSlideToggle).OnIsCheckedChanged(args);
}

void OnIsCheckedChanged(DependencyPropertyChangedEventArgs args)
{
    fillRectangle.Visibility = IsChecked ? Visibility.Visible :
                                           Visibility.Collapsed;

    slideBorder.HorizontalAlignment = IsChecked ? HorizontalAlignment.Right :
                                                  HorizontalAlignment.Left;

    if (IsChecked && Checked != null)
        Checked(this, new RoutedEventArgs());

    if (!IsChecked && Unchecked != null)
        Unchecked(this, new RoutedEventArgs());
}
}
```

The static property-changed handler calls an instance handler of the same name, which alters the visuals in the XAML just a little bit and then fires one of the two events. The only methods missing from the code above are the overrides of two *Manipulation* events. Here they are:

Silverlight Project: Petzold.Phone.Silverlight   File: TapSlideToggle.xaml.cs (excerpt)

```
protected override void OnManipulationStarted(ManipulationStartedEventArgs args)
{
    args.Handled = true;
    base.OnManipulationStarted(args);
}

protected override void OnManipulationCompleted(ManipulationCompletedEventArgs args)
{
    Point pt = args.ManipulationOrigin;
```

```
    if (pt.X > 0 && pt.X < this.ActualWidth &&
        pt.Y > 0 && pt.Y < this.ActualHeight)
        IsChecked ^= true;

    args.Handled = true;
    base.OnManipulationCompleted(args);
}
```

I decided to toggle the button only if the user presses the button and then releases the finger while it's still over the button, which is the common approach. The *OnManipulationStarted* override sets *Handled* to *true* to prevent the event from travelling further up the visual tree and in effect, to signal that the button is commandeering this particular manipulation. The *OnManipulationCompleted* override then checks if the *ManipulationOrigin* property is within the bounds of the control. If so, *IsChecked* is toggled:

```
IsChecked ^= true;
```

The TapSlideToggleDemo program tests it out. The content area defines two instances of *TapSlideToggle* and two *TextBlock* element to display their current state:

Silverlight Project: TapSlideToggleDemo   File: MainPage.xaml (excerpt)

```
<Grid x:Name="ContentPanel" Grid.Row="1" Margin="12,0,12,0">
    <Grid.RowDefinitions>
        <RowDefinition Height="Auto" />
        <RowDefinition Height="Auto" />
    </Grid.RowDefinitions>

    <Grid.ColumnDefinitions>
        <ColumnDefinition Width="*" />
        <ColumnDefinition Width="*" />
    </Grid.ColumnDefinitions>

    <TextBlock Name="option1TextBlock"
               Grid.Row="0" Grid.Column="0"
               Text="off"
               Margin="48"
               VerticalAlignment="Center" />

    <petzold:TapSlideToggle Name="slideToggle1"
                            Grid.Row="0" Grid.Column="1"
                            Margin="48"
                            HorizontalAlignment="Right"
                            Checked="OnSlideToggle1Checked"
                            Unchecked="OnSlideToggle1Checked" />

    <TextBlock Name="option2TextBlock"
               Grid.Row="1" Grid.Column="0"
```

```
                    Text="off"
                    Margin="48"
                    VerticalAlignment="Center" />

    <petzold:TapSlideToggle Name="slideToggle2"
                            Grid.Row="1" Grid.Column="1"
                            Margin="48"
                            HorizontalAlignment="Right"
                            Checked="OnSlideToggle2Checked"
                            Unchecked="OnSlideToggle2Checked" />
</Grid>
```

Each of the two *TapSlideToggle* instances has both its *Checked* and *Unchecked* events set to the same handler, but different handlers are used for the two instances. This allows each handler to determine the state of the button by obtaining the *IsChecked* property and accessing the corresponding *TextBlock*:

Silverlight Project: TapSlideToggleDemo   File: MainPage.xaml.cs (excerpt)

```
public partial class MainPage : PhoneApplicationPage
{
    public MainPage()
    {
        InitializeComponent();
        slideToggle2.IsChecked = true;
    }

    void OnSlideToggle1Checked(object sender, RoutedEventArgs args)
    {
        TapSlideToggle toggle = sender as TapSlideToggle;
        option1TextBlock.Text = toggle.IsChecked ? "on" : "off";
    }

    void OnSlideToggle2Checked(object sender, RoutedEventArgs args)
    {
        TapSlideToggle toggle = sender as TapSlideToggle;
        option2TextBlock.Text = toggle.IsChecked ? "on" : "off";
    }
}
```

And here's the result:

This button does not implement a unique visual appearance if the button is disabled. When *IsEnabled* is set to *false*, a control no longer gets user input automatically, but visually conveying this state is the responsibility of the control itself. Commonly, a semi-transparent black *Rectangle* overlays the entire control with a *Visibility* property set to *Collapsed*. When *IsEnabled* is true, the *Visibility* property of this *Rectangle* is set to *Visible*, in effect, "graying out" the visuals of the control.

Panels with Properties

I demonstrated how to write a custom panel in Chapter 9 but the panels were rather wimpy because they had no properties. Most panels have custom properties and some also define attached properties. Let's see how it works.

The Windows Presentation Foundation has a panel I often find useful called *UniformGrid*. As the name suggests, the *UniformGrid* divides its area into cells, each of which has the same dimensions.

By default, *UniformGrid* automatically determines a number of rows and columns by taking the ceiling of the square root of the number of children. For example, if there are 20 children, *UniformGrid* calculates 5 rows and columns (even though it might make more sense to have 5 rows and 4 columns, or 4 rows and 5 columns). You can override this calculation by explicitly setting the *Rows* or *Columns* property of *UniformGrid* to a non-zero number.

Almost always, I find myself setting either *Rows* or *Columns* to 1, in effect making a single column or row of equally sized cells. This is not like a *StackPanel* that continues off the screen if it has too many children, but more like a single-column or single-row *Grid* where every *RowDefinition* or *ColumnDefinition* has a *GridLength* set to *Star*, and hence allocates the same space.

My version of *UniformGrid* is called *UniformStack*. It doesn't have a *Rows* or *Columns* property but it does have an *Orientation* property—the same property defined by *StackPanel*—to indicate whether the children of the panel will be arranged vertically or horizontally.

Here's the portion of the *UniformStack* class that defines the single dependency property and the property-changed handler:

Silverlight Project: Petzold.Phone.Silverlight   File: UniformStack.cs (excerpt)

```
public class UniformStack : Panel
{
    public static readonly DependencyProperty OrientationProperty =
        DependencyProperty.Register("Orientation",
            typeof(Orientation),
            typeof(UniformStack),
            new PropertyMetadata(Orientation.Vertical, OnOrientationChanged));

    public Orientation Orientation
    {
        set { SetValue(OrientationProperty, value); }
        get { return (Orientation)GetValue(OrientationProperty); }
    }

    static void OnOrientationChanged(DependencyObject obj,
                                     DependencyPropertyChangedEventArgs args)
    {
        (obj as UniformStack).InvalidateMeasure();
    }

    . . .
}
```

The definitions of the dependency property and CLR property are straightforward. The property-changed handler casts the first argument to the class type, as usual, and then simply calls *InvalidateMeasure*. This is a method defined by *UIElement*, and it's basically telling the layout system: "Whatever you think you know about how big I am, forget it. I'm a whole different size." This call initiates the measure pass of layout from the root of the visual tree because the size of thid panel could affect parent classes. The measure pass is followed automatically by an arrange pass. (Layout passes are also initiated whenever the size of the panel changes, or when elements are added to or removed from the *Children* collection, or when an existing child changes size.)

There is also an *InvalidateArrange* method, which initiates just the second half of the layout process, but this is much rarer. Perhaps if you have a panel that dynamically moves its elements around without itself changing size you would have occasion to call *InvalidateArrange*.

The *InvalidateMeasure* method eventually causes a call to be made to *MeasureOverride*, and let's think for a moment what needs to be done.

Consider a *UniformStack* with a horizontal orientation. Suppose the panel has five children, and the *availableSize* offered to the panel has a *Width* of 400 and a *Height* of 200. Each child should be offered a size with a *Width* of 80 (1/5th the total available width) and a *Height* of 200. That's the panel's paradigm.

But what if the *Width* property of *availableSize* is infinite? What should happen in that case?

Well, it's not entirely clear. Certainly the panel has no choice but to offer to each child a *Width* of infinity. After that, one reasonable solution is to return a size from *MeasureOverride* with a *Width* that is five times the *Width* of the widest child.

That's what I do here:

Silverlight Project: Petzold.Phone.Silverlight   File: UniformStack.cs (excerpt)

```
protected override Size MeasureOverride(Size availableSize)
{
    if (Children.Count == 0)
        return new Size();

    Size availableChildSize = new Size();
    Size maxChildSize = new Size();
    Size compositeSize = new Size();

    // Calculate an available size for each child
    if (Orientation == Orientation.Horizontal)
        availableChildSize = new Size(availableSize.Width / Children.Count,
                                availableSize.Height);
    else
        availableChildSize = new Size(availableSize.Width,
                                availableSize.Height / Children.Count);

    // Enumerate the children, and find the widest width and the highest height
    foreach (UIElement child in Children)
    {
        child.Measure(availableChildSize);
        maxChildSize.Width = Math.Max(maxChildSize.Width, child.DesiredSize.Width);
        maxChildSize.Height = Math.Max(maxChildSize.Height, child.DesiredSize.Height);
    }
```

```
      // Now determine a composite size that depends on infinite available width or
    height
      if (Orientation == Orientation.Horizontal)
      {
          if (Double.IsPositiveInfinity(availableSize.Width))
              compositeSize = new Size(maxChildSize.Width * Children.Count,
                                       maxChildSize.Height);
          else
              compositeSize = new Size(availableSize.Width, maxChildSize.Height);
      }
      else
      {
          if (Double.IsPositiveInfinity(availableSize.Height))
              compositeSize = new Size(maxChildSize.Width,
                                       maxChildSize.Height * Children.Count);
          else
              compositeSize = new Size(maxChildSize.Width, availableSize.Height);
      }

      return compositeSize;
  }
```

The method begins by diving out if the panel has no children; this avoids division by zero later on.

An *availableChildSize* is calculated based on the *Orientation* property by ignoring the presence of infinity in the *availableSize* for the panel. (Infinity divided by the number of children will still be infinity, and that's what's required in that case.) The enumeration of the children calls *Measure* on each child with that *availableChildSize*. The logic involving the *DesiredSize* of the child also ignores infinite dimensions but instead accumulates a *maxChildSize*. This actually represents the width of the widest child and the height of the tallest child; it's possible that no single child has the same dimensions as *maxChildSize*.

The final calculation of *compositeSize* takes into account both *Orientation* and the possibility of an infinite dimension. Notice that *compositeSize* is sometimes based on one of the *availableSize* dimensions; this is normally not proper but the method does it only when it knows that dimension is not infinite.

The *ArrangeOverride* method calls *Arrange* on each child with the same size (called *finalChildSize* in the method) but with different *x* and *y* positions relative to the panel depending on orientation:

Silverlight Project: Petzold.Phone.Silverlight   File: UniformStack.cs (excerpt)

```
protected override Size ArrangeOverride(Size finalSize)
{
    if (Children.Count > 0)
```

```
    {
        Size finalChildSize = new Size();
        double x = 0;
        double y = 0;

        if (Orientation == Orientation.Horizontal)
            finalChildSize = new Size(finalSize.Width / Children.Count,
                                      finalSize.Height);
        else
            finalChildSize = new Size(finalSize.Width,
                                      finalSize.Height / Children.Count);

        foreach (UIElement child in Children)
        {
            child.Arrange(new Rect(new Point(x, y), finalChildSize));

            if (Orientation == Orientation.Horizontal)
                x += finalChildSize.Width;
            else
                y += finalChildSize.Height;
        }
    }

    return base.ArrangeOverride(finalSize);
}
```

Let's use the *UniformStack* to make a bar chart!

The QuickBarChart program actually uses three *UniformStack* panels:

Silverlight Project: QuickBarChart   File: MainPage.xaml (excerpt)

```
<Grid x:Name="ContentPanel" Grid.Row="1" Margin="12,0,12,0">
    <petzold:UniformStack Orientation="Vertical">

        <petzold:UniformStack x:Name="barChartPanel"
                              Orientation="Horizontal" />

        <petzold:UniformStack Orientation="Horizontal">

            <Button Content="Add 10 Items"
                    HorizontalAlignment="Center"
                    VerticalAlignment="Center"
                    Click="OnButtonClick" />

            <TextBlock Name="txtblk"
                       Text="0"
                       HorizontalAlignment="Center"
                       VerticalAlignment="Center" />
        </petzold:UniformStack>
    </petzold:UniformStack>
</Grid>
```

The first *UniformStack* with a *Vertical* orientation simply divides the content area into two equal areas. (See how much easier it is to use than a regular *Grid*?) The top half contains another *UniformStack* with nothing in it (yet). The bottom one contains a *UniformStack* with a *Horizontal* orientation for a *Button* and a *TextBlock*.

Clicking the *Button* causes the code-behind file to add 10 more *Rectangle* elements to the *UniformStack* named *barChartPanel*:

Silverlight Project: QuickBarChart   File: MainPage.xaml.cs (excerpt)

```
public partial class MainPage : PhoneApplicationPage
{
    Random rand = new Random();

    public MainPage()
    {
        InitializeComponent();
    }

    void OnButtonClick(object sender, RoutedEventArgs args)
    {
        for (int i = 0; i < 10; i++)
        {
            Rectangle rect = new Rectangle();
            rect.Fill = this.Resources["PhoneAccentBrush"] as Brush;
            rect.VerticalAlignment = VerticalAlignment.Bottom;
            rect.Height = barChartPanel.ActualHeight * rand.NextDouble();
            rect.Margin = new Thickness(0, 0, 0.5, 0);

            barChartPanel.Children.Add(rect);
        }

        txtblk.Text = barChartPanel.Children.Count.ToString();
    }
}
```

Notice that each *Rectangle* has a little half-pixel *Margin* on the right so there's at least some spacing between the bars. Still, I think you'll be surprised how many you can put in there before the display logic gives up:

Attached Properties

Attached properties are at first very mysterious. As you know from Chapter 9, here's how you might see them in XAML:

```
<Canvas>
    . . .
    <Ellipse Style="{StaticResource ellipseStyle}"
             Canvas.Left="116" Canvas.Top="92" />
    . . .
</Canvas>
```

That's straight out of the EllipseChain program.

Canvas.Left and *Canvas.Top* are attached properties. They are properties defined by *Canvas* that you set on children of the *Canvas*.

As I discussed in Chapter 9, there is actually nothing in *Canvas* named *Left* or *Top*. When setting these attached properties in code, you use two static methods defined by the *Canvas* class:

```
Canvas.SetLeft(ellipse, 116);
Canvas.SetTop(ellipse, 92);
```

Or you can use the *SetValue* method defined by *DependencyObject* and inherited by the *Ellipse* class to reference the static dependency properties defined by *Canvas*:

```
ellipse.SetValue(Canvas.LeftProperty, 116.0);
ellipse.SetValue(Canvas.TopProperty, 92.0);
```

This is the same *SetValue* methods that a class calls in a CLR property to set a dependency property.

You now know almost everything you need to define your own attached properties. The project named CanvasCloneDemo contains a class named *CanvasClone*. The class defines two *DependencyProperty* fields named *LeftProperty* and *TopProperty*:

Project: CanvasCloneDemo   File: CanvasClone.cs (excerpt)

```
public class CanvasClone : Panel
{
    public static readonly DependencyProperty LeftProperty =
        DependencyProperty.RegisterAttached("Left",
            typeof(double),
            typeof(CanvasClone),
            new PropertyMetadata(0.0, OnLeftOrTopPropertyChanged));

    public static readonly DependencyProperty TopProperty =
        DependencyProperty.RegisterAttached("Top",
            typeof(double),
            typeof(CanvasClone),
            new PropertyMetadata(0.0, OnLeftOrTopPropertyChanged));
    . . .
}
```

But notice the difference: Previously in this chapter, *DependencyProperty* objects were created with the static *DependencyProperty.Register* method. The *DependencyObject* fields in *CanvasClone* are created with the only other option, *DependencyProperty.RegisterAttached*. That makes them attached properties and allows them to be set on classes that did not define them.

Notice that the first argument to the *PropertyMetadata* constructor is explicitly a *double* so there won't be a runtime error because the C# compiler assumes the value is an *int*.

After defining the *DependencyProperty* fields, you need static methods to access the attached properties. These method names begin with *Set* and *Get* followed by the attached property names, in this case, *Left* and *Top*,

Project: CanvasCloneDemo   File: CanvasClone.cs (excerpt)

```
public static void SetLeft(DependencyObject obj, double value)
{
    obj.SetValue(LeftProperty, value);
}

public static double GetLeft(DependencyObject obj)
{
    return (double)obj.GetValue(LeftProperty);
}

public static void SetTop(DependencyObject obj, double value)
{
    obj.SetValue(TopProperty, value);
}

public static double GetTop(DependencyObject obj)
{
    return (double)obj.GetValue(TopProperty);
}
```

These methods get called either explicitly from code or implicitly from the XAML parser. The first argument will be the object on which the attached property is being set—in other words, the first argument will probably be a child of *CanvasClone*. The body of the method uses that argument to call *SetValue* and *GetValue* on the child. These are the same methods defined by *DependencyObject* to set and get dependency properties.

When these properties change, there will be a call to the property-changed handler defined in the *PropertyMetadata* constructor. The signature of this method is the same as a normal property-changed handler for regular dependency properties:

```
static void OnLeftOrTopPropertyChanged(DependencyObject obj,
                                       DependencyPropertyChangedEventArgs args)
{
    ...
}
```

Once again, the method is static. However, the first argument is not an object of type *CanvasClone*. It is a *child* of the *CanvasClone*. Or rather, it is *probably* a child of the *CanvasClone*. It's possible to call *CanvasClone.SetLeft* for an element that isn't actually a child of panel, and it's even possible for *CanvasClone.SetLeft* and the *OnLeftOrTopPropertyChanged* method to be called without any instance of *CanvasClone* in existence!

For this reason, the body of the method needs to use a little bit of caution. It calls the handy static *VisualTreeHelper.GetParent* method to obtain the parent of the *DependencyObject* argument and cast it to a *CanvasClone*:

Project: CanvasCloneDemo   File: **CanvasClone.cs** (excerpt)

```
static void OnLeftOrTopPropertyChanged(DependencyObject obj,
                                       DependencyPropertyChangedEventArgs args)
{
    CanvasClone parent = VisualTreeHelper.GetParent(obj) as CanvasClone;

    if (parent != null)
        parent.InvalidateArrange();
}
```

If the parent of the object that has called *CanvasClone.SetLeft* or *CanvasClone.SetTop* is truly a *CanvasClone*, then the method calls *InvalidateArrange* on the parent, which is the *CanvasClone*.

In the general case, when a panel handles a change in one of its attached properties, it will probably call *InvalidateMeasure* on the panel to initiate a complete recalculation of layout. However, as you can see in the following *MeasureOverride* method, the total size of *CanvasClone* doesn't change with the location of its children:

Project: CanvasCloneDemo   File: **CanvasClone.cs** (excerpt)

```
protected override Size MeasureOverride(Size availableSize)
{
    foreach (UIElement child in Children)
        child.Measure(new Size(Double.PositiveInfinity,
                               Double.PositiveInfinity));

    return Size.Empty;
}
```

It is part of the paradigm of a *Canvas* that it always returns zero from *MeasureOverride* regardless of its children, so *CanvasClone* does the same. *MeasureOverride* still needs to call *Measure* on all its children, or the children will have no size, but it calls *Measure* with infinite dimensions, forcing the child to assume as small a size as possible.

When the panel calls *InvalidateArrange* on itself, layout jumps right into the arrange pass with a call to *ArrangeOverride*: This method requires the panel to arrange the children on its surface. Essentially it gives each child a size and a location.

Project: CanvasCloneDemo   File: CanvasClone.cs (excerpt)

```
protected override Size ArrangeOverride(Size finalSize)
{
    foreach (UIElement child in Children)
        child.Arrange(new Rect(
            new Point(GetLeft(child), GetTop(child)), child.DesiredSize));

    return base.ArrangeOverride(finalSize);
}
```

ArrangeOverride calls its own static *GetLeft* and *GetTop* methods on each child to determine where the child should be positioned relative to itself. The size of each child is simply the *DesiredSize* the child originally calculated in the measure pass.

The XAML file in CanvasCloneDemo is the same as the one in the *EllipseChain* except that *Canvas* has been replaced with *CanvasClone*:

Project: CanvasCloneDemo   File: MainPage.xaml (excerpt)

```
<Grid x:Name="ContentPanel" Grid.Row="1">
    <local:CanvasClone>
        <local:CanvasClone.Resources>
            <Style x:Key="ellipseStyle"
                   TargetType="Ellipse">
                <Setter Property="Width" Value="100" />
                <Setter Property="Height" Value="100" />
                <Setter Property="Stroke" Value="{StaticResource PhoneAccentBrush}" />
                <Setter Property="StrokeThickness" Value="10" />
            </Style>
        </local:CanvasClone.Resources>

        <Ellipse Style="{StaticResource ellipseStyle}"
                 local:CanvasClone.Left="0" local:CanvasClone.Top="0" />

        <Ellipse Style="{StaticResource ellipseStyle}"
                 local:CanvasClone.Left="52" local:CanvasClone.Top="53" />
```

```
        <Ellipse Style="{StaticResource ellipseStyle}"
                local:CanvasClone.Left="116" local:CanvasClone.Top="92" />

        <Ellipse Style="{StaticResource ellipseStyle}"
                local:CanvasClone.Left="190" local:CanvasClone.Top="107" />

        <Ellipse Style="{StaticResource ellipseStyle}"
                local:CanvasClone.Left="263" local:CanvasClone.Top="92" />

        <Ellipse Style="{StaticResource ellipseStyle}"
                local:CanvasClone.Left="326" local:CanvasClone.Top="53" />

        <Ellipse Style="{StaticResource ellipseStyle}"
                local:CanvasClone.Left="380" local:CanvasClone.Top="0" />
    </local:CanvasClone>
</Grid>
```

With much elation, we discover that the display looks the same as the earlier program:

Chapter 12
Data Bindings

Suppose you want to let the user interact with a *Slider* but you also want a *TextBlock* to display its current value, such as in the ColorScroll program. No big deal. Just install a handler for the *ValueChanged* event of the *Slider*, and whenever the handler is called, get the *Value* property of the *Slider*, convert it to a string, and set the string to the *Text* property of the *TextBlock*.

Tasks such as this are so common that Silverlight provides a streamlined mechanism to perform them. This is called a *data binding*, or just *binding*. A data binding is a link between two properties of two objects, so that when one property changes, the other is updated with that change. The binding is optionally bidirectional, in which case a change in either property causes a change in the other.

Under the covers, a data binding works as you might expect: An event handler is installed so that one property is updated from another with a possible data conversion. Often you'll define this data binding entirely in XAML, which means you don't have to provide any code at all. Syntactically, it appears as if the transfer of data is occurring with no moving parts.

Data bindings are most easily demonstrated using two visual elements such as a *Slider* and a *TextBlock*, and that's where I'll begin. However, data bindings reveal much more power when providing links between visual elements and underlying data sources.

The goal in this chapter is to avoid explicit event handlers in the code-behind files, and only at the end of the chapter am I forced to use a couple. Of course, some *other* code is often required to support the data bindings in XAML, but much of this code can more properly be classified as business objects rather than user-interface elements.

Source and Target

In a typical data binding, a property of one object is updated automatically from a property of another object. The object providing the data—a *Slider*, for example—is considered to be the *source* of the data binding; the object receiving the data (such as the *TextBlock*) is the binding *target*.

The source of a data binding is usually given a name:

```
<Slider Name="slider" ... />
```

You can break out the target property as a property element and assign to it an object of type *Binding*:

```
<TextBlock ... >
    <TextBlock.Text>
        <Binding ElementName="slider" Path="Value" />
    </TextBlock.Text>
</TextBlock>
```

Use the *ElementName* property to indicate the name of the source element; use the *Path* property for the name of the source property, which is the *Value* property of the *Slider*. This type of binding is sometimes known as an *element-name* binding, because the binding source is a visual element that is referenced by name.

To make the syntax a little friendlier, Silverlight provides a markup extension for *Binding* where the whole thing is defined within a set of curly braces. (This is one of several markup extensions in Silverlight for Windows Phone. You encountered *StaticResource* in Chapter 7 and you'll see *TemplateBinding* in Chapter 16.) Here's the shorter syntax:

```
<TextBlock ... Text="{Binding ElementName=slider, Path=Value}" ... />
```

Notice that the *ElementName* and *Path* settings are separated by a comma, and that the *slider* and *Value* names are no longer in quotation marks. Quotation marks never appear within the curly braces of a markup extension.

The SliderBindings program includes this binding and lets you experiment with some variations. Everything is in the XAML file:

Silverlight Project: SliderBindings   **File: MainPage.xaml (excerpt)**

```
<Grid x:Name="ContentPanel" Grid.Row="1" Margin="12,0,12,0">
    <Grid.RowDefinitions>
        <RowDefinition Height="*" />
        <RowDefinition Height="*" />
        <RowDefinition Height="*" />
    </Grid.RowDefinitions>

    <Slider Name="slider"
            Value="90"
            Grid.Row="0"
            Maximum="180"
            Margin="24" />

    <TextBlock Name="txtblk"
               Text="{Binding ElementName=slider, Path=Value}"
               Grid.Row="1"
               FontSize="48"
               HorizontalAlignment="Center"
               VerticalAlignment="Center" />
```

```
    <Rectangle Grid.Row="2"
              Width="{Binding ElementName=slider, Path=Value}"
              RenderTransformOrigin="0.5 0.5"
              Fill="Blue">
        <Rectangle.RenderTransform>
            <RotateTransform x:Name="rotate"
                             Angle="90" />
        </Rectangle.RenderTransform>
    </Rectangle>
</Grid>
```

The page contains a *Slider* with a range from 0 to 180, a *TextBlock* with its *Text* property bound to the *Value* property of the *Slider*, and a *Rectangle* with its *Width* property bound to that same *Value* property. The *Rectangle* also has a *RotateTransform* that rotates the element by a constant 90°.

As you manipulate the *Slider*, the *TextBlock* displays the current value and the *Rectangle* height decreases and increases. (The *Binding* targets the *Width* property of the *Rectangle* but the *Rectangle* is rotated 90°.)

The order of the properties in the *Binding* markup extension doesn't matter. You can put the *Path* property first:

```
<TextBlock ... Text="{Binding Path=Value, ElementName=slider}"
```

In fact, if *Path* appears first, you can eliminate the "Path=" part and just use the property name:

```
<TextBlock ... Text="{Binding Value, ElementName=slider}"
```

Later in this chapter and in subsequent chapters, I will use this shortened syntax, but for element-name bindings I don't like it because it violates my sense of how the binding works. The *Binding* class *first* needs to find an element in the visual tree with the name of *slider*, and *then* it needs to use reflection to find the *Value* property in that element. I prefer the syntax where the order of the properties mimics the internal operation of the process:

```
<TextBlock ... Text="{Binding ElementName=slider, Path=Value}"
```

Why is this property of *Binding* called *Path* and not *Property*? After all, *Style* has a property named *Property*. Why not *Binding*?

The simple answer is that the *Path* can be a composite of multiple property names. For example, suppose the *Slider* did not have a name. You can indirectly refer to the *Slider* by knowing that it is the first item in the *Children* collection of the element named *ContentPanel*:

```
Text="{Binding ElementName=ContentPanel, Path=Children[0].Value}"
```

Or, going up higher in the visual tree,

```
Text="{Binding ElementName=LayoutRoot, Path=Children[1].Children[0].Value}"
```

The components of the path must be properties or indexers connected by periods.

Target and Mode

Bindings have a source and a target. The binding target is considered to be the property on which the binding is set. This property must always be backed by a dependency property. Always, always, always. This restriction is very obvious when you create a binding in code.

To try this out in *SliderBindings*, delete the binding on the *Text* property of the *TextBlock*. In the MainPage.xaml.cs file, you'll need a *using* directive for the *System.Windows.Data* namespace which contains the *Binding* class. In the constructor after the *InitializeComponent* call, create an object of type *Binding* and set its properties:

```
Binding binding = new Binding();
binding.ElementName = "slider";
binding.Path = new PropertyPath("Value");
```

The *ElementName* and *Path* properties reference the binding source. But look at the code to target the *Text* property of the *TextBlock*:

```
txtblk.SetBinding(TextBlock.TextProperty, binding);
```

The *SetBinding* method is defined by *FrameworkElement*, and the first argument is a dependency property. That's the target property. The target is the element on which you call *SetBinding*. You can alternatively set a binding on a target using the static *BindingOperations.SetBinding* method:

```
BindingOperations.SetBinding(txtblk, TextBlock.TextProperty, binding);
```

But you still need the dependency property. So this is yet another reason why the properties of visual objects should be depending properties. Not only can you style those properties, and target them with animations, but they need to be dependency properties to be targets of data bindings.

In terms of dependency property precedence, bindings are considered the same as local settings.

The *BindingOperations.SetBinding* method implies that you can set a binding on *any* dependency property. With Silverlight for Windows Phone, this is not the case. A binding target must always be a property of a *FrameworkElement*.

For example, you'll notice that the *Rectangle* element in MainPage.xaml has a *RotateTransform* set to its *RenderTransform* property. Try targeting the *Angle* property with the same binding that's set on the *Text* property of the *TextBlock* and the *Width* property of the *Rectangle*:

```
<RotateTransform x:Name="rotate"
                 Angle="{Binding ElementName=slider, Path=Value}" />
```

It looks fine, but it won't work. You'll get a *XamlParseException* at runtime. *Angle* is backed by a dependency property, all right, but *RotateTransform* does not derive from *FrameworkElement* so it can't be a binding target. (A *Binding* set on the *Angle* property of *RotateTransform* works under Silverlight 4, but Silverlight for Windows Phone is mostly Silverlight 3.)

If you're playing along, you'll want to remove that binding on the *Angle* property of *RotateTransform*, and any code that might have been added to MainPage.xaml.cs. The *Slider* has its *Value* property initialized to 90:

```
<Slider Name="slider"
        Value="90" ... />
```

The target of the binding is the *Text* property of the *TextBlock*:

```
<TextBlock Name="txtblk"
           Text="{Binding ElementName=slider, Path=Value}" ... />
```

Let's switch these around. Let's initialize the *Text* property of the *TextBlock* to 90:

```
<TextBlock Name="txtblk"
           Text="90" ... />
```

And let's make the binding target the *Value* property of the *Slider*:

```
<Slider Name="slider"
        Value="{Binding ElementName=txtblk, Path=Text}" ... />
```

At first this seems to work. The *Slider* thumb is initialized to its center to indicate the value of 90 it obtained from the *TextBlock*, and the *Rectangle* size is still bound to the *Slider*. However, when you manipulate the *Slider*, the *Rectangle* changes height but the *TextBlock* doesn't change at all. The *Binding* object on the *Slider* is looking for changes in the *Text* property of the *TextBlock*, and that's remaining fixed.

Now add a *Mode* setting to the binding on the *Slider* to indicate a two-way binding;

```
<Slider Name="slider"
        Value="{Binding ElementName=txtblk, Path=Text, Mode=TwoWay}" ... />
```

It works! The binding target is still considered to be the *Value* property of the *Slider*. Any changes to the *Text* property of the *TextBlock* will be reflected in changes to the *Value* property of the *Slider*, but any changes to the *Slider* will now also be reflected in the *TextBlock*.

You set the *Mode* property to a member of the *BindingMode* enumeration. The default *Mode* property is *BindingMode.OneWay*. Besides *BindingMode.TwoWay*, the only other option is *BindingMode.OneTime*, which only transfers data from the source to the target once.

Using this same technique, it's possible to establish a binding with the *Angle* property of the *RotateTransform*. Let's first restore the *TextBlock* to its original binding:

```
<TextBlock Name="txtblk"
           Text="{Binding ElementName=slider, Path=Value}" ... />
```

Now put a two-way binding on the *Slider* that references the *Angle* property of the *RotateTransform*:

```
<Slider Name="slider"
        Value="{Binding ElementName=rotate, Path=Angle, Mode=TwoWay}" ... />
```

And that works! The *Rectangle* element rotates as the *Slider* is manipulated:

Binding Converters

Perhaps as you were playing around with the SliderBindings program (or as you gaped in amazement at that screenshot), you were started to see that the *TextBlock* displays the *Slider* value sometimes as an integer, sometimes with one or two decimal points, but mostly in the full 15-digit glory of double-precision floating point.

Is there a way to fix that?

Yes there is. One of the properties of the *Binding* class is *Converter*, and the purpose of this property is to reference a class that converts data on its way from the source to the target and (if necessary) back the other way. Obviously, some implicit data conversion is being performed regardless as numbers are converted to strings and strings converted to numbers. But we can provide a little more explicit assistance to this conversion.

The *Converter* property of the *Binding* class is of type *IValueConverter*, an interface that requires only two methods named *Convert* and *ConvertBack*. *Convert* handles the data conversion from the source to the target, and *ConvertBack* handles the conversion going in the other direction for a *TwoWay* binding.

If you never intend to use the conversion class with two-way bindings, you can simply return *null* from *ConvertBack*.

To add a simple converter to SliderBindings, add a new class to the project and call it *TruncationConverter*. Actually the class is already in the project, and here it is:

Silverlight Project: SliderBindings   File: TruncationConverter.cs

```
using System;
using System.Globalization;
using System.Windows.Data;

namespace SliderBindings
{
    public class TruncationConverter : IValueConverter
    {
        public object Convert(object value, Type targetType,
                              object parameter, CultureInfo culture)
        {
            if (value is double)
                return Math.Round((double)value);

            return value;
        }

        public object ConvertBack(object value, Type targetType,
                                  object parameter, CultureInfo culture)
        {
            return value;
        }
    }
}
```

The value argument to the *Convert* method is the object passing from the source to the target. This method just checks if it's a *double*. If so, it explicitly casts it to a *double* for the *Math.Round* method.

You'll need to reference this class in MainPage.xaml, which means you'll need an XML namespace declaration:

```
xmlns:local="clr-namespace:SliderBindings"
```

The *TruncationConverter* class is then made a resource:

```
<phone:PhoneApplicationPage.Resources>
    <local:TruncationConverter x:Key="truncate" />
    . . .
</phone:PhoneApplicationPage.Resources>
```

You'll find these additions already in the MainPage.xaml file of the SliderBindings project.

The *Binding* markup extension then references this resource:

```
<TextBlock Name="txtblk"
           Text="{Binding ElementName=slider,
                          Path=Value,
                          Converter={StaticResource truncate}}" ... />
```

I've split the markup extension into three lines so the components are clearly visible. Notice that the *StaticResource* is another markup extension embedded in the first markup extension so the entire expression concludes with a pair of curly braces.

And now the number displayed by the *TextBlock* is truncated:

Be sure to reference the converter as a *StaticResource*. It is often very tempting to just set the *Converter* property of *Binding* to the key name:

```
<!-- This is wrong! -->
<TextBlock Name="txtblk"
           Text="{Binding ElementName=slider,
                          Path=Value,
                          Converter=truncate}" ... />
```

I still do that myself very often, and tracking down the problem can be difficult.

Defining the converter as a resource is certainly the most common approach to reference converters, but it's not the only way. If you use the element syntax of *Binding*, you can embed the *TrunctionConverter* class directly into the markup:

```
<TextBlock ... >
    <TextBlock.Text>
        <Binding ElementName="slider"
                 Path="Value">
            <Binding.Converter>
                <local:TruncationConverter />
            </Binding.Converter>
        </Binding>
    </TextBlock.Text>
</TextBlock>
```

However, if you have multiple references in the XAML file to this same converter, defining it as a resource is preferable because it allows the single instance to be shared.

TrucationConverter is actually a *terrible* data converter. Sure it does what it's supposed to do but it doesn't do it in a very versatile manner. If you're going to be calling *Math.Round* in a converter class, wouldn't it be better to have the option of rounding to a certain number of decimal places? Come to think of it, wouldn't it make more sense to allow all different kinds of formatting—not just of numbers but of other data types as well?

That magic is provided by a class in the Petzold.Phone.Silverlight library called *StringFormatConverter*:

Silverlight Project: Petzold.Phone.Silverlight   File: StringFormatConverter.cs

```
using System;
using System.Globalization;
using System.Windows.Data;

namespace Petzold.Phone.Silverlight
{
    public class StringFormatConverter : IValueConverter
    {
        public object Convert(object value, Type targetType,
```

```
                                          object parameter, CultureInfo culture)
        {
            if (targetType == typeof(string) && parameter is string)
                return String.Format(parameter as string, value);

            return value;
        }

        public object ConvertBack(object value, Type targetType,
                                  object parameter, CultureInfo culture)
        {
            return value;
        }
    }
}
```

Besides a *Converter* property, the *Binding* class also has a *ConverterParameter* property. The value of that property enters the *Convert* call as the *parameter* argument. The *Convert* method here assumes that *parameter* argument as a standard .NET formatting string that can be used in the *String.Format* call.

To use this converter in the SliderBindings program, you'll need a reference to the Petzold. Phone.Silverlight library. (That's already been done.) Already added to the file as well is an XML namespace declaration:

```
xmlns:petzold="clr-namespace:Petzold.Phone.Silverlight;assembly=Petzold.Phone.Silverlight"
```

Instantiate the *StringFormatConverter* in the *Resources* collection of the page:

```
<phone:PhoneApplicationPage.Resources>
    . . .
    <petzold:StringFormatConverter x:Key="stringFormat" />
</phone:PhoneApplicationPage.Resources>
```

You can now reference that converter in the *Binding* markup expression. Set the *ConverterParameter* to a .NET formatting string with one placeholder:

```
Text="{Binding ElementName=slider,
               Path=Value,
               Converter={StaticResource stringFormat},
               ConverterParameter=...}"
```

And as you start to type a .NET formatting string, you realize there's a problem. The standard .NET formatting strings involve the use of curly braces, and you're pretty sure that when the XAML parser attempts to decode a *Binding* markup expression, it's not going to appreciate unauthorized embedded curly braces.

The simple solution is to enclose the value of the *ConverterParameter* in single quotes:

```
Text="{Binding ElementName=slider,
               Path=Value,
               Converter={StaticResource stringFormat},
               ConverterParameter='{0:F2}'}"
```

The XAML parser and visual designer in Visual Studio doesn't care for this particular syntax either, but it's not a problem at runtime. If you want the designer to accept this, insert a space (or another character) after the first single quotation mark.

Because you know that the *ConverterParameter* becomes the first argument to a *String .Format* call, you can spruce it up a bit:

```
Text="{Binding ElementName=slider,
               Path=Value,
               Converter={StaticResource stringFormat},
               ConverterParameter='The slider is {0:F2}'}"
```

And here's the result:

Relative Source

Silverlight for Windows Phone supports three basic types of bindings categorized based on the source of the data. So far in this chapter you've seen *ElementName* bindings where the binding references a named element. Much of the remainder of this chapter uses the property *Source* rather than *ElementName* to reference a data source.

The third type of binding is called *RelativeSource*. In the Windows Presentation Foundation, *RelativeSource* is much more flexible than the version in Silverlight, so you may not be very impressed with this option. One of the purposes of *RelativeSource* is in connection with templates, as you'll see in Chapter 16. The only other option allows you to define a binding that references a property of the same element, known as *Self*. The following program shows the syntax:

Silverlight Project: BindToSelf   File: MainPage.xaml (excerpt)

```
<Grid x:Name="ContentPanel" Grid.Row="1" Margin="12,0,12,0">
    <StackPanel Orientation="Horizontal"
                HorizontalAlignment="Center"
                VerticalAlignment="Center">

        <TextBlock Text="{Binding RelativeSource={RelativeSource Self},
                                  Path=FontFamily}" />

        <TextBlock Text=" - " />

        <TextBlock Text="{Binding RelativeSource={RelativeSource Self},
                                  Path=FontSize}" />

        <TextBlock Text=" pixels" />
    </StackPanel>
</Grid>
```

The property *RelativeSource* is set to another markup extension containing *RelativeSource* and *Self*. The *Path* then refers to another property of the same element. Thus, the *TextBlock* elements display the *FontFamily* and *FontSize* of the *TextBlock*.

The "this" Source

Perhaps you have an application where you need to display many short text strings with borders around them. You decide you want to derive from *UserControl* to create a control named *BorderedText* that you can use like so:

```
<petzold:BorderedText Text="Ta Da!"
                      FontFamily="Times New Roman"
                      FontSize="96"
                      FontStyle="Italic"
                      FontWeight="Bold"
                      TextDecorations="Underline"
                      Foreground="Red"
                      Background="Lime"
                      BorderBrush="Blue"
                      BorderThickness="8"
```

```
CornerRadius="36"
Padding="16 4"
HorizontalAlignment="Center"
VerticalAlignment="Center" />
```

As you can see from the XML namespace prefix, this class is already in the Petzold.Phone. Silverlight library.

BorderedText derives from *UserControl*, and *UserControl* derives from *Control*, so we know that *BorderedText* will already have some of these properties through class inheritance. The properties that *BorderedText* needs to define on its own are *Text*, *TextDecorations*, *CornerRadius*, and perhaps a couple more to make it more flexible.

It seems likely that the BorderedText.xaml file will have a visual tree consisting of a *TextBlock* in a *Border*. Various properties of the *TextBlock* and this *Border* must be set from the *BorderedText* properties.

In the previous chapter, you saw one way to do this: The *ColorColumn* class defined properties named *Label* and *Value* and it used property-changed handlers in code to set the new values of these properties on elements in the visual tree. A rather simpler way is through data bindings.

The *BorderedText* code-behind file simply defines all the properties not available by virtue of descending from *Control*:

Silverlight Project: Petzold.Phone.Silverlight   File: BorderedText.xaml.cs

```
using System;
using System.Windows;
using System.Windows.Controls;

namespace Petzold.Phone.Silverlight
{
    public partial class BorderedText : UserControl
    {
        public static readonly DependencyProperty TextProperty =
            DependencyProperty.Register("Text",
                typeof(string),
                typeof(BorderedText),
                new PropertyMetadata(null));

        public static readonly DependencyProperty TextAlignmentProperty =
            DependencyProperty.Register("TextAlignment",
                typeof(TextAlignment),
                typeof(BorderedText),
                new PropertyMetadata(TextAlignment.Left));

        public static readonly DependencyProperty TextDecorationsProperty =
            DependencyProperty.Register("TextDecorations",
```

```
                        typeof(TextDecorationCollection),
                        typeof(BorderedText),
                        new PropertyMetadata(null));

        public static readonly DependencyProperty TextWrappingProperty =
            DependencyProperty.Register("TextWrapping",
                typeof(TextWrapping),
                typeof(BorderedText),
                new PropertyMetadata(TextWrapping.NoWrap));

        public static readonly DependencyProperty CornerRadiusProperty =
            DependencyProperty.Register("CornerRadius",
                typeof(CornerRadius),
                typeof(BorderedText),
                new PropertyMetadata(new CornerRadius()));

        public BorderedText()
        {
            InitializeComponent();
        }

        public string Text
        {
            set { SetValue(TextProperty, value); }
            get { return (string)GetValue(TextProperty); }
        }

        public TextAlignment TextAlignment
        {
            set { SetValue(TextAlignmentProperty, value); }
            get { return (TextAlignment)GetValue(TextAlignmentProperty); }
        }

        public TextDecorationCollection TextDecorations
        {
            set { SetValue(TextDecorationsProperty, value); }
            get { return (TextDecorationCollection)GetValue(TextDecorationsProperty)
; }
        }

        public TextWrapping TextWrapping
        {
            set { SetValue(TextWrappingProperty, value); }
            get { return (TextWrapping)GetValue(TextWrappingProperty); }
        }

        public CornerRadius CornerRadius
        {
            set { SetValue(CornerRadiusProperty, value); }
            get { return (CornerRadius)GetValue(CornerRadiusProperty); }
        }
    }
}
```

It's long but it's simple because it's only property definitions. There are no property-changed handlers. Here's the XAML file with the *Border* and the *TextBlock*:

Silverlight Project: **Petzold.Phone.Silverlight** File: **BorderedText.xaml**

```
<UserControl x:Class="Petzold.Phone.Silverlight.BorderedText"
             xmlns="http://schemas.microsoft.com/winfx/2006/xaml/presentation"
             xmlns:x="http://schemas.microsoft.com/winfx/2006/xaml"
             xmlns:d="http://schemas.microsoft.com/expression/blend/2008"
             Name="this">

    <Border Background="{Binding ElementName=this, Path=Background}"
            BorderBrush="{Binding ElementName=this, Path=BorderBrush}"
            BorderThickness="{Binding ElementName=this, Path=BorderThickness}"
            CornerRadius="{Binding ElementName=this, Path=CornerRadius}"
            Padding="{Binding ElementName=this, Path=Padding}">

        <TextBlock Text="{Binding ElementName=this, Path=Text}"
                   TextAlignment="{Binding ElementName=this, Path=TextAlignment}"
                   TextDecorations="{Binding ElementName=this, Path=TextDecorations}"
                   TextWrapping="{Binding ElementName=this, Path=TextWrapping}" />
    </Border>
</UserControl>
```

Notice that the root element is given a name:

```
Name="this"
```

You can give this root element any name you want, but it's traditional to use the C# keyword *this*, because within the context of the XAML file, *this* now refers to the current instance of the *BorderedText* class, so it's a familiar concept. The presence of this name means you can establish bindings from the properties of *BorderedText* to the properties of the elements of that make up its visual tree.

The file doesn't require bindings for the *Foreground* property or the various font-related properties because these are inherited through the visual tree. The one *TextBlock* property I was sad about losing in this control is *Inlines*, but *TextBlock* defines that property as get-only so you can't define a binding on it.

The BorderedTextDemo program tests the new control:

Silverlight Project: **BorderedTextDemo** File: **MainPage.xaml** (excerpt)

```
<Grid x:Name="ContentPanel" Grid.Row="1" Margin="12,0,12,0">
    <petzold:BorderedText Text="Ta Da!"
                          FontFamily="Times New Roman"
                          FontSize="96"
```

```
                                FontStyle="Italic"
                                FontWeight="Bold"
                                TextDecorations="Underline"
                                Foreground="Red"
                                Background="Lime"
                                BorderBrush="Blue"
                                BorderThickness="8"
                                CornerRadius="36"
                                Padding="16 4"
                                HorizontalAlignment="Center"
                                VerticalAlignment="Center" />
    </Grid>
```

Notification Mechanisms

For data bindings to work, the binding source must implement some kind of *notification mechanism*. This notification mechanism signals when the property value has changed so the new value can be retrieved from the source and transferred to the target. When you bind the *Value* property of a *Slider* to the *Text* property of a *TextBlock*, you're dealing with two dependency properties. Although you can't see it in the public programming interfaces, dependency properties provide this notification mechanism.

Connecting two visual elements with a data binding is certainly convenient, but the most powerful data bindings involve a target that is a visual element but a source that is not, and which instead is probably something commonly referred to as a *business object*.

And now a warning is required:

Sometimes when programmers learn a new and important feature of an operating system—such as the dependency properties I discussed in the previous chapter—they feel a need to use that feature everywhere, perhaps just to try it out and give it some exercise. With dependency properties, this is not such a good idea. Certainly you should use dependency properties when you're deriving from classes that already derive from *DependencyObject*, but you probably shouldn't derive from *DependencyObject* for the sole purpose of using dependency properties.

In other words: Don't start rewriting your business objects to use dependency properties!

Targets of data bindings must be dependency properties, but that is *not* a requirement for binding sources. Binding sources can be just regular old properties on regular old classes. However, if the source is changing, and you want the target updated with the current value of the source, the source must implement some kind of notification mechanism.

Almost always, business objects that serve as binding sources should implement the notification mechanism known as the *INotifyPropertyChanged* interface.

INotifyPropertyChanged is defined in the *System.ComponentModel* namespace—a clear indication that it transcends Silverlight and plays a very important role in .NET. This is how business objects provide notification that data has changed in some way.

INotifyPropertyChanged is also extremely simple, being defined like this:

```
public interface INotifyPropertyChanged
{
    event PropertyChangedEventHandler PropertyChanged:
}
```

A class can implement *INotifyPropertyChanged* simply by having a public event named *PropertyChanged*. In theory, the class needn't actually *do* anything with this event, but proper decorum mandates that the class fires this event whenever one of its properties changes.

The *PropertyChangedEventHandler* delegate is associated with a *PropertyChangedEventArgs* class that has a single public get-only property named *PropertyName* of type string. You pass the name of the property that's changed to the *PropertyChangedEventArgs* constructor.

Sometimes a class that implements *INotifyPropertyChanged* will have a protected virtual method named *OnPropertyChanged* with an argument of type *PropertyChangedEventArgs*. This isn't required but it's convenient for derivative classes. I do this in my examples because the method is a convenient place to fire the event.

Because business objects that implement *INotifyPropertyChanged* do not derive from *FrameworkElement*, they do not form part of the visual tree in a XAML file; usually they'll be instantiated as XAML resources or in the code-behind file.

A Simple Binding Server

I sometimes think of business objects that are intended to be referenced in XAML files through bindings as *binding servers*. They expose public properties and fire *PropertyChanged* events when these properties change.

For example, suppose you want to display the current time in a Windows Phone 7 application, and you want to be fairly flexible about what you display. Perhaps sometimes you only want to display seconds, and you want to do this entirely in XAML. For example, you might want a bit of XAML that says "The current seconds are … " followed by a number that changes every second. The technique I'll show you here can be extended to many other types of applications beyond clocks, of course.

Although you'll want to implement the visuals entirely in XAML, you're going to need some code—perhaps a class named simply *Clock* that has properties named *Year, Month, Day, DayOfWeek, Hour, Minute,* and *Second.* We'll instantiate this *Clock* class in a XAML file and access the properties through data bindings.

As you know, there already is a structure in .NET that has properties with the names *Year*, *Month*, *Day*, and so forth. It's called *DateTime*. Although *DateTime* is essential for writing the *Clock* class, it's not quite satisfactory for our purposes because the properties in *DateTime* don't dynamically change. Each *DateTime* object represents a particular immutable date and time. In contrast, the *Clock* class I'll show you has properties that change to reflect the current moment, and it will notify the external world about these changes through the *PropertyChanged* event

This *Clock* class is in the Petzold.Phone.Silverlight library. Here it is:

Silverlight Project: Petzold.Phone.Silverlight   File: Clock.cs

```
using System;
using System.ComponentModel;
using System.Windows.Threading;

namespace Petzold.Phone.Silverlight
{
    public class Clock : INotifyPropertyChanged
    {
        int hour, min, sec;
        DateTime date;

        public event PropertyChangedEventHandler PropertyChanged;

        public Clock()
        {
            OnTimerTick(null, null);

            DispatcherTimer tmr = new DispatcherTimer();
            tmr.Interval = TimeSpan.FromSeconds(0.1);
            tmr.Tick += OnTimerTick;
            tmr.Start();
        }

        public int Hour
        {
            protected set
            {
                if (value != hour)
                {
                    hour = value;
                    OnPropertyChanged(new PropertyChangedEventArgs("Hour"));
                }
            }
            get
            {
                return hour;
            }
        }
```

```csharp
public int Minute
{
    protected set
    {
        if (value != min)
        {
            min = value;
            OnPropertyChanged(new PropertyChangedEventArgs("Minute"));
        }
    }
    get
    {
        return min;
    }
}

public int Second
{
    protected set
    {
        if (value != sec)
        {
            sec = value;
            OnPropertyChanged(new PropertyChangedEventArgs("Second"));
        }
    }
    get
    {
        return sec;
    }
}

public DateTime Date
{
    protected set
    {
        if (value != date)
        {
            date = value;
            OnPropertyChanged(new PropertyChangedEventArgs("Date"));
        }
    }
    get
    {
        return date;
    }
}

protected virtual void OnPropertyChanged(PropertyChangedEventArgs args)
{
    if (PropertyChanged != null)
        PropertyChanged(this, args);
}
```

```
        void OnTimerTick(object sender, EventArgs args)
        {
            DateTime dt = DateTime.Now;
            Hour = dt.Hour;
            Minute = dt.Minute;
            Second = dt.Second;
            Date = DateTime.Today;
        }
    }
}
```

The *Clock* class implements *INotifyPropertyChanged* and therefore includes a public event named *PropertyChanged*. Near the bottom, a protected *OnPropertyChanged* method is also included and is responsible for firing the actual event. The constructor of the class installs a handler for the *Tick* event of the *DispatcherTimer* initialized to an interval of 1/10th second. The *OnTimerTick* handler (at the very bottom of the class) sets new values of the class's *Hour*, *Minute*, *Second*, and *Date* properties, all of which are structured very similarly.

For example, look at the *Hour* property:

```
public int Hour
{
    protected set
    {
        if (value != hour)
        {
            hour = value;
            OnPropertyChanged(new PropertyChangedEventArgs("Hour"));
        }
    }
    get
    {
        return hour;
    }
}
```

The *set* accessor is protected. The value is only set internally and we don't want external classes messing with it. The *set* accessor checks if the value being set to the property equals the value stored as a field; if not, it sets the *hour* field to the new value and calls *OnPropertyChanged* to fire the event.

Some programmers don't include the *if* statement to check that the property is actually changing, with the result that the *PropertyChanged* event is fired whenever the property is set, even if it's not changing. That's not a good idea—particularly for a class like this. We really don't want a *PropertyChanged* event reporting that the *Hour* property is changing every 1/10th second if it's really changing only every hour.

To use the *Clock* class in a XAML file, you'll need a reference to the Petzold.Phone.Silverlight library and an XML namespace declaration:

```
xmlns:petzold="clr-namespace:Petzold.Phone.Silverlight;assembly=Petzold.Phone.Silverlight"
```

When a binding source is not derived from *DependencyObject*, you don't use *ElementName* In the *Binding*. Instead, you use *Source*. The bindings we want to create set *Source* to the *Clock* object in the Petzold.Phone.Silverlight library.

You can insert a reference to the *Clock* class directly in the element form of *Binding*:

```
<TextBlock>
    <TextBlock.Text>
        <Binding Path="Second">
            <Binding.Source>
                <petzold:Clock />
            </Binding.Source>
        </Binding>
    </TextBlock.Text>
</TextBlock>
```

The *Source* property of *Binding* is broken out as a property element and set to an instance of the *Clock* class. The *Path* property indicates the *Second* property of *Clock*.

Or, more conventionally, you define the *Clock* as a XAML resource:

```
<phone:PhoneApplicationPage.Resources>
    <petzold:Clock x:Key="clock" />
    . . .
</phone:PhoneApplicationPage.Resources>
```

Then the *Binding* markup extension can reference that resource:

```
TextBlock Text="{Binding Source={StaticResource clock}, Path=Second}" />
```

Notice the embedded markup expression for *StaticResource*.

This approach is demonstrated in the TimeDisplay project, which uses a horizontal *StackPanel* to concatenate text:

Silverlight Project: TimeDisplay   File: MainPage.xaml

```
<Grid x:Name="ContentPanel" Grid.Row="1" Margin="12,0,12,0">
    <StackPanel Orientation="Horizontal"
                HorizontalAlignment="Center"
                VerticalAlignment="Center">
        <TextBlock Text="The current seconds are " />
        <TextBlock Text="{Binding Source={StaticResource clock},
                                  Path=Second}" />
    </StackPanel>
</Grid>
```

And here it is:

To re-emphasize: The binding target (the *Text* property of the *TextBlock*) must be a dependency property. That is required. To keep the target updated with changing values from the binding source (the *Second* property of *Clock*), the source should implement some kind of notification mechanism, which it does.

Of course, I don't need the *StackPanel* with the multiple *TextBlock* elements. Using the *StringFormatConverter* (which I've included as a resource in TimeDisplay with a key of "stringFormat" so you can experiment with it) I can simply include the whole text like so:

```
<Grid x:Name="ContentPanel" Grid.Row="1" Margin="12,0,12,0">
    <TextBlock HorizontalAlignment="Center"
               VerticalAlignment="Center"
               Text="{Binding Source={StaticResource clock},
                       Path=Second,
                       Converter={StaticResource stringFormat},
                       ConverterParameter='The current seconds are {0}'}" />
</Grid>
```

Now the *Binding* markup expression has *two* embedded markup expressions.

If you want to display several properties of the *Clock* class, you'll need to go back to using multiple *TextBlock* elements. For example, this will format the time with colons between the hours, minutes, and seconds and leading zeros for the minutes and seconds:

```
<Grid x:Name="ContentPanel" Grid.Row="1" Margin="12,0,12,0">
    <StackPanel Orientation="Horizontal"
                HorizontalAlignment="Center"
                VerticalAlignment="Center">
        <TextBlock Text="{Binding Source={StaticResource clock},
                          Path=Hour}" />
```

```
            <TextBlock Text="{Binding Source={StaticResource clock},
                                      Path=Minute,
                                      Converter={StaticResource stringFormat},
                                      ConverterParameter=':{0:D2}'}" />
            <TextBlock Text="{Binding Source={StaticResource clock},
                                      Path=Second,
                                      Converter={StaticResource stringFormat},
                                      ConverterParameter=':{0:D2}'}" />
        </StackPanel>
    </Grid>
```

As you can see, the three bindings all include the same *Source* setting. Is there some way that allows us to avoid the repetition? Yes there is, and the technique also illustrates an extremely important concept.

Setting the *DataContext*

FrameworkElement defines a property named *DataContext* that you can set to pretty much any object (in code) or generally a binding (in XAML). The *DataContext* is one of those properties that propagates down through the visual tree, at which point it can be combined with more local bindings. At the very least, the *DataContext* gives you a way to simplify individual bindings by eliminating repetition. In the broader view, DataContext is how you associate data with visual trees.

In this particular example, you can set the *DataContext* property on any element that is an ancestor to the *TextBlock* elements. Let's set it on the most immediate ancestor, which is the *StackPanel*:

```
<Grid x:Name="ContentPanel" Grid.Row="1" Margin="12,0,12,0">
    <StackPanel DataContext="{Binding Source={StaticResource clock}}"
                Orientation="Horizontal"
                HorizontalAlignment="Center"
                VerticalAlignment="Center">
        <TextBlock Text="{Binding Path=Hour}" />
        <TextBlock Text="{Binding Path=Minute,
                                  Converter={StaticResource stringFormat},
                                  ConverterParameter=':{0:D2}'}" />
        <TextBlock Text="{Binding Path=Second,
                                  Converter={StaticResource stringFormat},
                                  ConverterParameter=':{0:D2}'}" />
    </StackPanel>
</Grid>
```

Now the *StackPanel* has its *DataContext* set to a *Binding* element that references just the source of the binding—the *Clock* resource. All the children of that *StackPanel* don't need to reference that *Source*. It's merged in with the bindings on the individual *TextBlock* elements.

You can set the *DataContext* to a *Binding* object as I've done:

```
DataContext="{Binding Source={StaticResource clock}}"
```

Or in this case you can set the *DataContext* directly to the source:

```
DataContext="{StaticResource clock}"
```

Either is acceptable and you'll see both in my examples.

Once the *Source* property is removed from the individual *Binding* extensions, what begins to look more natural to me is for the "Path=" part of the individual bindings to be removed:

```
<Grid x:Name="ContentPanel" Grid.Row="1" Margin="12,0,12,0">
    <StackPanel DataContext="{Binding Source={StaticResource clock}}"
                Orientation="Horizontal"
                HorizontalAlignment="Center"
                VerticalAlignment="Center">
        <TextBlock Text="{Binding Hour}" />
        <TextBlock Text="{Binding Minute,
                            Converter={StaticResource stringFormat},
                            ConverterParameter=':{0:D2}'}" />
        <TextBlock Text="{Binding Second,
                            Converter={StaticResource stringFormat},
                            ConverterParameter=':{0:D2}'}" />
    </StackPanel>
</Grid>
```

Remember that the "Path=" part of the *Binding* markup extension can be removed only if the *Path* is the first item. Each of the bindings now seems to reference a particular property of the *DataContext*:

```
<TextBlock Text="{Binding Hour}" />
```

Here's the resultant display:

The *DataContext* is extremely useful when a page or a control is devoted to displaying the properties of a particular class. The *DataContext* can be set by code to switch between various instances of that class.

Although certainly not as common, you can also use *DataContext* with *ElementName* bindings. Here's the visual tree from the BorderText.xaml file you saw earlier:

```
<Border Background="{Binding ElementName=this, Path=Background}"
        BorderBrush="{Binding ElementName=this, Path=BorderBrush}"
        BorderThickness="{Binding ElementName=this, Path=BorderThickness}"
        CornerRadius="{Binding ElementName=this, Path=CornerRadius}"
        Padding="{Binding ElementName=this, Path=Padding}">

    <TextBlock Text="{Binding ElementName=this, Path=Text}"
               TextAlignment="{Binding ElementName=this, Path=TextAlignment}"
               TextDecorations="{Binding ElementName=this, Path=TextDecorations}"
               TextWrapping="{Binding ElementName=this, Path=TextWrapping}" />
</Border>
```

You can instead set the *DataContext* on the *Border* to a *Binding* with the *ElementName*, and then the remaining bindings are simplified considerably:

```
<Border DataContext="{Binding ElementName=this}"
        Background="{Binding Background}"
        BorderBrush="{Binding BorderBrush}"
        BorderThickness="{Binding BorderThickness}"
        CornerRadius="{Binding CornerRadius}"
        Padding="{Binding Padding}">

    <TextBlock Text="{Binding Path=Text}"
               TextAlignment="{Binding Path=TextAlignment}"
               TextDecorations="{Binding Path=TextDecorations}"
               TextWrapping="{Binding ElementName=this, Path=TextWrapping}" />
</Border>
```

Back to *Clock*: You may have noticed that I got a little lazy when coding the class and didn't define properties for the various components of the date, such as *Month* and *Year*. Instead, I simply defined a property named *Date* of type *DateTime*. The *OnTimerTick* handler assigns to that property the static property *DateTime.Today*, which is a *DateTime* object with the time set to midnight. That means that this *Date* property is not firing off *PropertyChanged* events every tenth second. It's only firing one at startup and then at the stroke of every midnight.

You can reference the individual properties of the *Date* property like this:

```
<Grid x:Name="ContentPanel" Grid.Row="1" Margin="12,0,12,0">
    <StackPanel HorizontalAlignment="Center"
                VerticalAlignment="Center">
        <StackPanel Orientation="Horizontal">
            <TextBlock Text="It's day number " />
            <TextBlock Text="{Binding Source={StaticResource clock},
                                      Path=Date.Day}" />
            <TextBlock Text=" of month " />
            <TextBlock Text="{Binding Source={StaticResource clock},
                                      Path=Date.Month}" />
        </StackPanel>
        <StackPanel Orientation="Horizontal">
```

```
            <TextBlock Text=" of the year " />
            <TextBlock Text="{Binding Source={StaticResource clock},
                                      Path=Date.Year}" />
            <TextBlock Text=", a " />
            <TextBlock Text="{Binding Source={StaticResource clock},
                                      Path=Date.DayOfWeek}" />
            < TextBlock Text="." />
        </StackPanel>
    </StackPanel>
</Grid>
```

Or, you can set a *DataContext* on the *StackPanel* as before and eliminate the "Path=" part of the bindings:

```
<Grid x:Name="ContentPanel" Grid.Row="1" Margin="12,0,12,0">
    <StackPanel DataContext="{StaticResource clock}"
                HorizontalAlignment="Center"
                VerticalAlignment="Center">
        <StackPanel Orientation="Horizontal">
            <TextBlock Text="It's day number " />
            <TextBlock Text="{Binding Date.Day}" />
            <TextBlock Text=" of month " />
            <TextBlock Text="{Binding Date.Month}" />
        </StackPanel>
        <StackPanel Orientation="Horizontal">
            <TextBlock Text=" of the year " />
            <TextBlock Text="{Binding Date.Year}" />
            <TextBlock Text=", a " />
            <TextBlock Text="{Binding Date.DayOfWeek}" />
            <TextBlock Text="." />
        </StackPanel>
    </StackPanel>
</Grid>
```

Either version displays two lines of text:

Date is a property of *Clock* of type *DateTime*, and *Day*, *Month*, *Year*, and *DayOfWeek* are all properties of *DateTime*. There is no formatting here beyond that provided by default calls to *ToString*. The *Day*, *Month*, and *Year* properties are displayed as numbers. The *DayOfWeek* property is of a member of the *DayOfWeek* enumeration, so you'll see actual text, such as Wednesday, but the text won't be localized. The *DayOfWeek* member names are in English so that's what's displayed.

You can also set a *DataContext* that references both the *Source* and the *Date* property, so the individual bindings just reference properties of *DateTime*:

```
<Grid x:Name="ContentPanel" Grid.Row="1" Margin="12,0,12,0">
    <StackPanel DataContext="{Binding Source={StaticResource clock},
                                      Path=Date}"
                HorizontalAlignment="Center"
                VerticalAlignment="Center">
        <StackPanel Orientation="Horizontal">
            <TextBlock Text="It's day number " />
            <TextBlock Text="{Binding Day}" />
            <TextBlock Text=" of month " />
            <TextBlock Text="{Binding Month}" />
        </StackPanel>
        <StackPanel Orientation="Horizontal">
            <TextBlock Text=" of the year " />
            <TextBlock Text="{Binding Year}" />
            <TextBlock Text=", a " />
            <TextBlock Text="{Binding DayOfWeek}" />
            <TextBlock Text="." />
        </StackPanel>
    </StackPanel>
</Grid>
```

Of course, there are lots of formatting options for dates documented with the *DateTimeFormatInfo* class in the *System.Globalization* namespace, so you can also make use of *StringFormatConverter*.

Suppose you want to include the name of the current month deep within a paragraph displayed using *TextBlock*. To use *TextBlock* to display a paragraph of text, you'll want to set the *TextWrapping* property to *Wrap*. But now you can't use *StackPanel* to concatenate multiple *TextBlock* elements. You need to include all the text in that single *TextBlock*, including the name of the month. How do you do it?

You will consider yourself a genius when you remember the *Run* class. You'll recall from the end of Chapter 8 how the *Run* class derives from *Inline* and allows you to specify formatting for a piece of text within an entire *TextBlock*. The *Run* class has a *Text* property, so it seems like an ideal way to embed the month name (or some other binding) in a longer paragraph:

```
<!-- This will not work! -->
<TextBlock TextWrapping="Wrap">
    This represents some long text that needs to display a month name of
    <Run Text="{Binding Source={StaticResource clock},
```

```
                     Path=Date,
                     Converter={StaticResource stringFormat},
                     ConverterParameter='{0:MMMM}'}" />
    and then continue with the rest of the paragraph.
</TextBlock>
```

This is exactly what you want, and the only problem is that it won't work! It won't work because the *Text* property of *Run* is not backed by a dependency property, and targets of data bindings must always be dependency properties.

It seems unfair that *Run* has this little problem, but frameworks are much like life, and life is not always fair.

Currently, you cannot do this little task entirely in XAML. You'll need to give the *Run* a name and assign the *Text* property from code.

Simple Decision Making

XAML is not a real programming language. It doesn't include anything like *if* statements. XAML isn't capable of making decisions.

But that doesn't mean we can't try.

As you may have noticed, the *Clock* class used the straight *Hour* property from *DateTime*, which is a 24-hour clock value. You might instead want a 12-hour clock and display the text "AM" or "PM" to indicate the morning or afternoon.

Normally you can do that by formatting the time (if the *Clock* class actually provided a *DateTime* object indicating the time) but suppose you want to be very flexible about how you display the AM and PM information—perhaps you'd prefer to display the text "in the morning" or "in the afternoon"—and you want to do it in XAML.

Here's a new class named *TwelveHourClock* that derives from *Clock*.

Silverlight Project: Petzold.Phone.Silverlight   File: TwelveHourClock.cs

```
using System;
using System.ComponentModel;

namespace Petzold.Phone.Silverlight
{
    public class TwelveHourClock : Clock
    {
        int hour12;
        bool isam, ispm;
```

```
public int Hour12
{
    protected set
    {
        if (value != hour12)
        {
            hour12 = value;
            OnPropertyChanged(new PropertyChangedEventArgs("Hour12"));
        }
    }
    get
    {
        return hour12;
    }
}

public bool IsAm
{
    protected set
    {
        if (value != isam)
        {
            isam = value;
            OnPropertyChanged(new PropertyChangedEventArgs("IsAm"));
        }
    }
    get
    {
        return isam;
    }
}

public bool IsPm
{
    protected set
    {
        if (value != ispm)
        {
            ispm = value;
            OnPropertyChanged(new PropertyChangedEventArgs("IsPm"));
        }
    }
    get
    {
        return ispm;
    }
}

protected override void OnPropertyChanged(PropertyChangedEventArgs args)
{
    if (args.PropertyName == "Hour")
```

```
        {
            Hour12 = (Hour - 1) % 12 + 1;
            IsAm = Hour < 12;
            IsPm = !IsAm;
        }

        base.OnPropertyChanged(args);
    }
}
}
```

The *TwelveHourClock* class defines three new properties, all triggering *PropertyChanged* events. These are *Hour12* and two Boolean properties, *IsAm* and *IsPm*. The override of *OnPropertyChanged* checks if the property being changed is *Hour* and, if so, calculates new values for these three properties, which themselves cause calls to *OnPropertyChanged*.

Because *isAm* is simply the logical negation of *isPM*, you may wonder why both properties are required. Because XAML itself can't perform a logical negation, having both properties available becomes extremely convenient.

Let's instantiate the *TwelveHourClock* class in a *Resources* collection and give it a key of "clock12":

```
<phone:PhoneApplicationPage.Resources>
    <petzold:TwelveHourClock x:Key="clock12" />
</phone:PhoneApplicationPage.Resources>
```

If you'd like XAML to display some text along the lines of "It's after 9 in the morning," you might begin like this:

```
<Grid x:Name="ContentPanel" Grid.Row="1" Margin="12,0,12,0">
    <StackPanel DataContext="{StaticResource clock12}"
                Orientation="Horizontal"
                HorizontalAlignment="Center"
                VerticalAlignment="Center">
        <TextBlock Text="It's after " />
        <TextBlock Text="{Binding Hour}" />
        <TextBlock Text=" in the morning." />
        <TextBlock Text=" in the afternoon." />
    </StackPanel>
</Grid>
```

This XAML has separate text strings for morning and afternoon, but at any time only one of them should be displayed depending on whether *IsAm* or *IsPm* is true. How is such a thing even possible?

Another converter is required, and this is also a converter that you'll use quite often. It's called a *BooleanToVisibilityConverter* and it assumes that the source value is a Boolean and the target is a property of type *Visibility*:

Silverlight Project: Petzold.Phone.Silverlight   File: BooleanToVisibilityConverter.cs

```
using System;
using System.Globalization;
using System.Windows;
using System.Windows.Data;

namespace Petzold.Phone.Silverlight
{
    public class BooleanToVisibilityConverter : IValueConverter
    {
        public object Convert(object value, Type targetType,
                              object parameter, CultureInfo culture)
        {
            return (bool)value ? Visibility.Visible : Visibility.Collapsed;
        }

        public object ConvertBack(object value, Type targetType,
                                  object parameter, CultureInfo culture)
        {
            return (Visibility)value == Visibility.Visible;
        }
    }
}
```

Add that class to the *Resources* collection:

```
<phone:PhoneApplicationPage.Resources>
    <petzold:TwelveHourClock x:Key="clock12" />
    <petzold:BooleanToVisibilityConverter x:Key="booleanToVisibility" />
</phone:PhoneApplicationPage.Resources>
```

Now bind the *Visibility* properties of the final two *TextBlock* elements to the *IsAm* and *IsPm* properties using the *BooleanToVisibilityConverter*. Here's the markup from the project AmOrPm:

Silverlight Project: AmOrPm   File: MainPage.xaml (excerpt)

```
<Grid x:Name="ContentPanel" Grid.Row="1" Margin="12,0,12,0">
    <StackPanel DataContext="{StaticResource clock12}"
                Orientation="Horizontal"
                HorizontalAlignment="Center"
                VerticalAlignment="Center">
        <TextBlock Text="It's after " />
        <TextBlock Text="{Binding Hour}" />
        <TextBlock Text=" in the morning."
                   Visibility="{Binding IsAm,
                                Converter={StaticResource booleanToVisibility}}"
/>
```

```
            <TextBlock Text=" in the afternoon."
                       Visibility="{Binding IsPm,
                                      Converter={StaticResource booleanToVisibility}}"/>
        </StackPanel>
    </Grid>
```

And it works:

Converters with Properties

It's not unreasonable to create a data-binding converter that is so specialized or so weird that it's only good for one particular application. For example, here's a class called *DecimalBitToBrushConverter*. This converter includes two public properties named *ZeroBitBrush* and *OneBitBrush*.

Silverlight Project: BinaryClock   File: DecimalBitToBrushConverter.cs

```
using System;
using System.Globalization;
using System.Windows.Data;
using System.Windows.Media;
```

```
namespace BinaryClock
{
    public class DecimalBitToBrushConverter : IValueConverter
    {
        public Brush ZeroBitBrush { set; get; }
        public Brush OneBitBrush { set; get; }

        public object Convert(object value, Type targetType,
                              object parameter, CultureInfo culture)
        {
            int number = (int)value;
            int bit = Int32.Parse(parameter as string);
            int digit = number / PowerOfTen(bit / 4) % 10;

            return ((digit & (1 << (bit % 4))) == 0) ? ZeroBitBrush : OneBitBrush;
        }

        public object ConvertBack(object value, Type targetType,
                                  object parameter, CultureInfo culture)
        {
            return null;
        }

        int PowerOfTen(int exp)
        {
            int value = 1;

            for (int i = 0; i < exp; i++)
                value *= 10;

            return value;
        }
    }
}
```

The *Convert* method expects a *value* argument of type *int*, and a valid parameter argument. When you set the *ConverterParameter* property in XAML to a string, it will come into the *Convert* method as an object of type *string*, at which point you must convert it manually into the desired type. (To override that behavior, you'd need to use property-element syntax for the *ConverterParameter* and specify the type using element tags.) This *Convert* method expects this string to represent another *int*, so it passes the string the *Int32.Parse*.

The *value* argument is a number, for example 127. The *parameter* argument, when converted to an *int*, is a bit position, for example, 6. The method essentially breaks the incoming number into decimal digits, in this example 1, 2 and 7, and then finds the digit in the specified bit position. The 7 of 127 corresponds to bit positions of 0 through 3; the 2 of 127 is bit positions 4 through 7; the 1 of 127 is bit positions 8 through 11.

If the bit in that bit position is 1, *Convert* returns *OneBitBrush*; if it's 0, *Convert* returns *ZeroBitBrush*.

I use this converter in a project called BinaryClock. The converter is referenced in a *UserControl* derivative called *BinaryNumberRow*. Notice how the two public properties of *DecimalBitToBrushConverter* are set right in the *Resources* collection, which also includes a *Style* for the *Ellipse*.

Silverlight Project: BinaryClock   File: BinaryNumberRow.xaml

```
<UserControl
  x:Class="BinaryClock.BinaryNumberRow"
  xmlns="http://schemas.microsoft.com/winfx/2006/xaml/presentation"
  xmlns:x="http://schemas.microsoft.com/winfx/2006/xaml"
  xmlns:petzold="clr-namespace:Petzold.Phone.Silverlight;assembly=Petzold.Phone.
Silverlight"
  xmlns:local="clr-namespace:BinaryClock">

    <UserControl.Resources>
        <Style x:Key="ellipseStyle" TargetType="Ellipse">
            <Setter Property="Width" Value="48" />
            <Setter Property="Height" Value="48" />
            <Setter Property="Stroke" Value="{StaticResource PhoneForegroundBrush}" />
            <Setter Property="StrokeThickness" Value="2" />
        </Style>

        <local:DecimalBitToBrushConverter x:Key="converter"
                                          ZeroBitBrush="{x:Null}"
                                          OneBitBrush="Red" />
    </UserControl.Resources>

    <petzold:UniformStack Orientation="Horizontal">
        <Ellipse Style="{StaticResource ellipseStyle}"
                 Fill="{Binding Converter={StaticResource converter},
                        ConverterParameter=6}" />

        <Ellipse Style="{StaticResource ellipseStyle}"
                 Fill="{Binding Converter={StaticResource converter},
                        ConverterParameter=5}" />

        <Ellipse Style="{StaticResource ellipseStyle}"
                 Fill="{Binding Converter={StaticResource converter},
                        ConverterParameter=4}" />

        <Ellipse Style="{StaticResource ellipseStyle}"
                 Stroke="{x:Null}" />

        <Ellipse Style="{StaticResource ellipseStyle}"
                 Fill="{Binding Converter={StaticResource converter},
                        ConverterParameter=3}" />

        <Ellipse Style="{StaticResource ellipseStyle}"
                 Fill="{Binding Converter={StaticResource converter},
                        ConverterParameter=2}" />
```

```
        <Ellipse Style="{StaticResource ellipseStyle}"
                Fill="{Binding Converter={StaticResource converter},
                                ConverterParameter=1}" />

        <Ellipse Style="{StaticResource ellipseStyle}"
                Fill="{Binding Converter={StaticResource converter},
                                ConverterParameter=0}" />
    </petzold:UniformStack>
</UserControl>
```

The body of the *BinaryNumberRow* visual tree is a horizontal *UniformStack* containing seven *Ellipse* elements. Each has a *Binding* that assigns only the *Converter* property to the *DecimalBitToBrushConverter* and a *ConverterParameter* that ranges from 0 for the *Ellipse* on the right to 6 for the *Ellipse* on the left. None of the bindings include *Source* or *Path* settings! These are obviously set elsewhere in the *DataContext* for the *BinaryNumberRow* instance.

The MainPage.xaml file of the BinaryClock project instantiates the *TwelveHourClock* object in its *Resources* section:

Silverlight Project: BinaryClock   File: **MainPage.xaml**

```
<phone:PhoneApplicationPage.Resources>
    <petzold:TwelveHourClock x:Key="clock12" />
</phone:PhoneApplicationPage.Resources>
```

The content area contains a vertically centered *StackPanel* with three instances of *BinaryNumberRow*:

Silverlight Project: BinaryClock   File: **MainPage.xaml**

```
<Grid x:Name="ContentPanel" Grid.Row="1" Margin="12,0,12,0">

    <StackPanel DataContext="{StaticResource clock12}"
            VerticalAlignment="Center">

        <local:BinaryNumberRow DataContext="{Binding Hour12}"
                            Margin="0 12" />

        <local:BinaryNumberRow DataContext="{Binding Minute}"
                            Margin="0 12" />

        <local:BinaryNumberRow DataContext="{Binding Second}"
                            Margin="0 12" />
    </StackPanel>
</Grid>
```

Notice the *DataContext* settings: The *StackPanel* has its *DataContext* set to the *TwelveHourClock* itself. Each of the *BinaryNumberRow* controls has a *DataContext* set to one of the properties of *TwelveHourClock*. This is why the *Binding* definitions in *BinaryNumberRow* only need to contain a *Converter* and *ConverterParameter*.

The result, of course, is a binary clock:

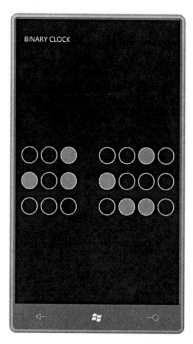

The time is, ummm, 12:58:06.

You might wonder if some of the *Binding* markup might be reduced even further. Considering that all the individual *Ellipse* elements have the same *Converter* setting, might that be moved to the first *DataContext* setting on the *StackPanel*? No it can't. The *Converter* and *ConverterParameter* settings must appear together in the same *Binding* definition.

Give and Take

The two binding services you've seen so far simply provide information. You can also create bindings in XAML that deliver data to the binding service and get back a result. As a very simple demonstration, let's look at a binding service that performs the momentous feat of adding two numbers together. I call it *Adder*.

Silverlight Project: Petzold.Phone.Silverlight   File: Adder.cs

```csharp
using System.ComponentModel;

namespace Petzold.Phone.Silverlight
{
    public class Adder : INotifyPropertyChanged
    {
        public event PropertyChangedEventHandler PropertyChanged;

        double augend = 0;
        double addend = 0;
        double sum = 0;

        public double Augend
        {
            set
            {
                if (augend != value)
                {
                    augend = value;
                    OnPropertyChanged(new PropertyChangedEventArgs("Augend"));
                    CalculateNewSum();
                }
            }
            get
            {
                return augend;
            }
        }

        public double Addend
        {
            set
            {
                if (addend != value)
                {
                    addend = value;
                    OnPropertyChanged(new PropertyChangedEventArgs("Addend"));
                    CalculateNewSum();
                }
            }
            get
            {
                return addend;
            }
        }

        public double Sum
        {
            protected set
```

```
                        {
                            if (sum != value)
                            {
                                sum = value;
                                OnPropertyChanged(new PropertyChangedEventArgs("Sum"));
                            }
                        }

                        get
                        {
                            return sum;
                        }
                    }

                    void CalculateNewSum()
                    {
                        Sum = Augend + Addend;
                    }

                    protected virtual void OnPropertyChanged(PropertyChangedEventArgs args)
                    {
                        if (PropertyChanged != null)
                            PropertyChanged(this, args);
                    }
                }
            }
```

When you add two numbers together, they can be called the *Augend* and the *Addend*, and that's what the two properties are named. Both properties are of type *double* and both are entirely public, and when either is set to a new value, it fires a *PropertyChanged* event and also calls a method named *CalculateNewSum*.

CalculateNewSum adds the *Augend* and *Addend* properties and sets the result to the *Sum* property. *Sum* is a little different because the *set* accessor is *protected*, so nobody external to this class can mess with the *Sum*, and that is how it should be.

The *SliderSum* project shows one way to use this binding service in a program. The *Resources* collection references two files from the Petzold.Phone.Silverlight library:

Silverlight Project: SliderSum   File: MainPage.xaml (excerpt)

```
<phone:PhoneApplicationPage.Resources>
    <petzold:Adder x:Key="adder" />
    <petzold:StringFormatConverter x:Key="stringFormat" />
</phone:PhoneApplicationPage.Resources>
```

In the content area, two *Slider* elements are positioned at the top and bottom, and a *TextBlock* occupies the larger interior:

Silverlight Project: SliderSum   File: MainPage.xaml (excerpt)

```xml
<Grid x:Name="ContentPanel" Grid.Row="1" Margin="12,0,12,0"
      DataContext="{Binding Source={StaticResource adder}}">
    <Grid.RowDefinitions>
        <RowDefinition Height="Auto" />
        <RowDefinition Height="*" />
        <RowDefinition Height="Auto" />
    </Grid.RowDefinitions>

    <Slider Grid.Row="0"
            Minimum="-100"
            Maximum="100"
            Margin="24"
            Value="{Binding Augend, Mode=TwoWay}" />

    <Slider Grid.Row="2"
            Minimum="-100"
            Maximum="100"
            Margin="24"
            Value="{Binding Addend, Mode=TwoWay}" />

    <TextBlock Grid.Row="1"
            HorizontalAlignment="Center"
            VerticalAlignment="Center"
            FontSize="48"
            Text="{Binding Sum,
                      Converter={StaticResource stringFormat},
                      ConverterParameter=' {0:F2} '}" />
</Grid>
```

Notice the *DataContext* on the *Grid*. Although the two *Slider* controls are providing values for the *Augend* and *Addend* properties, these *Augend* and *Addend* properties cannot be binding targets because they are not backed by dependency properties. The *Adder* must be the binding source and the *Slider* controls must be the binding targets, and that's why the two bindings have a *Mode* of *TwoWay*. The *Slider* bindings are set initially to their center positions from the default values defined by *Adder*, but thereafter, the *Slider* values are transferred to the *Augend* and *Addend* properties. The *TextBlock* is bound to the *Sum* property with some string formatting.

Suppose you want to display negative values in red. (You are probably an accountant.) By this time you probably know that a binding converter is involved. The converter can be generalized somewhat by testing whether the value going into the converter is greater than, equal to, or less than a certain criterion value. Each of the three possibilities can result in a different brush being returned from the converter. As in the converter in the BinaryClock project, this information can be provided through public properties on the converter class, like this:

Silverlight Project: Petzold.Phone.Silverlight   File: ValueToBrushConverter.cs

```csharp
using System;
using System.Globalization;
using System.Windows.Data;
using System.Windows.Media;

namespace Petzold.Phone.Silverlight
{
    public class ValueToBrushConverter : IValueConverter
    {
        public double Criterion { set; get; }
        public Brush GreaterThanBrush { get; set; }
        public Brush EqualToBrush { get; set; }
        public Brush LessThanBrush { get; set; }

        public object Convert(object value, Type targetType,
                              object parameter, CultureInfo culture)
```

```
        {
            double doubleVal = (value as IConvertible).ToDouble(culture);
            return doubleVal >= Criterion ? doubleVal == Criterion ? EqualToBrush :
                                                                      GreaterThanBrush

                                                                      LessThanBrush;
        }

        public object ConvertBack(object value, Type targetType,
                                  object parameter, CultureInfo culture)
        {
            return null;
        }
    }
}
```

Originally I wrote this converter to just cast the *value* argument to a *double*, but I later found a need to use the converter with other numeric data types, so I went for a more versatile conversion with an *IConvertible* method.

The SliderSumWithColor project adds this converter to the ever-growing *Resources* collection:

Silverlight Project: SliderSumWithColor   File: MainPage.xaml (excerpt)

```
<phone:PhoneApplicationPage.Resources>
    <petzold:Adder x:Key="adder" />
    <petzold:StringFormatConverter x:Key="stringFormat" />
    <petzold:ValueToBrushConverter x:Key="valueToBrush"
                    Criterion="0"
                    LessThanBrush="Red"
                    EqualToBrush="{StaticResource PhoneForegroundBrush}"
                    GreaterThanBrush="{StaticResource PhoneForegroundBrush}" />
</phone:PhoneApplicationPage.Resources>
```

The property settings on the *ValueToBrushConverter* indicate that values less than zero will be displayed in red; otherwise values are displayed in the *PhoneForegroundBrush* color.

Everything else is the same as in the previous program except that the *TextBlock* now has a *Binding* set on its *Foreground* property with the *ValueToBrushConverter*:

Silverlight Project: SliderSumWithColor   File: MainPage.xaml (excerpt)

```
<Grid ... >
    ...
    <TextBlock Grid.Row="1"
            HorizontalAlignment="Center"
```

```
                    VerticalAlignment="Center"
                    FontSize="48"
                    Text="{Binding Sum,
                                   Converter={StaticResource stringFormat},
                                   ConverterParameter=' {0:F2} '}"

                    Foreground="{Binding Sum,
                                         Converter={StaticResource valueToBrush}}" />
    </Grid>
```

It's actually quite exciting to see the color of the *TextBlock* become red knowing that there's no explicit event handler in the program making this change:

TextBox Binding Updates

The *Text* property of a *TextBox* can be a target of a data binding, but some potential problems are introduced. Once you allow the user to type anything into a *TextBox*, you need to deal with faulty input.

Suppose you want to write a program that solves quadratic equations, that is, solutions of the equation

$Ax^2 + Bx + C = 0$

To make the program most versatile, you'd probably supply three *TextBox* controls to allow the user to type in values of *A*, *B*, and *C*. You could then include a *Button* labeled "calculate" that obtains the two solutions from the standard equation:

$$x = \frac{-B \pm \sqrt{B^2 - 4AC}}{2A}$$

You'd then display the solutions in a *TextBlock*.

With what you know about data bindings (and considering the example of the *Adder* binding server), a somewhat different approach comes to mind. This approach retains the three *TextBox* controls and uses a *TextBlock* to display results. These controls are all bound to properties of the binding server.

So where does the *Button* go? Well, perhaps the *Button* isn't really needed.

To get started, here's a class from Petzold.Phone.Silverlight named *QuadraticEquationSolver*. It implements the *INotifyPropertyChanged* interface, has three properties named *A*, *B*, and *C*, and get-only properties named *Solution1* and *Solution2*. Two additional read-only properties are of type *bool* and named *HasTwoSolutions* and *HasOneSolution*.

```
Solution: Petzold.Phone.Silverlight   File: QuadaticEquationSolver.cs

using System;
using System.ComponentModel;

namespace Petzold.Phone.Silverlight
{
    public class QuadraticEquationSolver : INotifyPropertyChanged
    {
        Complex solution1;
        Complex solution2;
        bool hasTwoSolutions;
        double a, b, c;

        public event PropertyChangedEventHandler PropertyChanged;

        public double A
        {
            set
            {
                if (a != value)
                {
                    a = value;
                    OnPropertyChanged(new PropertyChangedEventArgs("A"));
                    CalculateNewSolutions();
                }
            }
            get
```

```
            {
                return a;
            }
        }

        public double B
        {
            set
            {
                if (b != value)
                {
                    b = value;
                    OnPropertyChanged(new PropertyChangedEventArgs("B"));
                    CalculateNewSolutions();
                }
            }
            get
            {
                return b;
            }
        }

        public double C
        {
            set
            {
                if (c != value)
                {
                    c = value;
                    OnPropertyChanged(new PropertyChangedEventArgs("C"));
                    CalculateNewSolutions();
                }
            }
            get
            {
                return c;
            }
        }

        public Complex Solution1
        {
            protected set
            {
                if (!solution1.Equals(value))
                {
                    solution1 = value;
                    OnPropertyChanged(new PropertyChangedEventArgs("Solution1"));
                }
            }

            get
            {
                return solution1;
            }
        }
```

```
public Complex Solution2
{
    protected set
    {
        if (!solution2.Equals(value))
        {
            solution2 = value;
            OnPropertyChanged(new PropertyChangedEventArgs("Solution2"));
        }
    }

    get
    {
        return solution2;
    }
}

public bool HasTwoSolutions
{
    protected set
    {
        if (hasTwoSolutions != value)
        {
            hasTwoSolutions = value;
            OnPropertyChanged(new PropertyChangedEventArgs("HasTwoSolutions"));
            OnPropertyChanged(new PropertyChangedEventArgs("HasOneSolution"));
        }
    }

    get
    {
        return hasTwoSolutions;
    }
}

public bool HasOneSolution
{
    get
    {
        return !hasTwoSolutions;
    }
}

void CalculateNewSolutions()
{
    if (A == 0 && B == 0 && C == 0)
    {
        Solution1 = new Complex(0, 0);
        HasTwoSolutions = false;
        return;
    }
```

```
            if (A == 0)
            {
                Solution1 = new Complex(-C / B, 0);
                HasTwoSolutions = false;
                return;
            }

            double discriminant = B * B - 4 * A * C;
            double denominator = 2 * A;
            double real = -B / denominator;
            double imaginary =
                Math.Sqrt(Math.Abs(discriminant)) / denominator;

            if (discriminant == 0)
            {
                Solution1 = new Complex(real, 0);
                HasTwoSolutions = false;
                return;
            }

            Solution1 = new Complex(real, imaginary);
            Solution2 = new Complex(real, -imaginary);
            HasTwoSolutions = true;
        }

        protected virtual void OnPropertyChanged(PropertyChangedEventArgs args)
        {
            if (PropertyChanged != null)
                PropertyChanged(this, args);
        }
    }
}
```

The *Solution1* and *Solution2* properties are of type *Complex*, a structure that is also included in the *Petzold.Phone.Silverlight* project but which doesn't implement any operations. The structure exists solely to provide *ToString* methods. (Silverlight 4 includes a *Complex* class in its *System.Numerics* namespace but this is not available in Silverlight for Windows Phone 7.)

Silverlight Project: Petzold.Phone.Silverlight   File: Complex.cs

```
using System;

namespace Petzold.Phone.Silverlight
{
    public struct Complex : IFormattable
    {
        public double Real { get; set; }
        public double Imaginary { get; set; }
```

```
        public Complex(double real, double imaginary) : this()
        {
            Real = real;
            Imaginary = imaginary;
        }

        public override string ToString()
        {
            if (Imaginary == 0)
                return Real.ToString();

            return String.Format("{0} {1} {2}i",
                                 Real,
                                 Math.Sign(Imaginary) >= 1 ? "+" : "-",
                                 Math.Abs(Imaginary));
        }
        public string ToString(string format, IFormatProvider provider)
        {
            if (Imaginary == 0)
                return Real.ToString(format, provider);

            return String.Format(provider,
                                 "{0} {1} {2}i",
                                 Real.ToString(format, provider),
                                 Math.Sign(Imaginary) >= 1 ? "+" : "-",
                                 Math.Abs(Imaginary).ToString(format, provider));
        }
    }
}
```

Complex implements the *IFormattable* interface, which means it has an additional
ToString method that includes a formatting string. This is necessary if you're going to use
numeric formatting specifications in *String.Format* to format these complex numbers, as
StringFormatConverter does.

The QuadraticEquations1 project is a first attempt at providing a user interface for this class.
The *Resources* collection of *MainPage* contains references to the *QuadraticEquationSolver*
class and two converters that you've seen before:

Silverlight Project: QuadraticEquations1   File: **MainPage.xaml** (excerpt)

```
<phone:PhoneApplicationPage.Resources>
    <petzold:QuadraticEquationSolver x:Key="solver" />
    <petzold:StringFormatConverter x:Key="stringFormat" />
    <petzold:BooleanToVisibilityConverter x:Key="booleanToVisibility" />
</phone:PhoneApplicationPage.Resources>
```

The content area has two nested *StackPanel* elements. The horizontal *StackPanel* contains three *TextBox* controls of fixed width with two-way bindings for typing in values of *A*, *B*, and *C*. Notice that the *InputScope* is set to *Number* for a specifically numeric keyboard.

Silverlight Project: QuadraticEquations1   File: MainPage.xaml (excerpt)

```
<Grid x:Name="ContentPanel" Grid.Row="1" Margin="12,0,12,0">
    <StackPanel DataContext="{Binding Source={StaticResource solver}}">
        <StackPanel Orientation="Horizontal"
                    HorizontalAlignment="Center"
                    Margin="12">

            <TextBox Text="{Binding A, Mode=TwoWay}"
                     InputScope="Number"
                     Width="100" />

            <TextBlock Text=" x" VerticalAlignment="Center" />
            <TextBlock Text="2" VerticalAlignment="Center">
                <TextBlock.RenderTransform>
                    <ScaleTransform ScaleX="0.7" ScaleY="0.7" />
                </TextBlock.RenderTransform>
            </TextBlock>
            <TextBlock Text=" + " VerticalAlignment="Center" />

            <TextBox Text="{Binding B, Mode=TwoWay}"
                     InputScope="Number"
                     Width="100" />

            <TextBlock Text=" x + " VerticalAlignment="Center" />

            <TextBox Text="{Binding C, Mode=TwoWay}"
                     InputScope="Number"
                     Width="100" />

            <TextBlock Text=" = 0" VerticalAlignment="Center" />
        </StackPanel>

        <TextBlock Text="{Binding Solution1,
                         Converter={StaticResource stringFormat},
                         ConverterParameter='x = {0:F3}'}"
                   HorizontalAlignment="Center" />

        <TextBlock Text="{Binding Solution2,
                         Converter={StaticResource stringFormat},
                         ConverterParameter='x = {0:F3}'}"
                   Visibility="{Binding HasTwoSolutions,
                                   Converter={StaticResource
booleanToVisibility}}"
                   HorizontalAlignment="Center" />
    </StackPanel>
</Grid>
```

The two *TextBlock* elements at the end display the two solutions; the second *TextBlock* has its *Visibility* property bound to the *HasTwoSolutions* property of *QuadraticEquationSolver* so it's not visible if the equation has only one solution.

Probably the first thing you'll notice is that typing a number into a *TextBox* has no effect on the solutions! At first it seems like the program is not working at all. Only when the *TextBox* you've been typing into loses input focus does the value get transferred to the *A*, *B*, or *C* property of the *QuadraticEquationSolver* class.

This behavior is by design. In the general case, controls could be bound to business objects over a network, and you probably don't want an object bound to a *TextBox* being updated with every little keystroke. Users make a lot of mistakes and perform a lot of backspacing and in some cases waiting until the user has finished is really the proper time to "submit" the final value.

In this particular program, that behavior is probably not what you want. To change it, you'll want to set the *UpdateSourceTrigger* property of the *Binding* in each of the *TextBox* controls to *Explicit*:

```
<TextBox Text="{Binding A, Mode=TwoWay,
                         UpdateSourceTrigger=Explicit}"
         InputScope="Number"
         Width="100" />
```

The *UpdateSourceTrigger* property governs how the source (in this case, the *A*, *B*, or *C* property in *QuadraticEquationSolver*) is updated from the target (the *TextBox*) in a two-way binding. The property is set to a member of the *UpdateSourceTrigger* enumeration. In the

WPF version of *UpdateSourceTrigger*, members named *LostFocus* and *PropertyChanged* are available, but in Silverlight the only two options are *Default* and *Explicit*.

Default means "the default behavior for the target control" which for a *TextBox* target means that the source is updated when the *TextBox* loses focus. When you specify *Explicit*, you need to provide some code that triggers the transfer of data from the target to the source. This could be the role of a *Button* labeled "calculate."

If you'd rather avoid that *Button*, you can trigger the transfer when the text changes in the *TextBox*, so in addition to setting the *UpdateSourceTrigger* property of *Binding*, you need to provide a handler for the *TextChanged* event of the *TextBox*:

```
<TextBox Text="{Binding A, Mode=TwoWay,
                         UpdateSourceTrigger=Explicit}"
         InputScope="Number"
         Width="100"
         TextChanged="OnTextBoxTextChanged" />
```

In the *TextChanged* event handler, you need to "manually" update the source by calling the *UpdateSource* method defined by *BindingExpression*.

Earlier in this chapter, I showed you how to call the *SetBinding* method defined by *FrameworkElement* or the static *BindingOperations.SetBinding* method to set a binding on a property in code. (The *SetBinding* method defined by *FrameworkElement* is just a shortcut for *BindingOperations.SetBinding*.) Both methods return an object of type *BindingExpression*.

If you haven't called these methods in code, you'll be pleased to learn that *FrameworkElement* stores the *BindingExpression* object so it can be retrieved with the public *GetBindingExpression* method. This method requires the particular property that is the target of the data binding, which is always, of course, a dependency property.

Here's the code for updating the source when the *TextBox* text changes:

```
void OnTextBoxTextChanged(object sender, TextChangedEventArgs args)
{
    TextBox txtbox = sender as TextBox;
    BindingExpression bindingExpression = txtbox.GetBindingExpression(TextBox.TextProperty);
    bindingExpression.UpdateSource();
}
```

Another problem with the *TextBox* is that the user can enter a character string that cannot be resolved to a number. Although you can't see it, a converter is at work converting the *string* object from the *TextBox* to a *double* to set to the *A*, *B*, or *C* property of *QuadraticEquationSolver*. This hidden converter probably uses the *Double.Parse* or *Double.TryParse* method.

If you'd like to catch exceptions raised by this converter, you can. You'll probably want to set two more properties of the *Binding* class to *true*, as shown here:

```
<TextBox Text="{Binding A, Mode=TwoWay,
                         UpdateSourceTrigger=Explicit,
                         ValidatesOnExceptions=True,
                         NotifyOnValidationError=True}"
          InputScope="Number"
          Width="100"
          TextChanged="OnTextBoxTextChanged" />
```

This causes a *BindingValidationError* event to be fired. This is a routed event, so it can be handled anywhere in the visual tree above the *TextBox*. Most conveniently in a small program, a handler for the event can be set right in the MainPage constructor:

```
readonly Brush okBrush;
static readonly Brush errorBrush = new SolidColorBrush(Colors.Red);

public MainPage()
{
    InitializeComponent();
    okBrush = new TextBox().Foreground;
    BindingValidationError += OnBindingValidationError;
}
```

Notice that the normal *Foreground* brush of the *TextBox* is saved as a field. Here's a simple event handler that colors the text in the *TextBox* red if it's invalid:

```
void OnBindingValidationError(object sender, ValidationErrorEventArgs args)
{
    TextBox txtbox = args.OriginalSource as TextBox;
    txtbox.Foreground = errorBrush;
}
```

Of course, as soon the *TextBox* text changes again, you'll want to restore that color, which you can do in the *OnTextBoxTextChanged* method:

```
void OnTextBoxTextChanged(object sender, TextChangedEventArgs args)
{
    TextBox txtbox = sender as TextBox;
    txtbox.Foreground = okBrush;
    ...
}
```

These two techniques—updating with each keystroke and giving a visual indication of invalid input—are combined in the QuadraticEquations2 project. Here's the XAML file:

Silverlight Project: QuadraticEquations2   File: MainPage.xaml (excerpt)

```
<Grid x:Name="ContentPanel" Grid.Row="1" Margin="12,0,12,0">
    <StackPanel DataContext="{Binding Source={StaticResource solver}}">
        <StackPanel Orientation="Horizontal"
                    HorizontalAlignment="Center"
                    Margin="12">
```

```
            <TextBox Text="{Binding A, Mode=TwoWay,
                                    UpdateSourceTrigger=Explicit,
                                    ValidatesOnExceptions=True,
                                    NotifyOnValidationError=True}"
                     InputScope="Number"
                     Width="100"
                     TextChanged="OnTextBoxTextChanged" />

            <TextBlock Text=" x" VerticalAlignment="Center" />
            <TextBlock Text="2" VerticalAlignment="Center">
                <TextBlock.RenderTransform>
                    <ScaleTransform ScaleX="0.7" ScaleY="0.7" />
                </TextBlock.RenderTransform>
            </TextBlock>
            <TextBlock Text=" + " VerticalAlignment="Center" />

            <TextBox Text="{Binding B, Mode=TwoWay,
                                    UpdateSourceTrigger=Explicit,
                                    ValidatesOnExceptions=True,
                                    NotifyOnValidationError=True}"
                     InputScope="Number"
                     Width="100"
                     TextChanged="OnTextBoxTextChanged" />

            <TextBlock Text=" x + " VerticalAlignment="Center" />

            <TextBox Text="{Binding C, Mode=TwoWay,
                                    UpdateSourceTrigger=Explicit,
                                    ValidatesOnExceptions=True,
                                    NotifyOnValidationError=True}"
                     InputScope="Number"
                     Width="100"
                     TextChanged="OnTextBoxTextChanged" />

            <TextBlock Text=" = 0" VerticalAlignment="Center" />
        </StackPanel>
        <StackPanel Name="result"
                    Orientation="Horizontal"
                    HorizontalAlignment="Center">

            <TextBlock Text="{Binding Solution1.Real,
                                    Converter={StaticResource stringFormat},
                                    ConverterParameter='x = {0:F3} '}" />
            <TextBlock Text="+"
                       Visibility="{Binding HasOneSolution,
                                    Converter={StaticResource
booleanToVisibility}}" />

            <TextBlock Text="&#x00B1;"
                       Visibility="{Binding HasTwoSolutions,
                                    Converter={StaticResource
```

```
booleanToVisibility}}" />

            <TextBlock Text="{Binding Solution1.Imaginary,
                                      Converter={StaticResource stringFormat},
                                      ConverterParameter=' {0:F3}i'}" />
        </StackPanel>
    </StackPanel>
</Grid>
```

You might also notice that I completely revamped the display of the solutions. Rather than two *TextBlock* elements to display two solutions, I use four *TextBlock* elements to display a single solution that might contain a ± sign (Unicode 0x00B1).

The code-behind file implements the updating and error handling:

Silverlight Project: QuadraticEquationSolver2   File: MainPage.xaml.cs

```
using System;
using System.Windows;
using System.Windows.Controls;
using System.Windows.Data;
using System.Windows.Media;
using Microsoft.Phone.Controls;

namespace QuadraticEquationSolver2
{
    public partial class MainPage : PhoneApplicationPage
    {
        readonly Brush okBrush;
        static readonly Brush errorBrush = new SolidColorBrush(Colors.Red);

        public MainPage()
        {
            InitializeComponent();
            okBrush = new TextBox().Foreground;
            BindingValidationError += OnBindingValidationError;
        }

        void OnTextBoxTextChanged(object sender, TextChangedEventArgs args)
        {
            TextBox txtbox = sender as TextBox;
            txtbox.Foreground = okBrush;

            BindingExpression bindingExpression =
                txtbox.GetBindingExpression(TextBox.TextProperty);
            bindingExpression.UpdateSource();
        }
```

```
        void OnBindingValidationError(object sender, ValidationErrorEventArgs args)
        {
            TextBox txtbox = args.OriginalSource as TextBox;
            txtbox.Foreground = errorBrush;
        }
    }
}
```

Here's a *TextBox* indicating that an entry is incorrect:

If you had written a quadratic equation solver for Windows Phone 7 prior to this chapter, the screen might looked pretty much the same, but I suspect the program would have been structured quite differently. I know that's the case if you wrote such a program for a code-only environment such as Windows Forms.

Notice how converting the program to a mostly XAML solution causes us to rethink the whole architecture of the program. It's always an interesting process to me how our tools seems to govern how we solve problems. But in some ways this is a good thing, and if you find yourself writing code specifically to use in XAML (such as binding services and data converters), I think you're on the right track.

Chapter 13
Vector Graphics

The world of two-dimensional computer graphics is generally divided between vector graphics and raster graphics—a graphics of lines and a graphics of pixels—a graphics of *draw* programs and a graphics of *paint* programs—a graphics of cartoons and a graphics of photographs.

Vector graphics is the visual realization of analytic geometry. Two-dimensional coordinate points in the form (*x, y*) define straight lines and curves. In Silverlight, these curves can be arcs on the circumference of an ellipse or Bezier curves, either in the customary cubic form or in a simplified quadratic form. You can "stroke" these lines with a pen of a desired brush, width, and style. A series of connected lines and curves can also define an enclosed area that can be filled with a brush.

Raster graphics (which I'll discuss in the next chapter) involves bitmaps. In Silverlight it is very easy to display a PNG or JPEG file using an *Image* element as I demonstrated as early as Chapter 4. But as I'll show you in the next chapter, it's also possible to generate bitmaps algorithmically in code using the *WriteableBitmap* class. The worlds of raster graphics and vector graphics intersect when an *ImageBrush* is used to fill an area, or when vector graphics are used to generate an image on a *WriteableBitmap*.

The *Shapes* Library

A Silverlight program that needs to draw vector graphics uses classes defined in the *System .Windows.Shapes* namespace, commonly referred to as the *Shapes* library. This namespace consists of an abstract class named *Shape* and six sealed classes that derive from *Shape*:

Object
      DependencyObject (abstract)
            FrameworkElement (abstract)
                Shape (abstract)
                      Rectangle (sealed)
                      Ellipse (sealed)
                      Line (sealed)
                      Polyline (sealed)
                      Polygon (sealed)
                      Path (sealed)

The *Shape* class derives from *FrameworkElement*, which means that these objects get touch input, participate in layout, and can have transforms. In Silverlight there is insufficient information to allow you to derive a class from *Shape* itself.

You've already seen *Rectangle* and *Ellipse*, but these are really two oddball classes in the realm of vector graphics because they don't contain any coordinate points. You can just stick an *Ellipse* in a *UserControl* and it fills the whole control. You can size the element, but positioning it at an arbitrary point requires a *Margin* or *Padding* property, or a *RenderTransform*, or putting it on a *Canvas* and using the *Left* and *Top* attached properties.

The other four classes of *Shape* are different; these allow you to position the elements with actual coordinate points. Although I'll discuss the *Path* class last, it is so versatile that it is pretty much the only class you need for all your vector graphics jobs. If you need to draw an arc or a Bezier spline, you'll be using the *Path* class.

Shape defines 11 settable properties that are inherited by all its descendants:

- *Fill* of type *Brush*
- *Stroke* of type *Brush*
- *StrokeThickness* of type *double*
- *StrokeStartLineCap* and *StrokeEndLineCap* of type *PenLineCap*
- *StrokeLineJoin* of type *PenLineJoin*
- *StrokeMiterLimit* of type *double*
- *StrokeDashArray* of type *DoubleCollection*
- *StrokeDashCap* of type *PenLineCap*
- *StrokeDashOffset* of type *double*
- *Stretch* property of type *Stretch*

You've already seen the first three properties in connection with *Rectangle* and *Ellipse*. The *Fill* property specifies the *Brush* used to fill the interior of the figure; the *Stroke* property is the *Brush* used to color the outline of the figure, and *StrokeThickness* is the width of that outline.

All the other properties can be used with *Rectangle* and *Ellipse* as well. Although the two enumerations (*PenLineCap* and *PenLineJoin*) allude to a *Pen*, there is no *Pen* class in Silverlight. Conceptually, the properties beginning with the word *Stroke* together comprise an object traditionally regarded as a pen.

Canvas and *Grid*

The *Line* class defines four properties of type *double* named *X1*, *Y1*, *X2*, and *Y2*. The line is drawn from the point (*X1*, *Y1*) to the point (*X2*, *Y2*) relative to its parent:

```
<Canvas Background="LightCyan">
    <Line X1="50" Y1="100"
          X2="200" Y2="150"
          Stroke="Blue" />
</Canvas>
```

Many of the examples in this program will be shown as a snippet of XAML and the corresponding image in a 480-square pixel area. At the end of the chapter I'll describe the program that created these images. For the printed page I've made the resolution of these images about 240 dots per inch so they are approximately the same size as what you would see on the actual phone.

The line begins at the coordinate point (50, 100) and ends at the point (200, 150). All coordinates are relative to an upper-left origin; increasing values of *X* go from left to right; increasing values of *Y* go from top to bottom.

The *X1, Y1, X2,* and *Y2* properties are all backed by dependency properties so they can be the targets of styles, data bindings, and animations.

Although the *Canvas* panel seems like a natural for vector graphics, you'll get the same image if you use a single-cell *Grid*:

```
<Grid Background="LightCyan">
    <Line X1="50" Y1="100"
          X2="200" Y2="150"
          Stroke="Blue" />
</Grid>
```

Normally when you use a *Canvas* you use the *Canvas.Left* and *Canvas.Top* attached properties to position elements within the *Canvas*. Those properties are not required with the *Line* because it has its own coordinates. You could use the attached properties with the *Line* but the values are compounded with the coordinates:

```
<Canvas Background="LightCyan">
    <Line X1="50" Y1="100"
```

```
            X2="200" Y2="150"
            Canvas.Left="150"
            Canvas.Top="100"
            Stroke="Blue" />
</Canvas>
```

Usually when you're working with elements that indicate actual coordinate positions, you'll use the *Canvas.Left* and *Canvas.Top* attached properties only for special purposes, such as moving an object relative to the *Canvas*.

Moreover, you'll recall that a *Canvas* always reports to the layout system that it has a size of zero. If you subject the *Canvas* to anything other than *Stretch* alignment, it will shrink into nothingness regardless of its contents.

For these reasons, I tend to put my vector graphics in a single-cell *Grid* rather than a *Canvas*.

If a *Grid* contains one or more *Line* elements (or any other coordinate-based elements), it will report a size that comprises the maximum non-negative *X* coordinate and the maximum non-negative *Y* coordinate of all its children. This can sometimes seem a little weird. If a *Grid* contains a *Line* from (200, 300) to (210, 310), the *Line* will report an *ActualWidth* of 210 and an *ActualHeight* of 310, and the *Grid* will be 210 pixels wide and 310 pixels tall, even though the rendered *Line* needs only a tiny corner of that space. (Actually, the *Line* and the *Grid* will be at least an extra pixel larger to accommodate the *StrokeThickness* of the rendered *Line*.)

Coordinates can be negative, but the *Grid* does not take account of negative coordinates. A negative coordinate will actually be displayed to the left of or above the *Grid*. I have spent much time thinking about this behavior, and I am convinced it is correct.

Overlapping and *ZIndex*

Here are two lines:

```
<Grid Background="LightCyan">
    <Line X1="100" Y1="300"
          X2="200" Y2="50"
          Stroke="Blue" />

    <Line X1="50"  Y1="100"
          X2="300" Y2="200"
          Stroke="Red" />
</Grid>
```

The second one overlaps the first one. You can see that more clearly if you go beyond the default 1-pixel thickness of the line using *StrokeThickness*:

```
<Grid Background="LightCyan">
    <Line X1="100" Y1="300"
          X2="200" Y2="50"
          Stroke="Blue"
          StrokeThickness="5" />

    <Line X1="50" Y1="100"
          X2="300" Y2="200"
          Stroke="Red"
          StrokeThickness="30" />
</Grid>
```

If you would prefer that the blue line be on top of the red line, there are two ways you can do it. You could simply swap the order of the two lines in the *Grid*:

```
<Grid Background="LightCyan">
    <Line X1="50" Y1="100"
          X2="300" Y2="200"
          Stroke="Red"
          StrokeThickness="30" />

    <Line X1="100" Y1="300"
          X2="200" Y2="50"
          Stroke="Blue"
          StrokeThickness="5" />
</Grid>
```

Or, you could set the *Canvas.ZIndex* property. Although this property is defined by *Canvas* it works with any type of panel:

```
<Grid Background="LightCyan">
    <Line Canvas.ZIndex="1"
          X1="100" Y1="300"
          X2="200" Y2="50"
          Stroke="Blue"
          StrokeThickness="5" />

    <Line Canvas.ZIndex="0"
          X1="50" Y1="100"
          X2="300" Y2="200"
          Stroke="Red"
          StrokeThickness="30" />

</Grid>
```

Polylines and Custom Curves

The *Line* element looks simple but the markup is a little bloated. You can actually reduce the markup for drawing a single line by switching from the *Line* to the *Polyline*:

```
<Grid Background="LightCyan">
    <Polyline Points="100 300 200 50"
              Stroke="Blue"
              StrokeThickness="5" />
    <Polyline Points="50 100 300 200"
              Stroke="Red"
              StrokeThickness="30" />
</Grid>
```

The *Points* property of the *Polyline* class is of type *PointCollection*, a collection of *Point* objects. In XAML you indicate multiple points by just alternating the *X* and *Y* coordinates. You can string out the numbers with spaces between them as I've done, or you can clarify the markup a little with commas. Some people prefer commas between the *X* and *Y* coordinates:

```
<Polyline Points="100,300 200,50" . . .
```

Others (including me) prefer to separate the individual points with commas:

```
<Polyline Points="100 300, 200 50"
```

The advantage of *Polyline* is that you can have as many points as you want:

```
<Grid Background="LightCyan">
    <Polyline Points="100 300, 200  50,
                      350 100, 200 250"
              Stroke="Blue"
              StrokeThickness="5" />

    <Polyline Points=" 50 100, 300 200,
                      300 400"
              Stroke="Red"
              StrokeThickness="30" />
</Grid>
```

Each additional point increases the total polyline by another line segment.

The *Polyline* does have one significant disadvantage that *Line* doesn't have: Because you're now dealing with a collection of *Point* objects, the individual points can't be targets of a style, or a data binding, or an animation. This is not to say that you can't *change* the *PointCollection* at runtime and have that change reflected in the rendered *Polyline*. You surely can, as I'll demonstrate in the GrowingPolygons program later in this chapter.

Although the *Polyline* can draw some simple connected lines, it tends to feel underutilized if it's not fulfilling its true destiny of drawing complex curves, usually generated algorithmically in code. The *Polyline* is always a collection of straight lines, but if you make those lines short enough and numerous enough, the result will be indistinguishable from a curve.

For example, let's suppose you want to use *Polyline* to draw a circle. Commonly, a circle centered at the point (0, 0) with a radius *R* is defined as all points (*x*, *y*) that satisfy the equation:

$$x^2 + y^2 = R^2$$

This is also, of course, the Pythagorean Formula.

But when generating points to draw a graphical circle, this formula tends to be a little clumsy: You need to pick values of *x* between −*R* and *R*, and then solve for *y* (keeping in mind that most values of *x* correspond to two values of *y*) and even if you do this in a systematic manner, you're going to get a higher density of points in the region where *x* is close to 0 than the region where *y* is close to 0.

A much better approach for computer graphics involves parametric equations, where both *x* and *y* are functions of a third variable, sometimes called *t* to suggest time. In this case that third variable is simply an angle ranging from 0 to 360°.

Suppose the circle is centered on the point (0, 0) and has a radius of *R*. The circle will be enclosed within a box where values of *x* go from −*R* on the left to +*R* on the right. In keeping with the Silverlight convention that increasing values of *y* go down, values of *y* range from −*R* on the top to +*R* on the bottom.

Let's begin with an angle of 0° at the rightmost edge of the circle, which is the point (*R*, 0), and let's go clockwise around the circle. As the angle goes from 0° to 90°, *x* goes from *R* to 0, and then *x* goes to −*R* at 180° and then goes back down to zero at 270° and back to *R* at 360°. This is a familiar pattern:

$$x = R \cdot \cos(\propto)$$

At the same time, the values of *y* go from 0 to *R* to 0 to −*R* and back to 0, or

$$y = R \cdot \sin(\propto)$$

Depending where the circle begins, and in what direction you go, you could have slightly different formulas where the sine and cosine functions are switched, or one or both or negative.

If you use different values of R for the two formulas, you'll draw an ellipse. If you want the circle centered at the point (C_x, C_y), you can add these values to the previous results:

$$x = C_x + R \cdot \cos(\alpha)$$

$$y = C_y + R \cdot \sin(\alpha)$$

In a program, you put those two formulas in a *for* loop that increments an *angle* value ranging from 0 to 360 to generate a collection of points.

How much granularity is required to make the resultant circle look smooth? In this particular example, it depends on the radius. The circumference of a circle is $2\pi R$, so if the radius is 240 pixels (for example), the circumference is approximately 1,500 pixels. Divide by 360° and you get about 4, which means that if you increment the angle in the *for* loop by 0.25°, the resultant points will be about a pixel apart. (You'll see later in this chapter that you can get by with a lot fewer points.)

Let's create a new projecvt. Bring up the MainPage.cs file and install a handler for the *Loaded* event to allow accessing the dimensions of the *ContentPanel* grid. Here are calculations for center and radius for a circle to occupy the center of a content panel and reach to its edges:

```
Point center = new Point(ContentPanel.ActualWidth / 2,
                         ContentPanel.ActualHeight / 2 - 1);
double radius = Math.Min(center.X - 1, center.Y - 1);
```

Notice the pixel subtracted from the calculation of the *radius*. This is to prevent the circle from being geometrically the same as the content area size. The stroke thickness straddles the geometric line so it would otherwise get cropped off at the edges.

Now create a *Polyline* and set the *Stroke* and *StrokeThickness* properties:

```
Polyline polyline = new Polyline();
polyline.Stroke = this.Resources["PhoneForegroundBrush"] as Brush;
polyline.StrokeThickness = (double)this.Resources["PhoneStrokeThickness"];
```

Calculate the *Point* objects in a *for* loop based on the formulas I've just showed you and add them to the *Points* collection of the *polyline*:

```
for (double angle = 0; angle < 360; angle += 0.25)
{
    double radians = Math.PI * angle / 180;
    double x = center.X + radius * Math.Cos(radians);
    double y = center.Y + radius * Math.Sin(radians);
    polyline.Points.Add(new Point(x, y));
}
```

Now add the *Polyline* to the *Grid*:

```
ContentPanel.Children.Add(polyline);
```

And here's the result:

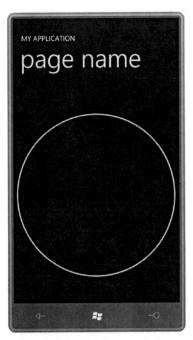

So big deal. We created a circle a hard way rather than an easy way. And it's not even a complete circle: Because the *angle* in the *for* loop didn't go all the way to 360, there's actually a little gap at the right side.

But instead of fixing that problem, let's do something a little different. Let's make the angle go all the way to 3600:

```
for (double angle = 0; angle < 3600; angle += 0.25)
```

Now the loop will go around the circle 10 times. Let's use that *angle* and the original *radius* value to calculate a *scaledRadius*:

```
double scaledRadius = radius * angle / 3600;
```

And use that *scaledRadius* value for multiplying by the sine and cosine values. Now the result is an Archimedian spiral:

Here's the complete class:

Silverlight Project: Spiral   File: MainPage.xaml.cs (excerpt)

```
public partial class MainPage : PhoneApplicationPage
{
    public MainPage()
    {
        InitializeComponent();
        Loaded += OnLoaded;
    }

    void OnLoaded(object sender, RoutedEventArgs args)
    {
        Point center = new Point(ContentPanel.ActualWidth / 2,
                                 ContentPanel.ActualHeight / 2 - 1);
        double radius = Math.Min(center.X - 1, center.Y - 1);

        Polyline polyline = new Polyline();
        polyline.Stroke = this.Resources["PhoneForegroundBrush"] as Brush;
        polyline.StrokeThickness = (double)this.Resources["PhoneStrokeThickness"];

        for (double angle = 0; angle < 3600; angle += 0.25)
        {
```

```
                double scaledRadius = radius * angle / 3600;
                double radians = Math.PI * angle / 180;
                double x = center.X + scaledRadius * Math.Cos(radians);
                double y = center.Y + scaledRadius * Math.Sin(radians);
                polyline.Points.Add(new Point(x, y));
            }
            ContentPanel.Children.Add(polyline);
        }
    }
```

It's not necessary to create the *Polyline* object in code: You could define it in XAML and then just access it to put the points in the *Points* collection. In Chapter 15 I'll show you how to apply a rotation animation to the spiral so that you can hypnotize yourself.

Caps, Joins, and Dashes

When you're displaying thick lines, you might want a little different appearance on the ends of the lines. These are known as line *caps*—"caps" like a hat. The available caps are members of the *PenLineCap* enumeration: *Flat* (the default), *Square*, *Round*, and *Triangle*. Set the *StrokeStartLineCap* property to one of these values for the cap at the beginning of the line, and set *StrokeEndLineCap* for the cap at the end. Here are *Round* and *Triangle* capping off a 30-pixel line:

```
<Grid Background="LightCyan">
    <Polyline Points=" 50 100, 300 200,
                       300 400"
              Stroke="HotPink"
              StrokeThickness="30"
              StrokeStartLineCap="Round"
              StrokeEndLineCap="Triangle" />
</Grid>
```

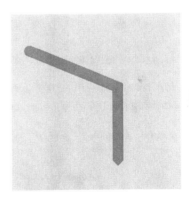

The difference between *Flat* and *Square* might not be obvious at first. To better clarify the difference, the following markup displays a thinner line over the thick line with the same coordinates to indicate the geometric start and end of the line:

```
<Grid Background="LightCyan">
    <Polyline Points=" 50 100, 300 200,
                       300 400"
              Stroke="HotPink"
              StrokeThickness="30"
              StrokeStartLineCap="Flat"
```

```
                    StrokeEndLineCap="Square" />

    <Polyline Points=" 50 100, 300 200,
                        300 400"
              Stroke="Black" />
</Grid>
```

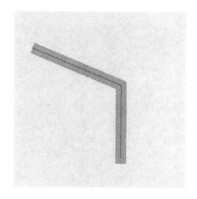

The *Flat* cap (at the upper left) cuts off the line at the geometric point. The *Square* extends the line for half the line thickness. My favorite caps are the rounded ones:

```
<Grid Background="LightCyan">
    <Polyline Points=" 50 100, 300 200,
                        300 400"
              Stroke="HotPink"
              StrokeThickness="30"
              StrokeStartLineCap="Round"
              StrokeEndLineCap="Round"    />

    <Polyline Points=" 50 100, 300 200,
                        300 400"
              Stroke="Black" />
</Grid>
```

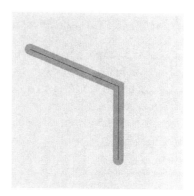

As you can see, they also extend the rendered size of the line by half the stroke thickness.

You can also specify what happens at the corners. Set the *StrokeLineJoin* property to a member of the *PenLineJoin* enumeration. Here's *Round*:

```
<Grid Background="LightCyan">
    <Polyline Points=" 50 100, 300 200,
                        100 300"
              Stroke="HotPink"
              StrokeThickness="30"
              StrokeStartLineCap="Round"
              StrokeEndLineCap="Round"
              StrokeLineJoin="Round" />

    <Polyline Points=" 50 100, 300 200,
                        100 300"
              Stroke="Black" />
</Grid>
```

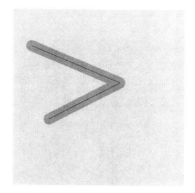

Or *Bevel*:

```
<Grid Background="LightCyan">
    <Polyline Points=" 50 100, 300 200,
                      100 300"
            Stroke="HotPink"
            StrokeThickness="30"
            StrokeStartLineCap="Round"
            StrokeEndLineCap="Round"
            StrokeLineJoin="Bevel" />

    <Polyline Points=" 50 100, 300 200,
                      100 300"
            Stroke="Black" />
</Grid>
```

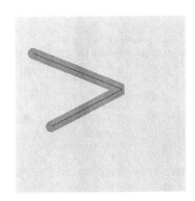

Or *Miter*, which is the default:

```
<Grid Background="LightCyan">
    <Polyline Points=" 50 100, 300 200,
                      100 300"
            Stroke="HotPink"
            StrokeThickness="30"
            StrokeStartLineCap="Round"
            StrokeEndLineCap="Round"
            StrokeLineJoin="Miter" />

    <Polyline Points=" 50 100, 300 200,
                      100 300"
            Stroke="Black" />
</Grid>
```

The *Miter* join has a little built-in problem. If the lines meet at a very sharp angle, the miter can be very long. For example, a 10-pixel wide line that makes an angle of 1° will have a miter point over 500 pixels long! To avoid this type of weirdness a *StrokeMiterLimit* property kicks in for extreme cases:

```
<Grid Background="LightCyan">
    <Polyline Points="50 230, 240 240,
                      50 250"
            Stroke="HotPink"
            StrokeThickness="30"
            StrokeStartLineCap="Round"
            StrokeEndLineCap="Round"
            StrokeLineJoin="Miter" />

    <Polyline Points="50 230, 240 240,
                      50 250"
            Stroke="Black" />
</Grid>
```

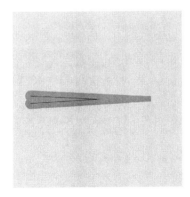

The default value is 10 (relative to half the *StrokeThickness*) but you can make it longer if you want:

```
<Grid Background="LightCyan">
    <Polyline Points="50 230, 240 240,
                      50 250"
              Stroke="HotPink"
              StrokeThickness="30"
              StrokeStartLineCap="Round"
              StrokeEndLineCap="Round"
              StrokeLineJoin="Miter"
              StrokeMiterLimit="50" />

    <Polyline Points="50 230, 240 240,
                      50 250"
              Stroke="Black" />
</Grid>
```

Here are two lines, one thick, one thin overlaying the thick line, with the same geometric points, going from the upper-left to the lower-left:

```
<Grid Background="LightCyan">
    <Polyline Points="100 100, 380 100,
                      380 380, 100 380"
              Stroke="HotPink"
              StrokeThickness="30"
              StrokeStartLineCap="Round"
              StrokeEndLineCap="Round"
              StrokeLineJoin="Round" />

    <Polyline Points="100 100, 380 100,
                      380 380, 100 380"
              Stroke="Black" />
</Grid>
```

You can make the line dashed by setting the *StrokeDashArray*, which is generally just two numbers, for example 1 and 1:

```
<Grid Background="LightCyan">
    <Polyline Points="100 100, 380 100,
                      380 380, 100 380"
              Stroke="HotPink"
              StrokeThickness="30"
              StrokeStartLineCap="Round"
              StrokeEndLineCap="Round"
              StrokeLineJoin="Round"
              StrokeDashArray="1 1" />

    <Polyline Points="100 100, 380 100,
                      380 380, 100 380"
              Stroke="Black" />
</Grid>
```

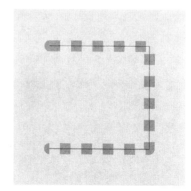

What this means is that a dash will be drawn for one-line thickness (30 pixels in this case), followed by a one-line thickness gap, and repeated until the end. As you can see, the caps are really handled a little differently; they are drawn or not drawn depending on whether they occur when a dash or a gap is in progress.

You can make the dashes longer by increasing the first number,

```
<Grid Background="LightCyan">
    <Polyline Points="100 100, 380 100,
                      380 380, 100 380"
              Stroke="HotPink"
              StrokeThickness="30"
              StrokeStartLineCap="Round"
              StrokeEndLineCap="Round"
              StrokeLineJoin="Round"
              StrokeDashArray="2 1" />

    <Polyline Points="100 100, 380 100,
                      380 380, 100 380"
              Stroke="Black" />
</Grid>
```

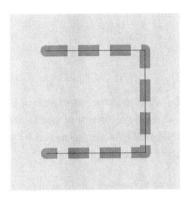

However, you'll probably also want to give the dashes their own caps. Set *StrokeDashCap* to a member of the *PenLineCap* enumeration, either *Flat* (the default), *Triangle*, *Square*, or *Round*, which is my preference:

```
<Grid Background="LightCyan">
    <Polyline Points="100 100, 380 100,
                      380 380, 100 380"
              Stroke="HotPink"
              StrokeThickness="30"
              StrokeStartLineCap="Round"
              StrokeEndLineCap="Round"
              StrokeLineJoin="Round"
              StrokeDashArray="2 1"
              StrokeDashCap="Round" />

    <Polyline Points="100 100, 380 100,
                      380 380, 100 380"
              Stroke="Black" />
</Grid>
```

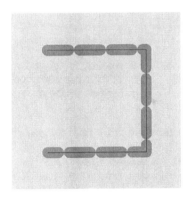

A little problem has arisen. Each of the dashes has acquired a rounded cap, so they've each increased in length on both ends by half the line thickness, and now the dashes actually touch. You need to fix that by increasing the gap:

```
<Grid Background="LightCyan">
    <Polyline Points="100 100, 380 100,
                      380 380, 100 380"
              Stroke="HotPink"
              StrokeThickness="30"
              StrokeStartLineCap="Round"
```

```
            StrokeEndLineCap="Round"
            StrokeLineJoin="Round"
            StrokeDashArray="2 2"
            StrokeDashCap="Round" />

    <Polyline Points="100 100, 380 100,
                      380 380, 100 380"
              Stroke="Black" />
</Grid>
```

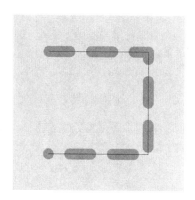

If you want to draw a dotted line with actual round dots, obviously you want to use the *Round* dash cap, and you want each dot to be separated by its neighbor by the dot width. The *StrokeDashArray* required for this job is somewhat non-intuitive. It's a dash length of 0 and a gap length of 2:

```
<Grid Background="LightCyan">
    <Polyline Points="100 100, 380 100,
                      380 380, 100 380"
              Stroke="HotPink"
              StrokeThickness="30"
              StrokeStartLineCap="Round"
              StrokeEndLineCap="Round"
              StrokeLineJoin="Round"
              StrokeDashArray="0 2"
              StrokeDashCap="Round" />

    <Polyline Points="100 100, 380 100,
                      380 380, 100 380"
              Stroke="Black" />
</Grid>
```

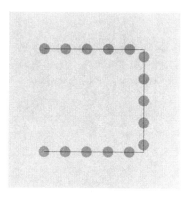

You can have more than two numbers. Here's a dot and dash configuration:

```
<Grid Background="LightCyan">
    <Polyline Points="100 100, 380 100,
                      380 380, 100 380"
              Stroke="HotPink"
              StrokeThickness="30"
              StrokeStartLineCap="Round"
              StrokeEndLineCap="Round"
              StrokeLineJoin="Round"
              StrokeDashArray="0 2 2 2"
              StrokeDashCap="Round" />

    <Polyline Points="100 100, 380 100,
                      380 380, 100 380"
              Stroke="Black" />
</Grid>
```

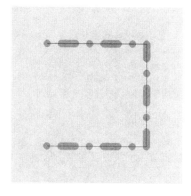

You don't even need an even number of numbers:

```
<Grid Background="LightCyan">
    <Polyline Points="100 100, 380 100,
                      380 380, 100 380"
            Stroke="HotPink"
            StrokeThickness="30"
            StrokeStartLineCap="Round"
            StrokeEndLineCap="Round"
            StrokeLineJoin="Round"
            StrokeDashArray="1 2 3"
            StrokeDashCap="Round" />

    <Polyline Points="100 100, 380 100,
                      380 380, 100 380"
            Stroke="Black" />
</Grid>
```

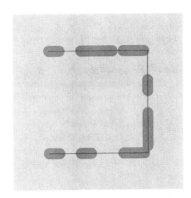

The other dash-related property is *StrokeDashOffset*, and it is also relative to the thickness of the line. This property lets you start the dashes in the middle of a dash, which makes the first dash (at the upper-left corner) smaller than the rest:

```
<Grid Background="LightCyan">
        <Polyline Points="100 100, 380 100,
                          380 380, 100 380"
                Stroke="HotPink"
                StrokeThickness="30"
                StrokeStartLineCap="Round"
                StrokeEndLineCap="Round"
                StrokeLineJoin="Round"
                StrokeDashArray="2 2"
                StrokeDashCap="Round"
                StrokeDashOffset="1" />

        <Polyline Points="100 100, 380 100,
                          380 380, 100 380"
                Stroke="Black" />
</Grid>
```

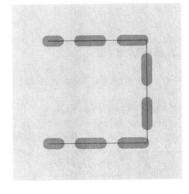

Or you can start with a gap:

```
<Grid Background="LightCyan">
    <Polyline Points="100 100, 380 100,
                      380 380, 100 380"
            Stroke="HotPink"
            StrokeThickness="30"
            StrokeStartLineCap="Round"
            StrokeEndLineCap="Round"
            StrokeLineJoin="Round"
            StrokeDashArray="2 2"
            StrokeDashCap="Round"
            StrokeDashOffset="3" />

    <Polyline Points="100 100, 380 100,
```

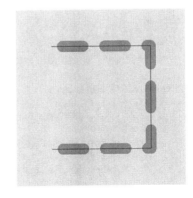

```
                                  380 380, 100 380"
                      Stroke="Black" />
    </Grid>
```

You can use a dotted line around an ellipse if you want:

```
<Grid Background="LightCyan">
    <Ellipse Width="400" Height="400"
             HorizontalAlignment="Center"
             VerticalAlignment="Center"
             Stroke="Red"
             StrokeThickness="23.22"
             StrokeDashArray="0 1.5"
             StrokeDashCap="Round" />
</Grid>
```

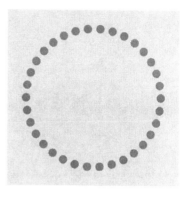

It's an unusual look, but you really have to experiment or do some calculations so you don't get half a dot in there.

Polygon and Fill

The *Polyline* that I've been using to demonstrate dotted lines is only three sides of a square:

```
<Grid Background="LightCyan">
    <Polyline Points="100 100, 380 100,
                      380 380, 100 380"
              Stroke="Red"
              StrokeThickness="20"
              StrokeStartLineCap="Round"
              StrokeEndLineCap="Round"
              StrokeLineJoin="Round"
              StrokeDashArray="0 2"
              StrokeDashCap="Round" />
</Grid>
```

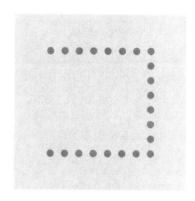

But if you set the *Fill* brush, the interior is filled as if the polyline describes a closed area:

```
<Grid Background="LightCyan">
    <Polyline Points="100 100, 380 100,
                      380 380, 100 380"
              Stroke="Red"
              StrokeThickness="20"
              Fill="Blue"
              StrokeStartLineCap="Round"
```

```
            StrokeEndLineCap="Round"
            StrokeLineJoin="Round"
            StrokeDashArray="0 2"
            StrokeDashCap="Round" />
</Grid>
```

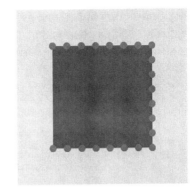

If you want the figure to be really closed, you can add another point to the *Points* collection that is the same as the first point, or you can use a *Polygon* rather than a *Polyline*:

```
<Grid Background="LightCyan">
    <Polygon Points="100 100, 380 100,
                     380 380, 100 380"
            Stroke="Red"
            StrokeThickness="20"
            Fill="Blue"
            StrokeStartLineCap="Round"
            StrokeEndLineCap="Round"
            StrokeLineJoin="Round"
            StrokeDashArray="0 2"
            StrokeDashCap="Round" />
</Grid>
```

Both elements have the same *Points* collection, but the *Polygon* is closed automatically if necessary.

Once you start filling enclosed area with *Polygon*, a question comes up about how the interior should be handled when boundary lines overlap. The *Polygon* class defines a property named *FillRule* that gives you a choice. The classic example is the five-pointed star. Here's the default *FillRule*, called *EvenOdd*:

```
<Grid Background="LightCyan">
    <Polygon Points="240  48, 352 396,
                     58 180, 422 180,
                     128 396"
            Stroke="Red"
            StrokeThickness="10"
            Fill="Blue"
            FillRule="EvenOdd" />
</Grid>
```

The *EvenOdd* algorithm determines if an enclosed area should be filled or not by conceptually taking a point in that area, for example, somewhere in the center, and drawing an imaginary line out to infinity. That imaginary line will cross some boundary lines. If it crosses an odd number of boundary lines, such as happens in the five points, then the area is filled. For an even number, like the center, the area is not filled.

The alternative is a *FillRule* called *NonZero*:

```
<Grid Background="LightCyan">
    <Polygon Points="240  48, 352 396,
                      58 180, 422 180,
                     128 396"
             Stroke="Red"
             StrokeThickness="10"
             Fill="Blue"
             FillRule="NonZero" />
</Grid>
```

The *NonZero* fill rule is a bit more complex because it takes account of the directions that boundary lines are drawn. If the boundary lines drawn in one direction balance out the boundary lines drawn in the opposite direction, then the area is not filled. In any interior area of this star, however, all the boundary lines go in the same direction.

Neither of these two *FillRule* options guarantees that all interior areas get filled. Here's a rather artificial figure that has an enclosed but unfilled area even with *NonZero*:

```
<Grid Background="LightCyan">
    <Polygon Points=" 80 160,  80 320,
                     240 320, 240  80,
                     400  80, 400 240,
                     160 240, 160 400,
                     320 400, 320 160"
             Stroke="Red"
             StrokeThickness="10"
             Fill="Blue"
             FillRule="NonZero" />
</Grid>
```

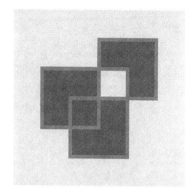

The *Stretch* Property

The only settable property defined by *Shape* that I haven't discussed yet is *Stretch*. This is similar to the same property in the *Image* element; you set it to a member of the *Stretch* enumeration, either *None* (the default), *Fill*, *Uniform*, or *UniformToFill*. Here's an innocent little *Polygon*:

```
<Grid Background="LightCyan">
    <Polygon Points="250 200, 250 210,
                     230 270, 230 260"
            Stroke="Red"
            StrokeThickness="4" />
</Grid>
```

Now here's the same *Polygon* with its *Stretch* property set to *Fill*.

```
<Grid Background="LightCyan">
    <Polygon Points="250 200, 250 210,
                     230 270, 230 260"
            Stroke="Red"
            StrokeThickness="4"
            Stretch="Fill" />
</Grid>
```

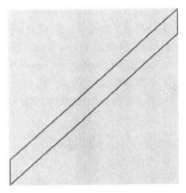

Regardless of the coordinates, it stretches to fill the container with a change in aspect ratio as well. To retain the aspect ratio, use *Uniform* or *UniformToFill* just as with the *Image* element.

You can probably see why the *Stretch* property of *Shape* isn't used very often in connection with vector graphics, but if you need a particular vector image to fill an area of arbitrary size, it's a welcome option.

Dynamic Polygons

As you've seen, when a property backed by a dependency property is changed at runtime, the element with that property changes to reflect that change. This is a result of the support for a property-changed handler built into dependency properties.

Certain collections will also respond to changes. *Collection* classes that derive from *PresentationFrameworkCollection* respond to changes when an object is added to or removed from a collection. A notification is funneled up to the element containing the collection. In some cases, changes to dependency properties in the members of the collection also trigger notifications. (Unfortunately, the exact nature of this notification process is hidden from the application programmer.) The *UIElementCollection* that the *Panel* classes uses for its *Children* property derives from this class, as does the *PointCollection* in *Polyline* and *Polygon*.

At runtime, you can dynamically add *Point* objects to the *PointCollection*, or remove them from the *PointCollection*, and a *Polyline* or *Polygon* will change.

The GrowingPolygons project has a MainPage.xaml file that instantiates a *Polygon* element and gives it a couple properties:

Silverlight Project: GrowingPolygons   File: MainPage.xaml (excerpt)

```
<Grid x:Name="ContentPanel" Grid.Row="1" Margin="12,0,12,0">
    <Polygon Name="polygon"
            Stroke="{StaticResource PhoneForegroundBrush}"
            StrokeThickness="{StaticResource PhoneStrokeThickness}" />
</Grid>
```

The code-behind file waits until the *Loaded* event is fired before determining the size of the content panel (just as in the Spiral program) and it begins by obtaining similar information. But the *OnLoaded* handler just adds two points to the *Points* collection of the *Polygon* to define a vertical line; everything else happens during *Tick* events of a *DispatcherTimer* (which of course requires a *using* directive for *System.Windows.Threading*):

Silverlight Project: GrowingPolygons   File: MainPage.xaml.cs (excerpt)

```
public partial class MainPage : PhoneApplicationPage
{
    Point center;
    double radius;
    int numSides = 2;

    public MainPage()
    {
        InitializeComponent();
        Loaded += OnLoaded;
    }

    void OnLoaded(object sender, RoutedEventArgs args)
    {
        center = new Point(ContentPanel.ActualWidth / 2 - 1,
                        ContentPanel.ActualHeight / 2 - 1);
        radius = Math.Min(center.X, center.Y);

        polygon.Points.Add(new Point(center.X, center.Y - radius));
        polygon.Points.Add(new Point(center.X, center.Y + radius));

        DispatcherTimer tmr = new DispatcherTimer();
        tmr.Interval = TimeSpan.FromSeconds(1);
        tmr.Tick += OnTimerTick;
        tmr.Start();
    }
```

```
void OnTimerTick(object sender, EventArgs args)
{
    numSides += 1;

    for (int vertex = 1; vertex < numSides; vertex++)
    {
        double radians = vertex * 2 * Math.PI / numSides;
        double x = center.X + radius * Math.Sin(radians);
        double y = center.Y - radius * Math.Cos(radians);
        Point point = new Point(x, y);

        if (vertex < numSides - 1)
            polygon.Points[vertex] = point;
        else
            polygon.Points.Add(point);
    }

    PageTitle.Text = "" + numSides + " sides";
}
}
```

Every second, the program replaces all but one of the *Point* objects in the *Points* collection of the *Polygon*. The first *Point* in the collection—which is the *Point* at the top center of the content area—is the only one that remains the same. In addition, the *Tick* handler adds a new *Point* object at the end of the collection. The result is a polygon that gains one new side every second:

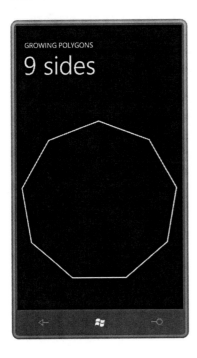

You can see for yourself how many points are needed before this polygon visually turns into a circle!

Notice that the program entirely replaces the *Point* object in the collection rather than attempting to modify the *X* and *Y* properties of the existing object in the collection. *Point* is a structure, and it implements no notification mechanism. There is no way for the *PointCollection* to know if a property of a particular *Point* in the collection has been changed. Only when the entire *Point* object is replaced does the *PointCollection* know about it.

If you're doing something like this is in a real application, you might want to detach the *PointCollection* from the *Polygon* when you're making a lot of changes to it. This prevents a long series of notifications firing that inform the *Polygon* that the *PointCollection* has changed. The code would look something like this:

```
PointCollection points = polygon.Points;
polygon.Points = null;

//...make changes to points collection

polygon.Points = points;
```

The *PointCollection* is detached by saving a reference to it and setting the *Points* property to *null*. When all changes have been made, the *PointCollection* is reattached to the *Polygon*, and the *Polygon* responds to the new collection of points.

The *Path* Element

Although *Line*, *Polyline*, and *Polygon* are all convenient and easy to use, their functionality is pretty much subsumed in the last of the *Shape* descendents, *Path*.

The *Path* class defines just one property of its own named *Data* of type *Geometry*, but geometries are a very important concept in Silverlight vector graphics. In general, a geometry is a collection of straight lines and curves, some of which might be connected to each other (or not) and might define enclosed areas (or not). In other graphics programming environments, the geometry might be called a graphics *path*. In Silverlight, *Path* is an element that uses a *Geometry* object for its *Data* property.

It's important to recognize that a *Geometry* object is nothing but naked coordinate points. There is no concept of brushes or line thickness or styles with a geometry. That's why you need to combine a *Geometry* with a *Path* element to actually render something on the screen. The *Geometry* defines the coordinate points; the *Path* defines the stroke brush and fill brush.

Geometry fits into the Silverlight class hierarchy like so:

Object
      DependencyObject (abstract)
          Geometry (abstract)
                  LineGeometry (sealed)
                  RectangleGeometry (sealed)
                  EllipseGeometry (sealed)
                  GeometryGroup (sealed)
                  PathGeometry (sealed)

Just as the *Path* element is pretty much the only *Shape* derivative you really need, the *PathGeometry* class is the only *Geometry* derivative you really need. But of course I'm going to discuss the others as well because they're often quite convenient. You can't derive from *Geometry* yourself.

Geometry defines four public properties:

- get-only static *Empty* of type *Geometry*

- get-only static *StandardFlatteningTolerance* of type *double*

- get-only *Bounds* of type *Rect*

- *Transform* of type *Transform*

The most useful are the last two. The *Bounds* property provides the smallest rectangle that encompasses the geometry and *Transform* allows you to apply a transform to the geometry (as I will demonstrate).

LineGeometry defines two properties of type *Point* named *StartPoint* and *EndPoint*:

```
<Grid Background="LightCyan">
  <Path Stroke="Maroon"
        StrokeThickness="4"
        StrokeDashArray="3 1">
    <Path.Data>
      <LineGeometry StartPoint="100 50"
                    EndPoint="300 150" />
    </Path.Data>
  </Path>
</Grid>
```

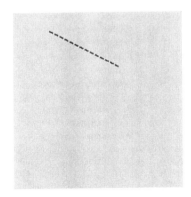

Notice how the duties are separated between *Geometry* and *Path*: The *Geometry* provides the coordinates; the *Path* provides all other rendering information.

LineGeometry may seem superfluous after the *Line* and *Polyline* elements, but unlike *Line* and *Polyline*, *LineGeometry* has two dependency properties of type *Point*, and these might be very useful as animation targets in some scenarios.

RectangleGeometry defines a property named *Rect* of type *Rect*, a structure that defines a rectangle with four numbers: two numbers indicate the coordinate point of the upper-left corner and two more numbers for the rectangle's size. In XAML you specify these four numbers sequentially: the *x* and *y* coordinates of the upper-left corner, followed by the width and then the height:

```
<Grid Background="LightCyan">
    <Path Stroke="Maroon"
          StrokeThickness="8"
          Fill="Green">
        <Path.Data>
            <RectangleGeometry
                Rect="100 50 300 200" />
        </Path.Data>
    </Path>
</Grid>
```

In this example, the bottom-right coordinate of the rectangle is (400, 250). In code, the *Rect* structure has three constructors that let you specify a *Point* and a *Size*, two *Point* objects, or a string of four numbers as in XAML: (*x, y, width, height*).

The *Bounds* property of *Geometry* is also of type *Rect*. For the *RectangleGeometry* above, *Bounds* would return the same values: (100, 50, 300, 200). For the *LineGeometry* in the previous example, *Bounds* would return (100, 50, 200, 100).

RectangleGeometry also defines *RadiusX* and *RadiusY* properties for rounding the corners:

```
<Grid Background="LightCyan">
    <Path Stroke="Maroon"
          StrokeThickness="8"
          Fill="Green">
        <Path.Data>
            <RectangleGeometry
                Rect="100 50 300 200"
                RadiusX="100"
                RadiusY="50" />
        </Path.Data>
    </Path>
</Grid>
```

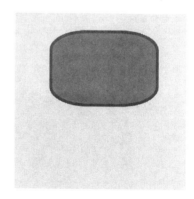

The *EllipseGeometry* also defines *RadiusX* and *RadiusY* properties, but these are for defining the lengths of the two axes. The center of the *EllipseGeometry* is provided by a property named *Center* of type *Point*:

```
<Grid Background="LightCyan">
    <Path Stroke="Maroon"
```

```
            StrokeThickness="8"
            Fill="Green">
        <Path.Data>
            <EllipseGeometry
                Center="250 150"
                RadiusX="150"
                RadiusY="100" />
        </Path.Data>
    </Path>
</Grid>
```

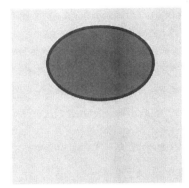

Specifying the center of a circle or ellipse to indicate its location is often a more convenient approach than specifying its upper-left corner (as with the *Ellipse* element)—particularly considering that ellipses don't have corners!

Here's a little exercise in interactive drawing called TouchAndDrawCircles. When you touch the screen, the program creates a new circle from a *Path* and an *EllipseGeometry*. As you move your finger, the circle gets larger. When you're finished, the circle is filled with a random color. If you then touch an existing circle, you can drag it around the screen.

In the MainPage.xaml file, the content grid is initially empty. The only change I've made is to give it a non-null *Background* so it can generate manipulation events:

Silverlight Project: TouchAndDrawCircles   File: MainPage.xaml (excerpt)

```
<Grid x:Name="ContentPanel" Grid.Row="1" Margin="12,0,12,0"
      Background="Transparent" />
```

The code-behind file has just a few fields to keep track of what's going on:

Silverlight Project: TouchAndDrawCircles   File: MainPage.xaml.cs (excerpt)

```
public partial class MainPage : PhoneApplicationPage
{
    Random rand = new Random();
    bool isDrawing, isDragging;
    Path path;
    EllipseGeometry ellipseGeo;
    . . .
}
```

The two Boolean fields indicate a current activity in progress. The *Path* field is only valid while drawing a new circle; the *EllipseGeometry* field is valid when drawing a new circle or moving an existing circle.

The override of the *OnManipulationStarted* method initiates a drawing or dragging operation but doesn't let more than one to be going on at any time. The *OriginalSource* property of the event arguments is either a *Path* element—which means that the user touched one of the existing circles and wants to move it—or the *ContentPanel*, which initiates a new drawing operation:

Silverlight Project: TouchAndDrawCircles   File: MainPage.xaml.cs (excerpt)

```
protected override void OnManipulationStarted(ManipulationStartedEventArgs args)
{
    if (isDrawing || isDragging)
        return;

    if (args.OriginalSource is Path)
    {
        ellipseGeo = (args.OriginalSource as Path).Data as EllipseGeometry;

        isDragging = true;
        args.ManipulationContainer = ContentPanel;
        args.Handled = true;
    }
    else if (args.OriginalSource == ContentPanel)
    {
        ellipseGeo = new EllipseGeometry();
        ellipseGeo.Center = args.ManipulationOrigin;
        path = new Path();
        path.Stroke = this.Resources["PhoneForegroundBrush"] as Brush;
        path.Data = ellipseGeo;
        ContentPanel.Children.Add(path);

        isDrawing = true;
        args.Handled = true;
    }

    base.OnManipulationStarted(args);
}
```

In the XAML file I set the *Background* of the *ContentPanel* to *Transparent* so it would generate *Manipulation* events. When the *OriginalSource* property is this *Grid*, so is the *ManipulationContainer*, and *ManipulationOrigin* is relative to the *Grid*. That's the point I need for defining the *Center* of this new *EllipseGeometry*.

For the dragging operation, the *OnManipulationDelta* override uses the *DeltaManipulation* property of the event arguments to modify the *Center* property of the *EllipseGeometry*:

Silverlight Project: TouchAndDrawCircles   File: MainPage.xaml.cs (excerpt)

```
protected override void OnManipulationDelta(ManipulationDeltaEventArgs args)
{
```

```
    if (isDragging)
    {
        Point center = ellipseGeo.Center;
        center.X += args.DeltaManipulation.Translation.X;
        center.Y += args.DeltaManipulation.Translation.Y;
        ellipseGeo.Center = center;

        args.Handled = true;
    }
    else if (isDrawing)
    {
        Point translation = args.CumulativeManipulation.Translation;
        double radius = Math.Max(Math.Abs(translation.X),
                                 Math.Abs(translation.Y));
        ellipseGeo.RadiusX = radius;
        ellipseGeo.RadiusY = radius;

        args.Handled = true;
    }

    base.OnManipulationDelta(args);
}
```

In contrast, for the drawing operation, the method modifies the *RadiusX* and *RadiusY* property of the *EllipseGeometry*. For this it uses the *CumulativeManipulation* property, which reports the entire manipulation since the *ManipulationStarted* event. The reason for the different property is simple: If the user initiates a drawing operation, and then moves a finger to the left or up, the translation factors will be negative. But these negative numbers must become a positive radius of the circle. It turns out to be easier taking the absolute value of the total translation factors rather than to modify existing dimensions.

When the finger lifts from the screen, the *OnManipulationCompleted* event is called for cleanup:

Silverlight Project: TouchAndDrawCircles   File: MainPage.xaml.cs (excerpt)

```
protected override void OnManipulationCompleted(ManipulationCompletedEventArgs args)
{
    if (isDragging)
    {
        isDragging = false;
        args.Handled = true;
    }
    else if (isDrawing)
    {
        Color clr = Color.FromArgb(255, (byte)rand.Next(256),
                                        (byte)rand.Next(256),
                                        (byte)rand.Next(256));
```

```
        path.Fill = new SolidColorBrush(clr);

        isDrawing = false;
        args.Handled = true;
    }

    base.OnManipulationCompleted(args);
}
```

For the dragging operation, cleanup is simple. But the drawing operation needs to conclude by giving the *Path* element a random *Fill* brush.

In actual use, you'll notice a little delay between the time your finger begins drawing or dragging a circle, and the screen reacts. This is a characteristic of the Manipulation events.

Geometries and Transforms

If you're using *EllipseGeometry* and you don't want the axes of the ellipse to be aligned on the horizontal and vertical, you can apply a *RotateTransform* to it. And you have a choice. Because *Path* derives from *UIElement*, you can set this *RotateTransform* to the *RenderTransform* property of the *Path*:

```
<Grid Background="LightCyan">
  <Path Stroke="Maroon"
        StrokeThickness="8"
        Fill="Green">
    <Path.Data>
      <EllipseGeometry Center="250 150"
                       RadiusX="150"
                       RadiusY="100" />
    </Path.Data>
    <Path.RenderTransform>
      <RotateTransform Angle="45"
                 CenterX="250"
                 CenterY="150" />
    </Path.RenderTransform>
  </Path>
</Grid>
```

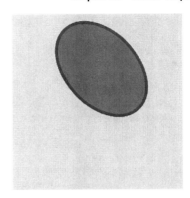

Notice that the *CenterX* and *CenterY* properties of *RotateTransform* are set to the same values as the *Center* point of the *EllipseGeometry* itself so that the ellipse is rotated around its center. When working with *Path* and *Geometry* objects, it's usually easier to specify actual transform centers rather than to use *RenderTransformOrigin*. Normally you set *RenderTransformOrigin* to relative coordinates, for example (0.5, 0.5) to specify the center, but look what happens when you try that in this case:

```
<Grid Background="LightCyan">
  <Path Stroke="Maroon"
        StrokeThickness="8"
        Fill="Green"
        RenderTransformOrigin="0.5 0.5">
    <Path.Data>
      <EllipseGeometry Center="250 150"
                       RadiusX="150"
                       RadiusY="100" />
    </Path.Data>

    <Path.RenderTransform>
      <RotateTransform Angle="45" />
    </Path.RenderTransform>
  </Path>
</Grid>
```

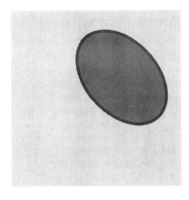

The problem here is that the *Path* element is large enough to accommodate an *EllipseGeometry* with a center at (250, 150) and a *RadiusX* of 150 and a *RadiusY* of 100, so the *Path* element must be at least about 400 pixels wide and 250 pixels tall. (It's actually a little larger due to the non-zero *StrokeThickness*.) The center of this *Path* is approximately the point (200, 125). In addition,, like other elements, the *Path* has default *HorizontalAlignment* and *VerticalAlignment* properties of *Stretch*, so it's really filling its container, in this case 480 pixels square, so the rotation is actually around the point (240, 240).

It's also possible to apply a transform to the *Geometry* object itself:

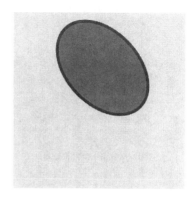

```
<Grid Background="LightCyan">
  <Path Stroke="Maroon"
        StrokeThickness="8"
        Fill="Green">
    <Path.Data>
      <EllipseGeometry Center="250 150"
                       RadiusX="150"
                       RadiusY="100">
        <EllipseGeometry.Transform>
          <RotateTransform Angle="45"
                           CenterX="250"
                           CenterY="150" />
        </EllipseGeometry.Transform>
      </EllipseGeometry>
    </Path.Data>
  </Path>
</Grid>
```

This appears to be exactly the same as the earlier example with the explicit *CenterX* and *CenterY* settings on the *RotateTransform*, but transforms can have rather different results depending whether they're applied to the *RenderTransform* property of the *Path* element or to the *Geometry* object.

The *RenderTransform* property has no effect on how the element is perceived in the layout system, but the *Transform* property of the *Geometry* affects the perceived dimensions. To see this difference, enclose a *Path* with an *EllipseGeometry* in a centered *Border*:

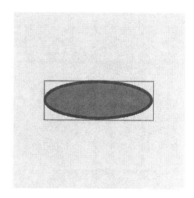

```
<Grid Background="LightCyan">
  <Border BorderBrush="Red"
          BorderThickness="3"
          HorizontalAlignment="Center"
          VerticalAlignment="Center">
    <Path Stroke="Maroon"
          StrokeThickness="8"
          Fill="Green">
      <Path.Data>
        <EllipseGeometry Center="150 50"
                         RadiusX="150"
                         RadiusY="50" />
      </Path.Data>
    </Path>
  </Border>
</Grid>
```

I deliberately set the *Center* of the *EllipseGeometry* to the same two values as *RadiusX* and *RadiusY* so the *Path* doesn't occupy any more space than that necessary to render the ellipse.

Now set the *RenderTransform* of the *Path* for rotation:

```
<Grid Background="LightCyan">
  <Border BorderBrush="Red"
```

```
                BorderThickness="3"
                HorizontalAlignment="Center"
                VerticalAlignment="Center">
        <Path Stroke="Maroon"
              StrokeThickness="8"
              Fill="Green">
            <Path.Data>
                <EllipseGeometry Center="150 50"
                                 RadiusX="150"
                                 RadiusY="50" />
            </Path.Data>
            <Path.RenderTransform>
                <RotateTransform Angle="90"
                                 CenterX="150"
                                 CenterY="50" />
            </Path.RenderTransform>
        </Path>
    </Border>
</Grid>
```

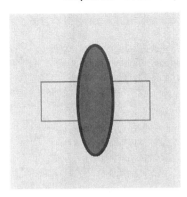

As was very clear early on in Chapter 8, the *RenderTransform* does not affect how an element is perceived in the layout system. The *Border* is still sizing itself based on the unrotated *Path*. Applying the transform to the *EllipseGeometry* produces quite a different result:

```
<Grid Background="LightCyan">
    <Border BorderBrush="Red"
            BorderThickness="3"
            HorizontalAlignment="Center"
            VerticalAlignment="Center">
        <Path Stroke="Maroon"
              StrokeThickness="8"
              Fill="Green">
            <Path.Data>
                <EllipseGeometry Center="150 50"
                                 RadiusX="150"
                                 RadiusY="50">
                    <EllipseGeometry.Transform>
                        <RotateTransform Angle="90"
                                         CenterX="150"
                                         CenterY="50" />
                    </EllipseGeometry.Transform>
                </EllipseGeometry>
            </Path.Data>
        </Path>
    </Border>
</Grid>
```

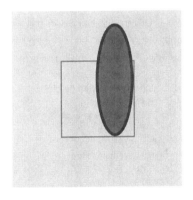

Well, that doesn't look right, either! What happened?

The *EllipseGeometry* defines an ellipse with a bounding box with an upper-left corner at the point (0, 0) and the lower-right corner at (300, 100). That's being rotated 90° around the point (150, 50). The bounding box of the rotated ellipse has an upper-left corner of (100, –100) and a lower-right corner of (200, 200). The *Border* is 200 pixels square to accommodate that lower-right corner, but the negative part sticks out of the top of the *Border*.

To make it work "correctly," the center of rotation needs to be set to the point (50, 50):

```
<Grid Background="LightCyan">
  <Border BorderBrush="Red"
          BorderThickness="3"
          HorizontalAlignment="Center"
          VerticalAlignment="Center">
    <Path Stroke="Maroon"
          StrokeThickness="8"
          Fill="Green">
      <Path.Data>
        <EllipseGeometry Center="150 50"
                         RadiusX="150"
                         RadiusY="50">
          <EllipseGeometry.Transform>
            <RotateTransform Angle="90"
                             CenterX="50"
                             CenterY="50" />
          </EllipseGeometry.Transform>
        </EllipseGeometry>
      </Path.Data>
    </Path>
  </Border>
</Grid>
```

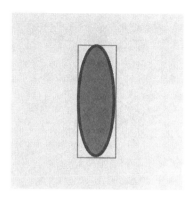

Another difference between the *RenderTransform* property of *Path* and the *Transform* property of *Geometry* is revealed when you use *ScaleTransform*. Let's begin with a little rectangle aligned at the left edge:

```
<Grid Background="LightCyan">
  <Path Stroke="Maroon"
        StrokeThickness="4"
        Fill="Green">
    <Path.Data>
      <RectangleGeometry
          Rect="2 220 40 40" />
    </Path.Data>
  </Path>
</Grid>
```

I've actually positioned the *RectangleGeometry* at the point (2, 220) so the *StrokeThickness* of the *Path* doesn't cause part of the rendered object to appear outside its confines.

Now apply a *ScaleTransform* to the *RectangleGeometry* to increase the width by a factor of 10:

```
<Grid Background="LightCyan">
  <Path Stroke="Maroon"
        StrokeThickness="4"
```

```
          Fill="Green">
    <Path.Data>
      <RectangleGeometry
          Rect="2 220 40 40">
        <RectangleGeometry.Transform>
          <ScaleTransform ScaleX="10" />
        </RectangleGeometry.Transform>
      </RectangleGeometry>
    </Path.Data>
  </Path>
</Grid>
```

The entire figure is 10 times wider, and the *RectangleGeometry* is now aligned at the point (20, 220). But something quite different happens when you apply the transform to the *Path* element:

```
<Grid Background="LightCyan">
  <Path Stroke="Maroon"
        StrokeThickness="4"
        Fill="Green">
    <Path.Data>
      <RectangleGeometry
          Rect="2 220 40 40" />
    </Path.Data>
    <Path.RenderTransform>
      <ScaleTransform ScaleX="10" />
    </Path.RenderTransform>
  </Path>
</Grid>
```

Now the thickness of the stroke at the left and right has also increased by a factor of 10!

Grouping Geometries

One of the descendent classes of *Geometry* is *GeometryGroup*. This allows you to combine one or more *Geometry* objects in a composite.

```
<Grid Background="LightCyan">
  <Path Stroke="Maroon"
        StrokeThickness="4"
        Fill="Green">
    <Path.Data>
      <GeometryGroup>
        <EllipseGeometry Center="200 150"
                         RadiusX="100"
                         RadiusY="50" />
        <RectangleGeometry
            Rect="200 150 100 100" />
      </GeometryGroup>
```

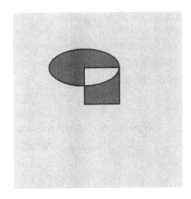

```
    </Path.Data>
  </Path>
</Grid>
```

Notice how the *FillRule* applies to this combination. Here's another:

```
<Grid Background="LightCyan">
  <Path Stroke="Maroon"
        StrokeThickness="4"
        Fill="Green">
    <Path.Data>
      <GeometryGroup>
        <RectangleGeometry
            Rect=" 40  40 200 200" />
        <RectangleGeometry
            Rect=" 90  90 200 200" />
        <RectangleGeometry
            Rect="140 140 200 200" />
        <RectangleGeometry
            Rect="190 190 200 200" />
        <RectangleGeometry
            Rect="240 240 200 200" />
      </GeometryGroup>
    </Path.Data>
  </Path>
</Grid>
```

The Versatile *PathGeometry*

LineGeometry, RectangleGeometry, EllipseGeometry, GeometryGroup—those are all convenient special cases of *PathGeometry*, certainly the most versatile of the *Geometry* derivatives. With *Path* and *PathGeometry* you can perform any vector graphics job that Silverlight allows.

PathGeometry defines just two properties of its own: the familiar *FillRule* and a property named *Figures* of type *PathFigureCollection*, a collection of *PathFigure* objects.

Conceptually, a *PathFigure* is a series of connected lines and curves. The key word here is *connected*. The *PathFigure* starts at a particular point, indicated by the *StartPoint* property, and then the *PathFigure* continues in a series of connected segments.

For these connected segments, *PathFigure* defines a property named *Segments* of type *PathSegmentCollection*, a collection of *PathSegment* objects. *PathSegment* is an abstract class, as shown here:

Object
       DependencyObject (abstract)
              PathSegment (abstract)
                     LineSegment (sealed)

> *PolyLineSegment* (sealed)
> *ArcSegment* (sealed)
> *QuadraticBezierSegment* (sealed)
> *PolyQuadraticBezierSegment* (sealed)
> *BezierSegment* (sealed)
> *PolyQuadraticBezierSegment* (sealed)

The *PathFigure* indicates a *StartPoint*. The first *PathSegment* object in the *Segments* collection continues from that point. The next *PathSegment* continues from where the first *PathSegment* left off, and so forth.

The last point of the last *PathSegment* in the *Segments* collection might be the same as the *StartPoint* of the *PathFigure* or it might not. To ensure that a *PathFigure* is closed, you can set the *IsClosed* property. If necessary, this will cause a straight line to be drawn from the last point of the last *PathSegment* to the *StartPoint* of the *PathFigure*.

PathFigure also defines an *IsFilled* property that is *true* by default. This property is independent of any *Fill* brush you might set on the *Path* itself. It's used instead for clipping and hit-testing. In some cases, Silverlight might perceive that an area is filled for purposes of clipping and hit-testing when that is not your intention. In that case, set *IsFilled* to *false*.

In summary, a *PathGeometry* is a collection of *PathFigure* objects. Each *PathFigure* object is a series of connected lines or curves indicated by a collection of *PathSegment* objects.

Let's look at the *PathSegment* derivatives in more detail.

LineSegment defines just one property on its own, *Point* of type *Point*. It just needs one *Point* object because it draws a line from the *StartPoint* property of *PathFigure* (if the *LineSegment* is the first segment in the collection) or from the end of the previous segment.

PolyLineSegment defines a *Points* property of type *PointCollection* to draw a series of connected straight lines.

Here's a *PathGeometry* with three *PathFigure* objects containing 3, 2, and 1 *PathSegment* objects, respectively:

```
<Grid Background="LightCyan">
  <Path Stroke="Blue"
        StrokeThickness="4"
        Fill="Green">
    <Path.Data>
      <PathGeometry>
        <PathFigure StartPoint="240 60">
          <LineSegment Point="380 240" />
          <LineSegment Point="100 240" />
          <LineSegment Point="240 60" />
        </PathFigure>

        <PathFigure StartPoint="240 150"
                    IsClosed="True">
```

```
            <LineSegment Point="380 330" />
            <LineSegment Point="100 330" />
        </PathFigure>

        <PathFigure StartPoint="240 240"
                    IsClosed="True">
            <PolyLineSegment
                Points="380 420, 100 420" />
        </PathFigure>
      </PathGeometry>
    </Path.Data>
  </Path>
</Grid>
```

The second and third figures are explicitly closed with the *IsClosed* property, but all three *PathFigure* collections are filled.

The *ArcSegment*

Things start getting tricky with *ArcSegment*. An arc is just a partial circumference of an ellipse, but because the *ArcSegment* must fit in with the paradigm of start points and end points, the arc must be specified with two points on the circumference of some ellipse. But if you define an ellipse with a particular center and radii, how do you specify a point on that ellipse circumference exactly without doing some trigonometry?

The solution is to define only the *size* of this ellipse and not where the ellipse is positioned. The actual location of the ellipse is defined by the two points.

I think we need an example. Here's a little line that begins at the point (120, 240) and ends at the point (360, 240).

```
<Grid Background="LightCyan">
  <Polyline Points="120 240, 360 240"
            Stroke="Black"
            StrokeThickness="6" />
</Grid>
```

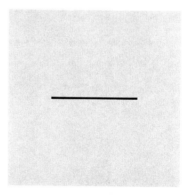

This line is just for reference. I want to draw an arc between these same two points. Now obviously there are an infinite number of arcs you can draw between these two points, but for any particular ellipse size, there are only four.

Let me demonstrate:

Suppose I want the two points to be connected by an arc on the circumference of a circle that has a radius of 144 pixels. Here's how you specify an *ArcSegment* of that size that goes between the points (120, 240) and (360, 240):

```
<Grid Background="LightCyan">
  <Polyline Points="120 240, 360 240"
            Stroke="Black"
            StrokeThickness="6" />

  <Path Stroke="Blue"
        StrokeThickness="2">
    <Path.Data>
      <PathGeometry>
        <PathFigure StartPoint="120 240">
          <ArcSegment Point="360 240"
                      Size="144 144" />
        </PathFigure>
      </PathGeometry>
    </Path.Data>
  </Path>
</Grid>
```

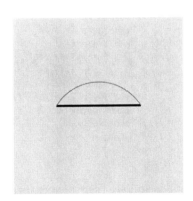

By default, arcs are drawn from the start point to the end point in a counter-clockwise direction. You can override that behavior by setting the *SweepDirection* property to *Clockwise*:

```
<Grid Background="LightCyan">
  <Polyline Points="120 240, 360 240"
            Stroke="Black"
            StrokeThickness="6" />

  <Path Stroke="Red"
        StrokeThickness="2">
    <Path.Data>
      <PathGeometry>
        <PathFigure StartPoint="120 240">
          <ArcSegment
              Point="360 240"
              Size="144 144"
              SweepDirection="Clockwise" />
        </PathFigure>
      </PathGeometry>
    </Path.Data>
  </Path>
</Grid>
```

In both those cases, the arc drawn between the two points is the shorter of two possibilities. Here's the result with the default *SweepDirection* of *CounterClockwise* but the *IsLargeArc* property set to *true*:

```
<Grid Background="LightCyan">
  <Polyline Points="120 240, 360 240"
```

```
                    Stroke="Black"
                    StrokeThickness="6" />

        <Path Stroke="Green"
              StrokeThickness="2">
          <Path.Data>
            <PathGeometry>
              <PathFigure StartPoint="120 240">
                <ArcSegment
                    Point="360 240"
                    Size="144 144"
                    IsLargeArc="True" />
              </PathFigure>
            </PathGeometry>
          </Path.Data>
        </Path>
    </Grid>
```

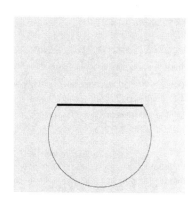

Finally, you can set both *IsLargeArc* to true and *SweepDirection* to *Clockwise*:

```
<Grid Background="LightCyan">
    <Polyline Points="120 240, 360 240"
              Stroke="Black"
              StrokeThickness="6" />

    <Path Stroke="Brown"
          StrokeThickness="2">
      <Path.Data>
        <PathGeometry>
          <PathFigure StartPoint="120 240">
            <ArcSegment
                Point="360 240"
                Size="144 144"
                IsLargeArc="True"
                SweepDirection="Clockwise"/>
          </PathFigure>
        </PathGeometry>
      </Path.Data>
    </Path>
</Grid>
```

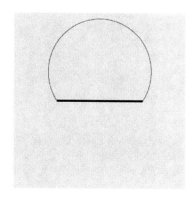

When you see them all together, you can get a better sense of how this works (at least on a conceptual level). Think of a circle of a particular size positioned so it meets the two points. You can fit the circle against those two points in one of two ways, and then go around the circle in one of two ways:

```
<Grid Background="LightCyan">
    <Polyline Points="120 240, 360 240"
              Stroke="Black"
              StrokeThickness="6" />

    <Path Stroke="Blue"
          StrokeThickness="2">
      <Path.Data>
```

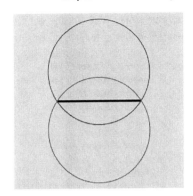

```
        <PathGeometry>
          <PathFigure StartPoint="120 240">
            <ArcSegment
                Point="360 240"
                Size="144 144" />
          </PathFigure>
        </PathGeometry>
      </Path.Data>
    </Path>

    <Path Stroke="Red"
          StrokeThickness="2">
      <Path.Data>
        <PathGeometry>
          <PathFigure StartPoint="120 240">
            <ArcSegment
                Point="360 240"
                Size="144 144"
                SweepDirection="Clockwise" />
          </PathFigure>
        </PathGeometry>
      </Path.Data>
    </Path>

    <Path Stroke="Green"
          StrokeThickness="2">
      <Path.Data>
        <PathGeometry>
          <PathFigure StartPoint="120 240">
            <ArcSegment
                Point="360 240"
                Size="144 144"
                IsLargeArc="True" />
          </PathFigure>
        </PathGeometry>
      </Path.Data>
    </Path>

    <Path Stroke="Brown"
          StrokeThickness="2">
      <Path.Data>
        <PathGeometry>
          <PathFigure StartPoint="120 240">
            <ArcSegment
                Point="360 240"
                Size="144 144"
                IsLargeArc="True"
                SweepDirection="Clockwise" />
          </PathFigure>
        </PathGeometry>
      </Path.Data>
    </Path>
</Grid>
```

This also works with an ellipse. The following markup is the same as the previous example except the *Size* property of the *ArcSegment* has been changed from (144, 144) to (200, 100):

```
<Grid Background="LightCyan">
  <Polyline Points="120 240, 360 240"
            Stroke="Black"
            StrokeThickness="6" />

  <Path Stroke="Blue"
        StrokeThickness="2">
    <Path.Data>
      <PathGeometry>
        <PathFigure StartPoint="120 240">
          <ArcSegment
              Point="360 240"
              Size="200 100" />
        </PathFigure>
      </PathGeometry>
    </Path.Data>
  </Path>

  <Path Stroke="Red"
        StrokeThickness="2">
    <Path.Data>
      <PathGeometry>
        <PathFigure StartPoint="120 240">
          <ArcSegment
              Point="360 240"
              Size="200 100"
              SweepDirection="Clockwise" />
        </PathFigure>
      </PathGeometry>
    </Path.Data>
  </Path>

  <Path Stroke="Green"
        StrokeThickness="2">
    <Path.Data>
      <PathGeometry>
        <PathFigure StartPoint="120 240">
          <ArcSegment
              Point="360 240"
              Size="200 100"
              IsLargeArc="True" />
        </PathFigure>
      </PathGeometry>
    </Path.Data>
  </Path>

  <Path Stroke="Brown"
        StrokeThickness="2">
    <Path.Data>
      <PathGeometry>
        <PathFigure StartPoint="120 240">
          <ArcSegment
```

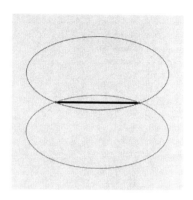

```
            Point="360 240"
            Size="200 100"
            IsLargeArc="True"
            SweepDirection="Clockwise" />
        </PathFigure>
      </PathGeometry>
    </Path.Data>
  </Path>
</Grid>
```

If you want to use an arc based on the circumference of an ellipse that does not have its axes parallel to the horizontal and vertical, you can set the final property of *ArcSegment*, which is *RotationAngle*.

```
<Grid Background="LightCyan">
  <Polyline Points="120 240, 360 240"
            Stroke="Black"
            StrokeThickness="6" />

  <Path Stroke="Blue"
        StrokeThickness="2">
    <Path.Data>
      <PathGeometry>
        <PathFigure StartPoint="120 240">
          <ArcSegment
              Point="360 240"
              Size="200 100"
              RotationAngle="36" />
        </PathFigure>
      </PathGeometry>
    </Path.Data>
  </Path>

  <Path Stroke="Red"
        StrokeThickness="2">
    <Path.Data>
      <PathGeometry>
        <PathFigure StartPoint="120 240">
          <ArcSegment
              Point="360 240"
              Size="200 100"
              SweepDirection="Clockwise"
              RotationAngle="36" />
        </PathFigure>
      </PathGeometry>
    </Path.Data>
  </Path>

  <Path Stroke="Green"
        StrokeThickness="2">
    <Path.Data>
      <PathGeometry>
        <PathFigure StartPoint="120 240">
          <ArcSegment
              Point="360 240"
```

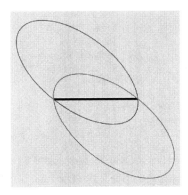

```
                    Size="200 100"
                    IsLargeArc="True"
                    RotationAngle="36" />
            </PathFigure>
          </PathGeometry>
        </Path.Data>
    </Path>

    <Path Stroke="Brown"
          StrokeThickness="2">
      <Path.Data>
        <PathGeometry>
          <PathFigure StartPoint="120 240">
            <ArcSegment
                Point="360 240"
                Size="200 100"
                IsLargeArc="True"
                SweepDirection="Clockwise"
                RotationAngle="36" />
          </PathFigure>
        </PathGeometry>
      </Path.Data>
    </Path>
</Grid>
```

In code, you can determine algorithmically the points on a circle where you want the arc to begin and end. That's the idea behind the SunnyDay program, which combines *LineSegment* and *ArcSegment* objects into a composite image. The MainPage.xaml file instantiates the *Path* element: and assigns all the properties except the actual segments:

Silverlight Project: SunnyDay   File: MainPage.xaml (excerpt)

```
<Grid x:Name="ContentPanel" Grid.Row="1" Margin="12,0,12,0">
    <Path Fill="Yellow">
        <Path.Data>
            <PathGeometry>
                <PathFigure x:Name="pathFigure"
                            IsClosed="True" />
            </PathGeometry>
        </Path.Data>
    </Path>
</Grid>
```

The *Loaded* event handler is then responsible for obtaining the size of the content area and calculating all the coordinates for the various path segments:

Silverlight Project: SunnyDay   File: MainPage.xaml.cs (excerpt)

```
public partial class MainPage : PhoneApplicationPage
{
    const int BEAMCOUNT = 24;
    const double INCREMENT = Math.PI / BEAMCOUNT;

    public MainPage()
    {
        InitializeComponent();
        Loaded += OnLoaded;
    }

    void OnLoaded(object sender, RoutedEventArgs args)
    {
        Point center = new Point(ContentPanel.ActualWidth / 2,
                                 ContentPanel.ActualHeight / 2);

        double radius = 0.45 * Math.Min(ContentPanel.ActualWidth,
                                        ContentPanel.ActualHeight);
        double innerRadius = 0.8 * radius;

        for (int i = 0; i < BEAMCOUNT; i++)
        {
            double radians = 2 * Math.PI * i / BEAMCOUNT;

            if (i == 0)
            {
                pathFigure.StartPoint = new Point(center.X, center.Y - radius);
            }

            LineSegment lineSeg = new LineSegment();
            lineSeg.Point = new Point(
                center.X + innerRadius * Math.Sin(radians + INCREMENT / 2),
                center.Y - innerRadius * Math.Cos(radians + INCREMENT / 2));
            pathFigure.Segments.Add(lineSeg);

            ArcSegment arcSeg = new ArcSegment();
            arcSeg.Point = new Point(
                center.X + innerRadius * Math.Sin(radians + 3 * INCREMENT / 2),
                center.Y - innerRadius * Math.Cos(radians + 3 * INCREMENT / 2));
            pathFigure.Segments.Add(arcSeg);

            lineSeg = new LineSegment();
            lineSeg.Point = new Point(
                center.X + radius * Math.Sin(radians + 2 * INCREMENT),
                center.Y - radius * Math.Cos(radians + 2 * INCREMENT));
            pathFigure.Segments.Add(lineSeg);
        }
    }
}
```

The result is a rather cartoonish sun:

Bézier Curves

Pierre Etienne Bézier (1910–1999) was an engineer at the French automobile company Renault from 1933 to 1975. During the 1960s the company started switching over from designing car bodies with clay to using computer-assisted design. The system required mathematical descriptions of curves that engineers could manipulate without knowing the underlying mathematics. From this work came the curve that now bears Pierre Bézier's name.

The Bézier curve is a spline, which is a type of curve used to approximate discrete data with a smooth continuous function. Silverlight supports the standard two-dimensional form of the cubic Bézier curve but also a quadratic Bézier curve that is somewhat simpler and faster, so I'll discuss that one first.

The quadratic Bézier curve is defined by three points, commonly denoted as p_0, p_1, and p_2. The curve starts at p_0 and ends at p_2. The point p_1 is known as a *control point*. The curve usually does not pass through p_1. Instead, p_1 functions like a magnet pulling the curve towards it. At p_0, the curve is tangent to (and in the same direction as) the line from p_0 to p_1, and at p_3 the curve is tangent to (and in the same direction as) the line from p_2 to p_3.

Perhaps the best way to become familiar with Bézier curves is to experiment with them. The QuadraticBezier program draws a single Bézier curve but lets you manipulate the three points to see what happens.

The XAML file assembles four *Path* elements and a *Polyline* in the single-cell *Grid*. The first *Path* is the quadratic Bézier itself. Notice that p_0 is provided by the *StartPoint* property of *PathFigure*, while p_1, and p_2 correspond to the *Point1* and *Point2* properties of *QuadraticBezierSegment*:

Silverlight Project: QuadraticBezier   File: **MainPage.xaml** (excerpt)

```xml
<Grid x:Name="ContentPanel" Grid.Row="1" Margin="12,0,12,0">
    <Path Stroke="{StaticResource PhoneForegroundBrush}"
          StrokeThickness="2">
        <Path.Data>
            <PathGeometry>
                <PathFigure x:Name="pathFig"
                            StartPoint="100 100">
                    <QuadraticBezierSegment x:Name="pathSeg"
                                            Point1="300 250"
                                            Point2="100 400" />
                </PathFigure>
            </PathGeometry>
        </Path.Data>
    </Path>

    <Polyline Name="ctrlLine"
              Stroke="{StaticResource PhoneForegroundBrush}"
              StrokeDashArray="2 2"
              Points="100 100, 300 250, 100 400" />

    <Path Name="pt0Dragger"
          Fill="{StaticResource PhoneAccentBrush}"
          Opacity="0.5">
        <Path.Data>
            <EllipseGeometry x:Name="pt0Ellipse"
                             Center="100 100"
                             RadiusX="48"
                             RadiusY="48" />
        </Path.Data>
    </Path>

    <Path Name="pt1Dragger"
          Fill="{StaticResource PhoneAccentBrush}"
          Opacity="0.5">
        <Path.Data>
            <EllipseGeometry x:Name="pt1Ellipse"
                             Center="300 250"
                             RadiusX="48"
                             RadiusY="48" />
        </Path.Data>
    </Path>

    <Path Name="pt2Dragger"
          Fill="{StaticResource PhoneAccentBrush}"
          Opacity="0.5">
        <Path.Data>
            <EllipseGeometry x:Name="pt2Ellipse"
```

```
                                    Center="100 400"
                                    RadiusX="48"
                                    RadiusY="48" />
            </Path.Data>
        </Path>
    </Grid>
```

The *Polyline* element draws a dotted line from the two end points to the control point.
The remaining three *Path* elements are "draggers," that is, they let you drag any of the three
points. The initial screen looks like this:

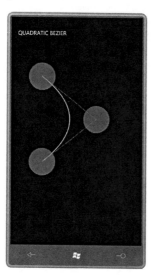

The code-behind file provides all the dragging logic. Because Silverlight for Windows Phone
does not support bindings for properties not defined by *FrameworkElement* derivatives, I
wasn't able to hook all the corresponding points together in the XAML file. Instead, they have
to be set individually in the *Manipulation* overrides:

Silverlight Project: QuadraticBezier   File: MainPage.xaml.cs (excerpt)

```
protected override void OnManipulationStarted(ManipulationStartedEventArgs args)
{
    if (args.OriginalSource == pt0Dragger ||
        args.OriginalSource == pt1Dragger ||
        args.OriginalSource == pt2Dragger)
    {
        args.ManipulationContainer = ContentPanel;
        args.Handled = true;
    }
    base.OnManipulationStarted(args);
}
```

```
protected override void OnManipulationDelta(ManipulationDeltaEventArgs args)
{
    Point translate = args.DeltaManipulation.Translation;

    if (args.OriginalSource == pt0Dragger)
    {
        pathFig.StartPoint = Move(pathFig.StartPoint, translate);
        ctrlLine.Points[0] = Move(ctrlLine.Points[0], translate);
        pt0Ellipse.Center = Move(pt0Ellipse.Center, translate);
        args.Handled = true;
    }
    else if (args.OriginalSource == pt1Dragger)
    {
        pathSeg.Point1 = Move(pathSeg.Point1, translate);
        ctrlLine.Points[1] = Move(ctrlLine.Points[1], translate);
        pt1Ellipse.Center = Move(pt1Ellipse.Center, translate);
        args.Handled = true;
    }
    else if (args.OriginalSource == pt2Dragger)
    {
        pathSeg.Point2 = Move(pathSeg.Point2, translate);
        ctrlLine.Points[2] = Move(ctrlLine.Points[2], translate);
        pt2Ellipse.Center = Move(pt2Ellipse.Center, translate);
        args.Handled = true;
    }
    base.OnManipulationDelta(args);
}

Point Move(Point point, Point translate)
{
    return new Point(point.X + translate.X, point.Y + translate.Y);
}
```

Being a quadratic, this version of the Bézier curve makes only a single turn, and it is extremely well behaved:

If you ever need them, the parametric formulas used to construct the quadratic Bézier are:

$$x(t) = (1-t)^2x_0 + 2t(1-t)x_1 + t^2x_2$$

$$y(t) = (1-t)^2y_0 + 2t(1-t)y_1 + t^2y_2$$

for t = 0 to 1, where $p_0 = (x_0, y_0)$ and so forth.

The cubic Bézier spline is more standard, and has two control points rather than just one. The curve is defined by four points commonly labeled p_0, p_1, p_2, and p_3. The curve begins at p_0 and ends at p_3. At p_0 the curve is tangent to (and in the same direction as) a line from p_0 to p_1, and at p_3 the curve is tangent to the line from p_3 to p_2. The parametric equations describing the curve are:

$$x(t) = (1-t)^3x_0 + 3t(1-t)^2x_1 + 3t^2(1-t)x_2 + t^3x_3$$

$$y(t) = (1-t)^3y_0 + 3t(1-t)^2y_1 + 3t^2(1-t)y_2 + t^3y_3$$

For the CubicBezier program I took a little different approach. In an attempt to simplify it just a bit, I defined a *UserControl* derivative named *PointDragger*. The PointDragger.xaml file defines a visual tree consisting of just a *Grid* containing a *Path* with an *Opacity* of 0.5 and an *EllipseGeometry* with no *Center* point:

Silverlight Project: CubicBezier   File: PointDragger.xaml

```
<UserControl
    x:Class="CubicBezier.PointDragger"
    xmlns="http://schemas.microsoft.com/winfx/2006/xaml/presentation"
    xmlns:x="http://schemas.microsoft.com/winfx/2006/xaml">

    <Grid x:Name="LayoutRoot">
        <Path Fill="{StaticResource PhoneAccentBrush}"
            Opacity="0.5">
            <Path.Data>
                <EllipseGeometry x:Name="ellipseGeometry"
                                 RadiusX="48"
                                 RadiusY="48" />
            </Path.Data>
        </Path>
    </Grid>
</UserControl>
```

The code-behind file defines a dependency property named *Point* of type *Point*, and fires a *PointChanged* event when the value changes. The property-changed handler is also responsible for setting the value on the *EllipseGeometry* defined in the XAML file:

Silverlight Project: CubicBezier   File: PointDragger.xaml.cs (excerpt)

```
public partial class PointDragger : UserControl
{
    public static readonly DependencyProperty PointProperty =
        DependencyProperty.Register("Point",
            typeof(Point),
            typeof(PointDragger),
            new PropertyMetadata(OnPointChanged));
     public event RoutedPropertyChangedEventHandler<Point> PointChanged;

    public PointDragger()
    {
        InitializeComponent();
    }

    public Point Point
    {
        set { SetValue(PointProperty, value); }
        get { return (Point)GetValue(PointProperty); }
    }

    ...

    static void OnPointChanged(DependencyObject obj,
                            DependencyPropertyChangedEventArgs args)
    {
        (obj as PointDragger).OnPointChanged((Point)args.OldValue,
                                        (Point)args.NewValue);
    }

    protected virtual void OnPointChanged(Point oldValue, Point newValue)
    {
        ellipseGeometry.Center = newValue;

        if (PointChanged != null)
            PointChanged(this,
                new RoutedPropertyChangedEventArgs<Point>(oldValue, newValue));
    }
}
```

The *PointDragger* class also handles its own *Manipulation* events, which (compared with the ones in QuadraticBezier) become very simple:

Silverlight Project: CubicBezier   File: PointDragger.xaml.cs (excerpt)

```
protected override void OnManipulationStarted(ManipulationStartedEventArgs args)
{
    args.ManipulationContainer = VisualTreeHelper.GetParent(this) as UIElement;
    args.Handled = true;
```

```
        base.OnManipulationStarted(args);
    }

    protected override void OnManipulationDelta(ManipulationDeltaEventArgs args)
    {
        Point translate = args.DeltaManipulation.Translation;
        this.Point = new Point(this.Point.X + translate.X, this.Point.Y + translate.Y);
        args.Handled = true;
        base.OnManipulationDelta(args);
    }
```

The MainPage.xaml file defines a *Path* with a *BezierSegment*, two dotted *Polyline* elements for the tangent lines, and four instances of *PointDragger*. The *BezierSegment* class defines properties named *Point1*, *Point2*, and *Point3* for the two control points and the endpoint:

Silverlight Project: CubicBezier   File: MainPage.xaml (excerpt)

```
<Grid x:Name="ContentPanel" Grid.Row="1" Margin="12,0,12,0">
    <Path Stroke="{StaticResource PhoneForegroundBrush}"
          StrokeThickness="2">
        <Path.Data>
            <PathGeometry>
                <PathFigure x:Name="pathFig"
                            StartPoint="100 100">
                    <BezierSegment x:Name="pathSeg"
                                   Point1="300 100"
                                   Point2="300 400"
                                   Point3="100 400" />
                </PathFigure>
            </PathGeometry>
        </Path.Data>
    </Path>

    <Polyline Name="ctrl1Line"
              Stroke="{StaticResource PhoneForegroundBrush}"
              StrokeDashArray="2 2"
              Points="100 100, 300 100" />

    <Polyline Name="ctrl2Line"
              Stroke="{StaticResource PhoneForegroundBrush}"
              StrokeDashArray="2 2"
              Points="300 400, 100 400" />

    <local:PointDragger x:Name="pt0Dragger"
                        Point="100 100"
                        PointChanged="OnPointDraggerPointChanged" />

    <local:PointDragger x:Name="pt1Dragger"
                        Point="300 100"
                        PointChanged="OnPointDraggerPointChanged" />
```

```
    <local:PointDragger x:Name="pt2Dragger"
                        Point="300 400"
                        PointChanged="OnPointDraggerPointChanged" />

    <local:PointDragger x:Name="pt3Dragger"
                        Point="100 400"
                        PointChanged="OnPointDraggerPointChanged" />
</Grid>
```

The initial screen looks like this:

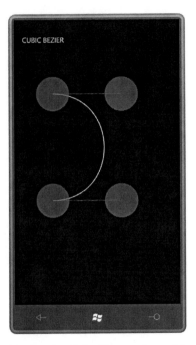

Notice the *PointChanged* event handlers on the *PointDragger* controls. Implementing that handler is pretty much the only thing left for MainPage.xaml.cs to do:

Silverlight Project: CubicBezier   File: MainPage.xaml.cs (excerpt)

```
void OnPointDraggerPointChanged(object sender,
                        RoutedPropertyChangedEventArgs<Point> args)
{
    Point translate = new Point(args.NewValue.X - args.OldValue.X,
                                args.NewValue.Y - args.OldValue.Y);

    if (sender == pt0Dragger)
    {
        pathFig.StartPoint = Move(pathFig.StartPoint, translate);
```

```
            ctrl1Line.Points[0] = Move(ctrl1Line.Points[0], translate);
        }
        else if (sender == pt1Dragger)
        {
            pathSeg.Point1 = Move(pathSeg.Point1, translate);
            ctrl1Line.Points[1] = Move(ctrl1Line.Points[1], translate);
        }
        else if (sender == pt2Dragger)
        {
            pathSeg.Point2 = Move(pathSeg.Point2, translate);
            ctrl2Line.Points[0] = Move(ctrl2Line.Points[0], translate);
        }
        else if (sender == pt3Dragger)
        {
            pathSeg.Point3 = Move(pathSeg.Point3, translate);
            ctrl2Line.Points[1] = Move(ctrl2Line.Points[1], translate);
        }
    }

    Point Move(Point point, Point translate)
    {
        return new Point(point.X + translate.X, point.Y + translate.Y);
    }
```

As you play around with the program, you might notice that the curve always stays confined within a four-side polygon defined by the two end points and the two control points. (It's called a "convex hull" in Bézier circles.). This version of the Bézier curve is a cubic, so the curve can make two turns:

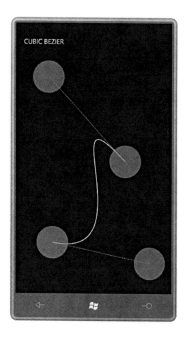

Besides *QuadraticBezierSegment* and *BezierSegment* to define single Bézier curves, you can also use *PolyQuadraticBezierSegment* and *PolyBezierSegment* for defining a series of Bézier curves. Each curve begins at the point the previous one ends. Each of these classes contains a property named *Points* of type *PointCollection*.

For *PolyQuadraticBezierSegment*, the number of *Point* objects in the *Points* collection must be a multiple of 2. The first, third, fifth, and so forth members of the collection are control points. For *PolyBezierSegment*, the number of points is a multiple of 3.

When connecting multiple Bézier curves, the end point of one curve becomes the begin point of the next curve. The composite curve is smooth at this point only if that point and the two control points on either side are collinear, that is, lie on the same line.

The Path Markup Syntax

Silverlight supports a type of "mini-language" that allows you to encode an entire *PathGeometry* in a string. The language consists of letters (such as M for Move, L for Line, A for Arc, and C for Cubic Bézier) that take the place of *PathFigure* and *PathSegment* objects. Each new *PathFigure* begins with a Move command. The syntax is described in the Graphics section of the online Silverlight documentation.

Here's an example:

```
<Grid Background="LightCyan">
    <Path Stroke="Maroon"
          StrokeThickness="4"
          Data="M 160 140 L 150 50 220 103
                M 320 140 L 330 50 260 103
                M 215 230 L 40 200
                M 215 240 L 40 240
                M 215 250 L 40 280
                M 265 230 L 440 200
                M 265 240 L 440 240
                M 265 250 L 440 280
                M 240 100
                A 100 100 0 0 1 240 300
                A 100 100 0 0 1 240 100
                M 180 170
                A 40 40 0 0 1 220 170
                A 40 40 0 0 1 180 170
                M 300 170
                A 40 40 0 0 1 260 170
                A 40 40 0 0 1 300 170" />
</Grid>
```

The Arc is probably the most complex syntax. It begins with the size of the ellipse, followed by a rotation angle, and then two flags, 1 for *IsLargeArc* and 1 for *Clockwise*, and concluding with the point. When drawing complete circles, you'll want to separate the circle into two halves and use two Arc commands (or two *ArcSegment* objects).

Besides using geometries for drawing you can use geometries for clipping. Here's the famous KeyholeOnTheMoon image:

This program makes use of the *Clip* property of type *Geometry*. *Clip* is defined by *FrameworkElement* so you can use the property to make any element or control visually non-rectangular in shape, and the Path Markup Syntax makes it look trivial:

Silverlight Project: **KeyholeOnTheMoon**   File: **MainPage.xaml (excerpt)**

```
<Grid x:Name="ContentPanel" Grid.Row="1" Margin="12,0,12,0"
      Background="{StaticResource PhoneAccentBrush}">
    <Image Source="Images/BuzzAldrinOnTheMoon.png"
           Stretch="None"
           Clip="M 120 95 L 90 265 L 220 265 L 190 95
                    A 50 50 0 1 0 120 95" />
</Grid>
```

I've also used Path Markup Syntax in the Analog Clock program. Here's what it looks like:

The visuals consist of five *Path* elements. The curves on the hour and minute hand are Bézier splines. The tick marks are dotted arc segments.

The XAML file defines a *Style* that's used for all five *Path* elements:

Silverlight Project: **AnalogClock**   File: **MainPage.xaml (excerpt)**

```
<phone:PhoneApplicationPage.Resources>
    <Style x:Key="pathStyle"
           TargetType="Path">
        <Setter Property="Fill" Value="{StaticResource PhoneAccentColor}" />
        <Setter Property="Stroke" Value="{StaticResource PhoneForegroundColor}" />
        <Setter Property="StrokeThickness" Value="2" />
        <Setter Property="StrokeStartLineCap" Value="Round" />
        <Setter Property="StrokeEndLineCap" Value="Round" />
        <Setter Property="StrokeLineJoin" Value="Round" />
        <Setter Property="StrokeDashCap" Value="Round" />
    </Style>
</phone:PhoneApplicationPage.Resources>
```

In an attempt to keep the graphics simple, I devised an arbitrary coordinate system. The clock graphics are drawn as if the width and height of the clock were 200 pixels, and the center were the point (0, 0). The clock graphics are thus bounded by X coordinates of –100 on the left and 100 on the right, and Y coordinates of –100 on the top and 100 on the bottom.

These arbitrary coordinates of the clock are in part defined by the explicit *Width* and *Height* settings of this nested *Grid*:

Silverlight Project: AnalogClock   File: MainPage.xaml (excerpt)

```
<Grid x:Name="ContentPanel" Grid.Row="1" Margin="12,0,12,0"
      SizeChanged="OnContentPanelSizeChanged">

    <!-- Draw clock on Grid with center at (0, 0) -->
    <Grid Width="200" Height="200">
        <Grid.RenderTransform>
            <TransformGroup>
                <ScaleTransform x:Name="scaleClock" />
                <TranslateTransform X="100" Y="100" />
            </TransformGroup>
        </Grid.RenderTransform>

        . . .

    </Grid>
</Grid>
```

The *TranslateTransform* shifts the whole *Grid* to the right and down. The upper-left coordinate of (–100, –100), for example, becomes (0, 0), and a coordinate of (100, 100) becomes (200, 200).

Notice the *SizeChanged* event handler set on the normal content grid. The code portion uses the actual size of the content area to set the *ScaleTransform* applied to the nested *Grid*. That scales the 200-pixel dimension to the actual size:

Silverlight Project: AnalogClock   File: MainPage.xaml.cs (excerpt)

```
void OnContentPanelSizeChanged(object sender, SizeChangedEventArgs args)
{
    double scale = Math.Min(args.NewSize.Width, args.NewSize.Height) / 200;
    scaleClock.ScaleX = scale;
    scaleClock.ScaleY = scale;
}
```

Here are the five paths:

Silverlight Project: AnalogClock   File: MainPage.xaml (excerpt)

```
<!-- Tick marks (small and large). -->
<Path Data="M 0 -90 A 90 90 0 1 1 0 90
                    A 90 90 0 1 1 0 -90"
```

```
            Style="{StaticResource pathStyle}"
            Fill="{x:Null}"
            StrokeDashArray="0 3.14159"
            StrokeThickness="3" />

    <Path Data="M 0 -90 A 90 90 0 1 1 0 90
                        A 90 90 0 1 1 0 -90"
          Style="{StaticResource pathStyle}"
          Fill="{x:Null}"
          StrokeDashArray="0 7.854"
          StrokeThickness="6" />

    <!-- Hour hand pointing up. -->
    <Path Data="M 0 -60 C 0 -30, 20 -30, 5 -20 L 5 0
                        C 5 7.5, -5 7.5, -5 -20 L -5 -20
                        C -20 -30, 0 -30 0 -60"
          Style="{StaticResource pathStyle}">
        <Path.RenderTransform>
            <RotateTransform x:Name="rotateHour" />
        </Path.RenderTransform>
    </Path>

    <!-- Minute hand pointing up. -->
    <Path Data="M 0 -80 C 0 -75, 0 -70, 2.5 -60 L 2.5 0
                        C 2.5 5, -2.5 5, -2.5 0 L -2.5 -60
                        C 0 -70, 0 -75, 0 -80"
          Style="{StaticResource pathStyle}">
        <Path.RenderTransform>
            <RotateTransform x:Name="rotateMinute" />
        </Path.RenderTransform>
    </Path>

    <!-- Second hand pointing up. -->
    <Path Data="M 0 10 L 0 -80"
          Style="{StaticResource pathStyle}">
        <Path.RenderTransform>
            <RotateTransform x:Name="rotateSecond" />
        </Path.RenderTransform>
    </Path>
```

The *StrokeDashArray* settings on the first two *Path* elements were carefully calculated to produce the pattern of 1-second and 5-second tick marks around the face of the clock. The other three *Path* elements have *RotateTransform* objects set to their *RenderTransform* properties. These *RotateTransforms* are reset every second from the code-behind file:

Silverlight Project: AnalogClock   File: MainPage.xaml.cs (excerpt)

```
public partial class MainPage : PhoneApplicationPage
{
    public MainPage()
```

```
    {
        InitializeComponent();

        DispatcherTimer tmr = new DispatcherTimer();
        tmr.Interval = TimeSpan.FromSeconds(1);
        tmr.Tick += new EventHandler(OnTimerTick);
        tmr.Start();
    }

    void OnTimerTick(object sender, EventArgs args)
    {
        DateTime dt = DateTime.Now;

        rotateSecond.Angle = 6 * dt.Second;
        rotateMinute.Angle = 6 * dt.Minute + rotateSecond.Angle / 60;
        rotateHour.Angle = 30 * (dt.Hour % 12) + rotateMinute.Angle / 12;
    }
    ...
}
```

How This Chapter Was Created

The little snippets of XAML and the pictures that accompany them began life with a concept that originated in the early days of the Windows Presentation Foundation. Although XAML was mostly designed to be compiled along with the rest of your source code, it was also reasonable to assume that programmers might want to convert XAML into objects (and objects into XAML) at runtime. For this purpose, the *System.Windows.Markup* namespace has a static method named *XamlReader.Load* for converting XAML into objects, and *XamlWriter.Save* for going the other way.

Only the first of those two static methods made it into Silverlight and Silverlight for Windows Phone. But that's the really useful one. Give *XamlReader.Load* a string containing some legal XAML—including the proper namespace declarations but excluding events assignments— and the method returns an object corresponding to the root element with all the other objects in the visual tree created as well.

One application of *XamlReader.Load* in WPF was an interactive programming tool that contained a *TextBox* to let you edit and enter XAML, and then displayed the resultant object. Of course, most of the time, as the user is editing a piece of XAML, it won't be legal, so the tool has to trap those errors and respond appropriately.

Several variations of this programming tool were written. The WPF Software Development Kit contained a version called XamlPad, and for my book *Applications = Code + Markup* (Microsoft Press, 2006), I created a version called XamlCruncher.

Later on, I enhanced XamlCruncher so it could present a type of slide show of little XAML files and their resultant objects. I used this for presentations about WPF programming, and I later rewrote the program for Silverlight.

The Petzold.Phone.Silverlight library contains the "guts" of the Windows Phone 7 version of XamlCruncher in a class derived from *TextBox*:

Silverlight Project: Petzold.Phone.Silverlight   File: XamlCruncherTextBox.cs (excerpt)

```
public class XamlCruncherTextBox : TextBox
{
    public event EventHandler<XamlCruncherEventArgs> XamlResult;

    public XamlCruncherTextBox()
    {
        this.AcceptsReturn = true;
        this.TextWrapping = TextWrapping.NoWrap;
        this.HorizontalScrollBarVisibility = ScrollBarVisibility.Auto;
        this.VerticalScrollBarVisibility = ScrollBarVisibility.Auto;

        TextChanged += OnTextBoxTextChanged;
    }

    void OnTextBoxTextChanged(object sender, TextChangedEventArgs args)
    {
        string xaml =
            "<UserControl " +
            " xmlns='http://schemas.microsoft.com/winfx/2006/xaml/presentation'\r" +
            " xmlns:phone='clr-namespace:Microsoft.Phone.Controls;" +
            "assembly=Microsoft.Phone'\r" +
            " xmlns:shell='clr-namespace:Microsoft.Phone.Shell;" +
            "assembly=Microsoft.Phone'\r" +
            " xmlns:system='clr-namespace:System;assembly=mscorlib'\r" +
            " xmlns:petzold='clr-namespace:Petzold.Phone.Silverlight;" +
            "assembly=Petzold.Phone.Silverlight'>\r" +
            "    " + this.Text + "\r" +
            "</UserControl>";

        UserControl ctrl = null;

        try
        {
            ctrl = XamlReader.Load(xaml) as UserControl;
        }
        catch (Exception exc)
        {
            OnXamlResult(new XamlCruncherEventArgs(exc.Message));
            return;
        }
```

```
        if (ctrl == null)
        {
            OnXamlResult(new XamlCruncherEventArgs("null result"));
            return;
        }

        OnXamlResult(new XamlCruncherEventArgs(ctrl));
    }

    protected virtual void OnXamlResult(XamlCruncherEventArgs args)
    {
        if (XamlResult != null)
            XamlResult(this, args);
    }
}
```

The *TextChanged* handler assumes that the *TextBox* contains a chunk of XAML that is appropriate as content for a *UserControl*. It wraps that text in *UserControl* tags with a bunch of namespace declarations—including the standard (and semi-standard) *phone*, *shell*, *system*, and *petzold*—and passes it to *XamlReader.Load*, which raises an exception of the XAML is not valid.

Whatever happens, the class fires a *XamlResult* event providing either the resultant *UserControl* or an error message in the following event arguments:

Silverlight Project: Petzold.Phone.Silverlight   File: XamlCruncherEventArgs.cs

```
using System;
using System.Windows;

namespace Petzold.Phone.Silverlight
{
    public class XamlCruncherEventArgs : EventArgs
    {
        public XamlCruncherEventArgs(UIElement element)
        {
            Element = element;
            Error = null;
        }

        public XamlCruncherEventArgs(string error)
        {
            Error = error;
            Element = null;
        }

        public UIElement Element { set; get; }

        public string Error { set; get; }
    }
}
```

I wrote two programs using the *XamlCruncherTextBox* class. The first is called simply XamlCruncher, and if you have an extreme amount of patience and diligence, you can actually type XAML into the program on your phone and see the results.

The patience and diligence involves the keyboard. Whether you're using a virtual keyboard or your phone's hardware keyboard, there's a lot of swapping between keyboard layouts for letters, numbers, and symbols. In particular, the hardware keyboard on the phone that I used for writing this book doesn't have angle brackets or an equal sign, which are absolutely necessary for XML, or curly braces, which is useful for XAML. These are accessible by pressing a Sym key, which invokes a special supplementary software keyboard that contains these symbols.

The XamlCruncher content area is divided in half with a *UniformStack*. Half the area contains the *XamlCruncherTextBox* with a *TextBlock* for error messages, and the other half is a *ScrollViewer* with a *Border* for hosting the resultant content:

Silverlight Project: XamlCruncher   File: MainPage.xaml (excerpt)

```
<Grid x:Name="ContentPanel" Grid.Row="1" Margin="12,0,12,0">
    <petzold:UniformStack Name="uniformStack">
        <Grid>
            <Grid.RowDefinitions>
                <RowDefinition Height="*" />
                <RowDefinition Height="Auto" />
            </Grid.RowDefinitions>

            <petzold:XamlCruncherTextBox
                    x:Name="txtbox"
                    Grid.Row="0"
                    FontSize="{StaticResource PhoneFontSizeSmall}"
                    FontFamily="Courier New"
                    TextChanged="OnTextBoxTextChanged"
                    XamlResult="OnXamlCruncherTextBoxXamlResult" />

            <TextBlock Name="statusText"
                    Grid.Row="1"
                    TextWrapping="Wrap" />
        </Grid>

        <ScrollViewer HorizontalScrollBarVisibility="Auto"
                    VerticalScrollBarVisibility="Auto">
            <Border Name="container" />
        </ScrollViewer>

    </petzold:UniformStack>
</Grid>
```

The code file has several tasks. Every time the text changes, it stores the new text in isolated storage. This allows you to work on a particular piece of XAML over several days or weeks as you become frequently frustrated and discouraged.

Silverlight Project: XamlCruncher   File: MainPage.xaml.cs (excerpt)

```
public partial class MainPage : PhoneApplicationPage
{
    IsolatedStorageSettings settings = IsolatedStorageSettings.ApplicationSettings;

    public MainPage()
    {
        InitializeComponent();
        Application.Current.UnhandledException += OnUnhandledException;

        string text;

        if (!settings.TryGetValue<string>("text", out text))
            text = "<Grid Background=\"AliceBlue\">\r    \r</Grid>";

        txtbox.Text = text;
    }

    protected override void OnOrientationChanged(OrientationChangedEventArgs args)
    {
        uniformStack.Orientation =
                ((args.Orientation & PageOrientation.Portrait) == 0) ?
                    System.Windows.Controls.Orientation.Horizontal :
                    System.Windows.Controls.Orientation.Vertical;

        base.OnOrientationChanged(args);
    }

    void OnTextBoxTextChanged(object sender, TextChangedEventArgs args)
    {
        settings["text"] = txtbox.Text;
    }

    void OnUnhandledException(object sender,
                        ApplicationUnhandledExceptionEventArgs args)
    {
        statusText.Text = args.ExceptionObject.Message;
        args.Handled = true;
    }

    void OnXamlCruncherTextBoxXamlResult(object sender, XamlCruncherEventArgs args)
    {
        if (args.Error != null)
        {
            statusText.Text = args.Error;
        }
```

```
        else
        {
            container.Child = args.Element;
            statusText.Text = "OK";
        }
    }
}
```

The *OnOrientationChanged* method changes the orientation of the *UniformStack* when the orientation of the screen changes. Because XamlCruncher is (marginally) easier to use with the hardware keyboard, it is usable in both portrait and landscape modes.

The program also attempts to handle unhandled exceptions. Particularly when animations are involved, it is possible for a piece of XAML to pass *XamlReader.Load* but then raise an exception later on.

You'll want to run this program without the Visual Studio debugger; otherwise, Visual Studio breaks when any exception occurs.

Here's a little sample:

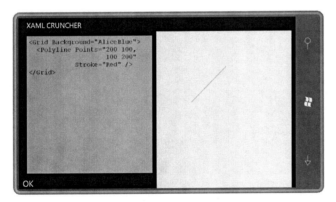

The VectorGraphicsDemos program (which is included with the source code for this chapter but not interesting enough to devote actual pages) incorporates the *XamlCruncherTextBox* control and includes a file containing all the little XAML snippets shown through this chapter. You can page through those files, see the resultant images, and edit them if you wish.

Chapter 14
Raster Graphics

In Chapter 4 I demonstrated how a Windows Phone 7 program can obtain bitmaps. These bitmaps can originate with the application itself, they can be downloaded from the Web, or they can come from the camera or from the phone's picture library. In this chapter I'll go beyond the task of *loading* bitmaps into the realm of *saving* bitmaps. You can save a bitmap in isolated storage, or in a special album of the picture library identified as "Saved Pictures."

If your program needs to save a bitmap, there's probably a good reason for it! Your application is probably creating a bitmap from scratch or modifying an existing bitmap in some way. These jobs involve the use of the exciting and powerful *WriteableBitmap* class.

The Bitmap Class Hierarchy

As you'll recall, you can display a bitmap in one of two ways: using the *Image* element or creating an *ImageBrush*. The *Source* property of the *Image* element and the *ImageSource* property of the *ImageBrush* are both of type *ImageSource*, a class occupying a very fundamental place in the region of the Silverlight class hierarchy devoted to bitmaps:

Object
    DependencyObject (abstract)
        ImageSource (abstract)
            BitmapSource (abstract)
                BitmapImage
                WriteableBitmap

ImageSource has only one descendent class and defines nothing public on its own, so it might seem a little superfluous. That's true in Silverlight but not in the Windows Presentation Foundation, where *ImageSource* is a parent to classes that define images derived from vector graphics as well as those involving raster graphics.

The remaining three classes are all defined in the *System.Windows.Media.Imaging* namespace.

BitmapSource defines two public get-only properties and one method:

- A *PixelWidth* property of type *int*.

- A *PixelHeight* property of type *int*.

- A *SetSource* method that has one argument of type *Stream*.

That *Stream* argument can be a file stream, a network stream, or a memory stream of some sort. But the *Stream* must provide bitmap data in either the JPEG or PNG file format. Once a bitmap has been created, it has a fixed size that cannot be changed.

The *BitmapImage* class expands on the functionality of *BitmapSource* by letting you reference a bitmap with a URI. *BitmapImage* defines the following:

- A constructor that accepts an argument of type *Uri*.

- A *UriSource* property of type *Uri*.

- A *CreateOptions* property.

- Three events that let you track downloading progress, and report upon success or failure

The *CreateOptions* property is of type *CreateOptions*, an enumeration with three members: *None*, *DelayCreation*, and *IgnoreImageCache*. The default is *DelayCreation*, which doesn't start loading an image until it's actually needed for rendering. The *IgnoreImageCache* is useful when a program knows that a previously loaded image has become invalid. You can combine *DelayCreation* and *IgnoreImageCache* with the C# bitwise OR operator.

By combining the features of *BitmapSource* and *BitmapImage*, the *BitmapImage* class lets you load a bitmap in JPEG or PNG format using either a *Stream* object or a *Uri* object. There is no facility to save bitmaps.

The *WriteableBitmap* class itself continues this trend. Taken by itself, *WriteableBitmap* does *not* including any facility to save bitmaps. However, the *WriteableBitmap* class does give you access to all the pixels that define the bitmap. Only one pixel format is supported, where each pixel is a 32-bit value. You can obtain the pixel bits from an existing bitmap, or set new pixel bits on a *WriteableBitmap* to define the image. Access to these pixel bits allows you a great deal of flexibility in how you save or load bitmaps. You can provide your own bitmap "encoder" to save pixel bits in a particular bitmap format, or your own "decoder" to access a file of a particular format and convert to the uncompressed pixel bits.

WriteableBitmap also provides a facility to "draw" images on the bitmap based on Silverlight elements. Although you can indeed draw *Button* elements and *Slider* elements on a bitmap, it's most common to use elements that derive from *Shape*. In other words, *WriteableBitmap* allows you to convert a vector drawing into a raster image.

Here are the constructors, methods, and property defined by *WriteableBitmap*:

- A constructor that accepts a *UIElement* and a transform.

- A constructor that accepts a pixel width and height.

- A constructor that accepts a *BitmapSource* object.

- A *Render* method that accepts a *UIElement* and a transform.

- An *Invalidate* method to update bitmap visuals.

- A property named *Pixels* of type *int* array.

Keep in mind that *WriteableBitmap* derives from *BitmapSource* rather than *BitmapImage*, so there is no facility in *WriteableBitmap* to load a bitmap from a URI. However, you can load a *BitmapImage* object from a URI and then create a *WriteableBitmap* from that using the third constructor I've listed.

WriteableBitmap lets you put images on the bitmap using two techniques:

- By rendering the visuals of any *UIElement* on the bitmap.

- By directly manipulating the pixel bits.

You can combine these techniques in whatever manner you want.

In addition, Windows Phone 7 provides several subsidiary methods that provide you with alternative ways to load JPEG files and to save them:

- A static *PictureDecoder.DecodeJpeg* method in the *Microsoft.Phone* namespace lets you load a JPEG file from a *Stream* but with a maximum *Width* and *Height*. This is useful if you know that a particular JPEG might be much larger than what you need to display on the phone. The method returns a *WritableBitmap*.

- An *Extensions* class in the *System.Windows.Media.Imaging* namespace has two extension methods to *WriteableBitmap*: *LoadJpeg* (which doesn't provide additional functionality over the *SetSource* method defined by *BitmapSource*) and *SaveJpeg*, which lets you alter the width and height of the image and specify a compression quality.

- The *SavePicture* method of the XNA *MediaLibrary* class lets you save a bitmap to the phone's picture library from a *Stream* or a *byte* array in JPEG format. You'll probably use this in conjunction with the *SaveJpeg* extension method with a *MemoryStream* intermediary, as I'll demonstrate towards the end of this chapter.

WriteableBitmap and *UIElement*

WriteableBitmap has two ways to get the visuals of a *UIElement* onto a bitmap. The first uses one of the constructors:

```
WriteableBitmap writeableBitmap = new WriteableBitmap(element, transform);
```

The *element* argument is of type *UIElement* and the *transform* argument is of type *Transform*. This constructor creates a bitmap based on the size of the *UIElement* argument as possibly modified by the *Transform* argument (which you can set to *null*).

The element and all its visual children are rendered on the bitmap. However, any *RenderTransform* applied to that element is ignored. Optionally taking account of that transform is the rationale behind the second argument. The resultant bitmap is based on the maximum horizontal and vertical coordinates of the transformed element. Any part of the element that is transformed into a negative coordinate space (to the left or above the original element) is cropped.

Here's a simple sample program. The content grid is given a background based on the current accent color. It contains a *TextBlock* and an *Image* element:

Silverlight Project: RecursivePageCaptures   File: MainPage.xaml (excerpt)

```
<Grid x:Name="ContentPanel" Grid.Row="1" Margin="12,0,12,0"
      Background="{StaticResource PhoneAccentBrush}">

    <TextBlock Text="Tap anywhere to capture page"
               HorizontalAlignment="Center"
               VerticalAlignment="Center" />

    <Image Name="img"
           Stretch="Fill" />
</Grid>
```

The *Image* element has no bitmap to display but when it does, it will ignore the bitmap's aspect ratio to fill the content grid and obscure the *TextBlock*.

When the screen is tapped, the code-behind file simply sets the *Image* element source to a new *WriteableBitmap* based on the page itself:

Silverlight Project: RecursivePageCaptures   File: MainPage.xaml.cs (excerpt)

```
public partial class MainPage : PhoneApplicationPage
{
    public MainPage()
    {
        InitializeComponent();
    }

    protected override void OnManipulationStarted(ManipulationStartedEventArgs args)
    {
        img.Source = new WriteableBitmap(this, null);

        args.Complete();
        args.Handled = true;
        base.OnManipulationStarted(args);
    }
}
```

When you first run the program, the screen looks like this:

Tap once, and the whole page becomes the bitmap displayed by the *Image* element:

Keep in mind that the *PhoneApplicationPage* object being captured has its *Background* property set to the default value of *null*, so that's why you see the original background of the content panel behind the captured titles. You can continue tapping the screen to recapture the page content, now including the previous *Image* element:

There is no sense in which these elements are "retained" by the bitmap in any way other than becoming part of the bitmap image.

The *WriteableBitmap* class also has a *Render* method with the same two arguments as the constructor I just demonstrated:

```
writeableBitmap.Render(element, transform);
```

You'll need to follow the *Render* call with a call to *Invalidate* to get the actual bitmap to reflect the visuals of the *element* argument:

```
writeableBitmap.Invalidate();
```

Obviously the *WriteableBitmap* must obviously already have been created at the time of these calls, so it already has a fixed size. Based on the size of the element and the transform, some (or all) of the element might be cropped.

If you try calling *Render* with a newly created *Button* element (for example) you'll probably discover that it doesn't work. A newly created *Button* element has a size of zero. You'll need to call *Measure* and *Arrange* on the element to give it a non-zero size. However, I have generally been unsuccessful in giving some elements a non-zero size even after calling

Measure and *Arrange*. The process seems to work a lot better if the element is already part of a visual tree. It works much better with *Image* elements and *Shape* derivatives.

Here's a program that obtains a square bitmap from the phone's picture library, and then chops it up into four quadrants, each of which is half the width and half the height of the original bitmap.

The content area of the SubdivideBitmap program contains a *TextBlock* and a *Grid* with two rows and two columns of equal size. Each of the four cells of this *Grid* contains an *Image* element with names that indicate the location in the grid: For example, *imgUL* is upper-left and *imgLR* is lower-right.

Silverlight Project: SubdivideBitmap   File: MainPage.xaml (excerpt)

```
<Grid x:Name="ContentPanel" Grid.Row="1" Margin="12,0,12,0">
    <TextBlock Name="txtblk"
               Text="Touch to choose image"
               HorizontalAlignment="Center"
               VerticalAlignment="Center" />

    <Grid HorizontalAlignment="Center"
          VerticalAlignment="Center">
        <Grid.RowDefinitions>
            <RowDefinition Height="*" />
            <RowDefinition Height="*" />
        </Grid.RowDefinitions>

        <Grid.ColumnDefinitions>
            <ColumnDefinition Width="*" />
            <ColumnDefinition Width="*" />
        </Grid.ColumnDefinitions>

        <Image Name="imgUL" Grid.Row="0" Grid.Column="0" Margin="2" />
        <Image Name="imgUR" Grid.Row="0" Grid.Column="1" Margin="2" />
        <Image Name="imgLL" Grid.Row="1" Grid.Column="0" Margin="2" />
        <Image Name="imgLR" Grid.Row="1" Grid.Column="1" Margin="2" />
    </Grid>
</Grid>
```

The code-behind file for the *MainPage* class is set up for a *PhotoChooserTask*: As required, the *PhotoChooserTask* object is defined as a field and the *Completed* event handler is attached at the end of the constructor:

Silverlight Project: SubdivideBitmap   File: MainPage.xaml.cs (excerpt)

```
public partial class MainPage : PhoneApplicationPage
{
    PhotoChooserTask photoChooser = new PhotoChooserTask();
```

```
    public MainPage()
    {
        InitializeComponent();
        photoChooser.Completed += OnPhotoChooserCompleted;
    }
    protected override void OnManipulationStarted(ManipulationStartedEventArgs args)
    {
        int dimension = (int)Math.Min(ContentPanel.ActualWidth,
                                      ContentPanel.ActualHeight) - 8;

        photoChooser.PixelHeight = dimension;
        photoChooser.PixelWidth = dimension;
        photoChooser.Show();

        args.Complete();
        args.Handled = true;
        base.OnManipulationStarted(args);
    }
    ...
}
```

The *OnManipulationStarted* override then calls the *Show* method of the *PhotoChooserTask* requesting a square bitmap using dimensions based on the size of the content panel. Eight pixels are subtracted from this dimension to account for the *Margin* property set on each *Image* element in the XAML file.

When the *Completed* event is fired by the *PhotoChooserTask*, the handler begins by creating a *BitmapImage* object based on the stream referencing the chosen bitmap. It then creates an *Image* element (named *imgBase*) to display the bitmap. Notice that this *Image* element is not part of a visual tree. It exists solely as a source for *Render* calls.

Silverlight Project: SubdivideBitmap   File: MainPage.xaml.cs (excerpt)

```
void OnPhotoChooserCompleted(object sender, PhotoResult args)
{
    if (args.Error != null || args.ChosenPhoto == null)
        return;

    BitmapImage bitmapImage = new BitmapImage();
    bitmapImage.SetSource(args.ChosenPhoto);

    Image imgBase = new Image();
    imgBase.Source = bitmapImage;
    imgBase.Stretch = Stretch.None;
```

```
// Upper-left
WriteableBitmap writeableBitmap = new WriteableBitmap(bitmapImage.PixelWidth / 2,
                                                 bitmapImage.PixelHeight / 2);

writeableBitmap.Render(imgBase, null);
writeableBitmap.Invalidate();
imgUL.Source = writeableBitmap;

// Upper-right
writeableBitmap = new WriteableBitmap(bitmapImage.PixelWidth / 2,
                                      bitmapImage.PixelHeight / 2);
TranslateTransform translate = new TranslateTransform();
translate.X = -bitmapImage.PixelWidth / 2;
writeableBitmap.Render(imgBase, translate);
writeableBitmap.Invalidate();
imgUR.Source = writeableBitmap;

// Lower-left
writeableBitmap = new WriteableBitmap(bitmapImage.PixelWidth / 2,
                                      bitmapImage.PixelHeight / 2);

translate.X = 0;
translate.Y = -bitmapImage.PixelHeight / 2;
writeableBitmap.Render(imgBase, translate);
writeableBitmap.Invalidate();
imgLL.Source = writeableBitmap;

// Lower-right
writeableBitmap = new WriteableBitmap(bitmapImage.PixelWidth / 2,
                                      bitmapImage.PixelHeight / 2);
translate.X = -bitmapImage.PixelWidth / 2;
writeableBitmap.Render(imgBase, translate);
writeableBitmap.Invalidate();
imgLR.Source = writeableBitmap;

txtblk.Visibility = Visibility.Collapsed;
}
```

The remainder of the *Completed* event handler creates four *WriteableBitmap* objects, each
½ the width and ½ the height of the original. (This calculation is based on the dimensions
of the *BitmapImage* and not the dimensions of the *Image*, which at this time will report a
zero size.)

Except for the first of the four *Render* calls, a *TranslateTransform* is also defined that shifts
to the left or up (or both) by half the bitmap dimension. Each call to *Render* is followed
by an *Invalidate* call. Each *WriteableBitmap* is then assigned to the *Source* property of the
appropriate *Image* element in the XAML file. The *Margin* property of those *Image* elements

separates them sufficiently to make it clear that we're now dealing with four separate *Image* elements:

Notice that the code uses a single *TranslateTransform* object. Normally you wouldn't want to share a transform among multiple elements unless you wanted the same transform to be applied to all elements. But here the *TranslateTransform* is only being used temporarily for rendering purposes.

Later in this chapter I'll show another approach to dividing a bitmap into pieces that has an application in a little game.

The Pixel Bits

The *Pixels* property of *WritableBitmap* is an array of *int*, which means that each pixel is 32 bits wide. The *Pixels* property itself is get-only so you can't replace the actual array, but you can set and get elements of that array.

A bitmap is a two dimensional array of pixels; the *Pixels* property of *WriteableBitmap* is a one-dimensional array of *int* values. The *Pixels* array stores the pixels of the bitmap starting with the top row and working down, and within each row from left to right. The number of elements in the array is equal to the product of the bitmap's pixel width and pixel height.

If *bm* is a *WriteableBitmap* object, then the number of elements in the *Pixels* property is *bm.PixelWidth* * *bm.PixelHeight*. Suppose you want to access the pixel in column *x* (where *x* ranges from 0 through *bm.PixelWidth* – 1) and row *y*, where *y* ranges from 0 to *bm.PixelHeight* – 1. You index the *Pixels* property like so:

```
bm.Pixels[y * bm.PixelWidth + x]
```

Silverlight for Windows Phone supports only one pixel format, sometimes denoted as PARGB32. Let me decode this format code working backwards:

The "32" at the end means 32 bits, or 4 bytes. That's the size of each pixel. The ARGB part indicates that the Alpha byte (opacity) occupies the high 8 bits of the 32-bit integer, followed by the Red byte, Green byte, and Blue byte, which occupies the bottom 8 bits of the integer.

If *A*, *R*, *G*, and *B* are all of type *byte*, you can create a 32-bit integer pixel value like so:

```
int pixel = A << 24 | R << 16 | G << 8 | B
```

The shifted values—implicitly converted to type *int*—are combined with the C# bitwise OR operator. You can obtain the components of an existing pixel value like so:

```
byte A = (byte)(pixel & 0xFF000000 >> 24);
byte R = (byte)(pixel & 0x00FF0000 >> 16);
byte G = (byte)(pixel & 0x0000FF00 >> 8);
byte B = (byte)(pixel & 0x000000FF);
```

When the Alpha channel byte is 255, the pixel is opaque. A value of 0 means completely transparent, and values in between indicate various levels of transparency.

In the PARGB32 pixel format, the P stands for "premultiplied," which means that if the Alpha value is anything other than 255, then the Red, Green, and Blue values have been already adjusted for the transparency indicated by that Alpha value.

To better understand this concept, let's look at an example involving a single pixel. Suppose you want the pixel to have the following color:

```
Color.FromArgb(128, 0, 0, 255)
```

That's blue with 50% transparency. When that pixel is rendered on a particular background surface, the color of the pixel must be combined with the existing colors of the surface. Drawn against a black background, the resultant RGB color is (0, 0, 128), which is the average of the blue pixel and the black background. Drawn against a white background, the resultant color is (127, 127, 255). Each of the three components is an average of the pixel and the surface.

With a transparency of anything other than 50%, the resultant color is a weighted average of the pixel source and the surface: The subscripts in the following formulas indicate the "result" of rendering a partially transparent "source" pixel on an existing "surface":

$$R_{result} = [(255 - A_{source}) \times R_{surface} + A_{source} \times R_{source}] \div 255$$

$$G_{result} = [(255 - A_{source}) \times G_{surface} + A_{source} \times G_{source}] \div 255$$

$$B_{result} = [(255 - A_{source}) \times B_{surface} + A_{source} \times B_{source}] \div 255$$

When a bitmap is rendered on an arbitrary surface, these calculations must be performed for each pixel.

Very often a single bitmap is rendered on different surfaces multiple times. The calculations shown above can be speeded up somewhat if the Red, Green, and Blue components of the pixels in the bitmap have already been multiplied by the Alpha channel. These pre-multiplied components are calculated like so:

$$PR_{source} = (A_{source} \times R_{source}) \div 255$$

and similarly for Green and Blue. The resultant formulas for rendering the bitmap have half the number of multiplications:

$$R_{result} = [(255 - A_{source}) \times R_{surface}] \div 255 + PR_{source}$$

Whenever you're working with the *Pixels* property of *WriteableBitmap*, you're dealing with pre-multiplied alphas. For example, suppose you want a pixel in the bitmap to have an RGB color value of (40, 60, 255) but with an Alpha value of 192. The ARGB value in the bitmap would be (192, 30, 45, 192). Each of the R, G, and B values have been multiplied by 192/255 or about 0.75.

In any pre-multiplied color value, the R, G, or B values should all be less than or equal to the A value. Nothing will "blow up" if any R, G, or B value is greater than A, but you won't get the level of transparency you want.

When working with ARGB color values *without* pre-multiplied alphas, there is a distinction between "transparent black," the ARGB color (0, 0, 0, 0), and "transparent white," the ARGB color (0, 255, 255, 255). With pre-multiplied alphas, the distinction disappears because transparent white is also (0, 0, 0, 0).

When you first create a *WriteableBitmap*, all the pixels are zero, which you can think of as "transparent black" or "transparent white" or "transparent chartreuse."

By directly writing into the *Pixels* array of a *WriteableBitmap* you can create any type of image you can conceive.

Comparatively simple algorithms let you create styles of brushes that are not supported by the standard *Brush* derivatives. The content area of the CircularGradient project consists solely of an *Image* element waiting for a bitmap:

Silverlight Project: CircularGradient   File: MainPage.xaml (excerpt)

```
<Grid x:Name="ContentPanel" Grid.Row="1" Margin="12,0,12,0">
    <Image Name="img"
           HorizontalAlignment="Center"
           VerticalAlignment="Center" />
</Grid>
```

The code-behind file for *MainPage* defines a rather arbitrary radius value and makes a square *WriteableBitmap* twice that value. The two *for* loops for *x* and *y* touch every pixel in that bitmap:

Silverlight Project: CircularGradient   File: MainPage.xaml.cs (excerpt)

```
public partial class MainPage : PhoneApplicationPage
{
    const int RADIUS = 200;

    public MainPage()
    {
        InitializeComponent();

        WriteableBitmap writeableBitmap = new WriteableBitmap(2 * RADIUS, 2 * RADIUS);

        for (int y = 0; y < writeableBitmap.PixelWidth; y++)
            for (int x = 0; x < writeableBitmap.PixelHeight; x++)
            {
                if (Math.Sqrt(Math.Pow(x - RADIUS, 2) + Math.Pow(y - RADIUS, 2)) <
RADIUS)
                {
                    double angle = Math.Atan2(y - RADIUS, x - RADIUS);
                    byte R = (byte)(255 * Math.Abs(angle) / Math.PI);
                    byte B = (byte)(255 - R);
                    int color = 255 << 24 | R << 16 | B;
                    writeableBitmap.Pixels[y * writeableBitmap.PixelWidth + x] =
color;
                }
            }

        writeableBitmap.Invalidate();
        img.Source = writeableBitmap;
    }
}
```

The center of the *WriteableBitmap* is the point (200, 200). The code within the nested *for* loops begins by skipping every pixel that is more than 200 pixels in length from that center. Within the square bitmap, only a circle will have non-transparent pixels.

If you connect that center point with any pixel in the bitmap, the line makes an angle with the horizontal axis. The angle of that line is obtained from the *Math.Atan2* method. The method then assigns values to the *R* and *B* variables based on this angle, creates a color value, and stores it in the *Pixels* array. A call to *Invalidate* then makes the actual bitmap image match these pixels, and the bitmap is set to the *Source* property of the *Image* element:

Vector Graphics on a Bitmap

You can combine the two approaches of drawing on a *WriteableBitmap*. The next sample displays a *Path* on a *WriteableBitmap* against a gradient that uses transparency so that you can see how the premultiplied alphas work.

I'm sure you remember the *Path* element from the end of the previous chapter that displayed a cat from a string in the Silverlight Path Markup Syntax. The goal of the VectorToRaster program is to make a bitmap of precisely the right size for that cat, and then put that cat in the bitmap.

The Path Markup Syntax for the cat is defined in a *Path* element in the *Resources* section of the MainPage.xaml file:

Silverlight Project: VectorToRaster   File: MainPage.xaml (excerpt)

```
<phone:PhoneApplicationPage.Resources>
    <Path x:Key="catPath"
          Data="M 160 140 L 150 50 220 103
                M 320 140 L 330 50 260 103
                M 215 230 L 40 200
                M 215 240 L 40 240
                M 215 250 L 40 280
                M 265 230 L 440 200
                M 265 240 L 440 240
                M 265 250 L 440 280
                M 240 100 A 100 100 0 0 1 240 300
                          A 100 100 0 0 1 240 100
                M 180 170 A 40 40 0 0 1 220 170
                          A 40 40 0 0 1 180 170
                M 300 170 A 40 40 0 0 1 260 170
                          A 40 40 0 0 1 300 170" />
</phone:PhoneApplicationPage.Resources>
```

This is not exactly the way I wanted to define the *PathGeometry* in the XAML *Resources* collection. I would have preferred defining the *PathGeometry* directly without a *Path*. But no matter how I tried it—setting the Path Markup Syntax string to the *Figures* property of a *PathGeometry* or putting the string between a *PathGeometry* start tag and end tag—I could not get it to work.

I'm using this *Path* element solely to force the XAML parser to acknowledge this string as Path Markup Syntax; the *Path* element won't be used for any other purpose in the program.

The content area consists of just an *Image* element awaiting a bitmap:

Silverlight Project: VectorToRaster   File: MainPage.xaml (excerpt)

```
<Grid x:Name="ContentPanel" Grid.Row="1" Margin="12,0,12,0">
    <Image Name="img"
           HorizontalAlignment="Center"
           VerticalAlignment="Center" />
</Grid>
```

Everything else happens in the constructor of the *MainPage* class. It's a little lengthy but well commented and I'll also walk you through the logic:

Silverlight Project: VectorToRaster   File: MainPage.xaml.cs (excerpt)

```
public MainPage()
{
    InitializeComponent();
```

```csharp
// Get PathGeometry from resource
Path catPath = this.Resources["catPath"] as Path;
PathGeometry pathGeometry = catPath.Data as PathGeometry;
catPath.Data = null;

// Get geometry bounds
Rect bounds = pathGeometry.Bounds;

// Create new path for rendering on bitmap
Path newPath = new Path
{
    Stroke = this.Resources["PhoneForegroundBrush"] as Brush,
    StrokeThickness = 5,
    Data = pathGeometry
};

// Create the WriteableBitmap
WriteableBitmap writeableBitmap =
    new WriteableBitmap((int)(bounds.Width + newPath.StrokeThickness),
                        (int)(bounds.Height + newPath.StrokeThickness));

// Color the background of the bitmap
Color baseColor = (Color)this.Resources["PhoneAccentColor"];

// Treat the bitmap as an ellipse:
//   radiusX and radiusY are also the centers!
double radiusX = writeableBitmap.PixelWidth / 2.0;
double radiusY = writeableBitmap.PixelHeight / 2.0;

for (int y = 0; y < writeableBitmap.PixelHeight; y++)
    for (int x = 0; x < writeableBitmap.PixelWidth; x++)
    {
        double angle = Math.Atan2(y - radiusY, x - radiusX);
        double ellipseX = radiusX * (1 + Math.Cos(angle));
        double ellipseY = radiusY * (1 + Math.Sin(angle));

        double ellipseToCenter =
            Math.Sqrt(Math.Pow(ellipseX - radiusX, 2) +
                    Math.Pow(ellipseY - radiusY, 2));

        double pointToCenter =
            Math.Sqrt(Math.Pow(x - radiusX, 2) + Math.Pow(y - radiusY, 2));

        double opacity = Math.Min(1, pointToCenter / ellipseToCenter);

        byte A = (byte)(opacity * 255);
        byte R = (byte)(opacity * baseColor.R);
        byte G = (byte)(opacity * baseColor.G);
        byte B = (byte)(opacity * baseColor.B);

        int color = A << 24 | R << 16 | G << 8 | B;

        writeableBitmap.Pixels[y * writeableBitmap.PixelWidth + x] = color;
    }
```

```
        writeableBitmap.Invalidate();

        // Find transform to move Path to edges
        TranslateTransform translate = new TranslateTransform
        {
            X = -bounds.X + newPath.StrokeThickness / 2,
            Y = -bounds.Y + newPath.StrokeThickness / 2
        };

        writeableBitmap.Render(newPath, translate);
        writeableBitmap.Invalidate();

        // Set bitmap to Image element
        img.Source = writeableBitmap;
}
```

The code begins by obtaining the *PathGeometry* from the *Resources* collection. Because it's
attached to a *Path* element, it normally wouldn't be usable for other purposes. That's why the
Data property of that *Path* element is assigned *null*. The *Path* element is now abandoned and
has no more role in this program.

The *Bounds* property defined by *Geometry* returns the *Rect* object indicating the coordinate
of the upper-left corner of the *PathGeometry*—in this case the point (40,50)—and its width
and height, in this case, 400 and 250, respectively. Notice that these values are strictly
geometric and do not take account of any non-zero stroke widths that may be present when
rendering the geometry.

The code then creates a *Path* element for this geometry. Unlike the *Path* element in
the *Resources* collection of the XAML file, this *Path* has an actual *Stroke* brush and
a *StrokeThickness* value of 5.

How large will the rendered geometry actually be? We know it will be at least 400 pixels wide
and 250 pixels tall. Beyond that, an *exact* calculation is difficult, but a *reasonable* calculation
is easy: If all the lines in the geometry are stroked with a thickness of 5, then the rendered
geometry will be 2.5 pixels more on the left, top, right, and bottom, or 5 pixels more than the
width and height of the geometry. This is the calculation used to create a *WriteableBitmap*
of the correct size. (This is *not* sufficient to account for miter joins, and might be a little more
than is needed for other line caps and joins, but the calculation is easy and usually adequate.)

Before rendering the *Path* on the *WriteableBitmap*, I want to give the bitmap a gradient
brush that is transparent in the center but the current accent color at the edges:

```
Color baseColor = (Color)this.Resources["PhoneAccentColor"];
```

The gradient actually might be more attractive the other way around (that is, transparent
at the edges) but I want you to see how close the bitmap comes to matching the size of the
rendered geometry.

At this point, two nested *for* loops take *x* and *y* though all the pixels of the bitmap. For each pixel, an *opacity* value is calculated ranging from 0 (transparent) to 1 (opaque):

```
double opacity = Math.Min(1, pointToCenter / ellipseToCenter);
```

This *opacity* value is used not only to calculate the Alpha byte but also as a pre-multiplication factor for the Red, Green, and Blue values:

```
byte A = (byte)(opacity * 255);
byte R = (byte)(opacity * baseColor.R);
byte G = (byte)(opacity * baseColor.G);
byte B = (byte)(opacity * baseColor.B);
```

Then it's just a matter of shifting all the color components into place and indexing the *Pixels* array:

```
int color = A << 24 | R << 16 | G << 8 | B;
writeableBitmap.Pixels[y * writeableBitmap.PixelWidth + x] = color;
```

At this point, the program is done referencing the *Pixels* array, so the actual image must be updated:

```
writeableBitmap.Invalidate();
```

Now the *Path* element named *newPath* must be rendered on the bitmap. This *Path* element has a *PathGeometry* with an upper-left corner at the point (40, 50) but the *WriteableBitmap* was sized only to account for the width and height of the geometry with non-zero stroke thickness. When rendering the *Path* on the *WriteableBitmap*, a *TranslateTransform* must shift left and up by the *X* and *Y* values of the rectangle obtained from the *Bounds* property of the *PathGeometry*. But then the *Path* also needs to be shifted a little right and down to accommodate the stroke thickness:

```
TranslateTransform translate = new TranslateTransform
{
    X = -bounds.X + newPath.StrokeThickness / 2,
    Y = -bounds.Y + newPath.StrokeThickness / 2
};
```

Now the *Path* can be rendered on the *WriteableBitmap*:

```
writeableBitmap.Render(newPath, translate);
writeableBitmap.Invalidate();
```

Here's the result:

The bitmap matches the geometry exactly at the bottom, but it's a little larger on the left and right. (Give those whiskers rounded ends and they'll come precisely to the edge.) The top of the bitmap is insufficient to accomodate the miter join of the ears. Make that a round join, and you'll see a better match. Try adding the following three assignments to the definition of *newPath*:

```
StrokeStartLineCap = PenLineCap.Round,
StrokeEndLineCap = PenLineCap.Round,
StrokeLineJoin = PenLineJoin.Round,
```

Now the bitmap is precisely right:

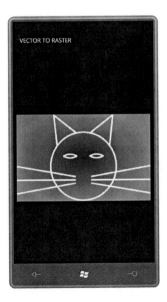

Images and Tombstoning

In the 1890s, American puzzle-make Sam Loyd popularized a puzzle that was invented a couple decades earlier and has since come to be known as the 15 Puzzle, or the 14-15 Puzzle, or (in France) *Jeu de Taquin*, the "teasing game." In its classic form, the puzzle consists of 15 tiles labeled 1 through 15 arranged randomly in a 4×4 grid, leaving one blank tile. The goal is to shift the tiles around so the numbers are sequential.

In computer form, this puzzle was one of the first game programs created for the Apple Macintosh, where it was called PUZZLE. A Windows version appeared in early versions of the Microsoft Windows Software Development Kit (SDK) under the name MUZZLE, where it was the only sample program in the SDK coded in Microsoft Pascal rather than C.

The version I'm going to show you does not use numbered tiles. Instead it lets you access a photo from the phone's picture library and chops that up into tiles. (The game becomes rather more difficult as a result.) As a bonus, the program shows you how to save images when an application is tombstoned.

The program's content area consists of a *Grid* named *playGrid* (used for holding the tiles) and two buttons:

Silverlight Project: JeuDeTaquin   File: MainPage.xaml (excerpt)

```xml
<Grid x:Name="ContentPanel" Grid.Row="1" Margin="12,0,12,0">
    <Grid.RowDefinitions>
        <RowDefinition Height="*" />
        <RowDefinition Height="Auto" />
    </Grid.RowDefinitions>

    <Grid.ColumnDefinitions>
        <ColumnDefinition Width="*" />
        <ColumnDefinition Width="*" />
    </Grid.ColumnDefinitions>

    <Grid Name="playGrid"
          Grid.Row="0" Grid.Column="0" Grid.ColumnSpan="2"
          HorizontalAlignment="Center"
          VerticalAlignment="Center" />

    <Button Content="load"
            Grid.Row="1" Grid.Column="0"
            Click="OnLoadClick" />

    <Button Name="scrambleButton"
            Content="scramble"
            Grid.Row="2" Grid.Column="1"
            IsEnabled="False"
            Click="OnScrambleClick" />
</Grid>
```

Seemingly redundantly, the XAML file also includes two buttons in the *Application*Bar also labeled "load" and "scramble":

Silverlight Project: JeuDeTaquin   File: MainPage.xaml (excerpt)

```
<phone:PhoneApplicationPage.ApplicationBar>
    <shell:ApplicationBar IsVisible="False">
        <shell:ApplicationBarIconButton x:Name="appbarLoadButton"
                                IconUri="/Images/appbar.folder.rest.png"
                                Text="load"
                                Click="OnLoadClick" />

        <shell:ApplicationBarIconButton x:Name="appbarScrambleButton"
                                IconUri="/Images/appbar.refresh.rest.png"
                                Text="scramble"
                                IsEnabled="False"
                                Click="OnScrambleClick" />
    </shell:ApplicationBar>
</phone:PhoneApplicationPage.ApplicationBar>
```

I couldn't get the randomizing feature to work when it was initiated from the *ApplicationBar*, but I left in the markup (and the code) and set *IsVisible* to *false*. Maybe someday the *ApplicationBar* will behave better.

The *MainPage* class in the code-behind file begins with some constants. The program is set up for 4 tiles horizontally and vertically but you can change those. (Obviously in Portrait mode, the program works best if VERT_TILES is greater than HORZ_TILES.) Other fields involve storing state information in the *PhoneApplicationService* object for tombstoning, and using the *PhotoChooserTask* for picking a photo.

The *tileImages* array is extremely important. This array stores all the *Image* elements for the tiles. At any time, one of the members of this array will be *null*, representing the empty space. That empty space is also indicated by the *emptyRow* and *emptyCol* indices.

Silverlight Project: JeuDeTaquin   File: MainPage.xaml.cs (excerpt)

```
public partial class MainPage : PhoneApplicationPage
{
    const int HORZ_TILES = 4;
    const int VERT_TILES = 4;
    const int MARGIN = 2;

    PhoneApplicationService appService = PhoneApplicationService.Current;
    PhotoChooserTask photoChooser = new PhotoChooserTask();
    Random rand = new Random();

    Image[,] tileImages = new Image[VERT_TILES, HORZ_TILES];
    bool haveValidTileImages;
```

```
    int emptyRow, emptyCol;
    int scrambleCountdown;

    public MainPage()
    {
        InitializeComponent();

        for (int col = 0; col < HORZ_TILES; col++)
        {
            ColumnDefinition coldef = new ColumnDefinition();
            coldef.Width = new GridLength(1, GridUnitType.Star);
            playGrid.ColumnDefinitions.Add(coldef);
        }

        for (int row = 0; row < VERT_TILES; row++)
        {
            RowDefinition rowdef = new RowDefinition();
            rowdef.Height = new GridLength(1, GridUnitType.Star);
            playGrid.RowDefinitions.Add(rowdef);
        }

        appbarScrambleButton = this.ApplicationBar.Buttons[1] as
ApplicationBarIconButton;

        photoChooser.Completed += OnPhotoChooserCompleted;
    }
    ...
}
```

In the constructor, the program initializes the *ColumnDefinition* and *RowDefinition* collections of the *Grid* that holds the tiles, and (as usual) sets a handler for the *Completed* event of the *PhotoChooserTask*.

When the user clicks the button labeled "load", the program determines how large each tile should be based on the width and height of the content area, the number of tiles, and the margin. This value is set to the *PixelWidth* and *PixelHeight* properties of the *PhotoChooserTask*:

Silverlight Project: JeuDeTaquin   File: MainPage.xaml.cs (excerpt)

```
void OnLoadClick(object sender, EventArgs args)
{
    int tileSize = (int)Math.Min(ContentPanel.ActualWidth / HORZ_TILES,
                                 ContentPanel.ActualHeight / VERT_TILES)
                 - 2 * MARGIN;

    photoChooser.PixelWidth = tileSize * HORZ_TILES;
    photoChooser.PixelHeight = tileSize * VERT_TILES;
    photoChooser.Show();
}
```

On return from the *PhotoChooserTask*, the event handler divides the bitmap into small square tiles and creates an *Image* element for each square. The SubdivideBitmap program earlier in this chapter showed how to chop up a bitmap into squares using the *Render* method of *WriteableBitmap*. This program instead does it by creating *WriteableBitmap* objects of the tile size, and then copying pixels into their individual *Pixels* arrays from the full-size returned bitmap:

Silverlight Project: JeuDeTaquin   File: MainPage.xaml.cs (excerpt)

```
void OnPhotoChooserCompleted(object sender, PhotoResult args)
{
    if (args.Error == null && args.ChosenPhoto != null)
    {
        BitmapImage bitmapImage = new BitmapImage();
        bitmapImage.SetSource(args.ChosenPhoto);
        WriteableBitmap writeableBitmap = new WriteableBitmap(bitmapImage);
        int tileSize = writeableBitmap.PixelWidth / HORZ_TILES;

        emptyCol = HORZ_TILES - 1;
        emptyRow = VERT_TILES - 1;

        for (int row = 0; row < VERT_TILES; row++)
            for (int col = 0; col < HORZ_TILES; col++)
                if (row != emptyRow || col != emptyCol)
                {
                    WriteableBitmap tile = new WriteableBitmap(tileSize, tileSize);

                    for (int y = 0; y < tileSize; y++)
                        for (int x = 0; x < tileSize; x++)
                        {
                            int yBit = row * tileSize + y;
                            int xBit = col * tileSize + x;

                            tile.Pixels[y * tileSize + x] =
                                writeableBitmap.Pixels[yBit *
                                        writeableBitmap.PixelWidth + xBit];
                        }
                    GenerateImageTile(tile, row, col);
                }

        haveValidTileImages = true;
        scrambleButton.IsEnabled = true;
        appbarScrambleButton.IsEnabled = true;
    }
}

void GenerateImageTile(BitmapSource tile, int row, int col)
{
    Image img = new Image();
    img.Stretch = Stretch.None;
    img.Source = tile;
    img.Margin = new Thickness(MARGIN);
```

```
            tileImages[row, col] = img;

            Grid.SetRow(img, row);
            Grid.SetColumn(img, col);
            playGrid.Children.Add(img);
        }
```

Actually creating the *Image* elements and adding them to the *Grid* is the responsibility of the *GenerateImageTile*, which also stores the *Image* elements in the *tileImages* array.

At this point, the tiles are not in a random order, but it's still possible to move them around. As you begin thinking about how tiles move, you'll discover that it's algorithmically much simpler than you might have initially guessed. Think about it in terms of the empty square. What tiles can be moved into that square? Only the tiles on the left, top, right, and bottom of that square, and those tiles can move in only one direction. This means that the user interface need only take account of taps and not bother with any type of tile sliding.

If you think about the game further, you'll see that you can move multiple tiles at once by tapping any tile in the same row or the same column as the empty square. There's absolutely no ambiguity.

Here's the entire manipulation logic:

Silverlight Project: JeuDeTaquin   File: MainPage.xaml.cs (excerpt)

```
protected override void OnManipulationStarted(ManipulationStartedEventArgs args)
{
    if (args.OriginalSource is Image)
    {
        Image img = args.OriginalSource as Image;
        MoveTile(img);
        args.Complete();
        args.Handled = true;
    }
    base.OnManipulationStarted(args);
}

void MoveTile(Image img)
{
    int touchedRow = -1, touchedCol = -1;

    for (int y = 0; y < VERT_TILES; y++)
        for (int x = 0; x < HORZ_TILES; x++)
            if (tileImages[y, x] == img)
            {
                touchedRow = y;
                touchedCol = x;
            }

    if (touchedRow == emptyRow)
    {
        int sign = Math.Sign(touchedCol - emptyCol);

        for (int x = emptyCol; x != touchedCol; x += sign)
        {
            tileImages[touchedRow, x] = tileImages[touchedRow, x + sign];
            Grid.SetColumn(tileImages[touchedRow, x], x);
        }
        tileImages[touchedRow, touchedCol] = null;
        emptyCol = touchedCol;
    }
    else if (touchedCol == emptyCol)
    {
        int sign = Math.Sign(touchedRow - emptyRow);

        for (int y = emptyRow; y != touchedRow; y += sign)
        {
            tileImages[y, touchedCol] = tileImages[y + sign, touchedCol];
            Grid.SetRow(tileImages[y, touchedCol], y);
        }
        tileImages[touchedRow, touchedCol] = null;
        emptyRow = touchedRow;
    }
}
```

The *MoveTile* method first determines the row and column of the tile that the user touched. For anything to happen, this row must be the row or the column with the empty square. (It can't be both.) Rather generalized *for* loops move multiple tiles up, down, left, or right.

The randomizing logic piggy-backs on this manipulation logic. When the "scramble" button is clicked, the program attaches a handler for the *CompositionTarget.Rendering* event:

Silverlight Project: JeuDeTaquin   File: MainPage.xaml.cs (excerpt)

```
void OnScrambleClick(object sender, EventArgs args)
{
    scrambleCountdown = 10 * VERT_TILES * HORZ_TILES;
    scrambleButton.IsEnabled = false;
    appbarScrambleButton.IsEnabled = false;
    CompositionTarget.Rendering += OnCompositionTargetRendering;
}

void OnCompositionTargetRendering(object sender, EventArgs args)
{
    MoveTile(tileImages[emptyRow, rand.Next(HORZ_TILES)]);
    MoveTile(tileImages[rand.Next(VERT_TILES), emptyCol]);

    if (--scrambleCountdown == 0)
    {
        CompositionTarget.Rendering -= OnCompositionTargetRendering;
        scrambleButton.IsEnabled = true;
        appbarScrambleButton.IsEnabled = true;
    }
}
```

The event handler calls *MoveTile* twice, once to move a tile from the same row as the empty square, and secondly to move a tile from the same column as the empty square.

This program also handles tombstoning, which means that it saves the entire game state when the user navigates away from the page, and restores that game state when the game is re-activated.

I managed to restrict game state to just a few fields: The *haveValidTileImages* field is *true* if the *tileImages* array contains valid *Image* elements; otherwise there's really nothing going on. The *emptyRow* and *emptyCol* fields are also crucial. Most important, of course, are the actual bitmaps that make up the tiles. Rather than save the entire *Pixels* array of each *WriteableBitmap*, I decided to save space by saving these images in a compressed JPEG format:

Silverlight Project: JeuDeTaquin   File: MainPage.xaml.cs (excerpt)

```
protected override void OnNavigatedFrom(NavigationEventArgs args)
{
    appService.State["haveValidTileImages"] = haveValidTileImages;

    if (haveValidTileImages)
    {
        appService.State["emptyRow"] = emptyRow;
        appService.State["emptyCol"] = emptyCol;

        for (int row = 0; row < VERT_TILES; row++)
            for (int col = 0; col < HORZ_TILES; col++)
                if (col != emptyCol || row != emptyRow)
                {
                    WriteableBitmap tile = tileImages[row, col].Source as
WriteableBitmap;
                    MemoryStream stream = new MemoryStream();
                    tile.SaveJpeg(stream, tile.PixelWidth, tile.PixelHeight, 0, 75);
                    appService.State[TileKey(row, col)] = stream.GetBuffer();
                }
    }
    base.OnNavigatedFrom(args);
}

...

string TileKey(int row, int col)
{
    return String.Format("tile {0} {1}", row, col);
}
```

For each *Image* element in the *tileImages* array, the program obtains the corresponding *WriteableBitmap* and creates a new *MemoryStream*. The extension method *SaveJpeg* allows saving the *WriteableBitmap* in JPEG format into the stream. The *GetBuffer* method of *MemoryStream* obtains a *byte* array that is simply saved with the other state information.

When the program returns from its tombstoned state, the process goes in reverse:

Silverlight Project: **JeuDeTaquin**   File: **MainPage.xaml.cs** (excerpt)

```
protected override void OnNavigatedTo(NavigationEventArgs args)
{
    object objHaveValidTileImages;

    if (appService.State.TryGetValue("haveValidTileImages", out objHaveValidTileImages)
  &&
        (bool)objHaveValidTileImages)
    {
        emptyRow = (int)appService.State["emptyRow"];
        emptyCol = (int)appService.State["emptyCol"];

        for (int row = 0; row < VERT_TILES; row++)
            for (int col = 0; col < HORZ_TILES; col++)
                if (col != emptyCol || row != emptyRow)
                {
                    byte[] buffer = (byte[])appService.State[TileKey(row, col)];
                    MemoryStream stream = new MemoryStream(buffer);
                    BitmapImage bitmapImage = new BitmapImage();
                    bitmapImage.SetSource(stream);
                    WriteableBitmap tile = new WriteableBitmap(bitmapImage);
                    GenerateImageTile(tile, row, col);
                }

        haveValidTileImages = true;
        appbarScrambleButton.IsEnabled = true;
    }

    base.OnNavigatedTo(args);
}
```

The method reads the *byte* buffer and converts into a *MemoryStream*, from which a *BitmapImage* and then a *WriteableBitmap* is created. The method then uses the earlier *GenerateTileImage* method to create each *Image* element and add it to the *Grid*.

It's important to keep in mind that this *byte* array used to save and restore the bitmap is very different from the *int* array available from the *Pixels* property of *WriteableBitmap*. The *Pixels* array has a value for every pixel in the bitmap, but the *byte* array is the compressed bitmap in JPEG format, with all the JPEG file information and headers and such.

Saving to the Picture Library

The remaining two programs in this chapter create images that you might want to save for posterity (if not prosperity). For example, a program might want to save a bitmap in isolated storage so the user can work on a particular image from session to session.

However, it is most valuable to the user to save a bitmap into the picture library on the phone. There is a special folder (or "album" as it's termed) called "Saved Pictures" specifically for this purpose. From the picture library, the user can view the resultant bitmap, or email it, or send it with a text message. The bitmap is also moved to the user's PC during normal synchronization, at which point it might be printed.

Access to the picture library is provided with the XNA libraries, but you can use those libraries from a Silverlight program. You'll need a reference to the Microsoft.Xna.Framework library, and a *using* directive for the *Microsoft.Xna.Framework.Media* namespace.

In your program, you create an instance of the *MediaLibrary* class. The *SavedPictures* property returns a *PictureCollection* with a *Picture* object for each item currently in the Saved Pictures album. These can be presented to the user with names.

The *MediaLibrary* class also contains a method named *SavePicture* that requires two arguments: a filename and a *Stream* referencing a bitmap in JPEG format. This *Stream* object is commonly a *MemoryStream* whose contents have been created by a call to the *SaveJpeg* extension method of *WriteableBitmap*.

The Monochromize program lets the user select a picture from the picture library. As soon as the program obtains the photo in the form of a *WriteableBitmap*, it accesses the *Pixels* property and converts it to monochrome. A Save button navigates to a screen that lets the user enter a filename and press OK; on navigation back to the program, the monochrome bitmap is saved to the picture library under that name.

The page in Monochromize that lets the user enter a filename is the Windows Phone 7 equivalent of a traditional save-file dialog box, and so I called it *SaveFileDialog*. It derives from *PhoneApplicationPage* and resides in the Petzold.Phone.Silverlight library.

I took a little different strategy to return filename information to the particular program that makes use of the *SaveFileDialog* page: When the user presses the "save" or "cancel" button, *SaveFileDialog* calls the *GoBack* method of the *NavigationService* object as usual, but during the subsequent *OnNavigagedFrom* override, it attempts to call a method in the program's main page called *SaveFileDialogCompleted*. For this reason, any page that navigates to *SaveFileDialog* should also implement the following interface:

Silverlight Project: Petzold.Phone.Silverlight   File: ISaveFileDialogCompleted.cs

```
namespace Petzold.Phone.Silverlight
{
    public interface ISaveFileDialogCompleted
    {
        void SaveFileDialogCompleted(bool okPressed, string filename);
    }
}
```

The content area of *SaveFileDialog* has the traditional *TextBox* with two buttons labeled "save" and "cancel":

Silverlight Project: Petzold.Phone.Silverlight   File: SaveFileDialog.xaml (excerpt)

```xml
<Grid x:Name="ContentPanel" Grid.Row="1" Margin="12,0,12,0">
    <StackPanel>
        <TextBlock Text="file name" />
        <TextBox Name="txtbox"
                 TextChanged="OnTextBoxTextChanged" />
        <Grid>
            <Grid.ColumnDefinitions>
                <ColumnDefinition Width="*" />
                <ColumnDefinition Width="*" />
            </Grid.ColumnDefinitions>

            <Button Name="saveButton"
                    Content="save"
                    Grid.Column="0"
                    IsEnabled="False"
                    Click="OnSaveButtonClick" />

            <Button Content="cancel"
                    Grid.Column="2"
                    Click="OnCancelButtonClick" />
        </Grid>
    </StackPanel>
</Grid>
```

The code-behind file also defines a public method named *SetTitle*. A program that makes use of *SaveFileDialog* can call that method to set the title of the page with the application name:

Silverlight Project: Petzold.Phone.Silverlight   File: SaveFileDialog.xaml.cs (excerpt)

```csharp
public partial class SaveFileDialog : PhoneApplicationPage
{
    PhoneApplicationService appService = PhoneApplicationService.Current;
    bool okPressed;
    string filename;

    public SaveFileDialog()
    {
        InitializeComponent();
    }

    public void SetTitle(string appTitle)
    {
        ApplicationTitle.Text = appTitle;
    }
```

```
        void OnTextBoxTextChanged(object sender, TextChangedEventArgs args)
        {
            saveButton.IsEnabled = txtbox.Text.Length > 0;
        }

        void OnSaveButtonClick(object sender, RoutedEventArgs args)
        {
            okPressed = true;
            filename = txtbox.Text;
            this.NavigationService.GoBack();
        }

        void OnCancelButtonClick(object sender, RoutedEventArgs args)
        {
            okPressed = false;
            this.NavigationService.GoBack();
        }
        ...
}
```

Notice also that the "save" button is disabled unless the *TextBox* contains at least
a one-character filename.

The navigation overrides need to handle a couple jobs. The *OnNavigatedTo* method checks
if the query string contains an initial filename. (The Monochromize program does not make
use of this feature, but the following program in this chapter does.) The methods also handle
tombstoning by saving the application title and any filename the user might have entered:

Silverlight Project: Petzold.Phone.Silverlight   File: SaveFileDialog.xaml.cs (excerpt)

```
protected override void OnNavigatedTo(NavigationEventArgs args)
{
    if (appService.State.ContainsKey("filename"))
        txtbox.Text = appService.State["filename"] as string;

    if (appService.State.ContainsKey("apptitle"))
        ApplicationTitle.Text = appService.State["apptitle"] as string;

    if (this.NavigationContext.QueryString.ContainsKey("FileName"))
        txtbox.Text = this.NavigationContext.QueryString["FileName"];

    base.OnNavigatedTo(args);
}

protected override void OnNavigatedFrom(NavigationEventArgs args)
{
    if (!String.IsNullOrEmpty(txtbox.Text))
        appService.State["filename"] = txtbox.Text;
```

```
        appService.State["apptitle"] = ApplicationTitle.Text;

        if (args.Content is ISaveFileDialogCompleted)
            (args.Content as ISaveFileDialogCompleted).
                                SaveFileDialogCompleted(okPressed, filename);

        base.OnNavigatedFrom(args);
    }
```

The most important part of *OnNavigagedFrom* is at the bottom of the method, where it checks if the page it's navigating to implements the *ISaveFileDialogCompleted* interface and if so, calls the *SaveFileDialogCompleted* method in that page.

In the Monochromize program itself, the content area in the XAML file contains only an *Image* element with no bitmap:

Silverlight Project: Monochromize   File: MainPage.xaml (excerpt)

```
<Grid x:Name="ContentPanel" Grid.Row="1" Margin="12,0,12,0">
    <Image Name="img" />
</Grid>
```

The *ApplicationBar* has two buttons for load and save:

Silverlight Project: Monochromize   File: MainPage.xaml (excerpt)

```
<phone:PhoneApplicationPage.ApplicationBar>
    <shell:ApplicationBar>
        <shell:ApplicationBarIconButton x:Name="appbarLoadButton"
                                IconUri="/Images/appbar.folder.rest.png"
                                Text="load"
                                Click="OnAppbarLoadClick" />

        <shell:ApplicationBarIconButton x:Name="appbarSaveButton"
                                IconUri="/Images/appbar.save.rest.png"
                                Text="save"
                                IsEnabled="False"
                                Click="OnAppbarSaveClick" />
    </shell:ApplicationBar>
</phone:PhoneApplicationPage.ApplicationBar>
```

In the code-behind file, the fields are few, and the only one that's really necessary is the *PhotoChooserTask*. (The *PhoneApplicationService* field is only a convenience, and after the program creates *WriteableBitmap* object, it is also stored as the *Source* property of the *Image* element.)

Silverlight Project: Monochromize   File: MainPage.xaml.cs (excerpt)

```
public partial class MainPage : PhoneApplicationPage, ISaveFileDialogCompleted
{
    PhoneApplicationService appService = PhoneApplicationService.Current;
    PhotoChooserTask photoChooser = new PhotoChooserTask();
    WriteableBitmap writeableBitmap;

    public MainPage()
    {
        InitializeComponent();

        appbarLoadButton = this.ApplicationBar.Buttons[0] as ApplicationBarIconButton;
        appbarSaveButton = this.ApplicationBar.Buttons[1] as ApplicationBarIconButton;

        photoChooser.Completed += OnPhotoChooserCompleted;
    }
    ...
}
```

Notice that the class implements the *ISaveFileDialogCompleted* interface.

Clicking the "load" button causes the *PhotoChooserTask* to be invoked; on return the *Completed* handler creates a *WriteableBitmap* and then changes every member of the *Pixels* array by applying standard weights to the Red, Green, and Blue values.

Silverlight Project: Monochromize   File: MainPage.xaml.cs (excerpt)

```
void OnAppbarLoadClick(object sender, EventArgs args)
{
    appbarSaveButton.IsEnabled = false;
    photoChooser.Show();
}

void OnPhotoChooserCompleted(object sender, PhotoResult args)
{
    if (args.Error == null && args.ChosenPhoto != null)
    {
        BitmapImage bitmapImage = new BitmapImage();
        bitmapImage.SetSource(args.ChosenPhoto);
        writeableBitmap = new WriteableBitmap(bitmapImage);

        // Monochromize
        for (int pixel = 0; pixel < writeableBitmap.Pixels.Length; pixel++)
        {
            int color = writeableBitmap.Pixels[pixel];
            byte A = (byte)(color & 0xFF000000 >> 24);
            byte R = (byte)(color & 0x00FF0000 >> 16);
            byte G = (byte)(color & 0x0000FF00 >> 8);
            byte B = (byte)(color & 0x000000FF);
```

```
            byte gray = (byte)(0.30 * R + 0.59 * G + 0.11 * B);

            color = (A << 24) | (gray << 16) | (gray << 8) | gray;
            writeableBitmap.Pixels[pixel] = color;
        }
        img.Source = writeableBitmap;
        appbarSaveButton.IsEnabled = true;
    }
}
```

The "monochromized" *WriteableBitmap* is set to the *Source* property of the *Image* element and the save button is enabled.

Pressing the save button navigates to the SaveFileDialog.xaml page in the Petzold.Phone .Silverlight library. As you've just seen, the *SaveFileDialog* class handles its *OnNavigatedFrom* override by calling the *SaveFileDialogCompleted* method in the class that it's navigating to:

Silverlight Project: Monochromize   File: MainPage.xaml.cs (excerpt)

```
void OnAppbarSaveClick(object sender, EventArgs args)
{
    this.NavigationService.Navigate(
            new Uri("/Petzold.Phone.Silverlight;component/SaveFileDialog.xaml",
            UriKind.Relative));
}

public void SaveFileDialogCompleted(bool okPressed, string filename)
{
    if (okPressed)
    {
```

```
            MemoryStream memoryStream = new MemoryStream();
            writeableBitmap.SaveJpeg(memoryStream, writeableBitmap.PixelWidth,
                                              writeableBitmap.PixelHeight, 0, 75);

            memoryStream.Position = 0;

            MediaLibrary mediaLib = new MediaLibrary();
            mediaLib.SavePicture(filename, memoryStream);
        }
    }
```

The *SaveFileDialogCompleted* method uses the filename entered by the user to write the bitmap to the pictures library. This happens in two steps: First the *SaveJpeg* method writes the *WriteableBitmap* to a *MemoryStream* in JPEG format. The *Position* on the *MemoryStream* is then reset, and the stream is saved to the pictures library.

The Monochromize program also handles tombstoning. The *OnNavigatedFrom* method uses the *SaveJpeg* extension method to write to a *MemoryStream* and then saves the *byte* array. This method is also responsible for calling *SetTitle* on the *SaveFileDialog* if navigating to that page:

Silverlight Project: Monochromize   File: MainPage.xaml.cs (excerpt)

```
protected override void OnNavigatedFrom(NavigationEventArgs args)
{
    if (writeableBitmap != null)
    {
        MemoryStream stream = new MemoryStream();
        writeableBitmap.SaveJpeg(stream, writeableBitmap.PixelWidth,
                                      writeableBitmap.PixelHeight, 0, 75);
        appService.State["jpegBits"] = stream.GetBuffer();
    }

    if (args.Content is SaveFileDialog)
    {
        SaveFileDialog page = args.Content as SaveFileDialog;
        page.SetTitle(ApplicationTitle.Text);
    }

    base.OnNavigatedFrom(args);
}
```

The *OnNavigatedTo* method is responsible for re-activating after tombstoning. The *byte* array is converted by to a *WriteableBitmap*, and the save button is enabled:

Silverlight Project: Monochromize   File: MainPage.xaml.cs (excerpt)

```
protected override void OnNavigatedTo(NavigationEventArgs args)
{
```

```
    if (appService.State.ContainsKey("jpegBits"))
    {
        byte[] bitmapBits = (byte[])appService.State["jpegBits"];
        MemoryStream stream = new MemoryStream(bitmapBits);
        BitmapImage bitmapImage = new BitmapImage();
        bitmapImage.SetSource(stream);
        writeableBitmap = new WriteableBitmap(bitmapImage);
        img.Source = writeableBitmap;
        appbarSaveButton.IsEnabled = true;
    }
    base.OnNavigatedTo(args);
}
```

Becoming a Photo Extras Application

Architecturally and functionally, the Posterizer program that concludes this chapter is similar to the Monochromize program. It lets the user select a photo from the picture library and to save it back in the Saved Pictures album. But the Posterizer program allows the user to reduce the bit resolution of each color independently (creating a poster-like effect) and for this it needs to display a row of *RadioButton* elements. The program must also retain the original unadulterated pixels array so it can restore the image to full color resolution.

In addition, Posterizer registers itself as a "photos extra" application, which means that it can be invoked by the user from the picture library itself.

For maximum convenience, I decided to implement the controls to select the bit resolution as an overlay:

The middle *ApplicationBar* button toggles the visibility of that overlay. The accent color is used to indicate the selected value in each column.

This overlay is a *UserControl* derivative called *BitSelectDialog*, and I'll discuss that control first. The visual tree just defines a *Grid* with three columns and nine rows:

Silverlight Project: Posterizer   File: BitSelectDialog.xaml (excerpt)

```
<Grid x:Name="LayoutRoot" Background="Transparent">
    <Grid.ColumnDefinitions>
        <ColumnDefinition Width="*" />
        <ColumnDefinition Width="*" />
        <ColumnDefinition Width="*" />
    </Grid.ColumnDefinitions>

    <Grid.RowDefinitions>
        <RowDefinition Height="Auto" />
        <RowDefinition Height="*" />
        <RowDefinition Height="*" />
        <RowDefinition Height="*" />
        <RowDefinition Height="*" />
        <RowDefinition Height="*" />
        <RowDefinition Height="*" />
        <RowDefinition Height="*" />
        <RowDefinition Height="*" />
    </Grid.RowDefinitions>
</Grid>
```

Each cell is a *TextBlock* and the code-behind file handles the manipulation logic to make them behave like radio buttons. The public interface to the class includes an event and a public property that stores the three current settings:

Silverlight Project: Posterizer   File: BitSelectDialog.xaml.cs (excerpt)

```
public event EventHandler ColorBitsChanged;
...
public int[] ColorBits { protected set; get; }
```

You may see a little flaw in this already. Although the set accessor for the *ColorBits* array is protected and the array cannot be replaced by an external class, the individual members of the array can be set, and there is no way for the class to know about it, let alone to fire the *ColorBitsChanged* event. But I allowed the flaw to exist rather than make the class more complex.

The class creates all the *TextBlock* elements in the constructor. Notice that the *ColorBits* array is initialized to contain three values of 2.

Silverlight Project: Posterizer   File: BitSelectDialog.xaml.cs (excerpt)

```
public partial class BitSelectDialog : UserControl
{
    Brush selectedBrush;
    Brush normalBrush;
    TextBlock[,] txtblks = new TextBlock[3, 9];

    ...

    public BitSelectDialog()
    {
        InitializeComponent();

        ColorBits = new int[3];
        ColorBits[0] = 2;
        ColorBits[1] = 2;
        ColorBits[2] = 2;

        selectedBrush = this.Resources["PhoneAccentBrush"] as Brush;
        normalBrush = this.Resources["PhoneForegroundBrush"] as Brush;
        string[] colors = { "red", "green", "blue" };

        for (int col = 0; col < 3; col++)
        {
            TextBlock txtblk = new TextBlock
            {
                Text = colors[col],
                FontWeight = FontWeights.Bold,
                TextAlignment = TextAlignment.Center,
                Margin = new Thickness(8, 2, 8, 2)
            };

            Grid.SetRow(txtblk, 0);
            Grid.SetColumn(txtblk, col);
            LayoutRoot.Children.Add(txtblk);

            for (int bit = 0; bit < 9; bit++)
            {
                txtblk = new TextBlock
                {
                    Text = bit.ToString(),
                    Foreground = bit == ColorBits[col] ? selectedBrush : normalBrush,
                    TextAlignment = TextAlignment.Center,
                    Padding = new Thickness(2),
                    Tag = col.ToString() + bit
                };

                Grid.SetRow(txtblk, bit + 1);
```

```
                    Grid.SetColumn(txtblk, col);
                    LayoutRoot.Children.Add(txtblk);

                    txtblks[col, bit] = txtblk;
                }
            }
        }
    }
```

Each *TextBlock* has a two-character string set to its *Tag* property to indicate the color and the number of bits associated with that element.

I also defined a public method that allows a program to initialize the three *ColorBits* values, changing the *TextBlock* colors in the process but not raising the *ColorBitsChanged* event. This was useful during re-activating from a tombstoned condition.

Silverlight Project: Posterizer   File: BitSelectDialog.xaml.cs (excerpt)

```
public void Initialize(int[] colorBits)
{
    for (int clr = 0; clr < 3; clr++)
    {
        txtblks[clr, ColorBits[clr]].Foreground = normalBrush;
        ColorBits[clr] = colorBits[clr];
        txtblks[clr, ColorBits[clr]].Foreground = selectedBrush;
    }
}
```

The *OnManipulationStarted* override decodes the *Tag* property from the touched *TextBlock* to determine the user's selection:

Silverlight Project: Posterizer   File: BitSelectDialog.xaml.cs (excerpt)

```
protected override void OnManipulationStarted(ManipulationStartedEventArgs args)
{
    if (args.OriginalSource is TextBlock)
    {
        TextBlock txtblk = args.OriginalSource as TextBlock;
        string tag = txtblk.Tag as string;

        if (tag != null && tag.Length == 2)
        {
            int clr = Int32.Parse(tag[0].ToString());
            int bits = Int32.Parse(tag[1].ToString());
```

```
            if (ColorBits[clr] != bits)
            {
                txtblks[clr, ColorBits[clr]].Foreground = normalBrush;
                ColorBits[clr] = bits;
                txtblks[clr, ColorBits[clr]].Foreground = selectedBrush;

                if (ColorBitsChanged != null)
                    ColorBitsChanged(this, EventArgs.Empty);
            }

            args.Complete();
            args.Handled = true;
        }
    }
    base.OnManipulationStarted(args);
}
```

Based on the information decoded from the *Tag* property of the touched *TextBlock*, the method can recolor that *TextBlock* (and the one becoming unselected), store a new value in the *ColorBits* array, and raise the *ColorBitsChanged* event.

In the *MainPage* class of the program itself, the content area includes a (by now familiar) *Image* element with no bitmap and this *BitSelectDialog* control:

Silverlight Project: Posterizer   File: MainPage.xaml (excerpt)

```
<Grid x:Name="ContentPanel" Grid.Row="1" Margin="12,0,12,0">

    <Image Name="img" />

    <local:BitSelectDialog x:Name="bitSelectDialog"
                           Visibility="Collapsed"
                           FontSize="{StaticResource PhoneFontSizeExtraLarge}"
                           HorizontalAlignment="Center"
                           VerticalAlignment="Center"
                           ColorBitsChanged="OnBitSelectDialogColorBitsChanged" />
</Grid>
```

Notice that the *BitSelectDialog* control has its *Visibility* property set to *Collapsed*.

The XAML file also contains three buttons in its *ApplicationBar*:

Silverlight Project: Posterizer   File: MainPage.xaml (excerpt)

```
<phone:PhoneApplicationPage.ApplicationBar>
    <shell:ApplicationBar>
```

```
                <shell:ApplicationBarIconButton x:Name="appbarLoadButton"
                                    IconUri="/Images/appbar.folder.rest.png"
                                    Text="load"
                                    Click="OnAppbarLoadClick" />

                <shell:ApplicationBarIconButton x:Name="appbarSetBitsButton"
                                    IconUri="/Images/appbar.feature.settings.rest.png"
                                    Text="set bits"
                                    IsEnabled="False"
                                    Click="OnAppbarSetBitsClick" />

                <shell:ApplicationBarIconButton x:Name="appbarSaveButton"
                                    IconUri="/Images/appbar.save.rest.png"
                                    Text="save"
                                    IsEnabled="False"
                                    Click="OnAppbarSaveClick" />
        </shell:ApplicationBar>
    </phone:PhoneApplicationPage.ApplicationBar>
```

In the code-behind file, the fields of the *MainPage* class include three variables that represent bitmaps: of type *WriteableBitmap*, *byte* array, and *int* array.

Silverlight Project: Posterizer   File: MainPage.xaml.cs (excerpt)

```
public partial class MainPage : PhoneApplicationPage, ISaveFileDialogCompleted
{
    PhoneApplicationService appService = PhoneApplicationService.Current;
    PhotoChooserTask photoChooser = new PhotoChooserTask();
    WriteableBitmap writeableBitmap;
    byte[] jpegBits;
    int[] pixels;

    public MainPage()
    {
        InitializeComponent();

        appbarLoadButton = this.ApplicationBar.Buttons[0] as ApplicationBarIconButton;
        appbarSetBitsButton = this.ApplicationBar.Buttons[1] as
ApplicationBarIconButton;
        appbarSaveButton = this.ApplicationBar.Buttons[2] as ApplicationBarIconButton;

        photoChooser.Completed += OnPhotoChooserCompleted;
    }
}
```

The *WriteableBitmap* field is the bitmap that is set to the *Image* element and displayed to the user. This is the bitmap that has its pixels adjusted for lower color resolution. The *jpegBits* array is the original file that the user loads from the picture library. Retaining the *jpegBits* array is very convenient for tombstoning, and ensures that the photo reconstituted after tombstoning is the same one that was originally loaded. The *pixels* array stores the unaltered pixels of the loaded bitmap, but this is *not* saved during tombstoning. Saving *jpegBits* rather than *pixels* requires much less storage.

When the user presses the "load" button, the *PhotoChooserTask* is invoked. During the *Completed* event, the program sets *jpegBits* from the *ChosenPhoto* stream, and then calls *LoadBitmap*.

Silverlight Project: Posterizer   File: MainPage.xaml.cs (excerpt)

```
void OnAppbarLoadClick(object sender, EventArgs args)
{
    bitSelectDialog.Visibility = Visibility.Collapsed;
    appbarSetBitsButton.IsEnabled = false;
    appbarSaveButton.IsEnabled = false;

    photoChooser.Show();
}

void OnPhotoChooserCompleted(object sender, PhotoResult args)
{
    if (args.Error == null && args.ChosenPhoto != null)
    {
        jpegBits = new byte[args.ChosenPhoto.Length];
        args.ChosenPhoto.Read(jpegBits, 0, jpegBits.Length);
        LoadBitmap(jpegBits);
    }
}

void LoadBitmap(byte[] jpegBits)
{
    // Create WriteableBitmap from JPEG bits
    MemoryStream memoryStream = new MemoryStream(jpegBits);
    BitmapImage bitmapImage = new BitmapImage();
    bitmapImage.SetSource(memoryStream);
    writeableBitmap = new WriteableBitmap(bitmapImage);
    img.Source = writeableBitmap;

    // Copy pixels into field array
    pixels = new int[writeableBitmap.PixelWidth * writeableBitmap.PixelHeight];

    for (int i = 0; i < pixels.Length; i++)
        pixels[i] = writeableBitmap.Pixels[i];

    appbarSetBitsButton.IsEnabled = true;
    appbarSaveButton.IsEnabled = true;
    ApplyBitSettingsToBitmap();
}
```

The *LoadBitmap* method then turns that *byte* array back into a *MemoryStream* for creating the *BitmapImage* and *WriteableBitmap*. This may seem like a roundabout way to create the bitmap, but it makes much more sense in conjunction with tombstoning.

The *LoadBitmap* method then makes a copy of the *Pixels* array of the *WriteableBitmap* as the *pixels* field. This *pixels* field will remain unaltered as the *Pixels* array of the *WriteableBitmap* is changed based on the user selection of bit resolution. The objective is to do nothing irrevocable. The user should always be able to select a greater color resolution after choosing a lower one.

The *ApplyBitSettingsToBitmap* called at the end of the *LoadBitmap* method is also called whenever the *ColorBitsChanged* event is fired by the *BitSelectDialog*. The visibility of that dialog is toggled on and off by the middle button in the *ApplicationBar*:

Silverlight Project: Posterizer   File: MainPage.xaml.cs (excerpt)

```
void OnAppbarSetBitsClick(object sender, EventArgs args)
{
    bitSelectDialog.Visibility =
        bitSelectDialog.Visibility == Visibility.Collapsed ?
            Visibility.Visible : Visibility.Collapsed;
}

void OnBitSelectDialogColorBitsChanged(object sender, EventArgs args)
{
    ApplyBitSettingsToBitmap();
}

void ApplyBitSettingsToBitmap()
{
    if (pixels == null || writeableBitmap == null)
        return;

    int mask = -16777216;    // ie, FF000000

    for (int clr = 0; clr < 3; clr++)
        mask |= (byte)(0xFF << (8 - bitSelectDialog.ColorBits[clr]))
                                << (16 - 8 * clr);

    for (int i = 0; i < pixels.Length; i++)
        writeableBitmap.Pixels[i] = mask & pixels[i];

    writeableBitmap.Invalidate();
}
```

The *mask* variable is built from the three bit-resolution values, and then applied to all the values in the pixels field to set all the values in the *Pixels* array of the *WriteableBitmap*.

The Posterizer program also does something a little special when the user presses the button to save the file to the picture library. The program wants to suggest to the user a filename of Posterizer followed by a three digit number higher than anything currently in the picture library. It obtains the saved pictures album through the *SavedPictures* property of the *MediaLibrary* and searches for matching filenames:

Silverlight Project: Posterizer   File: MainPage.xaml.cs (excerpt)

```
void OnAppbarSaveClick(object sender, EventArgs args)
{
    int fileNameNumber = 0;
    MediaLibrary mediaLib = new MediaLibrary();
    PictureCollection savedPictures = mediaLib.SavedPictures;

    foreach (Picture picture in savedPictures)
    {
        string filename = Path.GetFileNameWithoutExtension(picture.Name);
        int num;

        if (filename.StartsWith("Posterizer"))
        {
            if (Int32.TryParse(filename.Substring(10), out num))
                fileNameNumber = Math.Max(fileNameNumber, num);
        }
    }

    string saveFileName = String.Format("Posterizer{0:D3}", fileNameNumber + 1);

    string uri = "/Petzold.Phone.Silverlight;component/SaveFileDialog.xaml" +
                "?FileName=" + saveFileName;

    this.NavigationService.Navigate(new Uri(uri, UriKind.Relative));
}

public void SaveFileDialogCompleted(bool okPressed, string filename)
{
    if (okPressed)
    {
        MemoryStream memoryStream = new MemoryStream();
        writeableBitmap.SaveJpeg(memoryStream, writeableBitmap.PixelWidth,
                                    writeableBitmap.PixelHeight, 0, 75);
        memoryStream.Position = 0;

        MediaLibrary mediaLib = new MediaLibrary();
        mediaLib.SavePicture(filename, memoryStream);
    }
}
```

A program that modifies a photo from the picture library has the option of becoming a "photos extra" program. If so, the user can press a photo in the library, which brings up a menu including the item "extras." Pressing this item includes all the programs that have registered themselves as "photos extra" applications. Pressing one of these programs invokes the program with the photo already loaded.

Among the files in the program's project, the following is required:

Silverlight Project: Posterizer   File: Extras.xml

```xml
<Extras>
    <PhotosExtrasApplication>
        <Enabled>true</Enabled>
    </PhotosExtrasApplication>
</Extras>
```

The Properties for this file must indicate a Build Action of Content, and a Copy to Output Directory option of Copy Always.

The program must also be prepared to handle a special *OnNavigatedTo* call that indicates the selected photo.

Here are both navigation overrides. The *OnNavigatedFrom* method indicates either that the program is being tombstoned or that it's navigating to the *SaveFileDialog* object. If being tombstoned, the program must save both the current state of the color bit selection and (if it exists) the bitmap itself. If navigating to the *SaveFileDialog*, the method sets the title on the page.

Silverlight Project: Posterizer   File: MainPage.xaml.cs (excerpt)

```csharp
protected override void OnNavigatedFrom(NavigationEventArgs args)
{
    appService.State["colorBits"] = bitSelectDialog.ColorBits;

    if (jpegBits != null)
    {
        appService.State["jpegBits"] = jpegBits;
    }

    if (args.Content is SaveFileDialog)
    {
        SaveFileDialog page = args.Content as SaveFileDialog;
        page.SetTitle(ApplicationTitle.Text);
    }

    base.OnNavigatedFrom(args);
}
```

```
protected override void OnNavigatedTo(NavigationEventArgs args)
{
    if (this.NavigationContext.QueryString.ContainsKey("token"))
    {
        string token = this.NavigationContext.QueryString["token"];

        MediaLibrary mediaLib = new MediaLibrary();
        Picture picture = mediaLib.GetPictureFromToken(token);
        Stream stream = picture.GetImage();
        jpegBits = new byte[stream.Length];
        stream.Read(jpegBits, 0, jpegBits.Length);
        LoadBitmap(jpegBits);
    }
    else if (appService.State.ContainsKey("colorBits"))
    {
        int[] colorBits = (int[])appService.State["colorBits"];
        bitSelectDialog.Initialize(colorBits);
    }

    if (appService.State.ContainsKey("jpegBits"))
    {
        jpegBits = (byte[])appService.State["jpegBits"];
        LoadBitmap(jpegBits);
    }
    base.OnNavigatedTo(args);
}
```

The *OnNavigatedTo* method could indicate that the program was just invoked from the picture library. If so, then the *QueryString* dictionary of the *NavigationContext* will contain the special key string "token". The item corresponding to that string is then passed to the special *GetPictureFromToken* method of *MediaLibrary* to obtain a memory stream from which the JPEG file can be accessed.

I mentioned earlier that the *LoadBitmap* method was convenient when being re-activated from a tombstoned condition, and the logic near the bottom of the method proves it.

Chapter 15
Animations

Anima is a Latin word that translates vaguely as *vital force*, rather equivalent to the Greek word *psyche*. Introducing animation into our programs is therefore the process of giving dead (or *inanimate*) objects a little life and vigor.

In previous chapters you've seen how to change the location of elements on the screen through touch, or based on periodic *Tick* events from *DispatcherTimer*. You've also seen the *CompositionTarget.Rendering* event that lets your program perform animations by altering visuals in synchronization with the refresh rate of the video display.

Both the *DispatcherTimer* and *CompositionTarget.Rendering* can be very useful. But for most animation needs, it is easier and better to use Silverlight's built-in animation support. This support consists of over 50 classes, structures, and enumerations in the *System.Windows .Media.Animation* namespace.

Silverlight's animation library is easier than the alternatives in part because you can define animations in XAML. But these animations are also preferred to *CompositionTarget.Rendering* because several key types of animations exploit the Graphics Processing Unit (GPU) on the phone. These animations don't run in the user-interface thread; they run in a separate thread called the *compositor* or *render* thread.

Animations play a big role in control templates used to redefine the visuals of controls. Controls have *states*, such as the *Pressed* state associated with a *Button*, and all state transitions are based on animations. I'll discuss control templates in the next chapter.

Eventually, many programmers gravitate towards Expression Blend for defining animations and control templates. That's fine, but in this chapter I'm going to show you how to write animations by hand, and I'll also show you that valuable (but often neglected) technique of defining animations in code rather than XAML.

Frame-Based vs. Time-Based

Suppose you want to write a little program that rotates some text using the *CompositionTarget.Rendering* event. You can pace this animation either by the rate that video hardware refreshes the display, or by clock time. Because each refresh of the video display is called a *frame*, these two methods of pacing animation are referred to as *frame-based* and *time-based*.

Here's a little program that shows the difference. The content area of the XAML file has two *TextBlock* elements with *RotateTransform* objects set to their *RenderTransform* properties, and a *Button*:

Silverlight Project: FrameBasedVsTimeBased **File: MainPage.xaml** (excerpt)

```
<Grid x:Name="ContentPanel" Grid.Row="1" Margin="12,0,12,0">
    <Grid.RowDefinitions>
        <RowDefinition Height="*" />
        <RowDefinition Height="*" />
        <RowDefinition Height="Auto" />
    </Grid.RowDefinitions>

    <TextBlock Grid.Row="0"
            Text="Frame-Based"
            FontSize="{StaticResource PhoneFontSizeLarge}"
            HorizontalAlignment="Center"
            VerticalAlignment="Center"
            RenderTransformOrigin="0.5 0.5">
        <TextBlock.RenderTransform>
            <RotateTransform x:Name="rotate1" />
        </TextBlock.RenderTransform>
    </TextBlock>

    <TextBlock Grid.Row="1"
            Text="Time-Based"
            FontSize="{StaticResource PhoneFontSizeLarge}"
            HorizontalAlignment="Center"
            VerticalAlignment="Center"
            RenderTransformOrigin="0.5 0.5">
        <TextBlock.RenderTransform>
            <RotateTransform x:Name="rotate2" />
        </TextBlock.RenderTransform>
    </TextBlock>

    <Button Grid.Row="2"
            Content="Hang for 5 seconds"
            HorizontalAlignment="Center"
            Click="OnButtonClick" />
</Grid>
```

The code-behind file saves the current time in a field and then attaches a handler for the *CompositionTarget.Rendering* event. This event handler is then called in synchronization with the video frame rate.

Silverlight Project: FrameBasedVsTimeBased **File: MainPage.xaml.cs** (excerpt)

```
public partial class MainPage : PhoneApplicationPage
{
    DateTime startTime;
```

```
public MainPage()
{
    InitializeComponent();

    startTime = DateTime.Now;
    CompositionTarget.Rendering += OnCompositionTargetRendering;
}

void OnCompositionTargetRendering(object sender, EventArgs args)
{
    // Frame-based
    rotate1.Angle = (rotate1.Angle + 0.2) % 360;

    // Time-based
    TimeSpan elapsedTime = DateTime.Now - startTime;
    rotate2.Angle = (elapsedTime.TotalMinutes * 360) % 360;
}

void OnButtonClick(object sender, RoutedEventArgs args)
{
    Thread.Sleep(5000);
}
}
```

The rotation angle for the first *TextBlock* is increased by 0.2° every frame. I calculated this by knowing that the phone display is refreshed at 30 frames per second. Multiply 30 frames per second by 60 seconds per minute by 0.2° and you get 360°.

The rotation angle for the second *TextBlock* is calculated based on the elapsed time. The *TimeSpan* structure has a convenient *TotalMinutes* property and this is multiplied by 360 for the total number of degrees to rotate the text.

Both work, and they work approximately the same:

But if your phone is anything like my phone, you'll see that the frame-based animation lags a little behind the time-based animation, and the lag progressively gets larger and larger. Why?

The calculation for the frame-based animation assumes that the *CompositionTarget.Rendering* handler is called at the rate of 30 times per second. However, the phone I'm using for this book has a video refresh rate closer to 27 frames per second—about 27.35, to be more precise.

That's one problem with frame-based animation: It's dependent on the actual hardware. Your mileage may vary.

Here's another difference: Suppose the program suddenly needs to perform some job that hogs the processor. The FrameBasedVsTimeBased program simulates such a job with a *Button* that hangs the thread for 5 seconds. Both animations grind to a halt during this time because the calls to the *CompositionTarget.Rendering* handler are not asynchronous. When the revolutions start up again, the frame-based animation continues from where it left off; the time-based animation jumps ahead to where it would have been had the delay never occurred.

Whether you prefer one approach to the other ultimately depends on the application. Sometimes you really do need a frame-based animation. But if you ever need to use an animation to pace the hands of a clock or something similar, a time-based animation is essential; frame-based animations are just too unpredictable for the job.

The Silverlight animation library is all time-based. You specify what change you want over a particular period of time, and the Silverlight animation classes handle the rest.

Animation Targets

Animations in Silverlight work by changing a particular property of a particular object, for example the *Opacity* property of an *Image*. Changing that *Opacity* property over time makes the *Image* element fade in, or fade out, or fade in and out, depending on what you want.

The target of an animation must be a dependency property! Obviously that dependency property must be defined by a class that derives from *DependencyObject*.

The animation classes are distinguished by the *type* of the property that they animate. Silverlight animations can target properties of type *double*, *Color*, *Point*, and *Object*. (The inclusion of *Object* in this short list might seem to encompass all the others but you'll see shortly that the *Object* animations are quite restricted in functionality.)

Properties of type *double* are very common in Silverlight. They include *Opacity*, *Canvas.Left* and *Canvas.Top*, *Height* and *Width*, but also all the properties of the transform classes: *X* and *Y* of *TranslateTransform*, *ScaleX* and *ScaleY* of *ScaleTransform* and *Angle* of *RotateTransform*. Animating transforms is extremely common and one of the most efficient way to use animations.

Also in this chapter I'll show you how to use the *Projection* property defined by *UIElement* for creating 3D-like perspective effects.

But use your imagination: Whenever you come across a dependency property of type *double*, *Color*, or *Point*, think about how you might animate that property to create an interesting visual effect. For example, you can animate the *Offset* property in *GradientStop* objects to change gradient brushes over time, or you can animate the *StrokeDashOffset* property defined by *Shape* to make dots and dashes travel along lines. (Remind me to show you an example of that one!)

Animating properties of type *Color* is pretty much restricted to brushes: *SolidColorBrush*, *LinearGradientBrush*, and *RadialGradientBrush*.

Properties of type *Point* are fairly rare in Silverlight except among *Geometry* objects, and I'll show you a couple examples later in this chapter.

You'll use the classes *DoubleAnimation*, *ColorAnimation*, and *PointAnimation* to animate properties of type *double*, *Color*, or *Point* continuously from one value to another, and perhaps back again, either once or multiple times. (Even after many years of programming WPF and Silverlight, the name *DoubleAnimation* still suggests to me *two* animations. No! It's an animation that targets double-precision floating point properties.)

The *DoubleAnimation*, *ColorAnimation*, and *PointAnimation* classes have a property named *Easing* that you can set to an instance of one of a variety of classes that change the velocity of the animation either at the beginning or the end (or both) to make it more natural, and even to briefly "overshoot" the target value of an animation.

You can put together more complex animations using the classes *DoubleAnimationUsingKeyFrames*, *ColorAnimationUsingKeyFrames*, and *PointAnimationUsingKeyFrames*. These classes have a property named *KeyFrames* that is a collection of individual key frame objects that indicate what the value of the target property should be at a particular elapsed time.

For example, a *DoubleAnimationUsingKeyFrames* object can contain individual key frames of type *DiscreteDoubleKeyFrame* (to jump to a particular value at a particular time), *LinearDoubleKeyFrame* (to move with constant velocity so the property reaches a particular value at a particular time), *SplineDoubleKeyFrame* (which lets you define an animation that speeds up or slows down in accordance with a Bézier spline), and *EasingDoubleKeyFrame*, which lets you apply one of the *Easing* functions. Similar classes exist for *ColorAnimationUsingKeyFrames* and *PointAnimationUsingKeyFrames*.

In theory you can animate properties of type *Object*, but the only classes you have available are *ObjectAnimationUsingKeyFrames* and *DiscreteObjectKeyFrame*, which means that you're limited to jumping among discrete values. This is almost always used to animate properties of an enumeration type, such as *Visibility*.

Click and Spin

Suppose you want to enhance a button to give some extra visual feedback to the user. You decide you actually want a *lot* of visual feedback to wake up a drowsy user, and therefore you choose to spin the button around in a circle every time it's clicked.

Here are a few buttons in a XAML file:

Silverlight Project: ClickAndSpin   File: MainPage.xaml (excerpt)

```
<Grid x:Name="ContentPanel" Grid.Row="1" Margin="12,0,12,0">
    <Grid.RowDefinitions>
        <RowDefinition Height="*" />
        <RowDefinition Height="*" />
        <RowDefinition Height="*" />
    </Grid.RowDefinitions>

    <Button Content="Button No. 1"
            Grid.Row="0"
            HorizontalAlignment="Center"
            VerticalAlignment="Center"
            RenderTransformOrigin="0.5 0.5"
            Click="OnButtonClick">
        <Button.RenderTransform>
            <RotateTransform />
        </Button.RenderTransform>
    </Button>

    <Button Content="Button No. 2"
            Grid.Row="1"
            HorizontalAlignment="Center"
            VerticalAlignment="Center"
            RenderTransformOrigin="0.5 0.5"
            Click="OnButtonClick">
        <Button.RenderTransform>
            <RotateTransform />
        </Button.RenderTransform>
    </Button>

    <Button Content="Button No. 3"
            Grid.Row="2"
            HorizontalAlignment="Center"
            VerticalAlignment="Center"
            RenderTransformOrigin="0.5 0.5"
            Click="OnButtonClick">
        <Button.RenderTransform>
            <RotateTransform />
        </Button.RenderTransform>
    </Button>
</Grid>
```

Each of the buttons has its *RenderTransform* property set to a *RotateTransform*, and its *RenderTransformOrigin* set for the element center.

The *Click* event handler is responsible for defining and initiating the animation that spins the clicked button. (Of course, in a real application, the *Click* handler would also perform something important to the program!) The handler begins by obtaining the *Button* that the user touched, and the *RotateTransform* associated with that particular *Button*:

Silverlight Project: ClickAndSpin   File: MainPage.xaml.cs (excerpt)

```
void OnButtonClick(object sender, RoutedEventArgs args)
{
    Button btn = sender as Button;
    RotateTransform rotateTransform = btn.RenderTransform as RotateTransform;

    // Create and define animation
    DoubleAnimation anima = new DoubleAnimation();
    anima.From = 0;
    anima.To = 360;
    anima.Duration = new Duration(TimeSpan.FromSeconds(0.5));

    // Set attached properties
    Storyboard.SetTarget(anima, rotateTransform);
    Storyboard.SetTargetProperty(anima, new PropertyPath(RotateTransform.
AngleProperty));

    // Create storyboard, add animation, and fire it up!
    Storyboard storyboard = new Storyboard();
    storyboard.Children.Add(anima);
    storyboard.Begin();
}
```

Getting the animation going requires three steps:

1. Define the animation itself. The animation needed here will target the *Angle* property
   of a *RotateTransform*, and the *Angle* property is of type *double*, so that suggests
   a *DoubleAnimation*:

```
DoubleAnimation anima = new DoubleAnimation();
anima.From = 0;
anima.To = 360;
anima.Duration = new Duration(TimeSpan.FromSeconds(0.5));
```

This *DoubleAnimation* will animate a property of type *double* from a value of 0 to
a value of 360 in ½ second. The *Duration* property of *DoubleAnimation* is of type
Duration, and in code it is very common to set it from a *TimeSpan* object. But the
Duration property is not itself of type *TimeSpan* primarily due to legacy issues. You
can alternatively set the *Duration* property to the static *Duration.Automatic* value,
which is the same as not setting *Duration* at all (or setting it to *null*), and which creates
an animation with a duration of 1 second.

2. Set the attached properties. The *DoubleAnimation* must be associated with a particular
   object and property of that object. You specify these using two attached properties
   defined by the *Storyboard* class:

```
Storyboard.SetTarget(anima, rotateTransform);
Storyboard.SetTargetProperty(anima, new PropertyPath(RotateTransform.AngleProperty));
```

The attached properties are *Target* and *TargetProperty*. As you'll recall, when you set attached properties in code, you use static methods that begin with the word *Set*.

In both cases, the first argument is the *DoubleAnimation* just created. The *SetTarget* call indicates the object being animated (in this case *RotateTransform*), and the *SetTargetProperty* call indicates a property of that object. The second argument of the *SetTargetProperty* method is of type *PropertyPath*, and you'll note that I've specified the fully-qualified dependency property for the *Angle* property of *RotateTransform*.

3. Define, set, and start the *Storyboard*.

At this point, everything seems to be ready. But there's still another step. In Silverlight, animations are always enclosed in *Storyboard* objects. A particular *Storyboard* can have multiple children, so it is very useful for synchronizing multiple animations. But even if you have just one animation running by itself, you still need a *Storyboard*:

```
Storyboard storyboard = new Storyboard();
storyboard.Children.Add(anima);
storyboard.Begin();
```

As soon as you call *Begin* on the *Storyboard* object, the clicked button spins around in half a second, giving the user perhaps a little too *much* visual feedback.

Some Variations

I set the target property of the animation using the fully-qualified dependency property name:

```
Storyboard.SetTargetProperty(anima, new PropertyPath(RotateTransform.AngleProperty));
```

The alternative is using a string:

```
Storyboard.SetTargetProperty(anima, new PropertyPath("Angle"));
```

You might prefer that syntax because it's shorter, but it doesn't guarantee that you haven't misspelled the property name.

The advantage of using strings for property names is that you can stack property names in a pile. This allows you to animate a property of an object without referencing that object itself. For example, in the *Click* event handler above you can set the target of the animation to be the *Button* instead of the *RotateTransform*:

```
Storyboard.SetTarget(anima, btn);
```

The *RotateTransform* still needs to exist, and you still need to indicate that you're targeting the *Angle* property of that object, but look at how you do it:

```
Storyboard.SetTargetProperty(anima,
        new PropertyPath("(Button.RenderTransform).(RotateTransform.Angle)"));
```

This syntax—admittedly more common in XAML than in code—indicates that *RenderTransform* is a property of *Button*, and *Angle* is a property of *RotateTransform*, and the *RotateTransform* is set on the *RenderTransform* property. If the *RenderTransform* property is not set to a *RotateTransform* object, this will fail.

You can simplify the syntax a bit by removing the qualification of the *Angle* property:

```
Storyboard.SetTargetProperty(anima,
        new PropertyPath("(Button.RenderTransform).Angle"));
```

But this might be a little confusing. It looks like *Angle* is a property of *RenderTransform*, and it's really not. *Angle* is a property of a *RotateTransform* that's set on the *RenderTransform* property.

Regardless how you specify it, the animated property must be a dependency property.

The *Storyboard* class and the *DoubleAnimation* class are actually siblings, as the following class hierarchy shows:

Object
    DependencyObject (abstract)
        Timeline (abstract)
            DoubleAnimation
            DoubleAnimationUsingKeyFrames
            ColorAnimation
            ColorAnimationUsingKeyFrames
            PointAnimation
            PointAnimationUsingKeyFrames
            ObjectAnimationUsingKeyFrames
            Storyboard

Storyboard defines a *Children* property of type *TimelineCollection*, meaning that a *Storyboard* can contain not only animation objects but also other *Storyboard* objects to control a complex collection of animations. *Storyboard* also defines the attached properties that you use to associate an animation with a particular object and dependency property.

The *Timeline* class defines the *Duration* property that the program set to 0.5 seconds:

```
anima.Duration = new Duration(TimeSpan.FromSeconds(0.5));
```

You can also set the duration on the storyboard to something less than that:

```
storyboard.Duration = new Duration(TimeSpan.FromSeconds(0.25));
```

This will cause the animation to be truncated at 0.25 seconds. By default, the duration of a storyboard is the longest duration of its child timelines (in this case 0.5 seconds), and in most cases you don't want to override that.

Timeline also defines a *BeginTime* property that you can set on either the *Storyboard* or *DoubleAnimation*:

```
anima.BeginTime = TimeSpan.FromSeconds(1);
```

Now the animation doesn't start for a second.

The *AutoReverse* property is a Boolean with a default value of *false*. Try setting it to *true*:

```
anima.AutoReverse = true;
```

Now the button spins around 360° clockwise and then spins 360° counterclockwise. The total animation lasts for a second.

The *RepeatBehavior* property indicates how many times you want the animation to repeat itself:

```
anima.RepeatBehavior = new RepeatBehavior(3);
```

Now the button spins around three times for a total duration of 1.5 seconds. You can combine *RepeatBehavior* with *AutoReverse*:

```
anima.RepeatBehavior = new RepeatBehavior(3);
anima.AutoReverse = true;
```

Now the button spins around once, and then back, and then forward again, and then back, forward for the third time, and then back. Total duration: 3 seconds.

But perhaps that's not what you want. Perhaps you want the button to spin forward three times and then back three times. Easy enough. Just set *RepeatBehavior* on the animation:

```
anima.RepeatBehavior = new RepeatBehavior(3);
```

And set *AutoReverse* on the *Storyboard*:

```
storyboard.AutoReverse = true;
```

It's also possible to set *RepeatBehavior* in terms of time rather than a number:

```
anima.RepeatBehavior = new RepeatBehavior(TimeSpan.FromSeconds(0.75));
```

Now the button animation keeps repeating for the duration of the *RepeatBehavior* time. In this case, it will make 1½ revolutions and be left upside-down (unless *AutoReverse* is also set to *true* to bring it back to normal).

The *RepeatBehavior* property can also be set to the static *RepeatBehavior.Forever* value, but you probably don't want to use that in this particular example!

For the next several experiments, remove all the changes you might have made to the original program but change the duration of the animation to 5 seconds to see more clearly what's going on:

```
anima.Duration = new Duration(TimeSpan.FromSeconds(5));
```

You can sequentially click the three buttons and all the animations run independently. That's expected because all the animations are separate objects. But what happens when you click a button that's already in the middle of an animation? You'll discover that it starts over again from zero. You're basically applying a new animation that replaces the old animation, and the new animation always begins at 0° and proceeds to 360°. That's how the properties are defined:

```
anima.From = 0;
anima.To = 360;
```

Dependency properties such as the *Angle* property of *RotateTransform* have a *base value*, which is the value of the property when an animation is not active. There's actually a method defined by *DependencyObject* that lets you obtain this value: *GetAnimationBaseValue* can be called on any *DependencyObject* derivative with an argument set to a *DependencyProperty*, such as *RotateTransform.AngleProperty*.

If you call *GetAnimationBaseValue* for that *Angle* property, you'll get the value zero. Try commenting out the *From* property setting, leaving only the *To*:

```
// anima.From = 0;
anima.To = 360;
```

And it works. The animation animates the *Angle* property from its base value of zero to 360. But if you click the *Button* multiple times as the button is slowly spinning, something odd happens: It won't start over from 0 because there is no *From* property setting. But the velocity of the button slows down because each new animation starts from the current position of the button, so it has less distance to travel to reach 360 but the same amount of time to do it in.

But does it really work? After the animation has concluded, try clicking the button again. Nothing happens! The animation has left the *Angle* property at a value of 360, so there's nothing for subsequent animations to do!

Now try this:

```
anima.From = -360;
anima.To = null;
```

The *To* property setting might look a little strange since you probably assumed that *From* and *To* are of type *double*. They're actually nullable *double* values, and the default values are *null*. Setting the value to *null* is the same as not setting it at all. These settings work much like the original settings. Whenever you click the button, it jumps to the value of −360° and then is animated to its base value, which is 0.

Let's look at this one again:

```
// anima.From = 0;
anima.To = 360;
```

After the animation ends, the *Angle* property is left at the value of 360. That behavior is the result of the *FillBehavior* property defined by *Timeline*. By default, this property is set to the enumeration value *FillBehavior.HoldEnd*, which causes a property to be left at the animated value after the animation ends. Try this alternative:

```
// anima.From = 0;
anima.To = 360;
anima.FillBehavior = FillBehavior.Stop;
```

This setting causes the effect of the animation to be removed from the property. After the animation concludes, the *Angle* property reverts to its pre-animated value of 0. We can't actually see that property snap back, because 0° is the same as 360°, but it does. You can see the effect more clearly if you set the *To* value to 180.

An alternative to the *To* and *From* properties is *By*. Try this:

```
// anima.From = 0;
// anima.To = 360;
anima.By = 90;
anima.FillBehavior = FillBehavior.HoldEnd;
```

This setting of *FillBehavior* is the default value of *HoldEnd*. Each time you click the button, it advances by 90°. However, if you click it while it's moving, it will be animated 90° from that position, so it ends up in some odd angle. The *By* value is useful in some cases to progressively increment a property by a certain amount with each successive application of an animation.

XAML-Based Animations

Defining storyboards and animations in XAML is ostensibly easier than defining them in code, and for that reason you'll find the vast majority of Silverlight storyboards and animations in XAML. But there are some issues involving the sharing of resources.

Let's try to rewrite the ClickAndSpin program to use XAML for the storyboards and animations. The XamlClickAndSpin program has the following content area:

Silverlight Project: XamlClickAndSpin   File: MainPage.xaml (excerpt)

```xaml
<Grid x:Name="ContentPanel" Grid.Row="1" Margin="12,0,12,0">
    <Grid.RowDefinitions>
        <RowDefinition Height="*" />
        <RowDefinition Height="*" />
        <RowDefinition Height="*" />
    </Grid.RowDefinitions>

    <Button Name="btn1"
            Content="Button No. 1"
            Grid.Row="0"
            HorizontalAlignment="Center"
            VerticalAlignment="Center"
            RenderTransformOrigin="0.5 0.5"
            Click="OnButtonClick">
        <Button.RenderTransform>
            <RotateTransform x:Name="rotate1" />
        </Button.RenderTransform>
    </Button>

    <Button Name="btn2"
            Content="Button No. 2"
            Grid.Row="1"
            HorizontalAlignment="Center"
            VerticalAlignment="Center"
            RenderTransformOrigin="0.5 0.5"
            Click="OnButtonClick">
        <Button.RenderTransform>
            <RotateTransform x:Name="rotate2" />
        </Button.RenderTransform>
    </Button>

    <Button Name="btn3"
            Content="Button No. 3"
            Grid.Row="2"
            HorizontalAlignment="Center"
            VerticalAlignment="Center"
            RenderTransformOrigin="0.5 0.5"
            Click="OnButtonClick">
        <Button.RenderTransform>
            <RotateTransform x:Name="rotate3" />
        </Button.RenderTransform>
    </Button>
</Grid>
```

This is basically the same as the previous version except that all the *Button* elements and all the *RotateTransform* objects have been given names for easy reference.

The storyboards and animations are defined in the *Resources* collection of the page:

Silverlight Project: XamlClickAndSpin   File: MainPage.xaml (excerpt)

```xml
<phone:PhoneApplicationPage.Resources>
    <Storyboard x:Name="storyboard1">
        <DoubleAnimation Storyboard.TargetName="rotate1"
                         Storyboard.TargetProperty="Angle"
                         From="0" To="360" Duration="0:0:0.5" />
    </Storyboard>

    <Storyboard x:Name="storyboard2">
        <DoubleAnimation Storyboard.TargetName="rotate2"
                         Storyboard.TargetProperty="Angle"
                         From="0" To="360" Duration="0:0:0.5" />
    </Storyboard>

    <Storyboard x:Name="storyboard3">
        <DoubleAnimation Storyboard.TargetName="rotate3"
                         Storyboard.TargetProperty="Angle"
                         From="0" To="360" Duration="0:0:0.5" />
    </Storyboard>
</phone:PhoneApplicationPage.Resources>
```

Three buttons; three storyboards. Notice the attached properties:

```xml
<DoubleAnimation Storyboard.TargetName="rotate1"
                 Storyboard.TargetProperty="Angle"
                 From="0" To="360" Duration="0:0:0.5" />
```

To set the attached properties in code, you make calls to the static methods *Storyboard.SetTarget* and *Storyboard.SetTargetProperty*. In XAML you set the attached properties *Storyboard.TargetName* and *Storyboard.TargetProperty*. Notice the difference: The markup needs to reference a target object by name whereas code has access to the actual object itself.

Alternatively, the *Angle* property could be referenced through the *Button* object:

```xml
<DoubleAnimation Storyboard.TargetName="btn1"
                 Storyboard.TargetProperty="(Button.RenderTransform).(RotateTransform
.Angle)"
                 From="0" To="360" Duration="0:0:0.5" />
```

Or:

```xml
<DoubleAnimation Storyboard.TargetName="btn1"
                 Storyboard.TargetProperty="(Button.RenderTransform).Angle"
                 From="0" To="360" Duration="0:0:0.5" />
```

With this syntax, the *RotateTransform* objects do not require names.

Notice how the duration is defined. At least three numbers are required: hours, minutes, and seconds separated by colons. The seconds can have a fractional part. You can also preface hours with a number of days and a period.

I used *x:Name* rather than *x:Key* with the *Storyboard* resources to make them easier to reference in code. The handler for the button's *Click* event simply calls *Begin* on the appropriate object:

Silverlight Project: XamlClickAndSpin   File: **MainPage.xaml.cs** (excerpt)

```
void OnButtonClick(object sender, RoutedEventArgs args)
{
    if (sender == btn1)
        storyboard1.Begin();

    else if (sender == btn2)
        storyboard2.Begin();

    else if (sender == btn3)
        storyboard3.Begin();
}
```

Simple enough. But I'm probably not alone in desiring a way to define just one storyboard and animation in XAML rather than three. It seems like it should be possible to leave out the *Storyboard.TargetName* assignment in the XAML and call the *Storyboard.SetTarget* method in code once you know what button is involved. But you can't get around the fact that resources are shared, and if a particular *Storyboard* and *DoubleAnimation* are associated with one *Button*, they can't also be used with another *Button*. With one *Storyboard* and *DoubleAnimation* resource you couldn't have two buttons spinning at the same time.

Even if you could assure yourself that one *Button* would be stopped before another *Button* would begin, you still have to make sure that the storyboard is stopped as well, which means you need to call *Stop* on the *Storyboard* object. (Besides *Begin* and *Stop* methods, the *Storyboard* class also defines *Pause* and *Resume*, but they're not often used.)

A Cautionary Tale

In previous chapters I've showed you how to use *CompositionTarget.Rendering* for moving and changing visual objects in synchronization with the refresh rate of the video display. While certainly convenient for some scenarios, this feature of Silverlight should be used with discretion. If you're really interested in using *CompositionTarget.Rendering* for a full-fledged game loop, for example, perhaps it's time to start thinking about XNA.

The big problem is that sometimes *CompositionTarget.Rendering* does not work as well as you might anticipate. For example, you might remember the Spiral program from Chapter 13. Here is a program that attempts to use *CompositionTarget.Rendering* to rotate that spiral.

Silverlight Project: **RotatedSpiral**   File: **MainPage.xaml.cs** (excerpt)

```
public partial class MainPage : PhoneApplicationPage
{
    RotateTransform rotateTransform = new RotateTransform();

    public MainPage()
    {
        InitializeComponent();
        Loaded += OnLoaded;
    }

    void OnLoaded(object sender, RoutedEventArgs args)
    {
        Point center = new Point(ContentPanel.ActualWidth / 2 - 1,
                                 ContentPanel.ActualHeight / 2 - 1);
        double radius = Math.Min(center.X, center.Y);

        Polyline polyline = new Polyline();
        polyline.Stroke = this.Resources["PhoneForegroundBrush"] as Brush;
        polyline.StrokeThickness = 3;

        for (double angle = 0; angle < 3600; angle += 0.25)
        {
            double scaledRadius = radius * angle / 3600;
            double radians = Math.PI * angle / 180;
            double x = center.X + scaledRadius * Math.Cos(radians);
            double y = center.Y + scaledRadius * Math.Sin(radians);
            polyline.Points.Add(new Point(x, y));
        }
        ContentPanel.Children.Add(polyline);

        rotateTransform.CenterX = center.X;
        rotateTransform.CenterY = center.Y;
        polyline.RenderTransform = rotateTransform;

        CompositionTarget.Rendering += OnCompositionTargetRendering;
    }

    void OnCompositionTargetRendering(object sender, EventArgs args)
    {
        TimeSpan elapsedTime = (args as RenderingEventArgs).RenderingTime;
        rotateTransform.Angle = 360 * elapsedTime.TotalSeconds / 3 % 360;
    }
}
```

Most of this code is the same as the Spiral program, but notice the *RotateTransform* field. At the end of the *Loaded* handler, this *RotateTransform* is set to the *RenderTransform* property of the *Polyline* defining the spiral, and a handler is attached to the *CompositionTarget. Rendering* event. That event handler changes the *Angle* property of the *RotateTransform* to rotate the spiral once every 3 seconds.

There's nothing really wrong with this code, but if your phone is similar to my phone, the performance will be *terrible*. The screen will be updated only once or twice a second, and the resultant animation will seem very jumpy.

I'm going to tell you three ways to fix the problem and improve the performance. Fortunately, all three ways to fix the problem are general enough to be usable beyond this particular application.

Solution 1: **Simplify the graphics**. This spiral is a *Polyline* with 14,400 points. That is *way* more than sufficient. If you change the increment in the *for* loop from 0.25 to 5, the animation will be much smoother and the spiral itself will still seem round. The lesson: Fewer visual objects often result in better performance. Simplify your graphics and simplify your visual trees.

Solution 2: **Cache the visuals**. Silverlight is attempting to rotate a *Polyline* with very many individual points. It would find this job a lot easier if the spiral were a simple bitmap rather than a complex *Polyline*. You could make a *WriteableBitmap* of this graphic yourself and rotate that. Or you could let Silverlight do the equivalent optimization by simply setting the following property on *Polyline*:

```
polyline.CacheMode = new BitmapCache();
```

This instructs Silverlight to create a bitmap of the element and to use that bitmap for rendering. You shouldn't use this option for vector graphics that dynamically change. But complex graphics that are static within themselves, and which might be subjected to animations, are excellent candidates for bitmap caching. In XAML it looks like this:

```
CacheMode="BitmapCache"
```

Solution 3: **Use Silverlight animations instead of *CompositionTarget.Rendering***.

Let's rewrite the RotatedSpiral program with the same number of points in the *Polyline* and without explicit bitmap caching but replacing *CompositionTarget.Rendering* with a *DoubleAnimation*:

Silverlight Project: AnimatedSpiral   File: MainPage.xaml.cs (excerpt)

```
public partial class MainPage : PhoneApplicationPage
{
    public MainPage()
    {
        InitializeComponent();
```

```
        Loaded += OnLoaded;
    }

    void OnLoaded(object sender, RoutedEventArgs args)
    {
        Point center = new Point(ContentPanel.ActualWidth / 2 - 1,
                                 ContentPanel.ActualHeight / 2 - 1);
        double radius = Math.Min(center.X, center.Y);

        Polyline polyline = new Polyline();
        polyline.Stroke = this.Resources["PhoneForegroundBrush"] as Brush;
        polyline.StrokeThickness = 3;

        for (double angle = 0; angle < 3600; angle += 0.25)
        {
            double scaledRadius = radius * angle / 3600;
            double radians = Math.PI * angle / 180;
            double x = center.X + scaledRadius * Math.Cos(radians);
            double y = center.Y + scaledRadius * Math.Sin(radians);
            polyline.Points.Add(new Point(x, y));
        }
        ContentPanel.Children.Add(polyline);

        RotateTransform rotateTransform = new RotateTransform();
        rotateTransform.CenterX = center.X;
        rotateTransform.CenterY = center.Y;
        polyline.RenderTransform = rotateTransform;

        DoubleAnimation anima = new DoubleAnimation
        {
            From = 0,
            To = 360,
            Duration = new Duration(TimeSpan.FromSeconds(3)),
            RepeatBehavior = RepeatBehavior.Forever
        };

        Storyboard.SetTarget(anima, rotateTransform);
        Storyboard.SetTargetProperty(anima,
                              new PropertyPath(RotateTransform.AngleProperty));

        Storyboard storyboard = new Storyboard();
        storyboard.Children.Add(anima);
        storyboard.Begin();
    }
}
```

And it runs much smoother than the previous version.

Why the big difference? Surely on some level the Silverlight animations are making use of something equivalent to *CompositionTarget.Rendering*, right?

Actually, that's not true. It's pretty much true for the desktop version of Silverlight, but Silverlight for Windows Phone has been enhanced to make greater use of the phone's graphics processing unit (GPU). Although GPUs are customarily associated with hardware accelerations of complex texture processing and other algorithms associated with 3D graphics, Silverlight puts the GPU to work performing simple 2D animations.

Much of a Silverlight application runs in a single thread called the *UI thread*. The UI thread handles touch input, layout, and the *CompositionTarget.Rendering* event. Some worker threads are also used for jobs such as rasterization, media decoding, sensors, and asynchronous web access.

Silverlight for Windows Phone also supports a *compositor* or *render thread* that involves the GPU. This render thread is used for several types of animations of properties of type *double*, specifically:

- Transforms you set to the *RenderTransform* property

- Perspective transforms you set to *Projection* property

- *Canvas.Left* and *Canvas.Top* attached properties

- *Opacity* property

- Anything that causes rectangular clipping to occur

Animations that target properties of type *Color* or *Point* continue to be performed in the UI thread. Non-rectangular clipping or use of *OpacityMask* are also performed in the UI thread and can result in poor performance.

As a little demonstration, the UIThreadVsRenderThread project rotates some text in two different ways:

Silverlight Project: UIThreadVsRenderThread   File: MainPage.xaml (excerpt)

```xml
<Grid x:Name="ContentPanel" Grid.Row="1" Margin="12,0,12,0">
    <Grid.RowDefinitions>
        <RowDefinition Height="*" />
        <RowDefinition Height="*" />
        <RowDefinition Height="Auto" />
    </Grid.RowDefinitions>

    <TextBlock Grid.Row="0"
               Text="UI Thread"
               FontSize="{StaticResource PhoneFontSizeLarge}"
               HorizontalAlignment="Center"
               VerticalAlignment="Center"
               RenderTransformOrigin="0.5 0.5">
        <TextBlock.RenderTransform>
            <RotateTransform x:Name="rotate1" />
        </TextBlock.RenderTransform>
    </TextBlock>
```

```
<TextBlock Grid.Row="1"
           Text="Render Thread"
           FontSize="{StaticResource PhoneFontSizeLarge}"
           HorizontalAlignment="Center"
           VerticalAlignment="Center"
           RenderTransformOrigin="0.5 0.5">
    <TextBlock.RenderTransform>
        <RotateTransform x:Name="rotate2" />
    </TextBlock.RenderTransform>
</TextBlock>

<Button Grid.Row="2"
        Content="Hang for 5 seconds"
        HorizontalAlignment="Center"
        Click="OnButtonClick" />
</Grid>
```

The first *TextBlock* is rotated in code using *CompositionTarget.Rendering*. The second *TextBlock* is animated by the following *Storyboard* defined in the page's *Resources* collection:

Silverlight Project: **UIThreadVsRenderThread**   File: **MainPage.xaml** (excerpt)

```
<phone:PhoneApplicationPage.Resources>
    <Storyboard x:Name="storyboard">
        <DoubleAnimation Storyboard.TargetName="rotate2"
                         Storyboard.TargetProperty="Angle"
                         From="0" To="360" Duration="0:1:0"
                         RepeatBehavior="Forever" />
    </Storyboard>
</phone:PhoneApplicationPage.Resources>
```

The *MainPage* constructor starts the animation going and attaches a handler for the *CompositionTarget.Rendering* event.

Silverlight Project: **UIThreadVsRenderThread**   File: **MainPage.xaml.cs** (excerpt)

```
public partial class MainPage : PhoneApplicationPage
{
    DateTime startTime;

    public MainPage()
    {
        InitializeComponent();

        storyboard.Begin();
        startTime = DateTime.Now;
        CompositionTarget.Rendering += OnCompositionTargetRendering;
    }
```

```
    void OnCompositionTargetRendering(object sender, EventArgs args)
    {
        TimeSpan elapsedTime = DateTime.Now - startTime;
        rotate1.Angle = (elapsedTime.TotalMinutes * 360) % 360;
    }

    void OnButtonClick(object sender, RoutedEventArgs args)
    {
        Thread.Sleep(5000);
    }
}
```

I'm using the time-based logic for *CompositionTarget.Rendering* so the two animations move at the same rate. But press that button and you'll see something amazing: The *TextBlock* rotated by *CompositionTarget.Rendering* stops dead for five seconds, but the one powered by *DoubleAnimation* keeps right on going! That's the render thread working for you even though the UI thread is blocked.

If you're applying rotation and scaling to text, there's another setting you might want to know about. This is the attached property you set in XAML like this:

```
TextOptions.TextHintingMode="Animated"
```

The alternative is *Fixed*, which is the default. When you indicate that text is to be animated, certain optimizations for readability won't be performed.

Silverlight has three built-in features that can help you visualize performance issues. Although you can use these on the phone emulator, the emulator tends to run faster than the actual phone, so you're not getting a true view of performance anyway.

For more details about performance issues, you'll want to study the document "Creating High Performance Silverlight Applications for Windows Phone" available online The *Settings* class in the *System.Windows.Interop* namespace has three Boolean properties that can help you visualize performance. You access these three properties through the *SilverlightHost* object available as the *Host* property of the current *Application* object. These properties are considered so important that you'll find them set—and all but one commented out—in the constructor of the *App* class in the standard App.xaml.cs file.

Here's the first:

```
Application.Current.Host.Settings.EnableFrameRateCounter = true;
```

This flag enables a little display at the side of the phone showing several items:

- The frame rate (in frames per second) of the render thread (GPU)
- The frame rate (in frames per second) of the UI thread (CPU)

- The amount of video RAM in use in kilobytes

- The number of textures stored on the GPU

- The number of intermediate objects created for complex graphics

- The fraction of total screen pixels painted per frame

The first two items are the most important. When your program is running on the phone these two numbers should both be in the region of 30 frames per second. It is probably best to use these numbers (and the others) in comparative ways: Get accustomed to what the numbers are like in relatively simple programs, and then observe the changes as the program gets more complex.

The second diagnostics flag is:

```
Application.Current.Host.Settings.EnableRedrawRegions = true;
```

This flag is rather fun. Whenever the UI thread needs to rasterize graphics for a particular region of the video display, that region is highlighted with a different color. (These are sometimes called "dirty regions" because they need to be refreshed with new visuals.) If you see a lot of flickering over wide areas of the video display, the UI thread is working overtime to update the display. Optimally, you should be seeing very little color flashing, which is the case when the render thread is performing animations rather than the UI thread.

Here's the third flag:

```
Application.Current.Host.Settings.EnableCacheVisualization = true;
```

This flag uses a color overlay to highlight areas of the display that are cached to bitmaps. You might want to try this flag with the RotatedSpiral program (the version that uses *CompositionTarget.Rendering*). When you run the program as it's shown above, the whole display is tinted, meaning that the whole display needs to rasterized every time the *Polyline* changes position. That takes some times, and that's why the performance is so poor. Now set:

```
polyline.CacheMode = new BitmapCache();
```

Now you'll see the spiral in a tinted box, and the box itself is rotated. That's the cached bitmap.

Key Frame Animations

If you like the idea of giving the user some visual feedback from a button, but the 360° spin is just a bit too ostentatious, perhaps jiggling the button a little might be more polite. So you open a new project named JiggleButtonTryout and begin experimenting.

Let's start with just one *Button* with a *TranslateTransform* set to the *RenderTransform* property:

Silverlight Project: JiggleButtonTryout   File: MainPage.xaml (excerpt)

```
<Grid x:Name="ContentPanel" Grid.Row="1" Margin="12,0,12,0">
    <Button Content="Jiggle Button"
            HorizontalAlignment="Center"
            VerticalAlignment="Center"
            Click="OnButtonClick">
        <Button.RenderTransform>
            <TranslateTransform x:Name="translate" />
        </Button.RenderTransform>
    </Button>
</Grid>
```

In the *Resources* collection you'll want to define a *Storyboard*:

```
<phone:PhoneApplicationPage.Resources>
    <Storyboard x:Name="jiggleStoryboard">

    </Storyboard>
</phone:PhoneApplicationPage.Resources>
```

The code-behind file starts the animation when the button is clicked:

Silverlight Project: JiggleButtonTryout   File: MainPage.xaml.cs (excerpt)

```
void OnButtonClick(object sender, RoutedEventArgs args)
{
    jiggleStoryboard.Begin();
}
```

Perhaps the first thing you try is a *DoubleAnimation* that animates the *X* property of the *TranslateTransform*:

```
<Storyboard x:Name="jiggleStoryboard">
    <DoubleAnimation Storyboard.TargetName="translate"
                     Storyboard.TargetProperty="X"
                     From="-10" To="10" Duration="0:0:0.05"
                     AutoReverse="True"
                     RepeatBehavior="3x" />
</Storyboard>
```

The result looks vaguely OK, but it's not quite right, because the animation initially jumps the button to the left 10 pixels, and then the animation goes from left to right and back again three times. (Notice the XAML syntax for repeating the animation three times or "3x".) Then it stops with the button still 10 units to the left. You can see the problem more clearly if you change the offsets to –100 and 100, and the duration to ½ second.

One way to fix part of the problem is to set the *FillBehavior* to *Stop*, which releases the animation at the end, causing the button to jump back to its original position. But that creates another discontinuous jump at the end of the animation besides the one at the beginning.

To make this correct, we really need a couple different animations. We first want to animate from 0 to –10, then from –10 to 10 and back again a few times, and then finally back to zero. Fortunately, Silverlight has a facility to string animations like this in a sequence. It's called a key-frame animation, and the first step is to replace *DoubleAnimation* with *DoubleAnimationUsingKeyFrames*. Everything except the *TargetName* and *TargetProperty* doesn't apply in new approach:

```
<Storyboard x:Name="jiggleStoryboard">
    <DoubleAnimationUsingKeyFrames Storyboard.TargetName="translate"
                                   Storyboard.TargetProperty="X">

    </DoubleAnimationUsingKeyFrames>
</Storyboard>
```

When you're animating properties of type double, *DoubleAnimationUsingKeyFrames* is the only alternative to *DoubleAnimation*, but it gives you a lot more flexibility. The *DoubleAnimationUsingKeyFrames* class has children of type *DoubleKeyFrame*, and you have four choices:

- *DiscreteDoubleKeyFrame* jumps to a particular position
- *LinearDoubleKeyFame* performs a linear animation
- *SplineDoubleKeyFrame* can speed up and slow down
- *EasingDoubleKeyFrame* animates with an easing function

For now, I want to use *DiscreteDoubleKeyFrame* and *LinearDoubleKeyFrame*. Each keyframe object requires two properties to be set: a *KeyTime* and a *Value*. The *KeyTime* is an elapsed time from the beginning of the animation; the *Value* property is the desired value of the target property at that time.

To get a better view of what's happening, let's swing the button very wide, and let's do it slowly. At time zero, we want the value to be zero:

```
<DiscreteDoubleKeyFrame KeyTime="0:0:0" Value="0" />
```

This isn't actually required, because 0 is the value of the target property at the beginning of the animationanyway, but it doesn't hurt.

At the end of 1 second, let's set the value to be –100:

```
<LinearDoubleKeyFrame KeyTime="0:0:01" Value="-100" />
```

The use of *LinearDoubleKeyFrame* here means that in the duration from time zero to 1 second, the *X* property of *TranslateTransform* will change linearly from 0 to –100. The velocity is 100 units a second, so to keep the same velocity for the swing to 100, the next key time should be three seconds:

```
<LinearDoubleKeyFrame KeyTime="0:0:03" Value="100" />
```

This means that from an elapsed time of 1 second to an elapsed time of 3 seconds, the value changes from –100 to 100. Finally, another elapsed second brings it back to the starting position:

```
<LinearDoubleKeyFrame KeyTime="0:0:04" Value="0" />
```

If you try this out, you can see that the button moves left, then all the way right, then back to the center without any jumps in a total of 4 seconds. The total duration of a key-frame animation is the maximum *KeyTime* on all the key-frame objects.

Now let's perform that entire maneuver three times:

```
<Storyboard x:Name="jiggleStoryboard">
    <DoubleAnimationUsingKeyFrames Storyboard.TargetName="translate"
                                   Storyboard.TargetProperty="X"
                                   RepeatBehavior="3x">
        <DiscreteDoubleKeyFrame KeyTime="0:0:0" Value="0" />
        <LinearDoubleKeyFrame KeyTime="0:0:01" Value="-100" />
        <LinearDoubleKeyFrame KeyTime="0:0:03" Value="100" />
        <LinearDoubleKeyFrame KeyTime="0:0:04" Value="0" />
    </DoubleAnimationUsingKeyFrames>
</Storyboard>
```

The total show lasts for 12 seconds but without any discontinuities.

Now that the button has the desired behavior, the offsets can be reduced from 100 to 10:

```
<Storyboard x:Name="jiggleStoryboard">
    <DoubleAnimationUsingKeyFrames Storyboard.TargetName="translate"
                                   Storyboard.TargetProperty="X"
                                   RepeatBehavior="3x">
        <DiscreteDoubleKeyFrame KeyTime="0:0:0" Value="0" />
        <LinearDoubleKeyFrame KeyTime="0:0:01" Value="-10" />
        <LinearDoubleKeyFrame KeyTime="0:0:03" Value="10" />
        <LinearDoubleKeyFrame KeyTime="0:0:04" Value="0" />
    </DoubleAnimationUsingKeyFrames>
</Storyboard>
```

To bring the time values down to something reasonable, I want to show you a little trick. Often when you're developing animations you want to do run them very slowly to get them working correctly, and then you want to speed them up for the final version. Of course, you could go through and adjust all the *KeyTime* values, or you could simply specify a *SpeedRatio* on the animation, as in the version of the animation in the JiggleButtonTryout project:

Silverlight Project: JiggleButtonTryout   File: MainPage.xaml (excerpt)

```
<phone:PhoneApplicationPage.Resources>
    <Storyboard x:Name="jiggleStoryboard">
        <DoubleAnimationUsingKeyFrames Storyboard.TargetName="translate"
                                       Storyboard.TargetProperty="X"
                                       RepeatBehavior="3x"
                                       SpeedRatio="40">
            <DiscreteDoubleKeyFrame KeyTime="0:0:0" Value="0" />
            <LinearDoubleKeyFrame KeyTime="0:0:01" Value="-10" />
            <LinearDoubleKeyFrame KeyTime="0:0:03" Value="10" />
            <LinearDoubleKeyFrame KeyTime="0:0:04" Value="0" />
        </DoubleAnimationUsingKeyFrames>
    </Storyboard>
</phone:PhoneApplicationPage.Resources>
```

Each cycle of the key frames requires 4 seconds; this is repeated 3 times for a total of 12 seconds, but the *SpeedRatio* value of 40 effectively speeds up the animation by a factor of 40 so it's only 0.3 seconds total.

If you want to immortalize this effect in a custom control called *JiggleButton* for easy reusability, you have a few choices, none of which are entirely satisfactory.

You could derive from *UserControl* and incorporate the *Button* and the transform in that control. But to do this right would require reproducing all the *Button* properties and events as *UserControl* properties and events. Another approach involves a template. Perhaps the easiest option is to derive from *Button*, but in doing so you'd have to appropriate the *RenderTransform* property for this specific purpose, and the *RenderTransform* property would be unusable for other purposes.

Trigger on Loaded

The Windows Presentation Foundation has somewhat more flexibility than Silverlight in defining and using animations. WPF includes objects called *triggers*, which respond to event firings or to changes in properties and which can start animations going entirely in XAML, eliminating the need for the code-behind file to start the *Storyboard*. Triggers are largely gone from Silverlight—mostly replaced by the Visual State Manager that I'll discuss in the next chapter.

However, one trigger remains in Silverlight. This is a trigger that responds to the *Loaded* event. This allows you to define an animation entirely in XAML that automatically starts up when the page (or another element) is loaded.

The FadeInOnLoaded project contains the following XAML near the bottom of the page, right above the *PhoneApplicationPage* end tag. This is the traditional spot for event triggers:

Silverlight Project: FadeInOnLoaded   File: **MainPage.xaml** (excerpt)

```
<phone:PhoneApplicationPage.Triggers>
    <EventTrigger>
        <BeginStoryboard>
            <Storyboard>
                <DoubleAnimation Storyboard.TargetName="TitlePanel"
                                 Storyboard.TargetProperty="Opacity"
                                 From="0" To="1" Duration="0:0:10" />
            </Storyboard>
        </BeginStoryboard>
    </EventTrigger>
</phone:PhoneApplicationPage.Triggers>
```

The markup begins with a property-element tag for the *Triggers* property defined by *FrameworkElement*. The *Triggers* property is of type *TriggerCollection*, which sounds quite extensive and versatile, but in Silverlight the only thing you can put in there is an *EventTrigger* tag that is always associated with the *Loaded* event. This next tag is *BeginStoryboard*. This is the only place you'll see a *BeginStoryboard* tag in Silverlight. And now we get to something familiar: A *Storyboard* with one or more animations that can target any dependency object of any object on the page.

This one targets the *Opacity* property of the *TitlePanel*, which is the *StackPanel* containing the two titles at the top of the page. I made the animation 10 seconds long so you don't miss it. As the page is loaded, the titles fade into view:

The Silverlight documentation discourages the use of animations triggered in this way. Certainly the technique has limited use in real life. But it remains very popular for XAML-based demonstration programs with animations that run "forever." You can make an animation run forever (or to the limits of your toleration) with:

```
RepeatBehavior="Forever"
```

Although I've read that you can't put the markup with the *Triggers* property element on anything other than the root element of the page, in reality it's possible to define it on something a little closer to the actual objects being animated. I'll do that in the next several programs in this chapter so the visual tree in the content area and the animation are all together in one happy family.

All the visuals in the following program are in a centered *Grid* with a fixed 400-pixel square size. The *Grid* contains five concentric circles, all of which are *Path* elements whose *Data* properties are set to *EllipseGeometry* objects. Each *EllipseGeometry* has *RadiusX* and a *RadiusY* properties set to values that are 25 pixels longer than the next smallest object.

Silverlight Project: ExpandingCircles   File: MainPage.xaml (excerpt)

```
<Grid x:Name="ContentPanel" Grid.Row="1" Margin="12,0,12,0">
    <Grid Width="400" Height="400"
          HorizontalAlignment="Center"
          VerticalAlignment="Center" >

        <!-- The inner circle. -->
        <Path Name="pathInner"
              Stroke="{StaticResource PhoneAccentBrush}"
              StrokeThickness="12.5">
            <Path.Data>
                <EllipseGeometry x:Name="ellipse1"
                                 Center="200 200"
                                 RadiusX="0" RadiusY="0" />
            </Path.Data>
        </Path>

        <!-- All circles except the inner and outer. -->
        <Path Stroke="{StaticResource PhoneAccentBrush}"
              StrokeThickness="12.5">
            <Path.Data>
                <GeometryGroup>
                    <EllipseGeometry x:Name="ellipse2"
                                     Center="200 200"
                                     RadiusX="25" RadiusY="25" />
                    <EllipseGeometry x:Name="ellipse3"
                                     Center="200 200"
                                     RadiusX="50" RadiusY="50" />
                    <EllipseGeometry x:Name="ellipse4"
                                     Center="200 200"
                                     RadiusX="75" RadiusY="75" />
```

```
                    </GeometryGroup>
            </Path.Data>
        </Path>

        <!-- The outer circle. -->
        <Path Name="pathOuter"
              Stroke="{StaticResource PhoneAccentBrush}"
              StrokeThickness="12.5">
            <Path.Data>
                <EllipseGeometry x:Name="ellipse5"
                                 Center="200 200"
                                 RadiusX="100" RadiusY="100" />
            </Path.Data>
        </Path>

        <Grid.Triggers>
            <EventTrigger>
                <BeginStoryboard>
                    <Storyboard RepeatBehavior="Forever">
                        <DoubleAnimation Storyboard.TargetName="pathInner"
                                         Storyboard.TargetProperty="StrokeThickness"
                                         From="0" Duration="0:0:5" />

                        <DoubleAnimation Storyboard.TargetName="ellipse1"
                                         Storyboard.TargetProperty="RadiusX"
                                         From="0" To="25" Duration="0:0:5" />

                        <DoubleAnimation Storyboard.TargetName="ellipse1"
                                         Storyboard.TargetProperty="RadiusY"
                                         From="0" To="25" Duration="0:0:5" />

                        <DoubleAnimation Storyboard.TargetName="ellipse2"
                                         Storyboard.TargetProperty="RadiusX"
                                         From="25" To="50" Duration="0:0:5" />

                        <DoubleAnimation Storyboard.TargetName="ellipse2"
                                         Storyboard.TargetProperty="RadiusY"
                                         From="25" To="50" Duration="0:0:5" />

                        <DoubleAnimation Storyboard.TargetName="ellipse3"
                                         Storyboard.TargetProperty="RadiusX"
                                         From="50" To="75" Duration="0:0:5" />

                        <DoubleAnimation Storyboard.TargetName="ellipse3"
                                         Storyboard.TargetProperty="RadiusY"
                                         From="50" To="75" Duration="0:0:5" />

                        <DoubleAnimation Storyboard.TargetName="ellipse4"
                                         Storyboard.TargetProperty="RadiusX"
                                         From="75" To="100" Duration="0:0:5" />

                        <DoubleAnimation Storyboard.TargetName="ellipse4"
                                         Storyboard.TargetProperty="RadiusY"
                                         From="75" To="100" Duration="0:0:5" />
```

```
                      <DoubleAnimation Storyboard.TargetName="ellipse5"
                                       Storyboard.TargetProperty="RadiusX"
                                       From="100" To="125" Duration="0:0:5" />

                      <DoubleAnimation Storyboard.TargetName="ellipse5"
                                       Storyboard.TargetProperty="RadiusY"
                                       From="100" To="125" Duration="0:0:5" />

                      <DoubleAnimation Storyboard.TargetName="pathOuter"
                                       Storyboard.TargetProperty="Opacity"
                                       From="1" To="0" Duration="0:0:4.9" />
                  </Storyboard>
              </BeginStoryboard>
          </EventTrigger>
      </Grid.Triggers>
  </Grid>
</Grid>
```

That centered *Path* is also the element on which the *EventTrigger* is attached, and the *Storyboard* contains 12 *DoubleAnimation* objects, all of which run in parallel for 5 seconds. (The last one is actually 4.9 seconds, but I made that change to avoid a sporadic visual glitch.) The entire *Storyboard* is then repeated forever. All but two of these *DoubleAnimation* objects target the *RadiusX* and *RadiusY* properties of the five *EllipseGeometry* objects, making them 25 pixels larger—that is, as large as the base value of the next larger circle.

At the same time, the *Opacity* property of the outermost circle is animated to fade out, and the innermost circle has it *StrokeThickness* property animated to make it seem as if it grows from nothing. The overall visual effect is that circles seem to be generated from the center, and then disappear once they reach the outside:

The next program is called DashOffsetAnimation, and it uses a *Path* to draw an infinity sign in landscape mode. The infinity sign includes two semicircles (at the far left and far right), each of which is drawn using two Bézier splines based on a well-known approximation.

A single Bézier curve approximates a quarter circle very well. For a circle centered at the point (0, 0) with a radius of 100, the lower-right quarter-circle arc begins at the point (100, 0) and goes clockwise to end at the point (0, 100). You can approximate that arc with a Bézier curve that begins at the point (100, 0) and ends at the point (0, 100) with the two control points (100, 55) and (55, 100). Continue that same pattern—I think of it as the "Bézier 55" rule—to construct an entire circle from four connected Bézier curves. The approximation is so good that some graphics systems actually implement circles using this technique.

The *Data* definition used below is Path Markup Syntax that starts with an M ("move") and then a C ("cubic Bézier") with two control points and an end point. But then it switches to S ("smooth Bézier"), which requires only the second control point and the end point. The S automatically uses the previous Bézier to determine a first control point that is collinear with the start point and previous control point.

The *StrokeDashArray* is set with the two points 0 and 1.5 indicating a dash length of 0 and a gap of 1.5. However, the *StrokeDashCap* is set to *Round*, so the dots are round and are separated by half the thickness of the line.

Silverlight Project: **DashOffsetAnimation**   File: **MainPage.xaml (excerpt)**

```
<Grid x:Name="ContentPanel" Grid.Row="1" Margin="12,0,12,0">
    <Path Name="path"
          HorizontalAlignment="Center"
          VerticalAlignment="Center"
          Stroke="{StaticResource PhoneAccentBrush}"
          StrokeThickness="23.98"
          StrokeDashArray="0 1.5"
          StrokeDashCap="Round"
          Data="M 100     0
                C  45     0,     0   45, 0 100
                S  45   200,   100  200
                S 200   150,   250  100
                S 345     0,   400    0
                S 500    45,   500  100
                S 455   200,   400  200
                S 300   150,   250  100
                S 155     0,   100    0">

        <Path.Triggers>
            <EventTrigger>
                <BeginStoryboard>
                    <Storyboard>
                        <DoubleAnimation Storyboard.TargetName="path"
                            Storyboard.TargetProperty="StrokeDashOffset"
```

```
                                                 From="0" To="1.5" Duration="0:0:1"
                                                 RepeatBehavior="Forever" />
                        </Storyboard>
                    </BeginStoryboard>
                </EventTrigger>
            </Path.Triggers>
        </Path>
    </Grid>
```

This *DoubleAnimation* targets the *StrokeDashOffset* property of the *Path*, which is normally zero. This is the property that indicates the location in the sequence of dots, dashes, and gaps that is aligned with the beginning of the line. The result is that the dots seem to travel continuously around the figure.

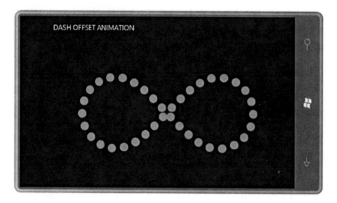

To avoid discontinuities when animating *StrokeDashOffset* in a closed path, the crucial number is the *StrokeThickness*. You want the total length of the line to be an integral multiple of the *StrokeDashArray* times the *StrokeThickness*. If *StrokeThickness* isn't anywhere close to the correct value, you'll see a kind of bubbling effect as partial dots are drawn; if it's very close to the correct value but not exact, you may see flickering.

AnimatedInfinity is another landscape program that uses that same Path Markup Syntax but colors the infinity sign with a *LinearGradientBrush* with the traditional colors of the rainbow:

Silverlight Project: AnimatedInfinity   File: MainPage.xaml (excerpt)

```
<Grid x:Name="ContentPanel" Grid.Row="1" Margin="12,0,12,0">
    <Path HorizontalAlignment="Center"
          VerticalAlignment="Center"
          StrokeThickness="25"
          Data="M 100    0
                C  45    0,    0  45, 0 100
                S  45  200,  100 200
                S 200  150,  250 100
```

```
                        S 345    0,   400    0
                        S 500   45,   500  100
                        S 455  200,   400  200
                        S 300  150,   250  100
                        S 155    0,   100    0">

        <Path.Stroke>
            <LinearGradientBrush SpreadMethod="Repeat">
                <LinearGradientBrush.Transform>
                    <TranslateTransform x:Name="translate" />
                </LinearGradientBrush.Transform>
                <LinearGradientBrush.GradientStops>
                    <GradientStop Offset="0.00" Color="Red" />
                    <GradientStop Offset="0.14" Color="Orange" />
                    <GradientStop Offset="0.28" Color="Yellow" />
                    <GradientStop Offset="0.42" Color="Green" />
                    <GradientStop Offset="0.56" Color="Blue" />
                    <GradientStop Offset="0.70" Color="Indigo" />
                    <GradientStop Offset="0.85" Color="Violet" />
                    <GradientStop Offset="1.00" Color="Red" />
                </LinearGradientBrush.GradientStops>
            </LinearGradientBrush>
        </Path.Stroke>
        <Path.Triggers>
            <EventTrigger>
                <BeginStoryboard>
                    <Storyboard>
                        <DoubleAnimation Storyboard.TargetName="translate"
                                         Storyboard.TargetProperty="X"
                                         From="0" To="625" Duration="0:0:2"
                                         RepeatBehavior="Forever" />

                    </Storyboard>
                </BeginStoryboard>
            </EventTrigger>
        </Path.Triggers>
    </Path>
</Grid>
```

The *Brush* defines a *Transform* property (although it's not often used), and this program sets it to a *TranslateTransform* and then animates it, making the colors continuously sweep across the figure:

You can also animate properties of type *Color*, which means you can animate brush colors. Here's a program that animates the *Color* properties in two *GradientStop* objects of a *LinearGradientBrush*:

Silverlight Project: GradientAnimation   File: **MainPage.xaml (excerpt)**

```
<Grid x:Name="ContentPanel" Grid.Row="1" Margin="12,0,12,0">
    <Grid HorizontalAlignment="Center"
          VerticalAlignment="Center">
        <TextBlock Text="GRADIENT"
                   FontSize="96"
                   FontWeight="Bold">
            <TextBlock.Foreground>
                <LinearGradientBrush>
                    <GradientStop x:Name="gradientStop1"
                                  Offset="0" Color="Red" />
                    <GradientStop x:Name="gradientStop2"
                                  Offset="1" Color="Blue" />
                </LinearGradientBrush>
            </TextBlock.Foreground>
        </TextBlock>

        <Grid.Triggers>
            <EventTrigger>
                <BeginStoryboard>
                    <Storyboard>
                        <ColorAnimation Storyboard.TargetName="gradientStop1"
                                        Storyboard.TargetProperty="Color"
                                        From="Red" To="Blue" Duration="0:0:11"
                                        AutoReverse="True"
                                        RepeatBehavior="Forever" />

                        <ColorAnimation Storyboard.TargetName="gradientStop2"
                                        Storyboard.TargetProperty="Color"
                                        From="Blue" To="Red" Duration="0:0:13"
                                        AutoReverse="True"
                                        RepeatBehavior="Forever" />
                    </Storyboard>
                </BeginStoryboard>
            </EventTrigger>
        </Grid.Triggers>
    </Grid>
</Grid>
```

The two animations are given prime-number periods of 11 seconds and 13 seconds so the overall cycle, including *AutoReverse*, lasts almost 5 minutes before it repeats.

Animating Attached Properties (or Not)

You can use Silverlight animations in a couple different ways to move an element around the screen. One way is to target a *TranslateTransform* set to the element's *RenderTransform* property. But programmers who are more comfortable with *Canvas* might want to animate the *Canvas.Left* and *Canvas.Top* attached properties. A special syntax is required to animate attached properties, but it's fairly simple.

This program defines a *Canvas* that is 450 pixels square, centers it in the content area, instantiates an *Ellipse* that is 50 pixels in size, and then moves that *Ellipse* around the perimeter of the *Canvas* in four seconds, repeated forever.

Silverlight Project: MoveOnCanvas   File: MainPage.xaml (excerpt)

```xml
<Grid x:Name="ContentPanel" Grid.Row="1" Margin="12,0,12,0">
    <Canvas Width="450" Height="450"
            HorizontalAlignment="Center"
            VerticalAlignment="Center">

        <Ellipse Name="ball"
                 Fill="{StaticResource PhoneAccentBrush}"
                 Width="50" Height="50" />

        <Canvas.Triggers>
            <EventTrigger>
                <BeginStoryboard>
                    <Storyboard RepeatBehavior="Forever">
                        <DoubleAnimationUsingKeyFrames
                                    Storyboard.TargetName="ball"
                                    Storyboard.TargetProperty="(Canvas.Left)">
                            <DiscreteDoubleKeyFrame KeyTime="0:0:0" Value="0" />
                            <LinearDoubleKeyFrame   KeyTime="0:0:1" Value="400" />
                            <DiscreteDoubleKeyFrame KeyTime="0:0:2" Value="400" />
                            <LinearDoubleKeyFrame   KeyTime="0:0:3" Value="0" />
                            <DiscreteDoubleKeyFrame KeyTime="0:0:4" Value="0" />
                        </DoubleAnimationUsingKeyFrames>

                        <DoubleAnimationUsingKeyFrames
                                    Storyboard.TargetName="ball"
                                    Storyboard.TargetProperty="(Canvas.Top)">
                            <DiscreteDoubleKeyFrame KeyTime="0:0:0" Value="0" />
                            <DiscreteDoubleKeyFrame KeyTime="0:0:1" Value="0" />
                            <LinearDoubleKeyFrame   KeyTime="0:0:2" Value="400" />
                            <DiscreteDoubleKeyFrame KeyTime="0:0:3" Value="400" />
                            <LinearDoubleKeyFrame   KeyTime="0:0:4" Value="0" />
                        </DoubleAnimationUsingKeyFrames>
                    </Storyboard>
                </BeginStoryboard>
            </EventTrigger>
        </Canvas.Triggers>
    </Canvas>
</Grid>
```

Notice that the *Storyboard.TargetName* is set to reference the *Ellipse* element, and the *Storyboard.TargetProperty* attributes are set to the strings "(Canvas.Left)" and "(Canvas.Top)". When targeting attached properties in an animation, put the fully-qualified property names in parentheses. Simple.

What isn't so simple—and you'll find the same problem with targeting *TranslateTransform*— is the complexity of moving an object in more than one dimension. You need to handle the *X* and *Y* coordinates separately, and this is often confusing. The approach I've used involves key frames. Both start with an unnecessary *DiscreteDoubleKeyFrame* that sets the property to zero, but the *DiscreteDoubleKeyFrame* objects and *LinearDoubleKeyFrame* objects alternate as the *Ellipse* makes it way around the edges of the *Canvas*.

It's usually much easier handling both X and Y coordinates in unison with *PointAnimation* or *PointAnimationUsingKeyFrames*. Of course, there are very few classes in Silverlight that define dependency properties of type *Point*, but those that do—in particular, the *Geometry* derivatives—are central to vector graphics.

Let's rewrite this program with a *DoubleAnimationUsingKeyFrames* to target the *Center* property of an *EllipseGeometry*:

Silverlight Project: MoveInGrid   File: MainPage.xaml (excerpt)

```
<Grid x:Name="ContentPanel" Grid.Row="1" Margin="12,0,12,0">
    <Grid Width="450" Height="450"
          HorizontalAlignment="Center"
          VerticalAlignment="Center">

        <Path Fill="{StaticResource PhoneAccentBrush}">
            <Path.Data>
                <EllipseGeometry x:Name="ballGeometry"
                                 RadiusX="25" RadiusY="25" />
            </Path.Data>
        </Path>

        <Grid.Triggers>
            <EventTrigger>
                <BeginStoryboard>
                    <Storyboard RepeatBehavior="Forever">
                        <PointAnimationUsingKeyFrames
                                    Storyboard.TargetName="ballGeometry"
                                    Storyboard.TargetProperty="Center">
                            <DiscretePointKeyFrame KeyTime="0:0:0" Value=" 25   25" />
                            <LinearPointKeyFrame   KeyTime="0:0:1" Value="425   25" />
                            <LinearPointKeyFrame   KeyTime="0:0:2" Value="425  425" />
                            <LinearPointKeyFrame   KeyTime="0:0:3" Value=" 25  425" />
                            <LinearPointKeyFrame   KeyTime="0:0:4" Value=" 25   25" />
                        </PointAnimationUsingKeyFrames>
                    </Storyboard>
                </BeginStoryboard>
```

```
            </BeginStoryboard>
          </EventTrigger>
        </Grid.Triggers>
    </Grid>
</Grid>
```

The coordinates have to be adjusted a bit because now we're positioning the center of the ball rather than its upper-left corner, but the progression of the animation is much clearer, and it's been reduced to one animation rather than two.

And now, the downside: Animations that target properties of type *Point* are *not* handled in the GPU on the render thread. If that's a concern, stick to animating properties of type *double*.

If you value fun more than performance, you can construct a *PathGeometry* using explicit *PathFigure*, *LineSegment*, *ArcSegment*, *BezierSegment*, and *QuadraticBezierSegment* objects, and every property of type *Point* can be an animation target.

Here's a program that stretches that concept to an extreme. It creates a circle from four Bézier splines, and then animates the various *Point* properties, turning the circle into a square and solving a geometric problem that's been bedeviling mathematicians since the days of Euclid:

Silverlight Project: SquaringTheCircle   File: **MainPage.xaml** (excerpt)

```
<Grid x:Name="ContentPanel" Grid.Row="1" Margin="12,0,12,0">
    <Path HorizontalAlignment="Center"
          VerticalAlignment="Center"
          Fill="{StaticResource PhoneAccentBrush}"
          Stroke="{StaticResource PhoneForegroundBrush}"
          StrokeThickness="3" >
        <Path.Data>
            <PathGeometry>
                <PathFigure x:Name="bezier1" IsClosed="True">
                    <BezierSegment x:Name="bezier2" />
                    <BezierSegment x:Name="bezier3" />
                    <BezierSegment x:Name="bezier4" />
                    <BezierSegment x:Name="bezier5" />
                </PathFigure>
                <PathGeometry.Transform>
                    <TransformGroup>
                        <ScaleTransform ScaleX="2" ScaleY="2" />
                        <RotateTransform Angle="45" />
                        <TranslateTransform X="200" Y="200" />
                    </TransformGroup>
                </PathGeometry.Transform>
            </PathGeometry>
        </Path.Data>
```

```xml
<Path.Triggers>
    <EventTrigger>
        <BeginStoryboard>
            <Storyboard RepeatBehavior="Forever"
                        AutoReverse="True" >
                <PointAnimation Storyboard.TargetName="bezier1"
                                Storyboard.TargetProperty="StartPoint"
                                From="0 100" To="0 125" />

                <PointAnimation Storyboard.TargetName="bezier2"
                                Storyboard.TargetProperty="Point1"
                                From="55 100" To="62.5 62.5" />

                <PointAnimation Storyboard.TargetName="bezier2"
                                Storyboard.TargetProperty="Point2"
                                From="100 55" To="62.5 62.5" />

                <PointAnimation Storyboard.TargetName="bezier2"
                                Storyboard.TargetProperty="Point3"
                                From="100 0" To="125 0" />

                <PointAnimation Storyboard.TargetName="bezier3"
                                Storyboard.TargetProperty="Point1"
                                From="100 -55" To="62.5 -62.5" />

                <PointAnimation Storyboard.TargetName="bezier3"
                                Storyboard.TargetProperty="Point2"
                                From="55 -100" To="62.5 -62.5" />

                <PointAnimation Storyboard.TargetName="bezier3"
                                Storyboard.TargetProperty="Point3"
                                From="0 -100" To="0 -125" />

                <PointAnimation Storyboard.TargetName="bezier4"
                                Storyboard.TargetProperty="Point1"
                                From="-55 -100" To="-62.5 -62.5" />

                <PointAnimation Storyboard.TargetName="bezier4"
                                Storyboard.TargetProperty="Point2"
                                From="-100 -55" To="-62.5 -62.5" />

                <PointAnimation Storyboard.TargetName="bezier4"
                                Storyboard.TargetProperty="Point3"
                                From="-100 0" To="-125 0" />

                <PointAnimation Storyboard.TargetName="bezier5"
                                Storyboard.TargetProperty="Point1"
                                From="-100 55" To="-62.5 62.5" />

                <PointAnimation Storyboard.TargetName="bezier5"
                                Storyboard.TargetProperty="Point2"
                                From="-55 100" To="-62.5 62.5" />
```

```
                    <PointAnimation Storyboard.TargetName="bezier5"
                                    Storyboard.TargetProperty="Point3"
                                    From="0 100" To="0 125" />
                </Storyboard>
            </BeginStoryboard>
        </EventTrigger>
    </Path.Triggers>
</Path>
</Grid>
```

Here's halfway between a square and a circle:

Splines and Key Frames

Three of the key-frame classes begin with the word *Spline*: *SplineDoubleKeyFrame*, *SplinePointKeyFrame*, and *SplineColorKeyFrame*. These classes have *KeyTime* and *Value* properties like the *Discrete* and *Linear* keyframes, but they also define a property named *KeySpline*. This property allows you to create a key frame that speeds up or slows down (or both) during its course but still ending at the correct value by the time *KeyTime* comes around. The change in velocity is governed by a Bézier spline.

KeySpline is a structure with two properties named *ControlPoint1* and *ControlPoint2* of type *Point*. The *X* and *Y* coordinates of each of these points must be between 0 and 1. A single

KeySpline object effectively describes a Bézier curve that begins at the point (0, 0) and ends at the point (1, 1) with these two control points. It is not possible to create an arbitrary Bézier curve under these constraints—for example, the curve can't make a loop—but you'll see you have a considerable amount of flexibility.

Conceptually, during the course of the key frame, the X coordinate of this spline represents normalized time, which changes linearly from 0 to 1. The Y coordinate is the normalized value of the animation, also changing from 0 to 1 but in a non-linear fashion.

Certainly the best way to get a feel for spline-based key frames is to experiment with them, and I have just the program. It's even called SplineKeyFrameExperiment:

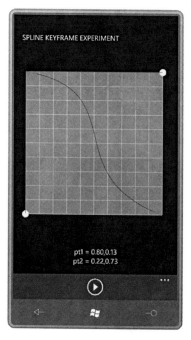

You can move the control points of the spline using the blue semi-translucent circles. The *ApplicationBar* has only one button labeled "animate":

Silverlight Project: SplineKeyFrameExperiment   File: MainPage.xaml (excerpt)

```
<phone:PhoneApplicationPage.ApplicationBar>
    <shell:ApplicationBar>
        <shell:ApplicationBarIconButton IconUri="/Images/appbar.transport.play.rest
.png"
                                        Text="animate"
                                        Click="OnAppbarAnimateButtonClick" />
    </shell:ApplicationBar>
</phone:PhoneApplicationPage.ApplicationBar>
```

When you press it, the white ball on the bottom of the grid moves linearly from left to right, representing the linear increase in time. The white ball at the right of the grid moves non-linearly from top to bottom based on the shape of the spline.

For purposes of simplicity, the layout of the screen is based on a grid with a fixed width and height of 400 pixels, so the program will need to be modified a bit for a smaller screen.

The content area begins with a gray 400-pixel square with horizontal and vertical grid lines every 40 pixels. Each grid line represents 0.1 units for displaying the spline.

Silverlight Project: SplineKeyFrameExperiment   File: MainPage.xaml (excerpt)

```xml
<Grid x:Name="ContentPanel" Grid.Row="1" Margin="12,0,12,0">
    <Grid.RowDefinitions>
        <RowDefinition Height="*" />
        <RowDefinition Height="Auto" />
    </Grid.RowDefinitions>

    <Grid Name="graphGrid"
          Grid.Row="0"
          HorizontalAlignment="Center"
          VerticalAlignment="Center">

        <!-- Background -->
        <Path Fill="#808080"
              Data="M 0 0 L 400 0, 400 400, 0 400 Z" />

        <!-- Horizontal lines -->
        <Polyline Stroke="{StaticResource PhoneForegroundBrush}"
                  Points="0 0 400 0" />
        <Polyline Stroke="{StaticResource PhoneForegroundBrush}"
                  Points="0 40 400 40" />
        <Polyline Stroke="{StaticResource PhoneForegroundBrush}"
                  Points="0 80 400 80" />
        <Polyline Stroke="{StaticResource PhoneForegroundBrush}"
                  Points="0 120 400 120" />
        <Polyline Stroke="{StaticResource PhoneForegroundBrush}"
                  Points="0 160 400 160" />
        <Polyline Stroke="{StaticResource PhoneForegroundBrush}"
                  Points="0 200 400 200" />
        <Polyline Stroke="{StaticResource PhoneForegroundBrush}"
                  Points="0 240 400 240" />
        <Polyline Stroke="{StaticResource PhoneForegroundBrush}"
                  Points="0 280 400 280" />
        <Polyline Stroke="{StaticResource PhoneForegroundBrush}"
                  Points="0 320 400 320" />
        <Polyline Stroke="{StaticResource PhoneForegroundBrush}"
                  Points="0 360 400 360" />
        <Polyline Stroke="{StaticResource PhoneForegroundBrush}"
                  Points="0 400 400 400" />
```

```
        <!-- Vertical lines -->
        <Polyline Stroke="{StaticResource PhoneForegroundBrush}"
                  Points="0 0 0 400" />
        <Polyline Stroke="{StaticResource PhoneForegroundBrush}"
                  Points="40 0 40 400" />
        <Polyline Stroke="{StaticResource PhoneForegroundBrush}"
                  Points="80 0 80 400" />
        <Polyline Stroke="{StaticResource PhoneForegroundBrush}"
                  Points="120 0 120 400" />
        <Polyline Stroke="{StaticResource PhoneForegroundBrush}"
                  Points="160 0 160 400" />
        <Polyline Stroke="{StaticResource PhoneForegroundBrush}"
                  Points="200 0 200 400" />
        <Polyline Stroke="{StaticResource PhoneForegroundBrush}"
                  Points="240 0 240 400" />
        <Polyline Stroke="{StaticResource PhoneForegroundBrush}"
                  Points="280 0 280 400" />
        <Polyline Stroke="{StaticResource PhoneForegroundBrush}"
                  Points="320 0 320 400" />
        <Polyline Stroke="{StaticResource PhoneForegroundBrush}"
                  Points="360 0 360 400" />
        <Polyline Stroke="{StaticResource PhoneForegroundBrush}"
                  Points="400 0 400 400" />
        ...
    </Grid>

    <TextBlock Name="txtblk"
               Grid.Row="1"
               TextAlignment="Center"
               Margin="0, 24" />
</Grid>
```

The *TextBlock* at the bottom is used to display the values of the two control points.

The markup below is for the Bézier curve that always begins at the upper-left of the grid, which represents the point (0, 0), and which ends at the bottom-right of the grid, representing the point (1, 1). The two control points (*Point1* and *Point2* of the *BezierSegment* object) are user-selectable.

This snippet of XAML also includes the two tangent lines from the end points to the control points. I would much prefer to bind the various properties of these elements to each other using data bindings, but in Silverlight 3 data binding targets must always be properties of elements, and these are properties of *PathSegment* derivatives.

Silverlight Project: SplineKeyFrameExperiment   File: MainPage.xaml (excerpt)

```
<!-- Bezier curve -->
<Path Stroke="{StaticResource PhoneBackgroundBrush}">
    <Path.Data>
```

```
            <PathGeometry>
                <PathFigure StartPoint="0 0">
                    <BezierSegment x:Name="bezierSegment"
                                   Point1="200 80"
                                   Point2="200 320"
                                   Point3="400 400" />
                </PathFigure>
            </PathGeometry>
        </Path.Data>
</Path>

<!-- Tangent lines -->
<Path Stroke="{StaticResource PhoneAccentBrush}">
    <Path.Data>
        <PathGeometry>
            <PathFigure StartPoint="0 0">
                <LineSegment x:Name="tangentLine1"
                             Point="200 80" />
            </PathFigure>
        </PathGeometry>
    </Path.Data>
</Path>

<Path Stroke="{StaticResource PhoneAccentBrush}">
    <Path.Data>
        <PathGeometry>
            <PathFigure StartPoint="400 400">
                <LineSegment x:Name="tangentLine2"
                             Point="200 320" />
            </PathFigure>
        </PathGeometry>
    </Path.Data>
</Path>
```

Here are the two little white balls that appear on the bottom and right, one representing time and the other representing the animated object:

Silverlight Project: SplineKeyFrameExperiment   File: MainPage.xaml (excerpt)

```
<!-- Balls -->
<Path Fill="{StaticResource PhoneForegroundBrush}">
    <Path.Data>
        <EllipseGeometry x:Name="timeBall"
                         RadiusX="10"
                         RadiusY="10"
                         Center="0 400" />
    </Path.Data>
</Path>

<Path Fill="{StaticResource PhoneForegroundBrush}">
```

```
    <Path.Data>
        <EllipseGeometry x:Name="animaBall"
                         RadiusX="10"
                         RadiusY="10"
                         Center="400 0" />
    </Path.Data>
</Path>
```

You can't see it when the program is inactive, but two lines—one horizontal and one vertical—connect the small balls with the spline curve. These lines track the spline curve when the small balls are moving:

Silverlight Project: SplineKeyFrameExperiment   File: MainPage.xaml (excerpt)

```
<!-- Tracking lines -->
<Line x:Name="timeTrackLine"
    Stroke="{StaticResource PhoneBackgroundBrush}"
    Y2="400" />

<Line x:Name="animaTrackLine"
    Stroke="{StaticResource PhoneBackgroundBrush}"
    X2="400" />
```

Finally, two semi-transparent circles respond to touch input and are used to drag the control points within the grid:

Silverlight Project: SplineKeyFrameExperiment   File: MainPage.xaml (excerpt)

```
<!-- Draggers -->
<Path Name="dragger1"
      Fill="{StaticResource PhoneAccentBrush}"
      Opacity="0.5">
    <Path.Data>
        <EllipseGeometry x:Name="dragger1Geometry"
                         RadiusX="50"
                         RadiusY="50"
                         Center="200 80" />
    </Path.Data>
</Path>

<Path Name="dragger2"
      Fill="{StaticResource PhoneAccentBrush}"
      Opacity="0.5">
    <Path.Data>
        <EllipseGeometry x:Name="dragger2Geometry"
                         RadiusX="50"
```

```
                         RadiusY="50"
                         Center="200 320" />
        </Path.Data>
    </Path>
```

The centers of these two *EllipseGeometry* objects provide the two control points of the *KeySpline* object. In the code-behind file, the constructor initializes the *TextBlock* at the bottom with the values, normalized to the range of 0 to 1:

Silverlight Project: SplineKeyFrameExperiment   File: MainPage.xaml.cs (excerpt)

```
public partial class MainPage : PhoneApplicationPage
{
    public MainPage()
    {
        InitializeComponent();
        UpdateTextBlock();
    }

    void UpdateTextBlock()
    {
        txtblk.Text = String.Format("pt1 = {0:F2}\npt2 = {1:F2}",
                            NormalizePoint(dragger1Geometry.Center),
                            NormalizePoint(dragger2Geometry.Center));
    }

    Point NormalizePoint(Point pt)
    {
        return new Point(pt.X / 400, pt.Y / 400);
    }
    ...
}
```

With the absence of data bindings in the XAML, the *OnManipulationDelta* override must modify two additional properties of type *Point* (plus the *TextBlock*) every time one of the semi-transparent circles is dragged:

Silverlight Project: SplineKeyFrameExperiment   File: MainPage.xaml.cs (excerpt)

```
protected override void OnManipulationDelta(ManipulationDeltaEventArgs args)
{
    Point translation = args.DeltaManipulation.Translation;

    if (args.ManipulationContainer == dragger1)
    {
        Point pt = new Point(Clamp(dragger1Geometry.Center.X + translation.X),
```

```
                                    Clamp(dragger1Geometry.Center.Y + translation.Y));

            dragger1Geometry.Center = pt;
            bezierSegment.Point1 = pt;
            tangentLine1.Point = pt;
            UpdateTextBlock();
        }
        if (args.ManipulationContainer == dragger2)
        {
            Point pt = new Point(Clamp(dragger2Geometry.Center.X + translation.X),
                                 Clamp(dragger2Geometry.Center.Y + translation.Y));

            dragger2Geometry.Center = pt;
            bezierSegment.Point2 = pt;
            tangentLine2.Point = pt;
            UpdateTextBlock();
        }

        base.OnManipulationDelta(args);
    }

    double Clamp(double input)
    {
        return Math.Max(0, Math.Min(400, input));
    }
```

When the button in the *ApplicationBar* is pressed, the program needs to set four different animations with identical *KeySpline* objects and then start the *Storyboard* going:

Silverlight Project: SplineKeyFrameExperiment   File: MainPage.xaml.cs (excerpt)

```
void OnAppbarAnimateButtonClick(object sender, EventArgs args)
{
    Point controlPoint1 = NormalizePoint(dragger1Geometry.Center);
    Point controlPoint2 = NormalizePoint(dragger2Geometry.Center);

    splineKeyFrame1.KeySpline = new KeySpline();
    splineKeyFrame1.KeySpline.ControlPoint1 = controlPoint1;
    splineKeyFrame1.KeySpline.ControlPoint2 = controlPoint2;

    splineKeyFrame2.KeySpline = new KeySpline();
    splineKeyFrame2.KeySpline.ControlPoint1 = controlPoint1;
    splineKeyFrame2.KeySpline.ControlPoint2 = controlPoint2;

    splineKeyFrame3.KeySpline = new KeySpline();
    splineKeyFrame3.KeySpline.ControlPoint1 = controlPoint1;
    splineKeyFrame3.KeySpline.ControlPoint2 = controlPoint2;

    splineKeyFrame4.KeySpline = new KeySpline();
    splineKeyFrame4.KeySpline.ControlPoint1 = controlPoint1;
```

```
    splineKeyFrame4.KeySpline.ControlPoint2 = controlPoint2;

    storyboard.Begin();
}
```

That storyboard is defined in the *Resources* collection of the page:

Silverlight Project: SplineKeyFrameExperiment File: MainPage.xaml (excerpt)

```
<phone:PhoneApplicationPage.Resources>
    <Storyboard x:Name="storyboard"
                SpeedRatio="0.25">
        <PointAnimation Storyboard.TargetName="timeBall"
                        Storyboard.TargetProperty="Center"
                        From="0 400" To="400 400" Duration="0:0:1" />

        <DoubleAnimation Storyboard.TargetName="timeTrackLine"
                         Storyboard.TargetProperty="X1"
                         From="0" To="400" Duration="0:0:1" />

        <DoubleAnimation Storyboard.TargetName="timeTrackLine"
                         Storyboard.TargetProperty="X2"
                         From="0" To="400" Duration="0:0:1" />

        <DoubleAnimation Storyboard.TargetName="animaTrackLine"
                         Storyboard.TargetProperty="X1"
                         From="0" To="400" Duration="0:0:1" />

        <PointAnimationUsingKeyFrames Storyboard.TargetName="animaBall"
                                      Storyboard.TargetProperty="Center">
            <DiscretePointKeyFrame KeyTime="0:0:0" Value="400 0" />
            <SplinePointKeyFrame x:Name="splineKeyFrame1"
                                 KeyTime="0:0:1" Value="400 400" />
        </PointAnimationUsingKeyFrames>

        <DoubleAnimationUsingKeyFrames Storyboard.TargetName="timeTrackLine"
                                       Storyboard.TargetProperty="Y1">
            <DiscreteDoubleKeyFrame KeyTime="0:0:0" Value="0" />
            <SplineDoubleKeyFrame x:Name="splineKeyFrame2"
                                  KeyTime="0:0:1" Value="400" />
        </DoubleAnimationUsingKeyFrames>

        <DoubleAnimationUsingKeyFrames Storyboard.TargetName="animaTrackLine"
                                       Storyboard.TargetProperty="Y1">
            <DiscreteDoubleKeyFrame KeyTime="0:0:0" Value="0" />
            <SplineDoubleKeyFrame x:Name="splineKeyFrame3"
                                  KeyTime="0:0:1" Value="400" />
        </DoubleAnimationUsingKeyFrames>

        <DoubleAnimationUsingKeyFrames Storyboard.TargetName="animaTrackLine"
```

```
                                        Storyboard.TargetProperty="Y2">
                <DiscreteDoubleKeyFrame KeyTime="0:0:0" Value="0" />
                <SplineDoubleKeyFrame x:Name="splineKeyFrame4"
                                      KeyTime="0:0:1" Value="400" />
            </DoubleAnimationUsingKeyFrames>
        </Storyboard>
    </phone:PhoneApplicationPage.Resources>
```

Try it out: If you set both control points to (1, 0) you get an animation that starts off slow and then gets very fast. Setting both control points to (0, 1) has the opposite effect. Set the first control point to (1, 0) and the second to (0, 1) and you get an animation that starts off slow, then gets fast, and ends up slow. Switch them and get the opposite effect.

Of course, you don't have to use the extremes. You'll probably want to find values that have a more subtle effect. You can simulate free fall with values of (0.25, 0) and (0.6, 0.2), for example. For an object moving up and decelerating from the effects of gravity, subtract each of those coordinates from 1.

Yes, I have an example.

The Bouncing Ball Problem

Here's some XAML designed for a large-screen phone that moves a ball up and down:

```
<Grid x:Name="ContentPanel" Grid.Row="1">
    <Path Fill="Red">
        <Path.Data>
            <EllipseGeometry RadiusX="25" RadiusY="25" />
        </Path.Data>

        <Path.RenderTransform>
            <TranslateTransform x:Name="translate" X="240" />
        </Path.RenderTransform>
    </Path>

    <Path Fill="{StaticResource PhoneAccentBrush}"
        Data="M 100 625 L 380 625, 380 640, 100 640 Z" />

    <Grid.Triggers>
        <EventTrigger>
            <BeginStoryboard>
                <Storyboard RepeatBehavior="Forever">
                    <DoubleAnimation Storyboard.TargetName="translate"
                                     Storyboard.TargetProperty="Y"
                                     From="50" To="600" Duration="0:0:1"
                                     AutoReverse="True"
                                     RepeatBehavior="Forever" />
                </Storyboard>
```

```
            </BeginStoryboard>
          </EventTrigger>
      </Grid.Triggers>
  </Grid>
```

There are two *Path* elements here. The first one is the red ball; the second is a "floor" on which the ball is supposed to bounce.

The ball has a *TranslateTransform* applied to it: the *X* property is fixed to keep the ball horizontally centered; the *Y* property is animated between 50 and 600 and back again. But it really doesn't look like it's bouncing because it has the same velocity throughout its movement. It doesn't obey the laws of physics. In the real world, obeying the laws of physics is pretty much mandatory, but in computer graphics, often more work is involved.

Getting a better bouncing effect is possible with a *DoubleAnimationUsingKeyFrames* object with a *SplineDoubleKeyFrame* that speeds up the ball as it's falling and slows it down as it's rising. These use the spline control points that approximate free fall:

```
<Storyboard RepeatBehavior="Forever">
    <DoubleAnimationUsingKeyFrames Storyboard.TargetName="translate"
                                   Storyboard.TargetProperty="Y">
        <DiscreteDoubleKeyFrame KeyTime="0:0:0" Value="50" />
        <SplineDoubleKeyFrame    KeyTime="0:0:1" Value="600"
                                 KeySpline="0.25 0, 0.6 0.2" />
        <SplineDoubleKeyFrame    KeyTime="0:0:2" Value="50"
                                 KeySpline="0.75 1, 0.4 0.8" />
    </DoubleAnimationUsingKeyFrames>
</Storyboard>
```

This is much better. But it's still not quite right, and the problem involves what happens when the ball hits the ground. The ball is at maximum velocity when it hits the ground, and then immediately it's at maximum velocity going in the opposite direction.

In reality, this is not the way it works. When the ball hits the ground, it decelerates and compresses somewhat, and then the decompression of the ball causes it to accelerate again. Can that be simulated? Why not?

Pausing the ball momentarily as it hits the ground is an additional key frame. I decided the ball will be compressed and uncompressed over the course of a tenth second (which is probably a bit exaggerated), so I adjusted the times somewhat:

```
<Storyboard RepeatBehavior="Forever">
    <DoubleAnimationUsingKeyFrames Storyboard.TargetName="translate"
                                   Storyboard.TargetProperty="Y">
        <DiscreteDoubleKeyFrame KeyTime="0:0:0" Value="50" />
        <SplineDoubleKeyFrame    KeyTime="0:0:1" Value="600"
                                 KeySpline="0.25 0, 0.6 0.2" />
        <DiscreteDoubleKeyFrame KeyTime="0:0:1.1" Value="600" />
        <SplineDoubleKeyFrame    KeyTime="0:0:2.1" Value="50"
                                 KeySpline="0.75 1, 0.4 0.8" />
    </DoubleAnimationUsingKeyFrames>
</Storyboard>
```

The *TranslateTransform* starts at time zero with a value of 50. Over the next second it goes to 600 while speeding up. Over the next 10th second, it remains at 600, and then goes back up to 50 during the next second. The new animation now lasts 2.1 seconds rather than 2 seconds.

Of course, by itself, this looks even worse. But let's add a *ScaleTransform* to the *Path* defining the ball:

```
<Path.RenderTransform>
    <TransformGroup>
        <ScaleTransform x:Name="scale" CenterY="25" />
        <TranslateTransform x:Name="translate" X="240" />
    </TransformGroup>
</Path.RenderTransform>
```

The untransformed center of the ball is the point (0, 0), and the two radii are 25 pixels, so the middle bottom of the ball is the point (0, 25). That's the point that touches the floor, and the point that should stay in the same spot during the *ScaleTransform*, which is the reason for setting *CenterY* to 25. *CenterX* is 0 by default.

Here are the two additional animations for momentarily flattening out the ball:

```
<Storyboard RepeatBehavior="Forever">
    . . .
    <DoubleAnimationUsingKeyFrames
                Storyboard.TargetName="scale"
                Storyboard.TargetProperty="ScaleX">
        <DiscreteDoubleKeyFrame KeyTime="0:0:1"    Value="1" />
        <SplineDoubleKeyFrame   KeyTime="0:0:1.05" Value="1.5"
                                KeySpline="0.75 1, 0.4 0.8" />
        <SplineDoubleKeyFrame   KeyTime="0:0:1.1"  Value="1"
                                KeySpline="0.25 0, 0.6 0.2" />
    </DoubleAnimationUsingKeyFrames>

    <DoubleAnimationUsingKeyFrames
                Storyboard.TargetName="scale"
                Storyboard.TargetProperty="ScaleY">
        <DiscreteDoubleKeyFrame KeyTime="0:0:1"    Value="1" />
        <SplineDoubleKeyFrame   KeyTime="0:0:1.05" Value="0.66"
                                KeySpline="0.75 1, 0.4 0.8" />
        <SplineDoubleKeyFrame   KeyTime="0:0:1.1"  Value="1"
                                KeySpline="0.25 0, 0.6 0.2" />
    </DoubleAnimationUsingKeyFrames>
</Storyboard>
```

Between 1 second and 1.05 seconds, the ball's width grows by 50% and its height decreases by a third. That's reversed over the next 0.05 seconds, at which point the ball is normal and it begins its upward path.

The final version of the BouncingBall program also applies a *RadialGradientBrush* to the ball:

Silverlight Project: BouncingBall   File: MainPage.xaml (excerpt)

```xaml
<Grid x:Name="ContentPanel" Grid.Row="1">
    <Path>
        <Path.Data>
            <EllipseGeometry RadiusX="25" RadiusY="25" />
        </Path.Data>

        <Path.Fill>
            <RadialGradientBrush GradientOrigin="0.35 0.35"
                                 Center="0.35 0.35">
                <GradientStop Offset="0" Color="White" />
                <GradientStop Offset="1" Color="Red" />
            </RadialGradientBrush>
        </Path.Fill>

        <Path.RenderTransform>
            <TransformGroup>
                <ScaleTransform x:Name="scale" CenterY="25" />
                <TranslateTransform x:Name="translate" X="240" />
            </TransformGroup>
        </Path.RenderTransform>
    </Path>

    <Path Fill="{StaticResource PhoneAccentBrush}"
          Data="M 100 625 L 380 625, 380 640, 100 640 Z" />

    <Grid.Triggers>
        <EventTrigger>
            <BeginStoryboard>
                <Storyboard RepeatBehavior="Forever">
                    <DoubleAnimationUsingKeyFrames
                            Storyboard.TargetName="translate"
                            Storyboard.TargetProperty="Y">
                        <DiscreteDoubleKeyFrame KeyTime="0:0:0" Value="50" />
                        <SplineDoubleKeyFrame   KeyTime="0:0:1" Value="600"
                                                KeySpline="0.25 0, 0.6 0.2" />
                        <DiscreteDoubleKeyFrame KeyTime="0:0:1.1" Value="600" />
                        <SplineDoubleKeyFrame   KeyTime="0:0:2.1" Value="50"
                                                KeySpline="0.75 1, 0.4 0.8" />
                    </DoubleAnimationUsingKeyFrames>

                    <DoubleAnimationUsingKeyFrames
                            Storyboard.TargetName="scale"
                            Storyboard.TargetProperty="ScaleX">
                        <DiscreteDoubleKeyFrame KeyTime="0:0:1"    Value="1" />
                        <SplineDoubleKeyFrame   KeyTime="0:0:1.05" Value="1.5"
                                                KeySpline="0.75 1, 0.4 0.8" />
                        <SplineDoubleKeyFrame   KeyTime="0:0:1.1"  Value="1"
                                                KeySpline="0.25 0, 0.6 0.2" />
                    </DoubleAnimationUsingKeyFrames>

                    <DoubleAnimationUsingKeyFrames
```

```
                                  Storyboard.TargetName="scale"
                                  Storyboard.TargetProperty="ScaleY">
                  <DiscreteDoubleKeyFrame KeyTime="0:0:1"    Value="1" />
                  <SplineDoubleKeyFrame   KeyTime="0:0:1.05" Value="0.66"
                                          KeySpline="0.75 1, 0.4 0.8" />
                  <SplineDoubleKeyFrame   KeyTime="0:0:1.1"  Value="1"
                                          KeySpline="0.25 0, 0.6 0.2" />
              </DoubleAnimationUsingKeyFrames>
          </Storyboard>
      </BeginStoryboard>
    </EventTrigger>
  </Grid.Triggers>
</Grid>
```

Here it is in action:

The Easing Functions

Defining key frames with splines is easy in one sense—there are only four numbers involved—but also hard: You need to approximate a certain desired effect with a Bézier spline, and that's not always obvious.

You might prefer something more "canned" that gives you an overall impression of adherence to physical law without requiring a lot of thought. This is the purpose of the animation *easing functions*. These are classes that derive from *EasingFunctionBase* with common types of transitions that you can add to the beginning or end (or both beginning and end) of your animations. *DoubleAnimation*, *PointAnimation*, and *ColorAnimation* all have properties named *EasingFunction* of type *EasingFunctionBase*. There are also *EasingDoubleKeyFrame*, *EasingColorKeyFrame*, and *EasingPointKeyFrame* classes.

EasingFunctionBase defines just one property: *EasingMode* of the enumeration type *EasingMode*, either *EaseOut* (the default, which uses the transition only at the end of the animation), *EaseIn*, or *EaseInOut*. Eleven classes derive from *EasingFunctionBase* and you can derive your own if you want to have even more control and power.

The project named TheEasingLife lets you choose among the eleven *EasingFunctionBase* derivatives to see their effect on a simple *PointAnimation* involving a ball-like object. The content area is populated with two *Polyline* elements and a *Path* but no coordinates are supplied; that's done in code.

Silverlight Project: TheEasingLife   File: MainPage.xaml (excerpt)

```xml
<Grid x:Name="ContentPanel" Grid.Row="1" Margin="12,0,12,0">
    <Polyline Name="polyline1"
            Stroke="{StaticResource PhoneForegroundBrush}" />

    <Polyline Name="polyline2"
            Stroke="{StaticResource PhoneForegroundBrush}" />

    <Path Fill="{StaticResource PhoneAccentBrush}">
        <Path.Data>
            <EllipseGeometry x:Name="ballGeometry"
                            RadiusX="25"
                            RadiusY="25" />
        </Path.Data>
    </Path>
</Grid>
```

The *Resources* collection contains a *Storyboard* with a *PointAnimation* targeting the *Center* property of the *EllipseGeometry*. The *PointAnimation* is given a *Duration* property but nothing else:

Silverlight Project: TheEasingLife   File: MainPage.xaml (excerpt)

```xml
<phone:PhoneApplicationPage.Resources>
    <Storyboard x:Name="storyboard"
            Completed="OnStoryboardCompleted">
        <PointAnimation x:Name="pointAnimation"
                Storyboard.TargetName="ballGeometry"
```

```
                            Storyboard.TargetProperty="Center"
                            Duration="0:0:2" />
        </Storyboard>
    </phone:PhoneApplicationPage.Resources>
```

Notice that a handler is set for the *Completed* event of the *Storyboard*. This *Completed* event is defined by *Timeline* and is often convenient for letting a program know when an animation has completed.

The *ApplicationBar* has two buttons for "animate" and "settings":

Silverlight Project: TheEasingLife   File: MainPage.xaml (excerpt)

```
<phone:PhoneApplicationPage.ApplicationBar>
    <shell:ApplicationBar>
        <shell:ApplicationBarIconButton IconUri="/Images/appbar.transport.play.rest.
png"
                                        Text="animate"
                                        Click="OnAppbarPlayButtonClick" />
        <shell:ApplicationBarIconButton IconUri="/Images/appbar.feature.settings.rest.
png"
                                        Text="settings"
                                        Click="OnAppbarSettingsButtonClick" />
    </shell:ApplicationBar>
</phone:PhoneApplicationPage.ApplicationBar>
```

The coordinates for the two *Polyline* elements and *EllipseGeometry* are set during the *Loaded* event handler based on the size of the content panel. The ball is intended to be animated between a *Polyline* at the top and a *Polyline* at the bottom; the actual points are stored in the *ballPoints* array. The direction (going down or going up) is governed by the *isForward* field.

Silverlight Project: TheEasingLife   File: MainPage.xaml.cs (excerpt)

```
public partial class MainPage : PhoneApplicationPage
{
    PointCollection ballPoints = new PointCollection();
    bool isForward = true;

    public MainPage()
    {
        InitializeComponent();
        Loaded += OnMainPageLoaded;
    }
```

```
        public EasingFunctionBase EasingFunction { get; set; }

        void OnMainPageLoaded(object sender, RoutedEventArgs args)
        {
            double left = 100;
            double right = ContentPanel.ActualWidth - 100;
            double center = ContentPanel.ActualWidth / 2;
            double top = 100;
            double bottom = ContentPanel.ActualHeight - 100;

            polyline1.Points.Add(new Point(left, top));
            polyline1.Points.Add(new Point(right, top));

            polyline2.Points.Add(new Point(left, bottom));
            polyline2.Points.Add(new Point(right, bottom));

            ballPoints.Add(new Point(center, top));
            ballPoints.Add(new Point(center, bottom));

            ballGeometry.Center = ballPoints[1 - Convert.ToInt32(isForward)];
        }
        . . .
}
```

Notice also the public property named *EasingFunction*. When you press the "animate"
button, the *Click* handler fills in the missing pieces of the *PointAnimation* (including the
EasingFunction property) and starts it going:

Silverlight Project: TheEasingLife   **File: MainPage.xaml.cs (excerpt)**

```
void OnAppbarPlayButtonClick(object sender, EventArgs args)
{
    pointAnimation.From = ballPoints[1 - Convert.ToInt32(isForward)];
    pointAnimation.To = ballPoints[Convert.ToInt32(isForward)];
    pointAnimation.EasingFunction = EasingFunction;

    storyboard.Begin();
}

void OnStoryboardCompleted(object sender, EventArgs args)
{
    isForward ^= true;
}
```

The *Completed* handler toggles the *isForward* value in preparation for the
next animation.

When you press the "settings" button, the program navigates to the *EasingFunctionDialog* page that lets you choose which easing function you want:

Silverlight Project: TheEasingLife   File: MainPage.xaml.cs (excerpt)

```
void OnAppbarSettingsButtonClick(object sender, EventArgs args)
{
    NavigationService.Navigate(new Uri("/EasingFunctionDialog.xaml", UriKind
.Relative));
}

protected override void OnNavigatedFrom(NavigationEventArgs args)
{
    if (args.Content is EasingFunctionDialog)
    {
        (args.Content as EasingFunctionDialog).EasingFunction = EasingFunction;
    }
    base.OnNavigatedTo(args);
}
```

When the *OnNavigatedFrom* override determines that a transition from *MainPage* to *EasingFunctionDialog* page is in progress, it transfers the contents of its *EasingFunction* property to *EasingFunctionDialog*, which also has a public *EasingFunction* property.

The content area of the EasingFunctionDialog.xaml file just has a *StackPanel* in a *ScrollViewer*:

Silverlight Project: TheEasingLife   File: EasingFunctionDialog.xaml (excerpt)

```
<Grid x:Name="ContentPanel" Grid.Row="1" Margin="12,0,12,0">
    <ScrollViewer>
        <StackPanel Name="stack" />
    </ScrollViewer>
</Grid>
```

In its *OnNavigatedTo* override, the dialog uses reflection to fill up the *StackPanel* with *RadioButton* elements. By the time *OnNavigatedTo* is called, the *EasingFunction* property already has a valid value set by the *OnNavigatedFrom* override in *MainPage*:

Silverlight Project: TheEasingLife   File: EasingFunctionDialog.xaml.cs (excerpt)

```
public partial class EasingFunctionDialog : PhoneApplicationPage
{
    public EasingFunctionDialog()
    {
        InitializeComponent();
    }
```

```
    public EasingFunctionBase EasingFunction { get; set; }

    ...

    protected override void OnNavigatedTo(NavigationEventArgs args)
    {
        // Create "None" RadioButton
        RadioButton radio = new RadioButton();
        radio.Content = "None";
        radio.IsChecked = (EasingFunction == null);
        radio.Checked += OnRadioButtonChecked;
        stack.Children.Add(radio);

        Assembly assembly = Assembly.Load("System.Windows");

        // Create RadioButton for each easing function
        foreach (Type type in assembly.GetTypes())
            if (type.IsPublic && type.IsSubclassOf(typeof(EasingFunctionBase)))
            {
                radio = new RadioButton();
                radio.Content = type.Name;
                radio.Tag = type;
                radio.IsChecked = (EasingFunction != null &&
                                   EasingFunction.GetType() == type);
                radio.Checked += OnRadioButtonChecked;
                stack.Children.Add(radio);
            }
        base.OnNavigatedTo(args);
    }
    ...
}
```

Notice how the *Tag* property of each *RadioButton* is a *Type* object indicating the *EasingFunctionBase* derivative associated with that button. When the user presses one of the *RadioButton* elements, that *Tag* property is used to make a new object of that type:

Silverlight Project: TheEasingLife   File: **EasingFunctionDialog.xaml.cs** (excerpt)

```
void OnRadioButtonChecked(object sender, RoutedEventArgs args)
{
    Type type = (sender as RadioButton).Tag as Type;

    if (type == null)
    {
        EasingFunction = null;
    }
    else
    {
        ConstructorInfo constructor = type.GetConstructor(Type.EmptyTypes);
        EasingFunction = constructor.Invoke(null) as EasingFunctionBase;
    }
}
```

Finally, when you're finished choosing the easing function you want, you press the Back button and the dialog's *OnNavigatedFrom* override is called. This responds by storing the current selection back in *MainPage*:

Silverlight Project: TheEasingLife **File: EasingFunctionDialog.xaml.cs** (excerpt)

```
protected override void OnNavigatedFrom(NavigationEventArgs args)
{
    if (args.Content is MainPage)
    {
        (args.Content as MainPage).EasingFunction = EasingFunction;
    }
    base.OnNavigatedFrom(args);
}
```

Keep in mind that these *EasingFunctionBase* derivatives have all default property settings, including the *EasingMode* property that restricts the effect only to the end of the animation. You'll find that a couple of these effects—specifically *BackEase* and *ElasticEase*—actually overshoot the destination. While this doesn't matter in many cases, for some properties it might result in illegal values. You don't want to set *Opacity* to values outside the range of 0 and 1, for example.

Animating Perspective Transforms

The types of transforms you set with *RenderTransform* are all examples of two-dimensional *affine* transforms. Affine transforms are very well behaved and just a little dull: Straight lines are always transformed to straight lines, ellipses are always transformed to ellipses, and squares are always transformed to parallelograms. Two lines that are parallel before the transform are still parallel after the transform.

Silverlight 3 introduced a new *UIElement* property named *Projection* that allows setting *non-affine* transforms on graphical objects, text, controls, and media. Non-affine transforms do not preserve parallelism.

The type of non-affine transform allowed in Silverlight 3 is still represented by a matrix multiplication, and it still has restrictions on what it can do. Straight lines are always transformed to straight lines, and a square is always transformed into a simple convex quadrilateral. By "quadrilateral" I mean a four-sided figure (also called a tetragon or quadrangle); by "simple" I mean that the sides don't intersect except at their vertices; by "convex" I mean that the internal angles at each vertex are less than 180 degrees.

This type of non-affine transform is very useful for creating *taper* transforms, where opposite sides of a square or rectangle taper somewhat in one direction. Objects appear to be somewhat three dimensional because part of the object seems further away from our eyes—an effect called a *perspective* projection.

In a sense, the *Projection* property gives Silverlight a little bit of "pseudo 3D." It's not a real 3D system because there's no way to define objects in 3D space, no concept of cameras, lights, or shading, and—perhaps most crucially—no clipping of objects based on their arrangement in 3D space.

Still, working with the *Projection* transform requires the programmer to begin thinking about three dimensions and especially about 3D rotation. Fortunately, the developers of Silverlight have made common and simple use of the *Projection* property fairly easy.

You can set this *Projection* property to one of two objects: You can be mathematical and flexible by using *Matrix3DProjection*, or you can do as I'll do here and take the easy way out with *PlaneProjection*. Although *PlaneProjection* defines twelve settable properties, you can pretty much limit yourself to six of them.

The three crucial properties of *PlaneProjection* are *RotationX*, *RotationY*, and *RotationX*, which you can set to angle values to cause rotation around the X axis (which extends in a positive direction from left to right), the Y axis (which extends from top to bottom), and the Z axis (which comes out of the screen towards the viewer).

You can anticipate the direction of rotation using the right-hand rule: Point your thumb in the direction of the positive axis. (For X, that's to the right, for Y it's down, for Z, it's toward you.) The curve that your other fingers make indicates the direction of rotation for positive rotation angles. Negative angles rotate in the opposite direction.

A composite rotation depends on the order in which the individual rotations are applied. When you use *PlaneProjection*, you are sacrificing some flexibility in these rotations. *PlaneProjection* always applies *RotationX* first, then *RotationY*, and finally *RotationZ*, but in many cases you only need set one of these properties. As with *RenderTransform*, *Projection* doesn't affect layout. The layout system always sees an untransformed and unprojected element.

RotationX, *RotationY*, and *RotationZ* are all backed by dependency properties, so they can all be animation targets, as demonstrated by the PerspectiveRotation program. The content area contains a *TextBlock* with a *PlaneProjection* object set to its *Projection* property, and three buttons:

Silverlight Project: PerspectiveRotation   File: MainPage.xaml (excerpt)

```
<Grid x:Name="ContentPanel" Grid.Row="1" Margin="12,0,12,0">
    <Grid.RowDefinitions>
        <RowDefinition Height="*" />
        <RowDefinition Height="Auto" />
    </Grid.RowDefinitions>
```

```
<Grid.ColumnDefinitions>
    <ColumnDefinition Width="*" />
    <ColumnDefinition Width="*" />
    <ColumnDefinition Width="*" />
</Grid.ColumnDefinitions>

<TextBlock Name="txtblk"
           Grid.Row="0" Grid.Column="0" Grid.ColumnSpan="3"
           Text="ROTATE"
           FontSize="{StaticResource PhoneFontSizeHuge}"
           Foreground="{StaticResource PhoneAccentBrush}"
           HorizontalAlignment="Center"
           VerticalAlignment="Center">
    <TextBlock.Projection>
        <PlaneProjection x:Name="planeProjection" />
    </TextBlock.Projection>
</TextBlock>

<Button Grid.Row="1" Grid.Column="0"
        Content="Rotate X"
        Click="RotateXClick" />

<Button Grid.Row="1" Grid.Column="1"
        Content="Rotate Y"
        Click="RotateYClick" />

<Button Grid.Row="1" Grid.Column="2"
        Content="Rotate Z"
        Click="RotateZClick" />
</Grid>
```

Three storyboards defined in the *Resources* collection are defined to animate the *RotationX,*
RotationY, and *RotationZ* properties of the *PlaneProjection* object:

Silverlight Project: PerspectiveRotation   File: MainPage.xaml (excerpt)

```
<phone:PhoneApplicationPage.Resources>
    <Storyboard x:Name="rotateX">
        <DoubleAnimation Storyboard.TargetName="planeProjection"
                         Storyboard.TargetProperty="RotationX"
                         From="0" To="360" Duration="0:0:5" />
    </Storyboard>

    <Storyboard x:Name="rotateY">
        <DoubleAnimation Storyboard.TargetName="planeProjection"
                         Storyboard.TargetProperty="RotationY"
                         From="0" To="360" Duration="0:0:5" />
    </Storyboard>

    <Storyboard x:Name="rotateZ">
```

```
        <DoubleAnimation Storyboard.TargetName="planeProjection"
                         Storyboard.TargetProperty="RotationZ"
                         From="0" To="360" Duration="0:0:5" />
    </Storyboard>
</phone:PhoneApplicationPage.Resources>
```

The buttons simply start the corresponding storyboards:

Silverlight Project: PerspectiveRotation File: **MainPage.xaml.cs (excerpt)**

```
void RotateXClick(object sender, RoutedEventArgs args)
{
    rotateX.Begin();
}

void RotateYClick(object sender, RoutedEventArgs args)
{
    rotateY.Begin();
}

void RotateZClick(object sender, RoutedEventArgs args)
{
    rotateZ.Begin();
}
```

Here's rotation around the Y axis:

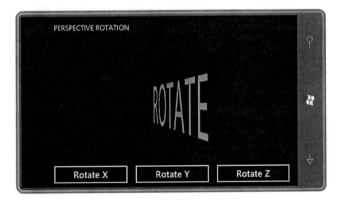

The animations are slow enough that you can click multiple buttons and see the interactions. It almost looks as if the text is tumbling through the weightlessness of space.

In 2D space, rotation is relative to a point; in 3D space, rotation is relative to a line, commonly referred to as an "axis of rotation." But the *PlaneProjection* class prefers to treat this center of rotation using three numbers—the properties *CenterOfRotationX*, *CenterOfRotationY*, and *CenterOfRotationZ*. In effect, these three numbers define a 3D point that remains unchanged during rotation. *CenterOfRotationX* does not affect rotation around the X axis, and similarly for the other two properties.

The *CenterOfRotationX* and *CenterOfRotationY* properties are relative coordinates based on the size of the element being rotated, where (0, 0) is the upper-left corner. The default values are 0.5, indicating the center of the element.

If you set *CenterOfRotationX* to 0, the *RotationY* property causes the element to rotate around its left side. If *CenterOfRotationY* is set to 1, then the *RotationX* property causes the element to be rotated around its bottom.

The *CenterOfRotationZ* property is in absolute coordinates—pixels, in other words—where 0 is the plane of the screen and positive coordinates come out of the screen toward the user. For purposes of its internal calculations, the viewer (you) is assumed to be 1000 pixels in front of the screen. In PerspectiveRotation, try setting the *CenterOfRotationZ* property of *PlaneProjection* to 200:

```
<TextBlock.Projection>
    <PlaneProjection x:Name="planeProjection"
                     CenterOfRotationZ="200" />
</TextBlock.Projection>
```

Now try the "Rotate X" and "RotateY" buttons: You'll see the text sweep around as if it's leaving the screen (where the Z coordinate is 0) and circling around a Z value of 200, curving in front of the viewer at a Z value of 400. A *CenterOfRotationZ* value greater than 500 will cause projections to stop working right. The projected object will get a Z value of 1000 and strike the viewer right on the nose.

The other properties of *PlaneProjection* cause translation in the X, Y, and Z directions: Conceptually, the *LocalOffsetX*, *LocalOffsetY*, and *LocalOffsetZ* properties are applied first, then the element is rotated, then *GlobalOffsetX*, *GlobalOffsetY*, and *GlobalOffsetZ* properties are applied.

Try setting *LocalOffsetX* or *GlobalOffsetX* to 200. In either case, the unrotated text is moved to the right by 200 pixels. But *GlobalOffsetX* is more like the whole screen shifting right. Try setting *LocalOffsetX* and rotate the text around the Y axis. The actual offset will begin at the right, and shift to the left, and then back to the right.

You can use animated projection transforms for small effects or for big effects. An example of a big effect is to change the way a new page in your program comes into view. The SweepIntoView program has a MainPage.xaml file containing just a little text:

Silverlight Project: SweepIntoView   File: MainPage.xaml (excerpt)

```
<Grid x:Name="ContentPanel" Grid.Row="1" Margin="12,0,12,0">
    <TextBlock Text="Touch to go to second page"
```

```
                     HorizontalAlignment="Center"
                     VerticalAlignment="Center" />
   </Grid>
```

The code-behind file uses touch to navigate to Page2.xaml:

Silverlight Project: SweepIntoView   File: MainPage.xaml.cs (excerpt)

```
protected override void OnManipulationStarted(ManipulationStartedEventArgs args)
{
    this.NavigationService.Navigate(new Uri("/Page2.xaml", UriKind.Relative));

    args.Complete();
    args.Handled = true;
    base.OnManipulationStarted(args);
}
```

For some variety (and to see more clearly what's happening) Page2.xaml colors its content
area with an accented background:

Silverlight Project: SweepIntoView   File: Page2.xaml (excerpt)

```
<Grid x:Name="ContentPanel" Grid.Row="1" Margin="12,0,12,0"
      Background="{StaticResource PhoneAccentBrush}">
    <TextBlock Text="Touch to go back"
               HorizontalAlignment="Center"
               VerticalAlignment="Center" />
</Grid>
```

The code-behind file also has an *OnManipulationStarted* override:

Silverlight Project: SweepIntoView   File: Page2.xaml.cs (excerpt)

```
protected override void OnManipulationStarted(ManipulationStartedEventArgs args)
{
    this.NavigationService.GoBack();

    args.Complete();
    args.Handled = true;
    base.OnManipulationStarted(args);
}
```

But what makes this program different is some additional markup in the Page2.xaml file. This ensures that the page just doesn't come on the stage in a sudden pop, but dramatically sweeps into view:

Silverlight Project: SweepIntoView   File: Page2.xaml (excerpt)

```
<phone:PhoneApplicationPage.Projection>
    <PlaneProjection x:Name="planeProjection"
                        CenterOfRotationX="0" />
</phone:PhoneApplicationPage.Projection>

<phone:PhoneApplicationPage.Triggers>
    <EventTrigger>
        <BeginStoryboard>
            <Storyboard>
                <DoubleAnimation Storyboard.TargetName="planeProjection"
                        Storyboard.TargetProperty="RotationY"
                        From="-90" To="0" Duration="0:0:01" />
            </Storyboard>
        </BeginStoryboard>
    </EventTrigger>
</phone:PhoneApplicationPage.Triggers>
```

The *PlaneProjection* is set to the *Projection* property of the whole *PhoneApplicationPage* element, and the animation is triggered when the page is first loaded. The animation makes the *RotationY* property go from –90 degrees to zero, with a *CenterOfRotationX* equal to zero. This causes the page to sweep in almost like a door:

Animations and Property Precedence

The sample code for this chapter includes a little program called ButtonSetAndAnimate that doesn't do anything particularly useful except to illustrate how animation fits into dependency property precedence.

The XAML file contains a *Slider* with a range of 0 to 100, a *TextBlock* showing the *Slider* value, and four buttons:

Silverlight Project: ButtonSetAndAnimate   File: MainPage.xaml (excerpt)

```
<Grid x:Name="ContentPanel" Grid.Row="1" Margin="12,0,12,0">
    <Grid.RowDefinitions>
        <RowDefinition Height="Auto" />
        <RowDefinition Height="*" />
        <RowDefinition Height="Auto" />
        <RowDefinition Height="Auto" />
        <RowDefinition Height="Auto" />
    </Grid.RowDefinitions>

    <Grid.ColumnDefinitions>
        <ColumnDefinition Width="*" />
        <ColumnDefinition Width="*" />
    </Grid.ColumnDefinitions>

    <TextBlock Grid.Row="0" Grid.Column="0" Grid.ColumnSpan="2"
            Text="{Binding ElementName=slider, Path=Value}"
            HorizontalAlignment="Center"
            Margin="24" />

    <Slider Name="slider"
            Grid.Row="1" Grid.Column="0" Grid.ColumnSpan="2"
            Minimum="0" Maximum="100"
            Orientation="Horizontal"
            VerticalAlignment="Center" />

    <Button Grid.Row="2" Grid.Column="0"
            Content="Set to 0"
            Click="OnSetToZeroClick" />

    <Button Grid.Row="2" Grid.Column="1"
            Content="Set to 100"
            Click="OnSetToOneHundredClick" />

    <Button Grid.Row="3" Grid.Column="0" Grid.ColumnSpan="2"
            Content="Animate to 50"
            HorizontalAlignment="Center"
            Click="OnAnimateTo50Click" />

    <Button Grid.Row="4" Grid.Column="0" Grid.ColumnSpan="2"
```

```
                        Content="Set Maximum to 25"
                        HorizontalAlignment="Center"
                        Click="OnSetMaxTo40Click" />
    </Grid>
```

Also in the XAML file is an animation that targets the *Value* property of the *Slider*.

Silverlight Project: ButtonSetAndAnimate   File: MainPage.xaml (excerpt)

```
<phone:PhoneApplicationPage.Resources>
    <Storyboard x:Name="storyboard">
        <DoubleAnimation Storyboard.TargetName="slider"
                         Storyboard.TargetProperty="Value"
                         To="50" Duration="0:0:5" />
    </Storyboard>
</phone:PhoneApplicationPage.Resources>
```

Handlers for the four buttons are in the code-behind file:

Silverlight Project: ButtonSetAndAnimate   File: MainPage.xaml.cs (excerpt)

```
public partial class MainPage : PhoneApplicationPage
{
    public MainPage()
    {
        InitializeComponent();
    }

    void OnSetToZeroClick(object sender, RoutedEventArgs args)
    {
        slider.Value = 0;
    }

    void OnSetToOneHundredClick(object sender, RoutedEventArgs args)
    {
        slider.Value = 100;
    }

    void OnAnimateTo50Click(object sender, RoutedEventArgs args)
    {
        storyboard.Begin();
    }

    void OnSetMaxTo40Click(object sender, RoutedEventArgs e)
    {
        slider.Maximum = 25;
    }
}
```

Here's the program:

You can manipulate the *Slider* with your finger and you can also use the topmost two buttons to set the *Slider* value to its minimum or maximum. So far, so good. Now click the "Animate to 50" button.

As the *Slider* is animated and moving to the center position, try overriding that movement with your finger or by pressing the "Set to 0" or "Set to 100" buttons. You can't do it. The animation has precedence over local settings, which means that the chart of dependency property precedence (last encountered in Chapter 11) must be supplemented by putting animations at the very top:

> **Animations** have precedence over
>
> **Local Settings** which have precedence over
>
> **Style Settings**, which have precedence over the
>
> **Theme Style**, which has precedence over
>
> **Property Inheritance**, which has precedence over
>
> **Default Values**

This is as it should be. Animations must have precedence over local settings or they wouldn't work on properties that are simply initialized to some value.

After the animation has concluded, you'll discover that you can now manipulate the *Slider* both manually and with the first two buttons. This behavior is not correct and not in accordance with documentation. With the default *FillBehavior* setting of *HoldEnd*, the *Slider* should actually be frozen after the animation has concluded. The *Slider* should continue to reflect the final value of the animation.

Is there something more powerful than animations? Yes there is, but it's probably not something you'd immediately consider, and you probably won't find any examples outside the realm of *Slider* and *ScrollBar*.

Set the *Slider* to its maximum value, and press the "Animate to 50" button again. As the *Slider* is approaching 50, click the "Set Maximum to 25" button. That sets the *Maximum* property of the *Slider* to 25 and immediately halts the animation. And once again, it seems logical. No matter what an animation does, it makes no sense whatsoever for a *Slider* to have a *Value* that is outside the range of *Minimum* and *Maximum*. This is an example of property coercion:

Property Coercion has precedence over

Animations which have precedence over

Local Settings which have precedence over

Style Settings, which have precedence over the

Theme Style, which has precedence over

Property Inheritance, which has precedence over

Default Values

In theory, values of templated properties also fit into this chart between local settings and style settings, but these are hard to differentiate, so this is the final version of this chart in this book.

Chapter 16
The Two Templates

Silverlight templates are visual trees of elements and controls defined in XAML. What makes these visual trees special is that they function as patterns or molds to create identical visual trees. Templates are almost always defined as resources, so they are shared, and they almost always contain bindings, so they can be associated with different objects and assume different appearances.

You'll use one type of template (the *DataTemplate*) to render objects that otherwise have no visual representation. Use another type (the *ControlTemplate*) to customize the visual appearance of controls. There's actually a third type (*ItemsPanelTemplate*) but this one is very simple and has a special use that I'll discuss in the next chapter.

The template is easily one of the most powerful features in Silverlight, and perhaps one of the most difficult. For that reason, many developers swear by Expression Blend to generate their templates. This chapter will demonstrate how to write templates by hand so you'll be in a better position to understand Expression Blend output if you later decide to go that route.

ContentControl and *DataTemplate*

In Chapter 10 I demonstrated how you can assign the *Content* property of a *ContentControl* derivative (such as a *Button*) to almost any object. If that object derives from *FrameworkElement* (such as *TextBlock* or *Image*), then the element is displayed inside the *ContentControl*. But you can also set the *Content* property to an object that does not derive from *FrameworkElement*. Here's the *Content* of a *Button* set to a *RadialGradientBrush*:

```
<Button HorizontalAlignment="Center"
        VerticalAlignment="Center">

    <RadialGradientBrush>
        <GradientStop Offset="0" Color="Blue" />
        <GradientStop Offset="1" Color="AliceBlue" />
    </RadialGradientBrush>

</Button>
```

Normally you'd set the *Foreground* property of a *Button* to a brush, or the *Background* property, or perhaps the *BorderBrush* property. But setting the *Content* property to a brush? What does that even mean?

If the object set to the *Content* property of a *ControlControl* does not derive from *FrameworkElement*, it is rendered with its *ToString* method, and if the class has no *ToString* override, the fully-qualified class name is displayed, so this particular *Button* looks like this:

This is not exactly something you want to use to show off your programming skills to your friends.

Here's the *Clock* class from Chapter 12 inside a *Button*:

```
<Button HorizontalAlignment="Center"
        VerticalAlignment="Center">

    <petzold:Clock />

</Button>
```

And this *Button* doesn't display much of value either:

Yet, there is a way to display this object intelligently. The solution is an object of type *DataTemplate* set to the *ContentTemplate* property of the *Button*. Here's the syntax with an empty *DataTemplate*:

```
<Button HorizontalAlignment="Center"
        VerticalAlignment="Center">

    <petzold:Clock />
```

```
    <Button.ContentTemplate>
        <DataTemplate>

        </DataTemplate>
    </Button.ContentTemplate>
</Button>
```

ContentTemplate is one of two properties defined by *ContentControl* and inherited by *Button*; the other property is *Content* itself.

And now all you need to do is supply a visual tree within the *DataTemplate* tags that contains bindings to properties in the *Clock* class:

```
<Button HorizontalAlignment="Center"
        VerticalAlignment="Center">

    <petzold:Clock />

    <Button.ContentTemplate>
        <DataTemplate>
            <StackPanel>
                <TextBlock Text="The time is:"
                            TextAlignment="Center" />
                <StackPanel Orientation="Horizontal"
                            HorizontalAlignment="Center">
                    <TextBlock Text="{Binding Hour}" />
                    <TextBlock Text=":" />
                    <TextBlock Text="{Binding Minute}" />
                    <TextBlock Text=":" />
                    <TextBlock Text="{Binding Second}" />
                </StackPanel>
            </StackPanel>
        </DataTemplate>
    </Button.ContentTemplate>
</Button>
```

The *Button* uses this visual tree to display the *Content* object. The bindings in this visual tree are often rather simple. The data bindings don't need a *Source* property because the *DataContext* associated with this visual tree is the object set to the *Content* property. The bindings shown here require only *Path* properties, and the "Path=" part of the *Binding* markup extension can be omitted.

The displayed time is dynamically updated. Of course, the bindings for the *Minute* and *Second* properties should really reference a string-formatting converter to always be displayed with two digits.

The existence of the *DataTemplate* means that you really *can* set the content of a *Button* to a *RadialGradientBrush* just as long as you define a visual tree that makes use of that brush in the *DataTemplate*:

```
<Button HorizontalAlignment="Center"
        VerticalAlignment="Center">

    <RadialGradientBrush>
        <GradientStop Offset="0" Color="Blue" />
        <GradientStop Offset="1" Color="AliceBlue" />
    </RadialGradientBrush>

    <Button.ContentTemplate>
        <DataTemplate>
            <Ellipse Width="100"
                     Height="100"
                     Fill="{Binding}" />
        </DataTemplate>
    </Button.ContentTemplate>
</Button>
```

Notice the *Fill* property setting of the *Ellipse*. It's just a *Binding* markup extension with no *Path* settings set. The *Fill* property doesn't want a particular property of the *RadialGradientBrush*. It wants the whole thing. Here's the *Button*:

You can use this technique with any *ContentControl* derivative, or even *ContentControl* itself.

Let's define that *DataTemplate* in the *Resources* collection of a MainPage.xaml files:

Silverlight Project: ContentControlWithDataTemplates   File: MainPage.xaml (excerpt)

```
<phone:PhoneApplicationPage.Resources>
    <DataTemplate x:Key="brushTemplate">
        <Ellipse Width="100"
                 Height="100"
                 Fill="{Binding}" />
    </DataTemplate>
</phone:PhoneApplicationPage.Resources>
```

Let's give the content panel of this page three *Button* instances, each with its
ContentTemplate property set to that resource, but with three different types of *Brush*
objects set to the *Content* property:

Silverlight Project: ContentControlWithDataTemplates   File: MainPage.xaml (excerpt)

```
<Grid x:Name="ContentPanel" Grid.Row="1" Margin="12,0,12,0">
    <StackPanel>
        <Button HorizontalAlignment="Center"
                ContentTemplate="{StaticResource brushTemplate}">
            <SolidColorBrush Color="{StaticResource PhoneAccentColor}" />
        </Button>

        <Button HorizontalAlignment="Center"
                ContentTemplate="{StaticResource brushTemplate}">
            <RadialGradientBrush>
                <GradientStop Offset="0" Color="Blue" />
                <GradientStop Offset="1" Color="AliceBlue" />
            </RadialGradientBrush>
        </Button>

        <Button HorizontalAlignment="Center"
                ContentTemplate="{StaticResource brushTemplate}">
            <LinearGradientBrush>
                <GradientStop Offset="0" Color="Pink" />
                <GradientStop Offset="1" Color="Red" />
            </LinearGradientBrush>
        </Button>
    </StackPanel>
</Grid>
```

Here's the result:

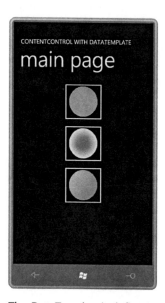

The *DataTemplate* is defined as a resource so it is shared among all *Button* controls. However, a separate visual tree based on that template is built for each *Button*. Somewhere within the visual tree for each *Button* is an *Ellipse* with a binding to the *SolidColorBrush* set to the *Content* property.

Sharing the *DataTemplate* among a few *Button* controls is convenient, but it doesn't really show off the sheer power of this technique. Imagine that you can define a *DataTemplate* for displaying the items in a *ListBox* or *ComboBox*. I'll show you how to do that in the next chapter.

Examining the Visual Tree

I've been mentioning visual trees. Let's look at a few.

The ButtonTree program lets you dump the visual tree for a rather conventional *Button* (one with its *Content* just set to text), a *Button* with its *Content* property set to an *Image* element, and two others with their *Content* properties set to the *RadialGradientBrush* and *Clock* (as shown in the examples above) together with a *ContentTemplate*. The program's content *Grid* displays each *Button* in a cell:

Silverlight Project: **ButtonTree**   File: **MainPage.xaml** (excerpt)

```
<Grid x:Name="ContentPanel" Grid.Row="1" Margin="12,0,12,0">
    <Grid.RowDefinitions>
        <RowDefinition Height="Auto" />
        <RowDefinition Height="Auto" />
        <RowDefinition Height="*" />
    </Grid.RowDefinitions>
```

```
<Grid.ColumnDefinitions>
    <ColumnDefinition Width="*" />
    <ColumnDefinition Width="*" />
</Grid.ColumnDefinitions>

<Button Grid.Row="0" Grid.Column="0"
        Content="Click to Dump"
        HorizontalAlignment="Center"
        VerticalAlignment="Center"
        Click="OnButtonClick" />

<Button Grid.Row="0" Grid.Column="1"
        HorizontalAlignment="Center"
        VerticalAlignment="Center"
        Click="OnButtonClick">
    <Image Source="ApplicationIcon.png"
           Stretch="None" />
</Button>

<Button Grid.Row="1" Grid.Column="0"
        HorizontalAlignment="Center"
        VerticalAlignment="Center"
        Click="OnButtonClick">
    <Button.Content>
        <RadialGradientBrush>
            <GradientStop Offset="0" Color="Blue" />
            <GradientStop Offset="1" Color="AliceBlue" />
        </RadialGradientBrush>
    </Button.Content>

    <Button.ContentTemplate>
        <DataTemplate>
            <Ellipse Width="100"
                     Height="100"
                     Fill="{Binding}" />
        </DataTemplate>
    </Button.ContentTemplate>
</Button>

<Button Grid.Row="1" Grid.Column="1"
        HorizontalAlignment="Center"
        VerticalAlignment="Center"
        Click="OnButtonClick">
    <Button.Content>
        <petzold:Clock />
    </Button.Content>

    <Button.ContentTemplate>
        <DataTemplate>
            <StackPanel>
                <TextBlock Text="The time is:"
                           TextAlignment="Center" />
                <StackPanel Orientation="Horizontal"
                            HorizontalAlignment="Center">
```

```
                    <TextBlock Text="{Binding Hour}" />
                    <TextBlock Text=":" />
                    <TextBlock Text="{Binding Minute}" />
                    <TextBlock Text=":" />
                    <TextBlock Text="{Binding Second}" />
                </StackPanel>
            </StackPanel>
        </DataTemplate>
    </Button.ContentTemplate>
</Button>

<ScrollViewer Grid.Row="2" Grid.Column="0" Grid.ColumnSpan="2"
              HorizontalScrollBarVisibility="Auto">
    <StackPanel Name="stackPanel" />
</ScrollViewer>
</Grid>
```

Way down at the bottom is a *StackPanel* inside a *ScrollViewer* for displaying the visual tree. The code-behind file uses the static *VisualTreeHelper* class for enumerating an element's children in a recursive method, and then displays their names in a hierarchical list:

Silverlight Project: ButtonTree   File: MainPage.xaml.cs (excerpt)

```
void OnButtonClick(object sender, RoutedEventArgs args)
{
    Button btn = sender as Button;
    stackPanel.Children.Clear();
    DumpVisualTree(btn, 0);
}

void DumpVisualTree(DependencyObject parent, int indent)
{
    TextBlock txtblk = new TextBlock();
    txtblk.Text = String.Format("{0}{1}", new string(' ', 4 * indent),
                                          parent.GetType().Name);
    stackPanel.Children.Add(txtblk);

    int numChildren = VisualTreeHelper.GetChildrenCount(parent);

    for (int childIndex = 0; childIndex < numChildren; childIndex++)
    {
        DependencyObject child = VisualTreeHelper.GetChild(parent, childIndex);
        DumpVisualTree(child, indent + 1);
    }
}
```

Click the button in the upper-left corner that has its *Content* set to text and the program displays the visual tree of the *Button*:

The *Border* element is no surprise; it's clearly visible in the actual *Button* as is the *TextBlock* used to display the text. The first *Grid* hosting the *Border* is obviously a single-cell *Grid*; later in this chapter you'll see the purpose of that *Grid*. The purpose of the *Grid* hosting the *TextBlock* is not so obvious. If you set the *Content* of the *Button* to an explicit *TextBlock*, that second *Grid* disappears, and the tree looks more like the one for the *Button* with its *Content* property set to an *Image* element:

The portion of the visual tree up to an including the *ContentPresenter* defines the appearance of the standard *Button*. (Soon you'll see how that's the part that can be replaced by setting the control's *Template* property to an object of type *ControlTemplate*.) Everything after the *ContentPresenter* is used to display the content of the *Button*. Here's the tree when the *Content* property is set to a *RadialGradientBrush* but the *ContentTemplate* is set to an *Ellipse* referencing that brush:

If you're familiar with control templates from the Windows Presentation Foundation or the web version of Silverlight, you undoubtedly expect to see the *ContentPresenter*. That's a *FrameworkElement* derivative used specifically for hosting content. It is the *ContentPresenter* that formats some objects as text in the absence of a *DataTemplate*, or actually applies a *DataTemplate*. But you may be a little puzzled about the *ContentControl*. I was puzzled as well for awhile. A *Button* derives from *ContentControl*, but that doesn't necessarily mean that the visual tree of a *Button* should contain another *ContentControl*! I'll have a little more to say about the peculiar appearance of *ContentControl* later in this chapter.

Finally, here's the visual tree resulting from the more extensive *DataTemplate* for displaying the *Clock* object:

For any control that derives from *ContentControl*, you now know how to define the portion of the visual tree following the *ContentPresenter*. Now let's see how you can redefine the top part of this visual tree.

ControlTemplate Basics

A *DataTemplate* allows you to customize the display of content in a *ContentControl*. The *ControlTemplate*—which you can set to the *Template* property of any *Control*—allows you to customize the appearance of the control itself—what's commonly referred to as the control "chrome." These two different purposes are summarized in the following table:

Property	Property Type	Purpose
Template	*ControlTemplate*	customizes display of control "chrome"
ContentTemplate	*DataTemplate*	customizes display of content

Keep in mind that the *ContentTemplate* property is defined by *ContentControl* and is only something you'll find only in classes that derive from *ContentControl*. But the *Template* property is defined by *Control*, and it's presence is perhaps the primary distinction between controls and *FrameworkElement* derivatives like *TextBlock* and *Image*.

Whenever you think you need a custom control, you should ask yourself if it is truly a new control you need, or if it's merely a new look for an existing control. For example, suppose you need a control that has a particular appearance, and when you tap it, it changes appearance, and then you tap it again, it goes back to the original appearance. This is a *ToggleButton* with just different visuals—a different *ControlTemplate*.

As with styles, very often templates are defined as resources. Also as with *Style*, *ControlTemplate* requires a *TargetType*:

```
<ControlTemplate x:Key="btnTemplate" TargetType="Button">
    . . .
</ControlTemplate>
```

It is very common to see a *Template* defined as part of a *Style*:

```
<Style x:Key="btnStyle" TargetType="Button">
    <Setter Property="Margin" Value="6" />
    <Setter Property="Template">
        <Setter.Value>
            <ControlTemplate TargetType="Button">
                . . .
            </ControlTemplate>
        </Setter.Value>
    </Setter>
</Style>
```

Notice that property-element syntax is used for the *Setter* that sets the *Template* property to an object of type *ControlTemplate*. Defining a template as part of a style is a very common approach because generally you want to set some properties of the control to make them more conducive with the template you're building. These *Setter* tags effectively redefine the default property values for the styled and templated control, but they can still be overridden with local settings on the actual control.

Let's create a custom *Button*. This new *Button* will retain the full functionality of the familiar *Button* except that you (the programmer) will have total control over its appearance. Of course, to keep it simple, the new *Button* won't look all that different from the normal *Button*! But it will show you the concepts involved.

Here's a standard *Button* with text content and alignment set so it takes up only as much space as it needs to display that content:

```
<Button Content="Click me!"
        HorizontalAlignment="Center"
        VerticalAlignment="Center">
</Button>
```

To experiment with the *ControlTemplate* with greatest ease, let's not define the *ControlTemplate* as a resource but break out the *Template* property as a property-element of the *Button* and set that to a *ControlTemplate*:

```
<Button Content="Click me!"
        HorizontalAlignment="Center"
        VerticalAlignment="Center">
    <Button.Template>
        <ControlTemplate TargetType="Button">

        </ControlTemplate>
    </Button.Template>
</Button>
```

As soon as you set the *Template* property to an empty *ControlTemplate*, the button itself disappears. A visual tree defining the appearance of the control no longer exists. That visual tree is what you'll be putting in the *ControlTemplate*. Just to make sure that we haven't done anything serious damaging, let's stick a *TextBlock* in the *ControlTemplate*:

```
<Button Content="Click me!"
        HorizontalAlignment="Center"
        VerticalAlignment="Center">
    <Button.Template>
        <ControlTemplate TargetType="Button">
            <TextBlock Text="temporary" />
        </ControlTemplate>
    </Button.Template>
</Button>
```

Now the *Button* consists solely of the word "temporary." It doesn't have any visual feedback when you touch it, but otherwise it's a fully functional button. It's seriously flawed, of course, because the *Button* should really be displaying "Click me!" but that will be fixed soon.

You can put a *Border* around the *TextBlock*:

```
<Button Content="Click me!"
        HorizontalAlignment="Center"
        VerticalAlignment="Center">
    <Button.Template>
        <ControlTemplate TargetType="Button">
            <Border BorderBrush="{StaticResource PhoneAccentBrush}"
                    BorderThickness="6">
                <TextBlock Text="temporary" />
            </Border>
        </ControlTemplate>
    </Button.Template>
</Button>
```

Here's what it looks like:

But it's really not a good idea to hard-code property values like this in the template, particularly if you're going to be sharing that template in multiple controls. It particularly doesn't make sense to hard-code *BorderBrush* and *BorderThickness* in the template because the *Control* class itself defines *BorderBrush* and *BorderThickness* properties, and if we really want a border around the button, we should set those properties in the *Button* rather than the template because we might want to share this template among multiple buttons and set different border brushes and border thickness.

So, let's move those properties from the template to the button itself:

```
<Button Content="Click me!"
        HorizontalAlignment="Center"
        VerticalAlignment="Center"
        BorderBrush="{StaticResource PhoneAccentBrush}"
        BorderThickness="6">
    <Button.Template>
        <ControlTemplate TargetType="Button">
            <Border>
                <TextBlock Text="temporary" />
            </Border>
        </ControlTemplate>
    </Button.Template>
</Button>
```

Unfortunately, now we've lost the properties in the visual tree of the template, so the border has now disappeared and it doesn't seem like much of an improvement. The border in the template in not automatically inheriting the properties of *BorderBrush* and *BorderThickness* set on the button. Those are not inheritable properties.

What we need is a binding so the properties of the *Border* in the template get set from properties in the *Button*. It's a special type of binding that has its own markup extension. It's called a *TemplateBinding*:

```
<Button Content="Click me!"
        HorizontalAlignment="Center"
        VerticalAlignment="Center"
        BorderBrush="{StaticResource PhoneAccentBrush}"
        BorderThickness="6">
    <Button.Template>
        <ControlTemplate TargetType="Button">
            <Border BorderBrush="{TemplateBinding BorderBrush}"
                    BorderThickness="{TemplateBinding BorderThickness}">
                <TextBlock Text="temporary" />
            </Border>
        </ControlTemplate>
    </Button.Template>
</Button>
```

What the *TemplateBinding* means is that the properties of this particular element in the visual tree of the template—specifically, the *BorderBrush* and *BorderThickness* properties of the *Border* element—are bound to values set on properties in the control itself. The *Button* now has a border colored with the accent brush:

The *TemplateBinding* is syntactically very simple. It always targets a dependency property in the visual tree of the template. It always references a property of the control on which the template is applied. There is nothing else that can go in the *TemplateBinding* markup extension. *TemplateBinding* is only found in visual trees defined within a *ControlTemplate*.

On the other hand, there is nothing all that special about *TemplateBinding*. It is actually a shortcut, and when you see the longer version, you'll be glad it exists. The attribute setting

```
BorderBrush="{TemplateBinding BorderBrush}"
```

is a short-cut for

```
BorderBrush="{Binding RelativeSource={RelativeSource TemplatedParent},
                      Path=BorderBrush}"
```

This binding is on a *Border*, and the *RelativeSource* syntax refers to another element in the tree relative to this *Border*. The *TemplatedParent* is the *Button* on which the template is applied, so the binding is referencing the *BorderBrush* of that *Button*. (Makes sense, no?) You'll want to use this alternative to *TemplateBinding* if you need to establish a two-way binding on a property in the template because *TemplateBinding* is one-way only and doesn't allow a *Mode* setting.

Back to the template at hand: Now that we've established a *TemplateBinding* on the *BorderBrush* and *BorderThickness*, another issue has arisen. Perhaps we've decided that we want this *Button* to have a border that is 6 pixels wide colored with the accent brush, but you'll only get those values if the *Button* contains explicit settings of the *BorderBrush* and *BorderThickness* properties. It would be nice if these properties did not need to be set on the *Button*. In other words, we want the *Button* to have default values of these properties that might be overridden by local settings.

This can be done by setting the desired default properties in a *Style*. For convenience, I've defined such a *Style* directly on the *Button*:

```
<Button Content="Click me!"
        HorizontalAlignment="Center"
        VerticalAlignment="Center">
    <Button.Style>
        <Style TargetType="Button">
            <Setter Property="BorderBrush" Value="{StaticResource PhoneAccentBrush}" />
            <Setter Property="BorderThickness" Value="6" />
        </Style>
    </Button.Style>

    <Button.Template>
        <ControlTemplate TargetType="Button">
            <Border BorderBrush="{TemplateBinding BorderBrush}"
                    BorderThickness="{TemplateBinding BorderThickness}">
                <TextBlock Text="temporary" />
            </Border>
```

```
            </ControlTemplate>
        </Button.Template>
</Button>
```

Now the template picks up some default values from the *Style* but those settings can be overridden by setting them locally on the button. (If you don't want the properties to be overridden by local settings—if you want the properties to always have specific values—then by all means hard-code them directly in the template.)

It is very common to define the *Template* property as part of a *Style*, like so:

```
<Button Content="Click me!"
        HorizontalAlignment="Center"
        VerticalAlignment="Center">
    <Button.Style>
        <Style TargetType="Button">
            <Setter Property="BorderBrush" Value="{StaticResource PhoneAccentBrush}" />
            <Setter Property="BorderThickness" Value="6" />
            <Setter Property="Template">
                <Setter.Value>
                    <ControlTemplate TargetType="Button">
                        <Border BorderBrush="{TemplateBinding BorderBrush}"
                                BorderThickness="{TemplateBinding BorderThickness}">
                            <TextBlock Text="temporary" />
                        </Border>
                    </ControlTemplate>
                </Setter.Value>
            </Setter>
        </Style>
    </Button.Style>
</Button>
```

Now the *Style* sets default values for properties also used by the template. Let's add a *Background* property to the *Border* and give it a default value as well:

```
<Button Content="Click me!"
        HorizontalAlignment="Center"
        VerticalAlignment="Center">
    <Button.Style>
        <Style TargetType="Button">
            <Setter Property="BorderBrush" Value="{StaticResource PhoneAccentBrush}" />
            <Setter Property="BorderThickness" Value="6" />
            <Setter Property="Background" Value="{StaticResource PhoneChromeBrush}" />
            <Setter Property="Template">
                <Setter.Value>
                    <ControlTemplate TargetType="Button">
                        <Border BorderBrush="{TemplateBinding BorderBrush}"
                                BorderThickness="{TemplateBinding BorderThickness}"
                                Background="{TemplateBinding Background}">
                            <TextBlock Text="temporary" />
                        </Border>
                    </ControlTemplate>
                </Setter.Value>
            </Setter>
```

```
        </Style>
    </Button.Style>
</Button>
```

On the other hand, perhaps we want our newly designed button to have rounded corners on the *Border*. We know that the *Button* does not define a *CornerRadius* property, so it can be set to an explicit value right in the template:

```
<Button Content="Click me!"
        HorizontalAlignment="Center"
        VerticalAlignment="Center">
    <Button.Style>
        <Style TargetType="Button">
            <Setter Property="BorderBrush" Value="{StaticResource PhoneAccentBrush}" />
            <Setter Property="BorderThickness" Value="6" />
            <Setter Property="Background" Value="{StaticResource PhoneChromeBrush}" />
            <Setter Property="Template">
                <Setter.Value>
                    <ControlTemplate TargetType="Button">
                        <Border BorderBrush="{TemplateBinding BorderBrush}"
                                BorderThickness="{TemplateBinding BorderThickness}"
                                Background="{TemplateBinding Background}"
                                CornerRadius="12">
                            <TextBlock Text="temporary" />
                        </Border>
                    </ControlTemplate>
                </Setter.Value>
            </Setter>
        </Style>
    </Button.Style>
</Button>
```

Here's what we're up to so far:

The button still displays the text "temporary" and it should really be displaying the text "Click me!" You might be tempted to put a *TextBlock* in there and set its *Text* property to a *TemplateBinding* of the *Content* property of the *Button*:

```
<TextBlock Text="{TemplateBinding Content}" />
```

This actually works in this example, but it's very, very wrong. The problem is that the *Content* property of the *Button* is of type *object*. We can set it to anything—an *Image*, a *Panel*, a *Shape*, a *RadialGradientBrush*, and then the *TextBlock* would have a little problem.

Fortunately, there is a class in Silverlight that exists specifically to display content in a *ContentControl* derivative. That class is called *ContentPresenter*. It has a property named *Content* of type object, and *ContentPresenter* displays that object regardless whether it's a text string or any other element:

```
<Button Content="Click me!"
        HorizontalAlignment="Center"
        VerticalAlignment="Center">
    <Button.Style>
        <Style TargetType="Button">
            <Setter Property="BorderBrush" Value="{StaticResource PhoneAccentBrush}" />
            <Setter Property="BorderThickness" Value="6" />
            <Setter Property="Background" Value="{StaticResource PhoneChromeBrush}" />
            <Setter Property="Template">
                <Setter.Value>
                    <ControlTemplate TargetType="Button">
                        <Border BorderBrush="{TemplateBinding BorderBrush}"
                                BorderThickness="{TemplateBinding BorderThickness}"
                                Background="{TemplateBinding Background}"
                                CornerRadius="12">
                            <ContentPresenter Content="{TemplateBinding Content}" />
                        </Border>
                    </ControlTemplate>
                </Setter.Value>
            </Setter>
        </Style>
    </Button.Style>
</Button>
```

Notice how the *Content* property of the *ContentPresenter* is bound to the *Content* property of the *Button*. The *ContentPresenter* has the distinct advantage of working for any kind of object. The *ContentPresenter* might create its own visual tree; for example, if the *Content* is of type string, then the *ContentPresenter* creates a *TextBlock* to display that string. The *ContentPresenter* is also entrusted with the job of building a visual tree to display content based on a *DataTemplate* set to the *Control*. For this purpose, the *ContentPresenter* has its own *ContentTemplate* property that you can bind to the *ContentTemplate* of the control:

```
<Button Content="Click me!"
        HorizontalAlignment="Center"
        VerticalAlignment="Center">
```

```
        <Button.Style>
            <Style TargetType="Button">
                <Setter Property="BorderBrush" Value="{StaticResource PhoneAccentBrush}" />
                <Setter Property="BorderThickness" Value="6" />
                <Setter Property="Background" Value="{StaticResource PhoneChromeBrush}" />
                <Setter Property="Template">
                    <Setter.Value>
                        <ControlTemplate TargetType="Button">
                            <Border BorderBrush="{TemplateBinding BorderBrush}"
                                    BorderThickness="{TemplateBinding BorderThickness}"
                                    Background="{TemplateBinding Background}"
                                    CornerRadius="12">
                                <ContentPresenter
                                    Content="{TemplateBinding Content}"
                                    ContentTemplate="{TemplateBinding ContentTemplate}" />
                            </Border>
                        </ControlTemplate>
                    </Setter.Value>
                </Setter>
            </Style>
        </Button.Style>
</Button>
```

These two *TemplateBinding* settings on *ContentPresenter* are so standard that they are not required to be explicitly set! They will be set for you. I feel more comfortable seeing them explicitly set, however.

You may recall that the *Control* class defines a property named *Padding* that is intended to provide a little breathing room around the control's content. Try setting the *Padding* property of the *Button*:

```
<Button Content="Click me!"
        HorizontalAlignment="Center"
        VerticalAlignment="Center"
        Padding="24">
    . . .
</Button>
```

Nothing happens. The visual tree in the template needs to accommodate this *Padding* property. It needs to leave some space between the *Border* and the *ContentPresenter*. How can this be done? One solution is to use a *TemplateBinding* on the *Padding* property of the *Border*. But if there's some other stuff in the *Border* besides the *ContentPresenter* that's not going to work right. The standard approach is to set a *TemplateBinding* on the *Margin* property of the *ContentPresenter*:

```
<ContentPresenter
        Content="{TemplateBinding Content}"
        ContentTemplate="{TemplateBinding ContentTemplate}"
        Margin="{TemplateBinding Padding}" />
```

You don't need to set a *Padding* value on the *Button* for this to have an effect. The theme *Style* for the *Button* defines a *Padding* value that seems to work well with this *Button*, even with the rounded *Border* corners.

Now try setting the *HorizontalAlignment* and *VerticalAlignment* properties of the *Button* to *Stretch*. These work fine, so that's something you don't have to worry about in the template. Similarly, you can set the *Margin* property of the *Button* and that's still recognized by the layout system.

But when you set the *HorizontalAlignment* and *VerticalAlignment* properties of the *Button* to *Stretch*, you'll discover that the content of the *Button* is at the upper-left corner:

Control defines two properties named *HorizontalContentAlignment* and *VerticalContentAlignment* that are supposed to govern how the content is aligned within the *ContentControl*. If you set these properties on the button, you'll discover that they don't work.

This tells us that we need to add something to the template to handle these properties. We have to align the *ContentPresenter* within the *Border* based on the *HorizontalContentAlignment* and *VerticalContentAlignment* properties. This is accomplished by providing *TemplateBinding* markup targeting the *HorizontalAlignment* and *VerticalAlignment* properties of the *ContentPresenter*:

```
<ContentPresenter
        Content="{TemplateBinding Content}"
        ContentTemplate="{TemplateBinding ContentTemplate}"
        Margin="{TemplateBinding Padding}"
        HorizontalAlignment="{TemplateBinding HorizontalContentAlignment}"
        VerticalAlignment="{TemplateBinding VerticalContentAlignment}" />
```

Again, this is very standard markup for a *ContentPresenter*. It's copy-and-paste stuff.

If you set the font-related properties or the *Foreground* property on the *Button*, you'll find that the text changes accordingly. These properties are inherited through the visual tree of the template and you don't need to do anything in the template to accommodate them. (However the theme *Style* for the *Button* explicitly sets the *Foreground*, *FontFamily*, and *FontSize* properties, so the *Button* itself cannot inherit these properties through the visual tree, and there is apparently nothing you can do in a custom *Style* to change this behavior.)

The Visual State Manager

All this time that the *Button* has been redesigned with a template, it has otherwise remained a fully-functional button and it's been generating *Click* events every time it's been tapped. The big problem is that the *Button* does not deliver visual feedback to the user. It has a customized visual appearance, but that appearance does not change.

There are really just two features that need to be added to this template to make it functionally and visually complete:

- The *Button* needs to provide visual feedback when the user presses it.

- The *Button* needs to indicate a disabled state if it's disabled.

These two features are related because they both involve changing the visuals of the control under certain circumstances. And the two features are also related because the solution involves a Silverlight feature called the Visual State Manager.

The Visual State Manager helps the developer deal with *visual states*, which are changes in control visuals that result from changes in properties (or other states) of the control. For the *Button* on Windows Phone 7, the relevant visual states correspond to the properties *IsPressed* and *IsEnabled*.

You can determine the visual states supported by a particular control by looking at the documentation for that control. In the first page of the *Button* documentation, you'll see the class defined with six attributes of type *TemplateVisualStateAttribute*:

```
[TemplateVisualStateAttribute(Name = "Disabled", GroupName = "CommonStates")]
[TemplateVisualStateAttribute(Name = "Normal", GroupName = "CommonStates")]
[TemplateVisualStateAttribute(Name = "MouseOver", GroupName = "CommonStates")]
[TemplateVisualStateAttribute(Name = "Pressed", GroupName = "CommonStates")]
[TemplateVisualStateAttribute(Name = "Unfocused", GroupName = "FocusStates")]
[TemplateVisualStateAttribute(Name = "Focused", GroupName = "FocusStates")]
public class Button : ButtonBase
```

These are the six visual states of the *Button*. Each of these states has a name, but notice also that each of them has a group name, either CommonStates or FocusStates.

Within any group, the visual states are mutually exclusive. One and only one visual state in each group currently applies to the *Button*. In the CommonStates group, either a button is Normal, or Disabled, or the mouse is hovering, or the button is pressed. You don't need to worry about combinations of these states. You don't have to come up with a special state for mouse hovering on a disabled button because those two states will never occur at the same time.

The code in the *Button* class is responsible for the button going into a particular state. It does this through calls to the static *VisualStateManager.GoToState* method. The template is responsible for responding to visual changes based on these states.

As Windows Phone 7 programmers, we have a somewhat easier job than template authors targeting Silverlight on the web. We don't have to worry about the two states in the FocusStates group, or the MouseOver state. That leaves Normal, Disabled, and Pressed.

Very often, additional elements are inserted into the template specifically for these visual states. When a control is disabled, the contents usually get grayer in some way regardless of the nature of the content—be it text, a bitmap, or something else. This suggests that a disabled state can be handled by putting a semi-opaque *Rectangle* on top of the entire control.

So let's put the entire visual tree of the template inside a single-cell *Grid* and add a *Rectangle* on top:

```
<ControlTemplate TargetType="Button">
    <Grid>
        <Border BorderBrush="{TemplateBinding BorderBrush}"
                BorderThickness="{TemplateBinding BorderThickness}"
                Background="{TemplateBinding Background}"
                CornerRadius="24">
            <ContentPresenter
                    Content="{TemplateBinding Content}"
                    ContentTemplate="{TemplateBinding ContentTemplate}"
                    Margin="{TemplateBinding Padding}"
                    HorizontalAlignment="{TemplateBinding HorizontalContentAlignment}"
                    VerticalAlignment="{TemplateBinding VerticalContentAlignment}" />
        </Border>

        <Rectangle Name="disableRect"
                   Fill="{StaticResource PhoneBackgroundBrush}"
                   Opacity="0" />
    </Grid>
</ControlTemplate>
```

Fortunately the new *Rectangle* has its *Opacity* set to 0 or it would block out the entire control! But if you set the *Opacity* to 0.6 (for example) it provides a proper dimming effect, regardless of control content.

Notice the color of the *Rectangle* is set as the PhoneBackgroundBrush resource. The *Button* has rounded corners so you don't want the *Rectangle* changing the color of whatever's behind the *Button* and visible through those corners. It's also possible to give the *Rectangle* the same corner rounding as the *Border* and you'll have a little more flexibility with the color.

Now that we have the *Rectangle* in there, all we need to do is find some way to change the *Opacity* from 0 to 0.6 when the visual state becomes Disabled.

The markup for the Visual State Manager always appears after the start tag of the top level element of the template, in this case the *Grid*. It begins with a *VisualStateManager* *.VisualStateGroups* tag within which can be multiple *VisualStateGroups* sections. I'll be ignoring the FocusStates group:

```
<ControlTemplate TargetType="Button">
    <Grid>
        <VisualStateManager.VisualStateGroups>
            <VisualStateGroup x:Name="CommonStates">

            </VisualStateGroup>
        </VisualStateManager.VisualStateGroups>
        . . .
    </Grid>
</ControlTemplate>
```

The *VisualStateGroup* tags enclose a series of *VisualState* tags for each of the visual states in that group:

```
<ControlTemplate TargetType="Button">
    <Grid>
        <VisualStateManager.VisualStateGroups>
            <VisualStateGroup x:Name="CommonStates">
                <VisualState x:Name="Normal" />
                <VisualState x:Name="MouseOver" />

                <VisualState x:Name="Pressed">

                </VisualState>

                <VisualState x:Name="Disabled">

                </VisualState>
            </VisualStateGroup>
        </VisualStateManager.VisualStateGroups>
        . . .
    </Grid>
</ControlTemplate>
```

The *VisualState* tag for the Normal state is empty because the template that's already been designed is for the normal button. But don't leave out the tag; otherwise the control won't return to its Normal state after being in another state. The MouseOver state won't be used; it too will remain empty.

Within the *VisualState* tags you indicate what you want to happen for that state. How do you do that? You might imagine doing it with a *Setting* tag as in a *Style*, and that would work well. But to allow you to be very much more flexible, the Visual State Manager lets you use animations instead, and because the animation syntax isn't very much more complex than the *Setting* syntax, the Visual State Manager actually *requires* you to use animations. Within the *VisualState* tags you'll put a *Storyboard* containing one or more animations targeting properties of named elements within the template. In many cases, these animations will have a *Duration* setting of 0 so that the visual state changes immediately. But you can have smoother state animations if you want. Here's an animation for the *Opacity* property of the *Rectangle* named *disableRect*:

```
<ControlTemplate TargetType="Button">
    <Grid>
        <VisualStateManager.VisualStateGroups>
            <VisualStateGroup x:Name="CommonStates">
                <VisualState x:Name="Normal" />
                <VisualState x:Name="MouseOver" />

                <VisualState x:Name="Pressed">

                </VisualState>

                <VisualState x:Name="Disabled">
                    <Storyboard>
                        <DoubleAnimation Storyboard.TargetName="disableRect"
                                         Storyboard.TargetProperty="Opacity"
                                         To="0.6" Duration="0:0:0" />
                    </Storyboard>
                </VisualState>
            </VisualStateGroup>
        </VisualStateManager.VisualStateGroups>
        . . .

    </Grid>
</ControlTemplate>
```

The animations in the Visual State Manager don't usually have *From* values so they just take off from the existing value. The empty *VisualState* tag for the Normal state effectively restores the *Opacity* value back to its pre-animation value when the state goes back to Normal.

The Pressed state presents some challenges. Usually a Pressed state is often rendered as a form of reverse video. In the web version of Silverlight, the *Button* template hard-codes a *LinearGradientBrush* for the background and changes properties of that brush for the Pressed state. Because the template is controlling the brush for the Normal state, it can easily change that brush for the Pressed state.

In the *Button* template being created here, the default *Foreground* color is set in the theme style for the *Button*, and a default *Background* color is set in the *Style* that the template is part of. If these properties aren't changed, the colors will be either white on black (with the "dark" theme) or black on white. But the properties can be changed with local property settings on the *Button*.

It would be great to have some kind of graphic effect to reverse the colors, but that's not available. We need to define animations to set new foreground and background colors for the Pressed state that will seem to reverse colors in the normal case, that is, when the foreground is set to the PhoneForegroundBrush resource and the background is PhoneBackgroundBrush, which means that the Pressed state can set *Foreground* to PhoneBackgroundBrush and *Background* to PhoneForegroundBrush.

Can we use a *ColorAnimation* for this job? We could if we knew that the *Foreground* and *Background* brushes were actually *SolidColorBrush* objects. But we don't know that. That means we need to use *ObjectAnimationUsingKeyFrames* objects to target the *Foreground* and *Background* properties themselves. The *ObjectAnimationUsingKeyFrames* can have children of only one type: *DiscreteObjectKeyFrame*.

Let's do the *Background* property first by giving the *Border* a name:

```
<Border Name="border"
        BorderBrush="{TemplateBinding BorderBrush}"
        BorderThickness="{TemplateBinding BorderThickness}"
        Background="{TemplateBinding Background}"
        CornerRadius="12">
```

That name allows the animation to target the *Background* property of *Border*:

```
<VisualState x:Name="Pressed">
    <Storyboard>
        <ObjectAnimationUsingKeyFrames Storyboard.TargetName="border"
                                       Storyboard.TargetProperty="Background">
            <DiscreteObjectKeyFrame KeyTime="0:0:0"
                                    Value="{StaticResource PhoneForegroundBrush}" />
        </ObjectAnimationUsingKeyFrames>
    </Storyboard>
</VisualState>
```

For the Pressed state, the animation changes the *Background* property of the *Border* element to the brush referenced as the PhoneForegroundBrush resource. Excellent!

Now let's add a similar animation to target the *Foreground* property of … of what? There is no element in this template visual tree that has a *Foreground* property!

It would be ideal if *ContentPresenter* had a *Foreground* property but it does not.

But wait a minute. What about *ContentControl*? *ContentControl* is basically just a *ContentPresenter* but *ContentControl* has a *Foreground* property. So let's replace *ContentPresenter* with a *ControlControl* and give it a name:

```
<ContentControl Name="contentControl"
                Content="{TemplateBinding Content}"
                ContentTemplate="{TemplateBinding ContentTemplate}"
                Margin="{TemplateBinding Padding}"
                HorizontalAlignment="{TemplateBinding HorizontalContentAlignment}"
                VerticalAlignment="{TemplateBinding VerticalContentAlignment}" />
```

Now it's possible to define the second animation for the Pressed state:

```
<VisualState x:Name="Pressed">
    <Storyboard>
```

```
...
        <ObjectAnimationUsingKeyFrames Storyboard.TargetName="contentControl"
                                   Storyboard.TargetProperty="Foreground">
            <DiscreteObjectKeyFrame KeyTime="0:0:0"
                                   Value="{StaticResource PhoneBackgroundBrush}" />
        </ObjectAnimationUsingKeyFrames>
    </Storyboard>
</VisualState>
```

And here's the pressed Button:

I will now declare this template to be completed! (And now you'll understand why the default template for the *Button* contains a *ContentControl*.)

Let's look at this entire *Style* and *ControlTemplate* in the context of a page. In the CustomButtonTemplate program, the *Style* is defined in the page's *Resources* collection. Mostly to reduce keep the lines lengths shorter than the width of the page, the *ControlTemplate* is defined as a separate resource and then referenced by the *Style*. Here's the *ControlTemplate* first followed by the *Style* referencing that template:

Silverlight Project: **CustomButtonTemplate**   File: **MainPage.xaml (excerpt)**

```
<phone:PhoneApplicationPage.Resources>
    <ControlTemplate x:Key="buttonTemplate" TargetType="Button">
        <Grid>
            <VisualStateManager.VisualStateGroups>
                <VisualStateGroup x:Name="CommonStates">
                    <VisualState x:Name="Normal" />
                    <VisualState x:Name="MouseOver" />
```

```xml
                <VisualState x:Name="Pressed">
                    <Storyboard>
                        <ObjectAnimationUsingKeyFrames
                                Storyboard.TargetName="border"
                                Storyboard.TargetProperty="Background">
                            <DiscreteObjectKeyFrame KeyTime="0:0:0"
                                Value="{StaticResource PhoneForegroundBrush}" />
                        </ObjectAnimationUsingKeyFrames>

                        <ObjectAnimationUsingKeyFrames
                                Storyboard.TargetName="contentControl"
                                Storyboard.TargetProperty="Foreground">
                            <DiscreteObjectKeyFrame KeyTime="0:0:0"
                                Value="{StaticResource PhoneBackgroundBrush}" />
                        </ObjectAnimationUsingKeyFrames>
                    </Storyboard>
                </VisualState>

                <VisualState x:Name="Disabled">
                    <Storyboard>
                        <DoubleAnimation Storyboard.TargetName="disableRect"
                                Storyboard.TargetProperty="Opacity"
                                To="0.6" Duration="0:0:0" />
                    </Storyboard>
                </VisualState>
            </VisualStateGroup>
        </VisualStateManager.VisualStateGroups>

        <Border Name="border"
                BorderBrush="{TemplateBinding BorderBrush}"
                BorderThickness="{TemplateBinding BorderThickness}"
                Background="{TemplateBinding Background}"
                CornerRadius="12">

            <ContentControl Name="contentControl"
                    Content="{TemplateBinding Content}"
                    ContentTemplate="{TemplateBinding ContentTemplate}"
                    Margin="{TemplateBinding Padding}"
                    HorizontalAlignment="{TemplateBinding
                                        HorizontalContentAlignment}"
                    VerticalAlignment="{TemplateBinding
                                        VerticalContentAlignment}" />
        </Border>

        <Rectangle Name="disableRect"
                Fill="{StaticResource PhoneBackgroundBrush}"
                Opacity="0" />
    </Grid>
</ControlTemplate>

<Style x:Key="buttonStyle" TargetType="Button">
    <Setter Property="BorderBrush" Value="{StaticResource PhoneAccentBrush}" />
    <Setter Property="BorderThickness" Value="6" />
```

```
            <Setter Property="Background" Value="{StaticResource PhoneChromeBrush}" />
            <Setter Property="Template" Value="{StaticResource buttonTemplate}" />
        </Style>
</phone:PhoneApplicationPage.Resources>
```

The content area contains a *Button* that references this *Style*, of course, but I wanted to test the enabling and disabling of the *Button* in a very interactive manner, so I added a *ToggleButton* to the page and set a binding targeting the *IsEnabled* property on the styled and templated *Button* from the *IsChecked* property of the *ToggleButton*.

But it didn't look quite right for the *ToggleButton* to be toggled on (that is, highlighted) when the regular *Button* was in its normal (that is, enabled) state. It occurred to me that what I really wanted was for the *ToggleButton* to actually say "Button Enabled" when the *ToggleButton* was toggled on and the *Button* was enabled, and for it to say "Button Disabled" when the *ToggleButton* was toggled off and the *Button* was disabled.

This is the beauty of templates. You can do something like this right in XAML without a whole lot of fuss and without any extra tools like Expression Blend.

Silverlight Project: CustomButtonTemplate   File: MainPage.xaml (excerpt)

```
<Grid x:Name="ContentPanel" Grid.Row="1" Margin="12,0,12,0">
    <Grid.RowDefinitions>
        <RowDefinition Height="*" />
        <RowDefinition Height="*" />
    </Grid.RowDefinitions>

    <Button Grid.Row="0"
            Content="Click me!"
            Style="{StaticResource buttonStyle}"
            IsEnabled="{Binding ElementName=toggleButton, Path=IsChecked}"
            HorizontalAlignment="Center"
            VerticalAlignment="Center" />

    <ToggleButton Name="toggleButton"
              Grid.Row="1"
              IsChecked="true"
              HorizontalAlignment="Center"
              VerticalAlignment="Center">
        <ToggleButton.Template>
            <ControlTemplate TargetType="ToggleButton">
                <Border BorderBrush="{StaticResource PhoneForegroundBrush}"
                        BorderThickness="{StaticResource PhoneBorderThickness}">

                    <VisualStateManager.VisualStateGroups>
                        <VisualStateGroup x:Name="CheckStates">
                            <VisualState x:Name="Checked">
```

```
                                <Storyboard>
                                    <ObjectAnimationUsingKeyFrames
                                            Storyboard.TargetName="txtblk"
                                            Storyboard.TargetProperty="Text">
                                        <DiscreteObjectKeyFrame KeyTime="0:0:0"
                                                        Value="Button Enabled" />
                                    </ObjectAnimationUsingKeyFrames>
                                </Storyboard>
                            </VisualState>

                            <VisualState x:Name="Unchecked" />

                        </VisualStateGroup>
                        </VisualStateManager.VisualStateGroups>

                        <TextBlock Name="txtblk"
                                Text="Button Disabled"/>
                    </Border>
                </ControlTemplate>
            </ToggleButton.Template>
        </ToggleButton>
    </Grid>
```

This *ToggleButton* here has what I think of as a single-purpose special-use ad hoc *ControlTemplate*, so it doesn't have a lot of extra frills. The visual tree consists entirely of a *Border* and a *TextBlock*. It ignores the *Content* property, and the *Text* property of the *TextBlock* is initialized with "Button Disabled". Everything else is done with visual states. In addition to the regular *Button* visual states, the *ToggleButton* also defines a CheckStates group with states Checked and Unchecked. These are the only states this template handles, and the animation for the Checked state sets the *Text* property of the *TextBlock* to "Button Enabled." Here it is in action with the *Button* disabled:

I didn't define a Disabled state for the *ToggleButton* because this is a template I intend to use only for this program, and I know that this *ToggleButton* will never be disabled.

Sharing and Reusing Styles and Templates

As you know, it's possible to derive one *Style* from another, in the process inheriting all the *Setter* objects. The new *Style* can add to those *Setter* objects or override them.

However, it is not possible to derive from a *ControlTemplate*. There's no way to reference an existing *ControlTemplate* and specify an additional piece of the visual tree, or a replacement for part of the visual tree. (It's hard enough imaging the mechanics or syntax of such a process.)

Generally if you want to apply some changes to an existing *ControlTemplate*, you obtain a copy of that entire template and begin editing it. These default templates are generally included with Silverlight documentation. (However, as I write this chapter, the Silverlight documentation contains only the templates for the web-based version of Silverlight and not those for Silverlight for Windows Phone.) Expression Blend also has access to the standard default templates.

If you need to share a *Style* or a *ControlTemplate* (or a *Style* containing a *ControlTemplate*) among multiple controls on a page, you simply put it in the *Resources* collection of the page. If you need to share the *Style* or *ControlTemplate* among multiple pages, put it in the *Resources* collection of App.xaml.

It is also possible to share resources among multiple applications. To share these resources you define them in a XAML file with a root element of *ResourceDictionary*. Here's such a file with the name SharedResources.xaml:

```
<ResourceDictionary
    xmlns="http://schemas.microsoft.com/winfx/2006/xaml/presentation"
    xmlns:x="http://schemas.microsoft.com/winfx/2006/xaml">

    <SolidColorBrush x:Key="brush" Color="Blue" />

    . . .

</ResourceDictionary>
```

The file probably has a lot more resources than just the *SolidColorBrush*. Each resource has an *x:Key* attribute, of course. You could create this file as part of a project, or you can add this existing file to a project. In either case, the Build Action in the properties window should indicate Page.

Now you can reference that file in the *Resources* collection in App.xaml:

```
<Application.Resources>
    <ResourceDictionary>
        <ResourceDictionary.MergedDictionaries>
```

```
<ResourceDictionary Source="SharedResources.xaml" />

  . . .

</ResourceDictionary.MergedDictionaries>

  . . .

</ResourceDictionary>
</Application.Resources>
```

Notice the *ResourceDictionary.MergedDictionary* property element used for referencing external *ResourceDictionary* objects.

Here's a different approach: You might want to define a custom style and template for an existing control, and then refer to that control with a new name rather than to explicitly reference the style. That too is possible.

Here's a program called FlipToggleDemo that includes a custom class named *FlipToggleButton* that derives from *ToggleButton*. But *FlipToggleButton* doesn't add any code to *ToggleButton*—just a *Style* and *ControlTemplate*.

In the FlipToggleDemo project, I added a new item of type Windows Phone User Control and I gave it a name of FlipToggleButton.xaml. This process creates a FlipToggleButton.xaml file and a FlipToggleButton.xaml.cs file for a class that derives from *UserControl*. But then I went into both files and changed *UserControl* to *ToggleButton* so *FlipToggleButton* derives from *ToggleButton*.

To keep things simple, I decided not to implement any state transitions for a disabled button, but to flip the button upside down for the Unchecked state. Here's the complete XAML file for the custom button, with indentation reduced to 2 spaces to avoid lines wider than the pages of this book:

Silverlight Project: FlipToggleDemo   File: FlipToggleButton.xaml

```
<ToggleButton x:Class="FlipToggleDemo.FlipToggleButton"
              xmlns="http://schemas.microsoft.com/winfx/2006/xaml/presentation"
              xmlns:x="http://schemas.microsoft.com/winfx/2006/xaml">
  <ToggleButton.Style>
    <Style TargetType="ToggleButton">
      <Setter Property="Template">
        <Setter.Value>
          <ControlTemplate TargetType="ToggleButton">
            <Border BorderBrush="{StaticResource PhoneForegroundBrush}"
                    BorderThickness="{StaticResource PhoneBorderThickness}"
                    Background="{TemplateBinding Background}"
                    RenderTransformOrigin="0.5 0.5">
              <Border.RenderTransform>
```

```
                <RotateTransform x:Name="rotate" />
            </Border.RenderTransform>

            <VisualStateManager.VisualStateGroups>
              <VisualStateGroup x:Name="CheckStates">
                <VisualState x:Name="Checked">
                  <Storyboard>
                    <DoubleAnimation Storyboard.TargetName="rotate"
                                     Storyboard.TargetProperty="Angle"
                                     To="180" Duration="0:0:0.5" />
                  </Storyboard>
                </VisualState>

                <VisualState x:Name="Unchecked">
                  <Storyboard>
                    <DoubleAnimation Storyboard.TargetName="rotate"
                                     Storyboard.TargetProperty="Angle"
                                     Duration="0:0:0.5" />
                  </Storyboard>
                </VisualState>
              </VisualStateGroup>
            </VisualStateManager.VisualStateGroups>

            <ContentPresenter Content="{TemplateBinding Content}"
                              ContentTemplate="{TemplateBinding ContentTemplate}"
                              Margin="{TemplateBinding Padding}"
                              HorizontalAlignment="{TemplateBinding
                                          HorizontalContentAlignment}"
                              VerticalAlignment="{TemplateBinding
                                          VerticalContentAlignment}" />
          </Border>
        </ControlTemplate>
      </Setter.Value>
    </Setter>
  </Style>
 </ToggleButton.Style>
</ToggleButton>
```

Usually when you're looking at XAML file, the bulk of the file is set to the *Content* property of the root element. Here the bulk of the file is set to the *Style* property of the root element. Notice that the *Style* object and the *ControlTemplate* object both have *TargetType* set to *ToggleButton* rather than *FlipToggleButton*. This is fine because neither references any properties specifically defined by *FlipToggleButton* because *FlipToggleButton* does not define any new properties.

The template itself is very plain vanilla, consisting of just a *Border* and a *ContentPresenter* with all the standard template bindings. But the *Border* also has its *RenderTransformOrigin* property defined and its *RenderTransform* property set to a *RotateTransform* object.

The two animations that flip the button upside down (for the Checked state) and back (for the Unchecked state) have non-zero times. The *DoubleAnimation* for the Checked state has no *From* value; it uses the base value of the property, which is zero. The *DoubleAnimation* for the Unchecked state has neither a *To* or *From* value! The animation starts at whatever value the *Angle* property of the *RotateTransform* happens to be—probably 180 but perhaps something lower if the animation to flip the button hasn't quite completed when the button is unchecked—and it ends at the base value, which is zero.

Here's the complete code-behind file for the custom control:

Silverlight Project: FlipToggleDemo   File: FlipToggleButton.xaml.cs

```
using System.Windows.Controls.Primitives;

namespace FlipToggleDemo
{
    public partial class FlipToggleButton : ToggleButton
    {
        public FlipToggleButton()
        {
            InitializeComponent();
        }
    }
}
```

The MainPage.xaml file of the project instantiates the custom button to test it out:

Silverlight Project: FlipToggleDemo   File: MainPage.xaml (excerpt)

```
<Grid x:Name="ContentPanel" Grid.Row="1" Margin="12,0,12,0">
    <local:FlipToggleButton Content="Flip Toggle"
                            HorizontalAlignment="Center"
                            VerticalAlignment="Center" />
</Grid>
```

Custom Controls in a Library

Generally when you create a custom control, you define some new properties for the control as well as a default *Style* and *ControlTemplate*, and you put that new control in a DLL for sharing among multiple applications. You can couple the code and *Style* as shown in the *FlipToggleButton* example, but a more standard approach for Silverlight libraries involves defining the *Style* in a special file named generic.xaml located in a directory named Themes. This generic.xaml file has a root element of *ResourceDictionary*.

Let's look at an example.

Suppose you conceive of a *ToggleButton* template something like the one in the CustomButtonTemplate project but much more generalized. Rather than just switch between two hard-coded text strings, you want to switch between two objects of any type. And not just switch—you want an object associated with the Checked state and an object associated with the Unchecked state to fade from one to the other. Your name for this new button is called *FadableToggleButton*.

As you think about it, you realize that the control needs to define a new property named *CheckedContent*, similar to the normal *Content* property. The *Content* property is the object displayed for the button's Unchecked state, and *CheckedContent* is displayed for the Checked state.

I defined this class in the Petzold.Phone.Silverlight library. The complete code for *FadableToggleButton* is here:

Silverlight Project: Petzold.Phone.Silverlight   File: FadableToggleButton.cs

```
using System.Windows;
using System.Windows.Controls.Primitives;

namespace Petzold.Phone.Silverlight
{
    public class FadableToggleButton : ToggleButton
    {
        public static readonly DependencyProperty CheckedContentProperty =
            DependencyProperty.Register("CheckedContent",
            typeof(object),
            typeof(FadableToggleButton),
            new PropertyMetadata(null));

        public FadableToggleButton()
        {
            this.DefaultStyleKey = typeof(FadableToggleButton);
        }

        public object CheckedContent
        {
            set { SetValue(CheckedContentProperty, value); }
            get { return (object)GetValue(CheckedContentProperty); }
        }
    }
}
```

This is the only C# code required to implement this control! There's not even a property-changed handler for this new *CheckedContent* property. It's just a *DependencyProperty* definition and a CLR property definition. Everything else is XAML.

But notice the constructor. If this code file were a *partial* class definition partnered with a XAML file, you'd see a call to *InitializeComponent* in the constructor. Instead, there's the following:

```
this.DefaultStyleKey = typeof(FadableToggleButton);
```

This statement indicates that this class has a default *Style* definition, and the *TargetType* of this *Style* definition is *FadableToggleButton*. To apply a default *Style* to instances of this class, Silverlight needs to find that *Style* definition. Where does it search?

Silverlight looks in a very special XAML file in the library. This XAML file is always named generic.xaml and it is always located in a directory named Themes of the DLL project. This is how a control gets a default theme style and template.

This generic.xaml file has a root element of *ResourceDictionary*. However the file is special in another way: The contents are regarded as resources but the *Style* elements don't require *x:Key* or *x:Name* attributes because they are referenced via the *TargetType*.

Here's the portion of the generic.xaml file in the Themes directory of Petzold.Phone. Silverlight that contains the default *Style* definition of the *FadableToggleButton* class:

Silverlight Project: Petzold.Phone.Silverlight   File: Themes/generic.xaml (excerpt)

```
<ResourceDictionary
        xmlns="http://schemas.microsoft.com/winfx/2006/xaml/presentation"
        xmlns:x="http://schemas.microsoft.com/winfx/2006/xaml"
        xmlns:local="clr-namespace:Petzold.Phone.Silverlight">

    <Style TargetType="local:FadableToggleButton">
        <Setter Property="Template">
            <Setter.Value>
                <ControlTemplate TargetType="local:FadableToggleButton">
                    <Grid>
                        <VisualStateManager.VisualStateGroups>
                            <VisualStateGroup x:Name="CommonStates">
                                <VisualState x:Name="Normal" />
                                <VisualState x:Name="MouseOver" />
                                <VisualState x:Name="Pressed" />

                                <VisualState x:Name="Disabled">
                                    <Storyboard>
                                        <DoubleAnimation Storyboard.TargetName="disableRect"
                                                         Storyboard.TargetProperty="Opacity"
                                                         To="0.6" Duration="0:0:0" />
                                    </Storyboard>
                                </VisualState>
                            </VisualStateGroup>

                            <VisualStateGroup x:Name="CheckStates">
```

```xml
              <VisualState x:Name="Checked">
                <Storyboard>
                  <DoubleAnimation Storyboard.TargetName="uncheckedContent"
                               Storyboard.TargetProperty="Opacity"
                               To="0" Duration="0:0:0.5" />
                  <DoubleAnimation Storyboard.TargetName="checkedContent"
                               Storyboard.TargetProperty="Opacity"
                               To="1" Duration="0:0:0.5" />
                </Storyboard>
              </VisualState>

              <VisualState x:Name="Unchecked">
                <Storyboard>
                  <DoubleAnimation Storyboard.TargetName="uncheckedContent"
                               Storyboard.TargetProperty="Opacity"
                               Duration="0:0:0.5" />
                  <DoubleAnimation Storyboard.TargetName="checkedContent"
                               Storyboard.TargetProperty="Opacity"
                               Duration="0:0:0.5" />
                </Storyboard>
              </VisualState>
            </VisualStateGroup>
        </VisualStateManager.VisualStateGroups>

        <Border BorderBrush="{StaticResource PhoneForegroundBrush}"
                BorderThickness="{StaticResource PhoneBorderThickness}"
                Background="{TemplateBinding Background}">

          <Grid Margin="{TemplateBinding Padding}">
            <ContentPresenter
                    Name="uncheckedContent"
                    Content="{TemplateBinding Content}"
                    ContentTemplate="{TemplateBinding ContentTemplate}"
                    HorizontalAlignment="{TemplateBinding
                                             HorizontalContentAlignment}"
                    VerticalAlignment="{TemplateBinding
                                             VerticalContentAlignment}" />

            <ContentPresenter
                    Name="checkedContent"
                    Opacity="0"
                    Content="{TemplateBinding CheckedContent}"
                    ContentTemplate="{TemplateBinding ContentTemplate}"
                    HorizontalAlignment="{TemplateBinding
                                             HorizontalContentAlignment}"
                    VerticalAlignment="{TemplateBinding
                                             VerticalContentAlignment}" />
          </Grid>
        </Border>

        <Rectangle Name="disableRect"
                   Fill="{StaticResource PhoneBackgroundBrush}"
                   Opacity="0" />
```

```
                </Grid>
            </ControlTemplate>
        </Setter.Value>
    </Setter>
  </Style>

  ...

</ResourceDictionary>
```

The *TargetType* for the *Style* is *FadableToggleButton*, and that's enough to allow Silverlight to find this *Style* definition that becomes the default theme for the *FadableToggleButton*. Within the *Border* is a single-cell *Grid* with two *ContentPresenter* elements, one with a *TemplateBinding* referencing the normal *Content* property, the other referencing the *CheckedContent* property. The *ContentPresenter* referencing the *CheckedContent* property has an initial *Opacity* of zero. The animations for the Checked and Unchecked states target the *Opacity* property of the *ContentPresenter* so that one fades out as the other fades in.

Although the *Content* properties of the two *ContentPresenter* elements are bound to two different properties of the *FadableToggleButton*, the *ContentTemplate* properties of both are bound to the same *ContentTemplate* property originally defined by *ContentControl*. If you set a *DataTemplate* to the *ContentTemplate* property of *FadableToggleButton*, then that same *DataTemplate* must apply to both the *Content* property and the *CheckedContent* property. In other words, this template implicitly assumes that the *Content* property and *CheckedContent* property are of the same types.

To test out this new control, I created a FadableToggleDemo program. The project contains a reference to the Petzold.Phone.Silverlight library and an XML namespace declaration for the library in MainPage.xaml. I added two bitmaps of the same size to an *Images* directory in the project. These bitmaps are referenced by *Image* elements set to the *Content* and *CheckedContent* properties of the button:

Silverlight Project: FadableToggleDemo   File: MainPage.xaml (excerpt)

```
<Grid x:Name="ContentPanel" Grid.Row="1" Margin="12,0,12,0">

    <petzold:FadableToggleButton HorizontalAlignment="Center"
                                 VerticalAlignment="Center">

        <petzold:FadableToggleButton.Content>
            <Image Source="Images/MunchScream.jpg"
                Stretch="None" />
        </petzold:FadableToggleButton.Content>

        <petzold:FadableToggleButton.CheckedContent>
            <Image Source="Images/BotticelliVenus.jpg"
                Stretch="None" />
```

```
        </petzold:FadableToggleButton.CheckedContent>

    </petzold:FadableToggleButton>

</Grid>
```

The *Content* property is set to an image from Edvard Munch's painting *The Scream*:

The *CheckedContent* property uses Botticelli's *Birth of Venus*:

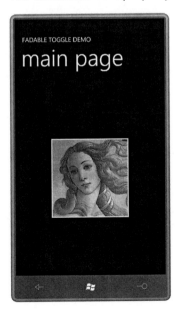

Variations on the Slider

As you might expect, the *Slider* has one of the more complex templates in all of standard Silverlight, and for that reason, it's important to get familiar with it—particularly if you're not a big fan of the default *Slider* template implemented in Windows Phone 7.

At first, a *Slider* does not seem to fit into the scheme of templates, primarily because it contains moving parts. How does this work exactly?

If you look at the documentation of *Slider*, you'll see the customary *TemplateVisualStateAttribute* tags, but also a collection of *TemplatePartAttribute* tags (rearranged somewhat here form their order in the documentation):

```
[TemplateVisualStateAttribute(Name = "Normal", GroupName = "CommonStates")]
[TemplateVisualStateAttribute(Name = "MouseOver", GroupName = "CommonStates")]
[TemplateVisualStateAttribute(Name = "Disabled", GroupName = "CommonStates")]
[TemplateVisualStateAttribute(Name = "Focused", GroupName = "FocusStates")]
[TemplateVisualStateAttribute(Name = "Unfocused", GroupName = "FocusStates")]
[TemplatePartAttribute(Name = "HorizontalTemplate", Type = typeof(FrameworkElement))]
[TemplatePartAttribute(Name = "HorizontalTrackLargeChangeDecreaseRepeatButton",
                Type = typeof(RepeatButton))]
[TemplatePartAttribute(Name = "HorizontalTrackLargeChangeIncreaseRepeatButton",
                Type = typeof(RepeatButton))]
[TemplatePartAttribute(Name = "HorizontalThumb", Type = typeof(Thumb))]
[TemplatePartAttribute(Name = "VerticalTemplate", Type = typeof(FrameworkElement))]
[TemplatePartAttribute(Name = "VerticalTrackLargeChangeDecreaseRepeatButton",
                Type = typeof(RepeatButton))]
[TemplatePartAttribute(Name = "VerticalTrackLargeChangeIncreaseRepeatButton",
                Type = typeof(RepeatButton))]
[TemplatePartAttribute(Name = "VerticalThumb", Type = typeof(Thumb))]
public class Slider : RangeBase
```

What this means is that the *Slider* expects its template to contain eight elements with the names of "HorizontalTemplate" and so forth. These are referred to as "parts" of the template. The "HorizontalTemplate" and "VerticalTemplate" parts need only be of type *FrameworkElement* (or derived from *FrameworkElement*) but other parts are required to be of type *RepeatButton* or *Thumb*.

The *RepeatButton* and *Thumb* are a couple of controls that I haven't yet had much occasion to use in this book. (They are both found in the *System.Windows.Controls.Primitives* namespace, a subtle suggestion that the controls are intended to be used in building other controls.) The *RepeatButton* is similar to a regular *Button* except that when you hold your finger on it, it fires repeated *Click* events. It's perfect for a *ScrollBar* or *Slider* and was probably invented specifically for that purpose.

The *Thumb* is a rather special control that reports how the user is trying to drag it. But if you can't quite figure out where the *Thumb* is located in the standard *Slider* on Windows Phone 7, that's because it's been pretty well hidden in the theme template. One of my goals here is to restore the *Thumb* to the *Slider*.

A control with parts (such as the *Slider*) overrides the *ApplyTemplate* method to be notified when a template has been set to its *Template* property. It then uses *GetTemplateChild* to find the elements with these particular names. It can attach event handlers to these elements, and otherwise manipulate these elements when the control is in use. (You'll see this process from the code perspective towards the end of this chapter.)

The standard *Slider* supports horizontal and vertical orientations, and the template actually contains two separate (and fairly independent) templates for these orientations. These two separate templates are enclosed in elements with the "HorizontalTemplate" and "VerticalTemplate" names. If the *Orientation* property of *Slider* is *Horizontal*, then the *Slider* sets the *Visibility* property of the "HorizontalTemplate" element to *Visible* and the *Visibility* property of "VerticalTemplate" element to *Collapsed*, and oppositely for the *Vertical* orientation.

When designing a new template for the *Slider*, the most straightfoward approach is to use a single-cell *Grid* to enclose the two templates. A nested *Grid* named "HorizontalTemplate" contains three columns with the two *RepeatButton* controls and a *Thumb*. Another nested *Grid* named "VerticalTemplate" has three rows.

Here's is what I think of as a "bare bones" template for *Slider* defined as a resource:

Silverlight Project: BareBonesSlider   File: MainPage.xaml (excerpt)

```
<phone:PhoneApplicationPage.Resources>
    <ControlTemplate x:Key="bareBonesSliderTemplate"
                    TargetType="Slider">
        <Grid>
            <Grid Name="HorizontalTemplate">
                <Grid.ColumnDefinitions>
                    <ColumnDefinition Width="Auto" />
                    <ColumnDefinition Width="Auto" />
                    <ColumnDefinition Width="*" />
                </Grid.ColumnDefinitions>

                <RepeatButton Name="HorizontalTrackLargeChangeDecreaseRepeatButton"
                        Grid.Column="0"
                        Content="-" />

                <Thumb Name="HorizontalThumb"
                        Grid.Column="1" />

                <RepeatButton Name="HorizontalTrackLargeChangeIncreaseRepeatButton"
                        Grid.Column="2"
                        Content="+" />
            </Grid>

            <Grid Name="VerticalTemplate">
                <Grid.RowDefinitions>
```

```
                    <RowDefinition Height="*" />
                    <RowDefinition Height="Auto" />
                    <RowDefinition Height="Auto" />
                </Grid.RowDefinitions>

                <RepeatButton Name="VerticalTrackLargeChangeDecreaseRepeatButton"
                              Grid.Row="0"
                              Content="-" />

                <Thumb Name="VerticalThumb"
                       Grid.Row="1" />

                <RepeatButton Name="VerticalTrackLargeChangeIncreaseRepeatButton"
                              Grid.Row="2"
                              Content="+" />
            </Grid>
        </Grid>
    </ControlTemplate>
</phone:PhoneApplicationPage.Resources>
```

The *Slider* template does not exactly require the two *RepeatButton* controls and the *Thumb* to be in a three-row or three-column *Grid*, but it's certainly the easiest solution. Notice that I rather whimsically assigned the *Content* properties of the *RepeatButton* controls to minus signs and plus signs depending on their role.

Let's focus on the *Horizontal* orientation: The *RepeatButton* to decrease values is in the first *Grid* cell with a width of *Auto*, and the *Thumb* is in the second *Grid* cell, also with a *Width* of *Auto*. The *Thumb* itself has a fixed width, but the *Slider* logic directly changes the width of the decreasing *RepeatButton* to reflect the *Value* property of the *Slider*. When *Value* is set to *Minimum*, this *RepeatButton* gets a width of zero. When *Value* is set to *Maximum*, the *RepeatButton* gets a width based on the entire control width minus the *Thumb* width.

The *Slider* changes the *Value* property (and consequently the relative size of the two *RepeatButton* controls) when the user presses a *RepeatButton* or physically moves the *Thumb*. (I'll discuss the *Thumb* control in more detail soon.)

The BareBonesSlider project continues by instantiating two *Slider* controls in its content area and applying the template:

Silverlight Project: BareBonesSlider   File: MainPage.xaml (excerpt)

```
<Grid x:Name="ContentPanel" Grid.Row="1" Margin="12,0,12,0">
    <Grid.RowDefinitions>
        <RowDefinition Height="Auto"/>
        <RowDefinition Height="*" />
    </Grid.RowDefinitions>
```

```
    <Slider Grid.Row="0"
            Orientation="Horizontal"
            Template="{StaticResource bareBonesSliderTemplate}" />

    <Slider Grid.Row="1"
            Orientation="Vertical"
            Template="{StaticResource bareBonesSliderTemplate}"
            HorizontalAlignment="Center" />
</Grid>
```

Here's what they look like after they've been moved a bit from their initial positions:

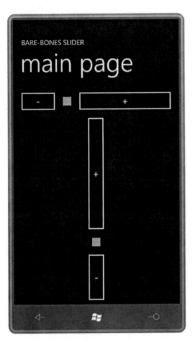

The *RepeatButton* looks just like *Button* and *Thumb* is a square surrounded by a transparent area.

Now that we know how to create a custom template for *Slider*, can we pretty this up a bit? Yes, and the key involves realizing that *RepeatButton* and *Thumb* derive from *Control*, which means they both have *Template* properties, and within the *Slider* template you can define new templates for *RepeatButton* and *Thumb* specifically for use in the *Slider* template.

Here's a fancier *Slider* that also incorporates template bindings for the *Background* and *Foreground* properties. Those properties are given default values in a *Style* that also incorporates the *ControlTemplate*. Shown here is only the outer *Grid* of the *ControlTemplate* object, which has its own *Resources* section for defining a very simple *ControlTemplate* for the *RepeatButton* and rather extensive templates for the horizontal and vertical *Thumb*:

Silverlight Project: AlternativeSlider   File: MainPage.xaml (excerpt)

```
<phone:PhoneApplicationPage.Resources>
    <Style x:Key="alternativeSliderStyle" TargetType="Slider">
        <Setter Property="Background"
                Value="{StaticResource PhoneBackgroundBrush}" />
        <Setter Property="Foreground"
                Value="{StaticResource PhoneForegroundBrush}" />
        <Setter Property="Template">
            <Setter.Value>
                <ControlTemplate TargetType="Slider">
                    <Grid Background="{TemplateBinding Background}">

                        <Grid.Resources>
                            <ControlTemplate x:Key="repeatButtonTemplate"
                                             TargetType="RepeatButton">
                                <Rectangle Fill="Transparent" />
                            </ControlTemplate>

                            <Style x:Key="horizontalThumbStyle"
                                   TargetType="Thumb">
                                <Setter Property="Width" Value="72" />
                                <Setter Property="Height" Value="72" />
                                <Setter Property="Template">
                                    <Setter.Value>
                                        <ControlTemplate TargetType="Thumb">
                                            <Border Background="Transparent">
                                                <Rectangle Margin="18 0"
                                                           RadiusX="6"
                                                           RadiusY="6"
                                                           Stroke="{StaticResource
                                                               PhoneAccentBrush}"
                                                           Fill="{TemplateBinding
                                                               Foreground}" />
                                            </Border>
                                        </ControlTemplate>
                                    </Setter.Value>
                                </Setter>
                            </Style>

                            <Style x:Key="verticalThumbStyle"
                                   TargetType="Thumb">
                                <Setter Property="Width" Value="72" />
                                <Setter Property="Height" Value="72" />
                                <Setter Property="Template">
                                    <Setter.Value>
                                        <ControlTemplate TargetType="Thumb">
                                            <Border Background="Transparent">
                                                <Rectangle Margin="0 18"
```

```
                                                              RadiusX="6"
                                                              RadiusY="6"
                                                              Stroke="{StaticResource
                                                                  PhoneAccentBrush}"
                                                              Fill="{TemplateBinding
                                                                  Foreground}" />
                                                </Border>
                                            </ControlTemplate>
                                        </Setter.Value>
                                    </Setter>
                                </Style>
                            </Grid.Resources>

                                    . . .

                        </Grid>
                    </ControlTemplate>
                </Setter.Value>
            </Setter>
        </Style>
    </phone:PhoneApplicationPage.Resources>
```

The *RepeatButton* template is just a transparent *Rectangle*. (You want the *Rectangle* to have a transparent *Fill* rather than a null *Fill* so it can receive touch input.) For the *Thumb* styles, however, I needed to redefine *Width* and *Height* properties. In the theme style, they're set at 48, which seemed a little low to me. I provided a *Border* with a transparent background for a touch target of the larger size, but the visual part is a little smaller to look more like a traditional *Slider* thumb.

The two *Grid* elements for the horizontal and vertical orientations each begins with a *Rectangle* that provides a kind of visual track. Each *RepeatButton* and *Thumb* references the *Style* for that control defined earlier:

Silverlight Project: AlternativeSlider   File: MainPage.xaml (excerpt)

```
<Grid Name="HorizontalTemplate">
    <Grid.ColumnDefinitions>
        <ColumnDefinition Width="Auto" />
        <ColumnDefinition Width="Auto" />
        <ColumnDefinition Width="*" />
    </Grid.ColumnDefinitions>

    <Rectangle Grid.Column="0" Grid.ColumnSpan="3"
               Height="8"
               Margin="12 0"
               Stroke="{TemplateBinding Foreground}"
               Fill="{StaticResource PhoneAccentBrush}" />
```

```
    <RepeatButton Name="HorizontalTrackLargeChangeDecreaseRepeatButton"
                  Grid.Column="0"
                  Template="{StaticResource repeatButtonTemplate}" />

    <Thumb Name="HorizontalThumb"
           Grid.Column="1"
           Style="{StaticResource horizontalThumbStyle}" />

    <RepeatButton Name="HorizontalTrackLargeChangeIncreaseRepeatButton"
                  Grid.Column="2"
                  Template="{StaticResource repeatButtonTemplate}" />
</Grid>

<Grid Name="VerticalTemplate">
    <Grid.RowDefinitions>
        <RowDefinition Height="*" />
        <RowDefinition Height="Auto" />
        <RowDefinition Height="Auto" />
    </Grid.RowDefinitions>

    <Rectangle Grid.Row="0" Grid.RowSpan="3"
               Width="8"
               Margin="0 12"
               Stroke="{TemplateBinding Foreground}"
               Fill="{StaticResource PhoneAccentBrush}" />

    <RepeatButton Name="VerticalTrackLargeChangeDecreaseRepeatButton"
                  Grid.Row="0"
                  Template="{StaticResource repeatButtonTemplate}" />

    <Thumb Name="VerticalThumb"
           Grid.Row="1"
           Style="{StaticResource verticalThumbStyle}" />

    <RepeatButton Name="VerticalTrackLargeChangeIncreaseRepeatButton"
                  Grid.Row="2"
                  Template="{StaticResource repeatButtonTemplate}" />
</Grid>
```

The content area of the program looks pretty much like the previous program except that the *Slider* controls reference this new style:

Silverlight Project: AlternativeSlider   **File: MainPage.xaml (excerpt)**

```
<Grid x:Name="ContentPanel" Grid.Row="1" Margin="12,0,12,0">
    <Grid.RowDefinitions>
        <RowDefinition Height="Auto"/>
        <RowDefinition Height="*" />
    </Grid.RowDefinitions>
```

```
    <Slider Grid.Row="0"
            Orientation="Horizontal"
            Style="{StaticResource alternativeSliderStyle}" />

    <Slider Grid.Row="1"
            Orientation="Vertical"
            Style="{StaticResource alternativeSliderStyle}"
            HorizontalAlignment="Center" />
</Grid>
```

And here they are:

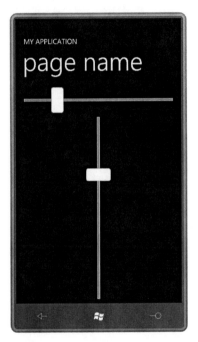

I decided to move this *Style* and *ControlTemplate* to Petzold.Phone.Silverlight as the default *Style* for a class named *AltSlider*. The class has no additional properties so the code file needs only identify the class that *AltSlider* derives from and what class should be used for locating the default *Style*:

Silverlight Project: Petzold.Phone.Silverlight   File: AltSlider.cs

```
using System.Windows.Controls;

namespace Petzold.Phone.Silverlight
{
    public class AltSlider : Slider
```

```
        {
            public AltSlider()
            {
                this.DefaultStyleKey = typeof(AltSlider);
            }
        }
    }
```

This default *Style* (including the *ControlTemplate*) is in generic.xaml. I won't show the whole thing here because it mostly repeats the *Style* definition from the AlternativeSlider project:

Silverlight Project: Petzold.Phone.Silverlight   File: Themes/generic.xaml (excerpt)

```
<ResourceDictionary
        xmlns="http://schemas.microsoft.com/winfx/2006/xaml/presentation"
        xmlns:x="http://schemas.microsoft.com/winfx/2006/xaml"
        xmlns:local="clr-namespace:Petzold.Phone.Silverlight">

    . . .

    <Style TargetType="local:AltSlider">
        <Setter Property="Background"
                Value="{StaticResource PhoneBackgroundBrush}" />
        <Setter Property="Foreground"
                Value="{StaticResource PhoneForegroundBrush}" />
        <Setter Property="Template">
            <Setter.Value>
                <ControlTemplate TargetType="local:AltSlider">
                    . . .
                </ControlTemplate>
            </Setter.Value>
        </Setter>
    </Style>

    . . .

</ResourceDictionary>
```

Of course, it's now necessary to test it. The AltSliderDemo project has a reference to the Petzold.Phone.Silverlight project, and an XML namespace declaration for it. The content area is similar to the past two programs:

Silverlight Project: AltSliderDemo   File: MainPage.xaml (excerpt)

```
<Grid x:Name="ContentPanel" Grid.Row="1" Margin="12,0,12,0">
    <Grid.RowDefinitions>
        <RowDefinition Height="Auto"/>
```

```
        <RowDefinition Height="*" />
    </Grid.RowDefinitions>

    <petzold:AltSlider Grid.Row="0"
                       Orientation="Horizontal"
                       Style="{StaticResource altSliderStyle}"/>

    <petzold:AltSlider Grid.Row="1"
                       Orientation="Vertical"
                       HorizontalAlignment="Center"
                       Style="{StaticResource altSliderStyle}" />
</Grid>
```

You'll notice these *AltSlider* controls have their *Style* properties set. What is that? That is a reference to a *Style* defined in the *Resources* collection of the page:

Silverlight Project: AltSliderDemo   File: **MainPage.xaml (excerpt)**

```
<phone:PhoneApplicationPage.Resources>
    <Style x:Key="altSliderStyle"
           TargetType="petzold:AltSlider">
        <Setter Property="Margin" Value="12" />
        <Setter Property="Background" Value="{StaticResource PhoneChromeBrush}" />
    </Style>
</phone:PhoneApplicationPage.Resources>
```

The only purpose of this *Style* is to demonstrate that defining a default *Style* for the *AltSlider* class does not negate the ability to set another *Style* later on, even one that overrides one of the properties in the original *Style*. Here's the program running:

The Ever-Handy Thumb

Where would the human race be without thumbs?

Several times in this book I've wanted to use the *Thumb* control. The most recent occasion was the SplineKeyFrameExperiment project in the previous chapter. Two chapters earlier, I even created a *PointDragger* control in the CubicBezier program to compensate for the lack of the *Thumb* control.

Thumb is not only a component of the *Slider* template: It can also be used as a general-purpose manipulable control for dragging with your finger around the screen. The problem is this: With its default template, the *Thumb* is ugly enough to be considered "unusable." It really needs a custom template.

Thumb derives from *Control*, defines an *IsDragging* method, and three events: *DragStarted*, *DragDelta*, and *DragCompleted*. A *CancelDrag* method lets you abort the process midway through.

The most important event is *DragDelta*, which comes with event arguments named *HorizontalChange* and *VerticalChange*, so you can think of the *Thumb* as a high-level interface to the *Manipulation* events—or at least when you're working solely with translation.

Here's the content area of the ThumbBezier program, which is similar to the CubicBezier program in Chapter 13 except that it positions four *Thumb* controls at the four points using *TranslateTransform*.

Silverlight Project: ThumbBezier   File: MainPage.xaml (excerpt)

```xml
<Grid x:Name="ContentPanel" Grid.Row="1" Margin="12,0,12,0">
    <Path Stroke="{StaticResource PhoneForegroundBrush}"
          StrokeThickness="2">
        <Path.Data>
            <PathGeometry>
                <PathFigure x:Name="pathFig"
                            StartPoint="100 100">
                    <BezierSegment x:Name="pathSeg"
                                   Point1="300 100"
                                   Point2="300 400"
                                   Point3="100 400" />
                </PathFigure>
            </PathGeometry>
        </Path.Data>
    </Path>

    <Polyline Name="ctrl1Line"
              Stroke="{StaticResource PhoneForegroundBrush}"
              StrokeDashArray="2 2"
              Points="100 100, 300 100" />
```

```
<Polyline Name="ctrl2Line"
          Stroke="{StaticResource PhoneForegroundBrush}"
          StrokeDashArray="2 2"
          Points="300 400, 100 400" />

<Thumb Name="pt0Thumb"
       Style="{StaticResource thumbStyle}"
       DragDelta="OnThumbDragDelta">
    <Thumb.RenderTransform>
        <TranslateTransform X="100" Y="100" />
    </Thumb.RenderTransform>
</Thumb>

<Thumb Name="pt1Thumb"
       Style="{StaticResource thumbStyle}"
       DragDelta="OnThumbDragDelta">
    <Thumb.RenderTransform>
        <TranslateTransform X="300" Y="100" />
    </Thumb.RenderTransform>
</Thumb>

<Thumb Name="pt2Thumb"
       Style="{StaticResource thumbStyle}"
       DragDelta="OnThumbDragDelta">
    <Thumb.RenderTransform>
        <TranslateTransform X="300" Y="400" />
    </Thumb.RenderTransform>
</Thumb>

<Thumb Name="pt3Thumb"
       Style="{StaticResource thumbStyle}"
       DragDelta="OnThumbDragDelta">
    <Thumb.RenderTransform>
        <TranslateTransform X="100" Y="400" />
    </Thumb.RenderTransform>
</Thumb>
</Grid>
```

All four *Thumb* controls share the same *DragDelta* event handler, which is pretty much the only responsibility of the code-behind file. You'll need a *using* directive for the *System .Windows.Control.Primitives* namespace for the *Thumb* and its event arguments.

Silverlight Project: ThumbBezier   File: MainPage.xaml.cs (excerpt)

```
void OnThumbDragDelta(object sender, DragDeltaEventArgs args)
{
    Thumb thumb = sender as Thumb;
    TranslateTransform translate = thumb.RenderTransform as TranslateTransform;
    translate.X += args.HorizontalChange;
    translate.Y += args.VerticalChange;
```

```
    if (thumb == pt0Thumb)
    {
        pathFig.StartPoint =
            Move(pathFig.StartPoint, args.HorizontalChange, args.VerticalChange);
        ctrl1Line.Points[0] =
            Move(ctrl1Line.Points[0], args.HorizontalChange, args.VerticalChange);
    }
    else if (thumb == pt1Thumb)
    {
        pathSeg.Point1 =
            Move(pathSeg.Point1, args.HorizontalChange, args.VerticalChange);
        ctrl1Line.Points[1] =
            Move(ctrl1Line.Points[1], args.HorizontalChange, args.VerticalChange);
    }
    else if (thumb == pt2Thumb)
    {
        pathSeg.Point2 =
            Move(pathSeg.Point2, args.HorizontalChange, args.VerticalChange);
        ctrl2Line.Points[0] =
            Move(ctrl2Line.Points[0], args.HorizontalChange, args.VerticalChange);
    }
    else if (thumb == pt3Thumb)
    {
        pathSeg.Point3 =
            Move(pathSeg.Point3, args.HorizontalChange, args.VerticalChange);
        ctrl2Line.Points[1] =
            Move(ctrl2Line.Points[1], args.HorizontalChange, args.VerticalChange);
    }
}

Point Move(Point point, double horzChange, double vertChange)
{
    return new Point(point.X + horzChange, point.Y + vertChange);
}
```

In a *Style* and *ControlTemplate* defined in the *Resources* collection, the *Thumb* is given an appearance much like the translucent round elements I used in the earlier program. The only visual element of the *ControlTemplate* is a *Path* with an *EllipseGeometry*:

Silverlight Project: ThumbBezier   File: MainPage.xaml (excerpt)

```
<phone:PhoneApplicationPage.Resources>
    <Style x:Key="thumbStyle" TargetType="Thumb">
        <Setter Property="HorizontalAlignment" Value="Left" />
        <Setter Property="VerticalAlignment" Value="Top" />
        <Setter Property="Template">
            <Setter.Value>
                <ControlTemplate TargetType="Thumb">

                    <Path Name="path"
```

```xml
        Fill="{StaticResource PhoneAccentBrush}"
        Opacity="0.5">
    <Path.RenderTransform>
        <ScaleTransform x:Name="scale" />
    </Path.RenderTransform>

    <Path.Data>
        <EllipseGeometry x:Name="ellipseGeometry"
                            RadiusX="48" RadiusY="48" />
    </Path.Data>

    <VisualStateManager.VisualStateGroups>
        <VisualStateGroup x:Name="CommonStates">
            <VisualState x:Name="Normal">
                <Storyboard>
                    <DoubleAnimation
                        Storyboard.TargetName="path"
                        Storyboard.TargetProperty="Opacity"
                        Duration="0:0:0.25" />
                    <DoubleAnimation
                        Storyboard.TargetName="scale"
                        Storyboard.TargetProperty="ScaleX"
                        Duration="0:0:0.25" />
                    <DoubleAnimation
                        Storyboard.TargetName="scale"
                        Storyboard.TargetProperty="ScaleY"
                        Duration="0:0:0.25" />

                </Storyboard>
            </VisualState>

            <VisualState x:Name="MouseOver" />
            <VisualState x:Name="Disabled" />

            <VisualState x:Name="Pressed">
                <Storyboard>
                    <DoubleAnimation
                        Storyboard.TargetName="path"
                        Storyboard.TargetProperty="Opacity"
                        To="0.75" Duration="0:0:0.25" />
                    <DoubleAnimation
                        Storyboard.TargetName="scale"
                        Storyboard.TargetProperty="ScaleX"
                        To="1.25" Duration="0:0:0.25" />
                    <DoubleAnimation
                        Storyboard.TargetName="scale"
                        Storyboard.TargetProperty="ScaleY"
                        To="1.25" Duration="0:0:0.25" />
                </Storyboard>
            </VisualState>
        </VisualStateGroup>
    </VisualStateManager.VisualStateGroups>
```

```
                    </Path>
                  </ControlTemplate>
                </Setter.Value>
            </Setter>
        </Style>
    </phone:PhoneApplicationPage.Resources>
```

The *Thumb* has a Pressed visual state, so this suggests that a feature can be added not present in the earlier programs: The *Thumb* can indicate that it's pressed and being dragged by growing a bit and by changing color. A few animations are all that's necessary to add this feature to the template.

Custom Controls

As you know, if you're creating controls that need only be used for special purposes in your own applications, the easiest approach is *UserControl*. Simply define a visual tree for the control in the XAML file.

You can also take a similar approach with *ContentControl*, except that the XAML file would contain a *Style* and *ControlTemplate* definition. The advantage of this approach is that you retain use of the *Content* property for the control's own purposes.

You can also derive from *Control*. This approach makes sense if the derived class is in a library, and you want the control to have a replaceable template. The default theme *Style* and *ControlTemplate* are in the library's generic.xaml file.

The Petzold.Phone.Silverlight library has an example of such a control named *XYSlider*. This control is intended to let the user move a *Thumb* around a two-dimensional surface; the control reports a location in a property name *Value* of type *Point*, but the two coordinates are normalized between 0 and 1 relative to the upper-left corner. This normalization relieves the control of defining *Minimum* and *Maximum* values like a regular *Slider*.

Besides a *Value* property, the *XYSlider* class also defines a *PlaneBackground* property of type *Brush*. This is the surface on which the *Thumb* moves, and you'll see shortly why it must be distinguished from the regular *Background* property of *Control*.

As the class attributes indicate, the class expects the template to have two elements: a *Canvas* named "PlanePart" and a *Thumb* named "ThumbPart":

Silverlight Project: Petzold.Phone.Silverlight   File: XYSlider.cs (excerpt)

```
[TemplatePartAttribute(Name = "PlanePart", Type = typeof(Canvas))]
[TemplatePartAttribute(Name = "ThumbPart", Type = typeof(Thumb))]
public class XYSlider : Control
```

```
{
    Canvas planePart;
    Thumb thumbPart;
    Point absoluteThumbPoint;

    public event RoutedPropertyChangedEventHandler<Point> ValueChanged;

    public static readonly DependencyProperty PlaneBackgroundProperty =
        DependencyProperty.Register("PlaneBackground",
            typeof(Brush),
            typeof(XYSlider),
            new PropertyMetadata(new SolidColorBrush(Colors.Gray)));

    public static readonly DependencyProperty ValueProperty =
        DependencyProperty.Register("Value",
            typeof(Point),
            typeof(XYSlider),
            new PropertyMetadata(new Point(0.5, 0.5), OnValueChanged));

    public XYSlider()
    {
        this.DefaultStyleKey = typeof(XYSlider);
    }

    public Brush PlaneBackground
    {
        set { SetValue(PlaneBackgroundProperty, value); }
        get { return (Brush)GetValue(PlaneBackgroundProperty); }
    }

    public Point Value
    {
        set { SetValue(ValueProperty, value); }
        get { return (Point)GetValue(ValueProperty); }
    }

    ...
}
```

A *Control* derivative is informed that its template has been built by a call to *OnApplyTemplate*. This is an appropriate time for the class to call *GetTemplateChild* with the names indicated in the attributes. It is considered proper behavior for the class to quietly accept the possibility that some parts might be missing, even if those parts are essential for the proper functioning of the control:

Silverlight Project: Petzold.Phone.Silverlight   File: XYSlider.cs (excerpt)

```
public override void OnApplyTemplate()
{
    if (planePart != null)
```

```
    {
        planePart.SizeChanged -= OnPlaneSizeChanged;
    }

    if (thumbPart != null)
    {
        thumbPart.DragDelta -= OnThumbDragDelta;
    }

    planePart = GetTemplateChild("PlanePart") as Canvas;
    thumbPart = GetTemplateChild("ThumbPart") as Thumb;

    if (planePart != null && thumbPart != null)
    {
        planePart.SizeChanged += OnPlaneSizeChanged;
        thumbPart.DragStarted += OnThumbDragStarted;
        thumbPart.DragDelta += OnThumbDragDelta;
        ScaleValueToPlane(this.Value);
    }

    base.OnApplyTemplate();
}
```

If the *Canvas* and *Thumb* are present, a handler is installed for the *SizeChanged* event of the *Canvas* and the *DragStarted* and *DragDelta* events of the *Thumb*.

The *SizeChanged* handler updates the location of the *Thumb* relative to the *Canvas*; the *DragDelta* handler updates the *Value* property of *XYSlider*:

Silverlight Project: Petzold.Phone.Silverlight   File: XYSlider.cs (excerpt)

```
void OnPlaneSizeChanged(object sender, SizeChangedEventArgs args)
{
    ScaleValueToPlane(this.Value);
}

void OnThumbDragStarted(object sender, DragStartedEventArgs args)
{
    absoluteThumbPoint = new Point(Canvas.GetLeft(thumbPart),
                                   Canvas.GetTop(thumbPart));
}

void OnThumbDragDelta(object sender, DragDeltaEventArgs args)
{
    absoluteThumbPoint.X += args.HorizontalChange;
    absoluteThumbPoint.Y += args.VerticalChange;

    Value = new Point(Math.Max(0,
                      Math.Min(1, absoluteThumbPoint.X / planePart.ActualWidth)),
                      Math.Max(0,
```

```
                          Math.Min(1, absoluteThumbPoint.Y / planePart.ActualHeight)));
    }

    void ScaleValueToPlane(Point point)
    {
        if (planePart != null && thumbPart != null)
        {
            Canvas.SetLeft(thumbPart, planePart.ActualWidth * point.X);
            Canvas.SetTop(thumbPart, planePart.ActualHeight * point.Y);
        }
    }
}
```

The property-changed handler for *Value* also updates the location of the *Thumb* and fires the *ValueChanged* event:

Silverlight Project: Petzold.Phone.Silverlight   File: XYSlider.cs (excerpt)

```
static void OnValueChanged(DependencyObject obj,
                           DependencyPropertyChangedEventArgs args)
{
    (obj as XYSlider).OnValueChanged((Point)args.OldValue, (Point)args.NewValue);
}

protected virtual void OnValueChanged(Point oldValue, Point newValue)
{
    if (newValue.X < 0 || newValue.X > 1 || newValue.Y < 0 || newValue.Y > 1)
        throw new ArgumentOutOfRangeException("Value",
            "Value property must be Point with coordinates between 0 and 1");

    ScaleValueToPlane(newValue);

    if (ValueChanged != null)
        ValueChanged(this,
            new RoutedPropertyChangedEventArgs<Point>(oldValue, newValue));
}
```

The default *Style* and *ControlTemplate* are in the generic.xaml file:

Silverlight Project: Petzold.Phone.Sivlerlight   File: Themes/generic.xaml (excerpt)

```
<Style TargetType="local:XYSlider">
  <Setter Property="Template">
    <Setter.Value>
      <ControlTemplate TargetType="local:XYSlider">
        <Border Background="{TemplateBinding Background}"
                BorderBrush="{TemplateBinding BorderBrush}"
                BorderThickness="{TemplateBinding BorderThickness}">
```

```
        <Canvas Name="PlanePart"
                Background="{TemplateBinding PlaneBackground}"
                Margin="48">
          <Thumb Name="ThumbPart">
            <Thumb.Style>
              <Style TargetType="Thumb">
                <Setter Property="Width" Value="96" />
                <Setter Property="Height" Value="96" />
                <Setter Property="Template">
                  <Setter.Value>
                    <ControlTemplate TargetType="Thumb">
                      <Path Name="path"
                            Stroke="{StaticResource PhoneForegroundBrush}"
                            StrokeThickness="{StaticResource
                                                  PhoneStrokeThickness}"
                            Fill="Transparent">
                        <Path.Data>
                          <GeometryGroup FillRule="Nonzero">
                            <EllipseGeometry RadiusX="48" RadiusY="48" />
                            <EllipseGeometry RadiusX="6" RadiusY="6" />
                            <LineGeometry StartPoint="-48 0" EndPoint="-6 0" />
                            <LineGeometry StartPoint="48 0" EndPoint="6 0" />
                            <LineGeometry StartPoint="0 -48" EndPoint="0 -6" />
                            <LineGeometry StartPoint="0 48" EndPoint="0 6" />
                          </GeometryGroup>
                        </Path.Data>
                      </Path>
                    </ControlTemplate>
                  </Setter.Value>
                </Setter>
              </Style>
            </Thumb.Style>
          </Thumb>
        </Canvas>
      </Border>
    </ControlTemplate>
  </Setter.Value>
 </Setter>
</Style>
```

A *Border* surrounds the whole control, and the *Canvas* named "PlanePart" is given a *Margin* that just so happens to be half the size of the *Thumb*. This allows the center of the *Thumb* to indicate a point on the plane while still remaining entirely within the control. Within the *ControlTemplate* for the *Control* is another *ControlTemplate* for the *Thumb* that forms a kind of bull's eye pattern.

The program is tested in a project named WorldMap. The content area contains an *XYSlider* with the *PlaneBackground* property set to an *ImageBrush* based on a map of the world:

Silverlight Project: WorldMap   File: MainPage.xaml (excerpt)

```
<Grid x:Name="ContentPanel" Grid.Row="1" Margin="12,0,12,0">
    <Grid.RowDefinitions>
        <RowDefinition Height="*" />
        <RowDefinition Height="Auto" />
    </Grid.RowDefinitions>

    <petzold:XYSlider Name="xySlider"
                      Grid.Row="0"
                      ValueChanged="OnXYSliderValueChanged">
        <petzold:XYSlider.PlaneBackground>
            <!-- Image courtesy of NASA/JPL-Caltech (http://maps.jpl.nasa.gov). -->
            <ImageBrush ImageSource="Images/ear0xuu2.jpg" />
        </petzold:XYSlider.PlaneBackground>
    </petzold:XYSlider>

    <TextBlock Name="txtblk"
               Grid.Row="1"
               HorizontalAlignment="Center" />
</Grid>
```

The code-behind file is devoted to handling the *ValueChanged* event from the *XYSlider* and converting the normalized *Point* to longitude and latitude:

Silverlight Project: WorldMap   File: MainPage.xaml.cs (excerpt)

```
public partial class MainPage : PhoneApplicationPage
{
    public MainPage()
    {
        InitializeComponent();
        DisplayCoordinates(xySlider.Value);
    }

    void OnXYSliderValueChanged(object sender,
                               RoutedPropertyChangedEventArgs<Point> args)
    {
        DisplayCoordinates(args.NewValue);
    }

    void DisplayCoordinates(Point point)
    {
        double longitude = 360 * point.X - 180;
        double latitude = 90 - 180 * point.Y;
        txtblk.Text = String.Format("Longitude: {0:F0} Latitude: {1:F0}",
                                   longitude, latitude);

    }
}
```

And here it is:

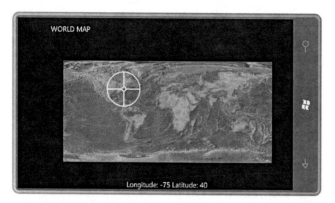

As you move the *Thumb* with your finger, the longitude and latitude values displayed at the bottom are updated. It's easy to imagine the WorldMap program being enhanced to obtain the phone's location and using that to initialize the position of the *Thumb*.

Chapter 17
Items Controls

There is still one major category of controls that I haven't discussed yet, and these are the derivatives of *Control* that begin with *ItemsControl*. This class hierarchy is complete beginning with that class:

Object
      DependencyObject (abstract)
          UIElement (abstract)
              FrameworkElement (abstract)
                  Control (abstract)
                      ItemsControl
                          Selector (abstract)
                              ListBox
                              ComboBox
                        TemplatedItemsControl (generic)
                              Panorama
                              Pivot
                              PivotHeadersControl
                      MapItemsControl

ItemsControl and its derivatives display collections of items. In addition, *Selector* and its derivatives implement properties and logic that allow the user to select one or more items from the collection. (I'll discuss the classes that derive from *TemplatedItemsControl* in the next chapter.)

Perhaps the most famous of these controls is *ListBox*, which has been in Windows-based environments for 25 years. The archetypal *ListBox* is a scrollable vertical list of items that you can navigate with the keyboard and mouse. (On Windows Phone 7 you use your fingers.) One (or optionally, more than one item) can be selected, visually indicated by highlighting and made available by the control. The *ComboBox* came a little later than the *ListBox*, so named because it combined a text-editing field and a drop-down *ListBox*.

What might not be as familiar to veteran Windows programmers is *ItemsControl*. *ItemsControl* often looks a lot like a *ListBox*, but it does not implement any selection logic. (It doesn't even implement its own scrolling, but that's easy to add.) The *ItemsControl* is simply for presentation purposes. Although *ItemsControl* is not *ListBox*, it still has an enormous value in Silverlight programming, and it is also useful if you'd prefer to implement your own selection logic.

I'll generally refer to *ItemsControl* and its derivatives as *items controls*—two words just like the name of this chapter. I have delayed discussing this family of controls until now because, in a very real sense, *ItemsControl* and *DataTemplate* were made for each other. You'll almost always define a *DataTemplate* for rendering the items in these controls.

Items Controls and Visual Trees

There are three basic ways to get items into an items control: code, XAML, and a data binding.

The code method is demonstrated by the ItemsControlsFromCode project. The program is intended to be displayed in a landscape orientation. It instantiates an *ItemsControl*, a *ListBox*, and a *ComboBox* in three columns of the content *Grid*:

Silverlight Project: ItemsControlsFromCode   File: MainPage.xaml (excerpt)

```
<Grid x:Name="ContentPanel" Grid.Row="1" Margin="12,0,12,0">
    <Grid.ColumnDefinitions>
        <ColumnDefinition Width="*" />
        <ColumnDefinition Width="*" />
        <ColumnDefinition Width="*" />
    </Grid.ColumnDefinitions>

    <ItemsControl Name="itemsControl" Grid.Column="0" />

    <ListBox Name="listBox" Grid.Column="1" />

    <ComboBox Name="comboBox" Grid.Column="2"
              VerticalAlignment="Top"
              Foreground="Black" />
</Grid>
```

I've added a couple property settings to the *ComboBox*. Aligning the control at the top of the cell works better with the drop-down feature. I also discovered that the default template for *ComboBox* has not been tweaked for the phone, so setting the *Foreground* property was necessary for the items to be displayed.

The code-behind file fills each of these controls with *FontFamily* objects:

Silverlight Project: ItemsControlsFromCode   File: MainPage.xaml.cs (excerpt)

```
public partial class MainPage : PhoneApplicationPage
{
    public MainPage()
    {
        InitializeComponent();
```

```
        FillItUp(itemsControl);
        FillItUp(listBox);
        FillItUp(comboBox);
    }

    void FillItUp(ItemsControl itemsControl)
    {
        string[] fontFamilies =
        {
            "Arial", "Arial Black", "Calibri", "Comic Sans MS",
            "Courier New", "Georgia", "Lucida Sans Unicode",
            "Portable User Interface", "Segoe WP", "Segoe WP Black",
            "Segoe WP Bold", "Segoe WP Light", "Segoe WP Semibold",
            "Segoe WP SemiLight", "Tahoma", "Times New Roman",
            "Trebuchet MS", "Verdana", "Webdings"
        };

        foreach (string fontFamily in fontFamilies)
            itemsControl.Items.Add(new FontFamily(fontFamily));
    }
}
```

The *Items* property defined by *ItemsControl* is of type *ItemCollection* and you can put pretty much anything in there that you want. If an object you put in the collection derives from *FrameworkElement* (such as a *Button*) then the element displays itself. Otherwise, the item's *ToString* method is used. Very conveniently, *FontFamily* has a *ToString* method that displays the *FontFamily* name:

Perhaps the first thing you'll notice about this program is that the *ItemsControl* doesn't scroll. If you want to scroll an *ItemsControl*, put it in a *ScrollViewer*.

The *ListBox* incorporates its own *ScrollViewer*. You use your fingers to both scroll and select an item, which is highlighted with the accent color, as Tahoma is highlighted here.

The *ComboBox* doesn't open until you touch anywhere in the control, and then the list appears:

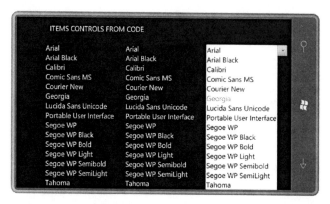

You see now why I set the *Foreground* property to Black. At first I set it to the *PhoneBackgroundBrush* resource but then I discovered that the *ComboBox* uses these same colors even with the Light theme.

Because *ComboBox* badly needs a *ControlTemplate* to fit in with the Windows Phone 7 aesthetics, I won't be describing the control in this book.

Much of this chapter involves defining templates for items controls, so it will be helpful to look at the visual trees of these three controls to get a sense of their internal architecture.

The ItemsControlsVisualTrees project is very similar to the ItemsControlsFromCode project except that it replaces the *ComboBox* with another *ItemsControl* (but this one in a *ScrollViewer*) and also includes a couple buttons. The program uses that second *ItemsControl* to display the visual trees associated with the first *ItemsControl* and the *ListBox*.

Here's the content area in the XAML file. To provide enough horizontal space to the *ItemsControl* used for displaying the visual trees, I've reduced the width of the first two columns:

Silverlight Project: ItemsControlsVisualTrees   File: MainPage.xaml (excerpt)

```
<Grid x:Name="ContentPanel" Grid.Row="1" Margin="12,0,12,0">
    <Grid.ColumnDefinitions>
        <ColumnDefinition Width="*" />
        <ColumnDefinition Width="*" />
        <ColumnDefinition Width="2*" />
    </Grid.ColumnDefinitions>

    <Grid.RowDefinitions>
        <RowDefinition Height="*" />
        <RowDefinition Height="Auto" />
    </Grid.RowDefinitions>
```

```
    <ItemsControl Name="itemsControl"
                  Grid.Column="0" Grid.Row="0" />

    <Button Content="Dump"
            Grid.Column="0" Grid.Row="1"
            Click="OnItemsControlDumpClick" />

    <ListBox Name="listBox"
             Grid.Column="1" Grid.Row="0" />

    <Button Content="Dump"
            Grid.Column="1" Grid.Row="1"
            Click="OnListBoxDumpClick" />

    <ScrollViewer Grid.Column="2" Grid.Row="0" Grid.RowSpan="2">
        <ItemsControl Name="dumpTreeItemsControl" />
    </ScrollViewer>
</Grid>
```

The code-behind file fills the first two controls with *FontFamily* objects again just as in the
first program:

Silverlight Project: ItemsControlsVisualTrees   File: MainPage.xaml.cs (excerpt)

```
public MainPage()
{
    InitializeComponent();

    FillItUp(itemsControl);
    FillItUp(listBox);
}

void FillItUp(ItemsControl itemsControl)
{
    string[] fontFamilies =
    {
        "Arial", "Arial Black", "Calibri", "Comic Sans MS",
        "Courier New", "Georgia", "Lucida Sans Unicode",
        "Portable User Interface", "Segoe WP", "Segoe WP Black",
        "Segoe WP Bold", "Segoe WP Light", "Segoe WP Semibold",
        "Segoe WP SemiLight", "Tahoma", "Times New Roman",
        "Trebuchet MS", "Verdana", "Webdings"
    };

    foreach (string fontFamily in fontFamilies)
        itemsControl.Items.Add(new FontFamily(fontFamily));
}
```

The class also includes handlers for the *Click* events for the two buttons and responds by dumping the visual tree of the corresponding items control:

Silverlight Project: ItemsControlsVisualTrees   File: MainPage.xaml.cs (excerpt)

```
void OnItemsControlDumpClick(object sender, RoutedEventArgs args)
{
    dumpTreeItemsControl.Items.Clear();
    DumpVisualTree(itemsControl, 0);
}

void OnListBoxDumpClick(object sender, RoutedEventArgs args)
{
    dumpTreeItemsControl.Items.Clear();
    DumpVisualTree(listBox, 0);
}

void DumpVisualTree(DependencyObject parent, int indent)
{
    TextBlock txtblk = new TextBlock();
    txtblk.Text = String.Format("{0}{1}", new string(' ', 4 * indent),
                                          parent.GetType().Name);
    dumpTreeItemsControl.Items.Add(txtblk);

    int numChildren = VisualTreeHelper.GetChildrenCount(parent);

    for (int childIndex = 0; childIndex < numChildren; childIndex++)
    {
        DependencyObject child = VisualTreeHelper.GetChild(parent, childIndex);
        DumpVisualTree(child, indent + 1);
    }
}
```

Here's the program displaying the visual tree for the *ItemsControl*:

The entire visual tree for an items control potentially incorporates several templates. This can be somewhat confusing, so perhaps a little review will help:

In some controls, such as *Slider*, the *ControlTemplate* defines the appearance of the entire control. The theme style for *Slider* defines a default *ControlTemplate* and you can define your own. That *ControlTemplate* might include other *ControlTemplate* definitions for the *ToggleButton* and *Thumb* that make up the *Slider*.

In *ContentControl* derivatives like *Button*, potentially two templates are present: a *ControlTemplate* defining the control's chrome, and a *DataTemplate* describing how the object set to the *Content* property is rendered in the control.

In *ItemsControl* derivatives, three types of templates are involved: A *ControlTemplate* for the control's chrome, an *ItemsPanelTemplate* for the panel it uses to host the items, and a *DataTemplate* that is applied to each item.

The visual tree for *ItemsControl* begins with the *ControlTemplate* for the control, and the default *ControlTemplate* for *ItemsControl* is simply an *ItemsPresenter*. This is a rather mysterious class that defines no public properties on its own. The *ItemsPresenter* is sometimes treated as a "placeholder" in a custom *ControlTemplate* for an items control.

The *ItemsPresenter* always uses a *Panel* derivative to display the items in the items control. In the default *ItemsControl* this is a *StackPanel* with a vertical orientation. This panel is replaceable by setting the *ItemsPanel* property defined by *ItemsControl* with an *ItemsPanelTemplate*. You'll see how to do this later in this chapter.

Following that are identical snippets of visual tree for each item in the collection beginning with a familiar element named *ContentPresenter*. As you'll recall from the last chapter, the *ContentPresenter* is the core of a *ContentControl*. This is the element responsible for hosting a *FrameworkElement* derivative, or converting a non-*FrameworkElement* derivative to text using its *TextString* method, or hosting an object using a visual tree based on a *DataTemplate* set to its *ContentTemplate* property. The *ContentPresenter* has the same role here but for each item individually.

In the *ItemsControl* being analyzed in this program, each item is displayed with a *TextBlock* within a single-cell *Grid*.

The visual tree for the *ListBox* is much more elaborate:

The visual tree begins with the default *ControlTemplate* for the *ListBox*. This tree begins with a *ScrollViewer*, which itself is a control so it has its own default *ControlTemplate* and its own visual tree starting with a *Border* and ending with the *ScrollContentPresenter*, which functions as the *ScrollViewer* engine. *ScrollViewer* is derived from *ContentControl* and within the *ControlTemplate* for *ListBox*, the *Content* of *ScrollViewer* is set to an *ItemsPresenter*, the same class that forms the entire default *ControlTemplate* of *ItemsControl*.

In the *ItemsControl* visual tree, the *ItemsPresenter* hosted a *StackPanel*; in the *ListBox* the *ItemsPresenter* hosts a *VirtualizingStackPanel*. Let me come back to that.

In the *ItemsControl* visual tree, each item is a *ContentPresenter*, a class familiar from the previous chapter. Here, each item is a *ListBoxItem*, which itself derives from *ContentControl*, and which has its own template, and its own *ContentPresenter*.

Why the difference? Why does *ListBox* need a special class named *ListBoxItem* to host each item but *ItemsControl* does not?

The answer is simple: Selection. Somebody has to handle the special display of a selected item in the *ListBox* and the *ComboBox*, and so there are classes for this purpose named *ListBoxItem* and *ComboBoxItem* (which derives from *ListBoxItem*). *ListBoxItem* derives from *ContentControl*—as you can see from the visual tree, it includes a *ContentControl* in its template, just like *Button*—but also defines an *IsSelected* property. The *ListBox* knows that its items are hosted by *ListBoxItem* controls so it is able to set that *IsSelected* property on the selected item, which the *ListBoxItem* template uses to highlight the item.

In the lingo of items controls, *ListBoxItem* is known as the *container* for items in the *ListBox*. These *ListBoxItem* containers are automatically created when the program adds items to the *ListBox*. The public interface to create and manage these containers is defined by *ItemsControl*, such as the *ItemContainerGenerator* property and several overridable methods for defining an alternative container class. But the subject of containers is beyond the scope of this book.

However, you may want to define a different *ControlTemplate* for *ListBoxItem*, perhaps to change the way that selected items are highlighted, but you might feel a little stymied because the *ListBoxItem* instances are created and maintained within this container logic. Fortunately, providing a custom *ControlTemplate* for *ListBoxItem* is easier than you might think: *ListBox* and *ComboBox* both define a property named *ItemContainerStyle* that you can set to a *Style* object that the *ListBox* applies to each *ListBoxItem* instance. Of course, this *Style* might include a *Setter* for the *Template* property. This is the easy approach. If you want *ListBox* to use a custom container class that you derive from *ListBoxItem*, then you need to get involved with the container-generator logic.

As you start looking at these visual trees—and keep in mind that in the general case each item will get its own visual tree defined by a *DataTemplate*—you may start worrying about the performance. Don't let the *DataTemplate* get too complex. One class that also helps performance is *VirtualizingStackPanel*, which only builds a visual tree for an object when that object needs to be displayed. You can derive your own virtualizing panels from *VirtualizingPanel*, but I'm afraid that topic is also beyond the scope of this book.

Customizing Item Displays

The second of the three approacesh to filling an items control requires explicitly defining the contents in XAML. The ItemsControlsFromXaml project uses this approach to fill an *ItemsControl* and two *ListBox* controls. The *Items* property defined by *ItemsControl* is the content property of the control, so in XAML all you need to do is put a bunch of objects between the begin and end tags of the particular items control.

In anticipation of formatting some strings in data bindings, a *StringFormatConverter* is included in the *Resources* collection of the program's MainPage.xaml file:

Silverlight Project: ItemsControlsFromXaml   File: **MainPage.xaml** (excerpt)

```
<phone:PhoneApplicationPage.Resources>
    <petzold:StringFormatConverter x:Name="stringFormat" />
</phone:PhoneApplicationPage.Resources>
```

The content area contains a three-column *Grid*:

Silverlight Project: ItemsControlsFromXaml   File: **MainPage.xaml** (excerpt)

```
<Grid x:Name="ContentPanel" Grid.Row="1" Margin="12,0,12,0">
    <Grid.ColumnDefinitions>
        <ColumnDefinition Width="*" />
        <ColumnDefinition Width="*" />
        <ColumnDefinition Width="*" />
    </Grid.ColumnDefinitions>

    ...

</Grid>
```

The first *Grid* cell contains a *ScrollViewer* hosting an *ItemsControl* which contains *Color* objects for all the colors defined in Silverlight:

Silverlight Project: ItemsControlsFromXaml   File: **MainPage.xaml** (excerpt)

```
<ScrollViewer Grid.Column="0">
    <ItemsControl>
        <Color>AliceBlue</Color>
        <Color>AntiqueWhite</Color>
        <Color>Aqua</Color>
        <Color>Aquamarine</Color>
        <Color>Azure</Color>
        ...
```

```
            <Color>Wheat</Color>
            <Color>White</Color>
            <Color>WhiteSmoke</Color>
            <Color>Yellow</Color>
            <Color>YellowGreen</Color>
    </ItemsControl>
</ScrollViewer>
```

Based on your experience of seeing what happens when you put a *Color* object in a *Button*, you can probably guess the result: a list of 141 hexadecimal color values. But at least it will be scrollable.

For a little variety, the second column of the *Grid* contains a *ListBox* with 141 *SolidColorBrush* objects:

Silverlight Project: ItemsControlsFromXaml   File: MainPage.xaml (excerpt)

```
<ListBox Grid.Column="1"
         DisplayMemberPath="Color">
    <SolidColorBrush Color="AliceBlue" />
    <SolidColorBrush Color="AntiqueWhite" />
    <SolidColorBrush Color="Aqua" />
    <SolidColorBrush Color="Aquamarine" />
    <SolidColorBrush Color="Azure" />
    ...
    <SolidColorBrush Color="Wheat" />
    <SolidColorBrush Color="White" />
    <SolidColorBrush Color="WhiteSmoke" />
    <SolidColorBrush Color="Yellow" />
    <SolidColorBrush Color="YellowGreen" />
</ListBox>
```

Again, from your experience with putting a *SolidColorBrush* object in a *Button*, you know that this will be even worse: All you'll get will be 141 instances of a text string with the fully-qualified class name "System.Windows.Media.SolidColorBrush".

But wait: Look at that property setting on the *ListBox*:

```
DisplayMemberPath="Color"
```

This property is defined by *ItemsControl*, and it allows you to specify one property of the items in the items control that you want used for display purposes. (Of course, it helps if all the items are of the same type, which is not otherwise a requirement.) With this property setting, *ListBox* will not display the *SolidColorBrush* object but will instead display the *Color* property of each *SolidColorBrush*, and the same hexadecimal values as the *ItemsControl*.

The third column is a *ListBox* done right. It has the same 141 *SolidColorBrush* items as the first *ListBox* but it also has a *DataTemplate* set to its *ItemTemplate* property that allows it to format the display of the items:

Silverlight Project: ItemsControlsFromXaml   File: MainPage.xaml (excerpt)

```
<ListBox Grid.Column="2">
    <ListBox.ItemTemplate>
        <DataTemplate>
            <StackPanel Orientation="Horizontal">
                <Rectangle Width="48" Height="36"
                           Margin="2"
                           Fill="{Binding}" />

                <StackPanel Orientation="Horizontal"
                            VerticalAlignment="Center">
                    <TextBlock Text="{Binding Color.R,
                                      Converter={StaticResource stringFormat},
                                      ConverterParameter=' {0:X2}'}" />
                    <TextBlock Text="{Binding Color.G,
                                      Converter={StaticResource stringFormat},
                                      ConverterParameter='-{0:X2}'}" />
                    <TextBlock Text="{Binding Color.B,
                                      Converter={StaticResource stringFormat},
                                      ConverterParameter='-{0:X2}'}" />
                </StackPanel>
            </StackPanel>
        </DataTemplate>
    </ListBox.ItemTemplate>

    <SolidColorBrush Color="AliceBlue" />
    <SolidColorBrush Color="AntiqueWhite" />
    <SolidColorBrush Color="Aqua" />
    <SolidColorBrush Color="Aquamarine" />
    <SolidColorBrush Color="Azure" />
    ...
    <SolidColorBrush Color="Wheat" />
    <SolidColorBrush Color="White" />
    <SolidColorBrush Color="WhiteSmoke" />
    <SolidColorBrush Color="Yellow" />
    <SolidColorBrush Color="YellowGreen" />
</ListBox>
```

In this *DataTemplate*, a *Rectangle* has its *Fill* property set to an empty *Binding*:

```
Fill="{Binding}"
```

This means that *Fill* is set to the particular item in the *ListBox*, which is of type *SolidColorBrush*. The three *TextBlock* elements have bindings that reference the *R*, *G*, and *B* properties of the *Color* property of the brush. Although this *ListBox* still displays hexadecimal numbers, it at least displays them with a modicum of class:

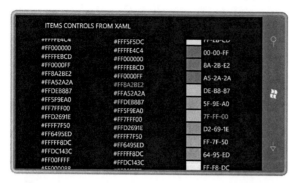

Defining a list of items for an items control entirely in XAML is fine for a small number of fixed items; the only reason I used this technique with the 141 *Color* values is because you can't generate them in Silverlight code by performing reflection on the *Colors* class. (The *Colors* class in Silverlight only defines 15 of these colors, so I wrote a WPF program instead that generated the markup that I then pasted into the Silverlight XAML file.)

If the items you want to put into an *ItemsControl* or *ListBox* in XAML are just text strings, you need to force the XAML parser to differentiate them. Perhaps the easiest solution is to define an XML namespace declaration for the *System* namespace:

```
xmlns:system="clr-namespace:System;assembly=mscorlib"
```

You can then explicitly delimit the items with *String* tags:

```
<ItemsControl>
    <system:String>Item Number 1</system:String>
    <system:String>Item Number 2</system:String>
    <system:String>Item Number 3</system:String>
    <system:String>Item Number 4</system:String>
    . . .
</ItemsControl>
```

In a similar way, you can explicitly fill an *ItemsControl* with numbers using *system:Double* tags. If you're using a *ListBox* rather than *ItemsControl*, you can separate string items with *ListBoxItem* tags:

```
<ListBox>
    <ListBoxItem>Item Number 1</ListBoxItem>
    <ListBoxItem>Item Number 1</ListBoxItem>
    <ListBoxItem>Item Number 1</ListBoxItem>
</ListBox>
```

Earlier I said that *ListBox* automatically generates *ListBoxItem* objects as containers. Won't this markup cause *ListBox* to wrap these *ListBoxItem* objects in additional *ListBoxItem* objects? Actually, no. Specifically to prevent this problem, *ItemsControl* defines a virtual method named *IsItemItsOwnContainerOverride*.

In the previous chapter I showed you a little chart that I hoped helped differentiate the two types of templates you can apply to a *ContentControl* derivative:

Property	Property Type	Purpose
Template	*ControlTemplate*	customizes display of control "chrome"
ContentTemplate	*DataTemplate*	customizes display of content

For an items control, there are three types of templates you can use, and another is indirectly available for *ListBox* and *ComboBox*. These are listed as you might encounter them from the top of the visual tree to the bottom

Property	Property Type	Purpose
Template	*ControlTemplate*	customizes display of control "chrome"
ItemsPanel	*ItemsPanelTemplate*	specifies *Panel* used to list items
ItemContainerStyle	*Style*	style of *ListBoxItem* or *ComboBoxItem*
ItemTemplate	*DataTemplate*	customizes display of item itself

ListBox Selection

Selector (the class from which *ListBox* and *ComboBox* derives) defines a *SelectedIndex* property that indicates the index of the selected item, or the value is –1 if no item is currently selected. *Selector* also defines a *SelectedItem* property, which is the item itself, or *null* if there's no selected item. If *SelectedIndex* is not equal to –1, *SelectedItem* is the same as the object returned from the *Items* property when indexed by *SelectedIndex*.

A *SelectionChanged* event is fired when the selection changes. This event implies that *SelectedItem* is a good choice for a binding source. *SelectedItem* is backed by a dependency property, so it can also serve as a binding target.

If a *ListBox* does not have its *SelectedIndex* or *SelectedItem* properties explicitly set, and the user has not yet touched the *ListBox*, *SelectedIndex* will be –1 and *SelectedItem* will be *null*. It's helpful to prepare for these eventualities.

The ListBoxSelection program allows a user to pick a *Color* and a *FontFamily* from two *ListBox* controls and displays some text using those selections. The *Resources* collection contains a standard binding converter and a *Style* for the *ListBox*:

Silverlight Project: ListBoxSelection   File: MainPage.xaml (excerpt)

```
<phone:PhoneApplicationPage.Resources>
    <petzold:StringFormatConverter x:Name="stringFormat" />

    <Style x:Key="listBoxStyle"
```

```
            TargetType="ListBox">
        <Setter Property="BorderBrush"
                Value="{StaticResource PhoneForegroundBrush}" />
        <Setter Property="BorderThickness"
                Value="{StaticResource PhoneBorderThickness}" />
        <Setter Property="HorizontalAlignment" Value="Center" />
        <Setter Property="Margin" Value="3" />
        <Setter Property="Padding" Value="3" />
    </Style>
</phone:PhoneApplicationPage.Resources>
```

All three elements are in a three-row *Grid*:

Silverlight Project: ListBoxSelection   File: MainPage.xaml (excerpt)

```
<Grid x:Name="ContentPanel" Grid.Row="1" Margin="12,0,12,0">
    <Grid.RowDefinitions>
        <RowDefinition Height="*" />
        <RowDefinition Height="*" />
        <RowDefinition Height="Auto" />
    </Grid.RowDefinitions>

    ...

</Grid>
```

The first *ListBox* contains a list of *SolidColorBrush* objects with the same *DataTemplate* used in the previous program to format the items:

Silverlight Project: ListBoxSelection   File: MainPage.xaml (excerpt)

```
<ListBox Name="brushListBox"
        Grid.Row="0"
        SelectedIndex="0"
        Style="{StaticResource listBoxStyle}">
    <ListBox.ItemTemplate>
        <DataTemplate>
            <StackPanel Orientation="Horizontal">
                <Rectangle Width="48" Height="36"
                           Margin="2"
                           Fill="{Binding}" />

                <StackPanel Orientation="Horizontal"
                            VerticalAlignment="Center">
                    <TextBlock Text="{Binding Color.R,
                                Converter={StaticResource stringFormat},
                                ConverterParameter=' {0:X2}'}" />
```

```
                    <TextBlock Text="{Binding Color.G,
                                  Converter={StaticResource stringFormat},
                                  ConverterParameter='-{0:X2}'}" />
                    <TextBlock Text="{Binding Color.B,
                                  Converter={StaticResource stringFormat},
                                  ConverterParameter='-{0:X2}'}" />
                </StackPanel>
            </StackPanel>
        </DataTemplate>
    </ListBox.ItemTemplate>

    <SolidColorBrush Color="AliceBlue" />
    <SolidColorBrush Color="AntiqueWhite" />
    <SolidColorBrush Color="Aqua" />
    <SolidColorBrush Color="Aquamarine" />
    <SolidColorBrush Color="Azure" />
    . . .
    <SolidColorBrush Color="Wheat" />
    <SolidColorBrush Color="White" />
    <SolidColorBrush Color="WhiteSmoke" />
    <SolidColorBrush Color="Yellow" />
    <SolidColorBrush Color="YellowGreen" />
</ListBox>
```

Notice that *SelectedIndex* is explicitly set to 0 so that the *ListBox* will have a valid *SelectedItem* at startup.

The second *ListBox* displays font families. I would have preferred using actual *FontFamily* objects but they cannot be created in XAML because *FontFamily* does not have a parameterless constructor. Instead, I stored the names as strings. *SelectedIndex* is initialized at 5, a number I chose pretty much at random.

When you see a *ListBox* displaying font families, do you expect the names to be displayed in the actual fonts? That's easy to implement with *DataTemplate*. Just bind both the *Text* and the *FontFamily* properties of a *TextBlock* to the items in the *ListBox*:

Silverlight Project: ListBoxSelection   File: MainPage.xaml (excerpt)

```
<ListBox Name="fontFamilyListBox"
         Grid.Row="1"
         SelectedIndex="5"
         Style="{StaticResource listBoxStyle}">
    <ListBox.ItemTemplate>
        <DataTemplate>
            <TextBlock Text="{Binding}"
                       FontFamily="{Binding}" />
        </DataTemplate>
    </ListBox.ItemTemplate>
```

```
        <system:String>Arial</system:String>
        <system:String>Arial Black</system:String>
        <system:String>Calibri</system:String>
        <system:String>Comic Sans MS</system:String>
        <system:String>Courier New</system:String>
        <system:String>Georgia</system:String>
        <system:String>Lucida Sans Unicode</system:String>
        <system:String>Portable User Interface</system:String>
        <system:String>Segoe WP</system:String>
        <system:String>Segoe WP Black</system:String>
        <system:String>Segoe WP Bold</system:String>
        <system:String>Segoe WP Light</system:String>
        <system:String>Segoe WP Semibold</system:String>
        <system:String>Segoe WP SemiLight</system:String>
        <system:String>Tahoma</system:String>
        <system:String>Times New Roman</system:String>
        <system:String>Trebuchet MS</system:String>
        <system:String>Verdana</system:String>
        <system:String>Webdings</system:String>
    </ListBox>
```

Because the items in the *ListBox* are strings rather than *FontFamily* objects, I wasn't sure the binding to *FontFamily* in the template would work, but it did.

The XAML file concludes with a *TextBlock* not in any template at all. Two of its properties are binding targets referencing the two *ListBox* controls:

Silverlight Project: ListBoxSelection   File: MainPage.xaml (excerpt)

```
<TextBlock Grid.Row="2"
           Text="Sample Text"
           FontSize="{StaticResource PhoneFontSizeExtraLarge}"
           HorizontalAlignment="Center"
           Margin="12"

           Foreground="{Binding ElementName=brushListBox,
                                Path=SelectedItem}"

           FontFamily="{Binding ElementName=fontFamilyListBox,
                                Path=SelectedItem}" />
```

When I was first developing this program, it seemed like the *FontFamily* binding in the *DataTemplate* was working fine but the *FontFamily* binding on the bottom *TextBlock* was causing a nasty runtime exception. I wrote a *StringToFontFamilyConverter* (which is still in the Petzold.Phone.Silverlight library) but the problem really seemed to be related to a *SelectedItem* value of *null* from the *ListBox*. Once I fixed that problem by explicitly initializing *SelectedIndex*, the binding problem disappeared.

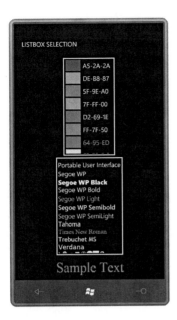

As you play with this program you'll see that the *TextBlock* changes height somewhat as the *FontFamily* changes. This has a ripple effect by causing changes to the two *ListBox* heights. A *ListBox* can also be susceptible to changes in width. If *HorizontalAlignment* is not *Stretch*, a *ListBox* will be only as wide as it needs to be, but because a *ListBox* uses a *VirtualizingStackPanel* by default, visual trees for items are created only as they are needed to be displayed. The *ListBox* might not know the width of its widest item at all times. It can be very disconcerting to see a *ListBox* change width as you scroll through the items!

For these reasons, a *ListBox* is often given an explicit width and height, or a specific width and height is imposed through a *Grid*.

Binding to *ItemsSource*

You've seen how to fill an items control through code or with a list in XAML. You can also set the items using the *ItemsSource* property defined by *ItemsControl*. The *ItemsSource* property is of type *IEnumerable* so you can pretty much use any collection type, including a simple array. However, if you're dealing with a collection where items can be added or removed dynamically, then it is very common to use the *ObservableCollection* class, which implements the *INotifyCollectionChanged* interface. The items control installs a handler for this event to be notified when the collection changes and then updates itself accordingly.

When working with data it is often necessary to provide a software layer between the actual objects you want to display and the user interface elements that display them. A plunge into the murky depths of model-view architectures is rather beyond the focus of this book. Instead I'll take a more relaxed approach and discuss simple intermediary classes sometimes referred to as *presenters*.

Let's create a *ColorPresenter* class that can fill up a *ListBox* with the 140 standard colors (excluding *Transparent*) by a single binding to *ItemsSource* and at the same time provide properties that allows displaying these colors in a more user-friendly manner.

It remains a mystery why the *Colors* class in Silverlight defines only 15 static properties of type *Color* instead of 141. That makes the *ColorPresenter* class rather awkward. I already had a WPF program that used reflection on the WPF *Colors* class, so I adapted that to generate the color names and values that I pulled into this class. Here they are in two static arrays in the *ColorPresenter* class in the Petzold.Phone.Silverlight library:

Silverlight Project: Petzold.Phone.Silverlight   File: ColorPresenter.cs

```
using System;
using System.Text;
using System.Windows.Media;

namespace Petzold.Phone.Silverlight
{
    public class ColorPresenter
    {
        static string[] colorNames =
        {
            "AliceBlue", "AntiqueWhite", "Aqua", "Aquamarine", "Azure",
            "Beige", "Bisque", "Black", "BlanchedAlmond", "Blue", "BlueViolet",
            "Brown", "BurlyWood", "CadetBlue", "Chartreuse", "Chocolate",
            "Coral", "CornflowerBlue", "Cornsilk", "Crimson", "Cyan",
            "DarkBlue", "DarkCyan", "DarkGoldenrod", "DarkGray", "DarkGreen",
            "DarkKhaki", "DarkMagenta", "DarkOliveGreen", "DarkOrange",
            "DarkOrchid", "DarkRed", "DarkSalmon", "DarkSeaGreen",
            "DarkSlateBlue", "DarkSlateGray", "DarkTurquoise", "DarkViolet",
            "DeepPink", "DeepSkyBlue", "DimGray", "DodgerBlue", "Firebrick",
            "FloralWhite", "ForestGreen", "Fuchsia", "Gainsboro", "GhostWhite",
            "Gold", "Goldenrod", "Gray", "Green", "GreenYellow", "Honeydew",
            "HotPink", "IndianRed", "Indigo", "Ivory", "Khaki", "Lavender",
            "LavenderBlush", "LawnGreen", "LemonChiffon", "LightBlue",
            "LightCoral", "LightCyan", "LightGoldenrodYellow", "LightGray",
            "LightGreen", "LightPink", "LightSalmon", "LightSeaGreen",
            "LightSkyBlue", "LightSlateGray", "LightSteelBlue", "LightYellow",
            "Lime", "LimeGreen", "Linen", "Magenta", "Maroon",
            "MediumAquamarine", "MediumBlue", "MediumOrchid", "MediumPurple",
            "MediumSeaGreen", "MediumSlateBlue", "MediumSpringGreen",
            "MediumTurquoise", "MediumVioletRed", "MidnightBlue", "MintCream",
            "MistyRose", "Moccasin", "NavajoWhite", "Navy", "OldLace", "Olive",
            "OliveDrab", "Orange", "OrangeRed", "Orchid", "PaleGoldenrod",
            "PaleGreen", "PaleTurquoise", "PaleVioletRed", "PapayaWhip",
            "PeachPuff", "Peru", "Pink", "Plum", "PowderBlue", "Purple", "Red",
            "RosyBrown", "RoyalBlue", "SaddleBrown", "Salmon", "SandyBrown",
            "SeaGreen", "SeaShell", "Sienna", "Silver", "SkyBlue", "SlateBlue",
            "SlateGray", "Snow", "SpringGreen", "SteelBlue", "Tan", "Teal",
            "Thistle", "Tomato", "Turquoise", "Violet", "Wheat", "White",
            "WhiteSmoke", "Yellow", "YellowGreen"
        };
```

```csharp
static uint[] uintColors =
{
    0xFFF0F8FF, 0xFFFAEBD7, 0xFF00FFFF, 0xFF7FFFD4, 0xFFF0FFFF,
    0xFFF5F5DC, 0xFFFFE4C4, 0xFF000000, 0xFFFFEBCD, 0xFF0000FF,
    0xFF8A2BE2, 0xFFA52A2A, 0xFFDEB887, 0xFF5F9EA0, 0xFF7FFF00,
    0xFFD2691E, 0xFFFF7F50, 0xFF6495ED, 0xFFFFF8DC, 0xFFDC143C,
    0xFF00FFFF, 0xFF00008B, 0xFF008B8B, 0xFFB8860B, 0xFFA9A9A9,
    0xFF006400, 0xFFBDB76B, 0xFF8B008B, 0xFF556B2F, 0xFFFF8C00,
    0xFF9932CC, 0xFF8B0000, 0xFFE9967A, 0xFF8FBC8F, 0xFF483D8B,
    0xFF2F4F4F, 0xFF00CED1, 0xFF9400D3, 0xFFFF1493, 0xFF00BFFF,
    0xFF696969, 0xFF1E90FF, 0xFFB22222, 0xFFFFFAF0, 0xFF228B22,
    0xFFFF00FF, 0xFFDCDCDC, 0xFFF8F8FF, 0xFFFFD700, 0xFFDAA520,
    0xFF808080, 0xFF008000, 0xFFADFF2F, 0xFFF0FFF0, 0xFFFF69B4,
    0xFFCD5C5C, 0xFF4B0082, 0xFFFFFFF0, 0xFFF0E68C, 0xFFE6E6FA,
    0xFFFFF0F5, 0xFF7CFC00, 0xFFFFFACD, 0xFFADD8E6, 0xFFF08080,
    0xFFE0FFFF, 0xFFFAFAD2, 0xFFD3D3D3, 0xFF90EE90, 0xFFFFB6C1,
    0xFFFFA07A, 0xFF20B2AA, 0xFF87CEFA, 0xFF778899, 0xFFB0C4DE,
    0xFFFFFFE0, 0xFF00FF00, 0xFF32CD32, 0xFFFAF0E6, 0xFFFF00FF,
    0xFF800000, 0xFF66CDAA, 0xFF0000CD, 0xFFBA55D3, 0xFF9370DB,
    0xFF3CB371, 0xFF7B68EE, 0xFF00FA9A, 0xFF48D1CC, 0xFFC71585,
    0xFF191970, 0xFFF5FFFA, 0xFFFFE4E1, 0xFFFFE4B5, 0xFFFFDEAD,
    0xFF000080, 0xFFFDF5E6, 0xFF808000, 0xFF6B8E23, 0xFFFFA500,
    0xFFFF4500, 0xFFDA70D6, 0xFFEEE8AA, 0xFF98FB98, 0xFFAFEEEE,
    0xFFDB7093, 0xFFFFEFD5, 0xFFFFDAB9, 0xFFCD853F, 0xFFFFC0CB,
    0xFFDDA0DD, 0xFFB0E0E6, 0xFF800080, 0xFFFF0000, 0xFFBC8F8F,
    0xFF4169E1, 0xFF8B4513, 0xFFFA8072, 0xFFF4A460, 0xFF2E8B57,
    0xFFFFF5EE, 0xFFA0522D, 0xFFC0C0C0, 0xFF87CEEB, 0xFF6A5ACD,
    0xFF708090, 0xFFFFFAFA, 0xFF00FF7F, 0xFF4682B4, 0xFFD2B48C,
    0xFF008080, 0xFFD8BFD8, 0xFFFF6347, 0xFF40E0D0, 0xFFEE82EE,
    0xFFF5DEB3, 0xFFFFFFFF, 0xFFF5F5F5, 0xFFFFFF00, 0xFF9ACD32
};

// Static constructor
static ColorPresenter()
{
    Colors = new ColorPresenter[140];

    for (int i = 0; i < 140; i++)
    {
        // Break down the color into components
        byte A = (byte)((uintColors[i] & 0xFF000000) >> 24);
        byte R = (byte)((uintColors[i] & 0x00FF0000) >> 16);
        byte G = (byte)((uintColors[i] & 0x0000FF00) >> 8);
        byte B = (byte)((uintColors[i] & 0x000000FF) >> 0);

        // Create a display name for the color
        StringBuilder builder = new StringBuilder();

        foreach (char ch in colorNames[i])
        {
            if (builder.Length == 0 || Char.IsLower(ch))
                builder.Append(ch);
            else
```

```
                    {
                        builder.Append(' ');
                        builder.Append(ch);
                    }
                }

                // Create a ColorPresenter for each color
                ColorPresenter clrPresenter = new ColorPresenter();
                clrPresenter.Color = Color.FromArgb(A, R, G, B);
                clrPresenter.Name = colorNames[i];
                clrPresenter.DisplayName = builder.ToString();
                clrPresenter.Brush = new SolidColorBrush(clrPresenter.Color);

                // Add it to the static array
                Colors[i] = clrPresenter;
            }
        }

        public static ColorPresenter[] Colors { protected set; get; }

        public Color Color { protected set; get; }

        public string Name { protected set; get; }

        public string DisplayName { protected set; get; }

        public Brush Brush { protected set; get; }

        public override string ToString()
        {
            return Name;
        }
    }
}
```

Towards the bottom you'll see the public instance properties that *ColorPresenter* exposes: *Color* of type *Color*, *Brush* of type *Brush*, but also *Name* of type *string*, and *DisplayName*. The *DisplayName* property converts the single-word camel-cased standard names to multiple words. For example "AliceBlue" becomes "Alice Blue".

ColorPresenter also exposes a public static property named *Colors*. This is an array of all 140 *ColorPresenter* objects. This array and all its contents are created in the class's static constructor.

If you were using *ColorPresenter* solely in code, you wouldn't need to create any additional instances of the class. You could simply access the static *ColorPresenter.Colors* property to get all 140 *ColorPresenter* objects.

However, Silverlight doesn't provide a way to access a static property in XAML without instantiating the class containing that property, so the ColorPresenterDemo project includes the *ColorPresenter* class in its *Resources* collection:

Silverlight Project: ColorPresenterDemo   File: **MainPage.xaml** (excerpt)

```
<phone:PhoneApplicationPage.Resources>
    <petzold:ColorPresenter x:Key="colorPresenter" />
    <petzold:StringFormatConverter x:Key="stringFormat" />
</phone:PhoneApplicationPage.Resources>
```

The instance of *ColorPresenter* created in the XAML file will not have any useful instance properties, but the program only needs the static *Colors* property.

The content *Grid* has just two rows: one for the *ListBox* and one for a *TextBlock* with bindings to the *ListBox*. Notice the *ItemsSource* property of the *ListBox* bound to the *Colors* property of the *ColorPresenter* resource. With this binding, the *ListBox* is filled with 140 objects of type *ColorPresenter* so the *DataTemplate* can have bindings to the *DisplayName* and *Color* properties of that class:

Silverlight Project: ColorPresenterDemo   File: **MainPage.xaml** (excerpt)

```
<Grid x:Name="ContentPanel" Grid.Row="1" Margin="12,0,12,0">
    <Grid.RowDefinitions>
        <RowDefinition Height="*" />
        <RowDefinition Height="Auto" />
    </Grid.RowDefinitions>

    <ListBox Grid.Row="0"
             Name="listBox"
             ItemsSource="{Binding Source={StaticResource colorPresenter},
                             Path=Colors}">
        <ListBox.ItemTemplate>
            <DataTemplate>
                <Grid>
                    <Grid.ColumnDefinitions>
                        <ColumnDefinition Width="Auto" />
                        <ColumnDefinition Width="Auto" />
                    </Grid.ColumnDefinitions>

                    <Rectangle Grid.Column="0"
                               Fill="{Binding Brush}"
                               Width="72" Height="48"
                               Margin="2 2 6 2" />

                    <StackPanel Grid.Column="1"
                                Orientation="Horizontal"
                                VerticalAlignment="Center">

                        <TextBlock Text="{Binding DisplayName}" />
```

```
                        <TextBlock Text="{Binding Color.R,
                                    Converter={StaticResource stringFormat},
                                    ConverterParameter=' ({0:X2}'}" />

                        <TextBlock Text="{Binding Color.G,
                                    Converter={StaticResource stringFormat},
                                    ConverterParameter='-{0:X2}'}" />

                        <TextBlock Text="{Binding Color.B,
                                    Converter={StaticResource stringFormat},
                                    ConverterParameter='-{0:X2})'}" />
                </StackPanel>
            </Grid>
        </DataTemplate>
    </ListBox.ItemTemplate>
</ListBox>

<TextBlock Grid.Row="1"
        FontSize="{StaticResource PhoneFontSizeExtraLarge}"
        HorizontalAlignment="Center"
        Margin="12"

        Text="{Binding ElementName=listBox,
                    Path=SelectedItem.DisplayName}"

        Foreground="{Binding ElementName=listBox,
                    Path=SelectedItem.Brush}" />
</Grid>
```

The *SelectedItem* property is also of type *ColorPresenter*, so the *TextBlock* can reference properties of *ColorPresenter* for the bindings to *Text* and *Foreground*:

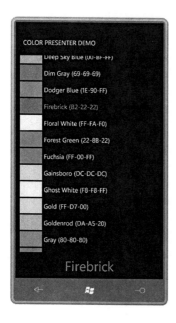

Putting these color names in your color-selection user interface is something you might consider. Familiarity with these names goes beyond programmers to anyone who's worked with colors in HTML, so the more sophisticated users of your application might have a very positive response to seeing these actual names on the screen.

Databases and Business Objects

Using a *ListBox* to display *Color* objects or *FontFamily* objects is fine for some special applications, but what are you going to put in *your* items control?

In general, you'll be filling an *ItemsControl* or *ListBox* with those vague but ubiquitous entities known as *business objects*.

For example, if you're creating an application that lets a user pick a hotel, it's likely you'll have a class named *Hotel*, and objects of *Hotel* will go into your *ListBox*. As a business object, *Hotel* is not going to derive from *FrameworkElement*. But it is very likely that *Hotel* will implement *INotifyPropertyChanged* so it can dynamically indicate a room rate that's just been reduced. Another business object will maintain a collection of *Hotel* objects, probably using *ObservableCollection* and implementing *INotifyCollectionChanged* to dynamically indicate changes when a new hotel opens its doors.

To get at least a little closer to a real-life example, I'm going to spend the remainder of the chapter focusing on programs that use a database of high school students. In these examples, the database is downloaded from a directory on my web site, but because I want to focus solely on the presentation of this data in this chapter, changes to properties of the *Student* class will be simulated locally.

The *http://www.charlespetzold.com/Students* directory of my Web site contains a file named students.xml that contains data on 69 students. The directory also contains lovely black-and-white photographs of all these students. These photographs are from high school yearbooks from El Paso, Texas for the years 1912 through 1914. The yearbooks are in the public domain and were graciously digitized by the El Paso Public Library and available on their Web site at *http://www.elpasotexas.gov/library/ourlibraries/main_library/yearbooks/yearbooks.asp*.

Among the source code for Chapter 17 is a library project named ElPasoHighSchool that contains several classes to read the XML file from my Web site and deserialize it into .NET objects.

Here's the *Student* class. It implements *INotifyPropertyChanged* and has several properties pertaining to the student, including name, sex, a filename referencing the photograph, and a grade point average:

Silverlight Project: **ElPasoHighSchool**   File: **Student.cs**

```
using System;
using System.ComponentModel;
```

```
namespace ElPasoHighSchool
{
    public class Student : INotifyPropertyChanged
    {
        public event PropertyChangedEventHandler PropertyChanged;

        string fullName;
        string firstName;
        string middleName;
        string lastName;
        string sex;
        string photoFilename;
        decimal gradePointAverage;

        public string FullName
        {
            set
            {
                if (fullName != value)
                {
                    fullName = value;
                    OnPropertyChanged("FullName");
                }
            }
            get
            {
                return fullName;
            }
        }

        public string FirstName
        {
            set
            {
                if (firstName != value)
                {
                    firstName = value;
                    OnPropertyChanged("FirstName");
                }
            }
            get
            {
                return firstName;
            }
        }

        public string MiddleName
        {
            set
            {
                if (middleName != value)
                {
```

```
                        middleName = value;
                        OnPropertyChanged("MiddleName");
                }
        }
        get
        {
                return middleName;
        }
}

public string LastName
{
        set
        {
                if (lastName != value)
                {
                        lastName = value;
                        OnPropertyChanged("LastName");
                }
        }
        get
        {
                return lastName;
        }
}

public string Sex
{
        set
        {
                if (sex != value)
                {
                        sex = value;
                        OnPropertyChanged("Sex");
                }
        }
        get
        {
                return sex;
        }
}

public string PhotoFilename
{
        set
        {
                if (photoFilename != value)
                {
                        photoFilename = value;
                        OnPropertyChanged("PhotoFilename");
                }
        }
```

```
            get
            {
                return photoFilename;
            }
        }

        public decimal GradePointAverage
        {
            set
            {
                if (gradePointAverage != value)
                {
                    gradePointAverage = value;
                    OnPropertyChanged("GradePointAverage");
                }
            }
            get
            {
                return gradePointAverage;
            }
        }

        protected virtual void OnPropertyChanged(string propChanged)
        {
            if (PropertyChanged != null)
                PropertyChanged(this, new PropertyChangedEventArgs(propChanged));
        }
    }
}
```

There will be one instance of the *Student* class for each student. Changes to any of these properties cause a *PropertyChanged* event to fire. Thus, this class is suitable as a source for data bindings.

The *StudentBody* class also implements *INotifyPropertyChanged*:

Silverlight Project: ElPasoHighSchool   File: StudentBody.cs

```
using System;
using System.Collections.ObjectModel;
using System.ComponentModel;
using System.Xml.Serialization;

namespace ElPasoHighSchool
{
    public class StudentBody : INotifyPropertyChanged
    {
        public event PropertyChangedEventHandler PropertyChanged;
        string school;
```

```
ObservableCollection<Student> students =
                        new ObservableCollection<Student>();

public string School
{
    set
    {
        if (school != value)
        {
            school = value;
            OnPropertyChanged("School");
        }
    }
    get
    {
        return school;
    }
}

public ObservableCollection<Student> Students
{
    set
    {
        if (students != value)
        {
            students = value;
            OnPropertyChanged("Students");

        }
    }
    get
    {
        return students;
    }
}

protected virtual void OnPropertyChanged(string propChanged)
{
    if (PropertyChanged != null)
        PropertyChanged(this, new PropertyChangedEventArgs(propChanged));
}
}
}
```

This class contains a property indicating the name of the school and an *ObservableCollection* of type *Student* to store all the *Student* objects. *ObservableCollection* is a very popular collection class in Silverlight because it implements the *INotifyCollectionChanged* interface, which means that it fires a *CollectionChanged* event whenever an item is added to or removed from the collection.

Before continuing, let's take a look at an excerpt of the student.xml file, which resides on my Web site:

File: http://www.charlespetzold.com/Students/students.xml (excerpt)

```
<?xml version="1.0" encoding="utf-8"?>
<StudentBody xmlns:xsi="http://www.w3.org/2001/XMLSchema-instance"
             xmlns:xsd="http://www.w3.org/2001/XMLSchema">
  <School>El Paso High School</School>
  <Students>
    <Student>
      <FullName>Adkins Bowden</FullName>
      <FirstName>Adkins</FirstName>
      <MiddleName />
      <LastName>Bowden</LastName>
      <Sex>Male</Sex>
      <PhotoFilename>
          http://www.charlespetzold.com/Students/AdkinsBowden.png
      </PhotoFilename>
      <GradePointAverage>2.71</GradePointAverage>
    </Student>
    <Student>
      <FullName>Alfred Black</FullName>
      <FirstName>Alfred</FirstName>
      <MiddleName />
      <LastName>Black</LastName>
      <Sex>Male</Sex>
      <PhotoFilename>
          http://www.charlespetzold.com/Students/AlfredBlack.png
      </PhotoFilename>
      <GradePointAverage>2.87</GradePointAverage>
    </Student>
    ...

    <Student>
      <FullName>William Sheley Warnock</FullName>
      <FirstName>William</FirstName>
      <MiddleName>Sheley</MiddleName>
      <LastName>Warnock</LastName>
      <Sex>Male</Sex>
      <PhotoFilename>
          http://www.charlespetzold.com/Students/WilliamSheleyWarnock.png
      </PhotoFilename>
      <GradePointAverage>1.82</GradePointAverage>
    </Student>
  </Students>
</StudentBody>
```

As you can see, the element tags correspond to properties in the *Student* and *StudentBody* classes. I created this file using XML serialization with the *XmlSerializer* class, and XML deserialization can convert it back into *Student* and *StudentBody* objects. That is the function of the *StudentBodyPresenter* class, which again implements *INotifyPropertyChanged*:

Silverlight Project: ElPasoHighSchool   File: StudentBodyPresenter.cs

```
using System;
using System.ComponentModel;
using System.IO;
using System.Net;
using System.Windows.Threading;
using System.Xml.Serialization;

namespace ElPasoHighSchool
{
    public class StudentBodyPresenter : INotifyPropertyChanged
    {
        public event PropertyChangedEventHandler PropertyChanged;

        StudentBody studentBody;
        Random rand = new Random();

        public StudentBodyPresenter()
        {
            Uri uri =
                new Uri("http://www.charlespetzold.com/Students/students.xml");

            WebClient webClient = new WebClient();
            webClient.DownloadStringCompleted += OnDownloadStringCompleted;
            webClient.DownloadStringAsync(uri);
        }

        void OnDownloadStringCompleted(object sender,
                                     DownloadStringCompletedEventArgs args)
        {
            StringReader reader = new StringReader(args.Result);
            XmlSerializer xml = new XmlSerializer(typeof(StudentBody));
            StudentBody = xml.Deserialize(reader) as StudentBody;

            DispatcherTimer tmr = new DispatcherTimer();
            tmr.Tick += TimerOnTick;
            tmr.Interval = TimeSpan.FromMilliseconds(100);
            tmr.Start();
        }

        public StudentBody StudentBody
        {
            protected set
            {
                if (studentBody != value)
                {
                    studentBody = value;
                    OnPropertyChanged("StudentBody");
                }
            }
```

```
            get
            {
                return studentBody;
            }
        }

        protected virtual void OnPropertyChanged(string propChanged)
        {
            if (PropertyChanged != null)
                PropertyChanged(this, new PropertyChangedEventArgs(propChanged));
        }

        void TimerOnTick(object sender, EventArgs args)
        {
            int index = rand.Next(studentBody.Students.Count);
            Student student = studentBody.Students[index];

            double factor = 1 + (rand.NextDouble() - 0.5) / 5;

            student.GradePointAverage =
                    Math.Max(0, Math.Min(5, Decimal.Round((decimal)factor *
                                            student.GradePointAverage, 2)));
        }
    }
}
```

The constructor of the *StudentBodyPresenter* class uses *WebClient* to access the students.xml file. As you'll recall, *WebClient* performs asynchronous web accesses, so it needs a callback to signal the program when it's completed. The *Deserialize* method of the *XmlSerializer* class then converts the XML text file into an actual *StudentBody* object, which is available as a public property to this class. When the *OnDownloadStringCompleted* callback sets that *StudentBody* property, the class fires its first and only *PropertyChanged* event.

The *OnDownloadStringCompleted* callback also starts up a *DispatcherTimer* that simulates changes to the data. Ten times a second, the *GradePointAverage* property of one of the students changes, causing the particular *Student* class to fire a *PropertyChanged* event. We hope very much to witness those dynamic changes on screen.

You can begin experimenting with this database by opening up a new Silverlight project, making a reference to the ElPasoHighSchool.dll library, and putting an XML namespace declaration in the MainPage.xaml file:

```
xmlns:elpaso="clr-namespace:ElPasoHighSchool;assembly=ElPasoHighSchool"
```

You then instantiate this the *StudentBodyPresenter* class in the *Resources* collection:

```
<phone:PhoneApplicationPage.Resources>
    <elpaso:StudentBodyPresenter x:Key="studentBodyPresenter" />
</phone:PhoneApplicationPage.Resources>
```

You can then put a *TextBlock* in the content area with a binding to that resource:

```
<Grid x:Name="ContentPanel" Grid.Row="1" Margin="12,0,12,0">
    <TextBlock HorizontalAlignment="Center"
               VerticalAlignment="Center"
               Text="{Binding Source={StaticResource studentBodyPresenter},
                          Path=StudentBody.School}" />
</Grid>
```

The screen indicates that the program is successfully downloading and deserializing the students.xml file:

Changing the binding path from StudentBody.School to StudentBody.Students indicates an *ObservableCollection*:

It's possible to access the *Count* property of the *ObservableCollection*:

```
<Grid x:Name="ContentPanel" Grid.Row="1" Margin="12,0,12,0">
    <TextBlock HorizontalAlignment="Center"
               VerticalAlignment="Center"
               Text="{Binding Source={StaticResource studentBodyPresenter},
                              Path=StudentBody.Students.Count}" />
</Grid>
```

And the *Students* collection can be indexed:

```
<TextBlock HorizontalAlignment="Center"
           VerticalAlignment="Center"
           Text="{Binding Source={StaticResource studentBodyPresenter},
                          Path=StudentBody.Students[23]}" />
```

This shows us that the *Students* collection contains objects of type *Student*:

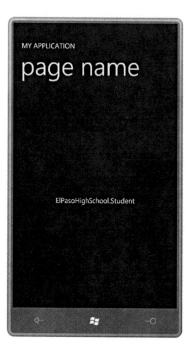

To avoid making this binding even longer, let's split it up by setting a *DataContext* on the content *Grid*. The *DataContext* is inherited through the visual tree and simplifies the binding on the *TextBlock*:

```
<Grid x:Name="ContentPanel" Grid.Row="1" Margin="12,0,12,0"
      DataContext="{Binding Source={StaticResource studentBodyPresenter},
                            Path=StudentBody}">
```

```
    <TextBlock HorizontalAlignment="Center"
               VerticalAlignment="Center"
               Text="{Binding Path=Students[23].FullName}" />
</Grid>
```

That binding references a particular student's name:

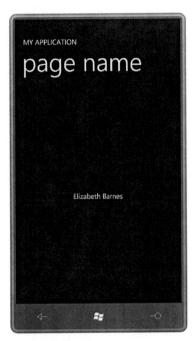

The binding can be simplified even more by eliminating the "Path=" part:

```
<TextBlock HorizontalAlignment="Center"
           VerticalAlignment="Center"
           Text="{Binding Students[23].FullName}" />
```

Now let's replace the *TextBlock* with an *Image* element referencing the *PhotoFilename* property of the *Student* class:

```
<Grid x:Name="ContentPanel" Grid.Row="1" Margin="12,0,12,0"
    DataContext="{Binding Source={StaticResource studentBodyPresenter},
                          Path=StudentBody}">

    <Image HorizontalAlignment="Center"
           VerticalAlignment="Center"
           Stretch="None"
           Source="{Binding Students[23].PhotoFilename}" />

</Grid>
```

And we get the photo successfully downloaded and displayed:

Now it's time to stop fooling around and put an actual *ListBox* in there:

```
<Grid x:Name="ContentPanel" Grid.Row="1" Margin="12,0,12,0"
      DataContext="{Binding Source={StaticResource studentBodyPresenter},
                            Path=StudentBody}">

    <ListBox ItemsSource="{Binding Students}" />

</Grid>
```

The *Students* property is of type *ObservableCollection*, which of course implements *IEnumerable*, which is all that *ListBox* really requires for its *ItemsSource*. But *ListBox* also determines if the object bound to *ItemsSource* can do a little more, for example, if it implements *INotifyCollectionChanged*, which *ObservableCollection* does. So if somehow a new *Student* were added to the collection, or other students were removed from the collection as they graduated, the *ListBox* would know about that and change the items it was displaying.

At the moment, the *ListBox* doesn't seem to be overjoyed with this data:

Whenever you see a *ListBox* or *ItemsControl* with a bunch of identical class names listed, don't despair. You should instead rejoice! Such a display shows that the *ListBox* has been successfully filled with items of the same type, and all it needs to display something meaningful is a *DataTemplate* or (if we're lazy) a *DisplayMemberPath* setting;

```
<Grid x:Name="ContentPanel" Grid.Row="1" Margin="12,0,12,0"
      DataContext="{Binding Source={StaticResource studentBodyPresenter},
                           Path=StudentBody}">

    <ListBox ItemsSource="{Binding Students}"
             DisplayMemberPath="FullName" />

</Grid>
```

Here it is:

Let's leave the *ListBox* like that for now, and instead focus on displaying the selected item from the *ListBox*.

By adding another row to the *Grid*, we can put a *TextBlock* down at the bottom of the display:

```
<Grid x:Name="ContentPanel" Grid.Row="1" Margin="12,0,12,0"
     DataContext="{Binding Source={StaticResource studentBodyPresenter},
                          Path=StudentBody}">
   <Grid.RowDefinitions>
      <RowDefinition Height="*" />
      <RowDefinition Height="Auto" />
   </Grid.RowDefinitions>

   <ListBox Grid.Row="0"
           Name="listBox"
           ItemsSource="{Binding Students}"
           DisplayMemberPath="FullName" />

   <TextBlock Grid.Row="1"
           FontSize="{StaticResource PhoneFontSizeLarge}"
           HorizontalAlignment="Center"
           Text="{Binding ElementName=listBox,
                         Path=SelectedItem.FullName}" />
</Grid>
```

Notice the binding on the *TextBlock*. The *SelectedItem* property of the *ListBox* is of type *Student*, so the binding path can reference a property of *Student*, such as *FullName*. Now when an item is selected from the *ListBox*, the *TextBlock* displays the item's *FullName* property:

Or, replace the *TextBlock* with an *Image* element:

```
<Grid x:Name="ContentPanel" Grid.Row="1" Margin="12,0,12,0"
      DataContext="{Binding Source={StaticResource studentBodyPresenter},
                            Path=StudentBody}">
    <Grid.RowDefinitions>
        <RowDefinition Height="*" />
        <RowDefinition Height="Auto" />
    </Grid.RowDefinitions>

    <ListBox Grid.Row="0"
             Name="listBox"
             ItemsSource="{Binding Students}"
             DisplayMemberPath="FullName" />

    <Image Grid.Row="1"
           HorizontalAlignment="Center"
           Stretch="None"
           Source="{Binding ElementName=listBox,
                            Path=SelectedItem.PhotoFilename}" />
</Grid>
```

You can now go through the *ListBox* and select an item to view that student's picture:

To view multiple properties of the selected item, you might want to put another *DataContext* definition on a *Border*:

```
<Grid x:Name="ContentPanel" Grid.Row="1" Margin="12,0,12,0"
      DataContext="{Binding Source={StaticResource studentBodyPresenter},
```

```
                                       Path=StudentBody}">
        <Grid.RowDefinitions>
            <RowDefinition Height="*" />
            <RowDefinition Height="Auto" />
        </Grid.RowDefinitions>

        <ListBox Grid.Row="0"
                Name="listBox"
                ItemsSource="{Binding Students}"
                DisplayMemberPath="FullName" />

        <Border Grid.Row="1"
                BorderBrush="{StaticResource PhoneForegroundBrush}"
                BorderThickness="{StaticResource PhoneBorderThickness}"
                HorizontalAlignment="Center"
                DataContext="{Binding ElementName=listBox,
                                      Path=SelectedItem}">


        </Border>
</Grid>
```

Within this *Border* can go a panel and elements with bindings that reference properties of the *Student* class. This is what I've done in the StudentBodyListBox program. The XAML file contains an XML namespace declaration for the ElPasoHighSchool library:

```
xmlns:elpaso="clr-namespace:ElPasoHighSchool;assembly=ElPasoHighSchool"
```

The *Resources* collection instantiates the *StudentBodyPresenter* class:

Silverlight Project: StudentBodyListBox   File: MainPage.xaml (excerpt)

```
<phone:PhoneApplicationPage.Resources>
    <elpaso:StudentBodyPresenter x:Key="studentBodyPresenter" />
</phone:PhoneApplicationPage.Resources>
```

Here's the content area:

Silverlight Project: StudentBodyListBox   File: MainPage.xaml (excerpt)

```
<Grid x:Name="ContentPanel" Grid.Row="1" Margin="12,0,12,0"
    DataContext="{Binding Source={StaticResource studentBodyPresenter},
                          Path=StudentBody}">
    <Grid.RowDefinitions>
        <RowDefinition Height="Auto" />
        <RowDefinition Height="*" />
        <RowDefinition Height="Auto" />
    </Grid.RowDefinitions>
```

```xml
<TextBlock Grid.Row="0"
           Text="{Binding School}"
           FontSize="{StaticResource PhoneFontSizeLarge}"
           HorizontalAlignment="Center"
           TextDecorations="Underline" />

<ListBox Grid.Row="1"
         Name="listBox"
         ItemsSource="{Binding Students}"
         DisplayMemberPath="FullName" />

<Border Grid.Row="2"
        BorderBrush="{StaticResource PhoneForegroundBrush}"
        BorderThickness="{StaticResource PhoneBorderThickness}"
        HorizontalAlignment="Center"
        DataContext="{Binding ElementName=listBox,
                              Path=SelectedItem}">
    <Grid>
        <Grid.RowDefinitions>
            <RowDefinition Height="Auto" />
            <RowDefinition Height="Auto" />
            <RowDefinition Height="Auto" />
        </Grid.RowDefinitions>

        <TextBlock Grid.Row="0"
                   Text="{Binding FullName}"
                   TextAlignment="Center" />

        <Image Grid.Row="1"
               Width="225"
               Height="300"
               Margin="24 6"
               Source="{Binding PhotoFilename}" />

        <StackPanel Grid.Row="2"
                    Orientation="Horizontal"
                    HorizontalAlignment="Center">
            <TextBlock Text="GPA=" />
            <TextBlock Text="{Binding GradePointAverage}" />
        </StackPanel>
    </Grid>

</Border>
</Grid>
```

Within the *Border* is a *Grid* with three rows, containing a *TextBlock* with a binding to the *FullName* property, an *Image* element, and a *StackPanel* to display the grade point average. Notice I've given the *Image* element a specific size based on my knowledge of the size of the images. This avoids a change in size of the *Image* element after it's able to download the photo.

You can now scroll through the *ListBox* and look at each student in detail

Wait a little while and you should be able to see a change in the grade point average. That's the beauty of *INotifyPropertyChanged* and dependency properties at work.

Fun with *DataTemplates*

For the remainder of this chapter, I want to switch from the *ListBox* to the *ItemsControl* to focus solely on presentation and navigation rather than selection. To play along, you can create a new project, set a reference to the ElPasoHighSchool library, and in the XAML file add an XML namespace declaration for that library and instantiate the *StudentBodyPresenter* class in the *Resources* collection as in the previous program. Here's an *ItemsControl* in a *ScrollViewer* that fills up the whole content *Grid*:

```
<Grid x:Name="ContentPanel" Grid.Row="1" Margin="12,0,12,0"
      DataContext="{Binding Source={StaticResource studentBodyPresenter},
                            Path=StudentBody}">
    <ScrollViewer>
        <ItemsControl ItemsSource="{Binding Students}"
                      DisplayMemberPath="FullName" />
    </ScrollViewer>

</Grid>
```

The *ScrollViewer* allows the contents to be scroll:

Replace the *DisplayMemberPath* with a *DataTemplate* to provide more extensive information, nicely formatted:

```
<Grid x:Name="ContentPanel" Grid.Row="1" Margin="12,0,12,0">
    <ScrollViewer>
        <ItemsControl ItemsSource="{Binding Students}">
            <ItemsControl.ItemTemplate>
                <DataTemplate>
                    <Border BorderBrush="{StaticResource PhoneAccentBrush}"
                            BorderThickness="1"
                            CornerRadius="12"
                            Margin="2">
                        <Grid>
                            <Grid.RowDefinitions>
                                <RowDefinition Height="*" />
                                <RowDefinition Height="*" />
                            </Grid.RowDefinitions>

                            <Grid.ColumnDefinitions>
                                <ColumnDefinition Width="Auto" />
                                <ColumnDefinition Width="*" />
                            </Grid.ColumnDefinitions>

                            <Image Grid.Row="0" Grid.Column="0" Grid.RowSpan="2"
                                   Source="{Binding PhotoFilename}"
                                   Height="120"
                                   Width="90"
                                   Margin="6" />
```

```
                                <StackPanel Grid.Row="0" Grid.Column="1"
                                            Orientation="Horizontal"
                                            VerticalAlignment="Center">
                                    <TextBlock Text="{Binding LastName}" />
                                    <TextBlock Text=", " />
                                    <TextBlock Text="{Binding FirstName}" />
                                    <TextBlock Text=", " />
                                    <TextBlock Text="{Binding MiddleName}" />
                                </StackPanel>

                                <StackPanel Grid.Row="1" Grid.Column="1"
                                            Orientation="Horizontal"
                                            VerticalAlignment="Center">
                                    <TextBlock Text="Grade Point Average = " />
                                    <TextBlock Text="{Binding GradePointAverage}" />
                                </StackPanel>
                            </Grid>
                        </Border>
                    </DataTemplate>
                </ItemsControl.ItemTemplate>
            </ItemsControl>
        </ScrollViewer>
    </Grid>
```

In this template, the height of the individual items is governed by the explicit *Height* setting on the *Image* element. To prevent the text from moving to the right as the photos are being loaded, an explicit *Width* setting is also provided. Here's the result:

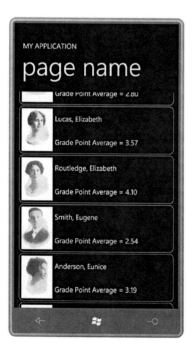

Sorting

In earlier displays of these students, I used the property of *Student* called *FullName* to display the student's name. You may have noticed that the students.xml file was actually sorted by this property, and that's the order in which the students appeared on the screen. Popular email programs display your contacts sorted by first name, so I figured it wasn't entirely a bad thing.

But in the most recent *DataTemplate*, I switched to using the *LastName*, *FirstName*, and *MiddleName* properties, and the unsorted display now looks very strange and just plain wrong.

How can this be fixed?

One approach is through code. It's possible for the *StudentBodyPresenter* class to re-sort the data after it's been downloaded. But you might prefer a more flexible approach. Perhaps your application needs to display data using different sort criteria at different times.

You can do that—and you can do it entirely in XAML—using a class called *CollectionViewSource* defined in the *System.Windows.Data* namespace. You'll use this class in conjunction with a *SortDescription* class defined in the *System.ComponentModel* namespace. Besides the reference and XML namespace declaration for the ElPasoHighSchool library, you'll need an XML namespace declaration for *System.ComponentModel*:

```
xmlns:componentmodel="clr-namespace:System.ComponentModel;assembly=System.Windows"
```

The whole *CollectionViewSource* can go in the *Resources* collection:

```
<phone:PhoneApplicationPage.Resources>
    <elpaso:StudentBodyPresenter x:Key="studentBodyPresenter" />

    <CollectionViewSource x:Key="sortedStudents"
                          Source="{Binding Source={StaticResource studentBodyPresenter},
                                   Path=StudentBody.Students}">
        <CollectionViewSource.SortDescriptions>
            <componentmodel:SortDescription PropertyName="LastName"
                                   Direction="Ascending" />
        </CollectionViewSource.SortDescriptions>
    </CollectionViewSource>

</phone:PhoneApplicationPage.Resources>
```

Notice how the *Source* property of the *CollectionViewSource* now references the *Students* property of the *StudentBody* property of the *StudentBodyPresenter*. This *Students* property is of type *ObservableCollection<Student>*. The *Source* of *CollectionViewSource* must be a collection.

The *SortDescription* object indicates that we want to sort by the *LastName* property in an ascending order. Since this *LastName* property is of type *string*, no additional code need be provided to support sorting.

The *Binding* can now be removed from the *DataContext* of the *Grid,* and the *Source* property of *ItemsControl* can now reference the *CollectionViewSource* resource:

```
<Grid x:Name="ContentPanel" Grid.Row="1" Margin="12,0,12,0">
    <ScrollViewer>
        <ItemsControl ItemsSource="{Binding Source={StaticResource sortedStudents}}">
            ...
        </ItemsControl>
    </ScrollViewer>
</Grid>
```

And now the display looks more alphabetically comforting:

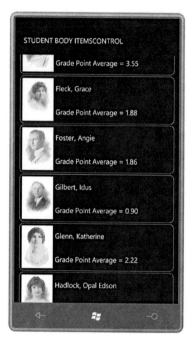

You can have multiple *SortDescription* objects in *CollectionViewSource.* Try this:

```
<CollectionViewSource x:Key="sortedStudents"
                      Source="{Binding Source={StaticResource studentBodyPresenter},
                                       Path=StudentBody.Students}">
    <CollectionViewSource.SortDescriptions>
        <componentmodel:SortDescription PropertyName="Sex"
                                        Direction="Ascending" />
        <componentmodel:SortDescription PropertyName="LastName"
                                        Direction="Ascending" />
    </CollectionViewSource.SortDescriptions>
</CollectionViewSource>
```

Now all the women are first, followed by the men.

Or alternatively, perhaps you want to display the names of the male students in *PowderBlue* and the female students in *Pink*. It's a rather antiquated convention, to be sure, but we are dealing with students who attended high school nearly 100 years ago! Regardless of the propriety of pink and blue, how would you do it?

Fortunately, the *Student* class has a property named *Sex*, which is set to a text string, either "Male" or "Female." Since we're dealing with data bindings in the *DataTemplate*, the obvious solution is a data converter, and fortunately the Petzold.Phone.Silverlight library has one that seems ideal:

Silverlight Project: Petzold.Phone.Silverlight   File: SexToBrushConverter.cs

```
using System;
using System.Globalization;
using System.Windows.Data;
using System.Windows.Media;

namespace Petzold.Phone.Silverlight
{
    public class SexToBrushConverter : IValueConverter
    {
        public Brush MaleBrush { get; set; }
        public Brush FemaleBrush { get; set; }

        public object Convert(object value, Type targetType,
                              object parameter, CultureInfo culture)
        {
            string sex = value as string;

            switch (sex)
            {
                case "Male": return MaleBrush;
                case "Female": return FemaleBrush;
            }

            return null;
        }

        public object ConvertBack(object value, Type targetType,
                                  object parameter, CultureInfo culture)
        {
            return null;
        }
    }
}
```

Like all data converters, it derives from *IValueConverter* and has two methods named *Convert* and *ConvertBack*. This converter also defines two properties named *MaleBrush* and *FemaleBrush*. These properties let us avoid hard-coding brushes in the code. The *Convert* method is the only one that's implemented: If the value coming in is "Male" it returns *MaleBrush* and if "Female" it returns *FemaleBrush*.

Let's put everything into one project. The StudentBodyItemsControl project has a reference to the Petzold.Phone.Silverlight library as well as ElPasoHighSchool. The *Resources* section instantiates the *StudentBodyPresenter*, the *CollectionViewSource* for sorting, and the *SexToBrushConverter*:

Silverlight Project: StudentBodyItemsControl   File: MainPage.xaml (excerpt)

```
<phone:PhoneApplicationPage.Resources>
    <elpaso:StudentBodyPresenter x:Key="studentBodyPresenter" />

    <CollectionViewSource x:Key="sortedStudents"
                          Source="{Binding Source={StaticResource
studentBodyPresenter},
                                           Path=StudentBody.Students}">
        <CollectionViewSource.SortDescriptions>
            <componentmodel:SortDescription PropertyName="LastName"
                                            Direction="Ascending" />
        </CollectionViewSource.SortDescriptions>
    </CollectionViewSource>

    <petzold:SexToBrushConverter x:Key="sexToBrushConverter"
                                 FemaleBrush="Pink"
                                 MaleBrush="PowderBlue" />
</phone:PhoneApplicationPage.Resources>
```

In the markup below I use five *TextBlock* elements to display the student's name—*LastName*, *FirstName*, and *MiddleName* with a comma and a space—and at least four of them need bindings targeting the *Foreground* property from the *Sex* property of the *Student* object, using this *SexToBrushConverter*. This same binding needs to be repeated four times.

Or, perhaps we can simplify the markup just a bit by enclosing all five *TextBlock* elements in a *ContentControl*. If the *Foreground* property on the *ContentControl* is set with a single binding, then the same property will be applied to each *TextBlock* based on property inheritance. That's what's done in the following *DataTemplate*, which is otherwise the same as the one you just saw:

Silverlight Project: StudentBodyItemsControl   File: MainPage.xaml (excerpt)

```
<Grid x:Name="ContentPanel" Grid.Row="1" Margin="12,0,12,0">
    <ScrollViewer>
        <ItemsControl ItemsSource="{Binding
                                    Source={StaticResource sortedStudents}}">
            <ItemsControl.ItemTemplate>
```

```xml
            <DataTemplate>
                <Border BorderBrush="{StaticResource PhoneAccentBrush}"
                        BorderThickness="1"
                        CornerRadius="12"
                        Margin="2">
                    <Grid>
                        <Grid.RowDefinitions>
                            <RowDefinition Height="*" />
                            <RowDefinition Height="*" />
                        </Grid.RowDefinitions>

                        <Grid.ColumnDefinitions>
                            <ColumnDefinition Width="Auto" />
                            <ColumnDefinition Width="*" />
                        </Grid.ColumnDefinitions>

                        <Image Grid.Row="0" Grid.Column="0" Grid.RowSpan="2"
                               Source="{Binding PhotoFilename}"
                               Height="120"
                               Width="90"
                               Margin="6" />

                        <ContentControl Grid.Row="0" Grid.Column="1"
                                        HorizontalAlignment="Left"
                                        VerticalAlignment="Center"
                           Foreground="{Binding Sex,
                           Converter={StaticResource sexToBrushConverter}}">

                            <StackPanel Orientation="Horizontal">
                                <TextBlock Text="{Binding LastName}" />
                                <TextBlock Text=", " />
                                <TextBlock Text="{Binding FirstName}" />
                                <TextBlock Text=", " />
                                <TextBlock Text="{Binding MiddleName}" />
                            </StackPanel>
                        </ContentControl>

                        <StackPanel Grid.Row="1" Grid.Column="1"
                                    Orientation="Horizontal"
                                    VerticalAlignment="Center">
                            <TextBlock Text="Grade Point Average = " />
                            <TextBlock Text="{Binding GradePointAverage}" />
                        </StackPanel>
                    </Grid>
                </Border>
            </DataTemplate>
        </ItemsControl.ItemTemplate>
    </ItemsControl>
  </ScrollViewer>
</Grid>
```

Adding the color is worth the effort, I think:

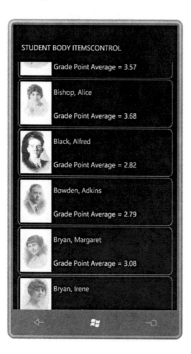

Changing the Panel

Internally, an *ItemsControl* uses an *ItemsPresenter* to display all the items, as you saw earlier in this chapter when looking at visual trees. One of the essential elements used to display the items is a panel of some sort. By default, this is a *StackPanel* (or, with *ListBox*, a *VirtualizingStackPanel*) with a vertical orientation. A vertical *StackPanel* is such a natural choice for this job that you may not think about replacing it.

But you can replace it. It's another template—but usually an extremely simple template—that you set to the *ItemsPanel* property defined by *ItemsControl*.

The HorizontalItemsControl project is much like the previous project. It has references and namespace declarations for Petzold.Silverlight.Phone and ElPasoHighSchool, and an identical *Resources* collection. The big difference is the use of a *StackPanel* with a horizontal orientation in the *ItemsControl*. The program also defines a rather different *DataTemplate* for each student and relies on a landscape orientation of the phone.

Because the *ItemsControl* is now displaying its items horizontally rather than vertically, the default behavior of *ScrollViewer* is all wrong. The *ScrollViewer* must be enabled for horizontal scrolling:

Silverlight Project: HorizontalItemsControl   File: **MainPage.xaml** (excerpt)

```xml
<Grid x:Name="ContentPanel" Grid.Row="1" Margin="12,0,12,0">

    <ScrollViewer VerticalAlignment="Center"
                  HorizontalScrollBarVisibility="Auto"
                  VerticalScrollBarVisibility="Disabled">
        <ItemsControl ItemsSource="{Binding
                                    Source={StaticResource sortedStudents}}">
            <ItemsControl.ItemTemplate>
                <DataTemplate>
                    <Border BorderBrush="{StaticResource PhoneAccentBrush}"
                            BorderThickness="1"
                            CornerRadius="12"
                            Margin="2">
                        <Grid>
                            <Grid.RowDefinitions>
                                <RowDefinition Height="Auto" />
                                <RowDefinition Height="Auto" />
                                <RowDefinition Height="Auto" />
                            </Grid.RowDefinitions>

                            <ContentControl Grid.Row="0"
                                            HorizontalAlignment="Center"
                                Foreground="{Binding Sex,
                                Converter={StaticResource sexToBrushConverter}}">

                                <StackPanel Orientation="Horizontal">
                                    <TextBlock Text="{Binding LastName}" />
                                    <TextBlock Text=", " />
                                    <TextBlock Text="{Binding FirstName}" />
                                    <TextBlock Text=", " />
                                    <TextBlock Text="{Binding MiddleName}" />
                                </StackPanel>
                            </ContentControl>

                            <Image Grid.Row="1"
                                   Source="{Binding PhotoFilename}"
                                   Height="240"
                                   Width="180"
                                   Margin="6" />

                            <StackPanel Grid.Row="2"
                                        Orientation="Horizontal"
                                        HorizontalAlignment="Center">
                                <TextBlock Text="GPA=" />
                                <TextBlock Text="{Binding GradePointAverage}" />
                            </StackPanel>
                        </Grid>
                    </Border>
                </DataTemplate>
            </ItemsControl.ItemTemplate>
```

```
            <ItemsControl.ItemsPanel>
                <ItemsPanelTemplate>
                    <StackPanel Orientation="Horizontal" />
                </ItemsPanelTemplate>
            </ItemsControl.ItemsPanel>

        </ItemsControl>
    </ScrollViewer>
</Grid>
```

Towards the bottom of the *ItemsControl* markup you'll see the *ItemsPanel* property set to an object of type *ItemsPanelTemplate*, which then encloses the *Panel* derivative you want to use.

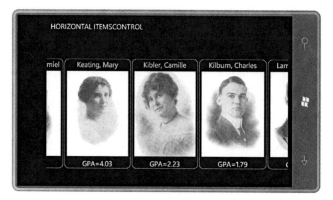

Not every type of panel is suitable for an items control. Generally you'll want to use a panel that organizes its children based on their order in its *Children* collection and not based on attached properties.

It is very common for programmers to create custom panels specifically for a *ListBox* or *ItemsControl*. Sometimes these panels take the form of circular organizations of children, or carousels. Toward the end of this chapter I'll show you an example of a custom panel to display these students.

The *DataTemplate* Bar Chart

With a combination of a *DataTemplate* and an *ItemsPanelTemplate*, you can make a *ListBox* or *ItemsControl* look like no other *ListBox* or *ItemsControl* you've ever seen.

Let's create a new project, and include references and XML namespace declarations for both the Petzold.Phone.Silverlight and ElPasoHighSchool libraries. Set properties in the root tag of MainPage.xaml for landscape. Put the *StudentBodyPresenter* in the *Resources* collection.

Here's an *ItemsControl* with no *ScrollViewer*. The *ItemsSource* is the *Students* property of the *StudentBodyPresenter* instance. The *ItemsPanelTemplate* is set to a *UniformStack* with a *Horizontal* orientation:

```
<Grid x:Name="ContentPanel" Grid.Row="1" Margin="12,0,12,0"
      DataContext="{Binding Source={StaticResource studentBodyPresenter},
                            Path=StudentBody}">

    <ItemsControl ItemsSource="{Binding Students}"
                  VerticalAlignment="Bottom">

        <ItemsControl.ItemsPanel>
            <ItemsPanelTemplate>
                <petzold:UniformStack Orientation="Horizontal" />
            </ItemsPanelTemplate>
        </ItemsControl.ItemsPanel>
    </ItemsControl>
</Grid>
```

With no *DataTemplate* the *ItemsControl* displays the fully-qualified class name as a string: "ElPasoHighSchool.Student." But with a *UniformStack* panel, every item gets the same amount of space so only the first "E" is visible:

This doesn't seem very promising, but let's set the *DataTemplate* to a *Rectangle* whose *Height* property is bound to the *GradePointAverage* property:

```
<ItemsControl ItemsSource="{Binding Students}"
              VerticalAlignment="Bottom">
    <ItemsControl.ItemTemplate>
        <DataTemplate>
            <Rectangle Fill="{StaticResource PhoneAccentBrush}"
                       Height="{Binding GradePointAverage}"
                       VerticalAlignment="Bottom"
                       Margin="1 0" />
        </DataTemplate>
    </ItemsControl.ItemTemplate>

    <ItemsControl.ItemsPanel>
```

```
        <ItemsPanelTemplate>
            <petzold:UniformStack Orientation="Horizontal" />
        </ItemsPanelTemplate>
    </ItemsControl.ItemsPanel>
</ItemsControl>
```

Notice how the *ItemsControl* itself is aligned at the bottom of the display, and each *Rectangle* is aligned at the bottom of the *ItemsControl*. The result is a bar chart:

Of course, the values of the *GradePointAverage* property only range between 0 and 5, so the bars are rather tiny. How can that problem be solved?

You might think about applying a *ScaleTransform* to the *Rectangle* with a constant vertical scaling factor of, say, 50. That was my first choice as well, but the results were unsatisfactory. It seemed as if the heights of the rectangles were being rounded to the nearest pixel before being scaled. So I abandoned that approach and wrote a new data converter:

Silverlight Project: Petzold.Phone.Silverlight   File: MultiplyConverter.cs

```
using System;
using System.Globalization;
using System.Windows.Data;

namespace Petzold.Phone.Silverlight
{
    public class MultiplyConverter : IValueConverter
    {
        public object Convert(object value, Type targetType,
                              object parameter, CultureInfo culture)
        {
            double multiplier;

            if (value is IConvertible &&
                    parameter is string &&
                        Double.TryParse(parameter as string, out multiplier))
            {
```

```
                    return (value as IConvertible).ToDouble(culture) * multiplier;
            }
            return value;
        }

        public object ConvertBack(object value, Type targetType,
                                  object parameter, CultureInfo culture)
        {
            double divider;

            if (value is IConvertible &&
                    parameter is string &&
                        Double.TryParse(parameter as string, out divider))
            {
                return (value as IConvertible).ToDouble(culture) / divider;
            }
            return value;
        }
    }
}
```

This converter multiplies the binding source by a factor provided as the converter parameter.
Define one of these in the *Resources* collection:

```
<phone:PhoneApplicationPage.Resources>
    <elpaso:StudentBodyPresenter x:Key="studentBodyPresenter" />
    <petzold:MultiplyConverter x:Key="multiply" />
</phone:PhoneApplicationPage.Resources>
```

Now reference the converter in the binding to multiply each value by 50:

```
<DataTemplate>
    <Rectangle Fill="{StaticResource PhoneAccentBrush}"
               Height="{Binding GradePointAverage,
                                 Converter={StaticResource multiply},
                                 ConverterParameter=50}"
               VerticalAlignment="Bottom"
               Margin="1 0" />
</DataTemplate>
```

And now it looks like a real bar chart:

What's more, as the *GradePointAverage* values dynamically change, the bars on the bar chart bounce up and down.

Do you remember the *ValueToBrushConverter* in the Petzold.Phone.Silverlight library? That converter allows us to color-code the bars so we're alerted to any student whose grade point average dips below 1 (for example). Here's the converter as it would appear in the *Resources* collection:

```
<petzold:ValueToBrushConverter x:Key="valueToBrush"
                               Criterion="1"
                               GreaterThanBrush="{StaticResource PhoneAccentBrush}"
                               EqualToBrush="{StaticResource PhoneAccentBrush}"
                               LessThanBrush="Red" />
```

Here's the new *DataTemplate*:

```
<DataTemplate>
    <Rectangle Fill="{Binding GradePointAverage,
                          Converter={StaticResource valueToBrush}}"

              Height="{Binding GradePointAverage,
                           Converter={StaticResource multiply},
                           ConverterParameter=50}"
              VerticalAlignment="Bottom"
              Margin="1 0" />
</DataTemplate>
```

As the teacher of these students, you'll be glad you implemented this feature because very soon you'll see that a few students are in danger of failing:

Is there a way to determine which students these are?

The GpaBarChart project shows one approach. It has the *StudentBodyPresenter* and two converters I mentioned defined as resources:

Silverlight Project: GpiBarChart   File: MainPage.xaml (excerpt)

```
<phone:PhoneApplicationPage.Resources>
    <elpaso:StudentBodyPresenter x:Key="studentBodyPresenter" />
    <petzold:MultiplyConverter x:Key="multiply" />
    <petzold:ValueToBrushConverter x:Key="valueToBrush"
                                    Criterion="1"
                                    GreaterThanBrush="{StaticResource PhoneAccentBrush}"
                                    EqualToBrush="{StaticResource PhoneAccentBrush}"
                                    LessThanBrush="Red" />
</phone:PhoneApplicationPage.Resources>
```

Most of the content area you've already seen but I also added a *Border* with the name "studentDisplay" floating near the top. This *Border* includes a couple *TextBlock* elements with their *Text* properties bound to the properties *FullName* and *GradePointAverage* under the assumption that the *DataContext* of this *Border* is an object of type *Student*. That's not normally the case, so the *Border* has its *Visibility* property initialized to *Collapsed*:

Silverlight Project: GpiBarChart   File: MainPage.xaml (excerpt)

```
<Grid x:Name="ContentPanel" Grid.Row="1" Margin="12,0,12,0"
      DataContext="{Binding Source={StaticResource studentBodyPresenter},
                            Path=StudentBody}">

    <Border x:Name="studentDisplay"
            BorderBrush="{StaticResource PhoneForegroundBrush}"
            BorderThickness="{StaticResource PhoneBorderThickness}"
            HorizontalAlignment="Center"
            VerticalAlignment="Top"
            Margin="24"
            Padding="12"
            CornerRadius="24"
            Visibility="Collapsed">
        <StackPanel>
            <TextBlock Text="{Binding FullName}"
                       HorizontalAlignment="Center" />
            <StackPanel Orientation="Horizontal">
                <TextBlock Text="GPA = " />
                <TextBlock Text="{Binding GradePointAverage}" />
            </StackPanel>
        </StackPanel>
    </Border>

    <ItemsControl ItemsSource="{Binding Students}"
                  VerticalAlignment="Bottom">
        <ItemsControl.ItemTemplate>
            <DataTemplate>
```

```
                <Rectangle Fill="{Binding GradePointAverage,
                                        Converter={StaticResource valueToBrush}}"

                           Height="{Binding GradePointAverage,
                                        Converter={StaticResource multiply},
                                        ConverterParameter=50}"
                           VerticalAlignment="Bottom"
                           Margin="1 0" />
            </DataTemplate>
        </ItemsControl.ItemTemplate>

        <ItemsControl.ItemsPanel>
            <ItemsPanelTemplate>
                <petzold:UniformStack Orientation="Horizontal" />
            </ItemsPanelTemplate>
        </ItemsControl.ItemsPanel>
    </ItemsControl>
</Grid>
```

The code-behind file fills in the missing logic. The page processes the *Touch.FrameReported* event. When the element directly behind the primary touch point is a *Rectangle*, the event handler obtains the *DataContext* of that *Rectangle*. That is an object of type *Student*. That object is then set to the *DataContext* of the *Border*. The *TouchAction* property is used to turn the *Visibility* on and off:

Silverlight Project: GpiBarChart   File: MainPage.xaml.cs (excerpt)

```
public partial class MainPage : PhoneApplicationPage
{
    public MainPage()
    {
        InitializeComponent();
        Touch.FrameReported += OnTouchFrameReported;
    }

    void OnTouchFrameReported(object sender, TouchFrameEventArgs args)
    {
        TouchPoint touchPoint = args.GetPrimaryTouchPoint(this);

        if (touchPoint != null && touchPoint.Action == TouchAction.Down)
            args.SuspendMousePromotionUntilTouchUp();

        if (touchPoint != null && touchPoint.TouchDevice.DirectlyOver is Rectangle)
        {
            Rectangle rectangle =
                    (touchPoint.TouchDevice.DirectlyOver as Rectangle);

            // This DataContext is an object of type Student
            object dataContext = rectangle.DataContext;
```

```
                studentDisplay.DataContext = dataContext;

                if (touchPoint.Action == TouchAction.Down)
                    studentDisplay.Visibility = Visibility.Visible;

                else if (touchPoint.Action == TouchAction.Up)
                    studentDisplay.Visibility = Visibility.Collapsed;
            }
        }
    }
```

As you run your fingers across the bars, you can see the student that each bar represents:

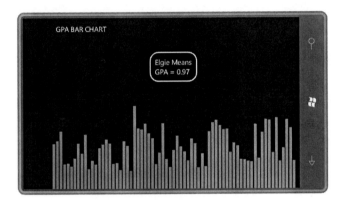

A Card File Metaphor

With the previous GpiBarChart program, in a sense we've managed to fit all the students onto a single screen, but the information is limited. Is there a way to get more information on the screen? One popular metaphor for displaying data is the card file. Normally only part of each card is visible but such a program also includes a facility for viewing an entire card.

In preparation for this job, I created a new panel in the Petzold.Phone.Silverlight library. In some ways this panel is similar to the *UniformStack* panel that I described in Chapter 9. Like *UniformStack*, this new panel gives all of its children an equal amount of space. But unlike *UniformStack*, this new panel actually overlaps its children if necessary to fit them all in the available space. For that reason, it's called *OverlapPanel*.

OverlapPanel defines an *Orientation* property and arranges its children either horizontally or vertically. If *OverlapPanel* is arranging its children horizontally, each child is positioned slightly to the right of the child before it, leaving the left-most sliver of the previous child visible. For a vertical orientation, the top of each child is visible.

If there are very many children, then that visible sliver will become very small. To make *OverlapPanel* more useful, it should be possible to specify that the sliver be at least a minimum height or width, even if that causes the contents of the panel to overrun the available space. In possibly going beyond the space available for it, the *OverlapPanel* behaves much like a regular *StackPanel*. A *ScrollViewer* will be necessary to view all the items.

OverlapPanel defines two properties, *Orientation* and *MinimumOverlap*:

Silverlight Project: **Petzold.Phone.Silverlight**   File: **OverlapPanel.cs** (excerpt)

```
public class OverlapPanel : Panel
{
    Size maxChildSize = new Size();

    public static readonly DependencyProperty OrientationProperty =
        DependencyProperty.Register("Orientation",
            typeof(Orientation),
            typeof(OverlapPanel),
            new PropertyMetadata(Orientation.Horizontal, OnAffectsMeasure));

    public static readonly DependencyProperty MinimumOverlapProperty =
        DependencyProperty.Register("MinimumOverlap",
            typeof(double),
            typeof(OverlapPanel),
            new PropertyMetadata(0.0, OnAffectsMeasure));

    public Orientation Orientation
    {
        set { SetValue(OrientationProperty, value); }
        get { return (Orientation)GetValue(OrientationProperty); }
    }

    public double MinimumOverlap
    {
        set { SetValue(MinimumOverlapProperty, value); }
        get { return (double)GetValue(MinimumOverlapProperty); }
    }

    static void OnAffectsMeasure(DependencyObject obj,
                                DependencyPropertyChangedEventArgs args)
    {
        (obj as OverlapPanel).InvalidateMeasure();
    }
    . . .
}
```

Changes to either of these two properties causes a call to *InvalidateMeasure*, which initiates a new layout pass.

The *MeasureOverride* method first enumerates through all its children to obtain the maximum child size. Of course, when you use *OverlapPanel* with an *ItemsControl* or *ListBox*, all the children will probably have the same size.

Silverlight Project: Petzold.Phone.Silverlight   File: **OverlapPanel.cs** (excerpt)

```
protected override Size MeasureOverride(Size availableSize)
{
    if (Children.Count == 0)
        return new Size(0, 0);

    maxChildSize = new Size();

    foreach (UIElement child in Children)
    {
        if (Orientation == Orientation.Horizontal)
            child.Measure(new Size(Double.PositiveInfinity, availableSize.Height));
        else
            child.Measure(new Size(availableSize.Width, Double.PositiveInfinity));

        maxChildSize.Width = Math.Max(maxChildSize.Width,
                                    child.DesiredSize.Width);

        maxChildSize.Height = Math.Max(maxChildSize.Height,
                                    child.DesiredSize.Height);
    }

    if (Orientation == Orientation.Horizontal)
    {
        double maxTotalWidth = maxChildSize.Width * Children.Count;
        double minTotalWidth = maxChildSize.Width +
                                MinimumOverlap * (Children.Count - 1);

        if (Double.IsPositiveInfinity(availableSize.Width))
            return new Size(minTotalWidth, maxChildSize.Height);

        if (maxTotalWidth < availableSize.Width)
            return new Size(maxTotalWidth, maxChildSize.Height);

        else if (minTotalWidth < availableSize.Width)
            return new Size(availableSize.Width, maxChildSize.Height);

        return new Size(minTotalWidth, maxChildSize.Height);
    }
    // Orientation = Vertical
    double maxTotalHeight = maxChildSize.Height * Children.Count;
    double minTotalHeight = maxChildSize.Height +
                            MinimumOverlap * (Children.Count - 1);

    if (Double.IsPositiveInfinity(availableSize.Height))
        return new Size(maxChildSize.Width, minTotalHeight);

    if (maxTotalHeight < availableSize.Height)
        return new Size(maxChildSize.Width, maxTotalHeight);

    else if (minTotalHeight < availableSize.Height)
```

```
            return new Size(maxChildSize.Width, availableSize.Height);

        return new Size(maxChildSize.Width, minTotalHeight);
    }
```

The method then splits into two different sections depending on the *Orientation* property. For example, for the vertical orientation (which I'll be using in the example below), the method calculates a *maxTotalHeight*, when all the children are side-by-side without overlap, and a *minTotalHeight*, when the children are overlapped to the maximum extent. If the available height is not infinite (a possibility handled separately), then the available height is either greater than *maxTotalHeight* or between *minTotalHeight* and *maxTotalHeight*, or less than *minTotalHeight*. If all the children can fit side-by-side in the available space, then that's the space requested. But the method never requests less height than it needs to display all the children.

The *ArrangeOverride* method is somewhat simpler. The *increment* value is the width or height of the sliver of each child that will always be visible:

Silverlight Project: Petzold.Phone.Silverlight   File: OverlapPanel.cs (excerpt)

```
protected override Size ArrangeOverride(Size finalSize)
{
    if (Children.Count == 0)
        return finalSize;

    double increment = 0;

    if (Orientation == Orientation.Horizontal)
        increment = Math.Max(MinimumOverlap,
            (finalSize.Width - maxChildSize.Width) / (Children.Count - 1));
    else
        increment = Math.Max(MinimumOverlap,
            (finalSize.Height - maxChildSize.Height) / (Children.Count - 1));

    Point ptChild = new Point();

    foreach (UIElement child in Children)
    {
        child.Arrange(new Rect(ptChild, maxChildSize));

        if (Orientation == Orientation.Horizontal)
            ptChild.X += increment;
        else
            ptChild.Y += increment;
    }

    return finalSize;
}
```

The StudentCardFile project has references to the Petzold.Phone.Silverlight and ElPasoHighSchool libraries. The MainPage.xaml file includes the *StudentBodyPresenter* in the *Resources* collection:

Silverlight Project: StudentCardFile   File: MainPage.xaml (excerpt)

```
<phone:PhoneApplicationPage.Resources>
    <elpaso:StudentBodyPresenter x:Key="studentBodyPresenter" />
</phone:PhoneApplicationPage.Resources>
```

The content area is rather simple, containing only a *ScrollViewer* and an *ItemsControl*. The *ItemsPanel* property of the *ItemsControl* references the *OverlapPanel* with two properties set:

Silverlight Project: StudentCardFile   File: MainPage.xaml (excerpt)

```
<Grid x:Name="ContentPanel" Grid.Row="1" Margin="12,0,12,0"
      DataContext="{Binding Source={StaticResource studentBodyPresenter},
                        Path=StudentBody}">
    <ScrollViewer>
        <ItemsControl ItemsSource="{Binding Students}">
            <ItemsControl.ItemTemplate>
                <DataTemplate>
                    <local:StudentCard />
                </DataTemplate>
            </ItemsControl.ItemTemplate>

            <ItemsControl.ItemsPanel>
                <ItemsPanelTemplate>
                    <petzold:OverlapPanel Orientation="Vertical"
                                          MinimumOverlap="24" />
                </ItemsPanelTemplate>
            </ItemsControl.ItemsPanel>
        </ItemsControl>
    </ScrollViewer>
</Grid>
```

The simplicity of the markup here is mostly a result of the *DataTemplate* property of the *ItemsControl* being set to another control named *StudentCard*.

StudentCard derives from *UserControl*. Deriving from *UserControl* is a common technique for creating a control to serve as a *DataTemplate*. If you ignore the ellipses (...) below, this is a very straightforward assemblage of a *TextBlock* and *Image* elements, with a collapsed *Rectangle* used as a dividing line:

Silverlight Project: StudentCardFile   File: StudentCard.xaml (excerpt)

```
<UserControl x:Class="StudentCardFile.StudentCard"
             xmlns="http://schemas.microsoft.com/winfx/2006/xaml/presentation"
             xmlns:x="http://schemas.microsoft.com/winfx/2006/xaml"
             FontFamily="{StaticResource PhoneFontFamilyNormal}"
             FontSize="{StaticResource PhoneFontSizeNormal}"
             Foreground="{StaticResource PhoneForegroundBrush}"
             Width="240" Height="240">

    ...

    <Border BorderBrush="{StaticResource PhoneAccentBrush}"
            BorderThickness="1"
            Background="{StaticResource PhoneChromeBrush}"
            CornerRadius="12"
            Padding="6 0">

        ...

        <Grid>
            <Grid.RowDefinitions>
                <RowDefinition Height="Auto" />
                <RowDefinition Height="Auto" />
                <RowDefinition Height="*" />
                <RowDefinition Height="Auto" />
            </Grid.RowDefinitions>

            <TextBlock Grid.Row="0"
                       Text="{Binding FullName}" />

            <Rectangle Grid.Row="1"
                       Fill="{StaticResource PhoneAccentBrush}"
                       Height="1"
                       Margin="0 0 0 4" />

            <Image Grid.Row="2"
                   Source="{Binding PhotoFilename}" />

            <StackPanel Grid.Row="3"
                        Orientation="Horizontal"
                        HorizontalAlignment="Center">
                <TextBlock Text="GPA = " />
                <TextBlock Text="{Binding GradePointAverage}" />
            </StackPanel>
        </Grid>
    </Border>
</UserControl>
```

The cards are listed down the left side of the display but only the top of each card is visible. Conveniently, the top of each card is a *TextBlock* displaying the student's name:

I set MinimumOverlap to a value sufficient to display this *TextBlock*. As you scroll down to the bottom, you'll see that the bottom card is entirely visible:

That's great if you want to look at the very last card, but rather deficient otherwise. What we need is a way to selectively bring a particular card into view. One approach might be to change the *Canvas.ZIndex* attached property of a particular card. Or, the whole deck of cards might be re-ordered to move a particular card to the topmost position.

I decided I wanted a selected card to slide out of the deck when it's touched, and then slide back when the card is touched again, or when another card is touched.

As you start integrating other code with *ScrollViewer*, you'll discover that *ScrollViewer* tends to hog the *Manipulation* events. Obviously *ScrollViewer* needs these *Manipulation* events for its own scrolling logic. But that makes it difficult for visual descendents of the *ScrollViewer* (such as these *StudentCard* elements) to process *Manipulation* events of their own for sliding in and out of the deck

For that reason, I decided that *StudentCard* would install a handler for the low-level *Touch. FrameReported* event, and to use that to toggle a dependency property named *IsOpen*. Here's that property in the *StudentCard* code-behind file:

```
Silverlight Project: StudentCardFile   File: StudentCard.xaml.cs (excerpt)

public partial class StudentCard : UserControl
{
    . . .
    public static readonly DependencyProperty IsOpenProperty =
        DependencyProperty.Register("IsOpen",
            typeof(bool),
            typeof(StudentCard),
            new PropertyMetadata(false, OnIsOpenChanged));
    . . .
    bool IsOpen
    {
        set { SetValue(IsOpenProperty, value); }
        get { return (bool)GetValue(IsOpenProperty); }
    }
    . . .
}
```

I'll show you the property-changed handler for *IsOpen* shortly.

When you touch one instance of *StudentCard*, it is supposed to slide out of the deck, but if another card is currently exposed, that card should slide back into the deck. If the *CardFile* class is to handle this logic on its own, each instance of *CardFile* needs access to all the other instances. For that reason, I defined a static field of type *List* to maintain these instances:

Silverlight Project: StudentCardFile   File: StudentCard.xaml.cs (excerpt)

```
public partial class StudentCard : UserControl
{
    static List<StudentCard> studentCards = new List<StudentCard>();
    ...
    public StudentCard()
    {
        InitializeComponent();
        studentCards.Add(this);
    }
    ...
}
```

Each new instance simply adds itself to the collection.

It also became apparent to me that each individual *StudentCard* instance does not need its own handler for the *Touch.FrameReported* event. All instances could share the same static handler installed in the static constructor and referencing static fields:

Silverlight Project: StudentCardFile   File: StudentCard.xaml.cs (excerpt)

```
public partial class StudentCard : UserControl
{
    ...
    static int contactTime;
    static Point contactPoint;
    ...
    static StudentCard()
    {
        Touch.FrameReported += OnTouchFrameReported;
    }
    ...
    static void OnTouchFrameReported(object sender, TouchFrameEventArgs args)
    {
        TouchPoint touchPoint = args.GetPrimaryTouchPoint(null);

        if (touchPoint != null && touchPoint.Action == TouchAction.Down)
        {
            contactPoint = touchPoint.Position;
            contactTime = args.Timestamp;
        }
        else if (touchPoint != null && touchPoint.Action == TouchAction.Up)
        {
            // Check if finger is directly over StudentCard or child
            DependencyObject element = touchPoint.TouchDevice.DirectlyOver;

            while (element != null && !(element is StudentCard))
                element = VisualTreeHelper.GetParent(element);
```

```
                    if (element == null)
                        return;

                    // Get lift point and calculate difference
                    Point liftPoint = touchPoint.Position;
                    double distance = Math.Sqrt(Math.Pow(contactPoint.X - liftPoint.X, 2) +
                                               Math.Pow(contactPoint.Y - liftPoint.Y, 2));

                    // Qualify as a Tap if distance < 12 pixels within 1/4th second
                    if (distance < 12 && args.Timestamp - contactTime < 250)
                    {
                        // Enumerate StudentCard objects and set IsOpen property
                        foreach (StudentCard studentCard in studentCards)
                            studentCard.IsOpen =
                                    (element == studentCard && !studentCard.IsOpen);
                    }
                }
            }
        }
        ...
    }
```

With a little experimentation, I determined that I wanted a tap to qualify as a touch and release with ¼ second where the touch point moves less than 12 pixels. That seemed to be about right and still allow flicks to be recognized by the *ScrollViewer*.

At the bottom of this method a *foreach* loop enumerates through all the *StudentCard* objects and sets the *IsOpen* property on each one. *IsOpen* is always set to *false* if the *StudentCard* is not the touched element, and *IsOpen* is also set to *false* if *IsOpen* is currently *true*. Otherwise, if the *StudentCard* object is the touched element, and *IsOpen* is currently *false*, then it's set to *true*. Of course, as a dependency property, *IsOpen* property-changed handlers will only be called if the property is truly changing.

I have not yet shown you the property-changed handler for the *IsOpen* property. As usual, the static version calls the instance version:

Silverlight Project: StudentCardFile   File: StudentCard.xaml.cs (excerpt)

```
public partial class StudentCard : UserControl
{
    ...
    static void OnIsOpenChanged(DependencyObject obj,
                                DependencyPropertyChangedEventArgs args)
    {
        (obj as StudentCard).OnIsOpenChanged(args);
    }
    ...
```

```
    void OnIsOpenChanged(DependencyPropertyChangedEventArgs args)
    {
        VisualStateManager.GoToState(this, IsOpen ? "Open" : "Normal", false);
    }
}
```

The instance version calls *VisualStateManager.GoToState*. Although the Visual State Manger is most frequently used in connection with controls and controls template, you can also use it with *UserControl* derivatives such as *StudentCard*. Calling *GoToState* is how you trigger a state change from code.

In the XAML file, the Visual State Manager markup must appear right after the topmost element in the visual tree. In the case of StudentCard.xaml, that's the *Border* element. Here's the rest of StudentCard.xaml (with some repetition from the previous excerpt) showing the Visual State Manager markup targeting a *TranslateTransform* set on the control itself:

Silverlight Project: StudentCardFile   File: StudentCard.xaml (excerpt)

```xml
<UserControl x:Class="StudentCardFile.StudentCard"
             xmlns="http://schemas.microsoft.com/winfx/2006/xaml/presentation"
             xmlns:x="http://schemas.microsoft.com/winfx/2006/xaml"
             FontFamily="{StaticResource PhoneFontFamilyNormal}"
             FontSize="{StaticResource PhoneFontSizeNormal}"
             Foreground="{StaticResource PhoneForegroundBrush}"
             Width="240" Height="240">

    <UserControl.RenderTransform>
        <TranslateTransform x:Name="translate" />
    </UserControl.RenderTransform>

    <Border BorderBrush="{StaticResource PhoneAccentBrush}"
            BorderThickness="1"
            Background="{StaticResource PhoneChromeBrush}"
            CornerRadius="12"
            Padding="6 0">

        <VisualStateManager.VisualStateGroups>
            <VisualStateGroup x:Name="CommonStates">
                <VisualState x:Name="Open">
                    <Storyboard>
                        <DoubleAnimation Storyboard.TargetName="translate"
                            Storyboard.TargetProperty="X"
                            To="220" Duration="0:0:1" />
                    </Storyboard>
                </VisualState>

                <VisualState x:Name="Normal">
```

```
                    <Storyboard>
                        <DoubleAnimation Storyboard.TargetName="translate"
                                         Storyboard.TargetProperty="X"
                                         Duration="0:0:1" />
                    </Storyboard>
                </VisualState>
                </VisualStateGroup>
            </VisualStateManager.VisualStateGroups>

            ...

        </Border>
    </UserControl>
```

When you tap one of the items, it slides out to reveal the full card:

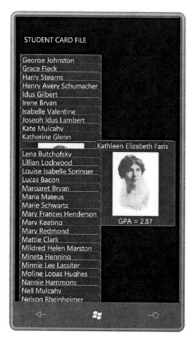

Throughout this chapter I've tried to do several different types of jobs entirely in XAML. That's not always possible; very often code is required, particularly for handling touch input.

But much of the required code doesn't *replace* the XAML: the code helps *support* the markup. These classes take the form of binding converters and custom panels that are referenced within the XAML file. In general, you should try to code *for* XAML and not *instead of* XAML, and you'll be a happier and better Silverlight and Windows Phone 7 programmer.

Chapter 18
Pivot and Panorama

Silverlight applications that need to present large amounts of information to the user have traditionally used a page-oriented navigation structure. On the phone, however, a division of your program into pages might not be the best approach. The phone's portrait form factor, the ease of multi-touch, and a recent emphasis on "fluid user interfaces" all suggest other types of layout. Two such alternatives are available in Windows Phone 7 in new controls named *Pivot* and *Panorama*.

Both *Pivot* and *Panorama* are in the Microsoft.Phone.Controls library and any program that uses these controls will need a reference to that DLL. The controls are defined in the *Microsoft.Phone.Controls* namespace with subsidiary components in *Microsoft.Phone.Controls.Primitives*, but it's unlikely you'll need those other classes unless you're customizing the controls.

Conceptually, *Pivot* and *Panorama* are very similar. Both controls provide a way to organize discrete components of your application horizontally in a virtual space that can be several times wider than the actual width of the phone. You move horizontally through the control simply by sweeping your finger across the screen. Although the *Pivot* and *Panorama* controls seem to be designed primarily for portrait mode, they can be used in landscape mode as well.

Compare and Contrast

Both *Pivot* and *Panorama* derive from *ItemsControl* by way of a class with a generic parameter:

```
public class TemplatedItemsControl<T> : ItemsControl where T : new(), FrameworkElement
```

This indicates an *ItemsControl* that is intended to be filled with objects of type *T*. Both *Pivot* and *Panorama* derive from *TemplatedItemsControl* with a type parameter set to *PivotItem* or *PanoramaItem*, respectively:

```
public class Pivot : TemplatedItemsControl<PivotItem>
public class Panorama : TemplatedItemsControl<PanoramaItem>
```

The *Pivot* control expects to contain items of type *PivotItem* while the *Panorama* control expects to contain items of type *PanoramaItem*. Both *PivotItem* and *PanoramaItem* derive from *ContentControl*. If you're filling the *Items* collection of a *Pivot* or *Panorama* object explicitly in XAML and code, you'll want to fill it with *PivotItem* or *PanoramaItem* items, because there's a crucial *Header* property you need to set on these controls. If you instead use a binding on the *ItemsSource* property defined by *ItemsControl*, these *PivotItem* and *PanoramaItem* objects are created for you behind the scenes, and you set the *Header* property through a template. (Don't worry: I'll have examples.)

To instantiate these controls in a XAML file you'll need an XML namespace declaration for the Microsoft.Phone.Controls library and namespace:

```
xmlns:controls="clr-namespace:Microsoft.Phone.Controls;assembly=Microsoft.Phone.Controls"
```

Perhaps the best way to explore these classes is to experiment with an actual example. The New Project dialog in Visual Studio allows you to create a project of type Windows Phone Pivot Application or Windows Phone Panorama Application, and you can surely experiment with those. For the demonstration programs in this chapter I took a different approach.

Here's a MainPage.xaml file from a project named PivotDemonstration. I created this project normally, that is, by selecting Windows Phone Application from the New Project dialog box. But then I deleted most of the contents of MainPage.xaml except the *PhoneApplicationPage* tags. I added the XML namespace declaration for "controls" (it's the widest one) and I replaced the contents of the page with a *Pivot* and four nested *PivotItem* children:

Silverlight Project: PivotDemonstration   File: MainPage.xaml (excerpt)

```
<phone:PhoneApplicationPage
    x:Class="PivotDemonstration.MainPage"
    xmlns="http://schemas.microsoft.com/winfx/2006/xaml/presentation"
    xmlns:x="http://schemas.microsoft.com/winfx/2006/xaml"
    xmlns:phone="clr-namespace:Microsoft.Phone.Controls;assembly=Microsoft.Phone"
    xmlns:shell="clr-namespace:Microsoft.Phone.Shell;assembly=Microsoft.Phone"
  xmlns:controls="clr-namespace:Microsoft.Phone.Controls;assembly=Microsoft.Phone.
Controls"
    xmlns:system="clr-namespace:System;assembly=mscorlib"
    xmlns:d="http://schemas.microsoft.com/expression/blend/2008"
    xmlns:mc="http://schemas.openxmlformats.org/markup-compatibility/2006"
    mc:Ignorable="d" d:DesignWidth="480" d:DesignHeight="768"
    FontFamily="{StaticResource PhoneFontFamilyNormal}"
    FontSize="{StaticResource PhoneFontSizeNormal}"
    Foreground="{StaticResource PhoneForegroundBrush}"
    SupportedOrientations="PortraitOrLandscape" Orientation="Portrait"
    shell:SystemTray.IsVisible="True">

    <controls:Pivot Title="PIVOT DEMONSTRATION">
        <controls:PivotItem Header="ListBox">
            ...
        </controls:PivotItem>

        <controls:PivotItem Header="Ellipse">
            ...
        </controls:PivotItem>

        <controls:PivotItem Header="TextBlock">
            ...
        </controls:PivotItem>
```

```
        <controls:PivotItem Header="Animation">
            . . .
        </controls:PivotItem>
    </controls:Pivot>
</phone:PhoneApplicationPage>
```

The *Pivot* control's *Title* property is set to "PIVOT DEMONSTRATION." By default, this title will appear in the same location and be the same size as the text displayed at the top of the normal Windows Phone page. (That's the text normally displayed by the *TextBlock* with the name *ApplicationTitle*.) Each of the four *PivotItem* controls has a *Header* property set; this text appears in the same location and is the same size as the customary *TextBlock* named *PageTitle*.

The *PivotItem* control derives from *ContentControl*, so you can put pretty much anything in those controls. I gave the first *PivotItem* a *ListBox* containing all the fonts available to Windows Phone 7 programs, including a simple *DataTemplate*:

Silverlight Project: PivotDemonstration   File: MainPage.xaml (excerpt)

```
<controls:PivotItem Header="ListBox">
    <ListBox FontSize="{StaticResource PhoneFontSizeLarge}">
        <ListBox.ItemTemplate>
            <DataTemplate>
                <TextBlock Text="{Binding}"
                           FontFamily="{Binding}" />
            </DataTemplate>
        </ListBox.ItemTemplate>

        <system:String>Arial</system:String>
        <system:String>Arial Black</system:String>
        <system:String>Calibri</system:String>
        <system:String>Comic Sans MS</system:String>
        <system:String>Courier New</system:String>
        <system:String>Georgia</system:String>
        <system:String>Lucida Sans Unicode</system:String>
        <system:String>Portable User Interface</system:String>
        <system:String>Segoe WP</system:String>
        <system:String>Segoe WP Black</system:String>
        <system:String>Segoe WP Bold</system:String>
        <system:String>Segoe WP Light</system:String>
        <system:String>Segoe WP Semibold</system:String>
        <system:String>Segoe WP SemiLight</system:String>
        <system:String>Tahoma</system:String>
        <system:String>Times New Roman</system:String>
        <system:String>Trebuchet MS</system:String>
        <system:String>Verdana</system:String>
        <system:String>Webdings</system:String>
    </ListBox>
</controls:PivotItem>
```

The *PivotItem* gives the *ListBox* an amount of space equal to the size of the page less the *Title* text and the *Header* text:

The *ListBox* is vertically scrollable, of course. Notice the *Header* text of the second *PivotItem* in a dimmed state next to the first one. That second *PivotItem* just displays an *Ellipse*:

Silverlight Project: PivotDemonstration   File: MainPage.xaml (excerpt)

```
<controls:PivotItem Header="Ellipse">
    <Ellipse>
        <Ellipse.Fill>
            <LinearGradientBrush>
                <GradientStop Offset="0" Color="{StaticResource PhoneAccentColor}" />
                <GradientStop Offset="0.5" Color="{StaticResource
PhoneBackgroundColor}" />
                <GradientStop Offset="1" Color="{StaticResource PhoneForegroundColor}"
/>
            </LinearGradientBrush>
        </Ellipse.Fill>
    </Ellipse>
</controls:PivotItem>
```

This clearly shows exactly how large an area the *PivotItem* is offering to its content:

The third *PivotItem* contains a *ScrollViewer* with a large *TextBlock* containing the opening paragraph from a well-known novel:

Silverlight Project: PivotDemonstration   File: MainPage.xaml (excerpt)

```
<controls:PivotItem Header="TextBlock">
    <ScrollViewer>
        <!-- from http://www.gutenberg.org/files/7178/7178-8.txt -->
        <TextBlock TextWrapping="Wrap">
            For a long time I used to go to bed early. Sometimes, when I had put out
            my candle, my eyes would close so quickly that I had not even time to
            say "I'm going to sleep." And half an hour later the thought that it was
            time to go to sleep would awaken me; I would try to put away the book
            which, I imagined, was still in my hands, and to blow out the light; I
            had been thinking all the time, while I was asleep, of what I had just
            been reading, but my thoughts had run into a channel of their own,
            until I myself seemed actually to have become the subject of my book:
            a church, a quartet, the rivalry between François I and Charles V. This
            impression would persist for some moments after I was awake; it did not
            disturb my mind, but it lay like scales upon my eyes and prevented them
            from registering the fact that the candle was no longer burning. Then
            it would begin to seem unintelligible, as the thoughts of a former
            existence must be to a reincarnate spirit; the subject of my book would
            separate itself from me, leaving me free to choose whether I would form
            part of it or no; and at the same time my sight would return and I
            would be astonished to find myself in a state of darkness, pleasant and
            restful enough for the eyes, and even more, perhaps, for my mind, to
            which it appeared incomprehensible, without a cause, a matter dark
            indeed.
        </TextBlock>
    </ScrollViewer>
</controls:PivotItem>
```

Once again, there's no issue with scrolling:

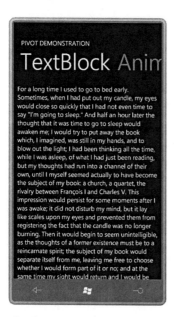

The final *PivotItem* contains a *TextBlock* with several animations applied:

Silverlight Project: PivotDemonstration **File: MainPage.xaml (excerpt)**

```xml
<controls:PivotItem Header="Animation">
    <TextBlock Text="Hello, Windows Phone 7!"
               HorizontalAlignment="Left"
               VerticalAlignment="Top"
               RenderTransformOrigin="0.5 0.5">
        <TextBlock.RenderTransform>
            <CompositeTransform x:Name="xform" />
        </TextBlock.RenderTransform>
    </TextBlock>

    <controls:PivotItem.Triggers>
        <EventTrigger>
            <BeginStoryboard>
                <Storyboard>
                    <DoubleAnimation Storyboard.TargetName="xform"
                                     Storyboard.TargetProperty="Rotation"
                                     From="0" To="360" Duration="0:0:3"
                                     RepeatBehavior="Forever" />

                    <DoubleAnimation Storyboard.TargetName="xform"
                                     Storyboard.TargetProperty="TranslateX"
                                     From="0" To="300" Duration="0:0:5"
                                     AutoReverse="True"
```

```
                                    RepeatBehavior="Forever" />

          <DoubleAnimation Storyboard.TargetName="xform"
                           Storyboard.TargetProperty="TranslateY"
                           From="0" To="600" Duration="0:0:7"
                           AutoReverse="True"
                           RepeatBehavior="Forever" />
        </Storyboard>
      </BeginStoryboard>
    </EventTrigger>
  </controls:PivotItem.Triggers>
</controls:PivotItem>
```

The animations make the *TextBlock* move and spin around:

Notice the header of the first *PivotItem* to the right of the active one. The animations are tailored for the approximate size of the content area of the *PivotItem* for the large screen in portrait mode. If you turn the phone or emulator sideways, the *TextBlock* will drift off the screen temporarily.

The PanoramaDemonstration program is extremely similar to PivotDemonstration. For the most part, every place in the MainPage.xaml file of PivotDemonstration where the word

"Pivot" occurs is replaced with the word "Panorama." Beyond that, the only other difference was the change in the *Title* property to lowercase:

Silverlight Project: **PanoramaDemostration**   File: **MainPage.xaml** (excerpt)

```
<controls:Panorama Title="panorama demonstration">
    <controls:PanoramaItem Header="ListBox">
        ...
    </controls:PanoramaItem>

    <controls:PanoramaItem Header="Ellipse">
        ...
    </controls:PanoramaItem>

    <controls:PanoramaItem Header="TextBlock">
        ...
    </controls:PanoramaItem>

    <controls:PanoramaItem Header="Animation">
        ...
    </controls:PanoramaItem>
</controls:Panorama>
```

Although *Pivot* and *Panorama* are conceptually very similar, they have rather different aesthetics. The next several screen shots show the two controls side-by-side with *Pivot* on the left and *Panorama* on the right. Notice how the *Title* is handled in the *Panorama*: It's much larger and suggests that it stretches to encompass all the other items:

Although I haven't done so here, generally you'll set the *Background* property of the *Panorama* control to an *ImageBrush* with a wide bitmap that spreads out behind the back. (On the phone, look at the Games, Marketplace, and Pictures applications to get some ideas.)

As a result of the large *Title*, the *Panorama* offers less vertical space for the content of each *PanoramaItem*. Slightly less horizontal space is available as well because the next item to the right is peaking through at the right edge.

You can navigate forwards or backwards through the *Pivot* and *Panorama* just by sweeping your finger to the right or left. With Panorama, sweeping your finger along the *Title* text feels very natural. With the *Pivot* (but not the *Panorama*) you can navigate to one of the other items by tapping its *Header* text:

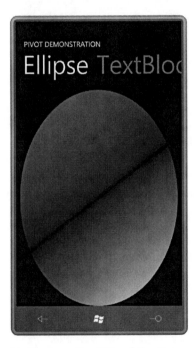 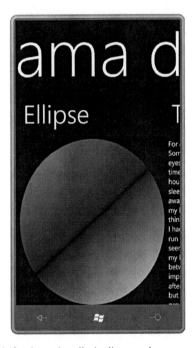

Notice how the *Title* of the *Panorama* has also shifted to visually indicate where you are in terms of the virtual width of all the content.

As you experiment with sweeping your finger across the screen, you'll discover that the *Pivot* and *Panorama* actually behave in very different ways: In both cases the *Header* texts are somewhat visually uncoupled from the actual items. With the *Pivot*, one item moves completely off the screen before the next item slides in; with the *Panorama*, you can see two items simultaneously. Here's a view in progress between two items:

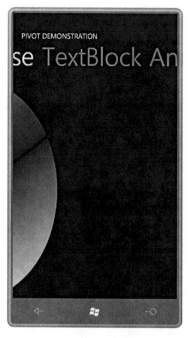 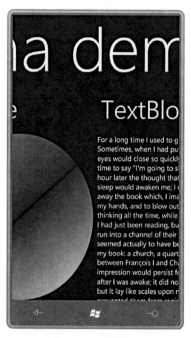

The *Panorama* gives a much better sense of a wide virtual screen through which a viewport is visible, particularly when used with a wide background bitmap. The *Pivot* seems more like it's occupying just the screen area and works by sliding individual items in and out of view.

The *Pivot* control defines several events that the *Panorama* control does not: *LoadingPivotItem, LoadedPivotItem, UnloadingPivotItem, UnloadedPivotItem*. These events signal when one item slips out of view and another item slips in. These events don't quite apply to the more fluid nature of the *Panorama*.

Both *Pivot* and *Panorama* define *SelectionChanged* events, as well as *SelectedIndex* and *SelectedItem*. The selection is considered to be the *PivotItem* or *PanoramaItem* in full view, and the event isn't fired until the item finishes sliding fully into place.

Both *Pivot* and *Panorama* define *TitleTemplate* and *HeaderTemplate* properties of type *DataTemplate* so if you use bindings to set the content of the control you can define a visual tree to indicate how the *Title* property and *Header* properties use the data.

The *HeaderTemplate* property is particularly important if you bind the *ItemsSource* property of *Pivot* or *Panorama* to a collection, in which case you aren't creating the *PivotItem* or *PanoramaItem* objects explicitly. You'll need this *HeaderTemplate* for a binding to set the *Header* text, but the template can consist solely of a *TextBlock*. You'll see an example later in this chapter.

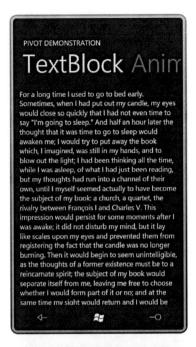

If you're feeling particularly adventurous, you can also define a whole new *ControlTemplate* for *Pivot* or *Panorama*. The *Pivot* template requires a *PivotHeadersControl* (which is a *TemplateItemsControl* of type *PivotHeaderItem*) and the *Panorama* template requires three *PanningLayer* objects. *PanningLayer* derives from *ContentControl*, and the *Microsoft.Phone*.

Controls.Primitives namespace includes *PanningBackgroundLayer* and *PanningTitleLayer* classes that derive from *PanningLayer*.

In the final view, we've circle back to the beginning. But in the *Panorama* control you can simultaneously see three *PanoramaItem* children: The *ListBox* is in full view, there's a little sliver of the *Ellipse* at the right, but look at that snippet of rotated text intersecting the "Comic Sans MS" item: That's the animation to the left.

Music by Composer

Once I started thinking about it, I realized that the *Pivot* control was the perfect choice for realizing a program I had long been contemplating. This program corrects what I perceive to be a major deficiency of portable music players such as the Zune and Windows Phone 7, so a little explanation is necessary:

As you may know, the landscape of music in the United States and Europe can be roughly divided into performer-centric music and composer-centric music. The performer-centric tradition has close ties with the rise and evolution of recording technologies and encompasses performers from (say) Robert Johnson (1911–1938) through Lady Gaga

(b. 1986). Performer-centric music consists predominantly of a musical form known as the *song*, generally several minutes in length, with a vocalist and instrumental accompaniment.

The composer-centric tradition is much older, stretching from (say) Claudio Monteverdi (1567–1643) through Jennifer Higdon (b. 1962), and encompasses very many different forms (for example, string quartet, piano concerto, symphony, and opera as well as songs) of widely varying lengths, styles, and instrumentation.

People who listen to composer-centric music generally prefer to organize their music by composer, and then within composer by composition, and within composition by performer. (As with the performer-centric tradition, the word *artist* is satisfactory for referring to the person or people playing the music.) The Zune desktop software allows you to enter composer information when downloading music and ripping CDs, but that information is not transferred with the files to portable devices such as the phone. Even if composer information was included in the music files transferred to the phone, it is not available through the public properties of the classes used to access the music.

To compensate for this deficiency, people who listen to composer-centric music often incorporate the composer's name in the album title followed by a colon, such as:

Mahler: Symphony No. 2

Many CDs of music in the composer-centric tradition rip with album titles in this format. For albums that have music of more than one composer, I've also adopted the convention of separating the composers' names with commas:

Adès, Schubert: Piano Quintets

Over the years I've ripped about 600 of my CDs to the PC, and most of them are identified in this way. When the music player lists the albums alphabetically by album title, the music is also listed alphabetically by composer, so that's a big help.

But I wanted more. I wanted a hierarchical structure based around the composer. I wanted to see the composers' names up front so I begin by selecting Schubert or Debussy or Messiaen.

So I decided to write a Windows Phone 7 program called MusicByComposer that takes this extra step. The program accesses the music library on the phone and—under the assumption that the album titles begin with one or more composer names followed by a colon—extracts the composers' names from the album titles. It then arranges the music by composer, where each composer becomes a *PivotItem*. The content of that *PivotItem* is a *ListBox* that lists all the albums containing music by that composer.

The MusicByComposer program begins with a screen that looks something like this:

You should recognize this as a standard *Pivot* control where each *PivotItem* is a composer. On my phone the first *PivotItem* displays albums by American composer John Adams (b. 1947). The other *PivotItem* headers you can see here are for British composer Thomas Adès (b. 1971) and German composer Johann Sebastian Bach (1685–1750).

If none of your music has a colon in the album title, all your albums will be listed under a single *PivotItem* with the header "Other".

The *PivotItem* for each composer contains a *ListBox* where each item includes the thumbnail album art, the album title (without the composer name) using the phone's current accent color, and the artist associated with the album in the foreground color.

Tapping any album brings you to a page for that album:

This is a standard *PhoneApplicationPage* with the standard two *TextBlock* items for the application title and the page title, but as you can see, the titles are the same size and in the same position as the *Pivot* control on the opening page. The larger album art is shown with the full album name and artist. Underneath is a *ScrollViewer* with an *ItemsControl* with all the tracks from the album. This screen has no touch interface except for scrolling: You control everything with the *ApplicationBar* buttons: go to the previous track, play and pause, and go to the next track. The currently playing track is indicated with the accent color and time progress.

After an application starts playing an album, it's normal in Windows Phone 7 for the album to play all the way through, even if the application ends or the phone's display shuts off. The MusicByComposer program allows you to navigate to other albums, but it will only shut off an existing album and play a new one if you press the middle button to pause the existing album and press again to play the album on the page.

The XNA Connection

As you'll recall from Chapter 4 and Chapter 14, a Silverlight program can get access to the phone's photo library for retrieving photos and saving them, but it needs to use an XNA class named *MediaLibrary* in the *Microsoft.Xna.Framework.Media* namespace. You need that same class—and other classes in that namespace—for accessing and playing music

Any program that uses *MediaLibrary* needs a reference to the Microsoft.Xna.Framework DLL; The MusicByComposer program also needs a reference to Microsoft.Phone.Controls for the *Pivot* control.

When you use XNA services to play music from a Silverlight application, some issues are involved. As described in the topic in the XNA documentation entitled "Enable XNA Framework Events in Windows Phone Applications," you need a class that calls the XNA static method *FrameworkDispatcher.Update* at the same rate as the video refresh rate, thirty times per second. The following class in the MusicByComposer project is basically the class shown in that documentation topic:

Silverlight Project: MusicByComposer   File: XnaFrameworkDispatcherService.cs

```
using System;
using System.Windows;
using System.Windows.Threading;
using Microsoft.Xna.Framework;

namespace MusicByComposer
{
```

```
public class XnaFrameworkDispatcherService : IApplicationService
{
    DispatcherTimer timer;

    public XnaFrameworkDispatcherService()
    {
        timer = new DispatcherTimer();
        timer.Interval = TimeSpan.FromTicks(333333);
        timer.Tick += OnTimerTick;
        FrameworkDispatcher.Update();
    }

    void OnTimerTick(object sender, EventArgs args)
    {
        FrameworkDispatcher.Update();
    }

    void IApplicationService.StartService(ApplicationServiceContext context)
    {
        timer.Start();
    }

    void IApplicationService.StopService()
    {
        timer.Stop();
    }
}
```

You'll need to instantiate that class in the *ApplicationLifetimeObjects* section of the App.xaml file. Notice the XML namespace declaration for "local":

Silverlight Project: MusicByComposer   File: App.xaml

```
<Application
    x:Class="MusicByComposer.App"
    xmlns="http://schemas.microsoft.com/winfx/2006/xaml/presentation"
    xmlns:x="http://schemas.microsoft.com/winfx/2006/xaml"
    xmlns:phone="clr-namespace:Microsoft.Phone.Controls;assembly=Microsoft.Phone"
    xmlns:shell="clr-namespace:Microsoft.Phone.Shell;assembly=Microsoft.Phone"
    xmlns:local="clr-namespace:MusicByComposer">

    <!--Application Resources-->
    <Application.Resources>
    </Application.Resources>

    <Application.ApplicationLifetimeObjects>

        <!-- Required for playing music from a Silverlight app -->
        <local:XnaFrameworkDispatcherService />
```

```
      <!--Required object that handles lifetime events for the application-->
      <shell:PhoneApplicationService
          Launching="Application_Launching" Closing="Application_Closing"
          Activated="Application_Activated" Deactivated="Application_Deactivated"/>
    </Application.ApplicationLifetimeObjects>
  </Application>
```

For testing purposes, the phone emulator has a music library that consists of a single album with three short songs, which is great for establishing basic album retrieval and playing logic, but it hardly gives the program a real workout.

For debugging a program running on the actual phone from Visual Studio, you'll need to exit the desktop Zune program (because it wants exclusive access to the music library) and instead run the Connect tool, WPDTPTConnect32 on 32-bit Windows or WPDTPTConnect64 on 64-bit Windows.

I also discovered another problem. When the program was deployed to the phone and running apart from Visual Studio, the program would report that the music library on the phone had no music.... except if I first ran an XNA program. I am told this is a bug in the initial release of Windows Phone 7, and I decided to work around this bug by making the program accessible from the Games hub on the phone. To do this I set the following attribute in the *App* tag of the WMAppManifest.xml file:

```
Genre="apps.games"
```

I also gave the program Background.png and ApplicationIcon.png images containing a portrait of perhaps the most famous individual in the composer-centric tradition.

The XNA Music Classes: MediaLibrary

An application that wants to play music under Windows Phone 7 uses classes from the *Microsoft.Xna.Framework.Media* namespace. You'll first need to access the music from the library, and for that you'll need a new instance of *MediaLibrary*, the same class you use to access the photo library.

The *MediaLibrary* class defines several get-only properties that let you access the music library in several standard ways. These properties include:

- *Albums* of type *AlbumCollection*, a collection of *Album* objects.

- *Songs* of type *SongCollection*, a collection of *Song* objects.

- *Artists* of type *ArtistCollection*, a collection of *Artist* objects.

- *Genres* of type *GenreCollection*, a collection of *Genre* objects.

Each of these collections contains all the music in your library but arranged in different ways. (The presence of a property called *Composer* of type *ComposerCollection* would have simplified my program considerably.)

For my purposes I found the *Albums* property of *MediaLibrary* the most useful. The *AlbumCollection* class is a collection of items of type *Album*, and *Album* has the following get-only properties (among others):

- *Name* of type *string*

- *Artist* of type *Artist*

- *Songs* of type *SongCollection*

- *HasArt* of type *bool*

If *HasArt* is true, you can call two methods, *GetAlbumArt* and *GetThumbnail*, both of which return *Stream* objects to access a bitmap with an image of the album cover. *GetAlbumArt* returns a bitmap of about 200-pixels square and *GetThumbnail* returns a bitmap of about 100-pixels square.

The *SongCollection* in an *Album* instance contains all the tracks on the album. (In the composer-centric tradition, the use of the word *song* to describe these album tracks doesn't make much sense if, for example, a track is actually a movement of a symphony, but the performer-centric prejudice of the XNA classes is something we're forced to live with.) The *Song* object has several get-only properties, among them:

- *Name* of type *string*

- *Album* of type *Album*

- *Artist* of type *Artist*

- *Duration* of type *TimeSpan*.

For organizing the music library by composer and for data binding purposes, I realized that I'd need a couple new classes. My *AlbumInfo* class is basically a wrapper around the XNA *Album* class:

Silverlight Project: MusicByComposer   File: AlbumInfo.cs

```
using System;
using System.Windows.Media.Imaging;
using Microsoft.Xna.Framework.Media;

namespace MusicByComposer
{
    public class AlbumInfo : IComparable<AlbumInfo>
    {
        BitmapImage albumArt;
        BitmapImage thumbnailArt;
```

```
    public AlbumInfo(string shortAlbumName, Album album)
    {
        this.ShortAlbumName = shortAlbumName;
        this.Album = album;
    }

    public string ShortAlbumName { protected set; get; }

    public Album Album { protected set; get; }

    public BitmapSource AlbumArt
    {
        get
        {
            if (albumArt == null && Album.HasArt)
            {
                BitmapImage bitmapImage = new BitmapImage();
                bitmapImage.SetSource(Album.GetAlbumArt());
                albumArt = bitmapImage;
            }
            return albumArt;
        }
    }

    public BitmapSource ThumbnailArt
    {
        get
        {
            if (thumbnailArt == null && Album.HasArt)
            {
                BitmapImage bitmapImage = new BitmapImage();
                bitmapImage.SetSource(Album.GetThumbnail());
                thumbnailArt = bitmapImage;
            }
            return thumbnailArt;
        }
    }

    public int CompareTo(AlbumInfo albumInfo)
    {
        return ShortAlbumName.CompareTo(albumInfo.ShortAlbumName);
    }
  }
}
```

This *AlbumInfo* class has a property of type *Album* and adds three more properties: The *ShortAlbumName* property is the name of the album with the composer or composers at the beginning stripped off. (For example, "Mahler: Symphony No. 2" becomes "Symphony No. 2".) This property is used in the *CompareTo* method at the bottom for sorting purposes. In the first of the two screen shots of MusicByComposer, you'll notice that the album names are sorted.

The *GetAlbumArt* and *GetThumbnail* methods of *Album* return *Stream* objects. For binding purposes, I expose two public properties of type *BitmapImage* but the class only creates these objects when the properties are first accessed, and then caches them for subsequent accesses.

The next class is *ComposerInfo*, which consists of the composer's name and a list of all the *AlbumInfo* objects containing music by that composer:

Silverlight Project: MusicByComposer   File: ComposerInfo.cs

```
using System;
using System.Collections.Generic;

namespace MusicByComposer
{
    public class ComposerInfo
    {
        public ComposerInfo(string composer, List<AlbumInfo> albums)
        {
            Composer = composer;
            albums.Sort();
            Albums = albums;
        }

        public string Composer { protected set; get; }

        public IList<AlbumInfo> Albums { protected set; get; }
    }
}
```

Notice that the *List* of *AlbumInfo* objects is sorted in the constructor.

The *MusicPresenter* class is responsible for accessing the phone's music library, obtaining all the albums, analyzing the album titles for the presence of composer names, and creating objects of type *ComposerInfo* and *AlbumInfo*. It does the main work in its instance constructor by storing the information in a dictionary with composer names used as keys that reference items of the type *List<AlbumInfo>*:

Silverlight Project: MusicByComposer   File: MusicPresenter.cs

```
using System;
using System.Collections.Generic;
using Microsoft.Xna.Framework.Media;

namespace MusicByComposer
{
```

```csharp
public class MusicPresenter
{
    // Static constructor
    static MusicPresenter()
    {
        if (Current == null)
            Current = new MusicPresenter();
    }

    // Instance constructor
    public MusicPresenter()
    {
        // Make this class a singleton
        if (MusicPresenter.Current != null)
        {
            this.Composers = MusicPresenter.Current.Composers;
            return;
        }

        MediaLibrary mediaLib = new MediaLibrary();
        Dictionary<string, List<AlbumInfo>> albumsByComposer =
                    new Dictionary<string, List<AlbumInfo>>();

        foreach (Album album in mediaLib.Albums)
        {
            int indexOfColon = album.Name.IndexOf(':');

            // Check for pathological cases
            if (indexOfColon != -1 &&
                // Colon at beginning of album name
                (indexOfColon == 0 ||
                // Colon at end of album name
                indexOfColon == album.Name.Length - 1 ||
                // nothing before colon
                album.Name.Substring(0, indexOfColon).Trim().Length == 0 ||
                // nothing after colon
                album.Name.Substring(indexOfColon + 1).Trim().Length == 0))
            {
                indexOfColon = -1;
            }

            // Main logic for albums with composers
            if (indexOfColon != -1)
            {
                string[] albumComposers =
                            album.Name.Substring(0, indexOfColon).Split(',');
                string shortAlbumName = album.Name.Substring(indexOfColon
+ 1).Trim();

                bool atLeastOneEntry = false;

                foreach (string composer in albumComposers)
                {
                    string trimmedComposer = composer.Trim();
```

```
                              if (trimmedComposer.Length > 0)
                              {
                                  atLeastOneEntry = true;

                                  if (!albumsByComposer.ContainsKey(trimmedComposer))
                                      albumsByComposer.Add(trimmedComposer,
                                                  new List<AlbumInfo>());

                                  albumsByComposer[trimmedComposer].Add(
                                                  new AlbumInfo(shortAlbumName, album));
                              }
                          }

                          // Another pathological case: Just commas before colon
                          if (!atLeastOneEntry)
                          {
                              indexOfColon = -1;
                          }
                      } .

                      // The "Other" category is for albums without composers
                      if (indexOfColon == -1)
                      {
                          if (!albumsByComposer.ContainsKey("Other"))
                              albumsByComposer.Add("Other", new List<AlbumInfo>());

                          albumsByComposer["Other"].Add(new AlbumInfo(album.Name, album));
                      }
                  }

                  mediaLib.Dispose();

                  // Transfer Dictionary keys to List for sorting
                  List<string> composerList = new List<string>();

                  foreach (string composer in albumsByComposer.Keys)
                      composerList.Add(composer);

                  (composerList as List<string>).Sort();

                  // Construct Composers property
                  Composers = new List<ComposerInfo>();

                  foreach (string composer in composerList)
                      Composers.Add(new ComposerInfo(composer, albumsByComposer[composer]));

                  Current = this;
              }

              public static MusicPresenter Current { protected set; get; }

              public IList<ComposerInfo> Composers { private set; get; }
      }
}
```

Only one instance of this class is required by the program. The music library will not change while the program is running, so there's no reason for this instance constructor to run again. For that reason, when the instance constructor is finished, it sets the static *Current* property equal to the instance of *MusicPresenter* being created. This first instance will actually be created from the static constructor at the very top of the class, and result in setting the *Composers* property (down at the bottom), which consists of a list of *ComposerInfo* objects. If the constructor is called again, it merely transfers the existing *Composers* property to the new instance.

Why not make *MusicPresenter* a static class and simplify it somewhat? Because *MusicPresenter* is used in data bindings in XAML files and an actual instance of a class is required for those bindings. However, code also needs to access the class and for that the static *MusicPresenter.Current* property is helpful.

This static constructor executes when the program first accesses the class, of course, but also when the program accesses the class again after it is revived from tombstoning. In this case, re-creating the data from the *MediaLibrary* is certainly easier than saving it all in isolated storage.

Displaying the Albums

When the program starts up, *MainPage* is displayed. The XAML file contains XML namespace declarations for "controls" (to access the *Pivot* control) and "local" (for *MusicPresenter*). The *Resources* collection instantiates *MusicPresenter*:

Silverlight Project: MusicByComposer   File: MainPage.xaml (excerpt)

```
<phone:PhoneApplicationPage.Resources>
    <local:MusicPresenter x:Key="musicPresenter" />
</phone:PhoneApplicationPage.Resources>
```

In the design view, Visual Studio will complain that it can't create an instance of *MusicPresenter*, and of course it can't because it would need access to the phone's (or the phone emulator's) music library.

Almost the entire visual tree of the page is a *Pivot* control:

Silverlight Project: MusicByComposer   File: MainPage.xaml (excerpt)

```
<Grid x:Name="LayoutRoot" Background="Transparent">
    <controls:Pivot Name="pivot"
                Title="MUSIC BY COMPOSER"
                ItemsSource="{Binding Source={StaticResource musicPresenter},
                                Path=Composers}">
```

```xml
            <controls:Pivot.HeaderTemplate>
                <!-- Objects of type ComposerInfo -->
                <DataTemplate>
                    <TextBlock Text="{Binding Composer}" />
                </DataTemplate>
            </controls:Pivot.HeaderTemplate>

            <controls:Pivot.ItemTemplate>
                <!-- Objects of type ComposerInfo -->
                <DataTemplate>
                    <ListBox ItemsSource="{Binding Albums}"
                            SelectionChanged="OnListBoxSelectionChanged">
                        <ListBox.ItemTemplate>
                            <!-- Objects of type AlbumInfo -->
                            <DataTemplate>
                                <Grid Background="Transparent">
                                    <Grid.ColumnDefinitions>
                                        <ColumnDefinition Width="Auto" />
                                        <ColumnDefinition Width="*" />
                                    </Grid.ColumnDefinitions>

                                    <Border Grid.Column="0"
                                            BorderBrush="{StaticResource
PhoneForegroundBrush}"

                                            BorderThickness="1"
                                            Width="100" Height="100"
                                            Margin="0 2 6 2">
                                        <Image Source="{Binding ThumbnailArt}" />
                                    </Border>

                                    <StackPanel Grid.Column="1"
                                            VerticalAlignment="Center">
                                        <TextBlock
                                            Text="{Binding ShortAlbumName}"
                                            Foreground="{StaticResource
PhoneAccentBrush}"

                                            TextWrapping="Wrap" />
                                        <TextBlock Text="{Binding Album.Artist.Name}"
                                            TextWrapping="Wrap" />
                                    </StackPanel>
                                </Grid>
                            </DataTemplate>
                        </ListBox.ItemTemplate>
                    </ListBox>
                </DataTemplate>
            </controls:Pivot.ItemTemplate>
        </controls:Pivot>
    </Grid>
```

This XAML file really shows off the power of templates and data binding. Remember that *Pivot* derives from *ItemsTemplate*, so it has an *ItemsSource* property that you can bind to a collection:

```
ItemsSource="{Binding Source={StaticResource musicPresenter},
                      Path=Composers}"
```

This means that the *Pivot* is filled with a collection of objects of type *ComposerInfo*. Internally, *Pivot* will generate objects of type *PivotInfo*, one for each *ComposerInfo* item. The *Header* property of each *PivotItem* needs to be bound to the *Composer* property of the corresponding *ComposerInfo* object. But the actual *PivotItem* object is being created behind the scenes! It is for this reason that *Pivot* defines a *HeaderTemplate* property:

```
<controls:Pivot.HeaderTemplate>
    <!-- Objects of type ComposerInfo -->
    <DataTemplate>
        <TextBlock Text="{Binding Composer}" />
    </DataTemplate>
</controls:Pivot.HeaderTemplate>
```

Don't worry about the formatting of the *TextBlock* object in this template: It magically gets the proper formatting, probably through property inheritance.

The *Pivot* class also defines an *ItemTemplate*. This is a *DataTemplate* that is used to generate the content of each *PivotItem*:

```
<controls:Pivot.ItemTemplate>
    <!-- Objects of type ComposerInfo -->
    <DataTemplate>
        <ListBox ItemsSource="{Binding Albums}"
                 SelectionChanged="OnListBoxSelectionChanged">
            . . .
        </ListBox>
    </DataTemplate>
</controls:Pivot.ItemTemplate>
```

This *DataTemplate* consists of a *ListBox* that lists all the albums associated with the composer represented by the *PivotItem*. The *ItemsSource* property of the *ListBox* is bound to the *Albums* property of the *ComposerInfo* object. This means that the *ListBox* is filled with a collection of objects of type *AlbumInfo*, which means the *DataTemplate* of the *ListBox* defines how each of those items is displayed:

```
<ListBox.ItemTemplate>
    <!-- Objects of type AlbumInfo -->
    <DataTemplate>
        . . .
    </DataTemplate>
</ListBox.ItemTemplate>
```

This *DataTemplate* references the *ThumbnailArt*, *ShortAlbumName*, and *Album* properties of *AlbumInfo*.

The first of the two screen shots of MusicByComposer shown earlier is entirely the result of the MainPage.xaml file and the data objects functioning as binding sources.

The code-behind file for *MainPage* is left with little to do except process the *SelectionChanged* event from the *ListBox* to navigate to AlbumPage.xaml:

Silverlight Project: MusicByComposer   File: MainPage.xaml.cs (excerpt)

```
public partial class MainPage : PhoneApplicationPage
{
    public MainPage()
    {
        InitializeComponent();
    }

    void OnListBoxSelectionChanged(object sender, SelectionChangedEventArgs args)
    {
        ComposerInfo composerInfo = pivot.SelectedItem as ComposerInfo;
        int composerInfoIndex = MusicPresenter.Current.Composers.IndexOf(composerInfo);

        AlbumInfo albumInfo = (sender as ListBox).SelectedItem as AlbumInfo;
        int albumInfoIndex = composerInfo.Albums.IndexOf(albumInfo);

        // Construct URI with two indices and navigate
        string destinationUri =
                String.Format("/AlbumPage.xaml?ComposerInfoIndex={0}&AlbumInfoInd
ex={1}",
                            composerInfoIndex, albumInfoIndex);

        this.NavigationService.Navigate(new Uri(destinationUri, UriKind.Relative));
    }
}
```

The query string consists of two indices: an index into the *Composers* collection of *MusicPresenter* to indicate the current *ComposerInfo* object, and an index into the *Albums* property of the *ComposerInfo* object to reference the selected *AlbumInfo*.

The code obtains the current *ComposerInfo* object being displayed through the *SelectedItem* property of the *Pivot* control. It was my original intention to save the *SelectedIndex* of the *Pivot* control during tombstoning so I could restore the *MainPage* display on reactivation. However, I experienced problems setting *SelectedIndex* on a newly created *Pivot* control, so I decided to abandon that amenity for now. This means that if the program is tombstoned, the *MainPage* always goes back to displaying the albums of John Adams.

The *Navigate* call instantiates an *AlbumPage* instance, which displays an album. *AlbumPage* is a normal *PhoneApplicationPage* derivative, with the normal two titles. (The page title is set to the composer's name from code.) The content area of the XAML file assumes that the *DataContext* of *AlbumPage* is set to an instance of *AlbumInfo*. (This is also set in code.) The first row of the content grid is the album art, album name, and artist. The second row is a *ScrollViewer* with an *ItemsControl* to display the songs:

Silverlight Project: MusicByComposer   File: AlbumPage.xaml (excerpt)

```xml
<Grid x:Name="ContentPanel" Grid.Row="1" Margin="12,0,12,0">
    <Grid.RowDefinitions>
        <RowDefinition Height="Auto" />
        <RowDefinition Height="*" />
    </Grid.RowDefinitions>

    <Grid.ColumnDefinitions>
        <ColumnDefinition Width="Auto" />
        <ColumnDefinition Width="*" />
    </Grid.ColumnDefinitions>

    <Border Grid.Row="0" Grid.Column="0"
            BorderBrush="{StaticResource PhoneForegroundBrush}"
            BorderThickness="1"
            Height="200" Width="200"
            Margin="0 0 6 0">

        <Image Source="{Binding AlbumArt}" />

    </Border>

    <StackPanel Grid.Row="0" Grid.Column="1"
            VerticalAlignment="Center">

        <TextBlock Text="{Binding Album.Name}"
                Foreground="{StaticResource PhoneAccentBrush}"
                TextWrapping="Wrap" />

        <TextBlock Text=" " />

        <TextBlock Text="{Binding Album.Artist}"
                TextWrapping="Wrap" />
    </StackPanel>

    <ScrollViewer Grid.Row="1" Grid.Column="0" Grid.ColumnSpan="2">
        <ItemsControl ItemsSource="{Binding Album.Songs}">
            <ItemsControl.ItemTemplate>
                <DataTemplate>
                    <local:SongTitleControl Song="{Binding}" />
                </DataTemplate>
            </ItemsControl.ItemTemplate>
        </ItemsControl>
    </ScrollViewer>
</Grid>
```

Notice that the *ItemsControl* that displays the songs has its *ItemsSource* property set to the *Songs* collection of the *Album* property of *AlbumInfo*. This *Songs* property is of type *SongCollection* and contains objects of the XNA class *Song*. Each *Song* object in that collection is the source of a binding to the *SongTitleControl* class that I'll show you soon.

AlbumPage.xaml also has an *ApplicationBar* for controlling the music player:

Silverlight Project: MusicByComposer   File: AlbumPage.xaml (excerpt)

```
<phone:PhoneApplicationPage.ApplicationBar>
    <shell:ApplicationBar>
        <shell:ApplicationBarIconButton IconUri="/Images/appbar.transport.rew.rest.
png"
                                        Text="previous"
                                        Click="OnAppbarPreviousButtonClick" />

        <shell:ApplicationBarIconButton x:Name="appbarPlayPauseButton"
                                        IconUri="/Images/appbar.transport.play.rest.
png"
                                        Text="play"
                                        Click="OnAppbarPlayButtonClick" />

        <shell:ApplicationBarIconButton IconUri="/Images/appbar.transport.ff.rest.png"
                                        Text="next"
                                        Click="OnAppbarNextButtonClick" />
    </shell:ApplicationBar>
</phone:PhoneApplicationPage.ApplicationBar>
```

The XNA Music Classes: *MediaPlayer*

To display music from the music library you use the XNA *MediaLibrary* and related classes. To actually play that music you use the static XNA *MediaPlayer* class.

The *MediaPlayer* class plays either a *Song* object, or all the songs in a *SongCollection*, or all the songs in a *SongCollection* beginning at a particular index. Those are the three variations of the static *MediaPlayer.Play* method.

You cannot create a *SongCollection* object yourself. You must always obtain an immutable *SongCollection* from one of the other classes (such as *Album*). This means that it's not a simple matter to let the user select a particular subset of an album, or to rearrange the tracks in some way. That would require the program to maintain its own list of *Song* objects, and to play them sequentially. I chose not to implement anything like that for this relatively simple demonstration program.

Besides *Play*, *MediaPlayer* also defines *Pause*, *Resume*, and *Stop* methods, as well as *MovePrevious* and *MoveNext* to move to the previous or next item in a *SongCollection*.

The crucial properties of *MediaPlayer* are all get-only:

■ *State*, which returns a member of the *MediaState* enumeration: *Playing*, *Paused*, or *Stopped*.

- *PlayPosition*, a *TimeSpan* object indicating the position within the currently playing song.

- *Queue*, a *MediaQueue* object that contains a collection of the *Song* objects in the currently-playing collection as well as an *ActiveSong* property.

From the *ActiveSong* property, you can obtain the *Album* object and other information associated with that song.

MediaPlayer also defines two events:

- *MediaStateChanged*

- *ActiveSongChanged*

The code-behind file for *AlbumPage* is responsible for actually playing the album. But first take a look at the parts of the class that perform what might be considered the "housekeeping" chores:

Silverlight Project: MusicByComposer   File: AlbumPage.xaml.cs (excerpt)

```
public partial class AlbumPage : PhoneApplicationPage
{
    // Used for switching play and pause icons
    static Uri playButtonIconUri =
                new Uri("/Images/appbar.transport.play.rest.png", UriKind.Relative);
    static Uri pauseButtonIconUri =
                new Uri("/Images/appbar.transport.pause.rest.png", UriKind.Relative);

    int composerInfoIndex;
    int albumInfoIndex;

    public AlbumPage()
    {
        InitializeComponent();
        appbarPlayPauseButton = this.ApplicationBar.Buttons[1] as
ApplicationBarIconButton;
    }

    protected override void OnNavigatedFrom(NavigationEventArgs args)
    {
        PhoneApplicationService.Current.State["ComposerInfoIndex"] = composerInfoIndex;
        PhoneApplicationService.Current.State["AlbumInfoIndex"] = albumInfoIndex;

        base.OnNavigatedFrom(args);
    }

    protected override void OnNavigatedTo(NavigationEventArgs args)
    {
        // Navigating from MainPage
```

```
            if (this.NavigationContext.QueryString.ContainsKey("ComposerInfoIndex"))
            {
                composerInfoIndex =
                    Int32.Parse(this.NavigationContext.QueryString["ComposerInfoIndex"]);
                albumInfoIndex =
                    Int32.Parse(this.NavigationContext.QueryString["AlbumInfoIndex"]);
            }

            // Reactivating from tombstoning
            else if (PhoneApplicationService.Current.State.ContainsKey("ComposerInfoInd
    ex"))
            {
                composerInfoIndex =
                    (int)PhoneApplicationService.Current.State["ComposerInfoIndex"];
                albumInfoIndex =
                    (int)PhoneApplicationService.Current.State["AlbumInfoIndex"];
            }

            ComposerInfo composerInfo = MusicPresenter.Current.
    Composers[composerInfoIndex];
            AlbumInfo albumInfo = composerInfo.Albums[albumInfoIndex];

            // Set page title and DataContext
            PageTitle.Text = composerInfo.Composer;
            this.DataContext = albumInfo;

            // Get the media state when it changes and also right now
            MediaPlayer.MediaStateChanged += OnMediaPlayerMediaStateChanged;
            OnMediaPlayerMediaStateChanged(null, EventArgs.Empty);

            base.OnNavigatedTo(args);
        }
        ...
    }
```

When being tombstoned, the *OnNavigatedFrom* method saves the two fields named *composerInfoIndex* and *albumInfoIndex*. These are the same two values that *MainPage* passes to *AlbumPage* in the navigation query string. The *OnNavigatedTo* method obtains those values either from the query string or the *State* property of the *PhoneApplicationService* to set the text of the *PageTitle* element (to display the name of the composer) and the *DataContext* of the page (so the bindings in AlbumPage.xaml work).

The *OnNavigatedTo* method also sets a handler for the *MediaPlayer.MediaStateChanged* event to maintain the correct icon image for the button that combines the functions of Play and Pause.

The event handler for that button turned out to be one of the trickier aspects of this class:

Silverlight Project: MusicByComposer   File: AlbumPage.xaml.cs (excerpt)

```
void OnAppbarPlayButtonClick(object sender, EventArgs args)
{
    Album thisPagesAlbum = (this.DataContext as AlbumInfo).Album;

    switch (MediaPlayer.State)
    {
        // The MediaPlayer is currently playing so pause it.
        case MediaState.Playing:
            MediaPlayer.Pause();
            break;

        // The MediaPlayer is currently paused...
        case MediaState.Paused:
            MediaQueue queue = MediaPlayer.Queue;

            // so if we're on the same page as the paused song, resume it.
            if (queue.ActiveSong != null &&
                queue.ActiveSong.Album == thisPagesAlbum)
            {
                MediaPlayer.Resume();
            }
            // Otherwise, start playing this page's album.
            else
            {
                goto case MediaState.Stopped;
            }
            break;

        // The MediaPlayer is stopped, so play this page's album.
        case MediaState.Stopped:
            MediaPlayer.Play(thisPagesAlbum.Songs);
            break;
    }
}

void OnAppbarPreviousButtonClick(object sender, EventArgs args)
{
    MediaPlayer.MovePrevious();
}

void OnAppbarNextButtonClick(object sender, EventArgs args)
{
    MediaPlayer.MoveNext();
}
```

Once a program calls *MediaPlayer.Play* on a *Song* or *SongCollection* object, the music keeps going even if the user exits that program or the phone shuts off the screen and locks the display. This is how it should be. The user wants to listen to the music regardless—even to the point where the battery completely runs down.

For that reason, a program should be very cautious about calling *MediaPlayer.Stop*, because calling that method will stop the music without allowing it to be resumed. I found no reason to call *MediaPlayer.Stop* at all in my program.

The user can also exit a program such as MusicByComposer and then return to it, and the user should also be allowed to navigate to different album pages without interfering with the playing music. Yet, the user should also have the option of switching from the music currently playing to the album currently in view. It seemed to me that these choices implied four different cases when the user presses the play/pause button:

- If music is currently playing, then the play/pause button displays the pause icon, and the currently playing music should be paused.

- If the player is stopped, then the play/pause button displays the play icon, and the album in view should be played.

- If the music is paused, then the play/pause button also displays the play icon. If the user is on the album page that's currently active, then the play button should just resume whatever was playing.

- However, if the music is paused but the user is on a *different* album page, then the play button should start playing the album on the current page.

In actual use, that logic seems to work well.

The only class you haven't seen yet is *SongTitleControl*, an instance of which is used to display each individual song on the album. *SongTitleControl* is also responsible for highlighting the currently playing song and displaying the elapsed time and total duration of that song.

SongTitleControl just derives from *UserControl* and has a simple visual tree:

Silverlight Project: MusicByComposer   File: SongTitleControl.xaml (excerpt)

```
<Grid x:Name="LayoutRoot">
    <StackPanel Margin="0 3">
        <TextBlock Name="txtblkTitle"
                   Text="{Binding Name}"
                   TextWrapping="Wrap" />

        <TextBlock Name="txtblkTime"
                   Margin="24 6"
                   Visibility="Collapsed" />
    </StackPanel>
</Grid>
```

In AlbumPage.xaml, the *SongTitleControl* contains a binding on its *Song* property, which means that *SongTitleControl* must define a dependency property named *Song* of the XNA type *Song*. Here's the definition of the *Song* property and the property-changed handlers:

Silverlight Project: MusicByComposer   File: SongTitleControl.xaml.cs (excerpt)

```
public static readonly DependencyProperty SongProperty =
    DependencyProperty.Register("Song",
        typeof(Song),
        typeof(SongTitleControl),
        new PropertyMetadata(OnSongChanged));

...

public Song Song
{
    set { SetValue(SongProperty, value); }
    get { return (Song)GetValue(SongProperty); }
}

static void OnSongChanged(DependencyObject obj, DependencyPropertyChangedEventArgs
args)
{
    (obj as SongTitleControl).OnSongChanged(args);
}

void OnSongChanged(DependencyPropertyChangedEventArgs args)
{
    if (Song != null)
        MediaPlayer.ActiveSongChanged += OnMediaPlayerActiveSongChanged;
    else
        MediaPlayer.ActiveSongChanged -= OnMediaPlayerActiveSongChanged;

    OnMediaPlayerActiveSongChanged(null, EventArgs.Empty);
}
```

If *Song* is set to a non-*null* value, then an event handler is set for the *MediaPlayer. ActiveSongChanged* event. That event is handled here:

Silverlight Project: MusicByComposer   File: SongTitleControl.xaml.cs (excerpt)

```
void OnMediaPlayerActiveSongChanged(object sender, EventArgs args)
{
    if (this.Song == MediaPlayer.Queue.ActiveSong)
    {
        txtblkTitle.FontWeight = FontWeights.Bold;
        txtblkTitle.Foreground = this.Resources["PhoneAccentBrush"] as Brush;
        txtblkTime.Visibility = Visibility.Visible;
        timer.Start();
    }
    else
    {
        txtblkTitle.FontWeight = FontWeights.Normal;
```

```
        txtblkTitle.Foreground = this.Resources["PhoneForegroundBrush"] as Brush;
        txtblkTime.Visibility = Visibility.Collapsed;
        timer.Stop();
    }
}
```

The *Text* property of *txtblkTitle* is handled with a binding in the XAML file. If the active song is the *Song* associated with this instance of *SongTitleControl*, then this *TextBlock* is highlighted with the accent color, the other *TextBlock* with the time information is made visible, and a *DispatcherTimer* is started:

Silverlight Project: MusicByComposer   File: SongTitleControl.xaml.cs (excerpt)

```
public partial class SongTitleControl : UserControl
{
    DispatcherTimer timer = new DispatcherTimer();
    ...
    public SongTitleControl()
    {
        InitializeComponent();
        timer.Interval = TimeSpan.FromSeconds(0.25);
        timer.Tick += OnTimerTick;
    }
    ...
    void OnTimerTick(object sender, EventArgs args)
    {
        TimeSpan dur = this.Song.Duration;
        TimeSpan pos = MediaPlayer.PlayPosition;

        txtblkTime.Text = String.Format("{0}:{1:D2} / {2}:{3:D2}",
                                (int)pos.TotalMinutes, pos.Seconds,
                                (int)dur.TotalMinutes, dur.Seconds);
    }
}
```

That *Tick* handler simply formats the duration of the song and the current position for display purposes.

I thought about shifting some of this code to XAML, which would require defining a property for the elapsed time, as well as using the Visual State Manager for ActiveSong and NotActiveSong states, and then bringing in the *StringFormatterConverter* for formatting the two *TimeSpan* objects. But for this particular application the code file seemed the simpler of the two approaches.

Although you've seen many ways in which XAML is very powerful, sometimes code is really the right solution.

Index

Symbols and Numbers

Charles Petzold

Charles Petzold has been writing about programming for Windows-based operating systems for 24 years. His books include *Programming Windows* (5th edition, Microsoft Press, 1998) and six books about .NET programming, including *3D Programming for Windows: Three-Dimensional Graphics Pro-gramming for the Windows Presentation Foundation* (Microsoft Press, 2007). He is also the author of two unique books that explore the intersection of computing technology, mathematics, and history: *Code: The Hidden Language of Computer Hardware and Software* (Microsoft Press, 1999) and *The Annotated Turing: A Guided Tour though Alan Turing's Historic Paper on Computability and the Turing Machine* (Wiley, 2008). Petzold lives in New York City. His website is *www.charlespetzold.com*.

Best Practices for Software Engineering

Collaborative Technologies—
Resources for Developers

**Inside Microsoft®
SharePoint® 2010**

Ted Pattison, Andrew Connell,
and Scot Hillier

ISBN 9780735627468

Get the in-depth architectural insights, task-
oriented guidance, and extensive code samples
you need to build robust, enterprise content-
management solutions.

**Programming for
Unified Communications
with Microsoft Office
Communications
Server 2007 R2**

Rui Maximo, Kurt De Ding,
Vishwa Ranjan, Chris Mayo,
Oscar Newkerk, and the
Microsoft OCS Team

ISBN 9780735626232

Direct from the Microsoft Office Communications
Server product team, get the hands-on guidance
you need to streamline your organization's real-time,
remote communication and collaboration solutions
across the enterprise and across time zones.

**Programming
Microsoft
Dynamics® CRM 4.0**

Jim Steger, Mike Snyder,
Brad Bosak, Corey O'Brien,
and Philip Richardson

ISBN 9780735625945

Apply the design and coding practices that
leading CRM consultants use to customize,
integrate, and extend Microsoft Dynamics
CRM 4.0 for specific business needs.

**Microsoft
.NET and SAP**

Juergen Daiberl,
Steve Fox, Scott Adams,
and Thomas Reimer

ISBN 9780735625686

Develop integrated, .NET-SAP solutions—
and deliver better connectivity, collaboration,
and business intelligence.

For C# Developers

Microsoft® Visual C#® 2010 Step by Step

John Sharp

ISBN 9780735626706

Teach yourself Visual C# 2010—one step at a time. Ideal for developers with fundamental programming skills, this practical tutorial delivers hands-on guidance for creating C# components and Windows–based applications. CD features practice exercises, code samples, and a fully searchable eBook.

Microsoft XNA® Game Studio 3.0: Learn Programming Now!

Rob Miles

ISBN 9780735626584

Now you can create your own games for Xbox 360® and Windows—as you learn the underlying skills and concepts for computer programming. Dive right into your first project, adding new tools and tricks to your arsenal as you go. Master the fundamentals of XNA Game Studio and Visual C#—no experience required!

CLR via C#, Third Edition

Jeffrey Richter

ISBN 9780735627048

Dig deep and master the intricacies of the common language runtime (CLR) and the .NET Framework. Written by programming expert Jeffrey Richter, this guide is ideal for developers building any kind of application—ASP.NET, Windows Forms, Microsoft SQL Server®, Web services, console apps—and features extensive C# code samples.

Windows via C/C++, Fifth Edition

Jeffrey Richter, Christophe Nasarre

ISBN 9780735624245

Get the classic book for programming Windows at the API level in Microsoft Visual C++®—now in its fifth edition and covering Windows Vista®.

Programming Windows® Identity Foundation

Vittorio Bertocci

ISBN 9780735627185

Get practical, hands-on guidance for using WIF to solve authentication, authorization, and customization issues in Web applications and services.

Microsoft® ASP.NET 4 Step by Step

George Shepherd

ISBN 9780735627017

Ideal for developers with fundamental programming skills—but new to ASP.NET—who want hands-on guidance for developing Web applications in the Microsoft Visual Studio® 2010 environment.

microsoft.com/mspress

For Visual Basic Developers

**Microsoft®
Visual Basic® 2010
Step by Step**

Michael Halvorson

ISBN 9780735626690

Teach yourself the essential tools and techniques for Visual Basic 2010—one step at a time. No matter what your skill level, you'll find the practical guidance and examples you need to start building applications for Windows and the Web.

**Microsoft Visual Studio® Tips
251 Ways to Improve Your
Productivity**

Sara Ford

ISBN 9780735626409

This book packs proven tips that any developer, regardless of skill or preferred development language, can use to help shave hours off everyday development activities with Visual Studio.

**Inside the Microsoft Build
Engine: Using MSBuild and
Team Foundation Build,
Second Edition**

Sayed Ibrahim Hashimi,
William Bartholomew

ISBN 9780735645240

Your practical guide to using, customizing, and extending the build engine in Visual Studio 2010.

**Parallel Programming
with Microsoft
Visual Studio 2010**

Donis Marshall

ISBN 9780735640603

The roadmap for developers wanting to maximize their applications for multicore architecture using Visual Studio 2010.

**Programming Windows®
Services with Microsoft
Visual Basic 2008**

Michael Gernaey

ISBN 9780735624337

The essential guide for developing powerful, customized Windows services with Visual Basic 2008. Whether you're looking to perform network monitoring or design a complex enterprise solution, you'll find the expert advice and practical examples to accelerate your productivity.

What do you think of this book?

We want to hear from you!

To participate in a brief online survey, please visit:

microsoft.com/learning/booksurvey

Tell us how well this book meets your needs—what works effectively, and what we can do better. Your feedback will help us continually improve our books and learning resources for you.

Thank you in advance for your input!

Stay in touch!

To subscribe to the *Microsoft Press®* *Book Connection Newsletter*—for news on upcoming books, events, and special offers—please visit:

microsoft.com/learning/books/newsletter

Breinigsville, PA USA
28 January 2011
254332BV00002B/39-798/P

9 780735 656673